EQUATIONS OF MOTION

Adventure, Risk and Innovation

The Engineering Autobiography of
William F. Milliken

B www.
BentleyPublishers
.com

EQUATIONS OF MOTION

Foreword by Dan Gurney v

Preface vii

Acknowledgments x

Chapter 2
Ski Mobile, rear view showing steerable rear ski and air rudder, 1927.

Section 1
Growing Up Down East 1911—1932

1	Old Town, Maine	2
2	Wheels, Skis and Propellers	24
3	Prelude to a Career	52
4	Designed, Built, Flew and Crashed	70

Chapter 7
Sitting in front of the MIT Aeronautical Laboratory with the torpedo plane model, 1935.

Section 2
An Engineer's Education 1932—1939

5	Tackling Tech	104
6	Noseover in Augusta	132
7	Wind Tunneling	140
8	Adventures with Tail Stall	150

Chapter 11
Al Reed, Chief of Flight Test and Chief Pilot, right, and WFM as Chief Flight Test Engineer and Assistant Head of Flight Test, 1940.

Section 3
War Effort 1939—1943

9	Pressurized Stratoliner	168
10	Last of the Clippers	192
11	Higher than Everest	208
12	Transcontinental Flight	246
13	Triumph and Tragedy	272

Chapter 15
About to leave on a PT-26 stalled flight test, 1947.

Section 4
Transition to Research 1944—1947

14	Secret Wing	300
15	Flight Dynamics	310

Section 5
Automobile Racing 1947—1956

Chapter 18
New name for the corner, 1948.

16 Entrée Bugatti... 354

17 Four-Wheel Drive.. 376

18 Milliken's Corner.. 398

19 Racing Takes Off... 412

20 The Big Bug at the Bridge................................. 428

21 Dynaflow Epic.. 436

22 Butterball Saga.. 468

Chapter 22
Butterball at start, Watkins Glen
Seneca Cup, 1955.

Section 6
Automotive Research 1956—2002

23 Camber Galore.. 492

24 Vehicle Dynamics.. 534

25 Transportation Research Division..................... 556

26 Milliken Research Associates, Inc..................... 582

27 Full Circle.. 610

Epilogue...632

Chapter 23
MX-1 Camber car, 1967.

Appendices

I   Research and Innovations............................... 635

II   SCCA Positions and Contributions................. 638

III   Al Reed.. 645

IV   Automotive Handling: Experiments and Results............. 646

V   Archie Butterworth FWD/AJB Letter............. 649

VI   Awards and Honors... 657

Editor's Note...658

Index 659

Figure Credits...681

Chapter 27
A turn around Goodwood in the
MX-1, 2002.

Bentley Publishers, a division of Robert Bentley, Inc.
1734 Massachusetts Avenue
Cambridge, MA 02138 USA   Information that makes
800-423-4595 / 617-547-4170   the difference®

BentleyPublishers™
.com

Copies of this book may be purchased from booksellers or directly from the publisher.

Bentley Stock No. GEMK
ISBN 0-8376-1348-5
09 08 07 06   6 5 4 3 2 1

The paper used in this publication is acid-free and meets the requirements of the National Standard for Information Sciences-Permanence of Paper for Printed Library Materials. ∞

Library of Congress Cataloging-in-Publication Data

Milliken, William F., 1911-
  Equations of motion : adventure, risk, and innovation : the engineering autobiography of William F. Milliken.
    p. cm.
  Includes index.
  ISBN-13: 978-0-8376-1348-2 ((hardcover) : alk. paper)
  ISBN-10: 0-8376-1348-5 ((hardcover) : alk. paper) 1. Milliken, William F., 1911- 2. Automobile engineers--United States--Biography. 3. Aeronautical engineers--United States--Biography. I. Title.

TL140.M547A3 2006
629.222092--dc22
[B]
                    2006023522

Equations of Motion by William F. Milliken
©2006 William F. Milliken
Bentley Publishers is a trademark of Robert Bentley, Inc.

Manufactured in the United States of America

Front endpaper: Old Town, Maine, 1923. Bill Milliken evaluates the chassis of the "Miller No. 1" pushcar before full bodywork is fitted.

Back endpaper: Mere Hall, England, 2002. Bill Milliken drives the restored 1932 FWD Miller, which he had driven in the 1948 Pikes Peak Hillclimb, the 1949 Watkins Glen Grand Prix and many other postwar events.

Foreword

When Bill Milliken sent me his book with the title *Equations of Motion* I hesitated for a few days to open it, fearing to be faced with a rather dry and complex treatise on physics and mathematics. Already in the first few chapters it became apparent to me, however, why Bill had chosen the title: He has spent a good part of his life in motion—as an accomplished and passionate ballroom dancer! And that is not the only surprise in this wonderfully entertaining book which spans over nine decades of Bill's fascinating career and life, and to which I have the great honor to contribute this foreword.

Sometimes in life you meet a person and for unknown reasons you feel an immediate connection, an inner sense tells you that you are on the same wavelength. That happened to me when I first met Bill Milliken almost 50 years ago at the U.S. Grand Prix at Watkins Glen, New York. We were kindred spirits, we both liked aviation and motor racing, we liked to know what made machines function and we did not hesitate to go out on a limb in the pursuit of our respective goals.

Dan Gurney at Watkins Glen, 1961.

Reading page after page I am happy to realize that unknowingly I have also shared a great many of his role models as well as his sense of curiosity, his sense of naughtiness and his relentless tenacity and passion. We both do not seem bothered in taking a chance of making fools of ourselves when tackling an unorthodox project.

Bill's life's journey preceded mine by 20 years starting in 1911. In the unfolding decades the world learned about telephones, radios, automobiles, motorcycles, trains, world wars, the Depression, television, atom bombs, the Cold War, computers, space flight, terrorism, laptops, the Internet—a fantastically grand canvas for living and learning. Bill has done just that becoming a pioneer in many fields including aircraft stability and control and the mathematics thereof, always pushing the envelope for greater understanding. His attitude in facing every challenge and not avoiding risks has an infectious appeal that is hard to resist.

Every long life has its ups and downs, and Bill has had his share. He coped with great fortitude and with his sense of humor intact, never lavishing much sympathy upon himself. He just kept swinging and acting like the Maine Yankee that he is.

Bill, it is a pleasure to know you and be called your friend. Your book will enlighten generations of young inventors and trailblazers to come.

With best wishes always,

Dan Gurney

This book is dedicated to
Barbara, Doug, Peter and Ann
in the order they came into my life.
Without them this book could
never have been written.

Bill Milliken

Preface

The fabric of life is woven from many threads that originate in one's heredity and the experiences of life. According to Reich,[1] the most basic character trait is the "red thread" which defines how the individual reacts, or defends himself, against the environment. This trait appears and reappears in different situations throughout life. It has nothing to do with the individual's physical appearance but is a prominent feature of his psychological outlook, determining his decisions and actions.

Because of my exposure at a young age to my father's adventurous career and my mother's memorable ancestry, my "red thread" is that of the heroic. I am fascinated by the hero's mode of action—taking a chance and, like Ulysses, pushing on regardless.

My early interests in auto racing and the pioneering oceanic flights reinforced this fundamental orientation while adding a creative urge which led to the development of my early ground vehicles and, in 1931, to my home-built M-1 airplane. Call this the "orange thread," the rising sun of creation which gets one out of bed in the morning, full of ideas and raring to go.

The men who pursued auto racing and long-distance flights became my heroes. In attempting to emulate them, accidents became a regular feature of my existence. As a result of the flight of my highly unstable airplane and hairy experiences with motorcycles, my curiosity focused upon vehicle stability and control.

At MIT I found a basic answer to this curiosity in G.H. Bryan's Equations of Motion, a powerful revelation and an identifiable thread in its own right. I think of these equations as a shining tool, a "yellow thread," if you will, that sheds light on many difficult dynamic problems.

As a child, I also knew anxiety and lonesomeness, having spent long and hopeless days alone with my mother while she struggled with depression. Thus I could empathize with the race drivers and flyers of my era who faced solitude and fear as regular components of their professions. I also began to recognize that resistance, inertia and sadness are inevitable in life, stalking ambition and achievement. However this "blue thread" is not all bad, as it gives one an appreciation for the problems others face, thus opening channels of communication and facilitating group accomplishment.

By the time I finished MIT, these four emotional threads were fully ingrained in my character.

Colored threads are at best only a graphic first-order analogy of the emotional structure of the individual. Those I have mentioned are nevertheless useful concepts for understanding the framework of this book and the relationships between its parts.

In this autobiography, I discuss specific events of my working life. As diverse as they appear, they are connected by an emotional consistency which gives my life a measure of wholeness. I have never believed life should be random. I have worked in a variety of venues—at home, in college, in small and large aircraft firms, at a major research laboratory and finally in my own company—but my emotional roots and threads have never changed, simply reappearing in different guises and energy levels. The discerning reader will find various combinations of these in each chapter.

---

[1] *Wilhelm Reich's theories are explicated by E. F. Baker in the psychology classic* Man in the Trap, *The American College of Orgonomy, 2000.*

There is virtue in connecting the dreams of youth with the realities of later years. I never thought I could recapture the childhood zest of driving the No. 1 Miller "push car" of 1923, but handling the Indy Miller in 1997 at Goodwood offered a stunning revival. My hairy test flights in World War II were *déjà vu* of my M-1 flight from Old Orchard Beach when I was 21. Life is never boring if one can re-experience as new the shining moments of childhood.

More importantly, by retaining strong identity with my earliest interests in race cars and airplanes, opportunities have arisen to contribute to the evolution of these machines. I feel indeed fortunate to have been a part of the research on aircraft dynamic stability and control and the introduction of aircraft technology to the automobile.

Life is finite, but the dream of immortality can be realized by adding something, however small, to the sum of human knowledge. By using our gifts and talents, following our stars while remaining faithful to our emotional heritage, we can leave worthwhile records of our achievements.

The creative life, working at what one loves, must surely be the best that life can offer. Those who have found it can survive endless struggle and disappointments. Their curiosity never wavers and retirement is not a part of their lexicon.

In today's complex world, the exercise of a creative life is seldom that of the single individual. Organization of specialists is frequently the norm. I hope I have fully acknowledged my associates and teachers and the pioneers to whom we owe so much. I think of Otto Koppen, George Bryan, Maurice Olley, J. B. Gates, Herman Glauert and the mathematical geniuses who preceded them.

We should also remember our heroes, the likes of John F. Stevens, Charles Lindbergh, Kingsford Smith, Tazio Nuvolari, Juan Manuel Fangio, Stirling Moss and Rudolf Caracciola, who peopled our inner world and inspired us by their daring. They are the source of our energy and our challenges.

Finally, life is so precious we should strive to think of it as a whole, a continuum, for it is our greatest adventure.

Bill Milliken, 2006

LINDBERGH FLIES ALONE

Alone? Is he alone at whose right side
rides Courage, with Skill within the
cockpit and Faith upon the left?

Does solitude surround the brave when
Adventure leads the way and
Ambition reads the dials?

Is there no company with him, for
whom the air is cleft by Daring
and the darkness made light
by Emprise?

True, the fragile bodies of his
fellows do not weigh down his plane.

True, the fretful minds of weaker
men are missing from his crowded cabin.

But as his airship keeps its course,
he holds communion with those
rare spirits that inspire to
intrepidity and by their sustaining
potency give strength to arm,
resource to mind, content to soul.

Alone? With what other companions
would man fly to whom
the choice were given?

> — *Editorial in the New York SUN, May 22, 1927*

*Enter by the narrow path
For the way is hard, that leads to life,
And those who find it are few.*

> — *Matthew 7:13*

Acknowledgments

After working together in Milliken Research for nearly 20 years, my son, Douglas, took over the management in 1996, giving me time to do something different. Never one to retire and anxious to remain active, this was an opportunity to reflect on my career and record some aspects of it. I decided to produce a story of my working life, as opposed to a more personal biography, though obviously with some overlap. Having been the co-author of two successful books on vehicle dynamics, I had some confidence in tackling another book and a realistic view of the effort involved.

Writing a book is a long, sustained, difficult and frequently frustrating task. In my case it couldn't have been done without the time, space, support and encouragement of my wife, Barbara, and my son, Doug. They not only provided the right atmosphere but made specific contributions in terms of proofing, typing and facilitating electronic communication. I can hardly thank them enough.

From the beginning, I decided that the book should not be ghost-written. I wanted it to have the authenticity of my own words because "I was there." To this end, I wrote the initial draft of each chapter by hand, having done the necessary research and developed an outline. There is a small print shop, Lazer Tree Grafics, at the foot of our street, operated by Terry and Rolf Hjalmarson. Terry deciphered my drafts and spelling to produce a readable typed copy which Rolf then delivered on disc. Working with Terry and Rolf these eight years has been a truly rewarding experience.

Having drafted over 20 chapters, it became time to look for an editor. For years I had dined at Le Chanteclair Restaurant in New York and formed a friendship with its proprietors, René and Maurice Dreyfus, augmented by our mutual interest in auto racing and Bugattis. I had an autographed copy of *My Two Lives* by René Dreyfus with Beverly Rae Kimes. This appealed to me as an outstanding biography. Beverly and I had met on only one occasion, so I had no reason to believe she would be interested in my book, but I called her anyway. This led to a meeting at her apartment in New York and an understanding that she would, in fact, do the editing and act as an editorial consultant. Since Beverly stands at the top of her profession as an author, editor and historian, her commitment added greatly to the book's quality and stature.

Several factors increased the difficulty of editing this book. First, the chapters were not written consecutively, thus leading to overlap and issues of connectivity. Second was my "no ghost" requirement and finally my own limitations as a writer of non-technical narrative. Beverly took all of these issues in stride and in addition helped to bring out the overall theme of the book. She faced up to the "ghost" by using my language as much as possible and insisting that I always had the last word. In reading the edited draft, I believe it is fair to say that it is not ghost-written but that it is vastly improved over my original draft. Together Beverly and I chose the photographs and drawings and keyed them to the text. We also assembled the additional illustrations for the folios. I am delighted to acknowledge her many contributions to the book.

Robb Ramsey has done all the new line drawings, graphics and sketches as he did for our technical books on vehicle dynamics. Getting back to regular meetings with Robb with his professional attitude for getting the figures "right," has been a real pleasure. Many thanks.

I feel indeed fortunate to have Bentley Publishers as the producer of this book. After an extensive telephone acquaintance with Michael Bentley, President, I spent two days at their fascinating headquarters in Harvard Square, Cambridge, Massachusetts. They also visited our facility in western New York. We reached mutual agreement in the objectives of the book and Joshua Davidson was designated as production editor. Bentley introduced a strong proviso to insure that technical concepts be made as intelligible as possible for the nontechnical reader and to increase the number of illustrations for the reader who likes to browse. Bentley also played a major role in the choice of title for the book.

Because of the variety of material covered and its time span, this book has not been an easy one to organize and present for publication. Josh Davidson and I struggled with various details to improve the flow for the reader. As production editor, Davidson has been assisted by a variety of specialists in page layout, cover design, art and publishing; notably, Terri Horning, Michael Lepera, Sarah Feldman, Jim Scott and Maurice Iglesias. I wish to fully acknowledge Michael Bentley and Joshua Davidson and their entire team in bringing this book to publication. Josh Davidson has also taken on the major role of promoting the sale of this book by obtaining appropriate reviews and presentations. Many thanks for an outstanding job.

Bob Richardson, who did the index for *Race Car Vehicle Dynamics* and *Chassis Design*, also did the index for this book. Furthermore he was retained to copyedit the entire book. I wish to acknowledge and thank him for the effort and enthusiasm he has brought to these tasks.

I am a great admirer of Dan Gurney and his career in motor racing and other pursuits--a great American in every respect. His Forword gave me the feeling that whatever effort went into this book was all worthwhile. I can't thank you enough, Dan.

Edward Kasprzak, our senior associate in Milliken Research Associates made valuable contributions to chapter 23 on the MX-1 camber car; certainly the most difficult chapter to review and proof.

Peter and Hannah Wright, great friends from Lotus days, have read and commented on early chapters and also the entire book. Since Peter is sort of my "latter day" technical role model, you can appreciate how valuable I view their comments and suggestions.

Doug Milliken and Donna Lewis have done a final "read through" to insure no major errors in the text. Many thanks.

My intent was to give proper credit for each photograph that appears in this book. In a few cases we have been unable to determine the photographer. I specifically want to acknowledge the following:

Ed Waterhouse, who provided nearly all the photo documentation of my early ground vehicles and younger years in Old Town. Valerie Osborne, Old Town Public Library, who supplied historic photos of Old Town and the environment in which I grew up. Cooper Milliken, photos of specific sites in Old Town. Ralph Jones, CAL Flight Research Department's official photographers, who left a complete record of our early race cars and also of some events at Watkins Glen. Kristine Kaske, Archive Division, (Smithsonian) National Air and Space Museum, who provided photos of early trans-oceanic flight aircraft. Jenny O'Neil, Curatorial Assistant, MIT Museum, for photos of my professors at MIT and the early wind tunnels. Harry Hleva, Igor I. Sikorsky Historical Archives for photos of Vought, Vought-Sikorsky aircraft and the Sikorsky Wind Tunnel. Karl Erickson, Owl's

Head Transportation Museum, Boeing Archives, Mike Walsh for photographs of FWD Miller and MX-1 at Goodwood and elsewhere, Karl Ludvigsen, Ludvigsen Library, for the remarkable photo of "Butterball" at Mt. Equinox, 1956, Pete de Beaumont for the outstanding photos of Type 54 at Bridgehampton, 1950, Charles Lytle for photos of numerous racing episodes, and Cam Angetsinger, Mark Steigerwald, Glenda Gephardt, Bill Green of the Watkins Glen Motor Racing Research Center for numerous photos and references. Also, special thanks to Dean and Don Butler, Mike Yust, Steve Havelock and Martin Walford for their help in many ways. *(Complete figure credits can be found on pages 681-683.)*

Much of my life has been associated with accomplishments of research teams. To the extent of memory and records, I have tried to list team members in the pages of this book. I have been fortunate to have encountered so many individuals in all branches of engineering and I wish to acknowledge their contributions to our accomplishments.

Finally, I want to thank my mother and father. In the midst of the Great Depression and other problems that beset them, they never failed to give me the love, time, support and financial help to pursue my own interests and insure that I had a fine education. My father made me aware that life can be a great adventure. Without my mother's help I don't believe I would have finished M-1 or met the University of Maine's entrance requirements.

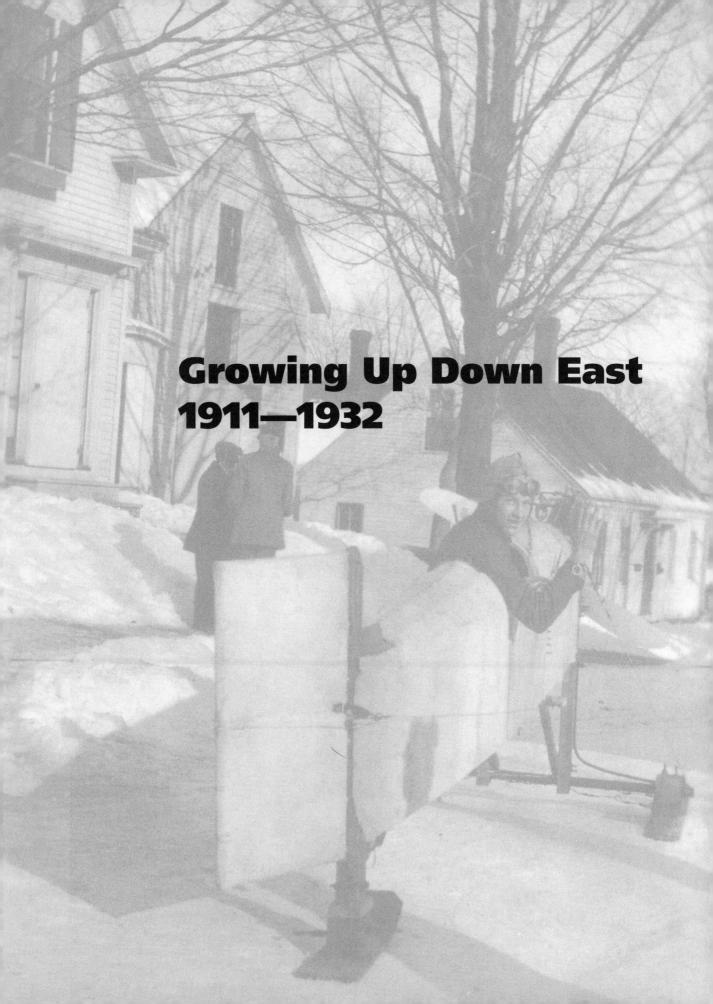

Growing Up Down East
1911—1932

Chapter 1

Old Town, Maine

> Something we feel should happen; we
> know not what, yet proceed in quest
> of it.
>
> – Robert Louis Stevenson
> ("A Gossip on Romance")

One of the great transportation challenges of the late nineteenth century was the completion of the railway system in the United States. My father, William Milliken, played a part in this accomplishment. Descended from Hugh Milliken, who emigrated from Scotland in 1680, he was born in 1876 in Portland, Maine. A recession ruined his chance for a college education but he was tutored in civil engineering and surveying. At 24 he went west to accept a position with the Great Northern Railway. This resulted from his introduction to the Great Northern's chief engineer John F. Stevens, who also was a native of Maine.

Initially, my father's job was superintending heavy construction work, beginning with the Verona-Marias cutoff of the Montana Central. By 1903 his talent for finding and surveying new routes was recognized, and he spent the major part of his railroad career as a "locating engineer."

Limitations of grade, the balancing of "cuts and fills," the need for tunneling, and the implications of snow and landslides, were among the factors to be considered in laying out a new railroad line. Taking a crew into the wilderness for months at a time presented all the hazards and logistical difficulties of exploration, as well as problems of health and morale for a small group of people living like mountain climbers, in harsh conditions and in close quarters. As the leader, my father selected the crew after judging their psychological ability to function in an effective and stable team. Finally, after the terrain had been surveyed, he prepared accurate maps and field reports to send back to the office for executive decision-making.

Prior to 1915, my father worked at "locating" for a variety of railways, including the Great Northern, the Northern Pacific, the

Old Town Railroad Station, where the circus arrived every summer.

Canadian Pacific, the Chihuahua and Pacific, the Oregon Trunk, the Chicago, Milwaukee and Puget Sound, the Grand Trunk Pacific and the Florida and Alabama Railroad. As his reputation grew, assignments came from British Columbia, Mexico and Alaska, where he was responsible for locating the Susitna Valley line of the Trans-Alaskan Railway.

MY MOTHER, ABBIE Cooper, also was born in 1876 and grew up in Old Town, Maine. She lived to be 100, dying at the 200th anniversary of the United States, having lived half our country's history. Following high school graduation she entered Westbrook Seminary (at that time a preparatory school for women) in Portland. Photographs show a strikingly beautiful woman—a "Gibson Girl"—tall, erect, slim-waisted, full figured,

Fig. 1-1
William Franklin Milliken, photographed in Maine circa 1920.

an oval face with high cheekbones, a direct and intelligent countenance. She walked and danced with a natural grace. My father fell blindingly in love when they met and pursued her relentlessly for the next ten years, taking the train to Old Town whenever he was in Portland. According to her diaries, they enjoyed each other's company at dances, concerts and dinners, but she had no interest in marriage.

Her real interest lay in a music career as a teacher and performer. She had studied piano at the Bangor School of Music and also at the Virgil School in Washington, D.C. Although very popular with a wide circle of friends, my mother had an artistic and sensitive nature and, in the parlance of the day, was "high strung" and prone to bouts of depression.

Fig. 1-2

William Milliken, associate G. F. Kuntz and their *mozo* (guide) during the 1904 locating trip to Mexico.

Contracting chicken pox in 1904, she broke out in a rash and boils, and feared she was heading for a nervous breakdown. Her physician recommended a month's vacation from the piano at a wilderness camp. That fall she literally "walked" herself back to health in the woods. Thereafter, whenever events overtook her she resorted to walking.

In 1906 my mother made the fateful decision of accepting my father's proposal of marriage, influenced perhaps by her approaching 30th birthday and the prevailing belief that a woman's place was in the home. According to a reliable witness, before walking downstairs for the ceremony in the front parlor of her parents' home she announced that she wanted to "run away."

Nevertheless, the first five years of their marriage apparently were happy and eventful. My father had arranged a honeymoon trip across the continent with stops at the best hotels, ending

Fig. 1-3
Abbie Cooper Milliken, photographed circa 1896.

at the famous Davenport Hotel in Spokane. They then went "on location" in British Columbia and Oregon. She learned to ride horseback, became proficient in working up maps of survey results, and acted as hostess to many top railway officials. My father had passes on most important railroads, so they always traveled in style.

IN 1910 MY MOTHER returned, pregnant, to her ancestral home in Old Town. I was born April 18, 1911. at 8:15 P.M.

Childbearing proved to be one of the most traumatic experiences of her life. She seemed totally unprepared, and my birth was long and difficult. (Seven years later, in her early forties, she would give birth to my brother Cooper.) The first four years of my life were spent with my mother in Old Town. In the evenings she played Chopin, Mozart, Strauss and the other romantic composers, leaving unforgettable memories as I drifted off to sleep.

Fig. 1-4
The Millikens (fourth and fifth from left) on a locating trip in Oregon.

Fig. 1-5
Camp headquarters. Here Abbie Milliken assisted her husband in working up the maps resulting from the survey.

Soon after I arrived, my father went back to work. Through letters and periodic visits home, my mother usually knew of my father's activities. While locating a line in Mexico,

Fig. 1-6
The Milliken home at 14 Oak Street in Old Town.

for example, he developed a rapport with a local farmer he needed for food supplies, and was surprised to discover he had befriended the famous bandit, Pancho Villa. Obviously another railway line would facilitate the business of train robbery, one source of Villa's income. But sometimes they lost touch. For example, my father contracted typhoid fever in Mexico and spent a month in a local hospital. By being careful of what he ate he managed to pull through, but as far as his wife and family knew he simply had disappeared.

My arrival posed a major problem for my parents. Accommodating a young child on a locating trip in the wilderness was not a practical option, and my father was forced to make a difficult decision. In 1915 he chose to come home to his family, leaving the work he loved so passionately. He soon joined George Hunt, the highly respected administrator of the Penobscot Indian Reservation, in establishing the firm of Hunt & Milliken for the manufacture of wooden handles. He never went west again.

In my hall bedroom, with its sloping ceiling, dark except for a thin shaft of light shining through the floor ventilator from the kerosene lamp in the room below, my father sat on the side of my bed and told me wondrous tales of adventure. I was four years old. His stories opened a window to the excitement life could hold. Among the stories he recounted in vivid detail was John Stevens' discovery of Marias Pass.

Marias Pass

By 1889, the Great Northern Railway had reached Havre, Montana, east of Glacier National Park. To compete with existing railways crossing the Rockies farther south, James J. Hill needed a direct route west to Spokane and thence to Seattle, but unless a pass could be discovered the Rockies were an impenetrable barrier. For years Indian legend had told of such a pass. Meriwether Lewis, of Lewis and Clark, had sought but failed to discover it from the west side. A determined Hill enlisted Stevens, who had a substantial reputation as a locating engineer. The search began in late autumn of 1889, at the onset of winter.

At Fort Assiniboine, a military post near Havre, Stevens was outfitted with a wagon, mule, saddle horse and supplies for the 180-odd-mile journey to a Blackfoot Indian Agency due west of Havre. If those Indians knew where a pass was, they showed little interest in divulging the location.

Stevens acquired snowshoes there and induced a Kalispell Indian to accompany him for the next stage. Heavy snow and severe weather were encountered near the foothills of

Fig. 1-7
William Milliken with his son and namesake during a visit home in 1912. I was four when father gave up railroad locating to return to Maine permanently.

the Rockies. The mule team was abandoned, and the two men proceeded on foot carrying food and blankets. Soon the Indian refused to go farther. Stevens left him with a small campfire and went on alone.

Two Medicine Creek flows eastward toward the Indian Agency along the route they had been following. It is fed by a number of creeks that flow down from the Continental Divide. Thus as he approached the Rockies, Stevens had a choice of several valleys leading into the mountains. He chose the more southern one. Struggling through snow and ice, he first reached a "false summit" and then walked straight into the pass at what he believed was the Continental Divide. Although late in the day, he continued into the valley on the western side to ensure this really was the Divide. After

Fig. 1-8a
Hunt & Milliken letterhead.

Fig. 1-8b
Drawing by cousin Bernice Breck of the company's factory where Peavy Cantdog handles and axe handles were manufactured.

As I grew older and experienced the heavy snows of a Maine winter, not infrequently walking to school in sub-zero temperatures, I often pondered the strength of character of a man like Stevens—alone at 5,000 feet on the Continental Divide in the Rockies, at night in the dead of winter, a temperature of 40 below, and miles from the nearest human.

Desperate situations with unpredictable outcomes often behoove one to ride them out. One of my father's own stories demonstrates this. As a railroad employee he enjoyed a travel pass that enabled him to ride on freights as well as passenger trains, and to choose his accommodations. On one freight train he chose to ride in the cab of the locomotive with the engineer and the fireman. The engineer, named Hood, was well known on the Great Northern for his competence and bravado, both of which he held in equal measure. He could couple the cars in the yard with hardly a jolt, but he also enjoyed setting record times whenever the opportunity arose.

Unfortunately, on this occasion Hood overran the designated siding, intentionally or inadvertently, and found himself heading for a collision with the regular Express, some miles ahead on the same track. In those days block signals and communication schemes were not universal, and unscheduled freight trains were charged with keeping the main line open. The only solution was to reach the next siding before the Express, which meant a maximum head of steam, full throttle, and hope for the best. As the train accelerated, the fireman and my father shoveled coal frantically to maintain steam pressure. Thanks to their long crank rods,

that he slogged back through the snow to the highest point of the pass and took aneroid readings. They indicated an altitude of 5,200 feet above sea level, well within the possibility of a railroad crossing without tunneling. Night had set in and the cold was intense, some 40 degrees below zero. He could not continue his return at night and any attempt to sleep would be fatal, so he tramped a path in the snow and walked back and forth until sunrise.

Stevens was the first white man to discover what would become known as Marias Pass, through which the Great Northern extended its westward construction to Spokane. Later he located the pass though the Cascades that bears his name, thus enabling the Great Northern to reach the coast and complete the northern transcontinental route.

these large steam locomotives were unbalanced in roll, and developed lateral oscillations that increased in frequency and amplitude as the engine speed increased. "Walking down the track" has been the phrase used since, as later investigation showed that the wheels on each side lifted off the rails. Only its huge inertial mass kept the locomotive from veering off the track. My father said that the rolling oscillation, frightening in itself, greatly added to the difficulty of shoveling coal into the firebox.

The wild ride continued. As they approached the next siding and reduced speed to enter it, smoke from the Express could be seen in the distance. Some of the freight cars still were on the main line as the two locomotives passed, but were dragged onto the siding just before the Limited barreled through.

My father told this story with such a sustained level of suspense that I always held my breath, wondering if they would make it.

Heroic Coopers

Adventurous tales came from my mother's side of the family, too. In 1849, at the age of 23, my grandfather William Ames Cooper (a descendant of Peter Cooper, who had arrived in this country in 1635) left for the California gold rush with a younger cousin. After a six-month sail on the good ship *Obed Mitchell* out of New Bedford, Massachusetts, they reached California. While rounding Cape Horn a terrific storm had been encountered that the captain predicted they would not survive. Grandfather, the older of the two boys, went to his cabin, lay down, and went to sleep. When he awoke the storm had abated. His full written account of the adventure still is in the family. My grandfather never found gold, but he took two more trips to California; one walking across the Isthmus of Panama, the other by transcontinental railway as a high school graduation trip for his oldest daughter, my Aunt Clara.

One of our most illustrious ancestors was General Peleg Wadsworth, who served under George Washington and was captured by the British. Imprisoned at Fort George in Castine, Maine, he used a hidden pocket knife to whittle out a circular exit from the wooden building, covering the crack with chewed-up bread. When a severe thunderstorm struck he forced the exit, struggled out, and ran down to the shore of Penobscot Bay where he hid in a hollow log. He finally rejoined the Continental Army. His daughter married Stevens Longfellow; one of their sons was Henry Wadsworth Longfellow, the poet.

According to family legend, in the winter of 1796–97 our ancestor Jesse Cooper and his friend Samuel Gray cut down the huge white pine trees that were used for two of the masts of the frigate *Constitution*. Thirty-six inches in diameter and nearly a hundred feet high, the trees were dragged by oxen to Sheepscot, and in the spring were floated down to Wiscasset to be towed by boat to Boston.

My grandmother Laura Augusta Cooper, born September 19, 1841, to Leonard and Abigail Cooper, lived her life in a large farmhouse that remains extant in Montville, Maine, some 40 miles from Old Town. Two of their eight children—Uncle Free (for Freeman) and Uncle Alex (for Alexander), as my mother referred to them, went into the carriage and sleigh business (Cooper Brothers–Carriage Makers) in West Searsmont, Maine. One took charge of the wood and paint shop, the other the foundry. The brothers became well known for the quality of their vehicles, which they sold as far west as Nevada. The Cooper Brothers sleigh, used in a record run from Portland to the Canadian border, was my first encounter with the intriguing business of record breaking.

THE HOME IN WHICH my brother Cooper and I grew up, and in which my mother lived her full 100 years, was built by my maternal grandfather. It had an attached barn on the first floor, in which he stalled two horses for deliveries from his meat and grocery store. Hay was delivered to the second floor "barn chamber" through a small door above the main front doors, with chutes to the stalls below. After my grandfather's death, when I was very young, the ground floor became a storage place for firewood and garden tools. The barn chamber became an attic and a treasure house with my grandfather's tools, family memorabilia and old trunks, all to be explored—except for one locked steamer trunk and the huge winter

Fig. 1-9
Milliken home, back yard. Abbie Milliken lived her full 100 years in this house.

sleeping bag used by my father that was neatly strapped up, never to be unrolled.

The barn was a playhouse too. A long wooden ladder hung from the ceiling about six feet above the floor, along with two trapeze-like swings my father had installed. My friend Paul "Peanut" Spruce and I would swing the length of the ladder hand-over-hand, or emulate circus performers, passing from one trapeze to the other, or chase each other down the hay chutes. In quiet moments on a summer's day, one could sit at the hay-loading door and dream.

Like many others in Old Town, our house left much to be desired in the way of comfort and convenience. Light was by kerosene lamp until my father personally wired the house for electricity in 1918 (although he always preferred the "softer" glow of a lamp for reading). The wood-burning kitchen stove was the primary source for cooking and heating water for the hot-water tank in the bathroom. In the early 1920s my father replaced the small wood-burning stove in the dining

room with an oil heater. Somewhat later he installed a Franklin stove in the parlor that proved to be a source of delight. None of the bedrooms was heated, and for "health reasons" bedroom windows always were wide open at night. One slept in flannel pajamas under feather comforters in beds warmed by heated soapstones. The floor in my room frequently was covered with snow from the howling winds of a winter storm. Central heating was not installed until a much later date.

That these conditions were inconvenient never occurred to me as a child, but they placed a further burden on a marriage that already was showing rifts. My mother abhorred cooking, housework and keeping the wood fires burning. Music remained her abiding interest. My father worked long hours at a business that held little of the challenge of his earlier career.

I was to experience the symptoms of their frustrations years before I could understand them. Night after night I crawled out of bed, pleading with them through the floor ventilator

Fig. 1-10
Milliken home, barn. In this winter scene note the attached barn with its high window in the barn chamber.

to stop arguing, and I remember spending dark days with my mother, depressed and endlessly crying.

To be exposed to so much unhappiness by parents who loved me dearly, though seldom expressing it in warm physical terms, was unsettling. I was confused by the conflicting signals. Nothing in my parents' behavior jibed with the heroic stories from both sides of the family. Because my mother viewed me as a weak and delicate child (perhaps a projection on her part), I spent a lot of time being treated for minor or imaginary illnesses. One of the "family doctors" was a fan of newfangled electrical alternatives to conventional medicine, and his office was filled with static spark generators, gas-filled tubes emitting purple heat waves and pulsating pads for electrical stimulation of the muscles. In my imagination it was another Frankenstein laboratory.

There was nothing in my environment to steer me into organized athletic activity, so I entered grade school with a lack of confidence in myself physically and became prey to all the bullies. I clearly remember the armistice celebrations of 1918, the parades, the fireworks, and burning the Kaiser in effigy. At the end of that year I became a victim of the influenza epidemic.

The remnants of our parents' marriage had a lifetime effect on both my brother and me as we pursued our individual careers. Cooper started his own architectural firm and designed several dozen elegant, modern residences throughout Maine. I worked in airplane flight test and aerodynamics, and later introduced aircraft technology into ground vehicles and race car handling. We hope that by our accomplishments we have given the memory of our parents the love they were unable to share with each other.

Way Down East

Following old Route 1 for about 150 miles, from Portland to 12 miles north of Bangor, brings one to an island in the Penobscot River that includes most of Old Town, part of Stillwater, and the original University of Maine campus. Marsh Island was first explored by the

French who sailed up the Penobscot River in the early 1600s, and it ultimately was acquired from the Abenaki Indians by John Marsh in 1777. More than a hundred years later, Old Town was established as an independent city.

Growing up, I was well aware of the Stillwater branch of the river flowing south on the west side via Gilman Falls to reunite with the main stream near the University. Like most youngsters, I was fascinated by the twin-lane covered wooden bridge connecting Old Town and Stillwater, its multiple diagonals going in both directions and the entire structure held together with wooden pegs. The highway bridge that crossed the main Penobscot River to Milford on the other side of town was more conventional, and figured prominently in our activities as we extended our bicycle range to Cold Stream Pond in Enfield.

Nineteenth-century Maine was a major center of the lumber industry. Old Town was at the southern border of a huge area of first-growth timber that was harvested in the winter at lumber camps distributed throughout northern Maine as far as the Allagash. Logs were loaded on sledges and dragged by oxen to frozen rivers and stream banks. In the spring they were floated down the Penobscot by a

complex of "booms." This was a huge and dramatic operation, replete with 30-foot-high log jams that were broken by the river men looking for the "key" logs.

One of the largest booms was the Argyle, a few miles north of Old Town which, according to one account, contained over six hundred acres of logs. Booms were preceded by the "drive," which collected the logs and organized their movement down the streams and branches into the main river. As explained in *Old Town, Maine—The First 125 Years—1840–1965:*

> The driving crew was divided into three parts—the head crew who kept the logs moving in front; the middle crew who kept the main body moving; and the rear group, the largest of all, who kept the rear moving and the shores free from any leftovers. This rear crew in bateaux was divided into seven men each and the head boatman was the boss. Among the well-known boatmen was Big Sabattus Mitchell who once ran his boat over Sourdnahunk Falls and lived to tell the tale. One of the big problems was transporting logs

Fig. 1-11
One of Old Town's two twin-lane wooden bridges; placing the two covered bridges together purportedly prevented horses from shying.

Fig. 1-12
Logging in Old Town. A log jam at Black Island Bridge above Indian Island.

across the lakes, where there was no current. In order to do this, the logs had to be boomed and hauled by a cable around a capstan on shore. Winding, sometimes all day and all night, on this capstan was one of the drivers' greatest tests of strength and endurance.

Once the logs were collected into the Argyle boom, the river men's task was completed and the driving boats raced the rest of the way to Old Town. As my mother well remembered, these rough, tough men, who had been cooped up in lumber camps during the winter, arrived in town with plenty of cash from their labors and wild for liquor and women.

To cope with this influx of logs, lumber mills dotted the area around Old Town and Bangor. The Penobscot was navigable up to the latter city, where great sailing ships were loaded with lumber for ports around the world.

Although much of the first-growth timber was gone by my childhood, many remnants of the lumbering era remained. My father dealt in long lumber at the sawmill he opened in 1929, and continued to manufacture handles, including those for the famous Peavy Cantdog.

This essential logger's tool was the invention of a Stillwater blacksmith, and for many years has been the tool of choice for handling logs. Pulp and paper mills also had become major wood-product users, and in those days Bangor still was a salt-water port with daily passenger boats to Boston, and ship chandlers could be found on the waterfront. In the 1920s Old Town was a city of only a few thousand, and one had only to walk a couple of miles in any direction to be in a dense forest.

Around Old Town

Over the years Old Town was served by a variety of railroads. The earliest line, inaugurated in 1836 and connecting Bangor and Old Town, has the distinction of being the first railway in New England and purportedly the second in the United States. It used two wood-burning Tom Thumb locomotives imported from England. After General Samuel Veazie, a local entrepreneur, acquired the line in 1854, its official name became the Bangor, Old Town and Milford line. The Old Veazie Railway, as the locals called it, ceased operation in 1870, but its route through the forest between Orono and Old Town remains, only partially overgrown. Early spring brought a

13

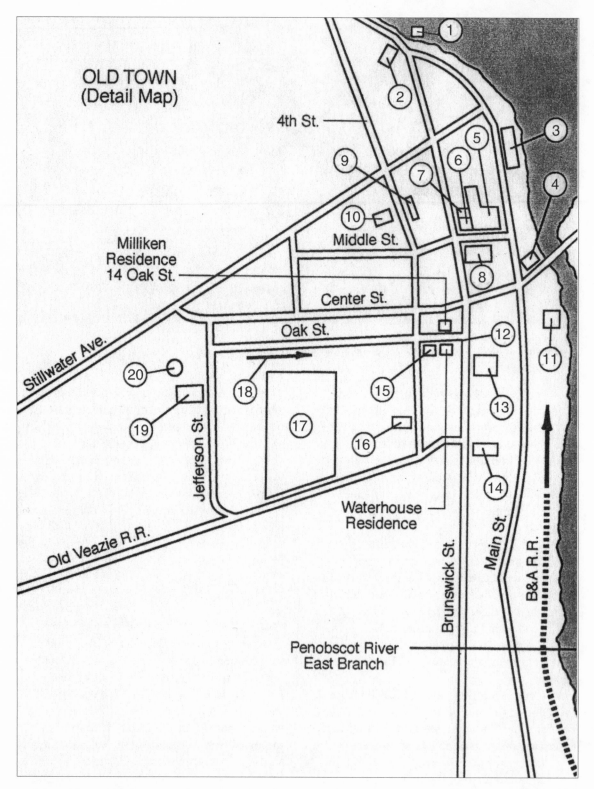

Fig. 1-13
Downtown Old Town, Maine, ca. 1920. 1) Indian Landing, 2) Indian Store, 3) Old Town Woolen Mill, 4) Chapman & Sons Machine Shop, 5) Old Town Canoe Company, 6) Firehouse, 7) Town Hall, 8) Carnegie Library, 9) Averill's Hedge, 10) Sam Gray's Garage (scene of M-l build), 11) Jordan Lumber Co., 12) Brown's Corner, 13) Helen Hunt Elementary School, 14) Convent School, 15) Cecil Godfrey residence, 16) Peanut Spruce residence, 17) Meadow (scene of skating and circus, 18) Academy Hill, 19) Academy Hill High School, 20) Water Tower. Map of Greater Old Town on p. 22.

Fig. 1-14
Old Town Canoe Company on right; Fire Department barn on left.

profusion of flowers alongside the path of the Old Veazie, and it was a delightful experience when the teacher took our kindergarten class for a hike along the route.

The Old Town Canoe Company was the principal business in town, and possibly the largest canoe manufacturer in the world at the time. Its wood and canvas canoes were derived from original Indian designs, and were painstakingly produced by skilled craftsmen in a labor-intensive operation. The White Canoe Company was much smaller, but well known for its specialized products. The Old Town Woolen Mill, built in 1898, employed a larger but less skilled workforce than Old Town Canoe. In a suburb the Penobscot Chemical and Fibre Company (PCF) made pulp products and was a large user of wood that was piled high in great pyramids. Its tall chimneys could be seen for miles, and if the wind was right plumes of pollutants and smell permeated Old Town. The PCF manager was a dignified gentleman who lived on the corner of our street and was always driven to work in a horse-drawn carriage. Among lesser businesses were the Jordan Lumber Company,

Sewell Civil Engineering and Surveying, Bickmore Gall Cure (a salve for horses, of local invention), Chapman & Sons Machine Shop, and Hunt & Milliken. The James W. Sewell Surveying Company, now in its third generation, became famous for aerial surveying. Today, Old Town Canoe remains a prominent producer of fiberglass canoes and boats, while continuing to meet the demand for wood and fabric canoes.

Ralph Chapman, the second-generation owner of Chapman & Sons Machine Shop, lived a few houses up Oak Street and was a close friend of my family. His shop was a complete facility, with its own design capability, pattern making and foundry. A self-educated first-class inventor, Ralph developed an electrically powered launch as a teenager, later producing an electrical muscle-stimulating massage machine known as the Morse Wave Generator, and an early automatic drafting machine. His most outstanding invention, a process for making paper plates directly from wet wood pulp, resulted in Old Town Pulp Products, a new industry that has been widely copied. When I became involved in making

Figs. 1-15a,b
Academy Hill High School and the standpipe alongside, its ladder an invitation for adventurous boys to climb.

which was part of Route 1 and one of the first concrete roads in New England.

The Flat ended at the top of Academy Hill, a mile-long steep hill into town leading onto Main Street near the east side of the Island. This was our site for coasting, on sleds, double runners, toboggans and bicycles. At the top of the hill was Academy Hill High School. Next to it was the 100-foot-high standpipe, the town's water supply, with an external ladder from bottom to top that was a perpetual challenge to climb and then hang by one hand from the top rung.

Northwest on Main Street, roughly paralleling the Penobscot River, was "Indian Landing" and the ferry to Indian Island Reservation. The Indians used bateaux, the shallow river craft pointed on both ends and propelled by oars, that had been developed during logging drives, for the trip that took all of 15 minutes. The Island was by far the largest in the Penobscot anywhere near Old Town. The Indian population, which was concentrated on the lower end, led a quiet life under its own chief and government. Their principal industry

small ground vehicles, I always could turn to Ralph Chapman for a machined part or design help. During World War II his company produced components for Wright Aeronautical aircraft engines.

BEFORE THE INTERSTATE, one approached Old Town from Stillwater on a two-mile straight stretch of road known as "The Flat,"

Fig. 1-16
Ferry to Indian Island.

was basket making and souvenirs, which were sold in an Indian store near the landing. One Abenaki family was especially well known. After training by his father on a footpath that ran around the edge of the Island, Andrew Sockalexis became a great long-distance runner and competed successfully in the Swedish Olympics in 1912. Louis Sockalexis probably was more famous as a baseball player, ironically with the Cleveland Indians. These legendary athletes still were much talked about when I was a child.

Beyond Indian Landing, on the outskirts of Old Town proper, was Bachelor's Field, so named for its eccentric owner. He lived with an aging mother in a huge house that I equated with the House of Shaws in Robert Louis Stevenson's *Kidnapped*. As kids we kept a respectful distance from the house, since Bachelor was reputed to shotgun trespassers with rock salt. The field itself, a large pasture sloping up to Blueberry Hill, was an ideal place to try out gliders. My father rented space there to store piles of long lumber from his adjacent sawmill. Just behind the mill lay the tracks of the Bangor and Aroostook Railway. Beyond that, along the river, was the old swimming hole on the site of the former Gray's sawmill. This was where I finally learned to swim, in murky waters filled with sawdust stirred up from the river bottom.

Although I never officially worked at Hunt & Milliken, I spent hours there assisting my father in bagging handles for shipment, and used the band saws and other machinery on my own vehicle projects. Because he had customers in Bangor, he and I frequently caught the noon Bangor and Aroostock steam train out of Old Town, arriving at the main central depot in Bangor, the terminus of trains from northern Maine and from the south. The locomotives all were steam powered, and I have vivid mental pictures of the arrival of the Bar Harbor Express from New York and Boston in the winter, encrusted in sleet and occasionally following a snowplow.

At the nearby Eastern Maine Steamship dock, a dingy ship chandler was a customer for my father's handles, so we often stopped there. Its eccentric owner was fond of spinning yarns of his sailing experiences. The place was low, with ancient roof beams, and filthy with the smell of tarred rope. I always thought the chandler must have been a pirate in his younger days.

Because my father was well liked in Old Town, neighbors dropped by his office routinely. The most fascinating were the Woodman brothers, both Civil War veterans and well into their eighties. One day, sitting by my father's desk in the office, Johnny Woodman began telling me about his experiences at the Battle of Gettysburg during Pickett's charge. At that time, this was a defining American military episode. I regret now that I was too young to appreciate the import of what he was telling me and missed the opportunity to quiz him further about it.

The railway disappeared beyond Blueberry Hill. There were no roads, only the railroad ties to walk on. With his keen sense of "locating," my father said it was a logical place for an airport and so it became, years later.

To complete the circuit around Old Town, we rode our bikes north on Gilman Falls Avenue, a gravel road in those days, to the Falls itself on the West Branch of the Penobscot, and then west to Stillwater. Or we could bear east along a high ridge called the Horseback that passed by Cy Green's horse race track, unused for most of the summer and a neat place for an impromptu bicycle or motorcycle race.

The Seasons

In the 1920s and 1930s seasons in Maine were clearly demarcated. When winter came, there was no doubt about it. After the first storm, a single-bladed sidewalk snowplow pulled by a draft horse left a narrow path on Oak Street with walls a couple of feet high on both sides. It was time to get out the skis and toboggans. The former were mostly homemade, with their tips bent upward in the "steamer" at the canoe factory. Toboggans were one-man size and more usable on snow than sleds with narrow runners.

My favorite sport was throwing a rope over the rear bumper of a passing car at the corner of Center and Fourth Street for a free ride up Academy Hill and down The Flat to Stillwater, the driver none the wiser. If The Flat was well plowed, mile-a-minute speeds were common and traveling that close to the ground was a real thrill. As Stillwater was approached I released my rope, drifted off to the side and waited for a return tow.

Jumping off rooftops into the snow was another high priority. Peanut Spruce was something of an expert in this endeavor. He could leap out our barn window, tuck into a somersault, and hit the snow feet first. Among the tallest barns was Dr. Porter's at the bottom of our backyard. It had a very steep pitched roof that ended some 30 feet off the ground. By maneuvering onto the roof at a lower point, we could launch ourselves from the peak, gain speed on the pitch and shoot off into space

Figs. 1-17a,b
Old Town winters. Bill Milliken in front of the barn and "ski jumping" in the backyard.

before the fall down to the snow field below. Once you left the peak you were committed.

On cold winter nights I hiked up to the top of Academy Hill with my toboggan and coasted down the natural chute of a dimly lighted sidewalk with high snow banks. The surface was icy and rough enough to add to the fun, and there was no stopping once you started. Walkers, sensing the situation, would climb up the sides.

During the winter big double-runners appeared on Oak Street for the coast down to the Helen Hunt School. These were heavy planks, up to 20 feet long, supported on two sleds, the front one steerable. The steersman, presumably the owner, sat up front and as many as fifteen kids piled on behind, including the last two or three who were the "pushers." A road surface beaten down by sleighs and delivery vehicles was ideal for a double-runner, which would pick up speed at an alarming rate. The turn at Brown's corner, a real sweeper, had to be negotiated with all the passengers leaning inward. Occasionally the double-runner rolled over in spectacular fashion, with a great tangle of passengers and much yelling and screaming. When I was very young my father made me a miniature double-runner, painted red, as a Christmas present. It accommodated three or four children and survives to this day in the Old Town Museum.

The river always froze during the winter. Blocks of ice were sawed out, packed in sawdust and stored in an ice house for delivery during the summer. Nobody had a refrigerator; instead everyone had a metal-lined wooden icebox. About once a week a horse-drawn wagon showed up, and the ice man picked up a 40-pound block with tongs and slung it over his leather-covered back. As he was doing this, the children rushed out to collect bits of ice from the tail board.

Not infrequently the river froze before the snows came, providing the opportunity for skating and iceboating. Probably because of river currents, the thickness of the ice varied, especially in early winter, and serious accidents resulted when a skater broke through. I was not much of a skater, and had one really close shave. Skating near the northern end of Indian Island, heading back to the Old Town side, I heard an ominous cracking behind me. Fortunately I had sense enough to keep skating as fast as possible until I was back on solid ice.

Most of the iceboats were powered by sail, but an ingenious employee of the Canoe company who lived near us constructed a motorized, air-propelled machine. I followed the development closely. The airboat proved to be very fast but had control problems. Despite this, the owner decided to take it on a long run upriver. Heading for a pier, he couldn't decide whether to pass on the left or right and ran into one of the abutments, demolishing the boat and nearly demolishing himself.

At the foot of Academy Hill, over toward the old Veazie, was a large meadow that tended to be marshy in the fall. Before the heavy snows it became a maze of frozen trails among patches of tall grass. With bonfires lit, skaters cruised out into the darkness, then back into the firelight. On a cloudless night, with the stars hanging low overhead, it was a magical sight. I was too young to have a partner, but the romance of skating arm-in-arm didn't escape me.

Winters never were dull. There were serious frozen snowball battles with the convent school, and attempts to build igloos and snow forts. One morning when I was eating breakfast, Peanut Spruce skied over and, feeling thirsty, went to our drinking water pump across the street. He placed one hand and his mouth on the spout and the other on the iron handle. He was stuck in three places until we came to his rescue with warm water.

Once the Sewall family gave a winter house party at their cottage on Pushaw Pond, ten miles out of Old Town. A group of us from junior high school were there. When the party ended in the early evening, the plan was to regather at their home for dancing and late-night refreshments. The journey to town was made in the Sewells' large toboggan, which they towed behind their car. The last man on the toboggan was Francis Lord, his legs locked alongside the person ahead of him. As the tow car accelerated, the passengers moved aft a bit and the seat of his pants slid off the end. By the time we reached Old Town, his tail was half frozen and his pants had worn through. Bare-assed he created a sensation, particularly among the young girls at the party.

Fig. 1-18
Old Town Trolley. The Millikens, father and son, took it to Bangor every December to see the toys at a department store.

Winter also brought Christmas. Every year my father and I visited the toy department on the top floor of Freese Department Store in Bangor. For years I was amazed at how Santa Claus could stock the very toys that had appealed to me. We usually made the trip on the electric trolley car, which made numerous stops in the 12 mile trip and took about an hour. Its swaying and lurching gave the impression we had traveled much farther. The seats were electrically heated, a joy in the winter if you were so fortunate as to get one and not have to make the trip as a straphanger.

With March and April came the renewal of interest in kites, spring break and the approach of summer. It also was maple syrup time, and heralded the appearance of Mr. Ham of West Old Town with light brown first-run syrup and maple candy.

SUMMER IN MAINE has its own special delights, and is a wonderful contrast to the rugged winters. Lengthening days and blue skies begged for an expansion of our bicycle and hitchhiking activities. Generally, however, I remember long, lazy afternoons and streets lined with stately elms along which one could wander

to the Carnegie Library and browse among the shelves. For one of the few times in my life, time moved slowly with no urgency. But even those days were punctuated with events like Chautauqua, the gypsies or the circus.

Arriving by train, the circus was packed into a number of special cars painted in bright colors and left on a siding near the station. We kids always were on hand to see the unloading, and to watch the parade to the tent site near Academy Hill. The wild animals rode in cages; the elephants walked. Putting up the big top and the sideshow tents was not to be missed. The circus was a one-night stand, which I saw from the bleachers with my folks. I was ready for bed by the time the circus wagons paraded back to the station with the steam calliope playing, Looking out the window I had that "journey proud" feeling that something mysterious had touched our lives and was disappearing as quickly as it came.

The arrival of the gypsies was mysterious. Nobody seemed to know where they came from, they just appeared with their decorated wagons. Rumors said they stole horses and even children, so there was a certain apprehension in town and parents kept an eye on their kids.

Fig. 1-19
Summers in Old Town included quiet afternoons at Carnegie Library.

The gypsies parked for a few days in the town square, sold souvenirs, and then one morning they were gone.

Most of the other traveling shows came by train, like the week's visit by the Chautauqua, and the one-night minstrel shows and plays that rented the town hall. "Polly of the Circus" was a great hit and even had a white horse on stage (probably on loan from the fire department). But it was the romantic implications that touched us preteen boys and put our imaginations into high gear.

Routine events that characterized summer months were the knife sharpener man, the extract peddler, and the hand-organ man and his monkey, who paraded up Fourth Street like a pied piper with a chain of children following behind. Then there was the unexpected, like the bull moose that casually walked the length of Main Street, or the overflow of the Penobscot River that brought down the railway bridge to Milford, forcing people to shop in canoes.

The era of jazz and the flapper, the Roaring Twenties, eventually reached conservative New England, and with it, the Charleston. In fox trots and waltzes couples danced close, even cheek to cheek, with the man leading and his partner following. With its high-speed gyrations, the Charleston was another activity altogether and became a feature of the dances that followed basketball games and the shows in the Town Hall. I decided it was my best hope for making out with the local gals. Night after night, with a hand-cranked Victrola and fortified by cranberry juice, I practiced in our kitchen. Soon I was good enough to acquire some outstanding partners, one an Indian girl. Together we came close to winning a contest in the Town Hall.

The Charleston was great exercise and improved my general dancing confidence. For years ballroom dancing was my primary way of securing female companionship. Ultimately I would dance in stellar venues all over the country: the Copley Plaza, the Statler and the Egyptian Room (Boston); the Georgian Room and Bowl at the Olympic Hotel (Seattle); the Fairmont (San Francisco); the Statler and Carlton (Washington); the Starlight Roof, Waldorf Astoria and Hawaiian Room at the Lexington (New York); and the Chamberlain (Old Point Comfort, Virginia). All wonderful memories that had their origin in Old Town.

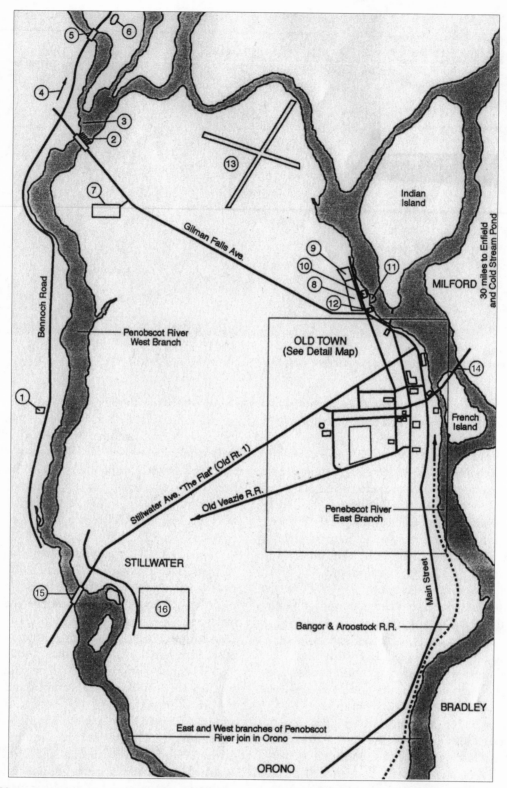

Fig. 1-20
Greater Old Town, Maine, ca. 1920. 1) Cooper Milliken residence [current], 2) Gilman Falls Dam, 3) Old Swimming Hole, 4) "Horseback," 5) Covered Bridge, 6) Cy Green's Horse Race Track, 7) Gray's Field (scene of Ralph Brown's airplane), 8) Bachelor's Field, 9) Blueberry Hill, 10) Hunt & Milliken Co., 11) Gray's Mill Swimming Hole, 12) Johnny Woodman residence, 13) Old Town Airport, 14) Bridge to Milford, 15) Covered bridge in Stillwater, 16) University of Maine campus.

Chapter 2

Wheels, Skis and Propellers

My first cousins, Eddie and Frank Waterhouse, lived in a large home across the street from us. Uncle Willie was a successful lawyer and insurance agent and, at one time, mayor of Old Town. Aunt Clara, my mother's older sister, was a semi-invalid who always claimed to have an upside-down stomach. She spent much time in their bedroom on the second floor, which became the central meeting place in the home.

Because we were only four months apart in age, Frank and I were inseparable as children, but by the time I turned nine my interests were shifting to those of Eddie, who was six years older. The collection of racing car pictures that covered the walls of his room fascinated me, and I think he recognized my mechanical inclinations. He also saw that I was socially less adept than his brother Frank, who played several musical instruments, was more popular with the girls and became president of our high school class. Without ever announcing it Eddie became a sort of mentor to me, turning my childhood lonesomeness into productive channels.

To my knowledge, no one else in town was interested in racing cars. Except for two years on the horse track at the Bangor Fair, automobile racing did not exist in Maine. The board track in Rockingham (New Hampshire) had not yet been built. I recently have wondered what sparked Eddie's race car enthusiasm. His sons Jonathan and Bill have no specific clues, nor does his brother Frank, although he notes that automobiles *per se* still were a source of some wonder during this period. Uncle Willie acquired his first automobile (an Overland) in 1914, when few people in Old Town owned one. He traded in the Overland for a Willys-Knight with a sleeve-valve engine, and during the early twenties bought a Packard Single Six. Thus

Aero-Triple-Cycle (1928), powered by Indian Scout motor with light airplane structure. One of my favorite machines.

All men dream, but the dreamers of the day act their dream with open eyes to make it possible.

– T. E. Lawrence

Fig. 2-1
Cousins Frank and William. Born four months apart, we were inseparable as children.

Fig. 2-2
A characteristic pose for Ed Waterhouse, a great reader and student all his life. Six years older than I, Ed interested me in race cars and became a mentor.

Eddie was exposed to cars from a young age. By late high school and college he was driving the family machine, which doubtless increased his popularity with the opposite sex, as well as his appreciation of cars in general.

During the summer months, the Waterhouses and the Millikens held Sunday picnics in Bar Harbor. Both families rode in the Willys-Knight, with Frank and me on the jump seats. We passed scores of chauffeur-driven cars

Fig. 2-3
The collection of race car pictures on the wall of Ed Waterhouse's room. This collection now resides in the Watkins Glen Motor Racing Research Library.

parked near the various churches in Bar Harbor—such varied makes as Minerva, Lancia, Isotta Fraschini, Rolls-Royce, Locomobile, Straker-Squire, Mercedes and Benz (the companies hadn't yet merged). They were owned by wealthy summer residents, and certainly would have excited Eddie's interest in automobiles, if not specifically in race cars. He was also exposed to the Marmon owned by the Cogswell family in town (with its manual exhaust cutout, it put out a great sound!) as well as the Stutzes owned by the Grays of the Old Town Canoe Company. For a time there was a Rolls-Royce agency in Bangor. Eddie always hung out at the two main garages in town, one run by Ted Swan, a contemporary, the other by the Sylvester brothers, all practical, versatile mechanics who we imagined would have done well at Indianapolis if given the chance.

Eddie's picture collection grew exponentially during his college years at the University of Maine when he discovered early copies of *Motor Age* in the dome of the old library. Soon clippings of the Vanderbilt Cup, Elgin and Santa Monica road races, among others, began to appear on the long wall of his bedroom.

These racing pictures must have captured my interest by or before 1920. I distinctly remember Jimmy Murphy's French Grand Prix win at Le Mans in 1921. The picture thumb-tacked on Eddie's wall was captioned, "Bringing home the bacon— America's first win in a European Road Race."

I spent hours with him discussing different race cars and drivers, or helping him cut out and tack up new pictures gleaned from the *Police Gazette*, *The New York Times* rotogravure section, or the two British magazines *Autocar* and *Motor.*

For years Eddie and I subscribed to the *Indianapolis*

Fig. 2-4
Duesenberg No. 4 with Maurice Burr and Ed Waterhouse, the constructors. I was the proud driver.

Fig. 2-5
Duesie No. 4. My Indianapolis pose.

Star during the month of May and bet milkshakes on the winner. In the twenties, Duesenbergs and Millers dominated the field.

At first we were strong fans of the Duesies but later switched allegiance to the Millers as they progressed from two-seater rear drive to the single-seater rears that eliminated the riding mechanic, then to the early front drives, and finally to four-wheel drive.

My First Specials

Eddie's enthusiasm distracted me from my problems at home. What young boy would not have been drawn to the thrills and pageantry of such a heroic, dangerous and adventurous sport? In 1922

Fig. 2-6
Our earliest "push car," the result of my fascination with Ed's race car interests. I was 8–9 years old.

Eddie decided to design a push car replica of a race car for me, and my life became focused for the first time. Our barn chamber was turned into a race shop. Using wood from the Old Town Canoe Company, he and his friend Maurice "Mossy" Burr built a Duesenberg reminiscent of Jimmy Murphy's French Grand Prix winner of 1921. It was a tight little two-seater carrying No. 4, and was followed in 1923

by a Miller bearing No. 1. Behind the wheel of these cars I was thrilled beyond words.

My decision to design my own was a logical progression. This absorbing work was carried on in the midst of more usual youthful adventures, and led to several action-packed years. During the summer months I passed up nearly all social activity. My parents were entirely supportive of these vehicle projects. Although I never gave it a thought at the time, they must have sensed I was laying the foundation for a career.

My diaries from the mid-twenties are a good record of my thinking and the progress of the projects. Ed was a prolific photographer, and from his photos and letters I can piece together what happened and when. In a way we were hobbyists building fairly elaborate toys, but the intensity of our interest and labor elevated it above pure play. Friends frequently would invite my parents to picnics down on the coast or other social outings, but I usually ducked out because it was so much more fun to spend the day working alone in the barn chamber.

The origins of this first design effort are somewhat obscure. My memory says my father had visited a relative engaged in a small woodworking business near Newport, Maine, and while there picked up wooden wheels or had them made. Studying the

Fig. 2-7
Staged accident with No. 4 Duesenberg, off the road and heading for a "rollover."

photograph, the steering wheel appears identical to the road wheels. Given these important parts, producing a simple vehicle of this kind was a small step.

With the exception of the baby-carriage wheels, I think Ed and Mossy did remarkably well with this two-seat Indianapolis car. Note the Duesenberg insignia on the radiator. Throughout the summer of 1922, coasting down hills or with a friend pushing, I won many imaginary races in this car and felt much closer to the drivers and events depicted in the pictures on Ed's walls. As fall approached, Ed and Mossy decided it was time for me to experience another aspect of racing: an accident. This event was staged on the bank by the corner of the Waterhouse garage. I tumbled out unhurt, a hero of sorts, and began to think that crashes were not

so bad after all, a belief that would be reinforced often in the future.

Early in January of 1923 I sent a photograph of No. 4 to the Duesenberg

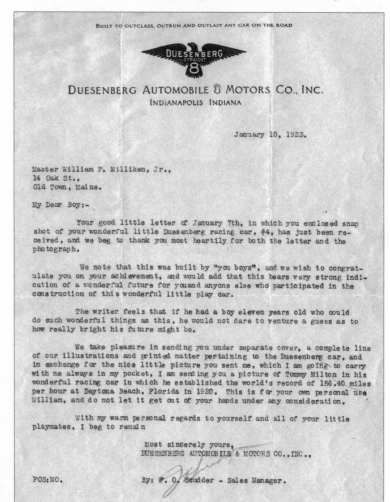

Fig. 2-8
Letter from Duesenberg Motor Co. after I sent them photos of our push car No. 4; Enclosed photograph with Duesenberg letter of Tommy Milton's record-breaking twin-engined car.

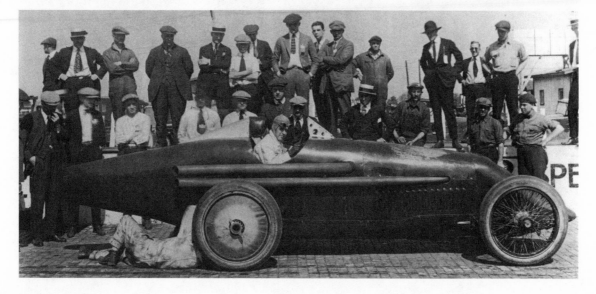

Fig. 2-9
Light car, 1923. Staged accident with "special effects." Frank threw the gravel (at top of picture) to produce some animation.

Company in Indianapolis and received a nice letter back from Sales Manager F. O. Scudder. He also sent a photo of Tommy Milton's world record car with the twin-engined Duesenberg straight eights, which I contributed to Ed's collection.

Later I sent the company a sketch of a rakish roadster that I imagined would look good on a Duesenberg chassis. Again, I received a nice acknowledgment, this time from Service Manager H. B. Blank.

While Ed and Mossy were thinking about a replica of a single-seat Duesenberg or Miller, I cranked out a light machine using some available wire wheels. Another accident was staged with this car, on the banking in front of the Waterhouse home. As the "director," Ed arranged for Frank to throw out a handful of dirt just as he took the photo. This certainly added the impression of speed to a static rendition and was not the last time we employed "special effects." I can't help but believe that this extensive exercise of the imagination in childhood was an asset to creative activity later in life.

I have the fondest memories of No. 1 Miller, which had elegant lines and even today

Fig. 2-10
No. 1 Miller. Mossy Burr on left and Ed Waterhouse. None of the real race cars I was to drive in later years produced the thrill of the No.1 Miller. It now resides in the Old Town Museum.

possesses the visual artistry of those great classic rear-drives. Like the one toy you always hoped Santa Claus would bring, this little car met all my aspirations.

Eddie and Mossy started construction on July 16. By the end of the month the chassis, axles, wheels, steering, and frames for the body were completed, and we slid the car down the ladder from the barn chamber to check out the steering. Testing at chassis stage was a common practice in the auto industry. We knew there were plenty of unbodied Duesenbergs running around Indianapolis and sought to emulate them. After testing, the car went back to the barn chamber for coachwork.

At that crucial point, cousin Frank decided to attend a two-week session at a YMCA summer camp in Enfield. In earlier years what Frank did, I did, and vice versa, so my folks insisted I go to camp too. I argued against it to no avail, and Eddie drove us up on August 3, dropping us off in the woods by the lake. To add to my misery, it was raining and dismal. After a few days we both were homesick, if for different reasons, and decided to run away.

Fig. 2-11
No. 1 Miller, top rear view.

Neither of us enjoyed the routine of getting up early, pulling on a wet bathing suit and plunging into cold water. We made it to the farm of family friends, where Doris Round

Fig. 2-12
The No. 1 Miller. Test of the steering and running gear before completing the body. This "push car" simulated the great rear-drive, single-seat Millers that swept Indianapolis.

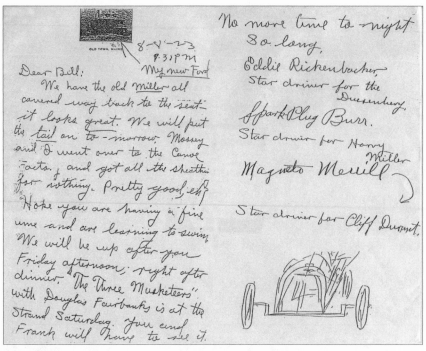

Fig. 2-13
Letter from Ed Waterhouse during the week I was in Enfield with Frank at the "horrible" YMCA summer camp.

Murphy, Ralph De Palma and Tommy Milton would stick it out. You can't quit now with only a week to go." I stayed. Eddie came up the next weekend and I drove the Willys-Knight most of the way home. Those few words had a lifetime of meaning for me. No matter how great the incentive to do otherwise, there are times when one must stay the course.

Miller No. 1 was finally completed and launched on August 27. With its white paint job and shiny black lettering, it looked stunning.

gave us a decent meal, and a phone call home brought a promise from Eddie to pick us up. Simultaneously, I received a letter from Eddie, noting exciting progress on the Miller.

When Eddie arrived, he took me aside as our stuff was being loaded into the car and said: "I know you don't like this place but you signed up for two weeks. I think Jimmy

Sometime the following month, when we got tired of pushing it around, Ed suggested we tow it behind the Willys. Whipping down Oak Street, we made the corner at Brunswick Street and accelerated up to 25 mph or so when the left front wooden wheel broke. The car collapsed on the axle with a violent pulse in the steering wheel and was enveloped in a cloud of

Fig. 2-14
No. 1 Miller, limit cornering. Pusher disappearing, top left.

Fig. 2-15
Waterhouse's Willys-Knight towing car. My early driving experience at the wheel.

dust as the axle dragged along the gravel road. I hung on and crawled out unhurt.

Giving serious thought to this incident, I concluded that if I wasn't willing to put up with accidents or tried too hard to avoid them, I would miss out on a lot in life.

Eddie Waterhouse entered the University of Maine in the fall of 1923. While he was still close by, his responsibilities and interests were expanding. We stayed very close, but I became the driving force behind the projects that ensued.

Gliders, 1924

In March of 1924 I constructed a hang glider with a 20-foot span and a 4-foot chord (80-square-foot area), using a bamboo frame covered with cotton cloth. Peanut Spruce and I carried it up to Bachelor's Field across from my father's mill. Blueberry Hill wasn't very high nor was there much wind. We had a lot of fun running down the hill but never took off. In hindsight I know why; if the glider and

"pilot" weighed 130 pounds and we could have achieved a lift coefficient of 0.5 (highly unlikely), we still would have needed a 35 mph relative wind. We concluded the wing area was too small and dismantled the glider in April.

Fig. 2-16
Shaw 2-½ hp motor and the Shaw Speedster.

Later I tried again with a much larger wing covered with shellacked paper, but it had a very poor airfoil shape. The test site this time was the high bank along the route of the old Veazie railroad, and a good wind was blowing. When Peanut rotated the wing to get some angle of attack before rushing down the bank, he was blown over backward and wrapped up in the wreckage. Following a rebuild, later attempts failed. As I learned more about aeronautics I concluded that the glider stalled at a very low angle of attack and produced a very high drag.

Shaw Single-Cylinder Engine, 1924

My first powerplant was a single-cylinder, 2-½ hp Shaw manufactured in Galesburg, Kansas, that I saw in a *Popular Mechanics* ad. Originally intended for bicycle use, the motor was designed to be clamped to the frame, driving the rear wheel via a narrow V-belt pulley. But Shaw also had designed and produced the components for a small, two-seat cyclecar using this engine: the Shaw Speedster. This vehicle had a flat, buckboard frame of five wooden slats, and the rear wheels were driven by V-belts through a countershaft that slid back and forth to tighten the drive belts, thus acting as a clutch. For 25 cents I bought the speedster plans, but the components were too expensive to consider. However, with help from my folks and saving every nickel over a couple of years,

I was able to order an available second-hand motor.

It arrived in October 1924 and was first installed on my bicycle. In theory one started the motor by pedaling the bicycle with a loose V-belt, and then tightening it up. But it was a cranky little engine, and even with Peanut Spruce pushing and priming the carburetor with ether from Dr. Preble (the lady physician next door), our success was intermittent.

In the next experiment we installed the engine on the No. 1 Miller, first with the idea of driving one rear wheel and later with a countershaft. By then it was November and working in the barn had become a chilly affair. Picking up again the following March, I finally admitted that the 2-½ hp (and unreliability) of the Shaw engine prohibited the construction of a successful powered vehicle.

Although 1924 was not a successful "vehicle year" with the failed glider attempts and the Shaw motor, there were compensations. Eddie and I were tracking automobile racing events, and my diary is filled with references to Tommy Milton, Harlan Fengler, Harry Hartz, Jimmy Murphy, Eddie Herne, and old-timers like Barney Oldfield and Eddie Rickenbacker. Four-wheel brakes were the latest thing, and Rolls-Royces were being built in Springfield, Massachusetts. Jimmy Murphy got the pole at Indy and the Boyer/Corum Duesenberg won. I found out that Harry Hartz had built and driven cyclecars in his youth in California—an

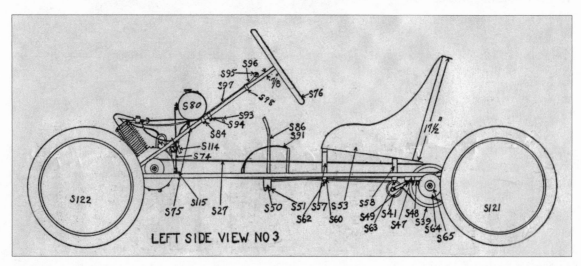

Fig. 2-17
Details of the Shaw Speedster.

incentive for me to push ahead on my own vehicle projects. For my birthday, my parents gave me a subscription to *Motor* magazine. Publicity about the 80-mph Wing Special single-seater excited people of all ages.

By now I was developing a side interest in airplanes. My friends and I also were expanding our bicycle excursions to Enfield 30 miles away, making it in four hours on our one-speeds and returning in three. My attention in school lagged as I dreamed of various adventures and became bored with studies. I knew I was heading for trouble and wrote in my diary, "If they send me to Mr. E. B. Williams (the Principal) I don't care. I'll stand on my own rights." Of course it happened and I had to spend a period each day in his office. It turned out that he was interested in sailboats and we had a great time discussing them. He never let on that I was not being punished.

On September 15, Jimmy Murphy was killed on the dirt track at the Syracuse Fair Grounds in upstate New York. Race accidents were common, and other race drivers had been killed, but Murphy had been a great favorite. Eddie and I felt a personal loss. For Christmas I got a pair of goggles to go with the cloth racing helmet my mother had made.

Fifth Car, 1925

One of Eddie's college fraternity brothers remembered seeing the remains of an Imp cyclecar in a junkyard near his home in Gray, Maine, and on spring break, he had it shipped by freight to Old Town. When the delivery notice arrived in early May, Peanut Spruce and I rushed down to the yard to collect it. The body and frame were missing but the wheels, brakes, front and rear axles, and some steering components were reasonably intact. The well-worn, flat tires were usable when taped to the rims. My mother took a deep breath as we dragged all these bits and pieces into the barn, but I viewed it as a great haul that would put an incremental jump into the vehicle projects— and I was right.

Producing a frame was the first task. My father had some well-seasoned, inch-thick clear hickory planks. I laid out frame rails for a wheelbase of about eighty inches, with a four-inch beam depth at the center tapering to two inches at each axle, with suitable kick-up over the axles. We cut the planks on the big band saw at the mill, then mounted the axles directly to the frame without springs. Using the Imp steering components and our own steering wheel, shaft and parts of the linkage, we cobbled up a steering arrangement. We had no conventional gearbox, so the steering was very direct with a fast ratio. It worked, but was a challenge to drive.

Still without a suitable engine, the best Peanut and I could do with this rig at the time was have it towed behind a car. Eddie was in college, so we had to look further. My mother had a live-in housekeeper who had a boyfriend who came around in the evening to "spoon" with her in the kitchen. With suitable compensation, he agreed to tow our newest creation. The athletic field at the middle school had a new cinder quarter-mile running track that was the pride and joy of the coach. School had just ended and the coach was not in evidence, so we used his track for our towing tests. We got up to 45 mph sliding around on the end of the tow rope. It was great sport and the closest thing to real racing I had experienced. Our tires left grooves in the track and, as usual, we were in trouble with the school authorities.

First Motorcycle, 1925

Word gets around in a small town, and in the fall of 1925 I heard of a motorcycle that might be for sale. It was a 1914 Excelsior Twin with a 74-cubic-inch engine, the "Harley Hog" of its day. I later learned this was the same model as Charles Lindbergh's first cycle, which he had driven to the top of Pike's Peak. The owner, Alvin Thompson, had used the Excelsior as a touring bike with a second seat, fenders, lights, etc. He took me for a ride and demonstrated that this machine was no slouch.

I wanted it more than anything I could remember, but I was 14 and my folks were adamant. Motorcycles were hazardous and my track record regarding accident avoidance hardly was exemplary. Nevertheless, I went to work and finally convinced my father to see the machine and find out its price. Thompson offered it for 15 dollars, so the cost was not

Fig. 2-18
My first motorcycle, a 1914 Excelsior. A temperamental but potent machine that I dearly loved.

prohibitive. Arguments with my parents went on for days. This was one of the toughest sales jobs I ever faced. But they finally gave in, and on October 19, 1925, I rolled the motorcycle into the barn.

The Excelsior promised to attract the attention of girls, but especially one girl in particular, Agatha, who returned every summer to her parents' camp in Enfield. My cousin Frank, Braley Gray (son of Old Town Canoe president Sam Gray) and I were equally smitten. I had named my bicycle for Agatha and regularly danced with her at socials. Frank, whose house was next to the one in which she was staying, created a tin-can communication system to her bedroom with a wire between the houses that I would periodically tear down.

One Sunday, when I heard that Braley Gray had left for Enfield on his bicycle, presumably to call on Agatha, I took off on in hot pursuit. Although handicapped by a flat front tire held on the rim by electrical tape, my bike was a

stripped-down affair, very light and racy, while Braley's was a new but heavy cruising machine. By nothing short of a heroic effort I caught up with him and we arrived at her cottage together. Her mother informed us that Agatha was boating with another suitor but invited us in, served us some soup and insisted we lie down and rest before beginning our long return journey. I learned that infatuation can be an exhausting business.

Although competitors, Frank and I were so desperate to see Agatha that we reluctantly decided to join forces. One day during the summer the Excelsior arrived and we decided to use the motorcycle to make the trip. Neither of us had the strength to kick-start it so we had to depend on coasting down a hill or organizing kids to push us. Starting that day was not helped by the dry cells we had fitted in place of the normal wet-cell motorcycle battery that no longer would hold a charge. Various kids came to our rescue. By the time the Excelsior boomed into life, we were at the end of the bridge to Milford. Once in high gear, we began really rolling and Frank, hanging onto my waist, was yelling to slow down. But I dared not. We made great time as we followed the river to Howland, but five miles short of Enfield rain came, and the engine quit on an uphill grade. Pushing was a tiring business. We hailed a passing truck whose driver agreed to tow me in while Frank rode in the cab with him. After a mile or so of a very rough ride, the rope broke and the Excelsior and I careered into a ditch. When Frank reached

Fig. 2-19
Agatha, the gal from out-of-town that we Old Town boys fell for. A great dancer.

Enfield he got out, thanked the driver and wondered where I was. We finally got together and pushed the bike to Enfield. Too exhausted to pursue the object of the trip, we discovered she was off as usual with another suitor in a canoe on the lake.

We left the bike in Enfield and hitchhiked home. I went back a week later to retrieve it. After five miles on the narrow woods-road cutoff, the engine quit in Passadumkeag. No one was around so I hid the bike in a shallow ditch and hitchhiked home. This was a weekend, and Eddie was back in Old Town. After picking up a supply of fresh dry cells, we drove back in the Packard. Between us we accomplished the push start, and I managed to get a foot on the pad and swing aboard. Amazingly, the Excelsior ran perfectly all the way home.

I cited this trip in some detail as it was typical of our experience with this tired and worn-out motorcycle.

ANOTHER EPISODE WAS SCARY. The Excelsior had a leaf spring front suspension connected to the axle by links. Leaning over the handlebars while pounding down The Flat one day, I glanced down and noticed the nut on one end of the axle was gone and the axle was well on its way out of the spring fork. Holding the

steering steady, I gingerly slowed down. Sudden action could have resulted in a nasty spill.

The following June the saga of the Excelsior as a complete motorcycle ended abruptly. Although a professional sport in Maine, harness racing also flourished as a gentleman's sport in small towns throughout the state. The wealthiest banker in Old Town, for example, maintained a trotter in his stable and exercised it in his racing gig on the local streets. His colorful racing silks and cap reminded me of some of the early sports car drivers; paraphernalia was more important than performance. The banker's home had a marvelously elaborate stone wall which we peered over as he was harnessing up for a spin. Every Decoration Day

Fig. 2-20
Wrecked Excelsior motorcycle after plunging down the embankment at Cy Green's track.

Fig. 2-21
My "staged" injury, being supported by Billy Danforth and Frank.

and Fourth of July he entered the local harness races. One long summer day loafing around the barn, Eddie, Frank, Billy Danforth (a summer visitor) and I decided to head out to Cy Green's race track near Pea Cove with the Excelsior. Eddie took the others in the Packard. The track always was dragged for smoothness before major holiday events, but lay fallow the rest of the year. With its small tower for the officials, the covered grandstand and surrounding board fence, this half-mile dirt oval was a magnetic attraction for those of us who longed to visit Indianapolis. We raced our bicycles around it, imagining all kinds of scenarios.

As usual, Eddie had his Kodak and did not have to wait long for something interesting to shoot. We took turns timing each other around the track. My temperamental motorcycle was on its best behavior, starting with an easy push, and as time wore on we became more competitive.

On what proved to be the last lap of the day I was running flat out in second gear.

Entering the second corner the throttle stuck open. I slid into the fence, one of the foot pegs struck a post, the attached guardrail let go—and we went catapulting off into the field below. The bike landed hard on the front end, ruining the front suspension, wheel, brake, handlebars, and other components. Having departed from the bike, I suffered no more than a bruise or two. Eddie got some good shots of the remains of the Excelsior, but as I was unhurt some "special effects" were in order. In the photo I am "supported" by Frank and Billy. Eddie was a great morale booster—no matter how dumb my mistake, he always sought to portray the hero.

Excelsior-Powered Three-Wheeler, 1926

I can't remember how the remains of the Excelsior were brought back to our barn. Perhaps my father hired a local farmer with a stake truck. We could never have done it with the Packard. The morning after, the parts were spread out on the barn floor. Like the

Fig. 2-22
The three-wheel Excelsior-powered car.

magician who surveys the broken pieces of the glass ball he has dropped, I was shattered. I'd worked so hard to acquire the Excelsior, and when it was on good behavior it was a thrill to ride. Fortunately I had my interest in racing to hang on to, a profession where thrills, spills, accidents and disappointments are endemic but the participants go on. The engine, clutch, rear wheel, suspension and drive of the Excelsior had survived the accident and in the corner of the barn was my fifth vehicle effort, a rolling, steerable chassis without an engine. Why not combine them into a unique three-wheeler with rear-mounted engine? The installation was completed by August 26 and the car ran a few days later.

In *The Youth's Companion,* a popular weekly publication, a column entitled the "Y. C. Lab" encouraged creative work by offering small monetary awards to anyone who could write up a project and submit it with photos

for consideration. One weekend I sent in a description of the three-wheeler with some of Eddie's photos, won the 49th Weekly $5 Award and had a very nice write-up in the magazine.

My folks were pleased. Even at that young age I realized that sponsors, which they were, must feel rewarded if sponsorship is to be continued. The Y. C. Lab was a great idea, creating a national competition among children with ideas. In principle it was similar to the

Fig. 2-23
Rear view of three-wheeler.

39

SAE Formula Car Competition in which college students design and build their own race cars, combining academic knowledge with practical experience.

49th Weekly $5 Award

AT last the workers on Cinderella have met a foeman worthy of their scrap-iron! They have met him in the person of William F. Milliken, Jr. (15), of Old Town, Me., the designer, fabricator and operator of the cycle car which you see illustrated above.

Few weekly-award projects have excelled Member Milliken's. Many of them have been different in technique, striving to be small scaled and precise, where his is epic and rakish. The difference is one in class, not excellence.

With his ability in automotive design, Member Milliken combines the art of taking good pictures and of writing good prose. For these reasons, we rely principally on him to relate the details of the cycle car. One interesting feature in its design is the extraordinary visibility of almost all parts. A careful glance reveals the ignition switch, the starting pedal, the timing gear chain, the gas supply pipe, the brake rod, the drive chain—almost everything, in fact, save the ''body by Fisher'' plate. The three-wheel design, it may be said, is quite popular in Europe at present.

Member Milliken built his cycle car because he wrecked his motorcycle. Thereby he has added materially to our good opinion of him. Can you have something, and prize it, and have the courage and perseverance to build something new out of the wreckage of it? You will need that ability some day, and so much the better for you if you can exhibit it in the fashion of Member Milliken. Many things get wrecked in life, you will find, besides motorcycles, and the grit to build something new out of the wreckage is not possessed by everyone.

But let us study Member Milliken's excellent description of specifications:

Fig. 2-24
My first Y. C. Lab Award.

Activities and Antics, 1926

Singling out the demise of the Excelsior and its use in the three-wheeler is no more a measure of the events covered by my diary for 1926 than a description of the Woolworth Building and Central Park gives one a feel for New York City. A few excerpts indicate that life was far from boring.

First, my mother always baked beans for Saturday night and in early March dropped the pot and was severely burned. Second, I was tracking Byrd's and Amundsen's attempts to fly to the North Pole and was glad when Byrd got there first. Third, in May, I finally taught myself to swim, which was one of the smarter things I ever did. Early each morning I rode my bike to the old swimming hole, stripped down, waded out as far as I dared and attempted to swim back to shore. Another lesson: the best things are not always easy.

Fires were a source of excitement. I remember three big ones during my teens. The first was in Bradley across the river where the only source of water was a small stream and a hand pumper. In pitch darkness eight men worked the two long handles, cursing and swearing, but getting enough water to the firemen to keep the fire from spreading. The next big conflagration was Sawyer's Garage. Earlier that day a Standard Oil tanker, filled to the hilt with gasoline, had driven into the garage for repairs. When the fire started, no one was inclined to drive this potential bomb out of the garage. Firemen and the public kept a reasonable distance away knowing that sooner or later there would be a huge explosion. They were not disappointed. The roof of the garage was shattered, and flames and debris shot upward, lighting the sky like a geyser.

Fires are a terrible thing, but as children we saw only the spectacular aspects. In the 1920s Old Town relied upon a steam-engined pumper mounted on wheels and propelled to the fire by four huge draft horses. To see it roll out of the fire barn in a hurry was a thrilling sight. The last big fire of that decade was McKinley Middle School. Because it began in early morning, no children or staff were present. In the sub-zero temperature, the hydrants were frozen and attempts to save the building in the gusty winds were unavailing. It burned to the ground and the area was strewn with pages of half-burned textbooks. To us it meant a brief vacation until other facilities could be organized.

Hazing by upper classmen was standard practice when one went from middle to high school. Naturally we sought to avoid it by traveling in groups or staying off the streets, but one evening six of us were hiding in our barn when the "enemy" got wise and started beating on the doors. My parents were not at home, and the barn was dark. Somehow the marauders got the door open and rushed in. Peanut and I beat on them with wooden swords as they climbed the stairs to the barn chamber. Suddenly, my father arrived, turned on the light in the barn and our attackers left in a hurry. Peanut and I knew they would be back, so we decided to get away by the small door in the back of the barn. When we jumped out, five or more kids landed on us and we were dragged downtown and dumped into the horse trough. As I wrote in the diary, "We got our money's worth!"

The last entry in my diary for 1926 was a poignant one for me. Eddie was leaving for a job at Aetna Insurance in Hartford, Connecticut. He put me in charge of his racing pictures and keeping up his book of clippings. How I hated to see him go.

Paul "Peanut" Spruce

Because of the tragic death of his parents in an accident, Peanut and his older sister

Fig. 2-25
Paul "Peanut" Spruce. My great companion during those early "vehicle" years in Old Town. He was a born stuntman, never failing to accept any challenge.

were brought up by an aunt and uncle who lived in Old Town on South Fourth Street, a few blocks from our home. An older brother was taken in by other relatives and lived in Camden. Aunt Maime was a devoted Catholic, warm and motherly, and a meticulous housekeeper; Uncle Eddie was a tall, fit individual who had survived the northern Maine logging camps and now was retired. Together they created a pleasant home.

Small, wiry and physically tough, Peanut had a gymnast's build. I always thought of him as a stuntman ready to accept or initiate any challenge. He didn't object to the nickname we had given him. A delightful aspect of his character was his quickness and surprising responses. We never were bored with Peanut because we never were quite sure what he would do next.

One Saturday afternoon Peanut suggested that we drop by the old Universalist Church that my folks attended. The plan was to play the organ; he would pump it and I would cope with the keyboard. The handle for the pump projected from the wall, high enough that two sawhorses and a plank had been erected for the pumpman. Peanut ascended to this platform and started vigorously pumping. Soon the church was filled with popular tunes of the day. Tiring of this activity, Peanut suggested we explore the mechanism of the organ, which he thought could be reached through a small door near the pipes. We squeezed through the narrow passage into a dusty, dark interior where the keys were connected to the valves on the pipes. The connections were made by long, thin, flat wooden reeds of varying lengths—a fascinating if ancient detail of construction. At that moment he slipped and I fell forward. God knows how many of the connections we broke but it was not a few. Scrambling out, we considered our next move. "Let's run up town and get some strong cord and repair the busted connections," Peanut said, adding, "We better hurry, someone might show up!" Twenty minutes later we were back fumbling around in the dark—not daring to light a match. Some of the valves were hard to reach and connecting a key with the right valve was chancy, but we did our best. Peanut suggested we attend the service the next day, but sit close to the door.

Sunday we hid in the bushes until most of the congregation had entered, then slid quietly into two seats near the door. The service began with an opening overture by the organist. Breathlessly, we heard the pumpman building up the air, and then came the first chaotic blast from the organ. The discords were unbelievable. The organist was all over the keyboard, pulling out stops, her feet running around on the foot pedals, trying to figure out what was wrong. On his elevated platform, the pumpman pumped madly, but in the excitement fell off the plank, crashing to the floor as the organ unwound.

Peanut grabbed my arm, "It's time to retreat!" We slipped out the door and ran as fast as we could down the street. This was not the only time I retreated from organized religion but was certainly the most memorable.

One year Old Town's movie theater, The Strand, ran a weekly serial thriller called "The Green Archer." Each episode ended with the hero in some desperate situation. The serial had great appeal for Peanut and me because not only was the Green Archer a superb stuntman, he was remarkably good with the women. Peanut and I held the belief that the way to attract girls was to perform daring feats. (Cousin Frank pursued a more subtle if conventional approach of music and flowers, which we later discovered was more successful.) Peanut decided that emulating the Green Archer would further his objective of becoming a hero to the local girls. To put his idea into action, he persuaded his aunt to create a tight-fitting costume, along with a face mask and a pointed hat that was an excellent replica of the Green Archer's attire. We made the bow and arrow.

Peanut elected to introduce the Green Archer at a dance social in the auditorium that was used for basketball games at Helen Hunt School. He would hide in the surrounding balcony and, at a given signal, jump up, run the length of the balcony to opposite the basketball net, leap the 15 feet or so to catch the rim with both hands and swing gracefully to the floor where he would take a bow. This seemed to us an ingenious idea certain to charm the fair sex. The dance was scheduled for seven o'clock; Peanut was waiting in the balcony by six. An hour to anticipate this difficult feat could not have been relaxing but he lay low and was undetected. The social started with the usual grand march and as the dancers moved back towards their seats, I put two fingers to my mouth and gave the whistle. The Green Archer stood up and started his run, as everyone below watched. With the bow held high in the air, he leapt over the railing but fell short of the basketball rim, catching it with only one hand and falling to the floor in a heap.

Fig. 2-26
Universalist Church, the scene of the organ episode with Peanut Spruce. My first encounter with organized religion.

There was little doubt among the crowd about who was behind the mask. One young girl shouted, "Huh, Peanut Spruce!" The Green Archer picked up his broken bow and arrow and stole away.

Not all of Peanut's stunts met such an unfortunate fate. Once on my second motorcycle, as we were driving through Brewer, his cap blew off and fell on the street directly in front of the fire station. As usual in the summertime, the firemen were sitting in front of the station enjoying the weather and the passing scene. Immediately sensing an opportunity, Peanut directed me to turn back and drive by his hat. Locking his legs around my waist, he swung down and picked it up. The firemen were delighted and gave us a good hand. Peanut couldn't resist the chance to improve on his performance and had me cruise by again as he stood up on the rear seat and climbed to a sitting position on my shoulders.

An artist on a bicycle, Peanut had developed a modest repertoire of stunts, but he had never driven a motorcycle. Once I had the big Excelsior, he was after me to let him try it. I could hardly turn him down. Since he had no experience in shifting gears, I put the bike in second gear and pushed him off. He disappeared around the corner at the foot of Oak Street. As he progressed around the block, we could hear the steady roar of the engine, but halfway up Bradbury Street, the roar became less pronounced and he did not reappear. We ran down the street. The motorcycle was down, its engine still running with the rear wheel spinning; Peanut was standing on one side surrounded by a pack of yapping and yowling dogs. As we approached, he made an attempt to escape, stepped on the rear wheel and was launched into the middle of the pack. Duly rescued, he was ready for another go.

Action first and thought afterwards was a flawed philosophy that frequently caught us out. Peanut had a close shave learning to swim at Gray's Mill. Out too far and making no progress toward shore, he was bobbing up and down until one of the other kids saw him, swam out and dragged him back, half drowned.

For all the pranks and humor in his younger years, Peanut was to live a responsible life as an adult. Following the death of his aunt and uncle he gravitated to Boston. With just a high school education he worked at such jobs as were available—once as an elevator operator at the Parker House. He lived in inexpensive quarters and contributed most of his earnings to support his brother's son in college. Whenever I passed through Boston, I looked him up at the hotel. He would accept no help, became ill and died in his early forties. His was a tragic life but a memorable one.

Ski Mobile, Winter of 1927

With my burgeoning interest in aviation, I began thinking about using my Excelsior engine to turn an air propeller. For practical experience I built the Ski Mobile during the winter of 1927. Three skis were fastened to a long, fabric-covered airplane-like fuselage: two in front and one on the rear, the former pivoting in pitch to assist in traveling over rough terrain. The single rear ski was steerable for directional control, assisted by an air rudder, both operated together

Fig. 2-27
Ski Mobile, airplane-like fuselage.

Fig. 2-28
Homemade propeller and adaption to the Excelsior engine.

by a rudder bar in the cockpit. I located the Excelsior engine, with the propeller mounted directly on the crankshaft, on the nose of the fuselage, producing in effect a wingless airplane on skis. When the engine could be persuaded to run in cold winter weather it proved to be fun.

The most interesting feature of the Ski Mobile was the crankshaft adapter for the propeller. This machining job was accomplished at Chapman's Foundry. The Excelsior motorcycle had a chain drive from the engine to the gearbox. The propeller adapter fit over the existing sprocket with torque taken by several bolts through the adapter and between the teeth of the sprocket. I doubt that a drawing was ever prepared; the machinist simply was given the Excelsior sprocket and the bolt circle diameter of the propeller flange.

Fig. 2-29
Ski Mobile (1927), rear view showing steerable rear ski and air rudder.

Indian Scout Motorcycle, 1927

My having survived the Excelsior evidently reassured my parents, because they were less resistant to my acquisition of another motorcycle. The 45-cubic-inch Indian Scout was a lighter, smaller machine of more recent vintage that had none of the starting problems of the Excelsior. It could be kick-started, and always ran. Even my father took a ride on back, although once was quite enough for him. Peanut Spruce and I made several trips on the Indian—one to Camden to see his brother. But on a picnic ride to Bar Harbor, we came to grief in Bangor following an encounter with a small farm truck delivering eggs. Peanut was catapulted over my head, landing on his backpack containing our lunch. The truck had swerved to avoid us and ran into an abutment alongside the entrance to the bridge. Between the eggs spilled from the crates and our lunch it was a messy business, ultimately

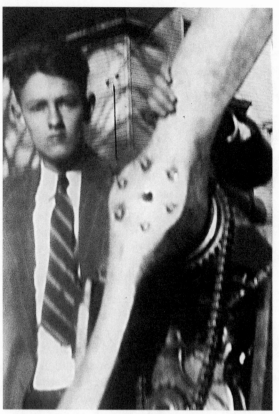

Fig. 2-30
Aero-Triple-Cycle, showing the "geared"-down
propeller drive which enabled a larger diameter
propeller and greater thrust.

Fig. 2-31
Aero-Triple-Cycle No. 1, start of initial test run.

involving my father to sort out a financial settlement. I was left with a nice reliable little engine sans motorcycle.

Aero-Triple-Cycle No. 1, 1928

The Aero-Triple-Cycle was an air-propelled hybrid. It was steered by a pair of front wheels, braked by a single wheel at the rear, and had a light, airplane-like structure. This 1928 machine served as my transition between ground and air vehicles. I felt it was a fairly unique concept, well integrated into a compact machine with a short, maneuverable wheelbase and a pert look. Of course, driver (pilot) vision was none too good, but it was exciting to watch the propeller whirling around and feel the slipstream on one's face. Its light construction and chain-driven propeller gave it a high-frequency vibration and the feeling of power.

On an overcast day with potential showers, Peanut and I rolled the Triple-Cycle out of

the barn for its initial trial. Having chocked the wheels, I climbed aboard and switched the ignition to "off." Peanut then pulled the propeller through a couple of revolutions and called out "contact." I switched on and set the throttle just off idle. He grasped the blade, swung his right leg across in the traditional fashion and pulled the blade down smartly. The engine backfired. Hanging on a fraction of a second too long, Peanut was picked up and tossed into the bed of zinnias that lined the driveway. As usual he was unhurt and ready to battle the engine again. This time it started and ran like a song. The chain drive that geared the propeller down to about half engine speed worked perfectly. Still on the chocks, I revved a few times and felt the structure come to life. As I held the rear brake on, Peanut removed the chocks, keeping clear of the propeller arc.

Easing the machine down the sloping driveway, I crossed the sidewalk into the street, opened the throttle and picked up

45

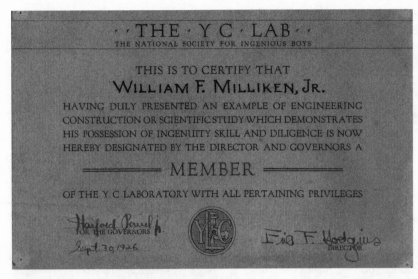

Fig. 2-32
The Aero-Triple-Cycle led to my full membership in the Y. C. Lab.

occasion a Chevrolet with a California top was on the right-hand side of the roadway. The combination of rain, poor visibility and my concentration on the handling of the machine led me to pass too close to the Chevy. The propeller chewed up the California top and my right front wheel struck the car, breaking the Triple-Cycle's axle support. A grinding stop followed. I have to say the responsibility was mine, but at the time I was mad as hell at

speed rounding Brown's corner. Peanut, who had been running after me, was left behind. As the rain began, visibility through the small windscreen became poor. In retrospect, I should have waited for better conditions but my enthusiasm took over. Now, it was rare for a car to park on Brunswick Street because the houses had long driveways, but on this

the owner of that Chevy. He, in turn, as the only owner of a California top in Old Town, was equally mad. My father settled with him for $100 and I went back to work repairing the Triple-Cycle. In due time I wrote up the Aero-Triple-Cycle, sent it to the Y. C. Lab and received a special award of $10 and full membership.

Fig. 2-33
Four-wheel car with Indian Scout engine, homemade clutch and countershaft drive.

Four-Wheel Cyclecar, 1928

With some help from Braley Gray, I removed the Indian motorcycle engine from the Aero-Triple-Cycle and built a four-wheel cyclecar that featured two developments, both of which worked well. The first was a countershaft in the drivetrain, the second a homemade clutch in which two wooden discs (about a foot in diameter) suitably faced with leather were forced together with a spring-loaded toggle. The frame was underslung to the axles with no suspension springs. We mocked up a radiator but never progressed to a full body.

Cecil Godfrey

No account of our vehicular activity would be complete without mention of Cecil Godfrey. Eddie, Mossy and I were not the only ones in the neighborhood engaged in construction projects. Cecil, who lived a few houses up Oak Street, came up with some very creative machines. We always referred to Cecil as the biggest liar in Penobscot County, but there was no gainsaying that he had a terrific imagination and was a skillful woodworker. He operated out of his father's single-car detached garage.

We always kept a good eye on each other's activities, but more from curiosity than for competitive reasons.

Cecil produced three notable vehicles. The first was his man-carrying kite. Unlike Alexander Graham Bell's Tetrahedral which actually soared aloft with a man, Cecil's was an enlarged version of the normal cruciform kite configuration. Its initial (and final) launch was from the third-floor fire escape of the Helen Hunt School during a thunderstorm. It broke its tether and disappeared westward.

His second vehicle, of which I have more than a few memories, was a sled that had the external appearance of a miniature submarine mounted on two conventional bobsleds, the front one steerable. As it neared completion Cecil commissioned me as test pilot (or whatever one calls the "steer-man" on a sub). Cecil was too tall to fit into his creation. When the time came for the launch, we hauled the submarine sled halfway up Academy Hill. Easing my way down through the "conning tower" and sliding into the commander's seat, I was surrounded by levers, knobs and handles, all reminiscent of a submarine's interior but none of them connected to anything. The crowning glory was a large steam gauge

Fig. 2-34
Sea sled at Pushaw Pond, an extreme design, only moderately successful.

Fig. 2-35
**Aero-Triple-Cycle No. 2, powered by Henderson four-cylinder
engine with Heath propeller adaptation.**

2 feet in depth, the sled was completely enclosed except for the operator's cockpit forward of the engine and propeller. I followed the construction daily as Cecil was nailing on the exterior planking. He had just about completed the upper deck when I noticed smoke coming up through the cracks between the planks. One of his friends was inside painting and waterproofing while lying on his back enjoying a cigarette. Cecil admitted that in his haste to finish, he had forgotten about his friend and was nailing him in.

Launched at Pushaw Pond, the sled immediately assumed a tail-down attitude. The engine/propeller unit was too far aft, and when moved forward for leveling, the propeller wound up in the middle of the operator's cockpit. Various modifications were made, but the sled never planed properly and finally was used as the floatation base for a diving tower. This episode was the inspiration for my one and only venture into watercraft. Powered by a 40-hp outboard engine, our sea sled proved a real bomb in a straight line but a handful to maneuver. To balance the boat one sat backward and as far forward as possible, while still within reach of the engine tiller. It probably was the most marginal of all the vehicles we toyed with.

centered on the panel in front of me, but also unconnected. Steering was by a sort of yoke that was relayed to the front sled. In keeping with the submarine motif, the only vision of the outside world was through a homemade periscope that was cleverly constructed of two mirrors. Feeling somewhat claustrophobic, I was pushed off and plunged down the hill trying to focus through the periscope, which was vibrating wildly with each bump. The trip ended in a mild but welcome crash.

Cecil's third machine, somewhat grander than those earlier, was a sea sled powered by a Le Rhône rotary aircraft engine with propeller. The power plant was mounted on a frame above the top deck. Probably 20–25 feet long, with a beam of 6–7 feet and a hull perhaps

Aero-Triple-Cycle No. 2, 1934

After the flight of my homebuilt airplane, the M-1 (described in Chapter 4), I constructed another Aero-Triple-Cycle using the four-cylinder Henderson engine and propeller from that airplane. It was a huge success, and much fun to operate. As the photos show, we ran it on the streets in Old Town and on the ¼-mile athletic track.

There would be tremendously creative years in the future, but none would be comparable to the unrestrained use of the imagination that guided the development of those early vehicles.

Fig. 2-36
Aero-Triple-Cycle on ¼-mile running track.

Fig. 2-37
Second Aero-Triple-Cycle, at full bore.

Home-built Vehicle Designs, 1921–1934

Vehicle	Year (my age)	Remarks
Duesenberg No. 5	1921 (10 yrs)	Later No. 4
Duesenberg No. 4 two-seater	1922 (11 yrs)	Built by Ed Waterhouse and Maurice Burr
Light car, no name	1923 (12 yrs)	Wire wheels
Miller No.1	1923 (12 yrs)	Built by Ed Waterhouse and Maurice Burr
Early driving experience	1923 (12 yrs)	Waterhouse's Overland
First glider	1924 (13 yrs)	Bamboo
Second glider, wood frame	1924 (13 yrs)	Poor airfoil shape
Shaw single-cylinder bicycle engine	1924 (13 yrs)	On bicycle On Miller No.1 with countershaft

Popular Mechanics "Penguin," first airplane attempt	1924 (13 yrs)	Planned to use Shaw engine
Fifth car, four-wheeler	1925 (14 yrs)	No engine initially, based on Imp cyclecar components
Excelsior motorcycle	1925 (14 yrs)	1914 model
Excelsior motorcycle	1926 (15 yrs)	Wrecked at Cy Green's racetrack
Fifth car converted to three-wheeler with Excelsior engine	1926 (15 yrs)	Y. C. Lab Award ($5.00)
M-1 airplane preliminary design started	1926 (15 yrs)	To use Excelsior engine and Brown's propeller experience
Ski Mobile	1927 (16 yrs)	Excelsior motor with propeller
Indian Scout motorcycle	1927 (16 yrs)	Wrecked with Paul Spruce
Aero-Triple-Cycle, No. 1	1927 (16 yrs)	Started, Indian Scout engine
Aero-Triple-Cycle, No. 1 three-wheeler, air propeller	1928 (17 yrs)	Completed, won second Y. C. Lab Award ($10.00)
Four-wheeled cyclecar, Indian Scout engine, countershaft, wooden disc clutch	1928–29 (17–18 yrs)	With Braley Gray
M-1 design and build	1928 (design—17 yrs), 1933 (flew—22 yrs)	
Aero-Triple-Cycle, No. 2 Henderson 4-cylinder engine used on M-1	Summer 1934 (23 yrs)	M-1 propeller, steered front wheels, single rear wheel

Chapter 3 ☙

Prelude to a Career

He is up and off with the east in his eyes
and all of his destiny in his hand.

– Nancy Byrd Turner
("The Ballad of Lucky Lindbergh")

Charles Lindbergh's transatlantic flight had a terrific impact on me, like a thunder clap, a hammer blow, a whip lashing. My reaction was visceral, not intellectual. I was one person one day and another the next. This occurred, as my diary reflects, while I was living through a further decline in my parents' relationship and feeling a strong recurrence of physical tension and concern. Lindbergh was a powerful role model for me, demonstrating that when skill and courage lead the way, adventure, success and acclaim surely must follow. This reinforced the early stories told to me by my father. Further, Lindbergh had done it alone, and deep inside I remained a lonely child. Inspired, I began a routine of physical exercise, increased my radius of hitchhiking—and resolved to build an airplane.

My intense interest in these pioneering long-distance over-water flights phased perfectly with my psychological state as well as my burgeoning interest in aircraft, and went far in establishing my fundamental outlook and philosophy.

During the summer of 1925, when my cousin Frank and I were visiting Knolton Small, a former schoolmate, in Augusta, his parents proposed we drive to Wiscasset to see the schooner *Bowdoin* before she set sail for Etah on the coast of northern Greenland. Her skipper, Donald MacMillan, had been a member of the expedition when Admiral Peary claimed to have reached the North Pole. The Department of the Navy supplied the steamship *Peary*, which carried three Loening amphibians for locating "land supposed to exist in the Polar Sea northwest of Etah." The Naval contingent was under a Lieutenant-Commander Richard E. Byrd, who was about to begin his career as an Arctic explorer. Unknown to the public, Byrd had

Lindbergh and *Spirit of St. Louis* in Paris, 1927.

been involved with the navigational aspects of the NC flying boats that had made the first crossing of the Atlantic, and was a strong promoter of naval aviation.

As alumni of Bowdoin College, MacMillan and Knolton's father were acquainted, and we were taken aboard the *Bowdoin* for a tour, after which we attended the outdoor departure ceremonies at which farewell speeches were made outlining the expedition's plans.

Byrd's championing of aircraft for Arctic exploration connected in my mind with the exciting railway surveying experiences of my father. From just a technically interesting machine the airplane became the key to unlimited pioneering and adventure. This romantic concept became a passionate dream that colored much of my subsequent thought and action.

After the Byrd/MacMillan encounter, I carefully followed every long-distance flight. One of the first, which also occurred in 1925, was the Ellsworth-Amundsen polar expedition by two Dornier-Wal seaplanes that flew from Spitzbergen and landed on the Polar Sea/Ice short of the Pole. After an heroic effort to take off from an iced runway, the two crews returned

to Spitzbergen in one aircraft. Details of that expedition were not published until 1928. That summer, when I worked on the Bangor-Boston ferry, I read an article portraying Amundsen as an Arctic expedition leader capable of maintaining an attitude of confidence in a desperate situation "though in no obnoxiously cheerful way."

Byrd's experience at Etah led him to organize his 1926 North Pole flight. Using a tri-motor Fokker on skis, he and Floyd Bennett began the non-stop round-trip flight from King's Bay, Spitzbergen, on May 9, 1926. On May 11–13, Amundsen, Ellsworth and Umberto Nobile made the trans-polar crossing from King's Bay to Point Barrow, Alaska, in the semi-rigid dirigible *Norge*. They also flew directly over the Pole, based on the best navigational techniques available at the time, and passed over vast areas of unexplored territory.

Attempting the Atlantic

The transatlantic flights, which soon followed, began with the incentive of the $25,000.00 Orteig Prize. A naturalized American citizen, Raymond Orteig had offered this prize in

Fig. 3-1
Sikorsky S-35 *Ville de Paris*, earliest contender for the Orteig prize, 1926. Crashed on takeoff attempt. Pilot René Fonck.

1919 for the first non-stop flight between New York and Paris to foster the relationship between his adopted country and his native France. Not until 1926 did improvements in technology and aircraft performance make it possible to accept this challenge. Entries came from both the United States and Europe, and were faithfully reported in *Aviation*. When the magazine arrived every Monday morning, I dropped everything and absorbed it from cover to cover.

First to reach the starting line was French WWI ace René Fonck with the Sikorsky S-35 *Ville de Paris*, a gigantic, specially constructed sesquiplane powered by three Gnome-Rhône Jupiter 425-hp engines. Built in the old Sikorsky hangar at Curtiss Field and elaborately fitted out, the heavily loaded plane carried a crew of four, in addition to Fonck: a co-pilot/navigator, mechanic and radio operator. During the takeoff attempt from Roosevelt Field on September 21, 1926, an auxiliary landing gear came loose (either inadvertently released or by failure) and began dragging. Fonck did not stop the takeoff attempt and went over the drop from Roosevelt to Curtiss Field whereupon the main gear failed. The airplane caught fire, and

mechanic Jacob Islamoff and radio operator Charles Clavier, who were in the main cabin, died in the flames. Fonck and Lawrence Curtiss managed to crawl to safety.

The next attempt occurred on May 8, 1927, when Charles Nungesser (another World War I ace) and François Coli took off from Le Bourget Field in Paris in the Levasseur biplane *L'Oiseau Blanc* (*The White Bird*), powered by a single Lorraine-Dietrich 450-hp engine. Dropping the landing gear to reduce air drag, the plan was to land on the hull-shaped bottom of the fuselage. Leaving Paris at 5:17 A.M., they were sighted over Fastnet, Ireland, at 10:10 and then disappeared over the Atlantic. Numerous theories have been put forth that they may have reached this continent, but nothing has ever been substantiated.

Meanwhile several aircraft were being prepared for the attempt in the United States. Commander Byrd was to fly a Fokker tri-motor, the *America*, sponsored by Wanamaker. The aircraft was constructed at the Fokker works in Hasbrouck Heights, New Jersey, under the direction of Anthony Fokker himself. Another early entrant was the famous Wright Bellanca, originally owned by Wright

Fig. 3-2
Fokker tri-motor *America*. Early contender for Orteig prize, 1927, by Commander Byrd and crew.

Fig. 3-3
Wright Bellanca *Columbia*, owned by Charles Levine of Columbia Aircraft, early competitor for Orteig prize. A very efficient aircraft which held the endurance record of over 50 hours, 1927.

Aeronautical to demonstrate its J-5 Whirlwind engine but now owned by Charles Levine and renamed *Columbia*. One of the most efficient aircraft of its time, this design was destined to play a prominent part in the pioneering trans-oceanic flights. A second tri-motor, the Keystone bomber *American Legion,* was being prepared for Noel Davis and Stanton Wooster. Then there was a late entrant by an unknown airmail pilot from St. Louis, Charles Lindbergh, who had tried to buy the *Columbia*, but now engaged Ryan Aircraft, a small firm in San

Diego, to construct a special machine for the attempt.

All this activity in the early months of 1927 was faithfully covered in *Aviation*. Delay was experienced in the Byrd camp when the Fokker was test flown with Tony himself at the controls, Byrd and Floyd Bennett aboard. The nose-heavy plane flipped over upon landing, putting Bennett out of the running and injuring Byrd. The *Columbia*, having set a new endurance record of over 50 hours, was involved in endless legal bickering and

Fig. 3-4
Ryan NYP ("New York–Paris") *Spirit of St. Louis*, built especially for the Orteig prize, flown solo by Charles Lindbergh, who set a transcontinental record from San Diego to Roosevelt Field, 1927.

complications centering around Levine's choice of crew.

Lindbergh's "Victory"

On May 12, 1927, Lindbergh, flying alone in *The Spirit of St. Louis,* arrived at Roosevelt Field after a one-stop record flight from San Diego. The repaired *America,* the *Columbia* and now *The Spirit of St. Louis* were, in theory at least, poised at the starting line. Byrd's actions were deliberate, he still was running tests and waiting for more ideal weather. The *Columbia* remained bogged down in red tape, to the desperation of designer Guiseppe Bellanca who naturally was anxious to see his aircraft reach Paris first. Only Lindbergh, flying solo, able to make his own decisions and with the simple objective of winning the Orteig Prize, was in a position to take advantage of a break in the weather over the North Atlantic.

At 7:54 A.M. on May 20th, he started his takeoff on the narrow runway at Roosevelt Field that Byrd had prepared for the *America.* The gravel strip was some 5,000 feet long, short by modern standards, and for the first time Lindbergh's aircraft was carrying a full load of fuel (460 gallons). The static thrust of the fixed-pitch propeller was so low that spectators had to push on the wing struts to start the plane rolling. With no vision directly forward and just the rudder for directional control, only Lindbergh's skill and experience made the takeoff possible. Clearing some wires at the end of the field by only 20 feet, Lindbergh was on his way to Paris. On May 21st at 10:22 P.M. he landed at Le Bourget Field after 33 hours 30 minutes in the air.

Such was the intensity of my interest in these transatlantic attempts that even today I can recall little events that occurred at the time and rekindle my feelings. As a dark horse, Lindbergh had burst upon the scene with little prior publicity, even in the aviation press. Conventional logic suggested the *Columbia* as the most likely winner of the Orteig Prize, and I remember how surprised I was when my Uncle Willie, reading a newspaper, remarked, "I'm betting on that fellow Lindbergh."

When a full-page picture of Lindbergh appeared in the *Times Supplement,* I pasted it

Fig. 3-5
Charles Lindbergh and mother at Roosevelt Field before his takeoff for Paris, 1927.

on the wall of my bedroom. For the first time I grasped the idea that I had some control of my life, that I could physically and mentally condition myself to a more adventurous existence. Standing in front of Lindbergh's picture, I would say over and over, "I will win, I will win." That Christmas my father gave me a copy of Lindbergh's book, *We,* which fully reinforced the image I had developed of this man of action who could set his own goals and strive against all odds to achieve them. Clearly, physical health and stamina were among the requisites for an active life, so I began with Walter Camp's exercises, the "Daily Dozen," and expanded this into running late at night regardless of the weather. A regimen of cold-water baths followed.

During June 4–6, 1927, the Bellanca *Columbia* with Clarence Chamberlain and Charles Levine flew from New York to Eisleben, Germany, establishing a new long-distance record. This was followed by Byrd's Fokker *America* on June 29–July 1 with a crew of Byrd, Bert Acosta, George Norville and Bernt Balchen, who reached Paris in zero/zero weather and returned to the coast effecting a water landing at Ver-sur-Mer after more than 43 hours in the air. All of the crew survived. Five more attempts to fly the Atlantic followed in 1927, of which only one was successful: William Brock and Edward Schlee in the Stinson-Detroit *Pride of Detroit*. Three disappeared into the Atlantic, while the last attempt, by George Halderman and Ruth Elder flying another Stinson-Detroiter, established a new over-water distance record before ditching in the ocean near a freighter.

Crossing the Pacific

In the Pacific, the first successful flight to Hawaii from the mainland USA was completed by Maitland and Hegenberger, who flew the tri-motored Fokker *Bird of Paradise* powered by the reliable Wright Whirlwind engines in a demonstration flight by the Air Corps. Less than a month later Smith and Bronte followed in the single-engined Travel Air *City of Oakland*. The first civilians to reach Hawaii, they crash-landed in Molokai, beating the Maitland/Hegenberger record, and walked away unhurt.

The famous Dole Derby, a $25,000 prize race from Oakland (California) to Hawaii, occurred on August 16, 1927. Three entrants crashed before reaching the starting line. Four entrants either crashed on takeoff or returned due to in-flight problems. Two took off successfully and were lost in the Pacific. One entrant who returned was later lost in searching for the two that had disappeared. The race was won by Goebel and Davis in the Travel Air *Woolaroc* which made the run in 26 hours 27 minutes. Jensen and Schluter came in second flying the Breeze monoplane *Aloha* in 28 hours 6 minutes after experiencing a navigational problem.

The disastrous results of the Dole Derby made it apparent that success in trans-oceanic flight required the best equipment, careful preparation and the most experienced pilots and navigators. The problems of heavy load takeoff, weather and navigation were ever present, the technologies for confronting them marginal. Nevertheless, there was no cessation of individuals who were willing to accept the challenge. The sidebar lists the major flight attempts over the Atlantic and the Pacific which I followed in those halcyon years up to the mid-1930s.

Thus in seven short years the Atlantic and the Pacific had been crossed and recrossed in a series of epic flights. What had started as a prize-winning sporting adventure turned into

---

Pioneering Trans-Oceanic Flights

By 1936 the following had been accomplished:

1. First solo non-stop flight, New York–Paris—Charles Lindbergh, 1927.
2. First non-stop flight and distance record, NewYork–Germany—Chamberlain and Levine, 1927.
3. New York to Tokyo in stages, including a North Atlantic crossing—Brock and Schlee, 1927.
4. New overseas distance record—Halderman and Ruth Elder, 1927.
5. First East-West flight across the Atlantic—The Breman Flyers, 1928 (crash landing in Labrador).
6. First woman to cross the Atlantic as a passenger, Newfoundland to Wales—Schultz, Gordon and Amelia Earhart. Also the first seaplane to cross the Atlantic, 1928.
7. First "successful" East-West crossing of the Atlantic, Ireland to Newfoundland—Kingsford-Smith and crew in the *Southern Cross*, 1930.
8. First Paris to New York non-stop flight—Costes and Bellonte, 1930.

continued on next page

9. New round-the-world record and North Atlantic crossing—Wiley Post and Harold Gatty, 1931.
10. First woman to cross the North Atlantic, solo—Amelia Earhart, Newfoundland to Ireland, 1932.
11. New round-the-world record, solo—Wiley Post, 1933.
12. First East-West crossing of the Atlantic by a woman, solo—Beryl Markham, England to Cape Breton, 1936.
13. First flight, mainland USA to Hawaii—Maitland and Hagenberger (U.S. Air Corps), 1927.
14. First civilian flight, mainland USA to Hawaii—Smith and Bronte, 1927.
15. First Pacific crossing, USA mainland to Australia (in three hops)—Kingsford-Smith and crew, 1928.
16. First trans-Pacific flight from Japan to USA mainland—Pangborn and Herndon, 1931.
17. First crossing of the Pacific from Australia to USA mainland—Kingsford-Smith and P. G. Taylor, 1934.

a pioneering movement toward trans-oceanic flying on a commercial basis. Lindbergh, while concentrating on the Orteig Prize, nevertheless sensed that his accomplishment was a door to aviation's unlimited future, in which he would later participate through survey flights for Pan American to the Orient, on the north and south Atlantic routes, in the Caribbean and also domestic transcontinental lines. From the beginning, Byrd had promoted the *America's* flight as a demonstration of an aircraft's long-range potential and refused to enter for the Orteig Prize. Kingsford-Smith's and P. T. Uln's long-held ambition was to establish a world airline connecting Australia with New Zealand, England and across the Pacific to the United States. They were successful in creating ANA (Australian National Airlines) but failed in their larger objective when Uln was lost in a trans-Pacific promotional flight and Smithy disappeared in a record-breaking attempt from England to Australia.

Fig. 3-6
Southern Cross, 1928.

Why did so many others with lesser vision attempt the hazards of these long over-water flights, with single-engine aircraft, when prize money, glory and fame had largely been exhausted by the earlier successful flights? It seems to me an undeniable characteristic of man is to seek and accept difficult challenges as a measure of his worth. We have an insatiable curiosity to know what it's like to be there. Hundreds of people still climb the Matterhorn and Mt. Everest long after the initial conquests. Most of the men who continued the long-distance flight attempts into the 1930s and beyond were experienced pilots from the ranks of barnstormers, fixed-base operators, the race, stunt and test pilot field and the military, and were well enough known to obtain sponsorship. These men, who made their living by flying, were realistic enough to be aware of the hazards involved. Interestingly, many of them, including Bernt Balchen and Clyde Pangborn, became key players in the Atlantic Ferry Operation (Air Transport Command) of military aircraft to Europe during WWII.

Fig. 3-7
Pangborn and Herndon, Bellanca, 1931.

Yet another exciting aspect of the great transoceanic flights was the interest they created in the design of the aircraft involved and in the engineers responsible for them. In those days, airplane design still was intimately connected with individual designers, men such as Igor Sikorsky and Giuseppe Bellanca, who often founded their own companies. By late 1928 I had developed an irresistible urge, augmented by reading Clarence Chamberlain's book *Record Flights*, to visit the airfields and aircraft factories of New York and New Jersey.

Stretching My Boundaries

The year following Lindbergh's flight, in mid June 1928, I began a summer job at Eastern Steamship Lines, which ran an overnight passenger service between Bangor and Boston. I was hired as cashier in the dining room on one of the company's two boats, the *Camden*. A captain on the line had married a school friend of my mother's, and my father frequently traveled the Boston-to-New York run as a guest in the captain's quarters. Having earlier begun to study the techniques of aerial navigation, which then was closely related to marine, I had plied Captain Crowell with questions about dead reckoning

Fig. 3-8
Kingsford-Smith and Taylor, *Lady Southern Cross*, 1934.

and celestial navigation. At night, steaming in the Atlantic some 15 or 20 miles offshore, I would lie on the top deck to study the constellations and imagine I was taking sextant shots on a long over-water flight.

I had the better part of the day to myself, either in Bangor or Boston. Fortunately, I was in the latter city in mid-June of 1928 when Amelia Earhart returned from her Newfoundland to Burry Port (Wales) flight with Wilmer Schultz in the twin-float Fokker *Friendship.* This was the first time a woman had flown across the Atlantic. I took the ferry to East Boston, hiked to the airfield, and got a spot close to the welcoming committee, which consisted of Commander Byrd and other celebrities. Later I listened to the welcoming speeches from the steps of the State Capitol.

But the principal adventure of that summer was quite unexpected. Those of us in the Steward's Department were quartered at the waterline, where we slept two-high in narrow bunks. It was stuffy, hot and smelly. If one opened a porthole when the ship was rolling, water poured in like an open hydrant. But the real problem was bedbugs. Most of us were covered with welts and scabs. After a routine medical check of the crew, Boston authorities concluded we all had smallpox and immediately put us into quarantine on Gallop's Island in the harbor for two weeks while we received smallpox shots and lived the life of Robinson Crusoe. For obvious reasons, Eastern Steamship Lines did not wish the presence of an epidemic on its boat to be made known, so none of our relatives was informed of our whereabouts. My parents were terribly concerned when their eldest son suddenly disappeared without a trace. Toward the end, only the black dining room waiters and I remained on the island. We became good friends and in the evening harmonized on popular tunes like "Old Man River."

My First Adventure

After my release, I returned home for a couple of weeks and made plans to hitchhike to Long Island, where Lindbergh's and most of the other great flights originated, and to visit aircraft factories there and in New Jersey. The aircraft had strong emotional appeal for me, while

the factory visits would satisfy my engineering interest.

The pleasures I experienced hitchhiking are difficult to explain, but they combined the reality of going some place, the anticipation of the unexpected, the complete separation from normal responsibilities and routines, and the uninterrupted opportunity to dream. The exciting objectives of this particular trip set it apart from all those preceding. I had been as far as Boston before, but now I was moving into new territory, doubling my radius of action. Years later I found that Walt Whitman's "Song of the Open Road" best expressed my feelings as I ventured forth from home on that crystal-clear day in Maine in the summer of '28. I had a small pack of extra clothes, a list of factories to visit, some friends' addresses, sandwiches for the day and 25 dollars in my pocket which, by staying with relatives and friends, would be more than enough for the trip. I felt totally self-sufficient and hadn't a care in the world.

Fig. 3-9
Amelia Earhart was the first woman to fly across the Atlantic in this Fokker tri-motor, *Friendship*, which was acquired from Commander Byrd and fitted with floats. With pilot Wilmer Shultz and flight mechanic Lou Gordon, they flew from Newfoundland to Burry Port, Wales, in 20 hours, 40 minutes, 1928.

There are different approaches to hitching a ride. One of the more common is to hold a sign aloft indicating one's destination and turning down rides that don't come close to it. My method was to walk along on the right-hand side of the road and hail cars as they came up behind. I'd accept lifts for any distance—short or long. It was more fun to keep moving and get some exercise between rides, and in the winter months walking was warmer than standing still. I tried to look presentable and since I was enjoying myself, I had no problem in creating a favorable impression. I consistently averaged 150 miles a day, and often much more.

BY LATE AFTERNOON of my first day out I was in Westbrook (near Portland) where I stayed overnight at the Brecks, relatives on my father's side. The following morning I leapt out of bed, proceeded through a series of exercises and topped off with a cold-water bath. Aunt Mabel had put up a lunch. Uncle Jimmie, the candy maker at the Longfellow Candy Shop in Portland, produced a pocket full of chocolates, and I was on my way.

Navigation was simple then. Thruways with convoluted exchanges didn't exist, and usually just one main road connected major cities. Old Route 1 followed the coast by Old Orchard Beach and York to the bridge at Portsmouth. That was the site of Thomas Bailey Aldrich's *Story of a Bad Boy*, about a bunch of kids who renovated some old cannon and fired them off in the middle of the night, to the consternation of the populace who envisioned the return of the British. Proceeding south one came to the old Newburyport Turnpike and on into Boston. Having spent every other day in Boston during my stint on the Bangor-Boston boat, I had no trouble getting through town on the subways and finding my way toward Springfield and thence down along the Connecticut River to Hartford.

Ed Waterhouse, then employed by Aetna, was expecting me at his apartment. We had a great reunion, a good meal and exchanged lots of motor racing news. Up to this point I'd spent less than a dollar of cash. The next morning Ed walked me to the road to New Haven and Bridgeport. From there on, things became more interesting.

The second ride out of Bridgeport took me to New York City, where I was dropped off in a large circle with streets radiating out, set in the midst of high buildings and with bright lights all around. I had no idea where I was; only later could I identify the place as Columbus Circle. It was about 9:00 in the evening. I had finished the last of Ed's sandwiches and was wondering where I'd spend the night. A policeman was standing nearby and I asked him about a rooming house in the area. He looked me over, asked a few searching questions, then pointed to a high brownstone building and said, "If you go in there and take the elevator to the fourth floor and turn right to the first apartment you will likely find a place to sleep." I followed his directions. My knock on the door was answered by a gaunt woman in a kimono holding a cigarette in one hand and a glass in the other. She seemed suspicious at first but finally announced that she had a bed. I wasn't quite sure whether she intended to share it with me, and was relieved when she showed me a cot in the next room that I could have for six bits (75 cents). She promised to wake me at 8:00 the next morning. I think she concluded, correctly, that I was a naive teenager visiting the big city for the first time. When I left she gave me a banana for breakfast. With directions to Penn Station I soon was on my way to Garden City on the Long Island Express train, wondering how "Mile a Minute Murphy" could have ridden a bicycle at such a speed on such a roadway.

In the Aeronautical Heartland

In 1928 Garden City, with its nearby flying fields of Curtiss, Roosevelt and Mitchell, was the center of aviation activity. I set up headquarters there above a barber shop where the proprietor had a bed and washstand for four bits a night. The next day I hitched to Curtiss/Roosevelt Field for one of the most memorable days I had ever experienced.

The two fields adjoined. Curtiss was the lower; the change in ground elevation between the two was known as the "hump." One runway on Roosevelt Field actually ended at the hump and was the site of René Fonck's catastrophic accident in the Sikorsky S-35 on

Fig. 3-10
The Lockheed Vega *Yankee Doodle* set a transcontinental record, Goebel (pilot) and Tucker (passenger), 1928. Goebel was the winner of the Dole Derby from California to Hawaii.

his transatlantic takeoff attempt. Roosevelt Field had a single hangar, the one Wanamaker used for Commander Byrd's transatlantic tri-motored Fokker *America*. Curtiss Field was lined on two sides with old wooden hangars.

The day before my arrival, Art Goebel had completed a record-breaking transcontinental flight in the Lockheed Vega *Yankee Doodle*. Crowds of people stood in front of the hangar watching the mechanics preparing the airplane for its return flight. I managed to slip under the rope and get a good look at the Vega, a high-wing, all-plywood cantilever monoplane and one of the cleanest designs of that period. She was painted a solid white with a hand-rubbed finish worthy of a Rolls-Royce.

In a nearby hangar was the huge Burnelli biplane with its airfoil-shaped fuselage, which *Aviation* magazine had reported carried a grand piano from New York to Washington. In still another hangar, one of the tallest on the field, was the Sikorsky Aircraft Company, where Igor Ivanovich Sikorsky was building aircraft on a "made-to-order" basis with the help of Russian immigrants like himself. I had no trouble wandering in and viewing a large twin-engined machine under construction.

Transatlantic attempts still were underway in 1928. At the time of my visit the Bellanca *Roma* was awaiting takeoff from Roosevelt Field at one end of the runway that had been prepared for Byrd's Fokker and also was used by Lindbergh. This so-called runway was really a gravel road 25–30 feet wide, reasonably smooth but not what one would think of as a runway today. The "hill" at the start of the runway, which Byrd had built to accelerate the *America* on its takeoff run, still was there. It last was used by George Haldeman and Ruth Elder in late 1927 in their Stinson-Detroit. All these overloaded planes had fixed-pitch propellers with low static thrust, and needed all the help they could get to start rolling.

I got a terrific charge out of the unique configuration of the *Roma*. It was a form of sesquiplane,[1] with the lower wing integrated into Bellanca's famous lift struts and retractable landing gear. Like all of Bellanca's creations it was aerodynamically

[1]*A variation on the biplane, the sesquiplane usually had a lower wing that was significantly smaller than the other wing, in span, chord or both. On occasion, the lower wing was only large enough to support the bracing struts for the upper wing. The name means "one-and-a-half wings."*

Fig. 3-11
This was one example of Burnelli aircraft with the airfoil-shaped fuselage. The concept never proved to be generally accepted, c. 1928.

Fig. 3-12
The *Roma* was the most advanced application of the Bellanca lift strut configuration, with a stub wing and retractable gear—a highly efficient and novel aircraft, 1928.

Fig. 3-13
The *Roma* after takeoff at Old Orchard Beach, 1928.

and structurally efficient. In reading Clarence Chamberlain's book *Record Flights,* I could sense the esteem that Bellanca enjoyed in aviation circles. I was to see him in person at Old Orchard Beach in Maine when Roger Q. Williams flew the *Pathfinder* across.[2]

Later that same Sunday, in the early evening, I had a unique experience. Wandering into what appeared to be a deserted hangar on Curtiss Field, I discovered the *Columbia*. This was the Whirlwind-engined Bellanca that Clarence Chamberlain and Charles Levine had flown from New York to Germany in 40-odd hours shortly after Lindbergh's New York to Paris. The *Columbia* was the greatest long-distance airplane of her day, and Lindbergh had tried to buy this aircraft for his transatlantic flight. Nosing around, I found the main cabin door unlocked and crawled up on the "shelf" of the big gas tank that took up the entire fuselage under the wing. The shelf was there so a pilot could get a little sleep during long-distance flights. Crawling forward and sliding down into the cockpit, I imagined what those 40 hours over the Atlantic and on to the Continent must have been like. Some might

remember that Levine, who was not much of a pilot but who owned the airplane, got into a spin over Germany early on the morning of the second day and Chamberlain, resting on the shelf, scrambled forward and finally pulled the airplane out. It had spun from about 18,000 feet to a couple of thousand. The plane picked up so much speed in the recovery that the rudder, with its large overhung balance, was almost torn off.

When it became too dark to prowl further, I began walking back toward Garden City on the straight road from Curtiss Field. This road was the one used by Lawrence Sperry to demonstrate *The Messenger*, the light biplane in which Sperry later was lost attempting to fly the English Channel. I soon obtained a lift into Garden City. Conversation revealed my driver was Bill Winston, an associate of Casey Jones but less flamboyant.

The next day I was back to visit the Curtiss Aeroplane and Motor Company located near the field. At that time it was the largest and best-equipped aircraft engineering and manufacturing facility in the United States. Glenn Curtiss still was there, and Ted Wright was chief engineer. In retrospect it seems amazing that I was given a full tour of the place—including the drafting room, shops and wind tunnel. I had written no letters

[2] *The* Roma *later used Old Orchard Beach for their record attempt. They got off safely but later returned due to engine trouble.*

Fig. 3-14
The Curtiss plant at Garden City produced some of the most notable military aircraft of the period and Navy and Army race planes. The famous D-12 engine and Reed metal propellers were developed there, c. 1930.

beforehand, just marched up to the front door and told them of my interest.

Curtiss was the first company to own and operate a wind tunnel, an open return facility of all-wood construction. Slotted wings, *à la* Handley-Page, were being tested. I assumed that this was in connection with the *Tanager*, which won the Guggenheim Safe Aircraft Competition. The tunnel was operated by Joe Muncey, who was to become the model shop superintendent at Cornell Aeronautical Laboratory. Many famous aircraft, including fighters, bombers, trainers and transporters, were built at this Garden City plant, as well as Schneider Cup and Pulitzer Trophy winners.

Before leaving my headquarters at Garden City I spent a day at Mitchell Field at the Army Air Base, and saw an airplane that I had seen pictures of in *Aviation*. This was the special Vought configured for Edward P. Warner's use as Secretary of the Navy.

On another day I stopped by Gates Aircraft where the *New Standard* was being built by Charles Healey Day, designer of the famous trainer used along with or slightly

after the Curtiss JN-4 Jenny. Gates Aircraft, located in what appeared to be a residential area on a quiet street surrounded by trees, was only large enough for the assembly of two or three airplanes at a time. I got there around noon, and was having difficulty getting past the receptionist, when a tall, rather informal man came in and offered to take me through the plant—none other than Charles Healey Day himself. He was most friendly and answered the many questions I had of a semi-technical nature. He subsequently married his receptionist, after building a special biplane to his own design for their round-the-world honeymoon.

I also hitchhiked out to College Point where Edo was building metal floats for such aircraft as the Fokker in which Schultz and Gordon flew Amelia Earhart across the Atlantic. Although prominent as a float manufacturer, Edo was a small operation. When I expressed an engineering interest I was shown around by chief engineer Korvin-Kroukovsky. Korvin was the author of an *Aviation* article on high-altitude airplanes that was written in simple, fundamental terms I had been able to understand, which I mentioned to him.

Following the Chamberlain/Levine flight to Germany, Levine had decided to get into aircraft manufacture himself and set up shop in Long Island City as Columbia Aircraft. A couple of French designers he had met at the time of the transatlantic flight were building an all-metal stressed-skin machine for him. One of the early uses of this construction in the United States, it was given a lot of space in the aviation technical press. I arrived there at noon on a Saturday and had no difficulty getting in. Just one stressed-skin metal job was on the floor. I overheard a conversation about static tests on a part of the structure that were to be run at New York University the following day. A couple of mechanics were mulling the possibility of ever getting a Sunday off while working at Columbia Aircraft.

The final day on Long Island found me at Valley Stream, a relatively new airfield where Curtiss did some experimental flying. I arrived there in an absolute downpour and slogged across the field, through mud and gravel, to the hangar. Only one aircraft was inside, but what a sight! It was the Curtiss-Bleeker helicopter, undergoing modification and development. Maitland Bleeker, a young engineering graduate from Cornell, had convinced Curtiss to build the original helicopter design that was the subject of his thesis. After wind tunnel studies, the company put up the unheard of sum of $100,000 to design and construct a prototype. Long before Sikorsky, the Curtiss-Bleeker helicopter was a pioneering design. Essentially it was four small airplanes chasing each other around. Each of its four wings was equipped with a horizontal tail and propeller. The pilot controlled the elevators which, in turn, rotated each wing assembly on a radial shaft. One can envision the complexity of the device, which consisted of a bewildering array of struts and tubing and bracing wires. Despite trying several

Fig. 3-15
Most aircraft companies in the 1920/30 period utilized university wind tunnels such as at MIT and New York University. Having its own wind tunnel and model-making capability set Curtiss apart and accounts, in part, for the success of its aircraft, c. 1930.

configurations, dynamic problems never were overcome and the project was abandoned when the stock market crashed in 1929.

Next, my base of operation moved to Ridgeway, New Jersey, where I stayed with friends of my folks for a few days. They had a beautiful home that was conveniently located to many of the aircraft companies in the area.

From Ridgeway, it was an easy hitchhike to Teterboro where Anthony Fokker had set up his American operations. His sizable factory was located at the old airfield. This also was Clarence Chamberlain's home base. A great expert on forced landings, Chamberlain kept in condition by operating from the short taxiway that ran alongside the Fokker plant. Anthony Fokker was on hand the day I visited, and no one could mistake him; he was in the middle of the activity. Fokker was riding high with his Tri-Motor and the Universal, among other aircraft. Their big wooden wings were under

Fig. 3-16
The fundamental problem of helicopters was reacting to the drive torque of the rotor system and controlling the cyclic moments produced by the rotating wings. Bleeker's solution had promise but was complex. The Sikorsky design of some years later used an articulated rotor and a controllable pitch propeller for yaw control driven by the rotor.

construction in one part of the factory, and the welded fuselages were coming down a sort of line in another section. The engineering office and drafting room were upstairs, although apparently Fokker did not spend much time there. He still was doing all of the test flying himself. One interesting aircraft I remember was an experimental amphibian. How impressive those big wooden wings were! I suppose the wings for the Tri-Motors were 70–80 feet in span; the center sections must have been over three feet in depth. Everything was done by hand and, in true Fokker tradition, the place was bedlam.

Following Teterboro I visited Hadley Field in New Jersey which still was an airmail base of operation. I went down there on a Sunday and found the hangar area crowded with sightseers. Local flying, joy rides and parachute jumps were going on. Most of the mail planes were De Havilland DH4s but there also was one of the new Pitcairn Mailwings, an open-cockpit biplane with a 225-hp Whirlwind engine. It was a really beautiful aircraft, built by the same man who brought the Cierva autogyro to this country. The Mailwing became famous when it was used by Howard Stark in the development of his 1-2-3 blind flying system. My final day was spent at Wright Aeronautical in Paterson, where the Whirlwind and subsequently the Cyclone engines were produced.

While I well recall the places I visited during the trip, for the life of me, I can't remember how I could have had enough clothes for the duration. I am certain I never sent anything ahead nor did I ever carry more than a small pack with me. I probably just kept wearing the same old shirt over and over again.

I left Boston on my way back to Old Town with one dollar in change still in my pocket.

Chapter 4 ⚶

Designed, Built, Flew and Crashed

M-1 side view, pilot at control, 1930.

On the early evening of September 5, 1933, a small monoplane took off from the curving sands of Old Orchard Beach and, after a brief but hectic flight, landed and nosed over. A meager result after nearly seven years of effort, perhaps, but the experience of conceiving, designing, building and flying an airplane almost solely on my own was extremely satisfying. Mine is believed to be the first home-built airplane in the state of Maine that actually flew, a fact that never occurred to me at the time.

By most standards the M-1 was a simple parasol monoplane. The story is worth telling only because of the circumstances surrounding its creation. Designed from a simplistic knowledge of aerodynamics and structures, built on a shoestring with elementary hand tools, the M-1 project never would have been completed except for the extraordinary inspiration of the heroic trans-oceanic flights of the time, and especially Lindbergh's successful solo New York to Paris flight.

Its flight characteristics displayed every form of aircraft instability and dramatically demonstrated how little I really knew. But the difficulty of translating theory into practice was instrumental in furthering my interest in a career in vehicle dynamics.

Well under way in late 1928 during my last year at Old Town High School, the M-1 project had begun two years earlier when I was 15. In terms of overall magnitude, duration and commitment, the M-1 far exceeded my earlier ground vehicles. Existing records indicate more than 2,100 hours of labor were expended, plus a lot of my mother's time in hand-sewing the fabric on the fuselage, wings and tail surfaces. The M-1 monopolized most of my spare time, as well as summer vacations, during my first three college years.

"The guy has an idea; he is testing it. If he thinks as an engineer, if it fails he will try to figure out why. With diligence the light will finally come on."

– Frank Winchell

Fig. 4-1
Curtiss Jenny, JN-4, the WWI trainer, popular with barnstormers.

A long gestation period and some preliminary starts preceded the M-1 becoming an ongoing endeavor. For several years my interest in aircraft had been evolving in parallel with my fascination with race cars. I have vague memories of the first Jenny barnstormers, the Shaw Flyers, landing on a hayfield across the river, performing stunts over Old Town to drum up business, and then giving rides for a dollar a minute. Three years later, in 1924, I built two gliders, both unsuccessful, followed by an attempt to construct a "Penguin" design published in *Popular Mechanics*, which finally was abandoned for lack of a suitable engine.

A World War I Avro 504K trainer with a rotary engine operated out of a pasture in Bangor called Godfrey's Field. This helped sustain my interest, as did the aeronautical collection in the Bangor Public Library. I must have read every reference in that collection from Lilienthal's *Bird Flight as a Basis of Aviation* to the Smithsonian Institution

Fig. 4-2
Bill Milliken in front of Helen Hunt Junior High School, circa 1924.

Proceedings covering the activities of the Wrights, Langley and Curtiss. I studied the controversy between the Smithsonian and the Wright brothers, in addition to the accounts of the 1914 flying of the reworked Langley Aerodrome in Hammondsport (New York) by Elwood "Gink" Doherty. There were wonderful flying adventures, like John Henry Mears's tale of his record-breaking round-the-world trip in a Fairchild, the first time an airplane had been used for overland sections. Further, I was gaining some experience in light structures and propeller design with the Aero-Triple-Cycle and the Ski Mobile. And then there was Brown's airplane.

Brown's Airplane

I was heading to my father's mill one day early in August 1924, when I was 13 years old. To avoid an encounter with the local bullies, I elected to run along the garden side of the Averills' cedar hedge, which ended abruptly at the rear

Fig. 4-3
Ralph Brown's homemade airplane. Side view, pilot about to taxi, circa 1924.

Fig. 4-4
Ralph Brown standing beside his motorcycle-engined airplane, 1924.

of a garage attached to a small house. Swerving through backyards to High Street, a window in the garage caught my eye. I stopped, peered in and looked incredulously at the engine and propeller end of a small airplane resting on conventional landing gear. Its cabane struts, wing center section above the single seat cockpit and four wing panels were leaning against the wall. The air-cooled vee-twin obviously was an adapted motorcycle engine. I ran around to the front, but found the garage doors locked. After a sleepless night I went back the next day to resolve the mystery.

The airplane was the creation of Ralph Brown. Brown had been hired as an efficiency expert at the Old Town Canoe Company.

73

His task was to cut costs by improving on the traditional "Indian way" of building wood and canvas canoes. During his first few years in town he had designed and constructed the small, single-place biplane, carefully tailoring it to fit into his 1-½ car garage. How he could have accomplished this without any kid in the neighborhood knowing is amazing. Few surprises in my youth equaled that of discovering Brown's airplane, right under my nose and only a mile from home. I now suspect that many of the components were built in the canoe factory after hours and assembled in the garage.

I never learned how Brown acquired his aircraft knowhow, but followed the final assembly stages and the initial flight attempt with deep interest. Because Old Town had no airport, Brown towed his machine, with wings detached, to Gray's Field. A pilot friend nosed over on his first takeoff attempt, ruining the propeller and causing other damage. Because Brown had accepted a prominent position at the Penn Yan Boat Company in New York State and soon would be leaving town, there were no further attempts.

During the next few weeks I hung around his place from morning to night, helping him disassemble and pack his machine for storage. He gave me the broken propeller, explaining its pitch calculations and fabrication. His biplane was an attractive, straightforward design that I always have believed would have flown successfully under the right circumstances. He offered to sell it for $200, a fortune to me at that time.

The Brown airplane provided a tremendous learning experience and was a definitive step along the way. The trigger for the M-1 project, however, was Lindbergh's 1927 crossing.

M-1 Preliminary Design and Preparations

Design is not a straightforward process, but a matter of trying this and trying that, making mistakes and using new knowledge. To quote automobile engineer Maurice Olley, "In design a straight line is the most awkward path between two points.... the entire history of mechanical engineering is of learning from failure. The prima donna type of mind is useless in engineering."

Converting a table in my bedroom for drafting use, I began by producing a side-view layout of a mid-wing, wire-braced monoplane. It used my old Excelsior vee-twin motorcycle engine, to which I had adapted a six-bolt propeller directly to the crankshaft. My diary says this occurred in late September of 1926. The brown wrapping-paper drawing still exists, and my initial renderings are reproduced in Figures 4-6 and 4-7. The fuselage construction was a conventional wire-braced wood truss. Steel tubing was not easily available to me, much less welding equipment, nor would I have had the experience to use it. A preliminary weight and balance study indicated that the center of gravity was much too far aft on the wings, so I modified my plan accordingly.

Shopping for materials at the Jordan Lumber Company on Water Street, and anticipating the need for a continuous source of clear straight-grained spruce, I sat down with the foreman and briefed him in some detail on the proposed project. This was a smart move because he became enthusiastic about participating and agreed to set aside the best spruce

Fig. 4-5
Excelsior twin-engine with direct-drive propeller adaptation.

as it came to stock. I agreed to forewarn him of particular size requirements for wing spars, ribs, gear, engine mount, etc. as fast as they could be determined. Now, more than 70 years later, I'm embarrassed to have forgotten his name. He never failed to produce the best wood, carefully cut or planed to specifications.

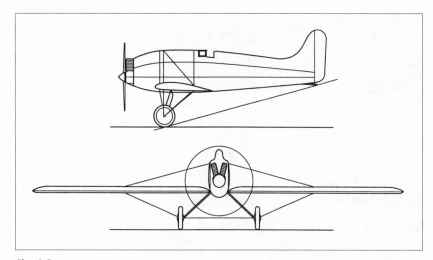

Fig. 4-6
Early layout of Excelsior twin-powered wire-braced low-wing monoplane, late 1926.

The fuselage longerons and uprights were 1-¼ by 1-¼ inches in section, routed slightly on all four sides. Working initially in our barn chamber, I completed the two fuselage sides, less wire bracing, in mid-October. By this time winter had set in, making it much too cold to continue. I had just about accepted a delay until spring when an unexpected solution appeared.

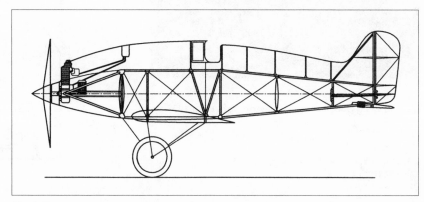

Fig. 4-7
Modified side-view layout with engine moved forward for improved balance.

NEXT TO HIS HOME on Fourth Street, Old Town Canoe Company proprietor Sam Gray had remodeled the second-story loft over his two-car garage into a recreation area. It was heated by a small wood stove next to a brick chimney. Measuring about 30 by 45 feet, and well lit by four windows and electrical fixtures, the loft included a ping-pong table, modest-sized work bench, cabinets, etc. The floor was smooth and painted a light gray. Braley Gray suggested I take over the loft, and after briefing his parents in some detail on the project they agreed. For the next seven years I was to pursue the M-1 build under ideal working conditions. The Grays were "patrons" of a high order. They never monitored progress or questioned when the airplane would be completed. I could come and go, day or night, and when there were long breaks during

the school year nothing was disturbed, so I could pick up wherever I had left off. The firewood supply was routinely replenished.

This was my first experience with such generosity, but by no means the last. I have concluded that human beings have an innate desire to be associated with potentially worthwhile projects, with the result that those who initiate a creative activity often will receive voluntary help and sponsorship. To me this cooperative spirit is a profound feature of our society.

My parents were totally supportive of the project. My consuming interest in the M-1 and preceding projects meant I didn't have paying jobs during summer vacations, and therefore little money of my own. My mother placed a hundred one-dollar bills, earned

Fig. 4-8a
Sam Gray's garage with second-story loft, circa 1927.

Fig. 4-8b
Layout of Sam Gray's garage and loft in which M-1 was constructed.

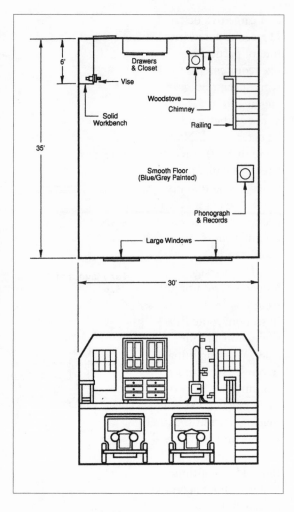

through her piano teaching, in an envelope from which I was free to draw. Despite my father's financially strapped business he helped whenever needed. For example, he paid the 40 dollars for the replacement engine. As the airplane reached completion, a check for $50 came from the local Rotary Club. Total cash outlay for the M-1 was less than $300.

To cut down on lonesome, solitary hours of work, I installed a hand-cranked Victrola in a corner of the loft so that friends could drop by after the movies for a few dance sets or to practice the Charleston. In a way it was like building an airplane in a dance hall.

Design Considerations

The evolution of the M-1 design was fixed by available material and tools. Before making my initial layout, I had acquired as much

information as possible on existing light planes, a number of which were quite sophisticated and had flown successfully. This data came from a variety of sources—sales literature, correspondence and descriptive articles in *The Aeroplane* and *Flight*. I tabulated this information for easy reference. (See Figure 4-9.) Early on, this data led me to question my Excelsior twin as a suitable powerplant because it only offered 15 hp, obviously marginal for most light planes. The switch from a wire-braced low-wing design to a strut-braced parasol was a later, more complex decision. Structural and aerodynamic considerations, and reported flight experience, suggested that the high-wing parasol configuration was a better choice for the M-1. Carrying all wing loads through the landing gear was critical to abandoning the original layout, in addition to the cost of tailored streamlined wires.

	WEIGHT		Wing Loading	Power Loading	H.P. Max	Span Cord	Aspect Ratio	AREAS					WEIGHTS					PERFORMANCE			Length	Airfoil
	Empty	Loaded						Wing	Aileron	Stab. Elevator	Fin	Rudder	Fuselage	L.Gear	Wing lbs per sq.ft.	Tail Surfaces	Engine	Top	L.S.	Climb, fpm		
Alco Ex. braced monoplanes	375	525	4.5	32.8	16	$\frac{26}{5}$	5.2	117	13.5	$\frac{15}{12}$	1.3	4.8					110	75	30	Range 400 m.	18'3"	Gotting 365
Heath Parasol High Wing Ex. braced monoplane	260	560	4.7	20.7	27	$\frac{2.5}{4.5}$	5.6	110	10	$\frac{5.5}{5.2}$	1	3.8					105	70	28	Range 120 m.	16'9"	Clark y
Lincoln Single Bay Biplane	370	600	5.6	17	35	$\frac{20}{2.75}$	7.3	110									105	80		800'	16'	U.S.A)s
Russel Ex. braced high wing monoplane	330	475	5.5	20.7	23	$\frac{24}{3.83}$	6.3	88				2.5			.75		125				14'6"	Clark
Heath Biplane (M.) Single Bay Biplane	325	500	3.2	31.3	16	$\frac{21.5}{4}$	5.4	172 app.	26	$\frac{13}{12}$	1.5	5.5	wt. without engine – 145 lbs.				110	60	29		15'5"	
Heath, Ford Single Bay Biplane	525	975	3.6	10.5	50	$\frac{26}{4}$	6.5	192	28	$\frac{17.5}{15}$	2	7					200	60	32	2000	18'8"	
Heath Baby Bullet Monoplane	235	535	8.9	16.7	32	$\frac{18}{3.5}$	5.1	60 app.	5	3	1	2.3					120	150	55	Ceiling 14,000	13'	St.Cyr 52
"Beetle" Single Bay Biplane	326	600	6.1	15.4	36	$\frac{18.5}{3}$	6.1	105	15'	8 sq.ft.							100	96	40	Range 300 m.	16'9"	
Tinson's Monoplane Plywood construction	245	400	8.3	15.4	28	$\frac{16.75}{3}$	5.6	42.5	7.8	$\frac{11.5}{5.3}$	1.5	2.6	28		1.38	10	100	94	52	600 ceiling 13,000	13'3"	
Tinson's Biplane Single Bay Biplane	349	525	6.1	17.5	30	$\frac{16.87}{2.56}$	6.6	85.8	14		1.3	4.7	30	22	1.15	15	100	80	40	400	15'	
Meteorplane (Irvin 20-25) Single Bay Biplane	240	440	4.5	18	25	20											64	90	30	400	14'	Irvin
Meteorplane (Motorcycle 9-15) Single Bay Biplane	265	441	4.5	28	15	20											100	60	30	300	14'	Irvin

Fig. 4-9
Comparative technical information of contemporary aircraft.

I could obtain material at the lumber company roughly cut or planed to size. Otherwise, I had no band saw, table saw, drill press or hand-held electric drill. Never having had the luxury of such tools, I hardly missed them and simply went ahead with the following:

- work bench and vise
- hand wood saw
- hand keyhole saw
- hand jig saw
- hack saw
- draw shave
- hand plane
- wood rasp
- several sizes of wood chisels
- wooden mallet
- ¼-inch hand-cranked drill
- metal files
- large tin snips
- pliers
- nail hammer
- peen hammer
- adjustable wrench
- T-square
- ¹/₁₆-inch scale
- "yo-yo" (spring-loaded tape measure).

The M-1 was a hand-built airplane in every sense of the word. Tool limitations made the project extraordinarily labor intensive. I overcame these limitations and maintained my determination in no small part because of the excitement and inspiration of the trans-oceanic record flights.

The M-1 project was all-consuming, and while I continued to work hard at math my other courses fell by the wayside. Sketching out details of the M-1 behind my geography book was more exciting than classwork, and at 4:30 every afternoon I hastened to Gray's loft for an hour or so before supper. In the evening I'd be back there or studying National Advisory Committee for Aeronautics (NACA)[1] reports, Diehl's *Engineering Aerodynamics* or Montieth's *Airplane Design*. On Friday evenings during the basketball season I'd sit in front of our Franklin stove reading aerodynamic reports until ten, and then slip down to the Helen

[1] *Congress founded NACA in 1915 as an independent government agency reporting to the President. NACA coordinated research and became a leader in wind-tunnel testing and airfoil development. NACA was incorporated into the National Aeronautics and Space Administration (NASA) after its creation in 1958.*

Hunt Auditorium for the dances after the games.

This routine led to progress on the M-1, but dismal report cards from high school. When graduation approached in June of '29, there was some question that my grades would meet the entry requirements of the Engineering School at the University of Maine, a state-supported college with low tuition (which was very important during the Depression). At that point my mother marched up Academy Hill. She knew all the high school teachers and made it clear to them that while I didn't fit into a conventional mold, I had something on the ball and was worth saving. Grades were adjusted so I could be accepted at the University. How fortunate I was to have a mother of such strong convictions. My own reaction at the time was that high school had been a waste of time, and I was determined to prove it by getting top grades in college. My mature feeling

now is that school systems should be able to accommodate children with varied interests. Surprisingly enough, I was elected to give the high school class oration. I chose the subject "The Interesting Career of a Genius Airplane Designer, Giuseppe M. Bellanca."

M-1 Build

Working through the winter of 1928–29 and the summers of '29 and '30, I completed the fuselage structure, landing gear, tail surfaces and controls, as shown in Figure 4-10 taken in August 1930. What a joy the summers were! I'd literally leap out of bed in the morning, slap some cold water on my face, grab a quick breakfast and take off on my bicycle for Gray's loft.

The wooden fuselage structure was internally braced with diagonal wires. Turnbuckles were in short supply, so I devised a simple fitting for using the threaded end on a

Fig. 4-10
M-1 fuselage, gear and tail surfaces, 1930. These are the original tail surfaces. I later installed a rudder with "aerodynamic" balance.

bicycle spoke as a light replacement. Conscious of weight, I put no floor in the cockpit, only heel plates made of ¼-inch plywood below the rudder bar and a plywood seat bottom, the back of which was a wide fabric belt with two attached cables running forward to the firewall to take the seat-back load.

An issue of *Flight* illustrated a simple way of approximating an ellipse with the arcs of three circles. Deciding that elliptical cross-sections would make a more attractive fuselage, I drew them up, jig-sawed the four segments out of plywood and taped them to the uprights and cross members. Thin longitudinal stringers then defined the fuselage shape.

The landing gear was simplicity itself. Elements of cost and availability dictated the use of small bicycle wheels, which I built up with wooden rims and hubs suitable for one-inch axle tubes, then covered them with fabric. Because the small tires dictated that the aircraft be flown from a smooth surface (certainly not from a hayfield), there was no need for shock struts, so I could get away with a rigid gear.

The two fixed spruce struts were draw-shaved to a streamlined section. The tops of the struts connected to the longerons at a point just below a substantial vertical member in the fuselage. The bottoms of the struts had U-shaped cuts in which the axle was located, and the axle was held in place with through bolts. Longitudinal loads were absorbed by substantial aircraft cables that ran forward and aft from the bottoms of the struts to points on the lower longeron. Diagonals in the plane of the struts took the side loads. Here I used aircraft hardware (turnbuckles and cable).

With the rigid gear, I later ran cables from the outboard ends of the axle to the outer attachments of the wing struts, a precautionary redundancy. To locate the inboard side of the wheels, fixed washers were welded onto the axle tube. Washers and through bolts located the outside of the wheel hubs and represented the only place where welding was used—accomplished at T. M. Chapman's Sons Co. for the total sum of six dollars. To complete the landing gear, a tail skid was made of three leaves of hardwood (like a laminated leaf spring) with an aluminum rubbing strip on the bottom. This was installed on the aft-most point on the fuselage. I had, of course, made an estimate of the fuselage attitude in static position.

Old Orchard Interlude

For a smooth takeoff area, Old Orchard Beach some 150 miles from Old Town seemed ideal. I often had visited the beach on hitchhiking trips, but the real incentive came from the use of the beach by several of the great transatlantic flight attempts. The first of these was *Old Glory*, the big single-engined Fokker of Bertaud, Hill and Payne that left for Rome on September 6, 1927. For some reason, probably the start of school, I missed being there but closely

Fig. 4-11
Old Glory, the single-engined Fokker flown from Old Orchard Beach by Bertaud, Hill and Payne. Lost in Atlantic. Part of the landing gear was found several hundred miles from Newfoundland.

Fig. 4-12
Calibrating the compasses on the Bernard *Yellow Bird* before takeoff from Old Orchard Beach, Maine, on its transatlantic flight, June 13, 1929.

followed the sobering outcome of the flight. Then in early June of 1929 word came that three Frenchmen – Lotti, LeFevre and Assolant – were planning to use the beach for a flight to Paris. I wasted no time hitchhiking to Old Orchard, but arrived while they were waiting for more favorable weather after an aborted takeoff. *The Yellow Bird* (*L'Oiseau Canari*) was the first airplane I saw poised at the start of a transatlantic attempt.

Walking down the beach from the northern end, I sighted her from some distance, bright yellow wings and fuselage gleaming in the sun. The plane was resting in the soft sand above tide line in front of Jones's hangar. (Jones, the equivalent of the FBO or Fixed Base Operator at conventional airports, had been a fixture at Old Orchard since the end of WWI.) The Bernard 191 was an impressive aircraft, aerodynamically clean by standards of the day. Her single, tapered cantilever wing was mounted near the top of the wooden monocoque fuselage, while the 600-hp liquid-cooled Hispano engine was nicely faired into the nose. The radiator extended below the fuselage just aft of the firewall. The tail surfaces also were cantilevered, and with the exception of the gear there were no external struts or wires. The pilot sat high up front between the engine and the wing; a small passageway led aft alongside the main tank to the spacious navigator/crew compartment, with an entry door on the left-hand side. Thanks to the low drag, the high wing loading and the amount of power, *Yellow Bird* could cruise much faster than earlier transatlantic aircraft.

Appearing compact, her size was deceptive. The cowling was off the engine and a mechanic was standing on a high stepladder checking out the power plant. It seemed to me the cockpit was at least ten feet off the ground. A small and friendly group of spectators surrounded the aircraft. Because there were no guards or fencing, one could wander around and peer into the open door of the main cabin. A navigator's table was on the right, radio equipment nearby, and a hatch opened in the roof for taking sextant observations. I could well imagine the concentration required for working up a star sight in rough air and under the general pressure of flight, and then plotting a position line using the Hydrographic Navigation Tables and logs for computation. There was also a large inspection door for access to the rear of the fuselage, which was to play a prominent role in the outcome of the flight.

Fig. 4-13
Bellanca *Green Flash,* **wrecked on takeoff at Old Orchard Beach, 1929. Roger Q. Williams pilot, Lon Yancey**
navigator.

In the vicinity of the aircraft, chatting among themselves, Assolant, Lotti and LeFevre were easy to identify from pictures I had seen. The French had not fared well in their early transatlantic ambitions. Fonck had crashed on takeoff, Nungesser and Coli had disappeared over the ocean, and by now Lindbergh and five others had flown across the Atlantic. Picking up the challenge, the all-French *Yellow Bird* was sponsored by Armand Lotti's hotel-owning father. He was the moving spirit and flight leader, and brought in the highly qualified Assolant and LeFevre as pilot and navigator. They had made one unsuccessful attempt at an East-West flight and, balked on their second try by a temporary French government prohibition against transatlantic takeoffs, had shipped their aircraft to the United States for a flight in the reverse direction.

The weather prognosis was so indefinite that after two days at the beach I returned from Old Orchard, but not before I visited Jones's hangar where another transatlantic aircraft, the Bellanca, was awaiting favorable weather for a flight to Rome. This was the *Green Flash,* to be flown by Roger Q. Williams and Lon Yancey, It would be wrecked when attempting a takeoff after the *Yellow Bird.* Bellanca himself, who closely followed all record flight attempts by his aircraft, was inspecting the *Green Flash* when I was there. Much too awed by his reputation, I watched him from a distance. Incidentally, Williams and Yancey were to return later with another Bellanca, a Pathfinder, and fly to Santander, Spain, when headwinds defeated their Rome objective.

On June 13, 1929, the weather pattern over the Atlantic changed for the better and the *Yellow Bird* crew decided to leave for Paris. They were carrying a fuel load of some 900 gallons. The takeoff was far from normal. Assolant had difficulty getting the tail up for takeoff and the run was much longer than anticipated. Once in the air the plane was difficult to trim for cruising flight. The cause of this puzzling behavior soon appeared when a stowaway, one Arthur Schreiber, came forward through the inspection door to the tail. His thoughtless, almost criminal, behavior had so unbalanced the aircraft it was a miracle it got off at all, and his additional weight ruined the chance of reaching Paris. It says a great deal for the humanity of the French crew that they accepted this burden and even included the stowaway in the reception upon finally reaching Paris after an enforced stop in Spain. The first Frenchmen to fly the Atlantic had run out of fuel some 28 hours 52 minutes after leaving Old Orchard. Years later I took my mother on a month's trip to Europe. We stayed at the Lotti Hotel in Paris where I conversed briefly with Armand Lotti, then the hotel manager, about his flight.

After the *Yellow Bird,* I went back to work on the M-1 with renewed enthusiasm.

Back at Gray's Loft

Sometime during the winter of 1930, probably before Christmas, I made the decision to go for the parasol, strut-braced configuration, and fabricated the cabane struts and the long wing struts. Now in my sophomore year at the University of Maine, the workload had lessened from that of my freshman year, and progress on M-1 was made over the winter. My mother completed the fuselage covering by late January 1931—a difficult task given the cockpit cutout and the changing cross-section approaching the

tail. Major progress during spring and summer involved the wing structure.

Based largely on published data for other light planes, I had decided early on to use a span of 25 feet and a chord of 4.5 feet. This gave an aspect ratio for a rectangular wing of about 5.5, and an area of 112 square feet. In those days the Clark Y wing section designed by Col. V. E. Clark, and used on Lindbergh's *Spirit of St. Louis,* was exceedingly popular. It had a flat bottom, well-rounded nose and no reverse curvature (ideal for fabric cover), plus good force/moment characteristics. The Variable Density Wind Tunnel at NACA Langley had come on line in 1925, enabling tests to be run at realistic Reynolds numbers that yielded reliable data. From NACA Report No. 352, Jacobs's and Anderson's "Large-Scale Aerodynamic Characteristics of Airfoils Tested in the Variable Density Tunnel" published in 1930, a maximum lift coefficient of 1.42 was obtained for a Clark Y model with an aspect

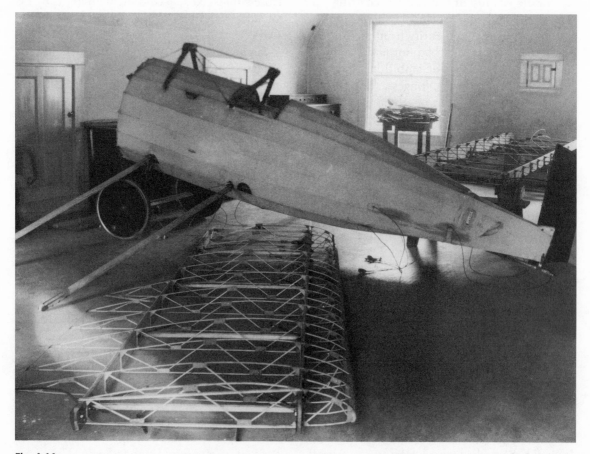

Fig. 4-14
I liked the looks of the elliptical fuselage, M-1.

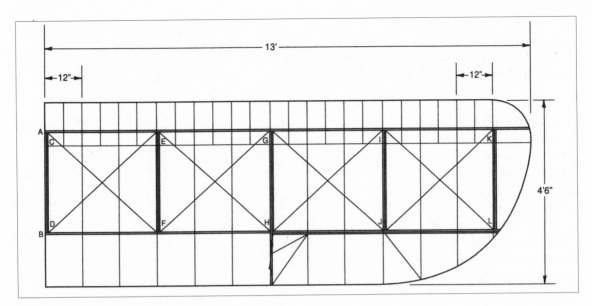

Fig. 4-15a
M-1 wing layout (showing ailerons).

Fig. 4-15b
M-1 completed wing structure, which is very conventional. Note compression members and wire shear bracing, circa 1930.

ratio of six. Assuming M-1 at 500 pounds gross weight (actually 475 pounds as flown), the landing speed could be calculated at about 35 mph.

During the summer of 1935 my mother sewed the fabric onto the wings. A millinery store downtown, run by two conservative spinster sisters, carried a good grade of unbleached cotton cloth, although not in the quantity we required. After convincing themselves that our use of the material was strictly moral, the sisters ordered another bolt or two. During that summer Old Town experienced an unprecedented heat wave, with temperatures in the eighties and high humidity. With no fans or air-conditioning the loft became a stifling place to work. My mother, a staunch New Englander who relished the long cold winters, suffered from heat all her life, but I don't remember her ever complaining during the weeks we worked together covering the wings and ailerons. So intense was my interest in the project that I was completely insensitive to what she must have been experiencing.

At first, we thought we could use the sewing machine at home to make a tightly fitting bag that could be worked onto the wing. For various reasons this proved impractical, so she had to resort to hand sewing. With the wing on sawhorses, a strip of fabric covering a few feet of span was wrapped around the wing and sewed at the trailing edge, then another strip sewed to this and the process was repeated. Kneeling, lying on a pillow or sitting on a box, my mother plied thimble and needle as if making a dress. My task was to assist by cutting and by keeping the fabric taut. The cutouts for the ailerons proved a major problem, and there were fittings on the wing that had to be worked around.

From my studies I was aware that one can't just "bag" a wing and dope the fabric. It must be tied down to the ribs. This is accomplished

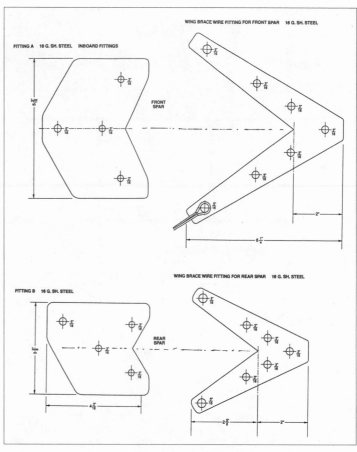

Fig. 4-16
Fittings for front and rear wing spars. An attempt to distribute the load into the spars.

by running a cord over the fabric on the top of a rib, then down each side of the rib and over the fabric on the bottom, all at a number of chord-wise stations. The long needle my father used for sewing up burlap bags to deliver axe handles was ideal for this purpose. Once the fabric was in place we set the wing up on its leading edge, with my mother on one side and me on the other, passing the needle and "thread" back and forth along the rib sides. This required some coordination, but we made light of it, carrying on a bantering conversation.

It took about six gallons of nitrate dope, acquired from the Johnson Aircraft and Supply Co. of Dayton, Ohio, to shrink and tighten the fabric. This was applied by brush after the rib stitching had been covered with tape. The last coat was aluminized to give the wings a silver color.

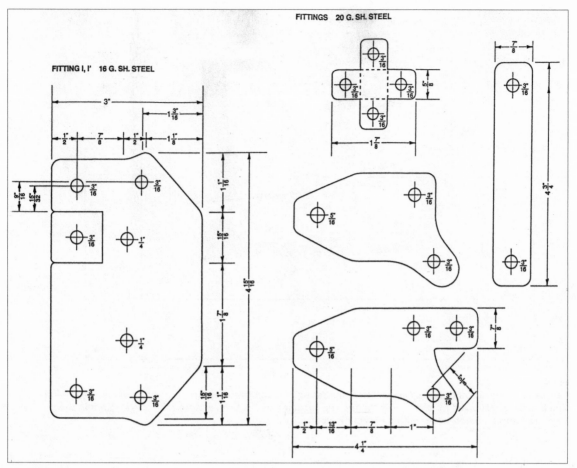

Fig. 4-17
More fittings, M-1.

Building M-1's Wings

The ordinates of the top and bottom of the airfoil in percent of chord were given in the NACA Report No. 352. Since I had already decided on the location of the rectangular cross-section of the spruce spars, it was easy to draw an accurate full-scale layout of the wing rib, then glue it to a 1-½-inch-thick plank planed for smoothness. Small locating blocks slightly less than ¼-inch (the height of the rib components) were screwed to it. This completed the so-called rib jig, which can be seen in one of the photos on the work table near the window. Gussets of thin plywood would be casein glued and tacked at each joint to hold the rib elements together.

Rib construction began after making up batches of carefully dimensioned quarter-by-quarter-inch rib elements and gussets shaped for the different joints. As any home builder can testify, rib making can be a long and tedious job. As each rib is removed from the jig, it must be turned over for gussets to be glued and tacked to the other side. The dimensions and locations of the spar openings have to be carefully held or all kinds of trouble can occur when the ribs are assembled on the spars. The ribs are attached to the spars with corner blocks to allow for some adjustment; nevertheless one cannot afford to be sloppy. To complete the wing structure five compression members were installed between the spars. They were diagonally braced to give the wing some fore and aft shear strength. A rounded leading edge was glued to the rib noses and a wire was fitted for the trailing edge. Wing tips were formed by a rounded tube of small diameter.

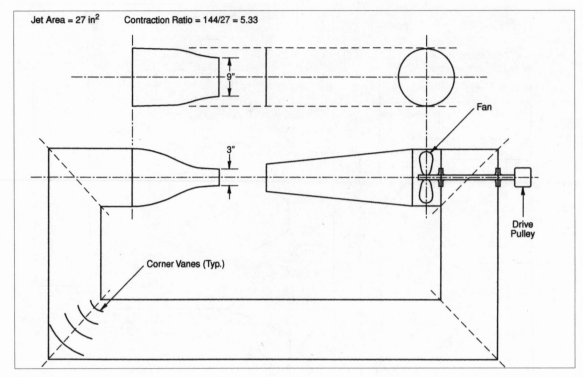

Jet Area = 27 in² Contraction Ratio = 144/27 = 5.33

9"

3"

Fan

Drive
Pulley

Corner Vanes (Typ.)

Fig. 4-18
Layout of the small wind tunnel I constructed and set up in the Physics Deptartment at the University of Maine. The fan design followed from propeller theory. The entrance and exit cones were fabricated from thin sheet steel. The return section was fiber board and plywood.

Looking back, I can see that one of the major time-consuming tasks in fabricating this wooden, non-welded aircraft was making the metal fittings required at all the major attachment points—cabane to fuselage, gear to fuselage, wing to cabane, wing struts to wings and fuselage, plus hinges for control surfaces, etc. All fittings were made from 16- or 20- gauge steel, thin enough to work with hacksaw, file and tin snips. For less stressed parts like control fittings I could get away with 24- gauge half-hard aluminum. In all cases I made simple sketches on brown wrapping paper, with dimensions and bolt hole locations and sizes specified.

At the University of Maine

My first two years studying Mechanical Engineering had given me the basics of mechanics and structures, and hence a confidence in those aspects of the M-1. Professor Weston was an inspiring teacher who not only presented the material but drilled it into his students: "The work done by the working forces minus the resistances is the change in kinetic energy!" I came away with a fundamental sense of mechanics. Similarly the design and drafting courses were exercises in "take the time and do it right." However, my knowledge of aerodynamics up to that point had come solely from home study of aerodynamic tests and NACA reports, and many of them were difficult because of my modest knowledge of mathematics.

For my third year at the University of Maine I transferred to Arts & Sciences to avoid the restrictions of the Mechanical Engineering curriculum. There I was able to take more advanced physics and mathematics courses (including logic), plus a practical course in slide rule use that enabled me to keep track of the decimal point! Better yet was the tutoring in aerodynamics and special projects by Dr. A. L. Fitch, head of the Physics Department. He agreed to spend one evening a week with me at his home reviewing a book on airscrew design by the British author Fage. For some time I

also had been struggling with a
highly theoretical book, *Aerofoil
and Airscrew Theory* by H. Glauert
of the British Research Center at
Farnborough, and I solicited help
from the Physics Department's
Professor Piston.

For a project that spring I
constructed a small open-throat
wind tunnel with closed return
from pictures of a model in a
NACA report. Figure 4-18 shows
the general arrangement and
dimensions. The cross-sectional
three-by-nine-inch area of the
jet was from memory, and the
wooden fan or propeller in the
entrance section was 14 inches in
diameter with high pitch and large
blade area. Built in sections in
our barn chamber using plywood,
fiber board and galvanized tin for
the entrance section, the tunnel
transitioned from a circular section
at the fan to the rectangular section
at the jet entrance. The exit cone
was a rectangular diffuser with a
small divergence angle. Turning
vanes of galvanized tin were located
in all corners. The tunnel was installed in the
University of Maine's Physics Department
shop and belt-driven by the electric motor
of the lathe. Speeds of up to 60 mph were
achieved in the working section and because of
the contraction ratio, the flow was reasonably
uniform. I investigated a variety of pitot tubes
fashioned from glass tubing and used them
to survey the jet. This was a great way to get
next to an airstream and experience Bernoulli's
equation as well as observe the flow with tufts
around miniature airfoils. To my knowledge
this was the first wind tunnel at the university.

Powering the M-1

Early in the M-1 design stage, after abandoning
use of the Excelsior twin as a power plant,
I began looking for a replacement engine.
On one of my hitchhiking trips in June of
1930 to explore the possibility of using Old
Orchard Beach for the M-1, I visited Pine

Fig. 4-19
**Henderson-Heath conversion. Note magnetos and oil sump. The
engine mount attaches at the junction between the bottom of the
crankcase and the oil sump.**

Point at the northernmost end of the beach.
Possibly through Harry Jones, I had learned of
a resident, Ira Snow, who owned a Henderson
four-cylinder air-cooled engine with the Heath
conversion complete with propeller. I suspect
he may have contemplated building a Heath
Parasol, the very popular light single-seater
from Heath Airplane Co. in Chicago. Ed Heath
had developed both the parasol design and the
conversion of the Henderson motorcycle engine
for use in it. The conversion consisted of an
extension to the crankshaft, modifications of
the crankcase, additional bearings, propeller
hub, etc., and camshaft modifications to
produce a reliable unit of some 27 horsepower
at 3,000 rpm. (See Figure 4-19.)

I gave Snow a ten-dollar down payment
and he agreed I could pay the balance of thirty
dollars when I took possession of the engine,
which he freighted to me via Maine Central
Railroad on June 13, 1933. Not only that, he
answered a number of questions regarding its
installation and operation.

Fig. 4-20
The four-cylinder Henderson motorcycle engine with the Heath conversion that provided a thrust bearing and crankshaft extension for the propeller hub. I designed and fabricated the propeller. The engine put out about 27 hp.

Early that summer, *Airplane Design—Aerodynamics* by Edward P. Warner, a former professor of aeronautical engineering at MIT, came to my attention at the Bangor Public Library. Part III of the book (which was published in 1927) was a comprehensive treatment of airplane stability, control and maneuverability. In those days stability and control were the most mysterious aspects of an aircraft's design, and even today they are a complex discipline whose complete analysis is highly mathematical. I had yet to be exposed to Professor Koppen's course at MIT and I certainly lacked the experience to realize that my original M-1 design, based largely on other light plane experience, probably was quite satisfactory. The M-1 was a very low-speed aircraft, which would minimize problems of control and stability. But even after my brief flight training at the Boeing School,[2] I had a genuine concern for its flying characteristics. I decided to take a few days off to study Warner's book, so I

One of my major tasks that busy summer was to design the engine mount, and make and install the cowling. Longitudinal (fore and aft) location of the engine, which was installed fairly high in the nose, was determined by the desired center-of-gravity in relation to the wing. The engine was mounted on two wooden beams extending forward of the firewall. It was braced by 22-gauge steel tubes $^5/_{16}$-inch in diameter that were flattened at the sides and drilled, with no welding. The cowling was made up of several single-curvature sections fastened together with a dozen or so small bolts. Once the engine was in place the various controls, throttle, spark and fuel lines were connected. A rectangular gas tank, soldered together with a filler neck and cap on top, was made to fit into the center of the wing above the cabane struts.

went up to a friend's camp on Cold Stream Pond where I could concentrate on it. Without tools to run *quantitative* analysis, I was forced to interpret the text in *qualitative* terms. In a device as complex as an airplane, where many requirements must be compromised, qualitative analysis has its hazards. Longitudinal stability, as Warner pointed out, can be enhanced with a forward center of gravity (CG) location relative to the wing chord. Lateral stability, the roll behavior of the airplane when side-slipped, is certainly desirable in moderation but in excessive amounts can lead to undesirable oscillatory behavior. Furthermore, the necessary amount of dihedral is greatly affected by the

[2] *In the summer of 1932, I completed a Private Ground and Flying Course at the Boeing School of Aeronautics in Oakland, CA. See Chapter 5.*

location of the wing on the fuselage, an effect difficult to determine except by wind tunnel tests. On an aircraft as small and slow as M-1, pilot control forces are almost never a problem, although some slow but highly maneuverable aircraft such as WWI Fokker fighters benefited from overhung aerodynamic balances on the control surfaces.

To make a long story short, I concluded that the M-1 would be a better flying machine if I shifted the CG to 20 percent on the wing chord by moving the engine forward, increased the dihedral, and provided the rudder with an overhung balance. These changes required rework of the engine mount, wing struts and rudder (which had to be recovered). They also taught me a harsh lesson and shortened the flying life of the M-1. These mistakes were the only major ones I made during the design of the aircraft. The CG should have been between

30–33 percent on this high-wing monoplane, its dihedral should have been around zero, and the rudder would have been much better with no overhung balance at all.

Years later I met E. P. Warner on a high-level aeronautical committee and mentioned that after reading his book I had made certain changes to the M-1, thereby creating a nearly unflyable aircraft. Before I could explain to him that the problem really was my qualitative interpretation, he said, "I have many things to account for in my life," a gesture of humility by one of our great aeronautical engineers and teachers. He went on to become a leading figure in international air regulations.

Pine Point Adventure

When I was trying to get a fix on use of the beach for the M-1 trials, a friend suggested I contact a relative of his in Saco near Old Orchard, to whom I wrote. He wrote back that a permit from the selectmen or the police department was necessary, and would be difficult to get during the summer season. I next contacted FBO Harry Jones, who came back with the discouraging answer that "no flying would be allowed on the beach unless the pilot and plane were licensed by the Department of Commerce." Since I intended to operate from the remote end of the beach near Pine Point, I decided to query Winslow Pillsbury, a nearby resident and proprietor of a lobster house called Pillsbury's Shore Dinners. He was more encouraging. If we took responsibility for any mishap that might occur, he knew of nothing that would prevent our use of the beach.

That was enough for me. I concluded that if one waited to get the approval of all dissenters, bureaucrats and conservatives, nothing would ever get done.

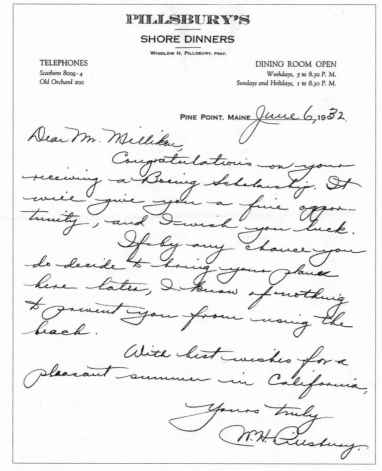

Fig. 4-21
Letter from Pillsbury that led me to Pine Point, June 6, 1932. Pillsbury was a real supporter of our venture.

In the course of a lifetime I have generalized this dictum to: "There are those who do the real work of the world, and the rest who hound them." I decided to go ahead with my plans to fly at Old Orchard Beach from a base at Pine Point.

To complete the work on the airplane, the fuselage and tail surfaces were painted red, and in good old Fokker fashion I stenciled MILLIKEN in large black letters sized to fit on the tapered fuselage. To avoid making another set of stencils for the other side, Milliken was reversed to NEKILLIM.

There remained the task of planning the transportation of the aircraft to Pine Point and setting up the remote base. Bill Miller, younger brother of Charlotte and Shirley Miller who were in my Old Town High class, had taken a genuine interest in the M-1. He hung around at the loft and provided help when needed, especially in mounting the 100-pound engine. Assembling the aircraft and operating at Pine Point obviously was a two-man job. Enthusiastic and competent, Bill Miller was the natural choice.

After preliminary assembly in the loft to insure that nothing had been overlooked, the plane was disassembled so the components could be taken out through a window. The wing chord just barely made it through, and the landing gear had to be taken off the fuselage. A truck had to be waiting because we had to leave early enough to reach Pine Point, 160 miles away, well before dark to set up our tent and get the aircraft under cover.

The tent, of large tarps laced together, was our own creation. A dozen tent poles as well as stakes were made at my father's mill. Tent area was 35 feet wide, 10 feet high in the middle and 20 feet deep, sufficient to house the entire aircraft with plenty of room for our sleeping bags and living quarters. To test our creation we erected the tent in Bill Miller's backyard, where it weathered at least one thunderstorm. Since we would be setting up on sandy soil beyond the tide line, the stakes were made long (1-½ to 2 feet). And, of course, we took along a regular sledgehammer to drive them in.

My father rented a suitable stakebed truck, whose owner lived on French Island. For 25 dollars he would make the trip to Old Orchard, unload us and return in the course of one day. Plans for our return trip were to be negotiated later. My father and brother Cooper wanted to be there so Mr. Pillsbury located a garage apartment within walking distance of our proposed campsite. This was to prove a great place for Bill and me to go for a meal and a shower, and to relax in more luxurious surroundings than a sleeping bag. In true expedition style I made up a list of everything that had to go, and added a checklist for assembling the aircraft. Perhaps overkill, but it was an exercise that would prove useful on many future occasions.

On the evening of Saturday, August 19, 1933, my father, Bill Miller, Peanut Spruce and I started loading the truck, which its owner/driver had parked in front of Gray's garage. He agreed to come back at 4:00 A.M. the next morning to begin the drive to Pine Point. Our first task, perhaps the most risky, was moving the fuselage and wings from the loft. We backed the truck as close to the front of the garage as possible, after which two of us in the loft gingerly eased the fuselage out the window while the other two stood on the truck to receive it. (The engine was packed separately.) The truck's bed was barely high enough to get away with this maneuver. We were well aware that hitting the window frame would severely damage the fuselage. Moving the wings was even dicier, as their chord (width) would only pass through the window on the diagonal. Once these were safely down we stopped, looked at each other, and heaved a sigh of relief.

My father's experience in loading supply wagons for long trips into the wilderness proved useful. Using my checklist, he came up with a packing sequence that protected the fragile airframe components from the heavy tent poles, engine and tool boxes by using softer items—the canvas tent, sleeping bags and clothing, etc.—as buffers. The truck was stiffly sprung and Maine roads were not all that smooth. As a further precaution, Bill and I decided to ride in back on the flatbed where we could monitor our load.

The heavy tent poles were laid on the floor, with the engine and tool boxes forward to the right, all well lashed down. The fuselage was

90

centered on the bed with firewall forward, resting on its wheels and tail skids, while the wings were tied against the left-hand side board with soft material in between. Tail surfaces, ailerons, cables and miscellaneous were distributed under and around the fuselage. Bill and I positioned ourselves behind the engine and the tools leaning against the right-hand side of the truck.

By 1:30 A.M. packing was completed and a tarp thrown over the top in case it rained. Bill Miller and Peanut left by bicycle, the former to catch a couple of hours of sleep. Walking home, my father and I found my mother still collecting and packing our food. In addition to hard-boiled eggs, bread, butter, jam and sandwiches, she had stuffed, baked and carefully packaged a full-sized chicken! With what we could purchase locally, we were set to survive a couple of weeks at camp.

A stickler for cleanliness, my mother insisted I take a bath before leaving. I'd been up for 19 hours and anticipated little sleep in the next 20, but rather than argue I got into a hot tub where I relaxed and dozed off for an hour.

As SCHEDULED, WE began the trek at 4:00 A.M. The route took us along the Penobscot River through Bangor to Hampden, where we branched off cross-country to Fairfield and Waterville on the old carriage road through the Dixmont Hills, Unity and Benton. As we lurched and swayed along, I thought of my bicycle trip to Boston. A single-track vehicle at pedaling speed gave a far smoother ride than this stiffly sprung truck that seemed to seek out every rut and bump. Apprehensive at first about damage to the aircraft, we gradually relaxed. To our delight, we were enjoying Maine's late-summer

best: gorgeous foliage, deep blue sky dotted with white cumulus clouds, and the sun beating down in between. It was an auspicious beginning. I winked at Bill. We were finally off on our long-planned adventure!

A brief stop was made at Waterville for a doughnut or two and coffee for the driver. The next 18 miles to Augusta followed the Kennebec River flowing down almost due south to the coast. When we passed the State Capitol on its promontory at Augusta at around 10:00 A.M., roughly half the trip was behind us. The road continued down along the Kennebec, through Gardiner and Richmond, finally connecting with Route 1, the old coastal road from Maine to Florida, in the Bowdoin College town of Brunswick. There was little traffic. In another 25 miles we approached Portland.

Fig. 4-22
Assembled aircraft in our tent at Pine Point, 1933.

Our driver, a good Catholic of French Canadian extraction, sighted a church in Falmouth and announced his intention of attending Sunday mass. Less than enthusiastic about the delay, but feeling we had made good progress, Bill and I laid down on the church lawn, munched a sandwich and rested for the next 45 minutes.

Journey resumed, we soon were passing the Maine Central Railway station in Portland, and the Western Promenade and waterway. By 3:00 P.M. we approached our destination. The gravel road leading down to the beach at Pine Point branches off Route 1 a few miles before West Scarborough. After a couple of miles we caught glimpses of the beach ahead. Pine Point is not a town and hardly was a community then, just a single general store and a number of scattered cottages joined by sandy strips that pass for roads. The north side of the Point itself is defined by a narrow inlet from the ocean bounded on the farther side by Prouts Neck, which juts out into the Atlantic.

Turning left at the general store, we passed Cutters Cottage and Pilllsbury's Shore Dinners. From previous visits I had in mind a site for our tent. Inland of the beach and tide line, a sort of plateau had been fashioned by the wind and sand and was now covered with scrub grass. By no means smooth, one or two low spots were filled with stagnant water from the last rain. Our tent site would be at the far end of the Point, on a high place close to the beach half a mile from Pillsbury's. I directed the driver across the firmer ground until we got there. He was anxious to leave on his return trip, so we quickly unloaded onto the grass. By 5:00 P.M. he was gone, and Bill and I were on our own. Not a soul around. We could have been at Kitty Hawk or on the surface of the moon.

ACCOMPANIED BY THE ROLLING overture of the ocean and the screeching of the gulls, we went to work. First we laid out the sections of the tent and laced them together. Then we spotted two corner poles and drove in the stakes, which held firmly. We soon had one end of the tent secured. The other followed and then some front and center support poles.

As evening approached we observed just enough cumulus clouds building up to suggest a thunderstorm. Rather than stop for supper we pushed on until everything was inside the tent and the tent itself tied down. Fortunately we had extra stakes and rope, and enough canvas to close off the back of the tent and most of the front. Our living space, with sleeping bags, clothes and food, was on the west side away from the beach. The aircraft, of course, still was disassembled. The wings were on the ground beside the fuselage, with engine, tools and control surfaces scattered around.

Fig. 4-23
Our crew at Pine Point, 1933. From left: Cooper Milliken (brother), WFM, my father and Bill Miller.

By the time we finished it was dark. We'd been up for nearly 36 hours, broken only by brief periods of rest, and we were tired. Opening the food box and fishing out some sandwiches, we poured some water into paper cups and had a brief respite before removing our sneakers and crawling into the sleeping bags, clothes and all.

A few hours later the storm struck with terrifying ferocity. With the first clap of thunder we were out of our sleeping bags scrambling for the flashlights. Confusion reigned. Except for

Fig. 4-24
Some of our visitors. From left: Bill Miller, Knowlton Small, Rod Averill. Pine Point, 1933.

Fig. 4-25
Assembled aircraft in front of tent. Pine Point, 1933.

occasional flashes of lightning the darkness was total, a blacker world than we ever had known. Battered by gusts from all sides, the swaying tent gave the impression it was ready to take off. Water and wind poured in through every opening, and the ground beneath us turned to mush. All this was accompanied by a crescendo of waves crashing against the embankment 30 feet away and the thunder and howling of the wind.

By the time we located the flashlights, instinct told us we'd better move with care if the airplane was going to survive this storm. Thrashing around in the dark we could damage the aircraft even if the tent survived. Soaked to the skin and unable to stand against the wind, we crawled outside to check the stakes and the ropes. They appeared to be holding thanks to their length and their redundancy.

This was no brief thunderstorm but a real Nor'easter that could last for hours. Back in the tent we monitored the situation periodically, did what we could to keep the tent standing, conserved the flashlights and hoped for the best. Simple in theory, but agonizing in a situation where action seemed demanded but was useless.

Huddling against the food box and the Victrola, which we had moved to a relatively dry corner of the tent, Bill took out a record in the dark without my knowledge and cranked up the player. It was crazy, of course, but it broke the tension and was one way to defy the storm.

Conversation was at minimum; we just sat there wet, cold and miserable. Then something happened that to this day seems miraculous. One of the heavy poles holding the back of the tent came loose and crashed down between the wings

Fig. 4-26
Initial engine run. Pine Point, August 29, 1933.

and the fuselage. A few inches either way and we would have packed up and gone home, the expedition ended and years of labor lost. It was not difficult to imagine that something more than luck was operating that night.

BY EARLY MORNING the storm had abated and good weather returned for the remainder of our stay. It was as if we had paid all our dues in that one thunderous night. Thanks to all the excitement we hardly realized that we had been going for 45 hours with only brief snatches of rest. By the time we crawled into our sleeping bags that evening we had been up over 60 hours. It took us a solid week to dry out everything, shore up the tent, assemble and inspect the aircraft, establish a daily routine, and last but not least learn how to cope with sand fleas by dousing ourselves with citronella and practically sealing ourselves into the sleeping bags.

My father and brother Cooper arrived at Pine Point on August 23rd and would stay to September 7th. There was also a steady stream of visitors from Old Town and locally. Peanut Spruce was one of the first to hitchhike over, showing up late one afternoon. We could see him approach from Pillsbury's Shore Dinners and pause at a stagnant pool of water left in a low spot by the storm. Instead of hiking around it, he stripped down to his BVDs, strapped his bundled clothes to the back of his neck and proceeded to swim across. His skinny frame in baggy BVDs had the look of an old-time movie comedy, and was fully appreciated by a couple of elderly ladies who had walked up the beach to see the airplane. His clothes had dragged in the water on his way over, and his struggle to rerobe was an inspired act of staged frustration. Rod Averill, the Buzzell girls, Braley Gray and other members of our gang also were visitors.

For all the company, the real charm of the place was its desolation. In the early morning I would hike to the inlet, which in my imagination was a sort of "Frenchman's Creek" where pirate ships could have hidden away or sallied forth. Seabirds were everywhere. As the sun came up I could look out to the east over the vast Atlantic. Somewhere out there, thousands of miles away, was the coast of Europe, the objective of the Atlantic flyers who had taken off from Old Orchard. Some of them had been lost, and the ghost-like mystery of their disappearances mingled with my romantic notions of those pioneering flights. To me this beach was sacred territory, and I never lost the feeling that my efforts to fly there were in some intangible way related to those historic takeoffs.

Clear for Taxi

By early Tuesday evening, August 29, we were ready for a first taxi run. The tide was out, the air was calm, and the sand was smooth and hard. We had fashioned a path from our campsite down to the beach, so we rolled the airplane out of the tent and chocked the wheels. While I climbed into the cockpit, Bill Miller stood by to swing the propeller. Never having started the engine before we went through the routine of priming and retarding the spark. With a single hefty pull the engine started and settled into idle, which surprised Bill and me. Based on other motorcycle engine experience we hardly expected this. I sat there for awhile at the chocks, warming it up and playing with the throttle. It revved nicely, hitting on all four cylinders. I was elated. That was a great little engine, so smooth it created hardly a ripple in the air frame.

After Bill removed the chocks I started to taxi slowly. The sand was soft and the bicycle tires started grooving down into it. As we approached the slope to the beach, the airplane slowed and I opened up the throttle to keep it moving. Suddenly the tail came up and the nose went down. I yanked back on the throttle, but too late. The propeller hit the sand, breaking one tip.

Without carefully analyzing the situation, I assumed the noseover was totally chargeable

Fig. 4-27
Starting to taxi to beach. WFM in cockpit. Pine Point, August 29, 1933.

Fig. 4-28
Broken propeller. About to hitchhike to Old Town to repair propeller. Pine Point, 1933.

with the configuration more closely related to small-aircraft practice, the noseover probably would not have occurred. In the event, I decided to repair or replace the propeller and avoid further taxiing in soft sand. Only later would flight experience drive home the lesson that an ounce of experience is worth pounds of qualitative theory.

Leaving Bill in charge of the camp and aircraft, I left for Old Town the next day carrying the propeller and the tip that had broken off. The hitchhiking was only fair. By evening I arrived in Augusta where I stayed overnight with the Smalls, reaching home by noon the next day. As I was about to start gluing up the laminations for a new propeller blank, our neighbor Ralph Chapman suggested I talk with his pattern maker at the Chapman Machine Shop.

Pattern making is a skilled art, and in this case it was practiced by a genuine craftsman. After studying the propeller and the broken end, he suggested gluing them back together. To accomplish this he cut several narrow slots lengthwise from the main blade into the broken end. In these he glued narrow strips of clear maple hardwood, planed to a close fit, and trimmed to the contour of the blade. The propeller was basically as good as new. All I had to do was cover the blade with doped fabric and rebalance it on the rig I had made earlier. Carving a new propeller would have taken two long days of draw shaving and sanding after the blank was ready, as well as setting up templates for the blade angles and

to the bicycle tires sinking into the soft sand. In fact it was the first indication that the changes I had made to "improve" flight stability had given me an aircraft with marginal pitch stability in taxiing. The CG was too far forward relative to the position of the main wheels, and the propeller's high thrust line added to the noseover moment. Nor was there enough airflow over the horizontal tail at taxiing speed to compensate with the elevator. Had I left the airplane as originally designed, airfoil shapes. By Saturday I was hitchhiking back to Pine Point, carrying the propeller and additional food supplies my mother had packed in a knapsack. In my absence, and during our whole stay at Pine Point, my father and brother were of great help in spelling Bill and me, so someone was at the campsite with the airplane at all times.

The Flight

On Sunday and Monday, September 3–4, we installed the propeller and generally checked the aircraft. The weather was not suitable for a flight attempt but was improving. On Tuesday everything came together. I had made up my mind there would be no more taxi tests; when

Fig. 4-29
Professional photo before flight (*Portland Press Herald*). Pine Point, September 5, 1933.

Fig. 4-30
Entering aircraft before flight. Note the aerodynamic balance on rudder. Pine Point, September 5, 1933.

Fig. 4-31
Engine warm-up before flight. Pine Point, September 5, 1933.

conditions were favorable we would go for a flight. While the tide still was high during the day, I reviewed the weight and balance calculations and, as a final check, put the scales under the tail skid. The CG was where

I thought it should be, about 20 percent on the wing chord. My calculations indicated the M-1 gross weight with me in it was 475 pounds, which is pretty light even today when you figure the engine weighed a little over 100 pounds and in those days I scaled about 120.

At 6:00 P.M. the aircraft was poised at the northern end of the beach, the Atlantic on the left and the full sweep of Old Orchard ahead. The tide was out, the beach was hard, and there was practically no wind: ideal conditions for a first flight. A few people were standing around and a press photographer from Portland took some nice pictures before the start. My father and Cooper had walked down the beach to a more advantageous viewing point.

I climbed into the cockpit, buckled up my old leather helmet and ran through a mental checklist. The first

Fig. 4-32
Aircraft on takeoff run. Pine Point, September 5, 1933.

flight of any airplane is a big moment and it's a somewhat bigger one if you have been the principal creator. Bill Miller gave our repaired propeller a healthy swing and the engine came to life. With it purring along at a nice fast idle and the wheels still held by the homemade chocks, I remember sitting there and thinking how thrilling it all was. I'd certainly had my apprehensions earlier that day, but once the point of commitment was reached they disappeared completely.

I pushed the throttle full forward. My impression was that the plane accelerated rapidly. To avoid a possible noseover I held the stick well back; afterwards the marks on the sand showed that the tail stayed on the ground for the first hundred yards. Once it came up and she was running free on the main gear, I accelerated to gain plenty of speed. When I finally eased back on the stick with this excess speed, the plane literally leapt off the ground and I found myself looking down, hanging on and wondering what to do next. I didn't have to wait long, because the excessive dihedral on the M-1, along with other flight characteristics, produced a phenomenal "Dutch roll" in which the aircraft went into an alarming oscillation in yaw, side-slipping and rolling. The rudder was so strongly overbalanced that if pushed in one direction it would go hard over. Longitudinally the aircraft had excessive stability and a relatively ineffective elevator. Most disconcerting of all were the low control forces. I'd soloed the Boeing 203 trainer in Oakland for eight hours and had thirteen hours of first-class dual instruction, but nothing in that experience seemed related to what I was experiencing in the M-1. If there was any connection at all it certainly did not reach my conscious level. Meanwhile my altitude was varying wildly and I realized that I had dropped from 500 feet above the beach down to about 30. For some reason I had been looking out the left side of the cockpit toward the water, too busy to swivel my head to the right, when I noticed how wide the beach appeared. At this altitude I could be close to the row of cottages near the tide line. I was. After the flight, a man rushed up to me saying that he had been shaving with a straight razor on his porch and nearly cut his throat as I sailed by a few feet away.

Fig. 4-33a
Professional photo before flight (*Portland Press Herald*).

After a mile or so I decided I'd better get down. Between the throttle and the elevator I managed to maneuver the wheels onto the ground, but as the machine slowed down with the throttle off, the tail started up. With the forward CG there wasn't enough elevator to keep the tail down. Furthermore, the stabilizer setting was slightly positive (i.e., nose up)—another design mistake. I poured on the power and took off again, the slipstream from the propeller blasting the tail down and restoring enough trim for flight.

Subsequently, I tried another landing at a higher speed with similar results. A third attempt at a still higher speed looked good but the tail came up so fast I couldn't catch it with the throttle. The nose struck the ground and the aircraft flipped over on its back in a maneuver so symmetrical that the wing tips hardly touched. Thinking of fire, I wasted no time in sliding out and putting some wet sand on the engine and carburetors.

Aftermath

I suppose I should have felt pretty disappointed at this outcome, but I really didn't. The machine had flown and I had flown in it. The satisfaction of having made it into the air by my own bootstraps, and surviving a hairy flight, more than outweighed the landing.

The M-1 gave me confidence that I could carry a long project through to a conclusion. It was also a lesson in the engineering process. In the future I would weigh state-of-the-art practice more heavily than theory unsubstantiated by quantitative testing. The M-1 experience gave me a more realistic view of the relative importance of control versus stability in vehicle design. When I read Warner's book I rated inherent stability as a highly desirable quality and was willing to modify my design in that direction. Most of the early pioneers of flight fell into that same trap, but not the Wrights, who emphasized control. The best handling results from plenty of control, modest amounts of stability and adequate damping of any oscillatory tendencies.

In time I came to realize that even though I viewed the project as a "one-man" effort, it never could have been completed without a great deal of outside help: my parents, the Grays, Jordan Lumber, Chapman Foundry, Old Town Canoe Company, the Rotary

Fig. 4-33b
Professional photo after flight. Bill Miller is in background. Pine Point, September 5, 1933.

Club. Bill Miller's enthusiastic help and companionship made the expedition to Pine Point an unforgettable experience. Thereafter I would more easily recognize, appreciate and acknowledge the team aspects of an engineering activity.

A number of local newspapers published accounts of the flight. Letters of congratulations arrived from friends and relatives, two from my cousins topping the list. Frank, the musician, wrote, "Congratulations on successful flight, Kitty Hawk-the second. Will have jazz band ready for return. Save piece of plane to exhibit to my pupils."

And from my great supporter, Ed Waterhouse, "Well, I see by the *Portland Press Herald* that you made your initial flight in a plane of your own construction and that you are still living; whether this is a matter which you ever doubted need not concern the world. After seeing you take off fence rails with dispatch with your then skinny chest, I didn't think a bit of a beach would phase you. Next time make it a two seater and I will go along as mechanic—like hell!"

My mother wrote a beautiful letter reflecting none of the concerns for which mothers are famous, saying in effect, you got away with it and can try again—and ending with, "Well, I'm just as pleased as pleased can be to think it flew and I'll help you make some more wings any time."

My father and Cooper returned home on September 7th. The truck returned on the 9th and I rode back to Old Town with the damaged aircraft, which I stored in our barn chamber. I went to work after college graduation and moved on, so there never was any occasion to repair and rework M-1, nor did it seem appropriate to do so. It was a significant episode in my early life and I was content to leave it at that.

The plane remained in the barn for 43 years, until my mother's death in 1976. Because of its pioneering history as an early home-built in the state, Jim Rockefeller, founder of Owls Head Transportation Museum of Rockland,

Maine, acquired and restored M-1, giving the plane a permanent home in the museum.

My father was to die a few years after the M-1 flight. I am eternally grateful we shared the Pine Point episode together. It was his kind of adventure.

Old Town Youth To Fly This Week In Plane Constructed From His Own Blueprints

William F. Milliken seated in the skeleton of the plane which he made from plans drawn when he was a high school pupil.

He isn't proving anything or trying something new, but he is having fun building his own plane. For four years he has kept his blue prints. For four years he has planned for his big day. And it will come this week for William F. Milliken when he assembles the airplane he constructed according to the blue prints made when he was a high school boy. (Only one detail has been changed. It was originally a low-wing type, since redesigned for high-wing.)

Always interested in aviation, at the end of his junior year at the University of Maine he accepted a three months' summer scholarship at the W. E. Boeing School of Aeronautics in Oakland, Cal., where he took up ground school work, airplane design and, with a student pilot's permit and, with a student pilot's permit after a few hours of flying, made his solo flight. He transferred from Maine to the Massachusetts Institute of Technology. Though he is taking an engineering course, he does include some work in the aeronautical division with courses under Prof. Dan Sayre, widely known at the East Boston Airport for his research work in meteorology, and instrument instruction under Stark Draper.

Young Milliken was particularly interested in Mr. Draper's motion pictures of the instrument board of a plane during different stunting maneuvers. The boys were supposed to be able to tell by the instruments' motions which stunt was being performed.

Mr. Milliken has another year at M. I. T. and before returning in the Fall he is applying theory and practice and his four-year-hope to fly the plane of his own design. He built it at his own home in Old Town, dis-

sembled it and sent it by truck to Pine Point last Sunday, along with canvas for a temporary hangar and camp, tent poles, a work bench, tools, fire extinguisher, sleeping bags, bathing suits, torchlights, citronella, a victrola and a roasted chicken. He also brought a young friend, Bill Miller of Old Town, to help out, and especially with the cooking.

The airplane is a high-winged parasol monoplane, single cockpit, with a rather deep fuselage for a tiny model, silver wings, and the name in large black lettering on the sides — "N E K I L L I M" — which is Milliken backwards. It weighs 470 pounds fully loaded, and has a four-cylinder, 27 h. p. rebuilt Henderson motor, formerly used in a Heath plane. The motor should have 3,000 revolutions, but more probably it will develop 2700, with a top speed of 70 M. P. H., landing from 30 to 35 M. P. H. and a stall of 34.

The hangar is at the far end of Pine Point, away from any cottages and the beach isolated, giving him an excellent opportunity to try it out, both taxiing and flying, provided he doesn't get cross-winds.

Fig. 4-34
Typical newspaper coverage. This was written by Meryl Cutter, who lived in a cottage at Pine Point near our tent. We became good friends.

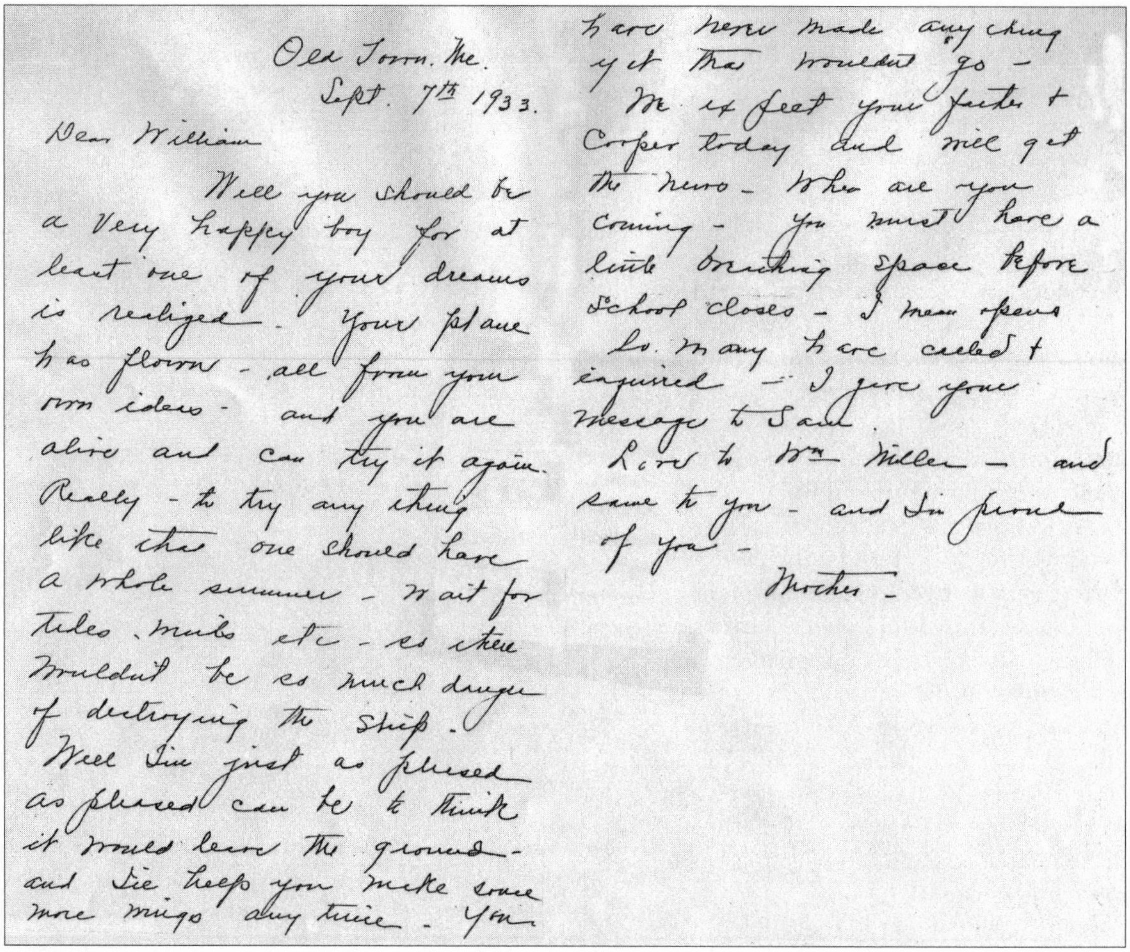

Old Town. Me.
Sept. 7th 1933.

Dear William

Well you should be a very happy boy for at least one of your dreams is realized. Your plane has flown - all from your own ideas - and you are alive and can try it again. Really - to try any thing like this one should have a whole summer - wait for tides, mails etc - so there wouldn't be so much danger of destroying the ship.

Well I'm just as pleased as pleased can be to think it would leave the ground - and Joe keeps you make some more things any time. You

have never made any thing yet that wouldn't go -

Me & feet your father & Cooper today and will get the news - When are you coming - you must have a little breathing space before school closes - I mean opens

So many have called & inquired - I gave your message to Saul.

Love to Wm Miller - and same to you - and I'm proud of you -

Mother -

Fig. 4-35
Mother's letter.

Fig. 4-36
Restored M-1 in Owl's Head Transportation Museum, circa 1990.

An Engineer's Education 1932–1939

Chapter 5

Tackling Tech

> "Today's stability and control engineers are generally astonished when they first see Bryan's Equations (of 1903 and 1911). Aside from notational differences, they are identical to those used in analysis of the most modern aircraft."
>
> – Malcolm Abzug
> – E. Eugene Larrabee
> (*Airplane Stability and Control*)

The agreement my parents and I had made when I entered the University of Maine was to get the engineering basics there and then go on to MIT for specialized courses in aircraft design. In early June of 1932, in preparation for the transfer, I visited Cambridge and had a long chat with Professor John Markham, who gave me a tour of the Aeronautical Department offices, class and drafting rooms, and the two wind tunnels located in the basement.

A temporary WW I facility behind the main aeronautical building housed the tunnel used by Jerome Hunsaker for his classic investigation, *Dynamical Stability of Aeroplanes*, published in June of 1914. As the founder of MIT's Laboratory of Aeronautical Engineering (part of the Naval Architecture Department until the establishment of the separate Department of Aeronautical Engineering in 1939), Hunsaker had been assisted by his students Donald Douglas (later CEO of Douglas Aircraft), T. H. Huff (Huff-Deland Aircraft) and V. E. Clark (designer of the famous Clark Y airfoil). They measured the coefficients, or mathematical derivatives, of the Bryan equations of motion for two model aircraft, one a Curtiss JN2 biplane trainer, and the other a similar aircraft designed by Clark with the objective of inherent stability. The steady-state forces and moments were measured with a conventional balance, while a dynamic (oscillatory) balance was designed for the dynamic terms.

I had borrowed a copy of Hunsaker's book from the Bangor Public Library. The report had given me my first insight into the mathematical theory of airplane stability and control and the character of motions—the longitudinal short period and phugoid oscillations, and the lateral spiral and "Dutch roll" modes. It also gave me some physical feel for the derivatives. To say I was thrilled to visit this

The Daniel Guggenheim Aeronautical Laboratory at MIT, built in 1928.

pioneering wind tunnel is an understatement. It connected my home studies with a significant source of aeronautical research, and also was the first of many historical connections I was to experience at MIT.

My visit to Cambridge was the first step of a summer adventure that happened by pure chance. As an off-campus student at the University of Maine, I seldom was involved in campus social activities and paid little attention to bulletin board notices. But the one in the Physics Building announcing the Third Annual W. E. Boeing Scholarships at the Boeing School of Aeronautics in California caught my eye. The top prize was a Master Ground and Flying Scholarship, with three choices for the second through fourth awards. The most interesting to me was the Private Ground and Flying Course (105 hours of ground school, 22 hours of flying).

I rushed home and over the next weekend wrote the essay required for the competition. Among the topics offered, I chose "Design in Relation to Speed of Aircraft," focusing on the virtues of speed with streamlining as the way to get it, using a few ideas from my observations of aircraft performance in the long-distance flights. Bill Stout of Ford Tri-Motor was among the well-known aeronautical figures on the judging committee.

Boeing Flight School

On May 28, 1932, a letter arrived from California indicating I had come in second. After telling my mother, who was very pleased in her restrained way, I jumped on my bicycle and rode up to my father's mill. He was quite overcome. This was one of the few occasions I saw my father cry. He had given up the career he loved to be with his family, and was now under extraordinary business stress. My success must have seemed a small ray of light among his many burdens.

There was never any question about my seizing the Boeing opportunity, only the best way of implementing it. Buying a secondhand Ford Model A roadster was deemed the best solution, and one was located that cost only a few hundred dollars. There had never been an

Fig. 5-1
Bill Milliken heading for California in the Model A Ford to attend the Boeing School of Aeronautics, summer of 1932.

automobile in my immediate family, but thanks to Ed Waterhouse I had some driving experience, so getting a license was only a formality. The prospect of driving my own car across the continent was exciting enough, but learning to fly at the end of the journey was a dream come true. It was like climbing up a rainbow and sliding down into a pot of gold at the other end.

During the 3,000-mile drive to Oakland, California, I did a lot of sightseeing and had more than my share of mishaps. The most memorable happened in Wisconsin. Reaching La Crosse in the early evening, I drove into town, missed a detour sign, proceeded up a slight embankment at the end of the street, and plunged down the other side into the Mississippi! With the front half of the car under water, I scrambled out over the rumble seat to be met by an amused crowd of young people exiting from a nearby movie theater. Soon a local fire truck showed up and hauled the car back up over the embankment. After the electricals dried out the engine reluctantly started, and the Model A and I continued west.

Following the Boeing school and my return to Maine I had a couple of weeks before reporting to MIT, during which I drove my father around to local business contacts. We then sold the Model A as too much of a luxury for our family to keep.

A FEW DAYS BEFORE the start of the term at MIT I hitchhiked to Boston to locate a place to live and complete all the transfer formalities, including loan and scholarship applications. Old Town is only 250 miles from Boston, and

Fig. 5-2
This is the Boeing trainer in which I soloed and completed the Private Flying Course, 1932.

I'd hitchhiked it so frequently I could almost guarantee making it in a day. On this occasion, leaving my ancestral home brought the realization that upon graduation I would return to Old Town only to visit. There was no aircraft industry in Maine, so I would have to seek my fortune elsewhere.

I knew I wanted a career in aviation, but never thought of it as "earning a living." I loved working, and had worked hard on vehicle projects since the age of ten, but never for money. In fact, working for money never become my paramount incentive. In midlife, when I changed from aircraft to automotive research, I did so simply because it seemed

Fig. 5-3
In the course of my solo flying I misjudged the landing flare and made a "hard" but non-destructive landing that earned this citation.

more exciting. In retrospect, I believe my father's romantic stories of his early railway-locating career strongly influenced my idea of work as a challenge and a pleasure.

Massachusetts Institute of Technology

Having spent the summer vagabonding my way across the continent and back, the idea of settling down to studies at a school as tough as MIT was not immediately appealing, and I arrived in Boston with some trepidation. Contrary to expectation, my first two years in Boston brought adventure of a different sort, in great intellectual and emotional explorations.

Designing and building the M-1 had given me such a strong interest in aerodynamics and aircraft structures that I arrived at MIT filled with questions and bubbling over with curiosity. To study with teachers like Otto Koppen and Manfred Rauscher was inspiring. But the transition from living at home in a small town where I had been exposed to a complex puzzle of influences, to being alone in a large city was not without some stress. Also, dealing with people, especially of the opposite sex, had been difficult for me in Maine.

In Boston all this was to change. These were the halcyon years of growth as I teetered toward a career and independence!

Because I had little interest in campus life, much less in joining a fraternity, my first task was finding a convenient and inexpensive place to live. MIT's main facility is in Cambridge, across the Charles River from Boston. The Aeronautical Laboratory was on Massachusetts Avenue on the west side of the MIT Great Dome. Being within walking distance of the school was my criterion, and I soon found a "room for rent" sign on an old brownstone at 278 Marlborough Street, a short walk from the Boston side of the Harvard Bridge (a.k.a. Mass. Ave. Bridge).

A stout, buxom woman named Mrs. Crosby showed me to a small second-floor bedroom with a semi-private bath down the hall. It was available for five dollars a week. Its furnishings included a narrow cot bed and chest of drawers on the right, a small desk on the opposite wall, and one comfortable stuffed chair near the French windows. Bed clothes, towels, soap and cleaning were up to the renter. I made a down payment and moved in.

In addition to meeting my simple requirements for a place to sleep and study, 278 Marlborough had a number of advantages. The Esplanade Restaurant was at the corner and always open for breakfast. Within a couple of blocks was a tailor shop, the entrance to the subway (to take me into downtown Boston or on to Lechmere to hitchhike home) and a post office for weekly mailing of my laundry to Old Town. The walk to MIT afforded some exercise, especially in winter months when sub-zero gales blew down the Charles River and crossing the bridge became a real challenge. (How often I was to pass walkers coming toward me on a blustery morning, with their hands over their ears or face, inquiring how much farther they had to go!)

Transferring credits from the University of Maine to MIT and setting up my course structure took patience and negotiation. Two terms of German language study were required in the Aeronautical Course. My high school experience with three foreign languages had been dismal, so the prospect of studying technical German was daunting. Professor Markham was sympathetic. He suggested I transfer into the Mathematics Department, which had many electives and offered the further advantage that I could fit in several postgraduate courses in aeronautics during my junior and senior years. Despite occasional moments of regret, I still doubt that becoming sufficiently proficient in a foreign technical language would have been of practical use.

THE DANIEL GUGGENHEIM FOUNDATION for the Promotion of Aviation was of immense significance to the development of our aircraft industry. Its major grants to selected universities assured a flow of highly trained aeronautical engineers, and fostered the development of centers of learning and research with close industrial ties. Both MIT and Caltech benefited from this. Built and commissioned in 1928, the Daniel Guggenheim Laboratory was a fully staffed and well-equipped educational facility when I arrived in the fall of 1932. Its establishment reflected MIT's long history of aeronautical research.

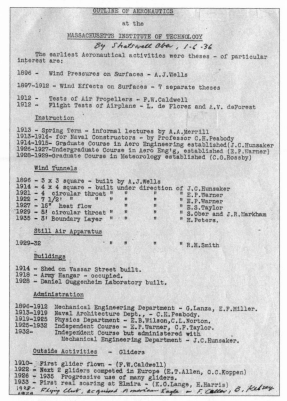

Fig. 5-4
Prof. Ober's outline History of Aeronautics at MIT. I arrived in the fall of 1932, having transferred from the University of Maine as a Junior.

The course outline includes some of the great names in aeronautical education, research, engineering and administration. Jerome Hunsaker's illustrious career dated back to the Navy NC flying boats, which were first to fly the Atlantic, and he was a pioneer in early stability research and teaching at MIT. He later headed the Mechanical Engineering Department and was a member of the National Advisory Committee for Aeronautics, among many other important government assignments. Frank Caldwell went on to hold an important position at Hamilton Standard Propeller Company. Professor Edward P. Warner was author of *Airplane Design*, editor of *Aviation* magazine, Assistant Secretary of the Navy for Aeronautics, worked in aircraft-handling specifications for Douglas Aircraft, and became the U.S. leader in international air traffic regulations. The Taylor brothers, Charles Fayette and Eddie (E. S.), became well known for their work at MIT's Engine Laboratory. C. F. wrote the definitive book *The Internal Combustion Engine in Theory and Practice*, and E. S. directed the Gas Turbine Laboratory, later becoming chief engineer of Wright Aeronautical and inventor of the dynamic balancer for radial aircraft engines. C. G. Rossby became renowned for his pioneering work in air mass analysis, E. T. Allen for his practice as an engineering test pilot on first flights of large aircraft and as head of Flight and Aerodynamics at Boeing. This was an all-star cast.

Still, although I felt privileged to be in their figurative company, my first few nights cooped up in that hall bedroom were depressing. Reading a book on the life of Harry Hawker, the first man to attempt a non-stop flight across the Atlantic, was all I needed to snap me out of my mood. Once classes began I never had a dull moment at MIT. An aeronautical treasure chest was opened for me, spewing out nuggets of aerodynamic information at bewildering rate.

My professors were the counterpart of "car men" in the automobile industry. Neither academic, managerial or financial types, nor trained teachers, these "airplane men" were primarily interested in how planes worked and how to design and test them. They had experience in aircraft engineering and were enthusiastic about it. Their inspirational lectures were laced with pertinent and amusing anecdotes of historical successes and failures in aircraft design. They were in touch with the industry through former students, through MIT's wind tunnel testing for East Coast aircraft companies, and through their consulting and research activity—all of which added reality to what they taught.

Like most new students at MIT, I had been exposed to "Tackling Tech," a scary account of the hazards confronting a student (i.e., how many would wind up at the infirmary at exam time or be expelled for poor performance). I wanted to enjoy my time there without ruining my health, so I adopted the following routine: in the evening the extensive notes taken at lectures would be rewritten into permanent notebook form, with questionable areas noted for further study, but at ten o'clock I would do something different, like hike or go to a movie. After I got to know some girls I usually went dancing until midnight. In my experience, MIT and ballroom dancing got on extremely well together.

My other relaxation was reading Dumas. For my birthday my father had given me a leather-bound, pocket-sized set of the D'Artagnan Tales—*The Three Musketeers, Twenty Years After, The Vicomte de Bragelonne (Ten Years Later), Louise de la Vallière* and *The Man in the Iron Mask*—that I carried around in my travels for years.

The Aeronautical Department

MIT's course structure in aeronautical engineering in the early 1930s created a generation of engineers that contributed to our superiority in the air during World War II, and from the dawn of the jet industry into space exploration. In my class alone were such innovators as George Schairer and Bill Cook, who were responsible for the aerodynamics of

Fig. 5-5
Prof. Shatswell Ober, who taught the first course in Aerodynamics of Airplane Design that focused on airplane performance prediction.

the Boeing Stratoliner, the B-17 series, B-29, B-47, 707 and B-52. Schairer ultimately became Boeing's corporate vice president for research, and Cook chief engineer of the Transport Division. Bob Mueller created the first electronic analog computer for analyzing aircraft motions and, as a member of MIT's Charles Stark Draper Laboratory, participated in developing the floating gyro for space navigation. Bob Seamans, also of the Draper Laboratory, was chief engineer of NASA during the early moon shots.

Professor Shatswell Ober

The first course I took at MIT was Ober's Aerodynamics of Airplane Design, which laid the foundation for calculating airplane performance. A mainstay in the Aero Department, Ober's background included a stint at NACA, but unlike other professors in the department he seldom engaged in consulting, publication or extracurricular activities. His sole interest seemed focused on the aero program, the wind tunnel work for industry and the placement of graduates in industry. Shats ("Obe" to all his friends) had the first office nearest the main entrance to the building, and when illustrious graduates like Jimmy Doolittle came back to visit they stopped there first. A soft-spoken man, his kindness and genuine concern for their problems made him a favorite of the students. After a brief discussion of lift and drag forces, Course 16.00 introduced the concept of force/moment coefficients. Four of them were empirical, with only the absolute having a substantial theoretical base. This was before the widespread adoption of absolute coefficients based on dynamic pressure that originally were developed in Germany. The next subject treated was airfoils, their general characteristics, figures of merit, test methods and the NACA Series. This was supplemented by a physical description of airflow around bodies, and pressure and velocity measurements in ideal and real flows. Starting from section characteristics, the airflow about finite wings was followed with a discussion of the vortex structure, downwash, induced drag and the effect of wing aspect ratio. The derivation of the early NACA Series airfoils was provided in detail, with test data plots showing the effect of thickness, camber, camber location, etc. Finally, devices such as flaps, slats and slots were presented. Biplanes still were extant, so the induced-drag theory was applied to the estimation of their characteristics.

Course 16.01 began with a discussion of friction drag, Reynolds number, and laminar and turbulent flow and transition, followed by parasitic and flat-plate drag, drag of various wing and engine installations, streamlined and bluff bodies, struts, wires, typical fuselages, landing gear and radiators, air-cooled engines and cowlings. The NACA cowling, a major advance over the Townsend ring, was beginning to see use as enhancing "propulsive efficiency" instead of propeller efficiency. Finally, horsepower and available-thrust curves were constructed for sea level and altitude conditions. Reference texts were Warner's *Airplane Design* (1927 edition), Diehl's *Engineering Aerodynamics* (1928 edition) and Weick's *Aircraft Propeller Design* (1930 edition).

All this was basic stuff, bolstered by simple engineering formulas for estimation purposes, by numerical ranges derived from experience, and by lots of practical problems. These introductory courses made the student aware of the wealth of knowledge available in NACA Reports, Technical Notes and Memoranda and the British R & M series. Arriving for my first job in industry at Chance Vought Aircraft, I found their techniques for performance estimation and analysis of flight test data lined up well with what I had been taught at MIT.

By the fall of 1939, when I joined Boeing, performance calculations and flight data analysis were considerably more complex. Boeing's Model 247, the first modern airliner (all metal, low-wing, multi-engined monoplane), had flown in 1933. This soon was followed by the Douglas DC-2 and DC-3 series (circa 1934), which utilized supercharged engines and controllable pitch, constant-speed propellers. The use of these aircraft in airline operation generated interest in economical cruise performance at altitude, and improved methods of prediction and testing. Much of this work was accomplished by the staff and graduates of GALCIT (Guggenheim Aeronautics Laboratory at the California Institute of Technology) including Dr. Theodore von Karman, Dr. Clark B. Millikan, W. C. Rockefeller, Dr. W. Bailey Oswald, Dr. Norton Moore, Albert C. Reed and others. Notable contributions were the "General Airplane Performance" report by Rockefeller (published as NACA Report No. 654, 1940) and "Airplane Performance Testing at Altitude" by Reed (*Journal of the Aeronautical Sciences,* February 1941). Thus in a few years the subject of airplane performance had progressed well beyond the basics I learned at MIT.

Professor John Markham

I next began two semesters of Aeronautical Laboratory given by Professor John R. Markham (16.62 and 16.63), each consisting of five wind tunnel experiments. The "five-foot" tunnel, as it was known, actually had a four-foot-diameter working section, with a closed throat and open return. The entrance cone decreased in size before merging with the parallel (in plan) working section. A honeycomb to straighten the airflow was located just before the working section. The exit cone (or diffuser) had a uniform taper of 4°, and the fixed-pitched four-bladed

Fig. 5-6
Prof. John Markham, who introduced the students to the "five-foot" wind tunnel in a two-semester series of experiments.

Fig. 5-7
Intake end of the 7½-foot open-return wind tunnel in the basement of the Aeronautics Building. The tunnel used for Professor Markham's course was similar but smaller (i.e., 5 feet).

Fig. 5-8
The fan at the exit end of the 7½-foot tunnel.

wooden fan was located at the end of the largest section. Supported on a steel framework, the tunnel was anchored to a concrete foundation. Its fan was powered by a 15-hp DC motor via a chain drive. The AC service to the building ran a DC generator, and motor speed was controlled by a Ward Leonard system with controls at the working section. Wind speeds of 60 mph were possible but 40 mph usually was used. This tunnel, typical of its era, was used for industry testing as well as student instruction.

The airspeed, or rather the dynamic pressure, q, was determined by measuring the difference between the pressure on the wall of the parallel section and that in the room. An alcohol manometer was used, after calibration with a pitot tube at various locations in the test section. Two types of balance were available. The NPL (British National Physical Laboratory) type, designed and constructed in England, consisted of a vertical spindle projecting into the tunnel through an oil seal, with the balance proper located outside and below the tunnel. The model was fixed to the top of the spindle. The spindle could be attached to a wing tip, with the model vertical, or it could be attached to the top or bottom of the fuselage, with the model horizontal. Depending upon the attitude of the model it was possible to measure lift and drag. Various moments were measured about the spindle axis only. Considerable experience was required for proper use of this balance.

In the second type of balance, the model was suspended upside-down by wires connected to electrical balance beams located outside and on top of the tunnel. Lift, drag and pitching moment could be measured by a suitable arrangement of wires. The balance beam carried a small electrical motor that moved a weight along the beam via a rotating screw. Balance was achieved when the end of the beam settled between two contacts that controlled the direction of rotation of the electric motor. Part of the course consisted of detailed familiarization with the two balances and their measurement possibilities.

Prof. Markham presided over all of the experiments, each with a group of three students. This was a hands-on operation with the lecture material integrated into the test description, setup, calibration, and the test itself. Each student was given the test data to work up and report on later.

I always have felt fortunate to have been introduced to wind tunnel technology by Johnny Markham, who spent a major part of his career in this field. Unlike Ober, he engaged in outside consulting, thus broadening his experience, and later was to play a part in the design and commissioning of the Wright Brothers tunnel at MIT (at the time a high-performance facility). Markham was also involved in the design of the 20-foot, full-scale tunnel at Wright Field commissioned by General Henry (Hap) Arnold, then head of the Army Air Corps. When Boeing decided to construct a high-speed subsonic tunnel, both Dr. Theodore von Karman and John Markham were retained as consultants. This was the fastest industrial tunnel in the United States, and to quote Karman, "greatly influenced the development" of such fast bombers as the B-47, the B-52, the KC-135, and later the high subsonic commercial jets. Markham was among the first to promote the use of strain-gauge balances.

As an instructor he had many attributes. Airplane design and aeronautics in general is all about airflow around bodies and the resulting forces. For most students the first encounter with real air and real forces is in the wind tunnel. Well aware of this, Markham made every effort to emphasize the physics of the situation. He frequently employed "tufts" on a model to show areas of separation, or "streamers" to demonstrate the downwash behind a wing or the angle of attack at the tail. He poked a long wand with a tuft of yarn taped to its end through a hole in the working section to show flow conditions at a particular point. I found it fascinating to observe the wing tip vortex and trace its progress downstream. Despite having conducted these experiments many times, Johnny never was bored; to the contrary, he exhibited a genuine enthusiasm.

The ten experiments (of the two semesters) covered a surprisingly large area of interest in the airplane design of that era, and are described at the end of this chapter:

Experiment I— USA 27 Airfoil Test
Experiment II—Test of C-100 Airplane Model
Experiment III—Test of TX-33 Airplane Model

Experiment IV—Test of TX-33 Airplane Model for Rolling and Yawing Moments Due to Yaw

Experiment V—Test of Airplane Model with Operating Propeller

Experiment VI—Lift and Drag of a Body from Pressure Distribution Measurements

Experiment VII—Thrust of Wind Tunnel Propeller of the five-foot Tunnel by Pressure Measurements

Experiment VIII—The Change in Airplane Pitching Moment from Power-on to Power-off Conditions

Experiment IX—Change in Downwash Due to Slipstream (from the Propeller)

Experiment X—Interference of Nacelle and Wing

Professor Manfred Rauscher

During the fall of 1932 a comprehensive course entitled Theoretical Aerodynamics (M43–M44) was presented by Prof. Manfred Rauscher. Given in two-hour sessions, it covered rigid-body dynamics and fluid mechanics, and was preparatory to the study of airplane stability and control that occupied the senior year.

A tall, blond Swiss national, Manfred Rauscher had come to MIT as an aeronautical engineering student in his late teens and soon demonstrated his technical abilities. In the summer of 1926 he prepared the illustrations, calculated tables and checked references for Edward P. Warner's *Airplane Design—Aerodynamics*, published the following year. Within a few years, while still in his late twenties, he was carrying a full instructor load. Rauscher stayed at MIT into the 1940s, then returned to Switzerland to become Professor of Aircraft Structures and Design at the Technische Hochschule, Zürich. In 1953 he published *Introduction to Aeronautical Dynamics*, based on his teaching experience at MIT and covering much the same material as Courses M43 and M44. Rauscher was thoroughly familiar with the technical literature and made frequent references to E. B. Wilson's *Aeronautics* and H. Glauert's *The Elements of Aerofoil and Airscrew Theory*.

An excellent lecturer with a great grasp of theory, Rauscher developed much of the course material on the blackboard without reference to notes. He also supplied mimeographed sheets to his students summarizing the contents of his lectures. I took voluminous class notes and created five bound sets (each a half-inch thick). Rauscher took the position that applied aerodynamics was covered in companion courses by Ober, Markham and Koppen and that his task was to stick to theory. Thus, his courses lacked the frequent references to aircraft design experience and homespun stories about flight that illuminated lectures in other courses. Design-oriented courses had very obvious objectives; theory is directed toward basic understanding. While I never developed into a really competent analyst, I found the insights into physical phenomena provided by theory to be of intense interest. I did well in Rauscher's courses. Although I would not have the occasion to apply much of the math, a general knowledge of the theory has been useful in directing R & D and in recognizing the value of analysis.

A brief summary of subjects covered in courses M43 and M44 by sections follows:

MIT Course Nos. M43, M44 Theoretical Aerodynamics; Rauscher Course Outline

Section I: Basic Mechanics

Weight vs. Mass

Vectors and their manipulation

Coordinate Systems, acceleration and velocity in different systems

Kepler's Laws

Universal Law of Gravitation

Impulse – Momentum relationship

Work and Kinetic Energy in several degrees of freedom

From particle equations to rigid bodies

continued on next page

Moment of Momentum
Dynamic equations, constant mass
Dynamic equations, variable mass (rockets)
Rocket propulsion, interplanetary rockets
Momentum theory of propellers

In summary, this section was a substantial review of classical mechanics.

Section II: Fluid Mechanics

Development of equations—assuming air is continuous and incompressible
Bernoulli's Equation
Bernoulli's Equation with compressible fluid
Velocity of Sound
Instruments based upon Bernoulli's Equation
Equation of Continuity
Unsteady motion
Velocity Potential
Equation of a Streamline
Examples of various flows
Concept of irrotational motion and Circulation
Equipotential lines
Vorticity
Kelvin's Equation
Sources and sinks
The Stream Function
Point vortex
Examples of flows around a cylinder
Doublets
Circulation
This section was a comprehensive review of the concepts of theoretical fluid dynamics.

Section III (continuation of Section II)

   This section began with the introduction to complex variables and the manipulation
of vectors. From there complex variables were used to develop relationships among the
components of flow velocity, the stream function and velocity potential. The principal
value of dealing with complex variables is that of transformation. If an irrotational flow
is transformed by the use of a complex function, it remains irrotational. Rauscher then
developed the process of transformation using the complex variable and considered a variety
of simple cases.
   Conformal transformation, in which the shapes of elementary figures remain unchanged,
was considered next. Since angles are preserved, the streamlines and equipotential lines
are transferred intact in the transformation from, say, a circle to an ellipse. I found this an
exciting capability. The problem of the "singular point," in which a small finite element
contracts to zero in the transformation, was discussed next. It was shown that the proper
placing of singular points is useful in many transformations. Once a transformation is
made, the pressures and velocities about the new figure are deduced from the stream
function and velocity potential. Section III concluded with a variety of transformations
short of the classical one of transforming a circle into an airfoil along with the flow field.

continued on next page

Section IV: Airfoil Theory

This section successively reviewed transformations from the circle to the ellipse, to streamlined struts, and to the symmetrical airfoil with sharp trailing edge, all of which depend on the location of the singular points on the circle.

The technique for introducing thickness and camber change then were developed. Graphical methods of producing Joukowski airfoils followed, as well as the means for adding in the flow fields at specified angles of attack. It then was possible to obtain the theoretical value of lift curve slope, lift and pitching moment, all in two dimensions. This section ended with a qualitative discussion of three-dimensional flow about airfoils of finite span.

By the time we had reached this stage of Rauscher's course in Theoretical Aerodynamics I began to realize what a monumental accomplishment it was. We had progressed from the classical hydrodynamic theory of the 19th century to the calculation of airfoil shapes, the flows about them at various angles of attack, and the associated pressure and velocity distributions. I began to see, for the first time, the miraculous workings of science—how abstract mathematics combined with physical concepts, often from a variety of different investigations, can be brought together to create a useful theory to predict the performance of a device as complex as an airfoil.

Section V: Mechanics of Solid Bodies

This section was developed as the basis for the differential equations of motion of the airplane. Starting with axis systems and particle theory, Rauscher worked up to angular momentum equations in terms of moments and products of inertia, defined the principal axes, ellipsoid of inertia, etc.—all for simple cases. He then developed the general three-dimensional case en route to Euler's equations.

For studying aircraft motions two sets of axes were used. The first was fixed in the aircraft with the origin at the CG. This set was assumed to be oriented along the three principal axes, so that the moments of inertia were constant and the products of inertia zero. It would be quite impossible in practice to deal with equations in which the moments of inertia were varying. The second set of axes was assumed to be coincident with the fixed airplane axes but momentarily fixed in inertial space. The motions of the aircraft axes are referenced to this space-fixed set. By this reference the angular momentum and applied forces can be determined for the aircraft. By dealing with small perturbations in this way, the aircraft can be tracked in maneuvers in space.

Furthermore, the perturbations enable definitions of control, stability and damping concepts so necessary for characterizing the motions. Because the airplane has a plane of symmetry, the motions in that plane (up and down, fore and aft and pitching) can be studied separately from the out-of-plane motions (rolling, yawing and sideslipping). The equations representing the in-plane motion are the *longitudinal* equations, those representing the out-of-plane, the *lateral* equations. Longitudinal equations are concerned with performance, ride, pitch control and stability. The lateral equations concern lateral maneuvering control and stability. Again it must be noted that the equations are for perturbations from an initial equilibrium or trim and they are linearized about a trim. Although appearing to be restricted in application, they have, in fact, successfully been applied to all regimes of flight, including stall and spin, provided they are initialized at an operating point.

Having derived Euler's equations and shown their application to aircraft stability and control, Rauscher had set the stage for Otto Koppen's classes.

Otto Koppen

Koppen's courses in airplane stability and control, and in airplane preliminary design (the latter, a drafting-room exercise), were the high points of my studies at MIT. Since the age of ten I had become increasingly fascinated with vehicle stability and control—from the performance and accidents of my early ground vehicles, my glider attempts, the early motorcycles, and the brief and hectic flight of the M-1. Reading had taught me the that the invention of the airplane required solving the control problem, that Lilienthal's fatal accident was due to loss of control and that the limited success of other aviation pioneers such as Ader, Langley, and Maxim also was related to control. As an automobile racing enthusiast, I could hardly avoid the conclusion that success in that field also was one of control at the limits of performance, a conclusion heavily reinforced by the death of Jimmy Murphy at the Syracuse dirt track in 1924.[1]

Through my studies of Hunsaker's work and Warner's book, I sensed that the fundamental answers to my questions about stability and control lay in a theoretical understanding of the airplane equations of motion, and a more extensive knowledge of the practical lessons learned from aircraft development and flight tests. Only after finishing several years of college was I able to comprehend the mathematics. My contacts with professional aircraft designers had been nil. I did know that the original equations of motion were the work of a Professor George Bryan in 1903, and I had seen his *Stability*

Fig. 5-9
Prof. Otto Koppen, who taught the airplane stability and control courses and the drafting-room exercises in airplane layout. Koppen was the first to introduce the full dynamic stability and control equations in American aeronautical education. He was also an aircraft designer of note.

in Aviation, published in 1911. I also sensed that the theoretical approach to stability and control had little influence on practical airplane design until WW I, and then largely in research circles.

Koppen's courses went far in satisfying my curiosity, and provided the inspiration and direction for my entire career. I came to know Otto on a first-name basis. His claim that as a young man he had considered a career as a professional baseball player was lent credence one day in the five-foot tunnel. He was standing on the platform in front of the open door to the working section. Several of us were inside the tunnel trying to remove a model that was fastened to the balance by taper pins. The pins refused to budge. In desperation, one of the technicians whacked one pin with a large hammer. The pin dislodged and whistled out of the working section door at fast-ball speed. Reflexively, Otto reached out and caught the pin as it hurtled by.

A student under E. P. Warner at MIT, where he became active in the glider club and competed in Europe in 1922, Otto subsequently worked at McCook Field, the Army Air Force technical base, and at the Ford Motor Company when Henry Ford became interested in building a small airplane. Inviting Koppen to his home for dinner to discuss it, Ford defined an airplane that would fit into his library as his criterion. Practical as usual, Otto pulled a yo-yo out of his pocket, measured the room and went on to design a small low-wing cantilever monoplane, powered with a three-cylinder air-cooled engine. The Flivver Plane, using a nickname for the Model T Ford, later established a long-distance record for a light aircraft. In time, Otto drifted back to MIT where he designed one of the earliest fiberglass prototypes. Otto and I journeyed

---

[1]*Murphy died on September 1, 1924, at the Syracuse dirt track when his car bounced off the inside railing several times before crashing through it.*

Fig. 5-10
L-R: WFM, Prof. Otto Koppen and Dr. Robert Mueller. In the background is my Curtiss-Wright Jr. airplane, which I sold to Mueller. Mueller was one of the early doctoral students in aeronautics and for his thesis developed the first analog computer based on the aircraft equations of motion. He was one of the brilliant members of the Draper Laboratory, which contributed so much to aircraft and space control and navigation systems.

experiences were used to drive the subject home.

In that era, treatment of airplane stability and control usually was confined to "statics," the steady-state forces and moments as measured in a wind tunnel. Koppen's coverage of statics was a mere preliminary to his full dynamic treatment of the equations of motion as put forth by the British Air Ministry Aeronautical Research Committee in its series of Reports and Memoranda (R & M). In the late 1920s and early 1930s this committee's research arm employed such greats as H. Glauert, S. B. Gates, L. W. Bryant and others. They engaged in laying a basis for predicting aircraft behavior in dynamic flight conditions, including both normal and stalled regimes. Koppen took full advantage of this work.

Otto's great strength as an instructor lay in the fact that he remained an airplane designer all his life. Nothing about his approach was academic. Mathematics *per se* was of no interest to him. His sole intent was to provide an understanding of airplane stability and control, and develop the tools for improving them. He accepted the complexities of the equations of motion as the best means to this end.

Koppen not only expounded on the theoretical fundamentals of stability and control, but he also brought to class recent and exciting cases from practice. For example, he pointed out that designers measure longitudinal stability "as the moment obtained by a given angle of attack change," whereas pilots think of stability "as the rate at which the airplane returns to equilibrium after a disturbance." Since these criteria do not give the same results, he developed a more comprehensive approach that brought these diverse criteria together. His class presentation

up to New Hampshire to see its first flight, made by Clarence Chamberlain of transatlantic fame. Before and during WWII Otto teamed up with a Boston investor group to build the Helio-plane, used by the Special Services for spy activity. They required an aircraft with exceptional low-speed performance and behavior.

Otto had a lifetime interest in stall behavior. A hands-on type, he flew on and off throughout his career. Following his retirement from MIT, and subsequent loss of his wife, Otto resumed flying. At an advanced age he bought a plane, reinstated his license, obtained instrument and seaplane ratings, and flew around the countryside visiting friends in the industry. Several years later, after he failed the flight physical, Otto bought a hot Japanese sports car and toured in it. We remained in touch throughout his life.

Otto's classes were small, relaxed and informal. Basic concepts were illustrated by simple physical analogies and numerical examples. Stories from aircraft design

Teaching Bryan's Equations of Motion

Before he could launch into applications, Otto first had to ensure that his students were well versed in the equations of motion. He provided typed notes summarizing their derivation in both dimensional and non-dimensional forms, and the procedure for their solution. Axis systems, nomenclature and sign conventions were established. The six equations (for three forces and for three moments), as noted earlier, naturally separated into two sets of three equations each for motion in the vehicle's plane of symmetry (longitudinal equations) and for motions outside the plane of symmetry (lateral equations). The equations were linearized for small displacements from equilibrium.

The applied forces and moments (the so-called unbalanced forces and moments) that cause the accelerations, velocities and motions of the aircraft were expanded in a "derivative format" which is best understood by its mathematical formulation of the change in any given force or moment component is a function of the linear and angular velocities along and about the reference axis system. Because the system is linear, the effects of the various velocities are additive and are proportional to the velocities. For example, in the unsymmetrical (out of the plane of symmetry) motions of the airplane, the velocity components of interest are r, the yawing velocity, p, the rolling velocity and v, the sideslip velocity. The moments and forces of interest are N, the yawing moment (torque), L, the rolling moment and Y, the lateral force. Changes in N, L, and Y are each a function of r, p and v. In the case of N, this may be written,

$$dN = \left(\frac{\partial N}{\partial r}\right)dr + \left(\frac{\partial N}{\partial p}\right)dp + \left(\frac{\partial N}{\partial v}\right)dv$$

where dN refers to the total change in N and dr, dp and dv, small changes in r, p, and v.

$$\left(\frac{\partial N}{\partial r}\right), \quad \left(\frac{\partial N}{\partial p}\right) \quad \text{and} \quad \left(\frac{\partial N}{\partial v}\right)$$

are the rates of change of N with respect for the velocity components r, p, and v. They are so-called "partial derivatives" because each contributes only partly to the total change in N (i.e., dN).

The important thing to note is that the behavior of the aircraft in its out-of-plane motion is defined mathematically by the numerical values of the set of derivatives of the lateral equations of motion—in this case,

$$N_r = \left(\frac{\partial N}{\partial r}\right), \ N_p = \left(\frac{\partial N}{\partial p}\right) \text{ and } N_v = \left(\frac{\partial N}{\partial v}\right)$$

and by comparable derivatives for the forces. More significantly, each derivative is understandable physically and can be measured in a conventional wind tunnel or with specialized test equipment. In general simple physical devices such as weather vanes and dashpots are analogous to the derivatives.

The first section of Otto's course covered longitudinal stability (motion in the plane of symmetry). In it he derived the longitudinal equations in dimensional and non-dimensional form, and exhaustively examined each derivative—how it is measured or calculated. Then he tackled the problems of control, such as the elevator control forces, control sensitivity, changes in trim with power, control required for landing, various control devices, control balances, etc.

led to the paper "Trends in Longitudinal Stability" published in the *Journal of the Aeronautical Sciences* in May 1936. Thus we were treated to his advanced thinking and encouraged to explore other applications ourselves.

Uncovering the Secrets of Stall

In 1927 a competition for a "safe" aircraft was initiated by Daniel Guggenheim and was won in 1929 by the Curtiss Tanager, a heavily flapped and slotted-winged aircraft. A few years later Eugene Vidal, the Department of Commerce's aeronautical director, issued a specification for a light airplane for use by his inspectors but directed toward private owners. Among the responses was the W-1, an airplane developed by Fred Weick of NACA, and a design proposed by Otto Koppen that exhibited a large vertical tail, the elimination of the rudder (two-control), good stall recovery, a new type of landing gear, etc. His approach was summarized in an article in *Aviation* magazine for September 1934.

Otto's treatment of the stall was an intellectual adventure that has fascinated me ever since. I will review it in some detail as a final example of his ability as a teacher and designer.

The story begins as a mystery and gradually unfolds to a solution. From the earliest days of the Wright brothers it was known that when a wing exceeds a certain angle of attack the smooth airflow over the top breaks down into turbulence and the lift of the wing decreases rapidly (i.e., the wing stalls). This normally occurs at an angle of about 18°. The typical result was loss of lateral control, a rapid rolling of the airplane, and entry into a spin. A logical solution was to avoid stalling, but inadvertent stalling was frequent and often proved fatal if it occurred close to the ground. Spin recovery techniques, when developed, lessened the danger of stalling if it occurred at some altitude. Nevertheless, stalling remained a major hazard. High angles of attacks are encountered in tight turns when the aircraft may stall, roll "over the top" and spin in a direction opposite to the initial turn.

The British Aeronautical Research Committee was first to tackle the stall problem with a comprehensive approach based on the equations of motion. One inspiration was the importation of Fokker-designed aircraft into England after World War I. Fokker airplanes were characterized by thick cantilever wings, long tails and flat-sided fuselages aft. The famous Fokker D-VII, a prominent fighter of the war, could be flown to a very high angle of attack and failed to roll off when stalled, recovering in a gentle pitching motion. As Fokker pilots reported, the plane could actually "hang on the propeller" in a controlled descent. Initial explanation of this behavior was the thick-wing characteristics, which certainly showed a more gentle breakaway when tested in the wind tunnel, but there were other contributing factors, as was discovered later.

In 1928 (sometime after the Fokker experience) Hawker Aircraft produced a conventional-appearing biplane fighter called the Hornbill. Pilots soon found this aircraft had exceptionally good stability in stalled flight. There was no easy answer why, so a major investigation was initiated by the Aeronautical Research Committee. The results of this investigation were reported in 1932 in R & M Nos. 1422 and 1519, by such outstanding researchers as S. B. Gates, L. W. Bryant, H. B. Irving and others. The lift curve was measured in the wind tunnel and in stalled glides to angles of attack of 25°, well beyond the peak lift (which occurred at about 17.5°). After the peak the lift fell off, but not suddenly as on most contemporary aircraft. Very careful flight measurements indicated that in smooth air the aircraft was slightly unstable when the angle of attack lay between 17.5° (the stall point) and 23°, but that at higher angles, up to about 30°, there was a region of stability. At that point the researchers tentatively concluded that "a happy adjustment" between the various derivatives of the equations of motion must be occurring.

From measurements on a rolling balance in the wind tunnel, and data from other tests, estimates were made of the Hornbill's derivatives in the unstable region (17.5°–23°) and the stable region (24°–30°). In the unstable region a spiral divergence occurred; in the stable region a disturbance resulted in a near dead-beat damping of an oscillation with no spiral divergence. (See Table 5.1).

Table 5.1. Hawker Hornbill Estimated Stability Derivatives

	α	l_p	n_p	l_r	n_r	y_v	μn_v	μl_v
Unstable	22.5°	1.2	0.5	4.0	-2.13	-0.26	13.4 – 16.6	-44
Stable	27.5°	0.9	-0.2	2.0	-1.60	-0.24	10.4 – 15.0	-44

Note: l_p *(for example) is an abbreviated notation for* $\partial l / \partial p$.

An examination of Table 5.1 indicates that with one exception, all of the derivatives change magnitude between the unstable and stable regions. The exception is n_p, the rate of change of yawing moment with rolling velocity, which not only changes magnitude but also changes its algebraic sign. But n_p is a small derivative, and it seemed incredible that it alone could account for the difference of the violent behavior of an ordinary aircraft at stall to the stable condition of the Hornbill. One only has to experience the stall of a normal aircraft as it whips over on one wing, noses down into a spin, and rotates rapidly about a nearly vertical axis (a terrifying maneuver to the uninitiated) to fully appreciate the Hornbill's exceptional behavior.

Hawker Hornbill Stability Analysis

Otto Koppen reviewed the British investigation of the Hornbill while adding his own more physical interpretation. As students we had reached the point where we could think in terms of the derivatives. Although most readers of this book are unlikely to have developed that facility, an understanding of the Hornbill's behavior is so fascinating I have decided to chance a description of it here.

There are four cases to compare:
1. Typical unstalled (normal aircraft)
2. Typical stalled (normal aircraft)
3. Hornbill at 22.5° angle of attack (unstable)
4. Hornbill at 27.5° angle of attack (stable)

In all cases assume a small initial roll (disturbance) to the right and then see whether the rolling moment derivatives oppose or amplify the initial roll disturbance. If they oppose it, the response is stable; if they amplify it, the response is unstable.

There are three rolling-moment components:
l_p, the damping in roll due to rolling velocity, p.
In unstalled flight this resists the initial rolling velocity, i.e., it generates a roll moment to the left.
l_r, the rolling moment due to yawing velocity, r.
Yawing velocity to the right gives a roll moment to the right.
l_v, the rolling moment due to sideslip velocity, v.
Sideslipping to the right gives a roll moment to the left.

There also are three yawing-moment components:
n_p, the yawing moment due to rolling velocity, p.
In unstalled flight-rolling to the right gives a yaw moment to the left.
n_r, the damping in yaw moment due to yawing velocity, r.
Yawing velocity to right gives a yawing moment to the left.
n_v, the yawing moment due to sideslip velocity, v.
Sideslipping to the right gives a yawing moment to the right.

continued on next page

For each of the four cases, we examine the algebraic signs of the derivatives and their moment components after the initial disturbance. For a normal unstalled aircraft, the result following a small initial rolling velocity to the right is:

Derivative	Moment Component	Direction of Moment	
n_p (−)	pn_p	yawing moment to left	(−)
n_r (−)	rn_r	yawing moment to right	(+)
n_v (+)	vn_v	yawing moment to right	(+)
l_p (−)	pl_p	rolling moment to left	(−)
l_r (+)	rl_r	rolling moment to left	(−)
l_v (−)	vl_v	rolling moment to left	(−)

Summary: The sum of the three rolling-moment components are to the left *and are opposed* to the initial rolling velocity. This is stable. The following table summarizes the rolling-moment components for all four cases.

	pl_p	rl_r	vl_v	
Normal unstalled	−	−	−	stable
Normal stalled	+	+	+	unstable
Hornbill at 22.5°	+	+	+	unstable
Hornbill at 27.5°	+	−	−	conditionally stable

At 27.5° the Hornbill is conditionally stable because

pl_p is small + unstable effect
rl_r is small − stable effect
vl_v is large − stable effect

i.e., rl_r and vl_v are likely greater than the negative damping in roll, pl_p.

In R & M 1519 entitled "Lateral Stability of an Aeroplane Beyond the Stall," Bryant, Jones and Pawsey (June 1932) present a remarkably comprehensive (and complex) analysis of the effect of various derivatives on stability under stalled conditions. First they establish from the theory that three conditions must be met, namely that R, T, and D_1 (three functions of the derivatives) must be positive for complete stability (i.e., no divergence or unstable oscillation). The boundaries between stability and instability are when $R = 0$, $T = 0$ and $D_1 = 0$. Calculating these boundaries for various combinations of derivatives can show areas of complete stability.

Figure 5-11 shows a typical set of plots drawn for one value of n_r, the yaw damping derivative, a typical value being −0.986. Each of the three plots is for a value l_p, the damping in roll, which changes sign at the stall as the lift curve falls off. When l_p is negative (below the stall), a true damping effect is achieved; when it is positive (above the stall), it accentuates any rolling disturbance and is a major destabilizing effect. On each figure the boundaries of stability ($R = 0$, $T = 0$ and $D_1 = 0$) are plotted, and the stable (positive) side of each boundary is indicated by +++. Complete stability is shown by the hatched area on the positive side of the three boundaries.

The first conclusion from these diagrams is that the stable area is largest when l_p is negative (as in unstalled flight). Stability still is possible when l_p is zero, but only a very small area of stability exists when l_p is positive (in stalled flight). In the latter case, almost all of the stable region occurs when n_p is negative.

continued on next page

It seems possible that the derivatives of equations of motion for the Hawker Hornbill fell in this small area, so that it was stable at 27.5°, when l_p was positive. The critical derivative is n_p, which, although very small, is negative (as estimated earlier).

In more physical terms, Koppen summarized the situation as follows: n_p, the yawing moment due to rolling, couples rolling and yawing. If, for example, the aircraft is beyond the point of stall and receives a rolling disturbance to the right, n_p produces a yawing moment to the left and the right wing moves forward. This produces a yawing velocity to the left and a sideslip to the right. These combine to initiate large rolling moments from l_r and l_v that counteract the unstable effect of l_p. This reaction also is closely related to pilot attempts to control the onset of stall by applying left (or "top") rudder when the wing starts down to the right. Therefore small changes in the yawing motions can dramatically change the balance of the rolling moments, and hence the rolling motion. Years later, at Cornell Aeronautical Laboratory, we were able to apply this idea via automatic control to stabilize an aircraft in stalled flight. Still more recently, with jet thrust control, aircraft have been flown at nearly 80° angle of attack.

The question still may be asked: what was it about the Hornbill's configuration that yielded a small negative value of n_p? Normally the derivatives are defined about axes fixed in the aircraft, but at angles of attack on the order of 30° it is more reasonable to define them about wind axes. The rest of the explanation must be related to the specific airfoil and biplane arrangement. Koppen studied ways to design every airplane with the right combination of derivatives to place it in the stable region beyond the stall, but without complete success. Nevertheless, his interest in stalled flight led to the development of larger vertical tails and longer tail lengths that have characterized many well-behaved aircraft.

Social Life at MIT

During my student years at MIT my social life centered in the city across the river. Today, with its huge student population, Boston is a teeming city of modern and ancient buildings, with sidewalk cafes giving a Parisian atmosphere. It is bursting with energy. How different from the Boston I knew in the early thirties! Distinguished by its quiet, unhurried

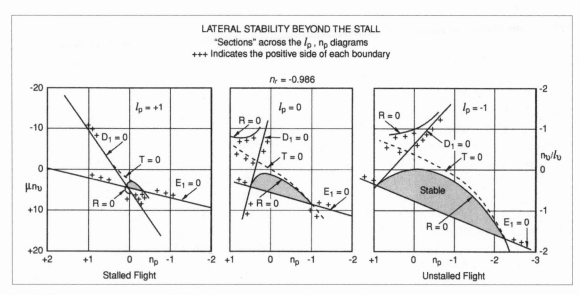

Fig. 5-11
This figure is based upon the British analysis of lateral stability beyond the stall.   123

charm, proud of its part in the American Revolution and complacent in its New England conservatism, Boston seemed distinct from other American cities and frequently was compared to those of England. Despite the questionable shenanigans of city hall under Mayor James Michael Curley, elected by a partisan and vocal Irish majority, the tenor of the city was set by the "Proper Bostonians." I saw no evidence of the Great Depression in Boston.

For a 21-year-old from a small town in Maine, Boston appeared as a romantic metropolis of tree-lined avenues and beautiful parks, sprinkled with fascinating shops, restaurants and theaters, all of which offered endless surprises and delights. But I lacked suitable female companionship to explore them. So after settling in at MIT, I decided to contact the only people I knew in Boston. On a weekend during Indian summer, when the wobbly brick sidewalks were strewn with fallen leaves and the crispness in the air foretold the end of autumn, I hiked eastward on Marlborough Street and turned south on Dartmouth toward Back Bay, where I came to a unique apartment complex called Trinity Court. A three-story structure with apartments around the four sides of the central court, it featured an ancient elevator that progressed at a dignified rate to the second floor. Stepping out put me directly in front of the apartment of Harry and Alice Clough.

My mother had become close friends with Alice while attending Westbrook Seminary. Alice married Harry Clough and her sister married Harry's brother. Both couples lived in Trinity Court and had a very close relationship into which I was always welcomed.

A Christian Science practitioner, Alice was the source of income for her family. Harry did the shopping and cooking. She confidently and effortlessly managed her role as head of the household, and he readily accepted his role and always was kind and hospitable to me. In the evening the entire clan frequently convened in front of a small coal fireplace in Harry and Alice's large sitting room, and Harry served tea and snacks. In addition to the family, a piano teacher who lived in a first-floor apartment usually was in attendance. The conversation,

centering on local politics or the many cultural events in Boston, was always lively despite frequent interruptions by trains passing through Back Bay Station close next door. Although well aware of MIT, the Cloughs had little curiosity about what went on there, so I never interjected anything about the exciting technical world to which I was being exposed. I accepted the Bostonian world they knew, enjoying their friendship and the social opportunity it offered. The only regret I had of the many hours I spent at the Cloughs was whether I ever adequately expressed how much I appreciated them. Their acceptance of me was complete and natural, like that of a child and parents, so I never felt as indebted as I should have.

I would occasionally stop by during the day when Alice was working with a client in the front room, and could hear her addressing the problem in a soft and reassuring manner. Although my grandmother had studied Christian Science in her later years, I knew nothing about it but surmised that Alice was an outstanding practitioner.

Unlike most of my acquaintances at MIT, Harry was possessed by neither ambition nor strong interests, and seemed to float through life accepting and enjoying what came his way. He never expressed strong emotions and did not appear to be suppressing them. From the perspective of the active life I was leading I could not understand Harry, but always found him a constant and pleasant companion.

One day, when I dropped by unannounced, a young woman stepped out of the front room. She was close to my age and dressed in a stylish suit. Upon noticing me, she stopped, smiled and waited for Alice to introduce us. Olga Sears was a commercial artist whose clientele included the best stores in Boston, for whom she did everything from window dressing to the design of advertising displays and announcements. After a brief conversation I suggested we have dinner, and silently hoped she liked ballroom dancing.

I assumed Olga was a relative of the Cloughs, but later suspected she was studying Christian Science with Alice. In the next two years we saw a great deal of each other, and I learned about her broken home and unhappy childhood.

Through the living allowance my folks provided me (and numerous small economies) I had enough cash to go dancing two or three times a week. With the full consent of the professor, I produced notes on aircraft stability and control for sale to students, which increased my discretionary fund. As long as I was doing well in my studies I felt no compunction about pursuing an entertainment program.

A member of a professional dance troupe as a teenager, Olga proved to be a sensational dance partner. In this Big Band era, fox trots and waltzes predominated, interspersed with an occasional Charleston or tango and, later, South American imports like the rumba. Olga could dance close or open, and faultlessly followed any improvised steps or variations. While I never thought of it as "going steady," we soon were dancing, dining, or both several times a week at the better restaurants and hotels—the Russian Bear, Parker House, Loch Ober, Egyptian Room, Statler and Copley—and, in the spring, when the weather was warm enough, at the outdoor plazas and patios. We never sat out a dance. At our favorite haunts the orchestra leaders got to know us. They always expected we would be first on the floor and played our favorite tunes.

Olga always seemed to be available. If I met her at the Cloughs after school and decided on an evening together, I rushed back to 278 Marlborough for a quick shave and change of clothes, and rushed back to meet her at her apartment. She gave no evidence of having other boyfriends. When close by, we walked to our destination; farther afield we used the subway. In the winter, when we danced late, we walked through the subway tunnels alongside the tracks, staying close to the wall should a train come barreling through. On warm nights in late spring we might wind up at the Egyptian Room, a short walk from Trinity Court. On the way back we would literally dance our way across the Square in front of Trinity Church, laughing and joking.

The Blue Ship Tea Room, down on the waterfront near Tea Wharf, was one of her discoveries. It was a charming little second-story restaurant that looked out across the harbor, and featured a friendly white cat and a piano-playing owner. Sitting by the open windows on sultry evenings, cooled by the breeze off the water, we would relax in its magic atmosphere.

For two years, Olga and I played like children in our carefree world of music, dancing and dining, hypnotized by romantic musical comedy tunes.[2] I never had seen my father put his arm around my mother, much less kiss her or give her a genuine hug. But Olga had a warm and affectionate nature, and never failed to demonstrate that when we arrived back at her apartment after an evening together.

In Old Town I must have been viewed by the local girls as a sort of amateur Tom Swift, but in Boston I was a student at MIT headed for a serious engineering career, which Olga respected. I had an equal respect for her burgeoning new career as a portrait artist.

Gradually I became infatuated with Olga, and she with me. Our relationship became more serious, with issues neither of us had confronted before. We were both highly career-oriented, and falling in love had no place in our plans. Marriage was something we never considered. Gradually we saw less and less of each other. But as I struggled to sort out my feelings and retain some sense of stability, I was learning that emotions have a powerful life of their own.

Although I have never believed Olga and I were right in the long term, I was fortunate to have experienced these feelings for the first time with a woman as sensitive as she was. In any event, romantic interludes are not made, they just happen. And when they do they should be appreciated.

After leaving Boston in 1936, I lost all contact with Olga until the sixties, when I saw her briefly. She was still pursuing her artistic career, had become a faculty member at the Boston Museum of Fine Arts and was living in a large warehouse building she had turned into a gallery of her own art. Olga never had

---

[2]Among our favorites were "Whispering," "Valencia," "Who," "Sunny," "Broadway Baby," "S'Wonderful," "I Got Rhythm," "Smoke Gets In Your Eyes," "Japanese Sandman" and "Melancholy Baby."

Graduation from MIT

While studying for final exams one morning around six o'clock, I was suddenly awakened by two burly workmen who pushed into my room and announced they had come to remove the furniture. My landlady, Mrs. Crosby, who owned the furniture, had a major disagreement with Mr. Maloof, who owned the building. She probably owed him rent money and was concerned he might attach her furniture, so she had decided to move out—bag and baggage. A huge van was parked out front and she was standing on the sidewalk directing operations. Most of the roomers decided to move out too, but three of us—a Mormon minister on the fourth floor, a female student on the third, and me on the second—decided to stick it out for another two weeks for reasons of convenience. We convinced the owner to leave the electricity on and the phones connected. I found an old mattress in the cellar that was comfortable enough, and a couple of boxes for table and chair. This domestic disruption didn't faze me. I passed the exams with flying colors. But a further problem arose.

I still was registered as a student in the Mathematics Department, while taking advantage of its many elective courses to effectively major in aeronautics. One of MIT's graduation requirements was a thesis. I chose long-range flight as my topic. Anticipating the home-built airplane movement exemplified by the EAA (Experimental Aircraft Association), I posed the question: "Could I design and construct, with my limited fabrication techniques, an airplane with a power plant of 40 horsepower that could fly nonstop 1,900 miles (equivalent to a flight from Newfoundland to England) with some margin of safety?"

In the thesis I first examined the history of record-breaking flights and the problems encountered with heavy load takeoffs, long-distance navigation, instrument flight with airplanes of various degrees of stability and emergency measures—all directed toward a set of design specifications.

I then proceeded to design an aircraft to meet the specs, including the choice of engine and an aircraft configuration, followed by all the detailed analysis of weight and balance, structures, three-view aerodynamics, wing design, fuel consumption, takeoff and range calculations, fuel system, aircraft stability analysis, etc.

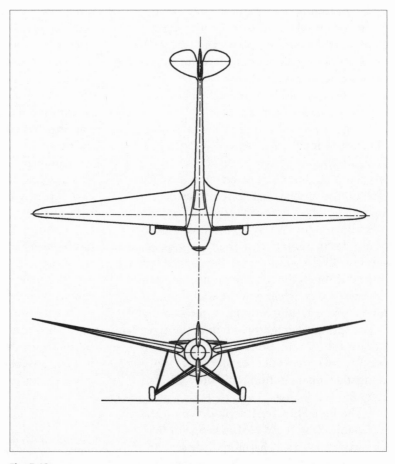

Fig. 5-12
Long Range Flight Design, front and top view.

The resulting design was a mid-wing monoplane with a highly tapered wing of aspect ratio 16, an NACA 2315 airfoil and an airship-shaped fuselage of optimum fineness ratio (about three) with a long tail boom. The novel features were a single cylindrical wing beam that also served as the main fuel tank, a droppable landing gear for drag reduction, and a spirally stable aircraft configuration for blind-flight assist and two-control (rudder only). The gross takeoff weight for a 1,900-mile flight (with fuel reserves) was 1,138 lbs., of which fuel and oil accounted for 500 lbs. Detailed power requirements and available-power curves were developed for a fixed-pitch propeller design, and various propeller drive ratios and range estimates were checked by the well-known Breguet formula.

All in all it was a reasonably complete preliminary design study and was accepted with favorable comments by my faculty advisors, Koppen, Rauscher and Ober. But it led to a major problem with the Mathematics Department. Its Academic Committee, which had raised no objections to my using electives to study aircraft design, now was confronted with approving a degree in mathematics for a student who had taken only the very few required math courses and was far from a math major. I was in deep trouble. There was no time to develop a mathematics thesis even if I had that capability, and my parents, who did not have the resources to finance another year at MIT, would be terribly disappointed if I failed to obtain a degree. At this juncture my professors in aeronautics—notably Ober, Koppen, Markham and Rauscher—said they would go to bat on my behalf with the Math Department but could not guarantee success. Graduation exercises were just a few days away, and I was told to attend and hope for the best. If they were successful I would be called to the platform to receive a diploma. I would not know the answer until the last moment.

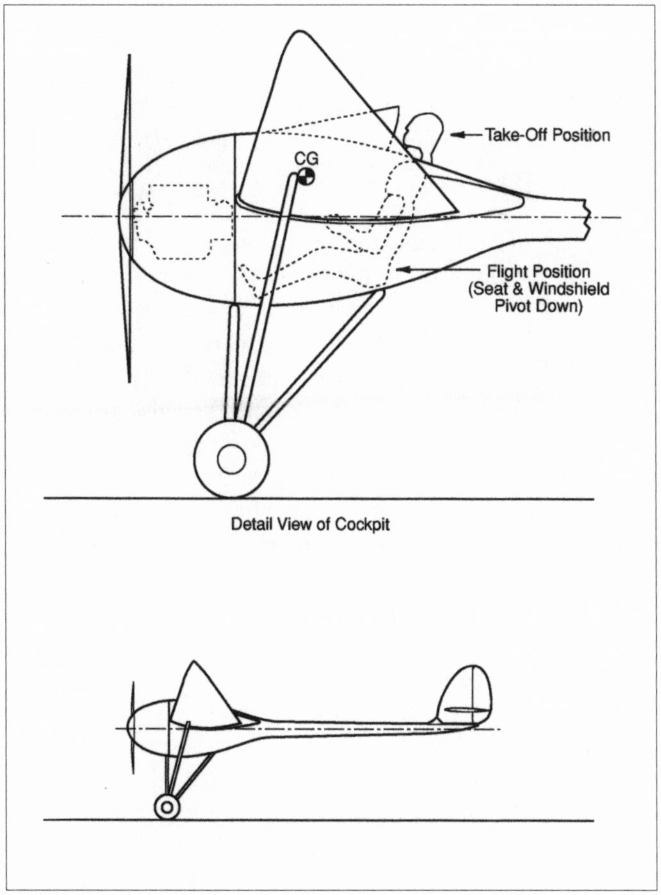

My folks could not afford to travel to Boston to attend the graduation ceremony, so they nominated my cousin, Ed Waterhouse, as the official family representative. I met Ed at Back Bay Station on one of Boston's oppressively hot days. Feeling it an imposition to require his attendance at this affair of questionable outcome, I took him to the Parker House to be fortified with mint juleps. Diplomas for the large graduating class were given out on an alphabetical basis, so there was plenty of time for me to build up a sweat. My name was finally called.

But the crowning event of that eventful day was a note from the Aeronautical Department Staff in which I was offered a job as a wind tunnel assistant for two years at $25 a week. In the depths of the Great Depression, obtaining work in one's specialty immediately upon graduation was an immeasurable gift that would allow me to pay off my loans and also establish contacts in the industry.

Detail View of Cockpit

Fig. 5-13
Long-Range Flight Design, side and cockpit detail.

127

MIT Course Nos. 16.62, 16.63 Aeronautical Laboratory; Markham Course Outline

Experiment I— USA 27 Airfoil Test

Plots of lift and drag coefficients, lift/drag ratio, moment coefficient about the leading edge and 1/4 chord, and center of pressure travel, all against angle of attack.

Experiment II—Test of C-100 Airplane Model

Plots of lift, drag and lift/drag ratio and pitching moment, all against angle of attack. The student was required to comment on stability, trim, minimum and maximum speed (given additional data), determination of angle of attack for cruise at 80 percent of V max and the ability of the aircraft to get the tail down on landing.

Experiment III—Test of TX-33 Airplane Model

Plot lift and drag curves as measured and corrected for tunnel-wall interference, pitching moment about CG for a given angle of attack, required and available horsepower, rate-of-climb curve, best rate of climb and climb speed, maximum angle of climb, etc.

Experiment IV—Test of TX-33 Airplane Model for Rolling and Yawing Moments Due to Yaw

The tests were run at zero- and 12-degree angles of attack. Results included developing equations for calculating the rolling, yawing and pitching moments about the body axis of the airplane, with final plots of rolling and yawing moments against yaw angle. This was a good exercise in axis transformation.

Experiment V—Test of Airplane Model with Operating Propeller

This test was performed with the wire balance, which enabled lift, pitching moment, drag (thrust) and motor torque to be measured. The experiment was run at one angle of attack and the propeller was operated at a constant rpm, so that V/nD[1] was varied by changes in true air speed (calculated from q). Results included thrust, torque and propeller efficiency versus V/nD, from which the maximum rpm and rate of climb were computed.

Experiment VI—Lift and Drag of a Body from Pressure Distribution Measurements

The body was a dome-shaped object mounted on a flat ground plane. Nine holes drilled from the top to the bottom on one side of the dome along a line cut by a vertical plane were attached to an alcohol manometer bank. Since the dome could be rotated about a vertical axis, it was possible to cover a large amount of the surface area. In fact, pressure measurements were made at 15-degree increments of rotation from zero degrees to 180 degrees (one assumed they also covered the same rotation in the opposite direction). The pressures as measured were normal to the surface. By appropriate corrections, the components of these pressures were obtained in the lift and drag direction and graphically summed to yield lift and drag of the body. The pressures were referenced to static in the tunnel, and the manometer readings had to be converted to pounds per square inch.

Experiment VII—Thrust of Wind Tunnel Propeller of the Five-foot Tunnel by Pressure Measurements

In this experiment pressures were measured in front and behind the propeller at a series of points along a radius from the centerline to the propeller tip. The pressures in front were below atmospheric as the air was sucked into the propeller and higher at the rear as the air was accelerated. Again, all measurements were done with an alcohol manometer. Various plots were made showing variation of the pressures along the blade radii and finally summed graphically to determine the thrust (at the tunnel operating speed of 40 mph).

---

[1] V/nD *is a parameter used in propeller analysis which essentially defines the angle of attack of the blade to the airstream.* (V = *forward velocity;* n = *rate of propeller rotation;* D = *propeller diameter.*)

Experiment VIII—The Change in Airplane Pitching Moment from Power-on to Power-off Conditions

The tests were done with the TX-33 model with a motor-driven propeller. The motor (propeller) was operated at a constant rpm (n). The V/nD, which determines the propeller performance, was varied by changing wind-tunnel airspeed. The power-off condition was simulated by removing the propeller.

This was a very clever experiment, illustrating that conditions can be realized in a wind tunnel that cannot be achieved in real flight, but that may prove useful. Many of these "wind-tunnel situations" could correspond to untrimmed or accelerated conditions in flight. The obvious example is a constraint system that permits the model to be held away from a real airplane pitching moment trim, which can be interpreted as measuring the stability moment that would attempt to return the disturbed airplane back toward trim. In general, wind tunnel tests can be run for combinations of independent variables whether they correspond to flight or not.

This experiment established a trim at α=0 degrees by adjusting the stabilizer and the wind speed, V (which changes V/nD) to approximately achieve, C_M=0 (about an assumed CG), T=D and L=W.[2] The student then measured the C_M at a series of angles of attack, for several speeds, i.e., for several V/nD and also ran one test with propeller off for C_M vs. α. This yielded a plot of C_M vs. α for a variety of V/nD. Given the V/nDs for level flight for various angles of attack of the real airplane, one can plot the real airplane moment curve. The power off (propeller removed) already corresponds to the real airplane. The data can be reduced to different CG locations.

Thus this experiment gave the student a better appreciation of the potential of wind tunnel testing.

Experiment IX—Change in Downwash Due to Slipstream (from the Propeller)

The downwash has two effects on the horizontal tail, namely a change in air velocity at the tail and a change in angle of attack. The propeller slipstream is superimposed on the wing and fuselage effects. This experiment was aimed at isolating these effects. The only simplification was to modify the model so that all of the tail was in the slipstream.

The following data were measured:

The pitching moments on the model about an assumed CG, for three angles of attack (0 deg., 6°, 12°) and four speeds (0, 15, 20, 25 mph) corresponding to V/nD values for constant, n. Each of these sets of runs was performed for conditions of stabilizer setting, with propeller running or removed, and horizontal tail on or removed.

Condition	Tail	Tail Setting	Propeller
C	on	+2°	off
A	on	+2°	running
D	on	−2°	off
B	on	−2°	running
F	off	—	off
E	off	—	running

From the above data the student was to deduce the following:

Rate of change of C_M with stabilizer angle for propeller turning and off, and for the two stabilizer angles. From these calculate the speed effect change at the tail due to the propeller (V_S^2/V^2).

---

[2]T = *thrust;* L = *lift;* W = *weight.*

From the tail on and off data, and the speed effect above, one could deduce the downwash angle change due to the slipstream. This experiment illustrated that some subtle effects can be determined from careful planning and reduction of test data.

Experiment X—Interference of Nacelle and Wing

A model engine nacelle for an air-cooled radial engine was tested on a wing in three locations: on high and short struts mounted above the wing, and in the wing leading edge. An improved nacelle (improved engine cowling) also was tested in the wing leading edge. The objective was to compare the drag and lift of the various nacelle locations over a range of angles of attack. The results generally confirmed more elaborate engine nacelle-wing studies by NACA.

I've reviewed the experiments in this course in some detail to illustrate how versatile a small low-speed wind tunnel can be. Until airplane speeds exceeded 200 mph, much of what the designer needed could be acquired in these low-speed facilities. This was especially true when the tunnel operator had long experience in the use of the facility and had compared the results with full-scale data. Ober and Markham had just such experience with the five-foot tunnel and were able, for example, to correct for low Reynolds number (RN) tests for stalling speed.

For some tests, of course, RN was less important. I remember one for a large four-engined Sikorsky flying boat and the accurate prediction of the stabilizer setting for first flight. Mike Gluhareff reported the setting had proven satisfactory. Many devices now used on high-performance aircraft originally were developed in small low-speed tunnels, e.g., the basic work on slots, slats, flaps and spoilers in NACA's 7-by-10 tunnel, and by Roger Griswold and Sikorsky in their modest facilities. With the addition of a moving ground plane (for race cars of low ride height), low-speed tunnels also have provided useful data for race cars up to nearly 200 mph performance.

Although I never have viewed myself as a wind-tunnel professional, during my aeronautical career I was involved with a variety of wind-tunnel facilities and tests, including the following:

1. The small tunnel that I built and installed in the Physics Department at the University of Maine.
2. The five-foot tunnel at MIT, where I ran model tests for Chance Vought, Sikorsky, etc. during my two years as assistant in the wind tunnel.
3. The 7-½-foot MIT tunnel, again performing tests for industry.
4. The Sikorsky Vertical Tunnel, running tests for Vought on a high-lift slotted flap developed by Roger Griswold called the "horsefeather."
5. The NACA Langley Propeller Research Tunnel, testing a large-scale model of the Vought XF4U-1 "Corsair" gullwing for slipstream effects.
6. The NACA Langley Full-Scale Tunnel, testing the Avion XP-79 flying wing.
7. The NACA Langley 7-by-10-foot tunnel, performing Avion XP-79 stability and control tests.
8. The GALCIT 10-foot wind tunnel, also for XP-79 stability and control tests.
9. The NACA Ames, 20-foot, High-Speed Tunnel, for additional XP-79 stability and control tests.
10. The five-foot tunnel at MIT, testing a model high-performance torpedo float plane designed by Kristian Østby, a student at MIT. He was a test pilot for the Norwegian Naval Air Force.
11. Development of a small automotive tunnel for Chevrolet/Chaparral R & D under Frank Winchell.
12. Testing bicycles in the CALSPAN Atmospheric Tunnel, with Doug Milliken as rider. He also has been involved in tests for the Olympic Bicycle team in the large GM automotive tunnel, and other bicycle tests at Texas A & M and MIT.

Chapter 6

Noseover in Augusta

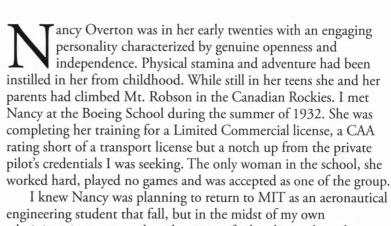

"A miss is as good as a mile."

– Sir Walter Scott

Nancy Overton was in her early twenties with an engaging personality characterized by genuine openness and independence. Physical stamina and adventure had been instilled in her from childhood. While still in her teens she and her parents had climbed Mt. Robson in the Canadian Rockies. I met Nancy at the Boeing School during the summer of 1932. She was completing her training for a Limited Commercial license, a CAA rating short of a transport license but a notch up from the private pilot's credentials I was seeking. The only woman in the school, she worked hard, played no games and was accepted as one of the group.

I knew Nancy was planning to return to MIT as an aeronautical engineering student that fall, but in the midst of my own administrative paperwork and trying to find a place to live, she was farthest from my thoughts. Walking into Walker Memorial, an on-campus dining room, I heard a voice call "Hi, Bill" from behind. Turning around, I hardly recognized Nancy. She was wearing a sweater and skirt instead of her flying jacket and jodhpurs. Finding a table, we engaged in some animated conversation and quickly recognized our mutual dilemma of adapting to the routine of university life.

As kindred spirits I suggested that we get together for dinner and dancing, to which she enthusiastically agreed. And so our friendship began around a fascination with flying and a love of dancing. Frequently, after independent study in the evening, we would meet at the Egyptian Room on Boylston Street for a few dance sets, usually talking nothing but aeronautics between them.

Early on, Nancy discovered the Little Madrid on a side street near the Boston Common. We regarded this as a private dine and

This shows the left-hand side of the airplane; the drop-off is on the left, November 11, 1932.

133

dance club, but it really was a speakeasy since Prohibition still was with us. Nancy had obtained membership credentials through friends, so we could drop by and dance with no cover charge. With her knock on a secluded back door a small slide opened and eyes peered out. Once she was recognized the door quickly opened, and as quickly closed behind us. A rather thinly clad coatroom girl unenthusiastically took Nancy's topcoat and my pony fur jacket, having learned from previous occasions that we seldom could afford to tip.

The club itself had a steamy atmosphere— low ceilings, darkened lights—right out of the Casbah. Although small by hotel standards, the floor was excellent for dancing. The band was on a slightly raised platform to the right, and a number of small tables lined the wall on the left. There was plenty of drinking but no evidence of a bar. Arriving early before the theater crowd, Nancy and I often had the dance floor to ourselves. One evening the five-piece band was warming up to the tune of "Sunny," from the Oscar Hammerstein and Jerome Kern musical of the same name. On a visit to the Crowells a couple of years before I had attended the Boston opening. That was my first exposure to a romantic musical, and the beginning of a lifelong addiction.

As we danced, all those feelings came back and I could hardly wait to initiate an adventure. Sitting down after the first set, I blurted out, "Nancy, I have a terrific idea! Why don't we fly up to Maine and see my folks. We could land in Bangor, which would take less than three hours." We had already located a fixed-base aircraft operator named E. W. Wiggins in Norwood, some 20 miles south of Boston, who operated a small but well-organized flight service engaged in training, repair and aircraft rental. The facility's manager, Joe Garsides, was about our age and had a great respect for aero students at MIT. To build up flight time and maintain proficiency, Nancy regularly rented an aircraft at Wiggins and I occasionally flew with her.

Adventure never was far from Nancy's heart, so she readily took to my idea. We settled on the details and the date that evening. We would leave on Armistice Day, November 11. Because we were enjoying a late fall it didn't occur to either of us that weather might be a problem,

or even that an open-cockpit airplane might be chilly. Such is the enthusiasm of youth!

A flight of that length would be child's play for an experienced pilot, but Nancy never had flown cross-country more than 25 miles, and that under the most favorable conditions. I never had flown in any airplane from Point A to Point B. Neither of us had experience in night flying or flying in instrument weather. I was thrilled by the prospect of this adventure, and imagined it as the beginning of a dramatic career of record-breaking flights in hero mode. The very route we would take carried a powerful emotional impact. Hitchhiking between Old Town and Boston had been my first real move toward independence and freedom. I knew every step of the way and wondered how it would look from several thousand feet above, and what it would be like to fly over my home town.

ON ARMISTICE DAY I got up early, dressed a bit more warmly than usual, had a good breakfast at the Esplanade café and hiked across Harvard Bridge, which carries Massachusetts Avenue across the Charles River, to fetch Nancy. With my old leather helmet in my jacket pocket I felt ready for anything. Nancy's undergraduate dorm, a distinctive serpentine structure designed by Alva Alto, was on Memorial Drive not far from MIT. Prompt as usual, she was in the lobby when I arrived. We had arranged for Joe Garsides to pick us up around nine-thirty at Tech Drug across from the Guggenheim Aeronautical Laboratory. The weather was favorable: a clear, crisp day with light wind and no sign of snow. Nevertheless, I could sense that Nancy was a bit apprehensive when she suggested we stop in the drug store for an extra cup of coffee before Joe arrived. While there I bought a dozen oranges. I always carried oranges on my motorcycle trips and had developed a technique for eating them with one hand.

Joe arrived a little late so it was after eleven before we pulled up on the ramp at Wiggins. On the apron in front of the hangar, checked out and ready to go, was the F-22. With its bright yellow fuselage and blue trim it looked like a tropical bird anxious to be off.

Manufactured by Fairchild in Hagerstown, Maryland, the F-22 was a beautiful aircraft. A

Fig. 6-1
The Fairchild F-22 with Menasco engine at E. W. Wiggins Flight Service, Norwood, circa 1932.

high-wing, strut-braced, parasol monoplane, it was a classic taildragger with two open cockpits, a widely spaced main gear and a tail wheel. It was powered by a four-cylinder air-cooled Wright Gipsy or similar engine (also see page 248, Figs. 12-1, 12-2). The F-22 normally was flown from the rear cockpit, but in the Wiggins plane the front cockpit also was equipped with a set of primary controls for student training.

According to Otto Koppen, Fairchild aircraft were universally renowned for their excellent flying and ground handling characteristics. A long tail length with a sizeable fin and rudder gave high damping of yawing motion, full-span narrow-chord ailerons provided excellent roll control with low stick forces, and the elevator and ailerons were actuated by low-friction push-pull control linkage (as opposed to cables). Good ground handling was facilitated by the wide-track gear, steerable tail wheel, and individual brake control at the rudder pedals. On our aircraft the brakes were operable from both cockpits.

Among the most basic of the various techniques for cross-country navigation is "dead reckoning." One draws the route on a map and the course direction is measured

relative to true north. Corrections are applied to yield a magnetic compass heading, including adjustments for wind drift. Progress along the course is estimated from the aircraft's speed, adjusted for head or following wind components. Although we carried Department of Commerce sectional maps, and had a dash-mounted compass in the rear cockpit, Nancy and I planned to "pilotage" our way to Bangor by following prominent features on the ground: the turnpike and the coastline to Portland and Brunswick, the Kennebec River to Augusta and Waterville, and the highway to Bangor. If we got lost we always could head east toward the coast, pick up the Penobscot River and follow it north to Bangor. This simple navigation required only that the weather be clear along the route. A final check at Wiggins indicated good visibility, modest winds and high clouds—in other words, VFR (Visual Flight Rules) conditions prevailed.

Shortly after noon Nancy climbed into the rear cockpit. With the wheels chocked and the switch off, I pulled the propeller through a couple of revolutions, leaving it horizontal. With another smart pull the engine started, and I scrambled up the step on the landing gear strut into the front cockpit. By twelve thirty-five we were airborne, heading for Boston at a thousand feet and still climbing.

Soon we could see the city's tallest building, Custom House Tower, standing alone above old Boston with its crooked streets and alleyways where patriots had walked and plotted. I couldn't help but think that flight gives one a grandstand seat for viewing history. From our vantage point we could see such landmarks as the Old North Church, Bunker Hill, Tea Wharf and the location of Paul Revere's home.

Off to the east, along the edge of the harbor, was Atlantic Avenue. Looking down I spotted two white steamships, like familiar twins, berthed along a wharf for the winter. I remembered my short summer job as dining room cashier on one of them, until an infestation of bedbugs was mistaken for smallpox.

As the F-22 was moving up the coast following the Old Newburyport Turnpike toward Portsmouth, I flashed back to my early hitchhiking experiences. I even found the spot in the road where, half frozen in the middle of a blizzard, I had gotten a lift in a big truck and made myself cozy in the banana blankets in back, munched a chocolate bar and enjoyed every minute of it. Passing directly over Hampton Beach, near Portsmouth, I picked out the summer home on Boar's Head where the Robinsons and their daughter Janet lived. I liked the Robinsons, but was more impressed that one of their close relatives was Arthur Nutt, designer of the famous Curtiss D-12 engine of early Schneider Cup fame. Just before 2:00 P.M. the white sands of Old Orchard Beach slid by beneath us.

Because we were getting cold, Nancy throttled back, yelling over the wind noise, and we decided to land at Portland to warm up and top off on fuel. In those days Portland's airfield was in Scarborough, just across the inlet from Pine Point. It wasn't much—just one short gravel runway, a very small hangar and a gas pump—but we were fortunate it was there. By the time we had warmed up in the hangar office and taken on gas, it was after two-thirty.

Augusta and Waterville, our last major checkpoints, were located on the Kennebec River. An hour later we sighted the capitol with its golden dome reflecting the sun's rays. Now

that we were on a more northerly course, the sun was abeam, directly off to our left and rather low in the west. Subliminally, I became aware that sunset might be sooner than we expected.

Augusta, city of hills, was like an old friend. I had explored it on several visits to the home of Knowlton Small, whose family summered in a quiet rustic cottage on Lake Cobbosseecontee, a few miles to the southwest. An inveterate sightseer, Knowlton suggested one day that we visit the muster field, a parade ground on a high bluff not far from the city center, whose longest dimension was roughly north and south. On the south side, next to the road, a sheer drop of more than one hundred feet led down to a gravel pit of broken rocks and boulders. The north side fell off less precipitously. A steep road led to the top of the field, and when we got there I could see that the surface was fairly level and reasonably smooth. In those days I looked at every hayfield as a possible landing field, and I could visualize getting in there under favorable circumstances.

As we crossed Augusta in the F-22 on the way up the Kennebec to Waterville, the bluff and the muster field were clearly visible. They drew my attention only as a pleasant memory.

Heading for Trouble

I don't know exactly when or where, but soon after that it became obvious to me that we were heading for serious trouble. I'd been keeping an eye on the sun, and remembered that its apparent motion speeds up as it nears the horizon. Although Waterville was only a few miles away, the distance from Waterville to Bangor was much greater. I hauled out the sectional chart and made a quick estimate. It would take about three quarters of an hour for that run by the direct route, and longer if we followed the highway. If we were to get over Bangor, which we could certainly see after sunset, finding the darkened field could be a problem. No lights marked its boundary. Like all the surrounding countryside it would appear as just another black area. Nor were the approaches good: telephone lines on one side and built-up residences on the other. At the rate the sun was moving I couldn't imagine making Bangor with any hope of landing safely.

Approaching Waterville, I backed off the throttle slowly so Nancy wouldn't think the engine had quit. Twisting around in the cockpit, I yelled, "Nancy, we're running out of daylight fast. We'll never make it to Bangor before dark." She raised her head above the cowling and replied, with typical directness, "What the hell can we do? I don't see any fields around here that we could get into."

All forest or small rocky fields on rough terrain, central Maine scarcely is the place for a forced landing, even in broad daylight. It didn't take a genius to realize that our only hope was the muster field, some 20 miles back. "Turn around, Nancy," I yelled, "let's get back to Augusta as fast as we can." She wasted no time rolling the airplane into a tight turn, descended a thousand feet with open throttle and headed back down the Kennebec. I could think of nothing better to do than toss the oranges over the side one at a time and watch them curve away toward the river. From the front cockpit I clearly saw the bluff, and with some arm signals managed to get Nancy lined up with the approach from the north side and into the prevailing wind. She came in well above stall with plenty of control and got the main wheels on the ground first, a nice landing but fast. We were rolling toward the drop-off—that hundred-foot precipice down to the gravel pit—at an alarming rate. Nancy was totally unfamiliar with the terrain in general, and the drop-off in particular. When it was apparent we couldn't stop in time, I jammed the throttle full forward and momentarily grabbed the stick to steady the airplane as we sailed out over the edge and could look down at that fearsome drop. I could hear Nancy cursing above the wind and engine noise. In any event I didn't have to tell her what we faced; she had seen it for herself. We were confronted with a tough call—to get into a very marginal field in the next few minutes without going over the edge or getting caught after dark, either of which promised to be fatal.

Someone later asked me what I was thinking, and I can assure you there was no time for reflection—it was all action, a race with the sun using whatever resources we had. Nancy was doing a great job of flying. She banked the airplane around into a turn for another try,

being careful to maintain a margin above stall in this downwind turn at low altitude and low speed. I could sense her well-coordinated turn. She was flying in a precise and professional manner under tremendously stressful circumstances. The next time we came in more slowly but still well above a three-point landing approach, maintaining margin for accelerating back up to flying speed if we needed to. And we did. Nancy poured on the coal when she realized that we could not stop in time.

By now the sun was halfway down on the horizon, creating a broad band of color sweeping from south to north. As we swung around for the third try I happened to look down. On the adjacent hillside was a huge cemetery with white slabs sticking up like a giant pincushion. We came in more slowly still, under some control, and thought we'd made it. Nancy got the power on at the last moment and we staggered out over the bluff. Both of us sensed the next try was it. The sun had now disappeared below the horizon into a narrow red band in the west. We were in that brief twilight. I could see the house and street lights coming on and the lighted capitol dome hazy in the distance. The gravestones were dark and ghostly.

This time Nancy touched down sooner and more slowly, still wheels first. After rolling a hundred feet or so, she got on the brakes, and taking the cue I followed suit with the front pedals. Between us we must have used up all the cable slack because the wheels locked up and slid along the ground. We were slowing fast but running out of elevator control to keep from pitching over. In a tail-high attitude we slid past the point where we could have attempted another takeoff and tried to go around again. This surely was the point of no return; it was either success or curtains. Suddenly and unexpectedly we struck some sort of declivity on the surface. The nose went down, shattering the propeller, as the airplane catapulted over its nose onto its back and crashed down on the vertical tail. After sliding a few feet, it came to a stop 30 feet from the drop-off!

I RIPPED OFF MY BELT the instant we hit and fell out onto the underside of the wing. Thinking of fire I slid back beneath the rear cockpit. Momentarily stunned, Nancy was

Fig. 6-2
This shows the right-hand side of the airplane after it flipped over. The drop-off is a short distance away on the right, November 11, 1932.

hanging on the belt. I reached up, found the release, and she came tumbling down into my arms. For a few minutes that seemed an hour, we were locked in a wordless embrace. As we hugged and hugged, I learned that those who survive a desperate situation together can experience a special kind of bonding. We were down, we had survived, we were safe and we had not failed each other. At that moment we were deliriously happy for no other reason than to be alive.

Soon we became conscious of our surroundings and discovered we were lying in about four inches of mud and water, which sent us into gales of laughter. The situation seemed sillier and sillier, sitting under a broken airplane, in complete darkness, on a remote and barren plateau. But as our eyes adjusted to the darkness, we found we were not alone. Some 20 or 30 people, hearing us circling around, had come up to the muster field and were arranged in a circle around the airplane, enjoying (or perhaps wondering at) our antics.

The spectators soon proved to be most helpful, and volunteered to keep the souvenir hunters away until we could get a crew from

Wiggins to take the airplane back to Norwood. They took us to a telephone to let my folks know what had happened, and later that evening to a bus bound for Bangor. Shortly before midnight we were at home in Old Town. Wiggins took a couple of months to repair the aircraft and Nancy's parents took care of the cost.

This account has been written more than 60 years after the event. To reinforce my memory I revisited the muster field during a vacation to Maine. Driving down from Lake Cobbosseecontee to the foot of the bluff, I noticed the road had been widened and there no longer was a gravel pit at the base. But the drop-off was every bit as scary, and certainly as high, as I remembered it. The muster field with extensions on the north and resurfaced with runways, now was Augusta's airport, not large but apparently adequate. The cemetery that had seemed so ghostly and unsettling as Nancy and I circled around in our landing attempts now was huge and spread out on the hillside.

For the reconstruction of our flight, I utilized a *World Almanac* to calculate the time of sunset, beginning and end of twilight at

Augusta (latitude 44.3 degrees north, longitude 69.8 degrees west) on November 11, 1932. New York, Montreal and Halifax sectional aeronautical maps (1995 edition) and an AAA Road Atlas (1994) also were used. Data on the Fairchild F-22 of that era was obtained from the CAA Type Certificate made available by the Experimental Aircraft Association (EAA) library.

What Really Matters

Nancy and I were not much for philosophizing. We assumed we had done something right and had been gifted with good luck. We were content to accept the old adage that "a miss is as good as a mile" without further analysis. Since narrow escapes are quite common in flying, one scenario might be the following: Arising through an unforeseen factor, a risk is detected before it becomes catastrophic. If there is enough information, or experience, available to make a remedial decision and time to take positive action, and if panic is avoided and the action avoids compounding the problem, and if sufficient feedback is available, success may be achieved albeit by a very small margin.

This scenario is common in the realm of "adventures" which, by definition, involve new experiences and a stretching of one's capabilities. The more novel the adventure the more likely there will be some unforeseen eventuality, with the ensuing risk. Even in Lindbergh's well-planned New York–Paris flight, his lack of sleep prior to leaving proved an unexpected risk. A careful reading of his book *Spirit of Saint Louis* indicates how close he came to losing consciousness. And who could have foreseen

that a stowaway would hide in the tail section of the *Yellow Bird*, making the heavily loaded takeoff an even more marginal affair.

The time from detection of a risk to its resolution can vary greatly. In Lindbergh's case it was hours, in our episode it was minutes, and in the case of the overloaded *Yellow Bird*, seconds. The response to the risk may depend upon skill, memory, analysis or (in Lindbergh's case) endurance and character. But the common controlling element is feedback, as in any control system problem.

Our risk came from a failure to realize how early the sun sets in that latitude late in the year, plus our several delays. Our daylight-time window was small but we rapidly sought out our best alternative and took action. Nancy's superb flying, precise and conservative, avoided a magnification of our problem, and we were favored by the feedback we received from the position of the sun and how well we were doing on each successive landing attempt. In effect, Nancy used all the available time to improve her approach and shorten the rollout. Whether we would have made it if the declivity had not flipped the airplane is arguable. We were slowing fast and might have stopped just short of the brink or, as we slowed down and lost elevator control, the airplane might have flipped on its own. In any narrow escape the element of chance cannot be totally discounted.

After we left MIT, I rarely saw or communicated with Nancy. But just before she died from Lou Gehrig's disease some years ago she wrote me a letter mentioning our flight to Maine. It confirmed for me the indelible connection that exists between those who have shared a life-threatening adventure.

Chapter 7 🦅

Wind Tunneling

"Prof. John Markham (MIT) contributed to the concept of Boeing's high-speed atmospheric tunnel, enabling accurate data production and quick advice for the designers. It was essential for the development of the swept wing 707 and all subsequent airliners."

– William H. Cook
(*The Road to the 707*)

That fall I reported for work. My desk in Ober's office was strategically located near the main entrance to the Guggenheim Aeronautical Laboratory, which was the receiving area for interesting visitors from old grads to celebrities. Professors Shats Ober and Johnny Markham occupied adjacent offices and the door between them always was open. Since my duties included technical liaison for wind-tunnel tests, data reduction, and assisting in the wind-tunnel classes, I was to see a lot of them.

In those days the Aero teaching staff was small and congenial. Koppen, Rauscher or Newell routinely dropped by at lunch time, whereupon we would all troop across the street to the Tech Drug Store for sandwiches. I got to know the three of them on a first-name basis. They were always ready to discuss any aspect of the aero sciences about which I might be curious.

Although my job title was "assistant in the wind tunnel," other duties included preparation of class material, guiding visitors through the facilities, assisting foreign students handicapped by language problems and participating in open-house days. I also had special assignments, such as preparing calculations or figures for publications in which the professors were involved. Ober, for example, was working on the fourth edition of *The Airplane and Its Engine,* a popular text he wrote with Chatfield and Taylor.

Those two years were a godsend for me. In addition to giving me the opportunity to meet industry representatives under actual working conditions, I was able to monitor Koppen's courses in aircraft stability and control, which enhanced my grasp of the subject. Further, I could attend courses I had missed, like Charles Stark Draper's instrumentation seminars.

Sikorsky S-43 being loaded onto the *Bergensfjord* for Norway.

A small-scale, non-powered, wooden model of Chance Vought's XSB2U-1 (a two-place Navy scout bomber) was one of the first industry wind-tunnel tests following my arrival. The test, on the wire balance in the five-foot tunnel, involved longitudinal stability and control, and flaps up and down with horizontal tail on and off. There were also some lateral/directional tests for yawing and rolling moments and aileron control. All measurements had to be reduced to wind axes and aerodynamic coefficients, and plotted. This was a big job with slide rule and trig tables. Vought was in a hurry, so Johnny, Obe and I worked simultaneously to get it out. Flaps still were somewhat of a novelty, and I found the results of especial interest. Another job was for a large four-engined Sikorsky seaplane, again tested, at very small scale, in the five-foot tunnel. The main reason for the test was to establish longitudinal trim conditions for first flight, and to ensure longitudinal stability and control. As noted earlier, the stabilizer setting for first flight on this aircraft was based on these wind tunnel tests, and proved satisfactory.

Assisting Markham in his student wind-tunnel courses proved pleasant and amusing. During the hot and muggy Indian summer that first year, when we were setting up the model and balance for his classes, Johnny occasionally suggested we cool off by sitting *in* the tunnel with the fan idling at a 5–10 mph breeze. A great raconteur, he entertained us with stories during these wind tunnel breaks.

A smattering of foreign students always was present in the Aero Department. That fall two Mongolian brothers, Yuck Poey Poon and Fuey Poey Poon, were taking the wind-tunnel course. Having been briefed on the standard airfoil test procedure, they were left to themselves to perform it. The plotted results were nothing short of remarkable. In place of the linear lift curve slope, the brothers had produced a jagged, saw-toothed result. Instead of maintaining the speed manometer at a set height by adjusting the rheostat on the fan motor control, they had found it convenient to simply adjust the manometer setting itself.

Numerous Air Force officers who had taken courses at MIT returned for visits whenever in the vicinity. Two I especially remember were Capt. Stevens of the early high-altitude balloon flights and Lt. Ben Kelsey of the Air Force Fighter Branch (a transcontinental record-setter in a Lockheed P-38). They would drop by unannounced, settle down in Ober's office and recount their adventures. The Aero staff learned a lot about the actual behavior of current military aircraft this way. A number of graduates appeared at early IAS (Institute of Aeronautical Sciences) conventions and organized a select dinner of MIT Aero staff and graduates that was referred to as "Viewing the Aeronautical Industry with Its Pants Down." At such dinners, aircraft research and development was discussed in a surprisingly open and non-competitive fashion.

Famous Visitors

Probably the most illustrious aeronautical graduate was Jimmy Doolittle, whose remarkable career was studded with firsts. By the time I met him he had won the Schneider Cup in a Curtiss seaplane in England (1924), the Thompson Trophy at the National Air Races (1930), and had established himself as an outstanding test, stunt and race pilot. He had also made the first "blind" flights out of Mitchell Field under Guggenheim Sponsorship (1929), and worked at the Air Force Center, McCook Field. Doolittle kept in touch with the Aero Department staff for years. His subsequent career included the IAS presidency (1940), the Tokyo raid (1942), and heading the 8th Air Force in World War II (1944).

One Saturday Roscoe Turner paid a visit to the Department. Having been forewarned, Ober, Markham and Koppen were on hand to show him around. As usual, he was wearing his self-styled uniform and arrived in full booming voice. Having flown into Boston, he asked about the weather conditions for his return flight. MIT ran no weather service but Prof. Rossby was a pioneer investigator of Air Mass Analysis. Turner was put in contact with one of Rossby's assistants, who stated that "good weather would probably hold, or it might be bad, but please don't quote me." Although Turner had none of the engineering status of Doolittle, his record of air race wins, and performance in the England-Australia event, were phenomenal.

Because of my great interest in long-range flight, I was thrilled to meet Clyde Pangborn in 1935. He came from the barnstorming era, survived as a stuntman and had flown everything. He was a "pilot's pilot." His greatest achievement still was in the future—the first trans-Pacific non-stop flight, which he made in a Bellanca from Japan to his hometown of Wenatchee, Washington. Pangborn participated in the North Atlantic ferry flights of American military aircraft to Europe during World War II. Unlike Turner, he was quiet and reserved and asked serious questions about the wind tunnel activity. In the course of conversation, I learned that he had flown into Boston in a Fairchild cabin plane (the folding-wing type used by John Henry Mears and Collier in their successful world flight) and that he intended to fly back to Hartford after his MIT visit. Noting my enthusiasm, he agreed that I could come along for the ride. I would say hello to my cousin Ed and hitchhike back.

DURING THE FALL AND SPRING TERMS of 1935–'36, I lived at 421 Marlborough Street in a front corner apartment on the fourth floor. Unlike Mrs. Crosby who had left me in the lurch at 278 Marlborough, Miss Spaulding, my new landlady, was friendly and genuinely concerned about her roomers. We became good friends. My brother Cooper also roomed at 421 when he attended MIT as an architectural student a few years later.

During and after my relationship with Olga I went through a difficult emotional period. Although I continued to see the Cloughs, it was some time before I developed other social activity and got back into the dance routine. Fortunately, during this transition, I was approached by Wiggins Airways of Norwood, Massachusetts, to design a small two-seat trainer tailored to its flight instruction activity. The decision was made with representative Joe Garsides, manager of the Wiggins Norwood base, for a design based on the Aeromarine AR-3 three-cylinder 50-hp air-cooled engine. The prototype would be built in the Wiggins shop, and would have a steel-tube fuselage frame with welded-up main wing spars, wood ribs and fabric covering. The general arrangement was that of a low-wing monoplane with fixed gear, well-streamlined pants and side-by-side seating. I went to some effort to ensure outstanding flying characteristics, and sacrificed a little performance by using a modified Göttingen 387 airfoil of 15 percent thickness (which was known to have exceptional stalling behavior), a fuselage tail length of more than half the wing span and a sizable vertical tail. Before Wiggins canceled the project for business reasons, I had completed the three-view, weight and balance analysis, and performance estimate. I also had estimated the longitudinal and lateral stability and control, elevator requirements for three-point landing, longitudinal trim, control sensitivities, etc. I was involved in detailed structural calculations at the time of cancellation.

This project proved a useful application of what I had been taught at MIT. Koppen's design course had taken us through most of the steps in creating an airplane layout and performance analysis. Joe Newell's courses provided a good dose of aircraft structure short of the all-metal full monocoque which was just coming on the scene. In many respects the Wiggins trainer had fewer design problems than the several designs required in Otto's courses.

My employment at MIT was for the school year, but fortunately I was offered a summer job. The Pratt & Whitney Aircraft Company of East Hartford, Connecticut, had invited Otto Koppen and Joe Newell to consult on the future characteristics of transport airplane design utilizing P&W air-cooled radial engines. The study emanated from George Mead at the highest level of United. Koppen and Newell planned to do layout and performance analyses, and I went along as draftsman. At that time transport aircraft design had not yet stabilized. Areas of controversy included required performance in terms of range, speed and altitude, aircraft size and number of engines, and such details as seating arrangements, space per passenger, baggage compartments, window sizes and aisle and headroom dimensions. One amusing aspect was the size and shape of the lavatories, which resulted in a number of proposed configurations with their pros and cons.

Otto ensured that the designs had adequate flight characteristics, while Newell proposed the structure and estimated weights. I did the three-view layouts. It was a fun deal from beginning to end. Early every Monday morning we left

143

Fig. 7-1
Lt. Kristian Østby (later Capt.) as he appeared at MIT as a temporary student.

for Hartford, and returned to Boston for the weekend. During the week we got to know many of P&W's engineering staff.

Lieutenant Kristian Østby, Royal Norwegian AF

One day early in the fall of 1934, I was introduced to Kristian Østby, a Norwegian who just had arrived at the Institute and was discussing course structure with Professor Ober. I sensed he was no rosy-cheeked student. Although in civilian dress, he had a military bearing and gave the impression of age and experience. Because he was having trouble with the English language, Ober recognized he might need more than the normal briefing and called me into the conversation.

We soon learned that Østby was a test pilot attached to the Royal Norwegian Aircraft factory, had the rank of lieutenant and was at MIT to enhance his piloting background

with a couple of semesters of aeronautical engineering. Although he was highly intelligent and an outstanding pilot, Østby's engineering qualifications for entry at MIT were marginal, made more so by the language problem. No attempt was made by Ober or Markham to make an issue of this; on the contrary they welcomed test pilots and military types as adding a reality component to the student group. Ober asked me to work informally to help Østby over technical and language difficulties which proved to be a rewarding experience for both of us.

Having gone to sea as a youngster, Østby transferred into naval aviation pilot training, flew as a civilian on an airline between Norway and Sweden, and finally became a test pilot at the Naval Air Base in Horten. He had wild tales to tell. On one occasion, while testing a prototype open-cockpit trainer with a wheel control (instead of the conventional stick), he pushed the plane into a steep dive to fully explore its performance, at which point the axle on the wheel caught under the instrument panel and the aircraft wound up inverted. Flying without a seat belt, Østby found himself hanging outside the aircraft while still clutching the wheel. When the axle broke loose, the aircraft completed the loop and he was thrown back into the cockpit, head first.

Østby knew many of the people I was aware of only from books and articles. I had read everything available on the use of aircraft for polar exploration, and was familiar with the Amundsen and Lincoln Ellsworth attempt to fly to the North Pole and Riiser-Larsen's dramatic takeoff after the forced landing. (Riiser-Larsen later commanded the Royal Norwegian Air Force.) Another name I was familiar with was Oskar Omdal, who flew with Amundsen and Umberto Nobile from Spitsbergen to Alaska in the airship *Norge*. Then, of course, there was Bernt Balchen, another Norwegian military pilot who flew across the Atlantic with Byrd shortly after Lindbergh's flight, and who was piloting the aircraft when it ditched at Ver-sur-Mer after more than 40 hours in the air. Balchen later made the first flight across the South Pole with Byrd in the Ford Tri-Motor, and was to go on to numerous exploits in World War II.

Fig. 7-2
Torpedo plane model, Østby's thesis project. A clean design for its era.

I found it fascinating to meet someone who knew Amundsen and was a close friend of these famous Norwegian pilots. For the next year and a half Østby and I spent countless hours together, often at his apartment near Harvard Square, where I learned to enjoy Norwegian food. He became popular with the students, who nicknamed him "Gen" (for General) or "The Gen." With a modest amount of help he did well in the courses, and I learned about life in old Norway.

One of the requirements for graduation, of course, was a thesis project. Of interest to the Royal Norwegian Air Force was a torpedo plane, so Gen and I did the layout and preliminary design of a twin-engined, twinfloat plane with a low wing of elliptical planform. The floats were mounted on streamlined cantilever struts below each nacelle. The pilot was located in a faired enclosure on the left side of the fuselage, and the torpedo operator sat in the nose for good vision. Overall, it was an attractive aircraft with good performance. A model shop near the Guggenheim Laboratory took our plans and produced a beautifully finished mahogany model with movable control surfaces, suitable for tests in the five-foot tunnel. The construction cost was $100.00. For a month, whenever the tunnel was not in use, we ran a series of tests that Gen worked up into an acceptable thesis.

A Hero Sails

Sometime early in 1936 Bernt Balchen, who had been working for Anthony Fokker in Teterboro, decided to return to Norway. He had been appointed Technical Advisor of the Norwegian Airline, Det Norske Luftfartselskap. He would take with him a Sikorsky S-43 amphibian to be used for experimental flights to London, Amsterdam and Stockholm before establishing regular service. Østby was set to sail with him on the *Bergensfjord* on August 1, 1936. The previous weekend I had driven the Ford Model A I had recently purchased to Old Town to bring my brother Cooper back for a visit. We accepted Gen's invitation to drive to New York for the send-off on their voyage.

Cooper and I left at 7:00 P.M. on the day before the sailing, met up with The Gen and some friends on Long Island, and finally got to bed at 3:00 A.M. in a YMCA. Up early the next morning, we drove to Brooklyn and located the *Bergensfjord* on the 30th Street wharf near fourth Avenue in the Upper Bay. Lashed down on its forward deck was the S-43 *Valkyrien*, with its wings removed and the Norwegian flag painted on its vertical fin and rudder. Gen greeted us at the gangplank and escorted us to the main cabin where Balchen was surrounded by a host of Norwegian friends and associates. The farewell party was an uproarious scene

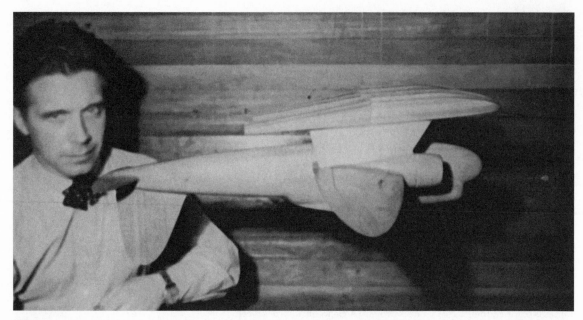

Fig. 7-3
Østby in the five-foot tunnel with the torpedo plane model on the wire balance for lift, drag and pitching moment tests.

with much drinking, back-slapping, laughter and joking. There was no question that this boisterous send-off was usual for a great Norwegian hero like Balchen. I was to run into this sort of "rioting" at Experimental Test Pilot conventions, but for a couple of staid New Englanders this first occasion was something of a revelation. We were introduced to Balchen and had a brief conversation. He exuded the physical strength, confidence and dash that I later was to associate with Grand Prix drivers.

As the time for departure approached, the crowd lined up at the dock, waving and cheering as the *Bergensfjord* got under way. Smoke poured from her funnels, and her whistle shook the air. It was an emotional moment as Gen waved good-bye and I experienced those "journey proud" feelings. Such scenes are rare these days. In our shrinking world the romance and mystery of distant places largely have disappeared.

After leaving MIT, Gen and I kept in touch for a number of years. With the onset of World War II, he was assigned to the Purchasing Commission attached to the Norwegian embassy in Washington. A captain by then, he was enjoying his high-level contacts with American aircraft firms.

Bob Mueller

For some time my financial situation had been augmented by selling detailed notes based on Koppen's classes to students. Otto had approved this scheme, and at $15 a set my notes were a good bargain. Since I monitored his courses I had contact with his students, most of whom needed all the help they could get. This was a seller's market. It also led to some related activity.

In those Depression days PhD students were a rarity. In fact, the only one I remember in the Aero Department was Bob Mueller. A one-off and a brilliant scientific type, he repaired old organs as a hobby and once was commissioned to renovate the organ in the Old North Church (of Paul Revere fame). For his PhD thesis Bob decided to design and construct an electrical analog, or simulator, of the dynamic longitudinal motions of airplanes. It is now believed to have been the *first* simulator of its kind. Starting with Bryan's Equations of Motion, his task was to devise their electrical counterparts. Although Mueller had no formal training in electrical engineering, he had a phenomenal grasp of physics fundamentals and could work from first principles. Defending his thesis before professors from both the Aero and

Electrical Engineering Departments revealed that he had, quite incidentally, derived several advanced laws of electrical engineering. Bob had little practical aeronautical experience, however, and solicited my help in establishing the numerical ranges of the stability and control derivatives.

A brief description of his device was published in the *Journal of the Aeronautical Sciences* for March 1936. In the discussion of his pioneering machine, Bob accurately predicted the virtues of electronic computers for solving dynamic problems. He wrote:

> The machine for solving the Equations of Longitudinal Stability uses a system of electrical elements (analogs). These are put together and rendered capable of adjustment so that the equations which indicate the behavior of various electrical currents with time may be made to look exactly like the Stability Equations, except for changes of scale. In a sense we have an "extremely flexible, fictitious airplane in the electrical realm."

In a subsequent paper, published in June of 1937 in the same journal, Mueller discusses a graphical solution for stability problems that reveals the type of thinking he used in developing his electrical simulator. Using vector diagrams, he worked through the effects of the various derivatives in their proper phase relationships to the forces and moments, and ultimately the frequencies and dampings. Thus he developed detailed physical insight into the interactions of the derivatives in the simultaneous solution of three differential equations. By so doing he derived approximate solutions that were of practical use. Following Mueller's thought processes gave one a physical feel for the details of a dynamic system.

Bob went on to become a prominent member of the Draper team that gave us the integrated gyro and inertial navigation systems used for space exploration. I remember visiting him at the Draper Lab. His desk was empty except for a blank pad and a pencil. He was thinking through a difficult problem from "first

Fig. 7-4
Sitting in front of the MIT Aeronautical Laboratory with the torpedo plane model, 1935.

principles." Bob Mueller was one of the most extraordinary individuals I met at MIT.[1]

During these two years I also monitored one of Stark Draper's instrument courses. Doc Draper already was a legend at the Institute for his work in the Powerplant Lab and for his grasp of servo control and feedback systems. A tremendous worker, a perpetual student,

[1] *After I sold my Curtiss-Wright Jr. airplane to Bob for a few hundred dollars, I lost contact with him for nearly 60 years. Following his stint with Draper, he literally disappeared. A few years ago he was "discovered," and we visited him at Schroon Lake in the Adirondacks. He was married, living in quiet retirement but still pondering difficult problems of interest to him (also see Chapter 5).*

Fig. 7-5
Bernt Balchen, returning to Norway as Technical Advisor to the Norwegian Airline.

Brothers Lecture in England, he analyzed their success in concise systems terms, a model of clear thinking.

Fair Game

There was so much creativity and excitement in the Aero Department in the 1935–40 period that one could fill a book, but I will close with the "Bird Coaster." The specialty of Dr. Richard H. Smith, the most academic member of the staff, was boundary layer flow, skin friction drag of streamlined airship shapes, etc., and their detailed mathematical description (which was to become of great interest as aircraft performance increased). Smith was greatly concerned with laminar flow and whether it existed at low Reynold's numbers (on birds, for example). Laminar-flow wind tunnels were not available, so he arranged to coast a frozen seagull attached to a rolling balance down a long wire located in the Mechanical Engineering facility at the Institute. A sensitive balance was designed and constructed in the Aero shop. By running the tests in the late evening he could be assured of perfectly calm air. The investigation proved difficult, because the slightest change in the seagull configuration produced significant changes in lift and drag. Later, live seagulls were used in the 7-½-foot tunnel between two screens to keep them out of the propeller. The lift/drag ratio could be determined by the angle of their glide path. With the wind on, the birds took off and soared for minutes. With undetectable changes in their wing shape, the glide paths changed all over the map. While the bird projects were inconclusive, they were certainly amusing.

and a record-holder for the number of courses taken, he also was a pilot and flew his own Curtiss Robin to California on vacation. His courses were exciting because much of the subject matter was new and the result of his current research. His analysis of the rate-of-climb instrument was completed only a few days before he presented it in class. Once he quoted Elmer Sperry saying "there is no law of the gyroscope," and then proceeded to develop a comprehensive theory for how it worked. Doc Draper asked his students to save the cardboard that came back with laundered shirts because it provided a convenient backing for his aeronautical maps. His talents were diverse. When asked to present the Wright

Chapter 8 ᗯ

Adventures with Tail Stall

> "Have you heard of the wonderful
> one-hoss shay that was built in such
> a logical way?"
>
> – Oliver Wendell Holmes
> ("The Deacon's Masterpiece")

As my job at MIT drew to a close in the late spring of 1936, it was time to put my excellent education to work. Hearing of an opportunity in New York City with a surplus aircraft exporter, I arranged for an interview but was unimpressed. The money was good, but the position had nothing to do with aircraft design. When I talked to Prof. Ober about it, he simply said, "That's no place for you—let me see what we can do about it." He and Johnny Markham phoned Paul Baker, an MIT Aero graduate and head of Flight and Aerodynamics at Chance Vought, the aircraft arm of United Aircraft located in East Hartford, Connecticut. An interview was arranged.

Hopping into my Model A, I headed south with the sun beating down, the wind in my hair (I had a stock of it in those days) and the anticipation of working in a real aircraft company. I was interviewed by Baker and his boss, Chief Engineer Rex Beisel. After a tour of the plant I was offered a job in Baker's department as an aerodynamicist, specializing in stability and control. It was a tremendous opportunity, with what seemed an enormous salary. No one could have launched a career under brighter circumstances, especially during that period. I felt extremely grateful to Ober, Markham and Baker.

Before reporting for work I had to settle in Hartford, which was a beautiful city with long tree-lined avenues. A large park-like city center had an exposition building that could have been transplanted from Vienna. A clean city of insurance companies and little industry, it reminded me of the "spotless town" of John Martin's children's books. Hartford had a safe, unhurried atmosphere, and a perpetual "long summer afternoon" feeling that was a nice contrast to the more

Hand-starting the Szekely engine on my Curtiss-Wright Junior—an unpleasant operation. Backfires were frequent, requiring constant attention.

intense and directed activity at Vought in East Hartford. There was one notable hotel, The Bond, with a restaurant, dance floor and nightly band.

Through Ed Waterhouse, who worked at Aetna, I located a good rooming house at 12 Marshall Street near his apartment. There was good bus service downtown and on to East Hartford, so I hardly needed a car. My Model A would be reserved for vacation trips to Maine. Ed was a great cook (I still think of his New England corn chowder) and I frequently had dinner with him. If he was going out for the evening, I'd settle down in his one comfortable chair to read one of his books on race cars, or the latest issues of *Autocar* or *Motor*. Neither of us had lost our intense interest in racing. On several occasions Ed tried to become connected with it, once approaching the AAA Contest Board for an administrative job. Unfortunately, it didn't happen.

Writing to his mother from Hartford, he explained why he wished he lived in Detroit:

> because though I might be lonely without knowing anyone, I could always go up to a proving ground and be happy listening to the roar of speeding cars. If I could ever be sure of getting a job there and knew it a couple of months beforehand, I think I could scrape together what it would take to go to England and France for a cheap visit. It would have to be in the summer, so I could take in some motor races.

He did attend a couple of Indy 500 races, got into the pit area and met some of his heroes, like Ralph De Palma. In his travels as an agent in New York State, he befriended Peter

Fig. 8-1
Paul Baker, head of Flight and Aerodynamics, Chance Vought Aircraft, circa 1938. He had heavy responsibilities on the ground and as chief test pilot, so we seldom saw him in this jovial mood. I kept in touch with Baker all his life. He lived well into his nineties.

Helck, the great motor racing artist, and visited his studio at Hale's Corner. But it seems sad that his entire working life was in insurance.

Working at Chance Vought

In 1936, United Aircraft consisted of Chance Vought, Pratt & Whitney Aircraft and Hamilton Standard, a manufacturer of propellers. The three companies were lined up side-by-side along a grassy airfield. Later Sikorsky merged with Chance Vought to form the Vought-Sikorsky Division of United Aircraft. Reportedly, Chance Vought and the Army Air Corps had become disenchanted with one another, so the company focused on producing aircraft for the Navy.

The Vought facility was a long four-story structure with offices fronting on the highway and the factory extending back to the airfield. There was a separate concrete hangar with apron, but no paved taxiways or runways. Baker's office was on the third floor center, directly over the ground floor lobby. To the right was the preliminary design layout group, consisting of Fred Dickerman and another draftsman. They later were joined by Charlie Zimmerman, formerly NACA, who came to develop the "Zimmer Skimmer." Beyond preliminary design was Rex Beisel's office. The detailed engineering groups bordered on the opposite side of Baker's office, and consisted of weights, structures, power plant, flutter, etc., and, of course, the airplane project engineers. A small secretarial and administrative unit was tucked away beyond Beisel's office. Engineering was organized on the dual modalities of "specialty" and "project" groups, from which were built the airplane project teams. This type of organization has proved so successful in designing complex aircraft that "platform

Fig. 8-2
Sikorsky plant in Bridgeport, Connecticut and the circular building that housed the wind tunnel. This is the site where Vought and Sikorsky were combined, and where the Corsair was produced during the war. Baker became chief engineer of Vought-Sikorsky.

teams" now are replacing the traditional automobile design approach.

Chance Vought was a self-contained engineering, development and manufacturing firm, capable of competing with such companies as Glenn L. Martin and Grumman. As a radial air-cooled engine manufacturer, P&W was second to none. Its only competitor was Wright Aeronautical in Paterson, New Jersey.

From my standpoint, the virtue of working at Vought was that every element for designing and building aircraft was under one roof, in a company of small size. Unlike the 40,000 engineers of modern military aircraft firms, Vought was more like a small principality. I knew all the project engineers and lead engineering specialists, and could follow the development of a design from its inception. Our Flight and Aerodynamics group played a prominent part in the determination of the aerodynamic configurations (including wind-tunnel testing), and also in the flight testing and development of finished prototypes. Unlike many members of the engineering department, we not only had a grandstand seat at the beginning and the finish, but a more than passing acquaintance with what went on in between.

Flight and Aerodynamics was very small. Baker sat at a large desk with his back to the window. Alongside him was Bill Schoolfield, a solid, conservative engineer with considerable analytical ability, whom I came to admire if not

become jealous of. Bill worked closely with the aircraft project engineers, and performed all manner of special assignments. Seniority made him Baker's first assistant, though he never had the title of assistant department head. My desk was at a right angle to Baker's and across from Gene Rohman, who sat against the wall near Schoolfield. Gene's job was twofold: he was the keeper of the flight test instrumentation, and also analyzed wind-tunnel data for lift and drag. Thus he provided the performance estimates for new design proposals. His major task was predicting the overall drag polar for a design, which he did by summing the Kxp's (flat-plate drag) of components, along with interference effects. He was very diligent at this, but in my opinion his results seldom were better than estimates of the overall drag coefficient from wind-tunnel tests, based upon frontal area. The proof of the pudding, of course, was the measured top speed of new and modified aircraft.

My job was stability and control (S & C) estimation. I was involved in planning and liaison for S & C wind-tunnel tests, and also was the engineer who went along on stability and control flight tests. To determine the sizes of tail surfaces and ailerons, aerodynamic balances, etc., I worked directly with aircraft project engineers in the detailed design areas. This was a lot of responsibility for a young engineer on his first job, but Baker and Schoolfield always were available as backup.

153

Lining the entire wall in back of my desk were bookshelves holding a complete collection of NACA reports, notes and memoranda, along with NACA annual volumes and British Reports & Memoranda (R & M) of the Aeronautical Research Committee. Other than wind-tunnel data from models of Vought aircraft, they were our primary sources of technical information. During my years at MIT I had collected miscellaneous information on aircraft stability and control, and had bound my class notes. All of these were in a wooden file drawer that I put alongside my desk. So for that era I had good sources of information.

Baker proved to be a tough boss, but very fair and intelligent. The unit was well disciplined, though it softened up a bit when he was away flying. I learned early on that he expected high engineering standards and the exercise of one's ingenuity. On one occasion, when he felt I was slipping, he yelled, "For Christ's sake, Milliken, get curious!" Until his death, Paul Baker remained as curious as ever. What an asset it was to have worked for such an individual at the beginning of my career!

The fourth member of Flight and Aerodynamics was Gene Rohman, who took

a little getting used to. He kept a large steam gauge on his desk, presumably as a paperweight, and when Baker was out he would toss it at me unexpectedly, yelling, "Catch it!" Except for the bullies at Old Town High, I hadn't run into antics like this before, and found the best tactic was to dodge. If I did catch the thing I hurled it back. We soon became reasonably good friends and worked well together.

Later the group was expanded by the addition of Lyman Bullard, a Navy-trained pilot who took over some of the flight load and was to do the XF4U-1 prototype flights. We occupied a double desk. Bull was a large six-foot-plus, strong-appearing individual—at least compared with me—so I figured I could safely kid him a bit and get away with it. One day I went too far and he literally came at me over the top of the desk. We later flew some very hazardous flights and sweated them out together.

The flight test instrumentation certainly was elementary by today's standards. One gadget slipped over the end of the pilot's stick had a spring element sliding in a scaled slot, with markings calibrated for control force. The stick position was measured by a "yo-yo," one end of which was attached to the

Fig. 8-3
SB2U-1 Vindicator, a shipboard Scout Bomber. Before my flight with Baker I was involved with model tests of it in MIT's five-foot wind tunnel.

Fig. 8-4
Carrier version of Vought XOS2U-1 Observation Scout. My adventures with tail stall took place on this version.

stick while the other clamped to the dash (for elevator position) or the cockpit side (for aileron position). The airspeed indicator was calibrated by a towed "trailing bomb"—a heavy streamlined body with stabilizing fins that could be lowered a hundred feet or so below the aircraft via a rubber-covered steel cable. It carried a pitot static head, and it was hoped the static pressure at that distance wasn't influenced by the aerodynamic flow field around the aircraft. We also used tufts and streamers for visualization, and the pilot and engineer maintained a record of subjective impressions of aircraft maneuvering behavior. Baker used a knee pad with 5 × 8 cards. In a single flight he could record a tremendous amount of data in very small script, which it was my job to unscramble. We also used "stops" on the controls so that well-defined step inputs could be used for response testing.

Military Projects

My first flight was on an SB2U-1 Vindicator dive bomber. (Eleven of these were on Midway in 1942, and while no match for the Zeros, they were involved in a successful attack on *Mikuma*, a Japanese heavy cruiser.) Baker and I had gone up to run an airspeed calibration with the trailing bomb. If the aircraft speed became

too high, the bomb would destabilize and begin a vertical oscillation of increasing amplitude. This occurred on the flight in question, but I was able to haul the bomb in as Baker slowed the airplane. On other occasions we had hairier experiences.

On one flight the amplitude of oscillation became so great that the bomb reached an altitude greater than the aircraft. As a safety precaution it became standard practice to carry cable snips for cutting the bomb loose if necessary. I heard about one flight in which they had to be used. The severed bomb went into a vertical dive of increasing speed, with cable whipping behind. The terminal velocity must have been high subsonic. It finally plunged through the roof of a farmhouse, ending up in the cellar and neatly threading the cable from top to bottom. Needless to say, repercussions followed and future flights were over unpopulated areas. I still retain memories of hauling this 40-pound monster back into the airplane with the cable jerking and the pilot yelling to hasten the process.

One day Gene Rohman suggested dropping the bomb from the third story of the Vought Building to see how far it would penetrate into the lawn. A pool was established at five dollars per person, winner take all. That the bomb burrowed in only up to the tail fins was a major disappointment. Incidentally, Gene won the bet.   155

During my years at Vought I was involved with two significant airplane developments: the XOS2U-1 Kingfisher and the XF4U-1 Corsair. The Navy specifications for the Kingfisher called for an observation-scout airplane that could be operated with wheels on a carrier, or as a single-float seaplane that could be catapulted from a battleship. These unique design requirements and associated problems posed a substantial challenge. The Corsair's inverted gullwing presented significant mechanical and aeronautical design challenges. It later became one of the highest performance fighters in the Pacific theater.

Developing the Kingfisher

For carrier operation, a modest landing speed was necessary, in addition to well-controlled behavior at low speed and a size that would fit into the ship's elevators. These requirements resulted in a compact, short-coupled low-wing monoplane with high-lift flaps and folding wings. It was realized from the beginning of the design that some advances in flap design and lateral control would be necessary.

Roger Griswold was an aerodynamics consultant from Old Lyme, Connecticut, who operated his own small, low-speed wind tunnel. He had devised a high-lift, multiple-slotted flap (the "slat" involved was called the "Horsefeather") with lift coefficients of well over 2.0. This impressive achievement had come to the attention of Vought's aerodynamic group. To do an independent check of Griswold's results on a larger scale model, Vought arranged a test in the Sikorsky wind tunnel in Bridgeport. It was my job to help plan and perform liaison for these tests. A rectangular planform model of suitable size was made at Vought.

The Sikorsky tunnel was unique: a *vertical* open-throat, closed-return configuration that was a circular annulus through which one had to pass on a bridge to reach the working section. One sat in this little room with the entrance cone projecting down from the ceiling and the exit cone a little above floor level. The airflow was from top to bottom, and the test model was supported on a wire or string balance at about eye level. This was an optimum arrangement for observing the model and probing the flow condition with a small tuft attached to a long, handheld wand. The tunnel was operated by Tony Fokker, nephew of the famous Dutch aircraft designer and industrialist. Although not a scientist, "Wind Tunnel Tony" was an extremely practical engineer capable of obtaining useful results in a hurry. We had a good working relationship. He spent hours in the tunnel, and had installed a comfortable chair for himself, frequently

Fig. 8-5
Float plane version of Vought XOS2U-1.

reading the newspaper during long, boring tests. One day, when we were running the Horsefeather tests, I wondered if the wind speed was on target. He reached down, balled up a section of newsprint, tossed it out into the air stream and timed its passage through the return section back to the working section. He then pronounced that the speed was "right on" and went back to reading.

The Sikorsky test confirmed Griswold's results, and Vought decided to use the Horsefeather flap on the XOS2U-1. Its section lift, as I recall, was about 2.30 with a 50° flap setting. To meet the stalling speed requirement, the decision was also made to droop the aileron 35° for the low-speed condition. I believe the next tests were run on a complete model at MIT.

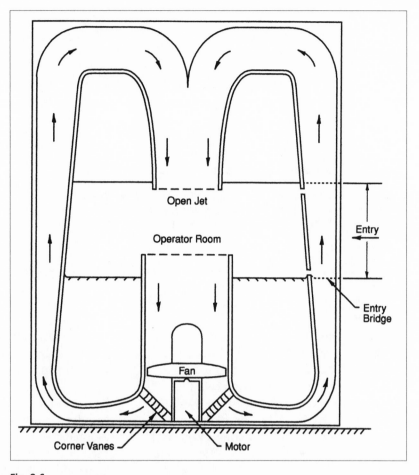

Fig. 8-6
Layout of the unique Sikorsky wind tunnel.

These included lift, drag and pitching moment, with various flap settings at different wing angles of attack and various elevator settings. Schoolfield did a masterful job of analyzing the test data. With the flaps full down, so much lift was produced that in level flight the airplane flew nose down. This caused the horizontal tail to operate at a high negative angle of attack. According to Baker, this was aggravated by the downwash from the slipsteam impinging on the inboard section of the flaps. The nose-down pitching moment on the aircraft was high with a large download on the tail for trim. It became apparent that the tail might stall, and if this happened the aircraft would rapidly pitch nose down. The only hope for recovery was to crank up the flaps.

The development phase for the lateral control system for the XOS2U-1 happened in 1937, a year after I had joined Vought. It had become apparent that ailerons drooped to 35° for lift would be unable to provide the necessary rolling moments for low-speed control. Consequently, studies in which I became involved explored the use of spoilers on the upper surface of the wings. Tests at Langley and elsewhere indicated that spoilers could not be near the wing leading edge because of the lag in response time, so they were located just ahead of the ailerons. They comprised a simple flap that hinged upward, spoiling the flow on the right-hand wing for a roll to the right, and vice versa for a roll to the left. The designers developed a clever "changeover mechanism" in which, as the flaps and ailerons went down, lateral control shifted progressively from the ailerons to the spoilers. This ingenious device was conceived with a cardboard model hinged with thumbtacks, but later was mocked-up in metal.

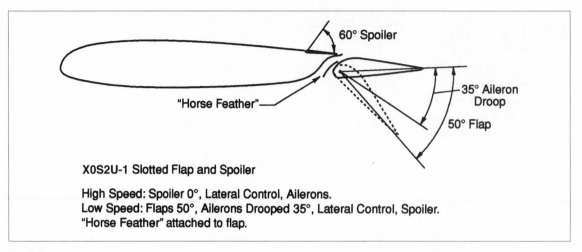

Fig. 8-7
Sketch of the high-lift "Horsefeather" flap and aileron, and the auxiliary spoiler control for low-speed operation, XOS2U-1.

In order to gain some flight experience with the flaps and spoilers, a Fairchild F-24 cabin plane referred to as the V-160 was acquired. Its wood and fabric construction could be modified with relative ease. Between June 16 and October 24, 1937, I made 40 flights with Baker, totaling 47.5 hours, testing a variety of configurations. The airplane had side-by-side seating with dual controls, so we alternated piloting and recording. I had a tendency to maintain a given speed in a maneuver by glancing at the airspeed indicator, but Baker beat it into me that sound and feel were more sensitive indicators. We did stability and lateral control tests, including control force measurements, stall tests with the bomb, etc. Plotting the data and summarizing progress followed each flight.

As the prototype XOS2U-1 Kingfisher was taking shape in early 1938, we wandered down to the shop at lunch time to follow its progress. Gene Rohman and I were involved with installing some instrumentation. It was, of course, an exciting experience to have followed an airplane design from inception to prototype. As the date for first flight grew closer, the activity and atmosphere intensified.

FIRST FLIGHTS, like the launching of a ship, are memorable events. While most vessels slip quietly into their element, the birth of an airplane can be far more traumatic. Taxi tests give some insight into the airframe and systems behavior, but reality comes with the commitment to full flight. Once the takeoff is begun in a high-performance military aircraft the likelihood is that it cannot be aborted, and the pilot is confronted with all the problems not predicted in the design process. (Computer-aided analytical techniques now have reduced the hazards of first flight.)

Carefully prepared for the initial flight of the XOS2U-1, Paul Baker was familiar with all the analysis and design of its aerodynamics and control, had done the flight testing on the V-160 of the unique features of the design and had tracked the project activity from the beginning. Unlike many so-called engineering pilots, Baker was an engineering professional who remained unhurried and unflappable under emotional pressure.

The initial flight of the XOS2U-1 was made on March 1, 1939, and lasted 26 minutes. The laconic comment in Baker's log book was "First Flight." Nonetheless, it was quite an occasion. Word had gotten around, and work in the shop ceased as the manufacturing people lined the field. All the top executives and design people hovered around the aircraft on the hangar apron—CEO C. J. McCarthy, Chief Engineer Rex Beisel, Project Engineers Frank Albright, John Lee and Jim Shoemaker, crew leader Jack Hospers, representatives from the Navy, etc. While the pilot was concentrating on the job he had to do, the executives were worrying about the business success of the airplane, and provided enough bad breath to last a month.

Finally, Baker taxied out and made a clean, no-fuss takeoff. When he returned in half an hour, the aircraft was surrounded by everybody anxiously awaiting his impressions, which were generally good. He was given a great hand, and all of us who had contributed felt satisfied that we had done our job well.

Flying solo, Baker managed a flight a day over the next week or so to explore the control and stall of XOS2U-1 in various configurations. His flight cards were filled with control force and position data, which kept me busy transcribing and plotting.

Tail Stall

Baker left for another flight late in the afternoon of the 10th of March. Everybody else in the office had left for the day, so I was alone when he returned. Appearing more intense than usual, he walked into the office, slapped his knee pad down on the desk and announced, "The tail stalled." He had recovered from a stall with full flaps and ailerons, and was easing on the power in a horizontal attitude, when with little warning the aircraft pitched over onto its back. Recognizing immediately that the horizontal tail had stalled, he got on the hand crank to reduce the flap and aileron angles. A hundred turns or so were required, and once accomplished the airplane wound up in a steep near-vertical dive from which a normal pull-up was required for recovery. Baker was unable to describe the gyrations that occurred before the recovery, except that the aircraft appeared to be oscillating about the vertical and losing altitude at a great rate. Luckily the stall had begun at a high altitude.

For the next several months our attention was totally focused on solving the tail stall problem. The day after the incident, Baker and I went up in the XOS2U-1 to calibrate the airspeed system using the trailing bomb. This work continued a few days later, followed by a flight for flow observations with yarn and streamers. As every aeronautical engineer knows, the lift of an airfoil is produced by

pressure differential between the lower and upper wing surfaces. The pressure field of the wing forces the air behind the wing downward in a "downwash." With its highly effective Horsefeather flaps, the downward airflow angle behind the wing was expected to be large, but I was astounded when the long streamers (tapes) attached to the wing appeared to trail downward at some forty-five degrees. Small yarn tufts (four to five inches in length) on the bottom of the horizontal tail and on the adjacent fuselage side also indicated the high negative angle of attack that the tail experienced when we approached the tail stall condition. The flow was by no means steady, and the aircraft was shaking in the buffeting flow. On two flights we ran stall tests with various flap settings and the trailing bomb to get an accurate assessment of the airspeeds. Testing of various modifications to the tail, such as a more rounded leading edge, a change in incidence, etc., continued throughout April and into May.

At that point two other activities were initiated. The first was to calculate the motions of the aircraft subsequent to the tail stall. Baker had only the foggiest idea of the gyrations that occurred while he was cranking the flaps up.

To this end Otto Koppen was brought in to help us set up the appropriate equations.[1] Gene Rohman and I were given the task of running a step-by-step integration, beginning at the point of tail stall. In this type of calculation, initial conditions are established from which the conditions are computed for a small time increment later. These then are used to calculate the condition at the end of the next time step, etc. The calculations are based upon the Bryan differential equations of motion derived from Newtonian mechanics. Analytical closed solutions for solving these large-amplitude motions were not available, nor were computers. We used our slide rules to calculate the incremental changes from step to step, and initially assumed a step size of 0.10 second. Having gone through perhaps 30 steps while plotting the motion variables, we realized we had chosen too large a step. All the variables

---

[1] *This was my first use in industry of Bryan's Equations of Motion, which would later be a feature of our research at Curtiss-Wright and Cornell Aeronautical Laboratory.*

showed increasing oscillations, which indicated unrealistic damping. Koppen had predicted this possible outcome, so we started over with a smaller step size (0.05 sec.). The calculations took a month. Every day we ground out steps and plotted them on our continuous charts of motion variables. These included angles of attack at the tail and wing, pitching velocity, normal acceleration, attitude of the aircraft etc. Although tedious, the work was enlightening as we tracked the culprit down. What we found was that the airplane pitched over on its back, stalling the wing in a negative direction, then rotated back, momentarily unstalling the wing. This motion was superimposed on the general flight path, which was effectively straight down. Conditions at the tail oscillated too, but the tail remained stalled until the flaps were retracted (a condition that we also simulated).

THE SECOND ACTIVITY in which I was involved was far from boring. The idea was to study the in-flight flow condition at the tail at the onset of tail stall. To sneak up on this condition and still recover before pitching over,

a mechanism for very rapidly raising the flaps and ailerons was installed in the rear cockpit. This consisted of a sizable inertia wheel, to which was attached a large hand crank geared to the retracting mechanism. Only 15–20 turns were required to fully retract the flaps. The operator knelt behind the device and used both hands on the crank handle. Bullard would fly the aircraft. My job was to be the crank man.

We practiced a bit on the ground. Our only communication in the air would be a two-inch flexible tube taped in a convenient location in the front cockpit so that Bullard could yell into it when he felt the tail was about to go. My end of the tube was taped to my parachute harness near one ear. I was correct in assuming that on approaching tail stall, Bullard's signal would be loud and clear. The tests were to be run with both canopies open, and a special seatbelt was rigged so I could continue to crank if I found myself in an inverted position.

Up we went to around 12,000 feet. Approaching tail stall with caution initially, Bull became more daring later. Toward the end we teetered on the brink until his booming

Fig. 8-8
Curtiss-Wright Junior with writer aboard, 1937.

voice told me to "crank it up," and I leapt into action as the aircraft shook, shuddered and started to pitch over. Both of us got a great charge out of this, and on the ground afterward talked about how that "son of a bitch nearly got away from us."

Some differences were found in the configurations we tested, but the final solution was arrived at later in July. This consisted of modifications to the tail itself, and spring-loaded flaps whose angle decreased as the airspeed increased. Baker's summary stated, "We increased the size of the horizontal tail slightly, increased the nose radius of the airfoil to get better stall angle tolerance, and inserted a *blow-up* spring in the flap actuation system that reduced the maximum flap angle. To the best of my knowledge no problems occurred in service."

Adventures with Junior

During my years at Vought, I arranged to continue private flying from Brainerd Field in Hartford, where I could rent both dual and solo time. After buying about five hours of instruction in aerobatics with a Capt. Samson in a Gates Standard powered by a Kinner five-cylinder air-cooled radial, I rented time on an Aeronca, a Kitty Hawk, and a Taylor Cub. In total this amounted to another 15 hours of solo time and 5.5 hours more of dual, during which I made a couple of cross-countries to Springfield, Massachusetts, just up the Connecticut River from Hartford. Renting a Taylor Cub in Norwood (Massachusetts), I flew up to Augusta, Maine, for the graduation celebration of my old friend Knowlton Small, and got caught in a snowstorm.

On August 7, 1937, I acquired a Curtiss-Wright Junior from a pilot who operated out of Brainerd Field. The price was $230. It was a minimal aircraft by any standards, especially when second- or third-hand. The Junior was a parasol monoplane, powered by a three-cylinder air-cooled 45-hp Szekely engine mounted near the trailing edge of the wing and swinging a wooden pusher propeller. The pilot sat in a tiny cockpit in front; a passenger seat was below the wing and just forward of the propeller arc. The

Fig. 8-9
Curtiss-Wright Junior showing aft-mounted three-cylinder Szekely engine/propeller unit. The engine is running in this photo, 1937. Note the unsprung air wheel.

fuselage extended back below the propeller to rather small vertical and horizontal tail surfaces. A tail dragger with a skid at the rear, its main gear was below the wing leading edge and consisted of two so-called "air wheels" (balloon tires). The gear was rigidly attached to the aircraft, with no shock absorbers.

Szekely engines were well known for throwing off cylinders, an eventuality from which my engine was protected by a cable running around the tops of the cylinders and tensioned with a turnbuckle.

The machine had plenty of wing, which was braced by struts running out from the fuselage. With a gross load officially stated as 405 pounds, the Curtiss Wright Junior had a phenomenally low landing speed—a sort of powered glider—and was a handful in rough air. The former owner was quite honest. The list of the problems he said I might encounter included overheating of the engine from continuous full throttle operation, resulting in warped or blown valves. Piston ring wear was common; squaring up the grooves in the pistons and installing oversized rings might be necessary. The engine oil system was not the best; the oil entrance through the hollow crankshaft was known to clog with chips shed from the engine's innards. The mica spark plugs never should be cleaned with gasoline. The fabric on top of the wing near the spar took a beating from the propeller slipstream and had to be watched for tears. The outer strut point bolts and fittings tended to wear excessively due to the hard landing gear. Finally, the former owner stressed the possibility of fire if inverted flight was attempted. In sum, the Curtiss Wright Junior wasn't much of an airplane, but it flew and I had some neat adventures with it. I always wondered who could have designed such a contraption, and found out when I went to work at Curtiss-Wright that Lloyd Child had been the project engineer. Lloyd no doubt was a great test pilot, but less creative in the design area.

I flew the plane solo and made a series of landings before I bought it. After taking ownership, I engaged Harry Beach, of the piloting staff at Brainerd, to demonstrate its stall/spin characteristics, after which I made several solo flights to become thoroughly

familiar with these characteristics. The stall was mild and controllable. The spin was in a straight-down attitude. That was a good characteristic, but different from other aircraft I'd flown in which the spin path seemed more helical. Sitting out in the nose and rotating at a great rate was a scary sensation.

Instrumentation was minimal and crude. An altimeter and oil pressure gauge were on the panel, but the airspeed indicator was a flat plate that stuck out in the wind, supported on a wire that moved against a spring. The position of the wire in a curved slot was a measure of the airspeed. The supporting wire was forever getting bent, so what you had was only an approximation of the airspeed at best. Approach to a stall was much better detected by other means.

ONE AFTERNOON soon after I bought the aircraft, I took off from Brainerd Field and arrived at Providence, Rhode Island, at 4:45 P.M. after a flight of 1 hr. 15 min. The date was August 25, 1937. I had a couple of weeks of vacation available, so was heading to Maine to see my folks. I pushed on to Norwood the same day, arriving at 6:00 P.M. My old friend Joe Garsides of Wiggins Airways helped me stake down the aircraft for the night and find a place to stay. The next morning I was off at 8:30 A.M., and reached Portland in 2 hr. 15 min. Hardly a fast aircraft, the C-W Junior was fun to fly in good weather.

The night before I had wired my brother suggesting he hitchhike to Augusta and meet me there. Cooper never had flown in an airplane. When I pulled up at the hangar in Augusta, Coop was standing there, all anticipation. It was high noon, with the sun beating down, the temperature in the high eighties, not a breath of wind, and the air as thin as tissue paper. Would the aircraft get off from that short runway at old Muster Field with the extra load?

After a brief lunch Cooper climbed into the rear seat and I started the takeoff, heading toward the drop-off that had been so scary when Nancy and I had landed there with the Fairchild a few years earlier. We became airborne near the edge and staggered out over the bluff, teetering near the stall. The Szekely

Fig. 8-10
L-R: Cooper Milliken, Ed Waterhouse and Rod Averill in Bradley, 1937.

was running flat-out but we were barely maintaining a few hundred feet of altitude over the city. Cooper leaned over the side of the cockpit to get a better view and, with the extra air drag, we lost 50 feet of altitude. I was too busy trying to keep us airborne to signal him to stay back in the cockpit. Getting clear of the city was a relief, but it was touch and go all the way to Bangor. This was the longest the Szekely ever ran at full throttle without something coming apart. Thrilled with the ride, Cooper said, "It was so good of you to fly so low over Augusta so I could see everything!"

In Bradley, across the Penobscot River from Old Town, was a hayfield large enough for the C-W Junior, so I landed there a few days later. Peanut Spruce had biked over and was waiting for me. After all the experiences we shared with my early vehicles and motorcycles, we were about to fly together—a dream come true. I taxied up by the road near the telephone poles and turned around. The wind was favorable and the pasture sloped toward the river, so we were airborne after a few hundred feet and banking toward Old Town. I throttled back so we could yell to each other. Paul was elated; never one to pass up a stunt, he would have been wing walking had we been in a biplane. Instead we enjoyed a three-dimensional rerun of our childhood. Beginning over Great Works, we flew the length of Main Street to the ferry for Indian Island and my father's mill. We then circled Blueberry Hill and Bachelor's Field, and came back over the Academy Hill School and the nearby water tower where Peanut had hung from the top of the 100-foot ladder to the delight of the students and the dismay of the teachers. We swooped low over the Convent School, remembering the famous snowball fights, and passed by the spire of the Catholic church, the highest building in Old Town— then back to the pasture in Bradley. This was the last adventure we were to share together.

163

On the return trip to Hartford, as I was nearing Nashua, New Hampshire, the engine started to slow down and I just managed to slip down to a landing at the edge of the field. The carburetor had iced up on a nice sunny but high humidity day. I sat there awhile until the ice melted and was on my way again.

My NEXT C-W JUNIOR ADVENTURE was a dinner date in September with girl I knew at Mt. Holyoke in Northhampton, an easy flight down the Connecticut River. I assumed there would be some place to land near the college but upon arrival in the late afternoon was unable to find one. Continuing to circle the campus, I saw what appeared to be an archery court on campus. I buzzed the place a couple of times. The approach was across open fields. The court itself was grassed and inviting but not very long, and a large dormitory blocked the other end. I would have to land very slow and short, so I decided to drag in on power, pull that off at the last minute and sideslip down. Everything worked according to plan except I was a little high and got into a steep sideslip which stalled the vertical fin. The rudder blew over and the aircraft struck the ground laterally at 90° yaw. The leading wing came up at the last moment due to ground effect. The plane slid sideways perhaps 15 feet on the grass and stopped, a fantastically short landing that never could have been done intentionally. One of the girls from the dormitory ran over and said, "Do you always land that way, Mister?" My girlfriend and I had a great evening, but there wasn't enough wind to take off, so I tied the Junior down, hitchhiked back to work in Hartford, and came back the next weekend to fly it out.

I generally hangared the Junior at Brainerd Field in Hartford, but occasionally flew it over to the field behind the plant in East Hartford so I could fly on weekends. One Saturday I took off and found myself a hundred feet over a tobacco field that was covered by netting supported on poles on 10-foot centers, when the engine quit due to carburetor icing. The rule is never to make a downwind turn at low speed and low altitude, but I couldn't see myself landing on all those poles, so I poked the nose down into a steep dive, turned back and made a fast downwind landing. After the ice melted and the engine was running well, I tried it again. The engine quit again and I went through the same procedure. With its low wing loading and glider-like properties, the Junior permitted maneuvers that would have been curtains with a higher performance aircraft.

SOCIAL LIFE IN HARTFORD was facilitated by a scarcity of single men. The Dickermans introduced me around when I first arrived at Vought, and I had a steady female companion. We frequently wound up in the evening dancing at The Bond Hotel. Not infrequently, Ed Waterhouse and Rod Averill showed up and I had to share my date with them. Of course, they disappeared just before I was stuck with the cover charge. After she and I broke up I moved into a rooming house on Eagle Street near the plant, and met a girl in East Hartford who was fond of horseback riding. My room was on the first floor and I always slept with the window beside the bed wide open. One Saturday I was awakened when her horse's head peered in. Later, caught necking in the town park, we were taken to the Justice of the Peace who turned out to be her father. After that my social life dwindled.

Developing the *Corsair*

As the XOS2U-1 moved into production, I became involved with the XF4U-1 Corsair, the famous inverted gullwing fighter. There are many stories about how the gullwing came about but my memory is as follows: Fred Dickerman had seen a photo of an aircraft with a small gull (to reduce the interference drag at the junction between wing and fuselage) produced by Heinkel in Germany. Vought submitted two designs to the Navy in the aircraft carrier fighter competition, one of them fairly conventional, the other with the inverted gullwing design. Among the rationalizations put forward at the time for the gull was a shorter landing gear. That was advantageous for several reasons, but altogether the gull was never truly justifiable. In fact, the design had not been fully analyzed before submission to the Navy, and I doubt

Fig. 8-11
Owner exiting the front cockpit, Bradley, 1937.

Fig. 8-12
With my Mt. Holyoke friend after my remarkable "sidewise" landing on the archery court.

Vought ever would have proposed it had they recognized the challenges it posed to development. We were surprised when the Navy went for the gull.

The details of the inverted gull design were staggering. The gear was attached at the bottom of the gull at the same place as the folding wing hinge *and* the oil cooler air inlet. The wing was basically single-spar, and the structures people wrestled with the design of the wing beam in that location. I remember something about there being 78 hand-reamed bolts in the spar cap.

In aerodynamics we had our own problems. The inboard portion of the gull was in the propeller slipstream, and with its large negative dihedral we could have a low or even negative rolling moment due to sideslip. Excellent low-speed, high-power handling is required of carrier-

165

Fig. 8-13
Original XF4U-1 Corsair.

based aircraft, and we were uncertain of this requirement with the inverted gull configuration. To get some information on the problem, a large-scale model with power plant and propeller was made of the gull, suitable for testing in the Propeller Research Tunnel at Langley Field. I was sent along to liaison the test and work with the tunnel staff during the summer months (and well before air conditioning was introduced at Langley). The temperature and humidity were high in the tunnel, and equally so in the barracks where I lived at the Field. The only saving grace was the devoted crew working under Abe Silverstein. I was there for a month and a half, during which we collected data on a variety of operating conditions that we tried to make sense of back in Hartford. The wing had a substantial amount of positive dihedral on the outer panels and finally proved satisfactory for carrier operations.

From the beginning there was interest in achieving a high roll rate with reasonable control forces. Roll rate requirements, in terms of the non-dimensional ratio $pb/2V$, were yet to be introduced, but some estimates of a desirable absolute roll rate were available. I was asked by Project Engineer Frank Albright to come up with suggestions for aileron dimensions, and estimates of rate and control forces. With the initial flap span, the length of the aileron was limited, and a reasonable roll rate required a wide chord. Even with a Frise balance on the nose, the control forces would be high.

I BELIEVE THE INITIAL CORSAIR FLIGHT was made with the aileron configuration I proposed, but I was not present when Bull made the first flight on XF4U-1 on May 29, 1940. I later ran into him at an aero meeting and asked about the aileron performance on that first flight. His answer was, "I couldn't move them." Walt Breuhaus, who later joined Baker's group, did extensive work on the ailerons, including larger span, linked tab and increased nose balance. Navy requirements for roll performance were finally met. While the XF4U-1 turned out to exceed the Navy's performance requirements, its success stems from arduous development to overcome a difficult design.

Because the company was interested in accumulating experience with a really high-speed aircraft, Vought tried to generate business with the Air Corps despite their earlier mutual disenchantment. To test some configurations, arrangements were made to rent "Time Flies," the machine that had been constructed by ex-Granville engineering staff members. A clean design with a retractable cockpit enclosure, the aircraft was flown to East Hartford but experienced trouble with the retractable gear. I have no recollection of much flight activity. This project did give me the opportunity, however, to visit the original Gee Bee Hangar in Springfield where the famous 711, winner of the Thompson Trophy piloted by Jimmy Doolittle, was stored.

War Effort
1939–1943

Chapter 9

Pressurized Stratoliner

Early in 1939 United Aircraft decided to consolidate its aircraft operations (Vought and Sikorsky) into a single facility located at the site of the Sikorsky plant in Bridgeport, Connecticut. Vought was engaged in several aircraft contracts for the Navy, including the F4U-5 gullwing fighter, and Sikorsky was producing large flying boats and amphibians for airline use as well as for the Navy. A distinguishing feature of the latter operation was that the key engineers under Igor Sikorsky were Russian. The decision to consolidate certainly was influenced by Sikorsky's concurrent development of a practical helicopter, which created an entirely new business, and by the expansion of aircraft production occasioned by World War II.

As a young employee, I was not aware of how the amalgamation of two such diverse entities as Vought and Sikorsky was supposed to take place, nor was I there long enough to find out. Although I had made the move from East Hartford to Bridgeport in May of '39, I was already planning to leave Vought.

A number of months earlier I began having a recurrence of physical tensions, disruption of sleep and other bodily patterns, and I was spending too much time at the local osteopath. There were multiple reasons for this, but I believed that the root cause lay in my inadequacy in handling engineering analysis. In this small Flight and Aerodynamics section, the ability to analyze wind tunnel data and develop performance predictions methods ranked high, and I lacked the patience to master and apply certain advanced mathematical techniques. These frustrations, and their consequent physical symptoms, led me to believe that my services were not fully appreciated and that I was underpaid. This was totally irrational.

Workmen on the fuselage fabrication, 307 Stratoliner. Boeing used every means for completing these aircraft, circa 1941.

"Out of this World"

– Anonymous

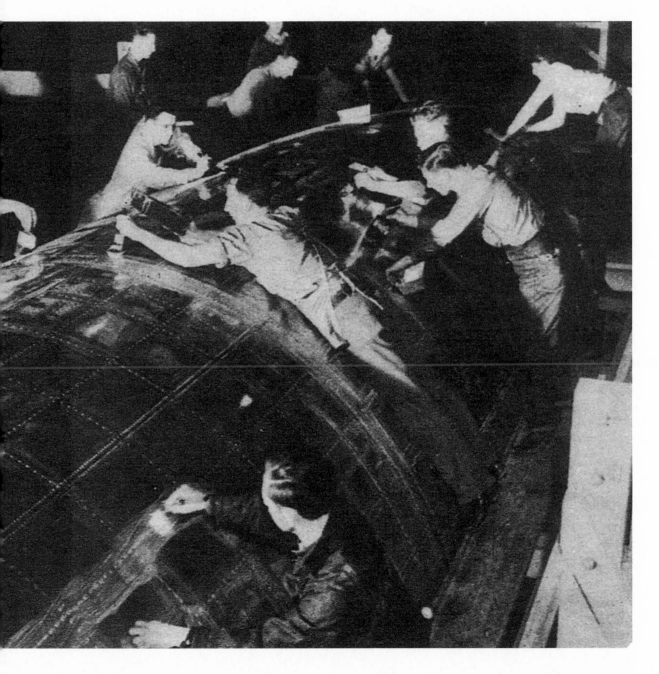

Fortunately I had confidence in my physical understanding of aircraft stability and control, and in my ability to handle flight situations that required decisive action. I also had sense enough to recognize the need for a change.

Looking West

My experience in California during the summer of '32, and my father's career in the Pacific Northwest, led me to gravitate toward employment at Boeing. In April of '39 I wrote to Frank Terdina in Seattle, and received the encouraging, although tentative, response that they were considering additions to their "aerodynamic unit." I also learned that the famous freelance test pilot Eddie Allen (E. T. Allen) had accepted the position of director of a new Flight and Aerodynamics Department at Boeing.

Earlier, in March of '38, the second production model Boeing 307 Stratoliner (the first pressurized four-engine transport) had crashed on a demonstration flight for KLM and TWA personnel. The directional stability at low speed with one engine out was suspected. Key Boeing engineering personnel went down with the aircraft, and Allen was invited to head a new flight test department.

He apparently presented convincing arguments for combining flight test and aerodynamics into a single organizational unit, separate from the established engineering design group but working closely with it.

As a consulting flight test pilot, Allen had flown several Boeing prototypes, including the 80A (a large transport biplane), the 247 (the first successful all-metal low-wing airliner), the 314 Clipper flying boat, and so forth. As a result he had plenty of experience in relating an aircraft's aerodynamic configuration to its flying qualities. His hairy initial flight of the prototype 314 Clipper with the single vertical tail was a classic example.

I had met Allen on two occasions. Once was through Otto Koppen at MIT, and later when he was employed by Vought to dive-test the SB2U to the Navy's 9g pullout requirement. Getting in on the ground floor of his new Flight and Aerodynamics Department was tremendously appealing, and in May '39 I sent a follow-up letter specifically addressed to Allen. After some delay I received a definitive offer by mail, to which I immediately telegraphed acceptance. Eddie's letter (Fig. 9.2) is indicative of his plans for his new organization, with which I was to be heavily involved over the next several years.

Fig. 9-1
Allen had flown earlier Boeing aircraft, including the Monomail passenger version. This was a pioneer low-wing monoplane with stressed skin construction.

A Final Round With Sikorsky

In order to be fair to Vought, and to take a little vacation, I agreed to report at the beginning of the second week in September. That was when Civil Aeronautics Authority (CAA) type approval tests of the improved Stratoliner were scheduled to begin. In the meantime, I was exposed to the early stages of the combined Vought-Sikorsky enterprise.

One of the great pioneering names in aviation, Igor Sikorsky dated back to the early days of the century in Russia. I was familiar with René Fonck's early Orteig prize entry of 1926, and knew that the loss of the S-35 sank Sikorsky Aircraft into another of the slumps that characterized its early struggles for survival. The S-36 and S-38 twin-engine amphibians resulted in business from the Navy as well as from Pan American, and ultimately led to a recapitalization of the company and the move to Bridgeport. The well-known four-engine clippers S-40 and S-42 followed, with which Pan American pioneered most of the world's over-ocean air routes. On my hitchhiking trip to Curtiss and Roosevelt Field I had visited the Sikorsky hangar. My knowledge of the company was further enhanced by attending tests in the Sikorsky Wind Tunnel during the "Horsefeather" flap development. I also read Sikorsky's autobiography, which was published in 1938. My brother Cooper gave me a copy for my 28th birthday.

Before relocating to Boeing, I rented a single room in an upstairs apartment in Milford, Connecticut, about a half-hour drive from the factory in my Model A Ford. The apartment belonged to Harold Inglish, who worked in the Vought engineering group. About my age, the Inglishes were a congenial couple and a good antidote to my depressed mood.

At Sikorsky, Tony Fokker introduced me around and I soon established a good rapport with members of the engineering staff. The Russian engineering philosophy was more intuitive than I had experienced at Vought, though generally backed up by analysis of the

---

BOEING AIRCRAFT COMPANY

Georgetown Station

SEATTLE, WASHINGTON

August 9, 1939   Address all Communications to the Company
                                                                          Not to Individuals

Mr. William F. Milliken
60 West Clark St.
Milford, Connecticut

Dear Mr. Milliken:

I must apologize for my long delay in answering your letters and your application. I have been very reluctant to do anything which might hamper Paul Baker in his department, although I was quite interested in securing your services in our department.

In the initial stages of our new department here, I have been very careful to select men who I felt would be permanent additions to the company and who would have an opportunity to advance to higher positions which could be rather clearly seen by them from the beginning. I would like very much to have you for work in stability and controllability and also for collaboration and active participation in our flight test program. Our new department here is organized in such a manner that there is no conflict between flight testing, aerodynamics and research, all of which are grouped together in a department separate from the general engineering department. Our program for the near future contemplates a serious effort to get our flight testing and aerodynamics on a common footing.

One of the new divisions of our work at present is performance calculations. We have been following Oswald's and Rockefeller's methods here with some use of Prof. Reid's new charts. Dr. Norton Moore from the University of California has been here during his summer vacation and has put our performance technique on a much more sound basis than it has ever been before. We are hoping to continue this standardization program in the direction of getting basic performance on all new aircraft.

I could offer you a starting salary of $2500.00 a year and assure you of increases almost immediately, depending upon the extent and character of your work.

Sincerely yours

E. T. Allen
Director of Flight
and Research

Fig. 9-2
Letter from Boeing.

Fig. 9-3
Prototype Sikorsky helicopter, constructed during the short period in which I worked for Vought-Sikorsky. This configuration led to the first practical helicopter.

details. Igor Sikorsky and his chief engineer, Mike Gluhareff, professed to have a design approach that included meditative thought and even dreams. On occasion this seemed to enable an advance into areas for which little scientific data were available. In his layout of *The Grand*, the first large Russian multi-engine aircraft (Petrograd, 1913), Sikorsky used a much higher aspect ratio for the wings than was common practice. The reduced span loading and lower induced drag were major contributors to the aircraft's success. This was years before the Prandtl induced-drag theory for predicting such a result. Similarly, I was told that Mike Gluhareff had proposed a highly swept wing for an advanced high-speed fighter design competition long before the virtues of sweep for high Mach numbers were understood.

But all was not intuitive. The core group of engineers surrounding Sikorsky also could

rapidly explore new ideas in their wind tunnel. Tony Fokker cited cases in which a design idea in the morning resulted in making and testing a model before the end of the day. If the preliminary results were promising more extensive testing might follow.

AT THIS TIME the development of the prototype Sikorsky helicopter was underway in a small shop adjacent to Vought Engineering, so we could observe its progress without being too intrusive. As early as 1909–1910, prior to his first successful airplane, Sikorsky had made two attempts to produce a workable helicopter. In the intervening years many inventors and some outstanding engineers had tried numerous helicopter configurations. Some of these left the ground for brief periods, but none with usable performance and satisfactory control. I had seen the Curtiss-Bleeker machine in Valley

Stream on my hitchhiking trip to Long Island, and knew about other helicopters such as the de Bothezat and the Berliner. One engineer/ inventor who made a substantial contribution was Juan de la Cierva, generally credited with the articulated rotor head and its practical application in the autogiro (now referred to as gyroplane) and later in the "jump" autogiro. Since no power was applied to the rotor in flight, the autogiro bypassed the problem of coping with rotor torque.

Although by no means an expert in these matters, it seemed to me Sikorsky's success lay in combining the elements of collective and cyclic pitch in an articulated rotor head, with a variable-pitch propeller at the rear of the fuselage for coping with rotor torque and to provide yaw control. By powering this rear propeller from the main rotor, control was retained even in autorotation flight subsequent to power plant failure (i.e., the main rotor would "windmill" and also drive the rear propeller). Like the Wright brothers, Sikorsky did not seek stability as much as control, and expected to have a fairly steep learning curve in flying his new machine.

Apart from its technical aspects, I was much impressed by the way Sikorsky organized his helicopter development. He used a small team of experienced individuals representing the specialties required—men who had worked together and who could communicate with a minimum of formal paperwork. In addition to Igor Sikorsky and Mike Gluhareff, there was Nikolsky (later a professor at Princeton) and probably Professor Sikorsky (a close relative of Igor) on the aerodynamics and rotor dynamics. Tony Fokker did the wind tunnel work, and several very experienced fabricators, led by Labensky, developed the transmission and the necessary testing apparatus. The entire development was funded by a modest allocation from United's board of directors. Sikorsky made the early flights himself, having mentally practiced hovering and forward flight while sitting in the prototype during construction. It was a classic example, on a smaller scale, of the project-oriented "Skunk Works" made famous by Clarence ("Kelly") Johnson at Lockheed.

On August 27 Harold Inglish drove me to Stratford, Connecticut, to pick up the 9:00

A.M. train for Montreal. I had decided to make the transcontinental trip to Boeing by rail, through the Canadian Rockies to Vancouver and thence down to Seattle. It would be my first opportunity to visit Banff and Lake Louise. Even though my life was wrapped up with aircraft, I loved train travel.

On to Boeing

My move to Seattle was not without qualms, and I remember thinking that I was in much the same situation as David Balfour when he left Essendean and sought his inheritance at the House of Shaws! [in *Kidnapped* by Robert Louis Stevenson]. However, the trip to Montreal proved a delightful beginning. The train wended its way north through New Haven, Meriden and Hartford, after which it followed the Connecticut River to Springfield, Northampton, Brattleboro and White River Junction. There it branched northwest to Burlington, north along historic Lake Champlain to St. Albans, and then to Montreal at the St. Lawrence. In effect, a south-to-north tour of scenic New England at a pleasant time of year, 370 miles as the crow flies, accomplished at the leisurely pace of about 40 mph including stops. As the sun beat through the window I began to relax for the first time in months. In early evening we rolled into the imposing Montreal railway station.

The Canadian Pacific ran a crack service over the 3,000-odd miles from Montreal to Vancouver, with transcontinental trains leaving daily for the five-day run to the coast. Large steam locomotives were employed, which were doubled up and even tripled for tackling the grades in the Rockies. Arriving at the gate that evening well in advance of departure time, I looked down the full length of the train, its dark red cars gleaming in the overhead lights, white smoke from the locomotive in the distance, and the rails shining silver in its headlight. It was hard to believe that those rails stretched unbroken across an entire continent and I was about to travel the length of them.

Having checked all but my hand luggage, I walked slowly down the train, past the lounge car and diner, to the Pullman in which I had reserved a lower berth. Anxious to lose none of the atmosphere, I remained on the platform as long as possible, observing the baggage handlers and the hustle-bustle of the passengers with their good-byes and well-wishes. Finally the conductor, watch in hand, raised his arm in the "all aboard signal." As I scrambled up the steps, I noted that the last passengers to rush down the platform and board the car were an attractive young woman and an older couple. I sensed, as did Grenfall Lorry when he "boarded the east-bound express in Denver" in that wonderful old romantic novel *Graustark*, that the trip was unlikely to be boring.

FOR THOSE WHO never have traveled on a steam train of that era, let me say that a lower berth was the ideal accommodation. One could lie alongside the window on a lengthy mattress which, with double blankets tucked in around the sides, made for a snug and toasty environment. With my head toward the front of the train and propped up on pillows, I enjoyed an endless procession of sights, sounds and motions as the train sped through the night. Lighted towns and stations, water towers, and other less distinct objects flashed by, accompanied by the rhythmic swaying of the car, the constant clicking of the wheels on the joints in the track and the distant "choo-choo-choo" of the engine. These relaxing, almost hypnotic, effects occasionally would be interrupted by a change in note as the train rumbled over a bridge or past a grade crossing, or more startlingly when an eastbound train thundered past on the adjacent track with a crescendo of noise and the strobe effect of the lighted rows of windows. The last thing I remember as I drifted off to sleep on that first night was the faint sound of the locomotive whistle as each grade crossing was approached—"toooo—toooo—to to."

Awakening the next morning after a sound night's sleep, I experienced a profound change in my emotional state. With no conscious effort on my part the depression, fears, anxieties and physical tension plaguing me suddenly had disappeared, replaced by a buoyant feeling of well-being, freedom and confidence. I was to experience mood changes in the future, but never again one so dramatic.

My good mood was further enhanced at breakfast in the dining car, where I had the good fortune to be seated at the table with the late boarders I had noticed earlier. They were Scottish, had been living in England and now were emigrating to Canada. They were full of news of the impending war with Germany, a revelation to me because in those days I seldom read a newspaper.

The young woman was about my age, and over the next few days we spent much time together in the dining and lounge cars, and on the open observation platform in back enjoying the view. As the train snaked its way up the foothills on its way to Banff the time passed pleasantly and quickly. My new Scottish friends were to spend some time there, and I decided to spend a week enjoying their company and hiking around Lake Louise. I wired Allen and he agreed because there were delays in the start of the Stratoliner's certification. While I was at Lake Louise, Great Britain and France declared war on Germany.

On our last evening together the young woman and I dined and danced at Chateau Lake Louise. With its wonderful view of the glacier this was a poignant end to a brief romantic interlude. On September 8th I was back on the train, which now rattled down through Revelstoke and Kicking Horse Canyon in the long descent to Vancouver. After that I boarded the steamer to Victoria, and then across Puget Sound to Seattle.

When the Vancouver–Seattle boat docked in Seattle on the 13th I was met by the Blakemores. Jack had worked with my father surveying branch routes for the Great Northern; he and his wife Cassa had reserved a temporary room for me at The Hungerford Hotel in downtown Seattle.

ON SEPTEMBER 15TH I REPORTED for work. In 1939 Boeing still was operating out of old Plant No. 1, a collection of buildings on the Duwamish Waterway, which runs south from Elliott Bay on the east coast of Puget Sound. Many of the early Boeing aircraft—the PW-9, FB-4, P-12 and F4B-4 fighters, the PB-1 patrol bomber, and the 40A commercial aircraft used for mail and passenger service—were produced in this facility. These were followed

Fig. 9-4
The Boeing aircraft Monomail airmail version.

Fig. 9-5
Boeing Plant 1, circa 1939. The building on the upper right, with the twin skylights, housed the engineering, administration and executive offices (the latter on the top floor). The large building in the center is Final Assembly. One of the early Clippers with the single vertical tail is about to be launched into the Duwamish Waterway, which connects on the left with Elliot Bay. The current Boeing Field on East Marginal Way is not shown on this photo.

by the Model 80 series large-transport biplanes, the low-wing cantilever "Monomail" monoplane that led to the B-9 bomber, and the Boeing 247, which was the first of the modern transport airliners. Plant No. 1 also was the home of the XB-15, a four-engine, long-range experimental Air Corps bomber, and the Model 299 prototype B-17. Because the plant was located on a waterway it was convenient for seaplane launching, and the original 314 Clipper and second series A314 were also built there. Boeing Field, with its long north-south runway, was located on the other side of the waterway, but farther south.

Arriving at the Administration Building, I was shown to the main engineering center, where 80-odd engineers and designers were at work, mostly at drafting tables. There were a few small offices for section heads and Allen had one on the south side near the windows.

I was somewhat awed by the impending interview with E. T. Allen. Over the course of his career thus far he had logged over 7,000 hours of the most hazardous kinds of flying imaginable, and was regarded by many here and abroad as the greatest "engineering-test pilot" of the time.

My apprehension was unwarranted. Allen proved to be one of the most unpretentious, friendly, mild-mannered individuals I had ever met. He was dressed in a comfortable unpressed tweed suit with a sloppily tied necktie, and was slightly balding. I judged him to be in his early forties. Exuding sincerity and enthusiasm, he outlined his objectives for the new Flight and Aerodynamics Department. His first concern had been to bring in two highly qualified individuals to head up the Aerodynamics and Flight Test branches. His choices were based on

Fig. 9-6
George S. Schairer, one of Boeing's great engineers. After the war he uncovered German research that showed the advantage of highly swept wings for high subsonic aircraft. Used on the 707, it set the trend for modern military and commercial transports. Schairer was a powerful influence on postwar Boeing designs, and became head of Boeing's research group.

knowledge obtained from working for various aircraft firms. First he signed on George S. Schairer to head Aerodynamics. As a teenager George had constructed prize-winning model aircraft, studied math and science at Swarthmore, and obtained a degree in aeronautics from MIT in 1932. He followed this with work for Consolidated Aircraft in San Diego, where he was involved with the Davis Wing development, and with general aerodynamics and seaplane design. On the first flight of the Boeing 314 Clipper with the single vertical tail and the built-in wing dihedral, Allen had a vivid example of Schairer's extraordinary talent and foresight. Though still a relatively young engineer (we were contemporaries at MIT), Schairer had wired Allen predicting a vicious Dutch roll characteristic. This actually occurred in flight, and nearly proved catastrophic. As I was to learn firsthand, everything about George was unique: his personality, his manner of speaking, his ability to interpret wind tunnel and towing tank tests and his almost mythical sense of aerodynamics.

ALLEN'S CHOICE TO HEAD the Flight Test Branch was Albert C. Reed. A Southern Californian, Al was a graduate of Cal Tech. According to Bill Sears's account, he had interrupted his graduate studies to fill a vacancy at the University of Minnesota in the Department of Aeronautical Engineering, where he was viewed as an expert in meteorology. At some stage he had trained as a military pilot, and joined Douglas Aircraft as an engineering test pilot. It was at Douglas that Allen and Reed became acquainted.

Allen made it clear that I was to report directly to Reed. As the first engineering employee in flight test (other than instrumentation and hangar personnel), I came in with seniority as principal flight test engineer, effectively becoming assistant head of flight test.

At the end of my interview I was introduced to Reed. In marked contrast to Allen, he was less straightforward, warm and open. I sensed immediately that our relationship would be at the technical and organizational level, untempered by social considerations. Reed's interests were in placing flight testing on a more efficient and quantitative basis. To that end he was excited by the early work of Oswald, Rockefeller, Moore and others at Cal Tech and Douglas, to which he had made some original contributions. I developed a strong respect for Reed's technical thinking, and also for his ability to analyze a situation and take immediate corrective action under the duress of flight emergencies. There were two occasions in which I am certain that his skill and presence of mind saved our lives. As a result of our first meeting I accepted Al as my superior, and would work wholeheartedly for him. This is not to say I was unaware of his controlling instincts, approaching the militaristic at times, and his over-enthusiasm for procedures.

Having officially started work, I was contacted by William H. Cook, another MIT aeronautical engineering graduate who had arrived at Boeing in July 1938. We had known each other at MIT, although not closely. Bill was involved with Stark Draper's activities in the instrument laboratory when I worked with Shats Ober and Johnny Markham in the wind tunnel. At Boeing, Cook had started on the drafting board but soon graduated to develop instrumentation for vibration measurements on the ill-fated 307. He became head of the Vibration and Flutter Group before transferring to Schairer's Aerodynamic Branch, where he was associated with wind tunnel instrumentation. By 1947 he was to make major contributions to Boeing's high-speed wind tunnel. From then to his retirement in 1974 he held major technical and administrative posts in nearly every aircraft and missile development project. He was one of the very small group of engineers responsible for Boeing's ascendancy to the pinnacle of modern jet transport design and production. Subsequent to his retirement he authored a definitive engineering history of the 707.

Prior to the war, Seattle fostered the pioneering atmosphere of the great Northwest and an iconoclastic sense of independence. Isolated from the southern California aircraft industry, Boeing did things its own way and was proud of it. Sometimes its engineering seemed too traditional, like using truss structures for wing beams instead of the newer stressed-skin approach. But in other respects Boeing leaped ahead of the conventional. No other aircraft company exhibited such risk-taking in terms of self-financing prototype aircraft that represented quantum advances in the state of the art. One thinks of the 299, prototype of the B-17, and the Dash-80, prototype of the 707 passenger jet and the KC-135 jet tanker. The Dash-80 (a.k.a. Model 367-80) also was the prototype for the 700 family of commercial and military jets. A sense of adventure seemed to permeate Boeing and gave it an aura of excitement.

Fig. 9-7
William H. Cook who, like Schairer, played a major role in Boeing aircraft designs. He held a number of responsible positions, including chief engineer of the Transport Division. Now retired, he and his wife still fly their own seaplane.

Stratoliner

When the prototype 307 Stratoliner crashed during a demonstration flight in 1938, it had stalled in a low-speed, single-engine-out maneuver. In the course of applying rudder to correct the stall, or in the ensuing spin, the rudder had locked hard over, the control forces being beyond the pilot's capability. Allen's aerodynamic section under Schairer later performed extensive wind tunnel tests at the University of Washington on a new design with an enlarged vertical tail and rudders, incorporating a long dorsal fin that would be effective at high yaw angles and thus prevent rudder lockover. Power boost had also been added. As a further means of improving stall behavior, fixed slots were provided in the leading edge of the outboard part of the wing. Flight tests prior to my arrival at Boeing had generally indicated the effectiveness of these measures.

On the day following my arrival, Reed and I visited the Boeing Experimental Hangar on the east side of Boeing Field along Marginal Way. As we approached the open doors of the hangar I was treated to a spectacular view of the 307, which essentially filled the hangar. Because of cabin pressurization, the fuselage was circular in cross-section right up to the nose. With the conventional gear the cockpit seemed 30 feet off the concrete. To me, the result was an almost scary appearance of an over-bloated whale.

In the course of exploring this monster we climbed up into the passenger compartment—a big, empty "tin can" of bulkheads, stringers and skin, with partial flooring and windows but no seats or upholstery. Workmen had removed the metal door on the left-hand forward side, and appeared to be covering the hole with fabric. I turned to Reed and asked why. Al replied, "A safety precaution. Aerodynamics wants a flight check on the effectiveness of the wing slots, so they requested we do some stalls with the slots covered up. On the remote chance of trouble, it would be easier to slash the fabric and bail out than to fumble with a metal door latch. Incidentally, it will be a good opportunity for you to get involved in the test program."

A FEW DAYS LATER we were at the hangar suiting up for the flight, with a minimum crew of Allen, Reed and me. I was to take 16-mm movies from a window in the passenger cabin of tufts installed on the upper wing surface behind the location of the slots (which now were sealed off with metal covers). Filming the movies would require some movement on my part, so I was assigned a snap-on chest pack that was hung near the emergency exit, which now was

Fig. 9-8
Original 307 configuration with small vertical tail and no dorsal fin. Aircraft is taking off from Boeing Field in a full-load climb. Gross weight was 45,000 lbs.; each Wright Cyclone engine generated 1,100-hp takeoff power. This is the first pressurized transport.

Fig. 9-9
After the loss of the prototype Stratoliner in a stall/spin accident in 1938, Eddie Allen became head of the Flight and Aerodynamics Department. His first task was to improve the 307 flight characteristics. He is shown with a powered model in the University of Washington wind tunnel. The model has the larger vertical tail and dorsal fin.

neatly covered with doped fabric. The pilots would use the regular seat-pack parachutes.

I stood up behind Allen. The aircraft was light and took off like a scared rabbit, and then settled into a rated power climb for 12,000 feet. After small single-engine aircraft, I found four engines and lack of soundproofing a bit uncomfortable, and resolved to use earplugs in the future. Approaching 12,000 feet, I scrambled back into the passenger compartment and got set with the camera.

The first stalls of the session in "clean" condition, flaps up and engine throttled back, gave some wing drop and loss of altitude but nothing spectacular. When the stall was initiated from a climb at rated power, such was not the case. As Allen pulled the nose up, higher and higher, buffeting set in followed by what seemed to be shaking of the entire airframe. The tufts on the wing were flickering wildly between straight up and pointing forward. I felt the airplane "go" as the wing on my side started down, but continued to concentrate on operating the camera, doing

whatever it took to keep the tufts in the field of view. Then, quite suddenly, I realized I was standing on the cabin wall with the ground straight down below. At this rate of roll I soon would be standing on the ceiling.

The power had been pulled off, but since recovery seemed by no means imminent I dropped the camera and crawled toward the cockpit for my chute. In an effort to unstall the aircraft as quickly as possible both pilots were pushing with their feet, not their hands, on the control wheel yokes. The aircraft made nearly a full turn in a sort of inverted spiral, and incipient spin, before the angle of attack came down and rudder could be applied to stop the rotation. The aircraft finally wound up in an almost vertical dive. Pulling out was a tricky business, because the speed was picking up at an alarming rate and large airplanes like the Stratoliner only are good for a few g's before coming apart, nor can they take excessive speed. Fascinated, I watched Allen ease the plane out of the dive, holding it close to the structural limit. Once she finally leveled out he said

Fig. 9-10a,b,c
Stratoliner model in University of Washington wind tunnel.

My reaction to this sort of flying was elation. There were moments of high tension but no lasting fear. I had responded rationally and was captivated by the superb piloting I had witnessed. Nothing courageous was involved here; I had wanted this so much that I spent no time pondering or imagining the risks. Perhaps I had considered the risks before and left them behind me. Test flying had so many elements of my childhood dreams of flying an ocean that I was filled with a sense of *déjà vu*. Back of it all, as I realized only years later, was my ego need, the old hero dream of doing something that would earn recognition.

FILLED WITH A SENSE of satisfaction, I went back that evening to the Olympic Grill, slouched down and relaxed on the comfortable cushions, and ordered a favorite meal of hardshell Dungeness crabs, an outside cut of roast beef, a glass of white wine and a dish of chocolate ice cream.

AS WE CONTINUED Stratoliner testing I began to settle into life in Seattle, leaving the Hungerford Hotel for a single bedroom in a private home on "First Hill" at 1410 Seneca Street. I lived there until January of 1942, when I moved into more luxurious accommodations a few blocks away at 908 Boren Avenue. I was far too busy to think in terms of an apartment or of doing my own housekeeping. My social life centered around the landmark Olympic Hotel near the center of downtown Seattle. The dark wood and paneling of the lobby and main dining room were subdued and elegant.

For practical purposes, the Olympic became my unofficial headquarters. Many

"enough of this" and we headed home. As a verification of the experience that Allen brought to this type of flight testing, subsequent inspection indicated that while a few rivets had popped, the airframe had not been seriously overstressed.

Fig. 9-11
Mockup for forward section of the 307 Stratoliner, showing the cockpit arrangement and some structural details.

of my friends (and even hotel employees) believed I lived there. As Boeing moved into war production our test flights became longer and more exhausting, frequently finishing well into the evening. No matter how late, I made it a practice to relax afterward over a good meal in the Olympic Grill or Georgian Room, after which I would hike up First Hill to catch as much sleep as possible.

Mine was mainly a life of work, but I didn't think of it as work because it was so exciting. As the pace of testing accelerated, I was frequently back at the plant on weekends, keeping up with flight planning and reporting. My only real diversion was ballroom dancing at the Olympic, either in the Georgian Room or, later, in the Olympic Bowl, both of which had excellent dance bands. The Blakemores had introduced me around and I made many friends at the plant, so I never was without a dance partner when I could get a Friday or

Saturday evening off. In due time I bought a standard Chevrolet sedan.

During my early months at Boeing all attention was focused on the Stratoliner. Until the reworked version passed CAA flight certification, no aircraft could be delivered to TWA, United or PAA, and hence paid for, since Boeing was on the ropes financially. It was made clear to me that the future of the company depended on the delivery of these aircraft. Winter weather in Seattle is far from propitious for flight test operations. Furthermore, the test pilots lacked proficiency in instrument flight and radio aids, and ground facilities were almost nonexistent. Even local weather prediction was unreliable, and we depended on the Krick Weather Service operating out of southern California. We flew whenever the weather was at all reasonable, and many times when it was very marginal.

181

Fig. 9-12
307 wing outboard of the No. 4 nacelle. The tip slots are in the leading edge, in front of the aileron.

Sometimes only a detailed familiarity with Seattle's appearance from the air got us safely back to the runway. If we could locate the large Rainier Beer sign we had it made; I still can sense our relief when that sign appeared through the rain and fog off the starboard side of the aircraft.

Many of the development flights involved only a minimum crew; others entailed specialized instrumentation and representatives from the design groups involved. It was my task to help prepare flight plans that would economize on test time while still allowing for the acquisition of the desired data. Stationed in the pilot's compartment, I had to coordinate these activities over the intercom while ensuring that the pilots were providing the desired flight and engine operating conditions. I remember one amusing episode in which the plan involved collection of information for heat and vent, pressurization, power plant, propeller feathering, engine restart, and aerodynamic data with various engines out. It is worth noting that on a four-engine aircraft, services such as pumps and generators are only available from specific engines, so the possibility for serious and unexpected confusion exists. Having started at 8,000 feet we gradually lost altitude as the test sequence progressed. Drifting down to under 1,000 feet, we rapidly descended toward the Sound when Allen suddenly turned to me and said, "Bill, I can't hold altitude, and I'm damned if I know which engines are throttled, feathered or running!"

One day our minimum crew went up for an extensive check of directional stability with the enlarged vertical tail and dorsal fin, including tests with various engines out, notably two on one side. In addition to standard instrumentation, a long boom had been installed on the nose of the fuselage, carrying a combined yaw vane and pitot tube, referred to as the "swiveling pitot." Data from this instrument was critical to the interpretation of the tests. When we found in the post-flight meeting that its performance was questionable (compared with data from the regular air speed indicators) a concern arose that we had lost the flight. Tempers were short because this was not a flight one wanted to repeat. Reed turned to me, "Call up Fred Woods [head of the Instrumentation Section, then at home] and read him the riot act." Fred was defensive, and our conversation had reached the yelling stage when Fred started to laugh. I asked why, and he replied, "My wife

that mine also had blanched, an involuntary reaction to an obviously desperate situation. Anyone who has been exposed to a first course in aircraft stability and control knows that sustained blind flight is not possible without instruments and proper training. Few aircraft are spirally stable and certainly not the Stratoliner in a rated power climb. Sooner or later the aircraft will diverge into a spiral, the pilot will lose orientation and the spiral will become a spin. Eddie Allen remained calm. He sat there concentrating, trying to maintain the aircraft at the speed and attitude it had prior to the loss of the instruments. Over the years Allen had subjectively evaluated dozens of aircraft and was famous for his ability to interpret control feel. I remember glancing over his shoulder, noting he was holding the wheel very lightly with his fingertips trying to sense the least change in the control force in elevator and ailerons. We were lucky that the air was reasonably smooth.

Characteristic of Reed, and observable on numerous occasions, was his concern for his own survival and his efforts to control his environment to that end. I remember after Pearl Harbor, when it was believed the Japanese might attack Seattle, and specifically Boeing, that Al's reaction was to obtain a pistol permit and carry a gun in his car at all times. This controlling aspect of his character, while scarcely endearing to his associates in normal circumstances, occasionally paid off handsomely. Reed possessed an uncanny ability to think analytically under duress, a faculty possessed by a number of great pilots. One thinks of Kingsford-Smith, in an uncontrollable spin in the Lockheed Altair at night in mid-Pacific, methodically going over every instrument and control in the cockpit, finally discovering that he inadvertently had switched on "down flaps."

I don't know how long it was before Reed shouted, "The swiveling total head tube—it's bigger and may not have iced up. Can we connect it up?" Normally there wouldn't have been a chance. The pitot-static heads connect to the pilot and co-pilot's instruments by small metal tubing with couplings over flared ends. They are behind the panels, and to get at them in a hurry, even with the proper size

open-end wrench, would have been well-nigh impossible.

Reed had the clearest idea of what was to be done and took the lead. After a struggle on the floor of the cockpit near the control pedestal, we finally located the lines involved and, with the help of pliers, made the connections. Allen remained riveted to the controls.

Reconstructing this story, one fact I am certain of is that when we finally connected the swiveling total head pitot tube into the system, *both* the pilot's and co-pilot's instruments became operative simultaneously. This says that the pilot and co-pilot systems were not plumbed separately to their separate pitot-static heads, as they would be in a production airplane. Instead they were ganged together, left to right total pressure, and left to right static pressure. This definitely was a temporary jury-rig, but not unreasonable. Any fuselage yaw would give different pressure readings from the two heads because they were located on opposite sides of the bulbous nose. Better to average them to begin with, before any calibration of the yaw effects. Therefore there was one line for total pressure and one line for static pressure coming back to the cockpit. Each line was connected to a three-way fitting, with lines running laterally to the pilot and co-pilot instruments. Breaking into the total-head line at the three-way fitting, and connecting it to the rubber tubing from the swiveling yaw total head, would provide pressure from the swiveling head to both the pilot's and co-pilot's instruments. Regarding static head, it would be sufficient to cut the line coming back to the three-way fitting, giving us cockpit static pressure at the instruments, which was close enough for a reference pressure.

When the instruments came back on Allen's efforts were vindicated. We had gained altitude but still were at a sensible airspeed. Although we still were in the clouds, a great sense of relief broke the tension. Reed exchanged positions with Haldeman in the co-pilot's seat. At an altitude of some 12,000 feet he turned around and instructed the Flight Engineer to turn on the cabin pressurization.

The third installment of our accident scenario was about to begin!

Fig. 9-15
Fuel dump demonstration. Colored water was used.

All of us heard Reed's instructions, but none of us remembered that the cabin door had been replaced by fabric. In a few minutes a tremendous explosion was followed by a rush of air as the fabric gave way and the cabin depressurized. I was holding onto the back of the pilot's seat and instinctively clung to it as my feet were swept out from under me. Everyone's reaction was different. Allen yelled that the rudder was gone, probably because the aircraft yawed as the air jetted out the side of the nose of the aircraft. An instant after the blast, Fred Wood literally slid into the cockpit crying, "What happened!" Bedlam reigned for a few moments, until the open door made apparent what we were experiencing. Al was the least verbal, perhaps chagrined by his initiation of cabin pressurization. For myself, I lost no time in grabbing my chest-pack parachute off the wall and snapping it on.

As if the gods had exposed us to all the hazards they could think of, we broke out into clear conditions minutes after the explosion. Still lost, we were on a westerly course toward the setting sun. A sizable city

and an airport appeared below us, that radio contact established was Wenatchee. Enough was enough, and Allen made the decision to land for the night. Parked on the ramp, I was standing by the nose of the aircraft when a mechanic from the local FBO (Fixed Base Operator) walked up. "Do you always fly with that big open hole in the aircraft?" he asked. I replied yes, that it was so much easier to bail out in an emergency.

The next day, loaded with Wenatchee apples, we flew back to Seattle. I handled the controls as co-pilot, with Al in the pilot's seat and Eddie dozing back in the cabin. All's well that ends well.

Certifying the Stratoliner

By late 1940 we were well into the Stratoliner CAA Certification Flights. George Haldeman established a CAA office at Boeing Field, and we adapted a program originally developed for transport aircraft to the new features of the Stratoliner. The CAA requirements were far from a hard quantitative specification, and much depended upon their interpretation. I always felt that Boeing was fortunate to have Haldeman assigned to the job. He recognized the difficult financial situation at Boeing, and the paramount need for Boeing to survive as a defense contractor. There never was a hint of the confrontations that have spoiled so many relations between government and industry representatives in recent years. On the contrary, there was great respect between Allen/Reed and Haldeman, in addition to a mutual determination to ensure that within the spirit of the CAA rules the Stratoliner would be a safe aircraft for airline use. Some difficult judgment calls arose, especially in the area of stability and control.

The practical utilization of a transport aircraft depends in part on the permissible range of location of the longitudinal center of gravity (CG). The larger the range, the more loading options are available to the operator. The CAA type certificate would specify this range, based on the limits established in our certification tests.

The CAA guidelines called for positive longitudinal stability throughout the allowable range of CG travel, with little clue as to the test conditions or how this was to be measured. It soon became apparent that one critical

condition for longitudinal stability was rated power climb-out after takeoff in the heavy-load condition with aft CG. This occurred at relatively low speed—around 140 mph indicated, with partial flaps. The unfavorable downwash reaction at the horizontal tail in this condition contributed to the marginal stability.

Academically, there are numerous aspects of stability that analysts deal with. These include the behavior of the aircraft with fixed or free control after a disturbance, static stability as derived from wind tunnel tests, or complete dynamic stability in which the frequency and damping of motion following a disturbance are assessed. There were standard criteria for all of these tests.

Thoroughly trained in aircraft stability and control theory by Otto Koppen at MIT, I had analyzed wind tunnel data and performed stability analyses at Chance Vought under Paul Baker's discipline, and had flown with him in stability control flight tests in small, single-engine aircraft. But now I was exposed to a far more complex situation, in which classical criteria of stability and control, while useful, were not in themselves decisive. The practical criterion in this real-life situation was subjective: how the pilot felt about his ability to control the aircraft and maintain trim in a

Fig. 9-16
Certified Stratoliner in flight. I was on board when this beautiful picture was taken, circa 1941.

climb-out with the CG aft. Would the average airline pilot have the capability to manage the aircraft at its rearward CG limit at night, in IFR (Instrument Flight Rules) weather and in rough air? Would the workload be excessive for a tired pilot? Could he handle an emergency such as an engine-out? Watching Allen and Haldeman, two highly experienced and responsible individuals, wrestle with all of the factors involved in establishing the limit was an education one does not receive in college. I began to appreciate the real world as opposed to an abstraction of it, a real world with all of its subtleties and nuances.

Grinding away in a rated power climb, with the aircraft alive and buffeting, Allen would introduce a slight out-of-trim disturbance, feel the control forces through the control friction, and observe the aircraft response and the "returnability." How marginal was it? How would it feel under less-than-favorable conditions? He would nudge the aircraft into turns and recoveries, suddenly throttling back on an outboard engine to simulate engine failure, and so forth. Everything so marginal. Then Haldeman would try it, after which the two men caucused to establish some uniformity of opinion.

At first, we'd load up the airplane at some aft CG, take off and run a flight evaluation at that condition. Later a better scheme was introduced, possibly suggested by Schairer, in which we took along a crew of some 15–20 passengers, each carrying 30–40 pounds of shot bags for a total weight of more than 3,000 pounds. The aircraft was without furnishings, so the full length of the cabin was available for moving this crew around in flight. Not only could we change the longitudinal CG, but we also had a way of obtaining a quantitative measure of the static stability to supplement the all-important judgments of the pilots. Suppose, for example, that with this crew forward we were at a CG that subjectively appeared as a possible aft limit. Moving the crew aft in effect applied a known pitching moment about that point, and by measuring the trim speed change, we could obtain a plot of pitching moment versus trim. The slope of this curve at the initial speed was a measure of the so-called "static stability," taking into account speed as

well as attitude effects (a more comprehensive measurement than normally is made in a wind tunnel with an unpowered model). In flight, this test could be performed with fixed control or free (force) control, the latter probably being more relevant to actual operation.

THE FLIGHTS WERE LONG and tiring, and we had to resolve the stability and control issue and get on to other CAA requirements. One flight went well into the evening, as our movable ballast was shifted farther and farther aft into the dark recesses of the cabin. In the well-lighted and heated cockpit up front the pilots were teetering on a final decision for the allowable aft CG. Over and over they attempted to simulate imagined airline operating conditions, and argued the consequences of aircraft or flight crew performance. We would climb for awhile, then descend to an initial altitude and start again, a sawtoothed affair. In the process we completely forgot about our human ballast. Allen was the first to remember, and told me to go back and see how our passengers were doing. I stumbled over the rear cockpit bulkhead into the dark cabin and felt my way along the wall, becoming colder and colder as I proceeded. I finally found our ballast huddled together against the spherical rear bulkhead, shot bags and parachutes piled on top for warmth. Embarrassed, we got our passengers into the cockpit two at a time to warm up as we headed back to Boeing Field.

Other tests on the CAA agenda were cabin explosive decompression, which proved rather tame after our unplanned decompression, and fuel dumping. In his book *The Road to the 707*, Bill Cook recorded this reminiscence:

Boeing was required to demonstrate . . . that [dumped] fuel missed the horizontal tail. A large pipe came out of the wing lower surface to expel the fuel. Instead of fuel, colored water was used for the test. The horizontal tail was painted with whitewash to detect any impingement of the colored water.

Eddie was in the left-hand pilot's seat and Al Reed was in the co-pilot's seat. The CAA observer on the cockpit jump seat was George Haldeman. When the 307 was ready to dump fuel, Al lowered the fuel dump pipe. George interrupted and said they were going upwind and he wanted to dump downwind. This offended Al Reed's technical sensibilities. He said emphatically, "I won't dump downwind!", an equally silly statement. Al imagined himself as a superior scientific test pilot, with all his Cal Tech education. Eddie hushed Al up, and told Al to turn downwind. Eddie then turned to George and said, "George, you can dump now." [For the non-technical reader, terms "upwind" and "downwind" are meaningless except in relation to the ground and have no bearing on the outcome of this fuel dumping test.]

FOLLOWING SUCCESSFUL COMPLETION of the CAA Certification Program, there were acceptance tests for the airline customers. These normally were quite routine, the airlines being anxious to acquire the aircraft and Boeing even more anxious to sell them. But one acceptance test for TWA proved far from routine.

TWA was interested in the possibility of a nearly blind landing, and had inserted in its contract a clause to fly the aircraft into the ground at a specified rate of descent without structural failure of the landing gear or damage to the aircraft. The figure that sticks in my mind was 500 feet per minute, a rate of descent that equaled 5.7 miles per hour, but it might have been more. The airline had sent its chief pilot, Tommy Tomlinson, to Seattle to accept the airplane, and he was adamant that a landing with this rate of descent had to be demonstrated. Tomlinson was something of a legend and was famous for his exploratory high-altitude flights to 25,000–30,000 ft. with rudimentary oxygen equipment. Rumor had it that the oxygen deprivation he had experienced left him a bit "punch-drunk." My own impression was of his determination that Boeing rigorously meet all aspects of the contract.

So it was that one Saturday, a beautiful spring day in Seattle, Al Reed, the flight engineer and I met with Tomlinson at the flight hangar. The single purpose of the flight was to demonstrate this fixed rate-of-descent landing. Tomlinson was to observe the gear from an aft seat in the passenger compartment while I recorded the rate of descent (indicated by the pilot's rate of climb instrument). Having convinced himself of the structural integrity of the landing gear, Tomlinson was to come forward to repeat the landing while he personally observed the instruments. There would be no fudging on Boeing's part.

Allen flew the demonstration. After takeoff he made a wide circle of the field, setting up for a landing from a long straight-in approach at the requisite rate of descent. The air was smooth and he held the rate precisely. I glanced outside to see the ground coming up at an alarming rate. Allen must have momentarily looked away from the instruments and thought so too, for he flared ever so slightly and the rate of descent fell to near zero at touchdown. Tomlinson sensed the flare, and came forward yelling "that will never do, try it again." So Allen made two more attempts with much the same results. Apparently he couldn't bring himself to crash into the ground at such a rate. Reed, ever impatient, said, "Let me do it"—so Allen turned over the controls. Down we came, Reed flying strictly on instruments, the needle seemingly glued to the required rate of descent. When we struck, all hell let loose. Standing behind the pilot, my knees buckled and I fell to the floor as the airplane bounced back up into the air. A large water tank on the wall of the lavatory bulkhead aft of the cockpit broke loose, crashing down with the sink and flooding the cockpit exit. As Reed poured on the power to avoid a further touchdown, Tomlinson literally slid into the cockpit, like snow avalanching from a pitched roof, yelling, "Don't do it again, boys, don't do it again!"

Convinced the gear must be damaged, no attempt was made to retract it as Allen radioed the hangar to report on the "landing" and decide the best course of action. Structural engineers from the landing gear section were called at home and rushed to the field. They were taken up in a small private aircraft to inspect the gear. All this gave us plenty of time to contemplate what would happen if one or both gears collapsed on landing, and to speculate on whether it would be better to attempt retraction and belly-in. However, the structural engineers could see no obvious damage, and the verdict was to make as smooth a landing as possible after circling the field to burn off excess fuel. Allen greased it in with his usual finesse. No gear or structural damage turned up in the following inspection, and Boeing's reputation for building substantial airplanes was reinforced. To the best of my knowledge TWA never indulged in such blind landings during its airline operation. Had they done so, the passengers would have felt they had gotten more than their money's worth.

THE STRATOLINER TESTS CONTINUED into the early months of 1941, by which time we had flown on serial numbers 1995 through 1998. We must have flown at least three more, probably 2001, 2002 and 2003, since a total of eight were delivered (five to TWA and three to PAA), and my record shows that we flew 2003 during May. PAA originally had ordered four, but never replaced the machine that was lost in the 1938 stall/spin accident.

Once the airlines had the Stratoliner they still were required by CAA to go through a series of so-called "proving flights" on regular routes before placing them in passenger service. These flights also served for crew training. On one such cross-country flight by TWA, with Haldeman on board and while flying in exceptionally bad weather, the carburetors (variously reported as on three or four engines) iced up with carburetor heat full-on. Over southern Colorado the pilot effected a landing on a plateau, damaging the gear and the cargo doors. Only one crew member was injured, a stewardess who jumped to the ground from the aft cabin door and broke her leg. When word reached Boeing there was unholy consternation about the level of carburetor heat that Boeing, as well as CAA, had deemed satisfactory. The only moral I ever have been able to draw from this incident is the wisdom of conducting proving flights under real airline operating conditions on actual routes. Flight testing at its very best is only a high-level simulation of ultimate operational reality.

For all its teething problems, the Stratoliner had a good airline service record. Five of them were commandeered by Air Transport Command for use on the Atlantic route during the war.[1]

[1] *The Stratoliner's history is described in some detail in* Legend and Legacy: The Story of Boeing and Its People *by Robert J. Serling.*

Chapter 10

Last of the Clippers

"They waft over from France
satin shoes for a dance.
Dim vases from old Cathay,
Topaz from Brazil,
silken lace from Saville,
and peacock from Mandalay"

– Bertha Lee Gardiner

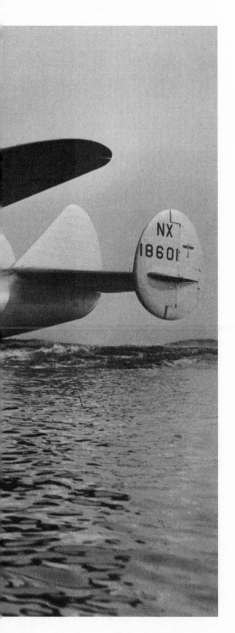

The last of the great over-ocean flying boats, the Boeing 314 Pan American Clipper, was a spectacular aircraft for a variety of reasons. Pan American Airways (PAA) had acquired an initial six from Boeing, and later exercised its option for six more. My flight experience occurred on the second series, the A-314s, during the first six months of 1941. Our task was to check out the aircraft for delivery. This was far from a major development program, but it did involve some interesting problems that had arisen in airline service.

At the outset I should say that flying on this aircraft was the most enjoyable way of earning a living I ever encountered. The low-altitude flights were neither long nor arduous. A small crew flew from a private dock on the west shore of Lake Washington, frequently taking off in mid-morning, anchoring offshore at noon for a box lunch onboard or an occasional swim, and then flying again in the afternoon. There was no taxiing on crowded runways, no waiting for tower instructions in cramped and stuffy cockpits, no oxygen lines to trip over, no uncomfortable parachute packs to sit on. Instead we flew in a palatial air yacht capable of transporting 80-odd passengers by day and 50 or so in berths at night across the long over-water air routes. Part of our delight as aeronautical engineers stemmed from the design of the aircraft. It was not the first of PAA's Clippers (preceded by Sikorskys and Martins), but it was the ultimate in luxurious appointments and unique features.

The sheer size of the 314 was impressive, especially its two-story height, the deep hull for the passengers, and the flight crew quarters, which were reached by a spiral staircase. Divided into separate areas, the passenger compartment comprised galley, lounge and bedrooms. At the aft end was the bridal suite, suitably outfitted for

The Boeing Clipper, second series, A-314 flying boat for Pan American Airways, 1941.

honeymooners and nicknamed "the tail suite" by our crew. We found it to be a convenient location for a stenotypist (usually Bill Talbott) and a mimeograph machine, so I could dictate the flight report and have it printed before the last landing of the day.

The flight deck, under and projecting forward of the giant wing, was more reminiscent of nautical than of aircraft practice. Pilots sat on a raised section at the forward end of a large room, perhaps 25 feet long, offering an excellent view over the nose and to the sides. On the left side of the deck was a full-sized navigator's table for hydrographic charts and work space, as well as a radio operator's station. The flight engineer was located on the right with a battery of engine instruments. These included complex fuel management controls that enabled fuel transfer between the numerous tanks. On both sides, just forward of the engineer's station, doors led to passageways into the leading edge of the wing. Aft of the

flight deck were sleeping quarters for an extra crew, topped by a transparent dome on the upper wing surface for taking sextant shots for celestial navigation.

The passageways in the wings allowed one to crawl all the way into the outboard nacelles. Four of the early Wright Cyclone R-2600 twin-row radial engines powered the 314. Each of these 14-cylinder air-cooled engines generated 1,500 horsepower at 2,400 rpm. The engine was known for its performance and reliability, and these qualities were further enhanced on subsequent versions. The carburetors, dual magnetos, and various pumps were located on the rear of the R-2600. They were accessible in flight from the passageways in the wings. Access was facilitated by a fabricated cone-shaped engine mount that surrounded the accessories, instead of the typical welded steel tube installation.

Crawling out into an outboard nacelle and kneeling behind the engine for takeoff was one of our hairier pastimes. One was subjected to a terrifying and painful sound, high heat from the exhaust shrouds, the vibrations of the wing and nacelle—all in all, a hellish experience. New members of the crew were inveigled into giving it a try. Once was enough. Even at cruise power in flight it was a horrifying environment.

THE EXTERNAL ASPECTS of the aircraft were just as distinctive, notably the three vertical tails. No story of the 314 would be complete without the tale of how they got there. When Eddie Allen flew the prototype in 1938 the plane sported only one vertical tail. Its wing design was a direct copy of Boeing's XB-15, a huge low-wing Air Corps bomber. Substantial dihedral had been built into the bomber's wings, certainly more geometric dihedral than for a high-winger such as the 314. George Schairer, then at Consolidated Aircraft, recognized

Fig. 10-1
As senior flight test engineer, I am standing on the dock near the Wright R-2600 Cyclone engines of 1,500 horsepower at 2,400 rpm.

from a photograph that the
314, with its small vertical
tail and large flat-sided hull
projecting forward of the
wing, would be directionally
unstable. This directional
instability also would couple
into the roll mode through the
excessive dihedral, to excite
a Dutch roll oscillation. (My
own experience with the M-1
had been a micro example of
a similar behavior.) Schairer
wired Allen urging him not
to fly the airplane. There
are various versions of what
happened next; what follows
is based on my memory of a
conversation I had with Eddie.

Fig. 10-2
Al Reed, co-pilot (left) and Bud Benton, crew chief. I am far right, carrying briefcase.

EDDIE WAS RELUCTANT to
fly the machine after receiving
the telegram, but realizing
that he was better qualified
than anyone else available he
agreed to go ahead. Boeing's
Earl Ferguson was co-pilot.
No sooner were they off the
water of Elliott Bay than the
directional instability set in,
and a large amount of rudder
was required to keep the
oscillation amplitude within
flyable bounds. At the same
time the roll mode was excited
to a less prominent degree.
Fortunately the rudder control
was reasonably effective,
but Eddie was all out on the
controls—a very considerable
physical effort. Possibly awed
by Allen's reputation as a
test pilot, Ferguson just sat
there until Eddie yelled at
him to "get on the controls
with me!" They had been
heading north but gradually
made a large 180- degree turn, partly through
their own efforts, partly inadvertently, and saw
Lake Washington ahead. When power was
reduced for landing, the instability abated and

Fig. 10-3
In discussion with Bud Benton.

a successful landing was made. There is a classic
photograph of Eddie standing at the dock
and looking up at the single vertical tail. The
expression on his face says it all. Subsequently,

Fig. 10-4
L-R: Bud Benton, WFM talking with Evan Nelson (back).

As long as they were in contact with the water they provided hydrostatic and/or hydrodynamic roll control. In normal flight their contribution was additional wing area and extra usable space in the aircraft. Proving unsatisfactory on the first series prototype, the hydrostabilizers were modified by extending their span and their angular relationship to the hull. They still proved marginal in service, especially in low-speed taxiing in cross winds where large destabilizing moments from the high dihedral of the wing were present. Once, in Spain, the aircraft rolled in a strong wind until the main wing tip entered the water. The story we got, perhaps exaggerated, was that the water was shallow and the wing tip struck bottom, thus averting a complete rollover. PAA registered a strong complaint to Boeing for further investigation of this problem before delivery of the second series.

two additional fins and rudders were added. Vastly improved, the airplane still was far from ideal in rough air.

Most seaplanes of that era utilized wingtip floats to stabilize the aircraft in roll while on the water below the speed where aileron control was effective. The 314 was unique in utilizing "stub sea wings," officially called hydrostabilizers, projecting out from the hull below the main wing and near the waterline.

NACA Testing

Thus in August 1940, George Schairer and I departed for NACA's Langley Laboratory with a model of the 314 for towing tank tests. As head

Fig. 10-5
The A-314 with its two additional fins, and rudders mounted on ends of the horizontal stabilizer, 1940.

of aerodynamics in Allen's department, George had full responsibility for planning and supervising the test program. Once the test program was underway I was to stay on to complete the routine work. I had joined Boeing 11 months earlier and this was to be my first, but not my last, experience at NACA's towing tank.

The only practical way to get to Langley Field was to fly into Washington D.C. and take the overnight boat for Old Point Comfort on the north shore of Hampton Roads, opposite the site of the *Monitor*

Fig. 10-6
Model with extra fins and rudders in University of Washington wind tunnel, 1940.

and *Merrimac* encounter. Next to the dock the Chamberlain Hotel, with its palatial southern dining room, swimming pools and dance band on the top floor, was the center of social activity in the Hampton area. After checking in there, we rented a car and drove out to NACA headquarters.

Towing Tank No. 1 was about six feet in depth, twenty-four feet wide and several hundred feet long. It was the longest water test facility in the United States. A large, rubber-tired carriage ran over the tank on carefully leveled steel tracks. Electrically powered, it could reach speeds of more than 50 mph. The

Fig. 10-7
Showing the hydrostabilizer or sea wing for roll control on the water, 1940.

entire tank was covered by an unheated shed, with an office/setup building attached to one end. The models on test were suspended from this carriage on various balances, depending upon the type of test. A multiple-component force balance was used for measuring the water forces on hulls at various attitudes and levels of immersion. Another balance allowed a dynamic model freedom in heave and pitch for studying porpoising tendencies.

Director of the hydrodynamic test facility was Starr Truscott, a heavyset, somewhat

Fig. 10-8
Showing sea wing during taxi test at low speed, 1940.

Fig. 10-9
Taxi test at higher speed, 1940.

ponderous individual who reigned over the facility with a quiet, imperturbable authority. His appearance and demeanor fit the clipper ship sea captain mold, distinctly nautical as befitted the manager of a towing tank facility. Assisted by his easygoing and much younger assistant, Jack Parkinson, he ran a tight ship. I took a genuine liking to Truscott, who became almost a father figure to me. He recognized that after George left I would be taking on a substantial responsibility, for which I had little technical background. I kept Starr up to date on the progress of our tests, used his office to phone reports back to Boeing and frequently went to lunch with him in the NACA dining room. Socially, as a bachelor, I was adopted by Parkinson and his wife.

NACA LANGLEY'S REPORTS, notes and memoranda were the main source of aeronautical research in the United States. They were invaluable for the aircraft industry and for organizations involved in aeronautical education. For a few cents, all these documents were available from the Government Printing Office. I certainly availed myself of them often in the past, and was very excited when Truscott or Parkinson pointed out, or occasionally introduced me to, such highly respected researchers as Abe Silverstein, Fred Weick, Bob Gilruth, Theodore Theodorsen, Oscar Seidman, Hartley Soulé, Carl Wensinger, Ira

Abbott, John Stack and Karl Kaplan, among many others.

OUR 314 TEST PROGRAM was to measure and plot the contact of the bow wave in relation to the under-surface of the hydrostabilizer as a function of the scaled speed of the model. Schairer suspected, and the tests later proved, that in a certain range of taxiing speed the trough of the bow wave fell well below the lower surface of the hydrostabilizer, which then offered little resistance to roll. We towed the model at a series of constant speeds in the scaled-speed range where difficulty had been encountered full scale. Only low speeds were involved so aerodynamic forces were negligible, and we could assume that the attitude of the hull was determined by hydrodynamic effects alone. The speed control of the carriage was so satisfactory that the wave configuration remained steady, and a probe was used for direct measurement of the distance from the under-surface of the hydrostabilizer to the water. Measurements were taken in the chordwise direction of the stabilizer, and for at least two span-wise stations. The probe was a calibrated wire that passed through vertical holes in the stabilizer and down to the water. In running the tests, one lay on a platform beside the model close to the water surface, and manually adjusted the wire until the point just touched the surface. The distance then was read

Fig. 10-10
Model tests at NACA Langley showing sea wing largely out of water, bow high and bow wave low, 1940.

Fig. 10-11
Model test at NACA Langley, bow low and sea wing in the water, 1940.

and recorded. This laborious process had to be repeated hundreds of times to cover the speed range of interest. By the middle of September, being subjected to the spray while riding on the carriage in the unheated towing tank became a chilly affair. Winter flying suits were worn but we had to get along without gloves. I

worked in shifts with Parkinson and other tank technicians to get the job done.

Although long under the impression that a flap or other device might have been tested to improve the effectiveness of the hydrostablizer, a recent conversation with George convinced me that the principal result was to convince Pan American that sustained taxiing in the speed range where the hydrostabilizer was ineffective had to be avoided. The flight crews were so warned and trained.

At the completion of the test program I was sent to New York to report the results directly to PAA at their headquarters in the Chrysler Building. I met with Andre Priester and John Borger. Priester's reputation as a tough engineering administrator was known throughout the industry. My memory is that he minced no words. He listened to my report of the tank test and immediately called Boeing (probably Well Beall) to indicate his pleasure that the tank tests had been made, and said that PAA would initiate appropriate action based upon them.

RETURNING TO SEATTLE, I found much more interest in the towing tank test than I had expected. Invited to give a lecture to the Seattle section of the Institute of the Aeronautical Sciences on October 30, I accepted with considerable trepidation, but enjoyed it. Of course George was on hand. We had some good action movies of the test and a lively discussion afterwards.

Fig. 10-12
Announcement of lecture I gave in Seattle on our tests at Langley on A-314 in the towing tank, 1940.

Fig. 10-13
Preparing for test on Lake Washington, 1941.

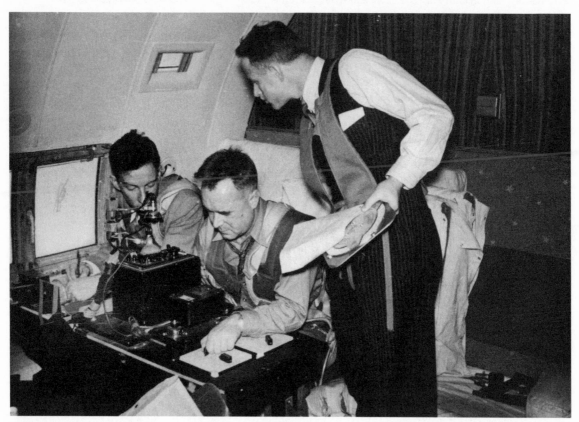

Fig. 10-14
Test station in main cabin with instrumentation. L-R: Bill Cook, Bob Patton and Al Reed (standing), 1941.

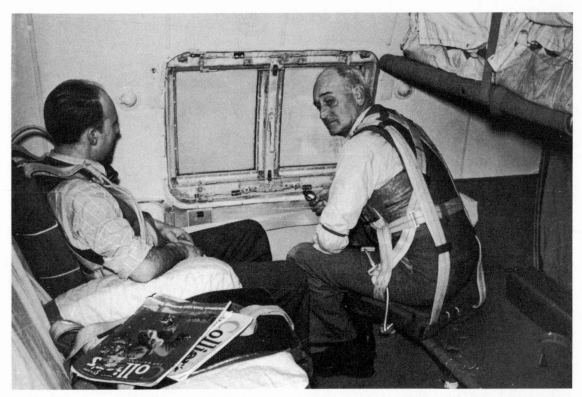

Fig. 10-15
Another test station with Messrs. Keeble and Hyde, instrumentation engineer and alternative co-pilot, 1941.

The flight test program of the second series began in January 1941. Like the first series, the seaplanes were built in Plant No. 1, then taken through the Duwamish Waterway into the Sound. Thunderstorms made getting the first of these aircraft out into Elliott Bay a hazardous operation, and maintenance crews stayed with the seaplane all night. My records show the first flight was made on January 15, followed by a second flight nine days later, with final flights of the last of the series in May and June. Each completed seaplane was flown to Lake Washington for our checkout and test program.

SEAPLANES ARE PRONE to two kinds of pitching oscillations: a low-angle wobble, uncomfortable but generally not serious, and a high-angle porpoising in which the aircraft can literally leap out of the water under hydrodynamic and aerodynamic forces. Porpoising can be quite serious. The phenomena had been investigated at Langley on a model of the 314. What happened depended on the depth and location of the main step on the hull, as well as the shape of the afterbottom. According to Schairer, the conclusion was if the water runs parallel to the afterbottom (at a certain attitude of the hull) the tail would be sucked down and the wing pitched up, creating enough aerodynamic lift to heave the seaplane out of the water. This obviously was very undesirable, especially so if it occurred on a landing attempt or in rough water. Moving the step aft had proved effective on the 314.

One of our tests to investigate porpoising was the measurement of pressure on the afterbottom behind the step. My task was to read and record the pressure gauge measurements on a high-attitude landing. I braced myself between the bulkheads and stringers on the floor, expecting a fairly rough ride. I was not disappointed. The noise and vibration when the hull struck the water were unbelievably severe, and for a moment I thought the structure was breaking up. I don't remember the recorded pressures, but acting on such a large area the total hull forces must have been enormous.

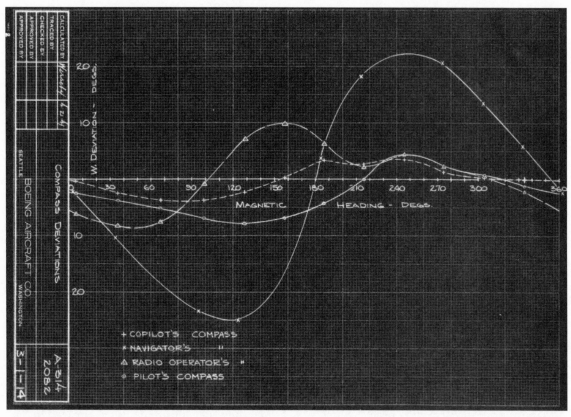

Fig. 10-16
Typical compass calibrations, A-314. The large deviations are due to magnetized steel wing spars, 1941.

Fig. 10-17
Eddie Allen crawling out of cockpit window to direct the mooring, 1941.

Fig. 10-18
Takeoff, sea wings and forward hull well clear of the water, 1941.

Another task performed on each A-314 was running a flight calibration of the master compass. The compasses were exposed to large deviations from the steel wing beams, which were magnetized in the earth's magnetic field during the construction process. Ed Wersebe of the Flight Division devised a shadow pin technique. Uncalibrated, the errors were huge.

As the tests were completed, we flew each 314 to Astoria, Oregon, near the outlet of the Columbia River, where it was officially delivered to a PAA crew. This was an enjoyable exercise.

ONE WEEKEND Capt. Harold Gray, chief pilot of PAA's Atlantic Division, showed up in Seattle. Although officially his visit was to check out the delivery schedule, he obviously was anxious to fly the A-314. As a prominent pilot and customer representative, his opinion of the second series airplane was important. Eddie organized a Saturday night dinner party for him at the Olympic Hotel, which several engineers and pilots from our Flight Section attended. Gray fit perfectly into the ideal pilot mold; articulate and friendly, he created a relaxed atmosphere for an evening filled with stories of flying adventures and close shaves.

On Sunday, a glorious day in Seattle, we met at the lake with a small crew. After making some high-speed taxi runs to check out general behavior on the water, Gray took off and explored the aircraft flight characteristics, including stall approaches, then engaged in a series of landings, takeoffs, tight circles, landings and so on. His performance was inspiring. Every landing, and Gray must have made a dozen of them, was perfectly executed and seemingly effortless. I stood behind him, fascinated. As he slowly came back on the yoke, at just the right height and airspeed, the big bird would swoosh onto the water with a smooth transition of the load from the wing to the hull.

On a future visit to PAA in New York, Harold invited me to dinner at his home on Long Island. I remember the occasion for the congeniality of his wife and the architecture of his home, distinctly modern by standards with which I was familiar. Harold Gray went on to become head of the Atlantic Division, and finally CEO and chairman of Pan American.

THE 314 CLIPPER, with its 3,500-mile range, had an excellent record during the war. Several were operated by the British. One PAA Clipper was over the Pacific at the time of Pearl Harbor. To avoid contact with the Japanese, it worked its way back to the East Coast via Australia, New Zealand, India, Africa

Fig. 10-19
A-314 in service, flying over Washington (Washington Monument on the left), 1941.

Fig. 10-20
XPBB-1, prototype Navy patrol boat. It featured a sharp bow, deep step and large vertical tail, with remarkable handling in flight and on the water, 1941.

and the South Atlantic to Natal and finally to New York, a distance of nearly 30,000 miles. Clippers also participated in getting American expatriates out of France when Germany invaded. Anaïs Nin writes of the flight in her famous diary.

Based on experience with the 314 Clipper, Boeing bid for and won a Navy contract for a twin-engine patrol flying boat, the XPBB-1, which was launched in July 1942. It had been thoroughly tank and wind tunnel tested at model scale. Its features were wingtip floats

Fig. 10-21
XPBB-1 on takeoff, 1941.

(instead of hydrostabilizers), a very deep step, sharp bow (underbody entrance) and a very large vertical tail. Its water and flight characteristics were so ideal that no faults were noted on the first flight and we went right into our long-range test plan. This accomplishment must be credited to George Schairer. However the Navy was committed to PBYs, and XPBB-1 never went into production.

Because of my fascination with the early pioneering flights, I never have been able to empathize with flying the ocean in a jet, as efficient and convenient as the trip might be. Cruising at 40,000 feet, largely isolated from the weather and from the ocean, assisted by electronic aids that eliminate navigational uncertainly and with jet engines of unimaginable reliability, the risk and the challenge are largely gone. In a sense it is like climbing the Matterhorn with fixed ropes. The biggest thrill I've yet experienced on a transatlantic jet was an approach to Kennedy during which the pilot announced, "We are now over the site of Roosevelt Field, where it all started." As a romantic, I empathized with the 314 Clipper, the first step in the commercialization of the oceanic routes. With this airplane, I could sense ancestral roots. Unpressurized, frequently flying close to the ocean, powered by piston engines, cruising at 180 mph, subjected to the storms and vagaries of the weather, and dependent on piloting skills and the uncertainties of celestial navigation—many elements of the great pioneering flights remained. I am eternally grateful to have crossed paths with the second series of that great flying boat.

Chapter 11 🦅

Higher than Everest

According to the Flight Plan, the aircraft was in a heavy-load condition with CG well aft. As we approached for landing, I watched Allen carefully—would he put her down three-point or grease her in wheels first? Throttled back but by no means dead stick, we were heading directly for the end of the runway when, only a few feet up, he initiated the flare, forcefully hauling back on the wheel with both hands. With perfect timing, he was about make an ideal three-pointer. At that point I observed a curious phenomenon. Although he was pulling back as hard as he could on the control wheel column, it was, in fact, slowly moving forward. What I was seeing was a classic example of "fixed or position" control longitudinal instability with "free or force" control stability. Once the flare was initiated it increased by itself, taking less and less elevator to trim at the increasing angle of attack, while the control forces still were building up. The pilot was completely unaware of all this, demonstrating again that control force—i.e., feel—is his primary cue.

On this B-17B, one of the early models of this famous series, the pilot's control first actuated the servo tab on the elevator, after which his applied force went directly to the elevator. In the situation described he had run out of tab control.

This was my first flight on a B-17, which probably took place in early 1940 a few months after my arrival at Boeing. From then on I became heavily involved in the continuous flight development program of models B through G, which continued to the end of the war in Europe. The Stratoliner, the A-314 and XPBB-1 flying boats made for exciting interludes in our testing activities, but were of limited priority and extent compared to the ongoing B-17 development. Until the B-29 came along the B-17 consumed most of our energy.

**Boarding through the cockpit door, 1941.
L-R. Al Reed, Dick McGline, Bill Milliken.**

"One finds a stimulation here unknown elsewhere—a world not of land and sea but of crystal air and sky and space."

– Richard Halliburton
(*The Royal Road to Romance*)

Dr. Theodore von Karman

One memorable flight on B-17C No. 1 took place in the summer of 1940. For some time the Tacoma Narrows Bridge had been acquiring a reputation for disturbing motions of its roadway. These were noticed by many users and led to the nickname of "Galloping Gertie." The bridge design was characterized by its long, narrow center span and shallow roadway. On this day a strong wind of about 40 mph was blowing through the narrows between the Olympic Peninsula and the mainland, west of Tacoma. Before takeoff, word reached us that the bridge had been undergoing some phenomenal excursions and traffic had been stopped. The large vertical and torsional motions of the roadway could clearly be seen. We circled several times, and then saw the bridge disintegrate, with major sections breaking loose and falling away. The event led to my introduction to Dr. Theodore von Karman of Cal Tech.

A few weeks after the collapse, Eddie announced that von Karman, an old friend of his, planned to visit Seattle. Even in those days von Karman was a notable figure in aeronautics, and Eddie made plans to entertain him, inviting several of us to dinner at a genuine German *rathskeller*. During dinner von Karman gave his analysis of the bridge failure. He said it was similar to wing flutter, where the twisting of the wing induced lift forces that coupled into bending, producing an oscillation of increasing amplitude and eventual structural failure. My recollection is that by using dimensionless analysis, von Karman was able to identify the wind velocity for catastrophic "flutter" of the bridge, using the general wing flutter diagram. Having analyzed the problem, he came up with a variety of corrections, some structural and some aerodynamic, that since have been applied to other suspension bridges.

Von Karman's long life was characterized by notable scientific, educational and organizational achievements. As a teacher at Cal Tech he was second to none. He was one of the creators of Aerojet and rocket technology, became Chief Scientist of the U.S. Army Air Force, and initiated AGARD—an international organization for aeronautical research and development centered in Paris. Although my contacts with him were casual, I remember attending a major international aeronautical meeting in Rome in which he took a group of us to the audience he had with Pope Pius XII. We stood around in an anteroom as His Holiness talked briefly to each of us in our own language, after which he gave us each a medal he had blessed. Speaking with an engineer from Turkey (a devout Catholic), the Pope passed on without presenting him with a medal—purely an oversight. The Turk exhibited concern, and finally blurted out, "You forgot to give me a medal!" The Pope turned around, and with a magnificent smile said, "For that, my good man, you shall have two!"

B-17 Origins

The prototype B-17, Boeing model 299, had flown some four years before the start of World War II in Europe. As background for my B-17 experiences, the following history of the type is abstracted from Tom Collison's *Flying Fortress* and other definitive sources. Collison points out that Boeing had prior experience in the construction of all-metal, low-wing monoplanes with retractable landing gear including the single Monomail prototype, the B-9 bomber, and the 247D transport. Furthermore, Boeing was involved in a three-year design/construction contract for the XB-15, a very large, one-of-a-kind, four-engine bomber for the Army Air Corps. The XB-15 made its initial flight on October 15, 1937. Three-engine high wing monoplanes, such as the Fokker and Ford/Stout, had been around since the twenties, but the XB-15 was an early example of a four-engine, low-wing type.

Thus Boeing's bid in the Army Air Corps high-performance bomber competition was for a lowwing, all-metal, four-engine bomber.

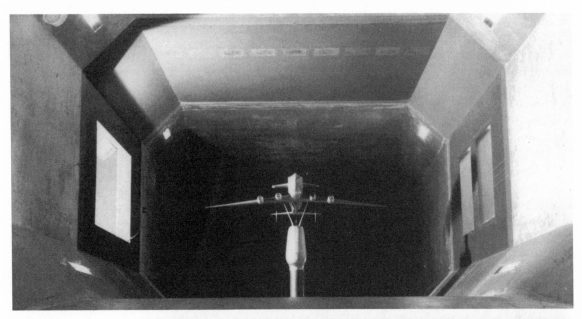

Fig. 11-1a,b,c
The Boeing Model 299, the prototype of the B-17, was extensively tested in the atmospheric wind tunnel at the University of Washington. It had relatively small tail surfaces and used tab control to move the surfaces.

211

Its competitors' bids were for twin-engine aircraft.

Boeing's greatest successes also have been its greatest gambles, and the 299 was no exception. The 299 stretched Boeing's financial stability, but it was a terrific airplane. It first flew on July 28, 1935, and less than a month later set a record on a non-stop flight from Seattle to Wright Field in Dayton, Ohio.

For years, Air Corps pioneers Billy Mitchell, Generals "Hap" Arnold, Carl "Tooey" Spaatz, and Ira Eaker had been promoting a philosophy of high-altitude daylight bombing. Potentially the B-17 could become the chosen instrument, but this achievement was in the future when the 299 landed in Dayton. Progress came to a temporary halt two months later when the 299 was demolished in a crash on takeoff. The elevator "gust lock" was on, a pure pilot oversight. The following is a brief summary of the B-17 saga prior to my arrival at Boeing:

Y1B-17—In January 1936, 13 aircraft were ordered for service test. Capt. John Corkille (whom I later would meet and fly with) was assigned by the Army Air Corps to flight check each one coming off the line (July 1936 to March 1937). Twelve were used for training at the Langley Field Air Force Base, while one stayed at Wright Field. Colonel Olds used Y1B-17s in his goodwill flight to Argentina in February 1938, and two of them broke the non-stop transcontinental record.

Y1B-17A—There was only one with this designation, used at Wright Field for a highly significant development. Initially intended for static test, it wound up as the test bed for the GE turbocharger installation, the key to the B-17's high-altitude performance. The B-17B and all subsequent types were turbocharged.

B-17B—In November 1937 a production order for 39 aircraft was placed with Boeing. The first one was flown by Corkille on June 27, 1939, and delivered to the Air Corps two days later. Numerous records fell to the B-17Bs, including load, speed and altitude.

B-17C—In the fall of 1939 an order for 38 aircraft was placed for delivery in 1940. It was evident by then that the USA might be drawn into the conflict in Europe. Flown by the British, the B-17C was the first to see action over Europe. The results were devastating, and revealed several shortcomings in aircraft performance and armament.

B-17D—A major order for B-17Ds was received in early 1940. All of the models through the B-17D had the original small vertical tail, servo tab operated tail surfaces, no top or tail turrets, .30 caliber machine guns and minimum armor plate protection for the crews.

B-17E—The British experience with the B-17C led to a major improvement program, initiated by the Air Force at Boeing. The E had a much larger vertical tail, designed in Schairer's aerodynamic section and based on wind tunnel tests. The servo tabs were eliminated and replaced by aerodynamically balanced surfaces. The vertical tail was extended into a long dorsal fin for coping with the high yaw angles that could be encountered in engine-out situations. The vertical tail was reminiscent of that of the improved Stratoliner. Other changes to the E included more firepower (tail, top and bottom turrets) and armor protection for the crew. It was a heavier aircraft. Many more changes occurred in the F and G models (the latter added a chin turret), but the basic configuration of the E remained to the end of the war.

The original 299 was powered by Pratt & Whitney R-1690 engines of 750 hp, but all of the B-17s were powered by versions of Wright R-1820 radials. The R-1820-39 G-series engines, rated at 930 hp, were used on the YB-17. The Y1B-17A turbocharged version, B-17B and early C and D models had R-1820-51 engines rated at 1000 hp, while subsequent B-17 models C through E were variously equipped with by R-1820-65, -73, and -91 engines rated at 1,200 hp. B-17F, G and H used 1,200 hp R-1820-97 engines, and a small number of B-17H were equipped with R-1820-93 engines rated at 1350 hp.[1]

---

[1] *The writer is indebted to Graham White's* Allied Aircraft Piston Engines of World War II *for this summary of B-17 engines.*

Fig. 11-2
B-17E flying over Seattle, circa 1940. "X" marks the site of the Olympic Hotel, my unofficial headquarters. The aerodynamic configuration of the Model E remained to the end of the war.

Our Objective

While the modifications to the E and subsequent models required many hours of development and proving flights, they did not define the major task confronting our Flight Test Section. That was made clear in a meeting in Eddie Allen's office early in April of 1940.

Allen pointed out that although the Y1B-17A (the test bed for the GE turbochargers) had indeed reached nearly 35,000 feet during a development flight, subsequent B-17 operation had been confined to altitudes of generally less than 15,000 feet. The production aircraft were not capable of reliable, routine operation at 35,000 feet. The Air Corps needed that capability for daylight bombing, and Boeing was charged with achieving it. Specifically, Reed was told to find out what the problems were and work with Boeing Engineering and our suppliers to overcome them. In short, make the B-17 a serviceable operational aircraft at 35,000 feet.

The approach was clear enough to us—take a B-17 and start climbing until one system or another acted up, then take it from there. But

first we had to learn how to live and work at high altitude. The B-17 was unpressurized, and we knew nothing at all about the use of oxygen or the aircraft heating system.

Mayo Clinic

Research soon led us to a paper by Drs. Boothby, Lovelace and Bulbulian of the Mayo Clinic, who had developed the BLB oxygen mask for emergency use by airline pilots. This mask featured a rebreather bag that collected the high-oxygen content of initial exhaled breath for reuse on the next breath, thus conserving oxygen. Their conclusions, based on test subjects in pressure-chamber tests, indicated that it is not the absolute oxygen content in the air, but the partial pressure of oxygen in the lungs, that counts. When breathing air at sea level, oxygen contributes about 21 percent partial pressure; when breathing pure oxygen at a simulated 35,000 feet altitude, the oxygen partial pressure is comparable. Figure 11-3, redrawn in 1941 from the Mayo Clinic data by Ken Luplow, one of our flight engineers, shows the alveolar oxygen tension (i.e.,

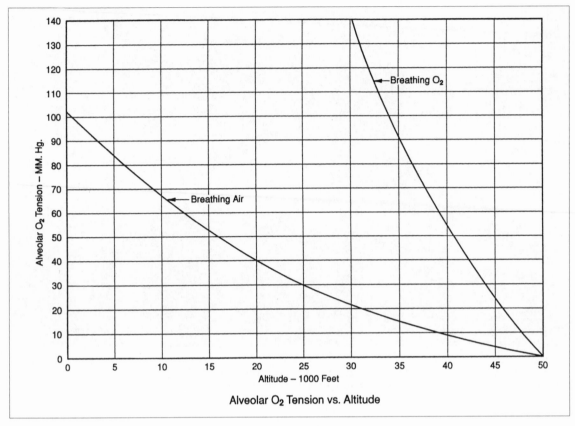

Alveolar O$_2$ Tension vs. Altitude

Fig. 11-3
This set of curves was abstracted from a paper by Boothby, Lovelace and Bulbulian, all of the Mayo Clinic, who developed the BLB oxygen mask. It shows the partial pressure of oxygen in the lungs when breathing air and when breathing pure oxygen. The key to survival at altitude is the partial pressure of oxygen. These curves show that on pure oxygen the partial pressure at 34000 feet equals that of breathing air at sea level. Unlike some reports, breathing pure oxygen is healthy. If our pilots had a hangover (for any reason) we'd put them on oxygen for half an hour and they were back in business!

partial pressure) in millimeters of mercury for breathing air and pure oxygen. It shows that the sea-level partial pressure in air can be achieved by pure oxygen at close to 34,000 feet.

By late April, Reed and I were on our way to the Mayo Clinic to get checked out in its pressure chamber and learn all we could about the use of oxygen. Upon arrival, we met with the group that developed the BLB mask. Walter Boothby, a distinguished physiologist, was the senior member of the team. His theoretical and experimental research provided the foundation for their developments. Dr. Randolph (Randy) Lovelace was equally comfortable in medical, military, government and engineering circles and I sensed immediately that he was the entrepreneurial leader of the group. The first head of the Aeromedical Laboratory at Wright Field, he later established the Lovelace Clinic in

New Mexico, where he was a prominent adviser to the NASA space program. Dr. Bulbulian, who completed the BLB trio, was a quiet, unpretentious professional medical technician whose expertise was essential in the fabrication of the prototype masks.

This was an exciting atmosphere. Recognized as a center of know-how for high-altitude operation, the Mayo Clinic attracted a diverse group of individuals from mountain climbers to aviators. At a cocktail party at Boothby's home on the evening of our arrival, I was hobnobbing with some military reps from Wright Field when Lovelace walked in with aviatrix Jackie Cochran on his arm.

The next day I received a substantial briefing, then moved to the pressure chamber. It was a steel tank, perhaps six feet in diameter and eight feet long with conical ends, one of which had a small pressure-tight hatch. Randy directed the proceedings, "To avoid any symptoms of the bends, we'll put you on pure oxygen for 20 minutes before getting into the chamber. By reducing the nitrogen in the blood an aeroembolism can be avoided." In due time I crawled through the hatch, reconnecting my mask to the farther regulator. A medical technician joined me on the bench seat, hooked up his oxygen regulator, and the hatch was closed. I noticed there were standby masks for both of us. An intercom provided communication between the subject, the technician and the outside world. Peering thorough a small window on the wall opposite me, Randy announced, "Well, here we go. We'll climb at about 1,000 feet per minute to 25,000 feet with a brief stop at 15,000." In my experience with Lovelace, I was to find him conservative in his concern for the individual undergoing training.

At 15,000 feet Randy's voice came through again, "Take the mask off for a while and see how you feel." My only symptom after several minutes was slight nausea. Handwriting on a pad seemed normal. At 25,000 feet useful consciousness without oxygen is reduced to a few minutes for average individuals. In my case, removing the mask resulted in a tendency toward deep breathing and a feeling of anxiety, both of which disappeared when back on oxygen. "Now we'll go to 30,000 feet and practice some emergency procedures. First remove your mask, then locate the standby mask and put it on. Be deliberate, you have a good minute to accomplish it." This proved to be easy. The next exercise was more difficult. My companion removed his mask and just sat there. The idea was to observe his plight, grab his standby mask, place it on his face (ensuring a good fit and headband adjustment) and then check the setting of his oxygen regulator. "Avoid haste and nervousness. Breathe

Fig. 11-4
Jackie Cochran and her husband, Floyd Odlum, circa 1940. Cochran directed WASP (Women's Airforce Service Pilots program) during the war. She was a Harmon Trophy winner and probably our greatest woman pilot, with numerous race wins and records, including supersonic ones.

normally. Don't lose your own oxygen supply by accidentally yanking the tube off the regulator," Lovelace counseled. Then we repeated the procedures at 35,000 feet.

On subsequent days we made further ascents and practiced a bailout from 35,000 feet by switching from the regular mask to a mouthpiece attached to a bailout bottle carried on the subject's suit. The bailout bottle then had to be turned on. In theory a regular mask would blow off in a free fall, while a mouthpiece might survive. I always wondered if I would breathe through my mouth in a real event.

To experience the feeling of anoxia, we removed our masks at various altitudes for brief periods, noting symptoms such as lack of coordination, degradation in handwriting and

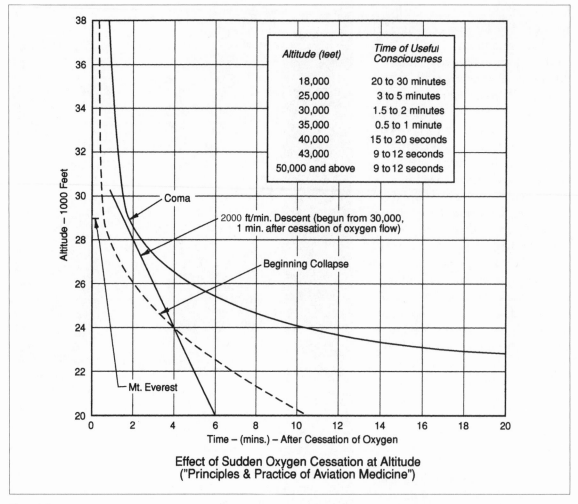

Altitude (feet)	Time of Useful Consciousness
18,000	20 to 30 minutes
25,000	3 to 5 minutes
30,000	1.5 to 2 minutes
35,000	0.5 to 1 minute
40,000	15 to 20 seconds
43,000	9 to 12 seconds
50,000 and above	9 to 12 seconds

Effect of Sudden Oxygen Cessation at Altitude
("Principles & Practice of Aviation Medicine")

Fig. 11-5
At 35,000 feet one has about a minute's worth of consciousness after loss of oxygen. For that reason we always paired off crew members and had standby oxygen masks with full flow of oxygen. We carried a huge supply of oxygen at high pressure in the bomb bay. There were plenty of occasions when this policy paid off.

bluing of the nails. People respond differently to oxygen deprivation.

On one occasion I actually passed out in flight at about 16,000 feet, but have no idea of how long my oxygen tube had been disconnected from the regulator.

Oxygen Policy

The training at Mayo was invaluable. Even at that stage Al and I realized that sooner or later we would need additional flight crews to keep up with the B-17 activity. We decided to promote a pressure chamber at Boeing and establish an oxygen use policy for high-altitude operation, one that would ensure crew safety and effectiveness. The general elements of this conservative policy were:

- Exercise on pure oxygen before a flight.
- Avoid the bends, or symptoms thereof, through denitrogenation.
- Avoid gradual performance degradation, and maintain mental alertness, by the use of oxygen even at lower altitudes.
- Provide standby oxygen masks in each compartment, with full flow of oxygen.
- Provide all crew members with bailout oxygen equipment.
- Use the pressure chamber to train all crew members in proper use of oxygen equipment and in emergency procedures.

Learning from the Mountains

The Mayo experience interested me in the use of oxygen by mountain climbers. At the time of our B-17 high-altitude development, Mt. Everest had yet to be climbed, and it was easy to speculate that advances in oxygen equipment during the war could facilitate that accomplishment.

The oxygen problem for climbers is quite different from that of aviators. Although a climber is not exposed to bends from rapid ascents, and has the possibility of acclimatization, he does have to carry his own oxygen supply.

The earliest use of oxygen on Everest was during the British Expedition of Finch and Bruce in 1922. Prior to leaving England, Finch had been tested in a pressure chamber.

At 28,873 feet simulated altitude without oxygen he was barely conscious, with a rapid heartbeat and pounding in the head. After taking oxygen orally through a tube, he felt fine at 27,889 feet, and "survived" to 29,857 feet. Thus he was convinced of oxygen's virtues. The equipment he took to Everest consisted of four oxygen cylinders attached to a light frame slung on the back. They weighed 44 pounds. With oxygen at 1,700 psi, and using an oral-nasal mask, Finch and Bruce made a surprisingly rapid ascent to 27,300 feet from about 25,500 feet. They also reached to 27,000 feet without oxygen, by which time they were nauseated and severely cold.

In the British Expedition of 1924, Norton and Somervell established a record for ascent without oxygen that was to stand until 1978. Together they reached 28,125 feet, and Norton continued on alone for another 600 feet. They felt they had reached "the physical limit of the world." The same year, Mallory and Irvine used oxygen equipment weighing 27 pounds, a considerable improvement over Finch's 1922 equipment. They were last sighted moving at a respectable pace at an estimated altitude of 28,200 feet. Then they vanished. In 1933 Harris and Wager discovered an ice axe at 27,725 feet, under the "first step," that only could have belonged to Mallory or Irvine. Conjecture that this was the site of a fatal accident was dispelled when Mallory's body was found elsewhere in 1999. Now the question is whether they reached the top.

Two decades later, on May 29, 1953, New Zealand beekeeper Edmund Hillary and Sherpa Tenzing Norgay, using much-improved oxygen equipment, reached the summit of Everest for the first time. Interestingly, some subsequent climbers, notably Reinhold Messner, objected to the use of oxygen on philosophical grounds, believing reliance should be placed solely on one's own capabilities. Following experimentation over a period of years in acclimatization and rates of deterioration, Messner and Habeler climbed Everest by the South Col route without oxygen in 1978. Two years later, Messner climbed Everest solo via the North Col/North Face route. Bivouacking at 25,590 and 26,900 feet, he reached the top near collapse, but after an hour started the descent and made it safely down. Since then more than 60 people have climbed Everest without oxygen.

Fig. 11-6
Bailout oxygen, 1940. A small bottle of oxygen at high pressure was attached to the uniform. It used a mouthpiece because that was thought more likely to survive a parachute descent.

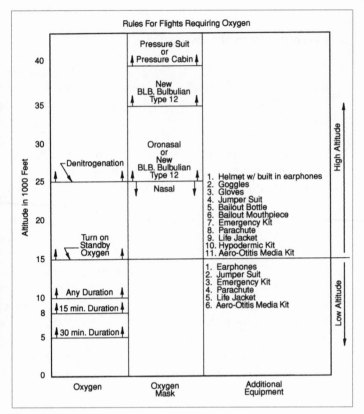

Fig. 11-7
Rules for Flights Requiring Oxygen, illustrated in this figure and the next. We defined anything up to 15,000 feet as low altitude, and anything above that as high altitude. We stuck to these rules religiously.

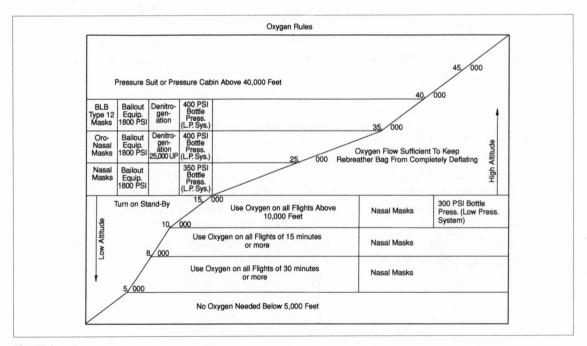

Fig. 11-8
Another depiction of our oxygen rules.

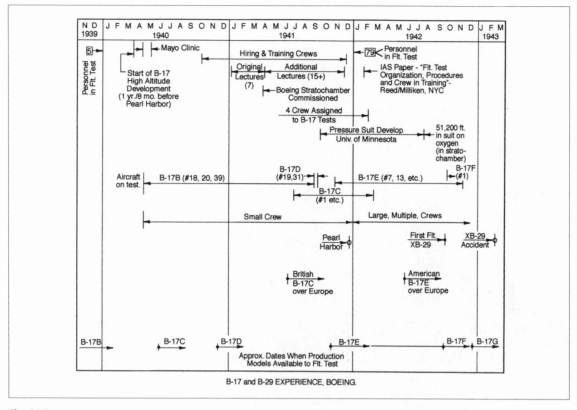

Fig. 11-9
Timeline of our B-17 (and B-29) development testing, which involved numerous B-17 models with minimum and large crews. It shows the test sequence from B-17B through to B-17G.

To implement this policy we installed large commercial oxygen bottles in the bomb bay. We had enough high-pressure oxygen to afford to be lavish and have the regulators of the standby masks turned full on. In an emergency one could slap on a standby mask and have oxygen immediately. There are situations at high altitude where one has used up a good part of his "time of useful consciousness" before he or his companion detects trouble. Therefore time is of the essence. Figures 11-7 and 11-8 indicate the developed policy.

All commercial and most military aircraft are now pressurized, and oxygen equipment is available only for rare emergency use. Even homebuilt planes are being pressurized, so mountaineers and flyers no longer are totally dependent on oxygen. Such is progress.

In retrospect, our oxygen experience in the B-17 program is somewhat unique, occurring in that historical wartime window when high altitude bombing was totally dependent on the use of oxygen.

B-17 High-Altitude Flight Crew Development

Upon our return from the Mayo Clinic in May 1940, an intensive B-17 high-altitude program began, 18 months before Pearl Harbor. This program would continue until the advent of the XB-29 in late 1942. The small B-17 crews were made up of original members from Reed's Flight Test department. Allen was the pilot on these flights, Reed was co-pilot, and I was chief flight test engineer. Frequently joining us were Ed Wersebe and Chuck Blaine from Flight Test, and Orin Johnston and others from Fred Wood's instrumentation section.

It was almost immediately apparent that we would need four or five B-17s on test simultaneously, with crews of as many as ten

Fig. 11-10
Al Reed, chief of flight test and chief pilot, right, and WFM as chief flight test engineer and assistant head of flight test, circa 1940. The airplane in the background is B-17C, No. 1.

time being of the essence, we were forced to lower the university educational standards and do our own specialized training.

The final group of 24 junior flight-test engineers, was largely recruited from undergraduates at the University of Washington, who had two years of college engineering training, some private flying experience such as primary or secondary CPT (Civilian Pilot Training), some shop or hands-on mechanic training and were 25 years or younger, and single.

It was a good bargain for them, because if they were not employed in a defense industry these young men were prime targets for the draft. Furthermore, flight testing has an aura of adventure and risk that many found hard to resist.

Our specialized training took place in a downtown hotel. The basic series of lectures proved so successful that we later developed a further 20. Subjects covered include flight planning procedures, manual flight recording, flight photo recorders, operation of potentiometers in flight, manometers and pressure measurements, power plant testing, turbocharging, elements of aerodynamics, high-altitude physiology, oxygen equipment and use, bailout from high altitude and familiarization with B-17E systems.

THROUGHOUT THIS RECRUITMENT/training effort I was enthusiastically assisted by Bill Talbott, chief administrative assistant and head of our secretarial and stenographic group. His office was next to mine in the new Boeing Engineering Building. Bill helped defuse the pressure under which we were all working by a variety of amusing and distracting antics. One morning he insisted I reverse the procedure for tying my four-in-hand necktie. With some effort I learned his proposed technique, and have been stuck with it ever since. On another

engineers per airplane. I was assigned to plan and carry out the recruitment and training program, which would include oxygen training in the Boeing Stratochamber which would be commissioned early in 1941.

OUR FIRST THOUGHT was that engineering schools should establish a course option aimed at meeting the need for junior flight-test engineers. This would include training in the theory of aircraft performance and stability, control testing, power plant and aircraft instrumentation, some actual flying experience, etc. A survey indicated some interest, but universities had a limited conception of how flight testing was carried out in industry. With

Fig. 11-11
Early in the B-17 flight test program we had little instrumentation, and flew with a minimum crew. In this picture Eddie Allen was first pilot (on left) and Al Reed was co-pilot. I am recording some 30 instrument readings every minute in this rated power climb without use of oxygen. We still were trying to get to 15,000 ft. without experiencing engine or propeller problems.

occasion he promoted the idea that "survival" depended upon one's ability to break out of well-developed habits. For example, could we spend one day at the office and never take a step forward, which was difficult to accomplish while attempting to appear natural to our associates.

On another morning I glanced through the glass that divided our offices and saw Talbott interviewing an absolutely gorgeous blonde. I picked up the phone, "Talbott, just hire her." He looked back with an "Oh-no" expression, imperceptibly moving his head from side to side. Exasperated, I suggested that his job was

Abnormally High Forces

Even using low-temperature grease, the effects of low temperature on the long cable runs resulted in stiff-feeling flight controls. The pilots complained that the problem never was completely solved. One B-17E on long-term test assignment had abnormally high aileron forces. One day, after some 40 hours of flying, the controls suddenly loosened up and remained so. The mystery was solved when, for an unrelated reason (possibly due to fuel leakage), the wing was opened up. A 12-foot plank used by the fabricator to back up the rivets had been left in the wing and lay on top of an aileron cable until the cable sawed its way through it.

on the line. He threw up his hands, hired her, and assigned her to me. From a well-to-do socialite family in Seattle, she wanted to contribute to the war effort after receiving minimal stenographic training. Gorgeous and friendly she was, but helpless as a secretary. We knew we had to discharge her, but neither of us could muster the courage. Fortunately she attracted a steady parade of young engineers from the department, among them a young lieutenant on loan from the Navy office who, following a rapid courtship, married her.

By January 1942 the Flight Test section had grown to nearly 80 people including, of course, an expansion of the instrumentation group under Fred Woods, and an analysis group under Sid Silber. Specific positions are listed on page 245.

The B-17E had come on line, and much of our test work was being done on that model. Junior flight engineers were assigned to four crews as indicated in Table 11-1.

We also had engineers Steve Umpleby and Vince North, and pilots Bob Lamson and Bob Robbins.

Several of these young engineers would have outstanding careers at Boeing, among them Jack Steiner, Ken Luplow, Jim Fraser, Marvin Michael, Lamson, and Robbins. Steiner

Fig. 11-12
The "morning meeting" to discuss flight plans for the day. Depending on the test schedule, the meeting could involve a sizable number of crew members.

was intimately associated with the 727 from inception to production, and later became vice-president of product development in the Transport Division, where he made major contributions to the 737 and 747 programs. Ken Luplow wound up in technical sales, and was involved in the 707 European promotion effort. He later became director of international affairs (in sales). Lamson, Robbins and Fraser became senior test pilots, with careers extending from B-17 to B-47. Incidentally, Jim was the co-pilot on the B-17 flight in which Randy Lovelace made his parachute jump from 40,000 feet. Michael made a career in production and test piloting.

Table 11-1. B-17E Flight Test Crew Roster

	Crew 1	*Crew 2*	*Crew 3*	*Crew 4*
Crew Leader	Wersebe*	Michael	Blaine*	Steiner
Asst. Crew Leader	Luplow	Bradley	Whitworth	Gius
Jr. Flt. Engineer	Stolz	Leonard	Strom	Erchinger
"	R. Bennett	Schutt	Shemet	Olason
"	Nelson	Smith	Maxfield*	O'Leary
"	Hungerford	Webber	L. Bennett	Lake
"	Basel*	Bertagna	Zerega	Fraser

*Killed in the XB-29 accident of February 18, 1942; see Chapter 13.

Up and Up

The B-17 high-altitude development was intense, exciting and satisfying. Nearly every flight was marked by some unique event—a mechanical failure, an oxygen incident or some crazy, unexpected, frequently humorous happening. But despite these incidents we kept pushing up the reliable operational altitude.

Solutions to airframe and engine problems, experienced and documented by our crews, led to wide-ranging responses by Boeing engineering and by suppliers. On many flights representatives of Wright Aeronautical, General Electric, AirResearch, Hamilton Standard, etc., were on board as crew members.

The low temperatures (ca. –40 degrees F/C) at altitude pointed up a number of challenging problems. Engine oil congealed in exposed places like the propeller dome, which reduced feathering control, and in the oil coolers, which starved the engine and raised operating temperature. Flight and engine controls became very stiff, the airframe and instrument pickups iced, wing flaps, rudder and bomb bay doors malfunctioned and the cabin heating/defrosting system was overwhelmed. The low static air pressure led to shorts in the ignition system, carburetor malfunction and turbocharger overspeeding.

Fig. 11-13
Instrument panel in the pilot's compartment.

Memorable Flight Experiences in the B-17

An early B-17B flight in the summer of 1940 began well. We had our minimum crew (Allen, Reed and me) and were climbing steadily at rated power. The weather was propitious, the remains of some stratus clouds surrounding Mr. Rainier far below and only a hint of cirrus clouds drifting by above. I was perched on a jury seat behind the control console, with a large aluminum data board on my lap and a stopwatch in my left hand. Each minute I recorded some 30 instrument readings on flight and engine operating conditions—altitude, indicated airspeed, outside air temperature and (for all four engines) manifold air pressure, RPM, BMEP (Brake Mean Effective Pressure), fuel pressure, fuel/air ratio, oil pressure, oil temperature, cylinder head temperature, turbo rpm, and so forth.

As I made the rounds, I was pleased to note our passing the 20,000-foot mark, the first time we had approached that altitude without some system problem. A few minutes later, as if the thought had fathered the event, the turbo on No. 3 inboard engine went into violent overspeed, the result of malfunction of the waste gate control.

Almost immediately the exhaust turbine wheel disintegrated, spewing its buckets like shrapnel, horizontally in all directions. The bottom of the nacelle was leveled off as if by a buzzsaw, and stray buckets penetrated the fuselage and even the horizontal tail. The

223

wheel hub and rim separated into segments, one cutting a clean rectangular slot some 4.5 by 1.5 inches out of a propeller blade on No. 3 engine. Fortunately, the slot started at the trailing edge of the blade, or we surely would have lost the propeller. Had that happened, we probably would have lost the engine because of the ensuing imbalance. When the propeller was shipped back to East Hartford, Hamilton Standard engineers were astounded that the blade was in one piece, and considered it to be an example of the "impregnability" of their products. I had an emotional retake some months later when I visited the company and saw it exhibited in their lobby.

Turbo overspeed failure is as close to machine gun fire as I ever hope to get. There is no warning before the shattering, tearing noise as the buckets rip into the structure, and engine power is rapidly lost as the manifold pressure drops to near ambient for that altitude. In the course of our B-17 program we had four or five overspeed failures. One never got used to them. My instinctive reaction was to pull in my shoulders and duck. I must say, however, that turbine failure is an impressive demonstration of how critical that unit is to the B-17 performance at altitude. When the wheel goes, the engine power goes to hell with it.

Oil congealing at the low temperatures of high altitude was another problem that was not easily resolved. It was especially troublesome in the propeller pitch control, and in the functioning of the engine oil coolers. The pitch of the hydraulically controlled Hamilton Standard propeller was mechanically adjusted by the movement of a piston in the dome on the hub, which in turn was activated by oil pressure. Oil not circulated by frequent pitch changes could congeal in the dome, pitch regulation would be lost and the propeller would go to the flat-pitch stop. The ability to feather the propeller also might be lost due to the solid plug of congealed oil in the dome.

ON A FLIGHT IN MID-1941, again with our minimum crew, we had worked our way up to over 30,000 feet. The outside air temperature that day was close to the magic –40 degrees F/C.[2] With little warning the propeller on an inboard engine went into flat pitch. The pilots did the right thing, quickly throttling back and hitting the feather button, but to no avail. We were confronted with a windmilling propeller locked in flat pitch. Thankfully, we were at a low indicated airspeed when it happened, so the windmilling

Fig. 11-14
The Boeing Stratochamber. It was commissioned in 1941 and was used to train our crew members in simulated high-altitude conditions. In the lower left photo, Bill Talbott and I are looking through the window at a flight test engineer undergoing wartime oxygen training. The manometer tubes for measuring pressure are in front of us.

[2] *–40 degrees is the temperature at which the Fahrenheit and Centigrade scales intersect.*

revs were within engine structural limits, but how were we going to get down? Any appreciable increase in speed during a descent would result in the engine coming apart. On the other hand, we were not far above stall speed and a stall/spin was to be avoided at all costs. Teetering in a small maneuvering envelope, Eddie played it with his usual finesse. With great care he worked the aircraft back and forth between the brink of stall and the speed of excessive engine rpm. Shuddering and buffeting, we gradually mushed down in altitude. Other more drastic measures like playing with the flaps or gear or the operating engines might have been tried, but Eddie sensed that the course he took was conservative and would work. Finally, of course, we got to a low enough altitude (and high enough ambient temperature) to feather the prop and come home on three engines. The congealing problem finally was solved by increased oil circulation and insulating muffs.

Fig. 11-15
L-R: Ed Wersebe, Chuck Blaine and WFM undergoing denitrogenation before a "flight" in the pressure chamber.

ON SEVERAL FLIGHTS we had drastic problems with the engine oil coolers. Oil congealing in those radiators stopped the normal oil flow, and huge quantities of oil then would be pumped overboard through the overflow relief valve, striking the horizontal tail and building up in great frozen gobs. On one occasion, at more than 20,000 feet, the lump of frozen oil on the stabilizer was over a foot in depth and width. This disturbed the airflow and resulted in severe buffeting of the horizontal stabilizer and elevator. The oil was frozen so solidly that it still was intact after landing.

At that time we were working with two competing manufacturers, Harrison and AirResearch, both of whom were anxious to receive the production order for oil coolers for the B-17E. Their representatives made a number of flights with us, sweating out the solution to this problem. AirResearch was finally chosen as the principal production contractor, which established the company as a major supplier.

Tough Decisions

In this period of a single small crew, evening flights were necessary to keep up with developments. To take some of the flying load off Allen, who also was carrying heavy administrative responsibilities, Verne Hyde, an experienced and highly respected pilot in his fifties, who had been flying in the vicinity of Seattle for years, was brought in.

On one memorable flight he was co-pilot to Reed. We took off around 8:00 P.M. under good weather conditions but with a high broken overcast of clouds. I don't remember the specific purpose of the flight, although it probably was related to our perpetual ignition/harness problem, which resulted in misfiring

225

Fig. 11-16
We could train as many as six people at a time. The engineer on the left is checking his writing skills, which deteriorate rapidly with loss of oxygen, 1941.

and engine roughness at altitude. We climbed above 15,000 feet, passing through the broken cloud layer and coming out into a clear sky peopled with stars, the cloud tops faintly lit by a rising moon. I was busy with my usual instruments, but the sight was so gorgeous and ethereal that we exchanged appreciative glances before settling into the task at hand.

To stay in the general Seattle area we had been flying a few minutes on each leg of a triangular course. At the completion of the test, we started looking for a break in the cloud layer, but in the last hour a solid overcast had developed. No radio ranges of help were operating in the Seattle area, and our navigation was purely dead reckoning. Test pilots of that era generally were not adept at instrument flying, even if adequate ground facilities had been available.

Looking for a hole at 15,000 feet or so, Reed became increasingly more apprehensive and agitated. Mt. Rainier is more than 14,000 feet high, and since we didn't know where we were, or what the winds at altitude might have done to our position, he envisioned our plowing into the mountain. Reed finally decided that our best alternative to chancing a descent through the

Fig. 11-17
Headquarters of the flight test engineers (Room 313) near my office.

overcast was to bail out, head the abandoned aircraft for the Rockies, and hope for the best. He yelled back to me that I should go first, and opened the bomb bay doors just aft of the cockpit. As I looked down through those open doors, the prospect was chilling. I might land in the freezing waters of Puget Sound, or in the Cascades wilderness, or find myself sliding down the side of a building in Seattle. While the pilot is the captain of the ship, my neck is my own. I hesitated, considering my chances and trying to decide whether Reed's idea was the best course to follow.

Fig. 11-18
Smaller meeting involved analysis of the flight data handled in Sid Silber's section. Sid is seated to the right.

During that interval Verne Hyde came up with a better solution after studying the cloud layer below. By the light of the moon he discerned two areas that seemed slightly lighter than the rest, and concluded they must be the lights of Seattle and Tacoma, faintly visible through a "not so thick" cloud layer. He further noted that one area was larger than the other, and convinced Reed to line up on the two and descend through the clouds between them. The bomb bay doors slammed shut. We went on instruments, emerging in a few moments almost directly over Boeing Field with the lights of Seattle shimmering below and welcoming us home. We spiraled down to a landing. A younger, less stable and experienced pilot than Verne might have accepted Reed's decision without question. I learned that when a hasty decision is not necessary, every alternative should be carefully considered. It was late in the evening when I had my usual dinner at the Olympic Grill. It tasted extraordinarily good.

Oxygen Oddities

As we gradually increased the operating altitude, I began to experience associated physical symptoms. Well aware of the danger of the bends, we ran long lines from the aircraft oxygen regulators so we could exercise on pure oxygen on the ramp for 45 minutes before a flight. With the exception of occasional pain in the arm and leg joints, there were no cases of acute bends. However, I soon learned that the lowered ambient pressure at altitude could produce gas pains if one had eaten too fast, or too much, or not easily digestible food. The flights were long, frequently four hours, and soon I settled into a routine of eating appropriately beforehand. This discipline has proven beneficial in high-stress situations, and in subsequent life. On one amusing flight, however, I got caught out.

Just as we left the ramp, a crew member handed me a piece of hard candy. Without thinking I lifted my oxygen mask and popped it into my mouth. It proved to be a continuous gas generator from zero to 35,000 feet. For the Guinness Book of Records I think I can claim to have produced the longest continuous fart in history.

I ALSO EXPERIENCED SORE THROATS from breathing dry oxygen for long periods. Not sure at that time of the cause, I visited a young nose and throat doctor across the street from the Olympic, who convinced me to have my tonsils removed. Appearing at his office on the appointed day, his assistant gave me a local anaesthetic, which proved so relaxing and euphoric that I could hardly keep my hands off

227

Fig. 11-19
Exercising on pure oxygen before a high-altitude flight, 1941. Note the long oxygen lines running to each crew member. I am standing next to the nurse, on the left.

Fig. 11-20
About to board a B-17, 1941. Marvin Michael is third from left, Ed Wersebe fifth. Al Reed is behind the Boeing mechanic, on right.

Fig. 11-21
Winter flying suits, taken in the flight hangar. L-R: Chuck Blaine, Al Reed, Ed Wersebe, Bill Milliken, 1941. Most of the test aircraft were heated, so we seldom wore these outfits. Blaine and Wersebe were lost in the XB-29 accident (see Chapter 13, "Triumph and Tragedy").

her. Led into his office, I waited in a straight-backed chair until he came in, handed me an elongated metal dish to catch the gore, fished a knife out of his breast pocket and proceeded to remove my tonsils. After dabbing a little antiseptic on the wounds, he suggested I get a good meal as I might have a sore throat for a few days. I ate an enormous meal at the Olympic, and began a painful week. Since then I never have had a sore throat of any consequence.

On one flight my oxygen mask was connected by a long line to the regulator in the bombardier's compartment in the nose of the aircraft. Standing behind Allen, and moving around to read the instruments, I pulled the line off the regulator. I have no idea when it

occurred, but at around 15,000 feet I began to feel a little woozy and sick to my stomach, finally passing out and falling to the floor. With the line reconnected, I got up and continued to record the instruments as if nothing had happened. What finally convinced me I had passed out was the time gap in the recorded data, and the dust I had picked up on my uniform while rolling around on the floor.

LACK OF OXYGEN can be a painless and insidious way of losing consciousness. On flights with large crews we always paired off. On one occasion the junior flight engineer, who had passed out, swore at the post-flight meeting that he had functioned perfectly

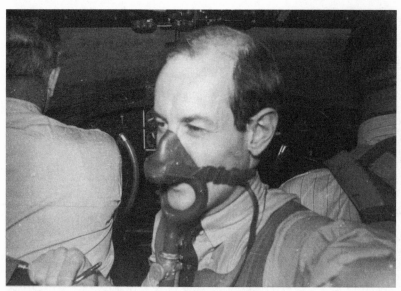

Fig. 11-22
WFM with nasal mask, only used for relatively low altitude.

throughout the flight, until confronted with his data sheets. They were filthy, wrinkled, and covered with "winged heel" prints matching perfectly the heels of his shoes!

When flying with large crews, the activity was coordinated by intercom from the cockpit, and it was my job to keep checking with the various stations. If no response or gibberish followed, the pilot would put the plane into a steep dive for lower altitude until things were sorted out. There were just enough of these irregularities to give us concern. Was there anything that could be done for a crew member who had been off oxygen for, say, more than a half minute at 35,000 feet? The medical people suggested that an injection of sodium benzoate might save a life. Playing it conservatively, we arranged to have hypodermic equipment installed at each station, and the flight engineers were trained in its use. No one was enthusiastic, and the crew reasonably insisted that Al and I go through the same training. Appearing at Boeing Medical, I was directed to a white room to await the nurse. On the table lay a hypodermic needle of a size used on livestock.

In an emergency, flight engineers were instructed to jab the needle through the clothing into the buttocks of the recumbent crew member, which was so appealing to the younger engineers that on occasion they did it without an impending emergency.

Occasionally, I would catch a flight on a production model as an observer or co-pilot. A new pressure carburetor was to be introduced into production, and prototypes had been installed on one aircraft. As our flight test load was so great, our Air Corps representative, Col. Corkille,[3] offered to make the check flight and I went along for the ride.

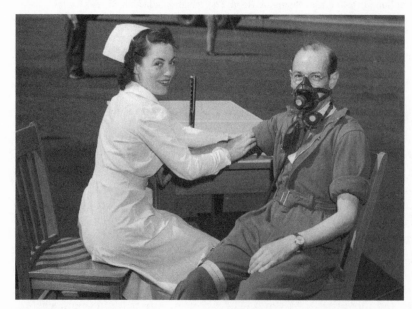

Fig. 11-23
Nurse checking blood pressure before a high-altitude flight. Do you wonder that I didn't mind such elaborate medical attention?

[3]*John D. Corkille was a legendary figure at Boeing. He later went on active duty in the North African campaign and died there.*

We taxied out to the end
of the runway, where
he carefully ran up each
engine. Takeoff seemed
routine, but I noticed
he lost no time pulling
the aircraft up into a
steep climb. Suddenly,
at perhaps 500 feet,
No. 4 engine coughed,
cut out, came in again.
One could deduce that
if one engine acted up
on these carburetors the
other three might follow.
But with Corkille the
deduction and action
were simultaneous. Still
in a climb, he rolled
the airplane into the
tightest turn and circle
of Boeing Field I was
ever to experience.

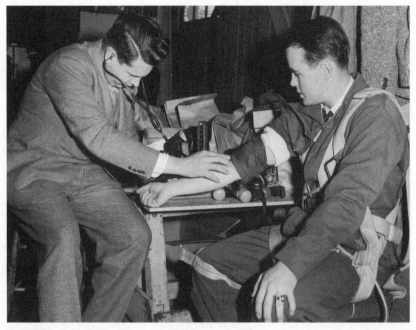

Fig. 11-24
Dr. Russell and Chuck Blaine.

Coming low over the surrounding buildings, he
approached in a steep turn, leveling off at the
last moment to land on the runway we just had
left a few minutes before. As we taxied back, all
of the engines were rough, cutting in and out.
Had the flight continued, we might have been
forced to attempt a landing in a built-up area or
abandon the aircraft at a very low altitude.

Mission Accomplished

Early in 1942, I flew back to New York
City to present a paper at the Institute of
the Aeronautical Sciences entitled "Flight
Test Organization, Procedures and Crew
Training," that I had co-authored with Al
Reed. It summarized the B-17 testing activity
of the preceding two years. Our primary goal
of providing the Air Force with a bomber
capable of routine operation at 35,000 feet
had been met, and American crews now were
hammering on Germany in daylight raids.
From a spasmodic operation involving one
airplane, we had progressed to a large flight-
test program capable of fielding four large
crews with adequate instrumentation and
analysis capability. At that time this was state-
of-the-art.

A large portion of our testing had been
at high altitude. By 1942 we had established
records of man-hours on oxygen at 30,000 to
35,000 feet. During an eight-month period two
crews had flown nearly 70 hours at over 30,000
feet. Many of the flights were four hours long,
with two hours of testing at 35,000 feet. Our
training and operational procedures were viewed
by the industry as standards of good practice.

In an internal memorandum that addressed
developing a pressure suit for altitudes above
35,000 feet, Reed and I summarized the
status of high-altitude testing at other aircraft
facilities, confirming that Boeing's progress had
been quite exceptional. Pratt & Whitney's flight
section, for example, had made a very limited
number of climbs up to 35,000 feet, but had
done no level work at that altitude. The Wright
Aeronautical test group made even fewer climbs
to these altitudes. Vought-Sikorsky never had
exceeded 30,000 feet in its flight testing. The
Grumman experience was essentially the same.
The Glenn L. Martin Company had done little
test flying above 20,000 feet, which was also the
case for the Curtiss Propeller Flight Section at
Caldwell, New Jersey. The Army Air Corps at
Wright Field, while occasionally making climbs
to 35,000 feet, had conducted practically no

231

Fig. 11-25
L-R: Dorman, Harlen, Michael, Merrill, Luplow and Strom, 1941. This crew lost half the horizontal stabilizer of a B-17 in a high-g maneuver, and were forced to abandon the aircraft and parachute down. The aircraft wound up cutting a swath through a forest, much to the delight of the property owner, who had wanted to clear the area for farming.

extended test work above 25,000 feet. The Navy still was in the process of developing suitable oxygen equipment. Doing little flight testing at altitudes exceeding 25,000 feet, it had experienced several serious accidents. Our information indicated that West Coast companies, other than ours, had done very little test flying at altitudes over 25,000 feet, although Lockheed was contemplating it.

The meager amount of test flying at high altitudes had not been due to a lack of incentive or lack of tests to be run at these altitudes, nor to a lack of airplanes capable of reaching these altitudes. As a matter of fact, several of the companies mentioned had outlined large test programs at altitudes exceeding 25,000 feet specifically requested by the Air Corps or the Navy. Almost without exception, the difficulties of high-altitude test flying were associated with the lack of proper equipment and properly

trained crews. Our accomplishments at high altitudes had been the result of adequate forethought, preparation and training. Our policy had been to obtain the best equipment possible, to thoroughly acquaint ourselves with its use and to educate our crews in the basic physiology associated with high-altitude flight. At all times we approached the subject from a conservative standpoint. Furthermore, we made a continual effort to keep abreast of the most recent developments in the field.

In two years no major accidents to either aircraft or personnel had occurred; flying personnel suffered from nothing more than slight cases of airsickness, aero-otitus or temporary anoxia. Approximately 40 chamber ascents were made for the purpose of checking out personnel for high-altitude flights. Sixty-seven different people performed the simulated emergency procedures at altitudes of 30,000 feet and 35,000 feet. Twenty-two made two or more chamber ascents during which, after proper denitrogenation, climbs were made at an average rate of 2,500 feet per minute to 30,000 feet, and 1,500 feet per minute up to 35,000 feet. Several cases of aeroembolism symptoms were observed, all traceable to improper denitrogenation, but none was noted in flight. Gas pains were slightly more common, but it seldom was necessary to discontinue a chamber ascent because of this difficulty. In several cases difficulty in equalizing pressure in the ears and sinuses was encountered when descending, necessitating a reduction in the rate of descent or its temporary cessation.

Six complete simulated bailout descents were made in the chamber from an altitude of 35,000 feet, using the standard bailout mouthpiece and bottle.

The simulated bailout usually was carried only as far as changing from the normal mask to the bailout mouthpiece. During the course of the chamber work, 39,000 feet was reached with the standard type BLB oral-nasal mask. Using the new BLB Bulbulian Type 12 mask, five crew members ascended to above 40,000 feet. For practical purposes, 40,000 feet was considered the absolute limit for both chamber and airplane use with the new Type 12 mask.

THE B-17E BENEFITED enormously from all this high-altitude test work. Every important system on this airplane had been test-flown on earlier models of B-17s, including the power-plant systems, structural features, aerodynamic refinements, stability and control, and items associated with armament and the military use of the aircraft. When the prototype B-17E emerged from the factory it was, in all important respects, a "production aircraft." No long period of service operation was required to prove its vital components.

Flying jet transports at 30,000–40,000 feet now is so commonplace that it is difficult to describe the

sensation of reaching these altitudes on oxygen alone, after months of trying, or later on a single flight.

I vividly remember the first time we climbed to 35,000 feet without any sort of mechanical trouble, our radial engines generating rated power for over 50 minutes as we passed through broken layers and then into sunshine. Off in the distance there were wisps of cirrus clouds, sparkling ice crystals set in a sky of deep blue. I thought I could see the curve of the earth. On the way up I had been plotting the outside air temperature (O.A.T.) against altitude. In my first course in meteorology at MIT I had been told that the temperature in the stratosphere was constant, and when my curve went straight up we were there. I slapped Eddie on the back and held up the plot for both pilots to see. Thumbs up, we exchanged

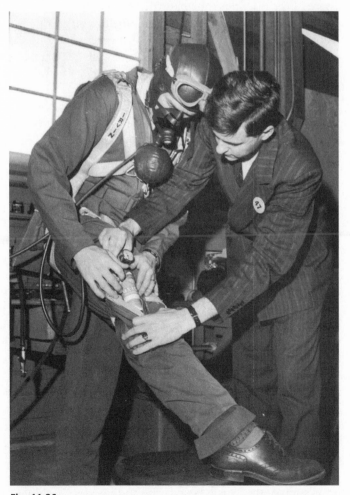

Fig. 11-26
Ed Wersebe checking out Everett Denton's bailout oxygen bottle.

broad grins. On this day the stratosphere was at 35,000 feet and the outside temperature was near the magical minus 40 degrees where the Fahrenheit and Centigrade scales come together.

Other airmen had been to these altitudes before, but we still were in a select company and experienced the elation of pioneering. Almost directly over Boeing Field we made radio contact with our station at the hangar, noting that we were seven miles away. "In which direction?" came back the answer. "Straight up, straight up, straight up!"

I remember thinking we were over a mile higher than Mt. Everest, on pure oxygen and feeling fine. Recently I had occasion to reread Lindbergh's account of running out of oxygen at over 35,000 feet while testing a P-47 fighter. Going into a vertical dive before losing consciousness, he finally recovered at 15,000 feet. He, too, had trained at Mayo, and was well aware of the brief time one has without oxygen: either oxygen is restored in a half-minute or you risk brain damage or worse. In a B-17 we never could descend like a fighter, but we were well prepared in other respects, with lots of stored oxygen and standby masks. I was to put in over 50 hours at about 35,000 feet—a working week in those days, and while I was conscious of the risks I have no memory of any real concern. Everything that's really worthwhile in this world is a calculated risk—whether it's getting married, having children or pursuing the work you love. After a long and successful flight my only feeling was how lucky I was to be there, to have helped pulled it off, to have had that experience.

Visit from a Lancaster

There also were some welcome breaks in the routine. One day early in 1942, Eddie announced that Capt. Clyde Pangborn was to visit Seattle in a British Lancaster bomber for inspection and flight by Boeing technical personnel. I was to go along and jot down Allen's impressions of its flying qualities. This was a great opportunity. Pangborn, a pioneer trans-oceanic flyer, was one of my heroes and a legendary figure in the flying world. My initial impression of the Lanc was of its size and interior arrangement. It seemed to stand much higher than a B-17, and its fuselage seemed deeper and narrower, with long bomb bays and a markedly different arrangement for pilot and crew. While Eddie flew the plane I stood in the passageway on the right, taking notes on 3" × 5" cards.

Before the Lancaster evaluation, Allen and Reed had subjectively evaluated the flying characteristics of the B-17E. Based on their comments, I produced the write-up for the Pilot's Handbook, which is on page 244 at the end of this chapter. Prior to the war, pilot handbooks prepared by the aircraft manufacturer frequently tended to soft-pedal marginal flying characteristics, believing it detrimental to sales. But during the war a high level of honesty prevailed. It is interesting to compare the flight characteristics of the Lancaster and the B-17, both highly successful bombardment aircraft. (*Eddie Allen's evaluation of the Lancaster is on page 243 of this chapter.*)

Jump from 40,000 Feet

It was early in 1942 when Col. Randy Lovelace, then in charge of the Air Force's Aeromed Laboratory at Wright Field, flew back to Boeing for his pioneering parachute jump from 40,000 feet. The air war was moving to higher altitudes, and crew members would need to know how to bail out of damaged aircraft. What were the problems of parachuting under these temperature and altitude conditions? Lightly loaded, one of our B-17s was capable of over 40,000 feet and was ideal for this parachute jump. The jump would be made out of the bomb bay with a "static line" that would yank the ripcord when Lovelace was well clear of the aircraft.

Reed selected the crew members, and to my consternation I was not included among them. I felt this was a "bonus" flight that I had earned, but Reed was adamant. The crew joining Reed as pilot were Jim Fraser as co-pilot and a member or two from AF Aeromed Laboratory as well as Lovelace. Although he later apologized to me, Reed never explained how he arrived at the crew composition. Perhaps he felt that, as the most senior individual in Flight after himself, I should be responsible for things on the ground during his absence. That would have been fallacious reasoning, because we had made many flights together. One thing is certain: Al was operating at a very high stress level. His wife, Florence, was a semi-invalid, and other problems hardly made for a solid home life. Like all of us, Al was experiencing sore throats and fatigue from the stress of long flights. Seldom appearing at the office until after our morning meeting, he became more dictatorial and critical than usual.

On the evening before the jump we convened at the Olympic Georgian Room for dinner, an occasion to remember for its pilots' talk and congeniality. As we finished dessert, Lovelace opened a small vial and swallowed two pills that I recognized immediately, and was sure he would have a sound night's sleep. A few weeks earlier, when I had been dispatched to Washington, D.C., on assignment, Eddie suggested I take United's DC-3 Sleeper plane which left Seattle early in the evening, to arrive

at the Capitol the next day. He recommended I have a stewardess give me a couple of the new Mayo sleeping tablets. After a nice meal out of Portland, Oregon, I crawled into the narrow upper berth, disrobed, snuggled down and rang for the stewardess. Taking the pills, I went into a sound sleep. When the plane became weathered-in in Omaha in the middle of the night, I remember the stewardess shaking me to get dressed. I pulled my shorts on, then fell asleep again. Another shaking, socks on, sleep again, etc. I have no recollection of leaving the berth or the airplane, but I do remember waking up at four in the afternoon in the lobby of a downtown hotel in Omaha after my best night's sleep in years.

Lovelace made the parachute jump over the Moses Lake area. The opening shock was great enough to render him unconscious, although I've often wondered if some oxygen deficiency

Fig. 11-27
L-R: Al Reed, Dr. Lovelace, Jim Fraser and Dr. Gagge (Harvard Medical) before Lovelace's parachute jump from 40,000 feet, circa 1942.

might also have been involved. He lost one glove and experienced severe frostbite. The B-17 circled him on the way down, noting that he returned to consciousness before landing. One of our pilots in a small airplane picked him up and brought him back to Seattle. Some months later, when I called on him at Wright Field, Lovelace still was working with a rubber ball to overcome the effects of the frostbite. He ultimately was successful in returning to surgical work (see page 267).

Christmases Away from Home

Before my employment at Boeing, I routinely spent Christmas at home in Maine. My first Christmas in Seattle was delightful. Allen had invited me to his home to play the part of Santa Claus for his young family. At 135 lbs, I never could have pulled that off without a generous amount of padding. Eddie and his young wife were exceptional hosts. He had a knack for storytelling, and I enjoyed hearing about his adventures in the Andes, on the airmail route, and his numerous "first flights" of well-known aircraft. He also had a great love of music and an outstanding record collection. This Christmas became a most pleasant memory.

The next Christmas, 1940, I flew back to Maine on Trans-Canada's Lockheed 14s, their "Pony Express" run, through violently rough air. The only other passenger, a girl about my age, was at least as scared as I was. We huddled together and in that environment became close if not good friends. I later visited her at her father's ranch in Montana.

WHEN CHRISTMAS 1941 CAME around I had no specific plans. Pearl Harbor cast a cloud over festivities, and there was concern about a Japanese raid on Seattle and Boeing. Having opened a few presents on Christmas morning, I started looking for something to do to stave off loneliness, and thought that Bill Talbott might enjoy a flight in the Fairchild F-22 I had bought in early 1940. His response to my call was, "Great idea, could we fly across Puget Sound to Bremerton and drop off some presents for my relatives?" We agreed to meet at the airport.

He arrived with a number of packages, a large stuffed turkey and a homemade parachute fashioned from a sheet. The idea was to locate his relatives' place and drop the gifts into their backyard. The weather was none too warm and there was a low overcast. After I stuffed Talbott into the front cockpit and surrounded him with his packages, he cradled the turkey in his arms and we took off. At a few hundred feet we started across the Sound. I was none too happy traversing that stretch of icy water at low altitude in marginal weather while feeling the cold of an open cockpit, but Talbott seemed jovial enough, occasionally twisting his head around and giving me a big smile.

I decided to maintain as much altitude as possible by flying close to the jagged base of the overcast, which presented a sort of inverted mountainous topography with bits of low-hanging cloud, ridges and valleys. About halfway across, with no warning, we suddenly lost all visibility as we plowed into one of those stringy, detached masses. I hauled off the throttle and put the nose down to get back in the clear. Talbott, who could only assume the engine had quit, let out a yell, stood up, leaned over the cowling and was about to cast the turkey into the Sound. "Oh no, no, no!" I yelled at the top of my lungs. He hesitated and finally retreated back into the cockpit as I shoved the throttle forward. It was a close shave, at least for the turkey.

We located his relatives' place and made a low pass over the backyard as Talbott threw out his cargo. The parachute failed to open, unfortunately, and the boxes and turkey bounced on the frozen ground, but I saw no more. Santa could have done no better. We started back across the Sound and, half frozen, landed at Boeing Field. I concluded there was no better way to avoid being bored and lonesome.

NINETEEN FORTY-TWO got off to a good start with a letter from Ed Waterhouse, who had introduced me to Dumas' great historical novels. I still carried around the leather-bound set my father had given me on my 24th birthday, to which I turned whenever the going got tough or without adventure. On this occasion Ed wrote, "Was thinking yesterday that your birthday is in the offing—so pulled out the 'bible' and read that chapter wherein M. Le Compte de la Fere tells Louis the XIV how D'Artagnan captured Gen. Monk single-handed and how he himself had gotten Charles back on his throne. What could they have done with a B-17! I pictured D'Artagnan as the pilot, Porthos, of course, would be the gunner, Aramis with his scientific knowledge, the navigator. Somehow Planchet would have to master the radio, Grimmard the rear gun. Monseqton assisting Porthos and undoubtedly Basin would comprise the ground crew—a bit timid for the air!"

I was 31 years old, reasonably comfortable with myself and deliriously happy with my job at Boeing. Every day seemed like a new and enchanting beginning. Our multiple large crews now were a standard fixture, flying B-17E, -F and -Gs to 35,000 feet and above on oxygen, and planning was underway for XB-29's early flights. It was one of the most eventful of my years at Boeing, and it never occurred to me that it would not go on forever.

Pressure Suit

Late in 1941 Al and I had initiated development of a pressure suit that, in theory at least, would enable flights to altitudes well beyond those on oxygen alone.

The idea of a pressure suit arose in conversation with Professor John Ackerman of the University of Minnesota, an associate of Al's when he taught meteorology there. Unlike some previous and more recent pressure suits, our concept did not replace the use of oxygen, but merely supplemented it.

In September of 1941 I dictated a memorandum to Eddie Allen over Al's signature entitled "Pressurized Suits for High-Altitude Flying," in which we made the case that operation on pure oxygen above 35,000 feet is marginal. I said: "The slope of the curve when breathing pure oxygen is so steep that an increase in altitude

from 35,000 to 40,000 feet changes the alveolar oxygen pressure by an amount equivalent to a change in altitude from 3,500 feet to 12,500 feet for a person breathing air. Any slight leak in the mask or hyperventilation is dangerous at 35,000 feet and intolerable at higher altitudes."

Certainly we had been to 40,000 feet (and even higher) on pure oxygen, but extended testing there was far more risky than at 35,000 feet. We next made the case for the need for testing at 40,000 feet and above, pointing out that a pressurized suit is a desirable safeguard for pressurized military aircraft that might be battle-damaged at high altitude. Finally, we summarized the history of pressure suits, noting that suits with pressurized internal air were cumbersome, heavy and generally severely limited the movements of the wearer. This referred to Wiley Post's suit and those of Swain

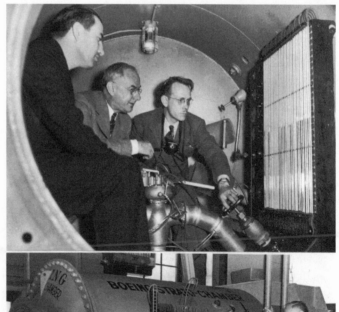

Fig. 11-28
Dr. Lovelace, Dr. Boothby and Jim Cooper (Boeing), checking out the Boeing Stratochamber before the pressure suit tests, circa 1942.

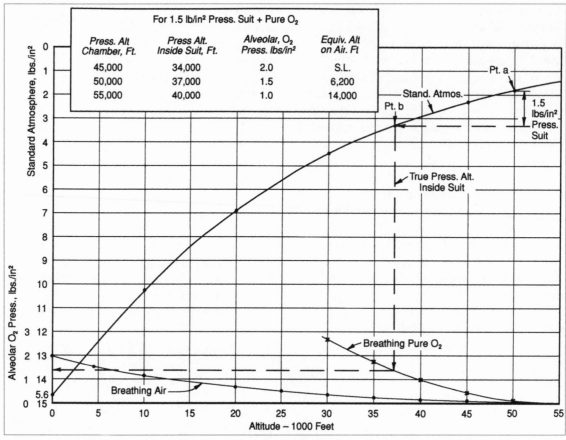

For 1.5 lb/in² Press. Suit + Pure O₂

Press. Alt Chamber, Ft.	Press Alt. Inside Suit, Ft.	Alveolar, O₂ Press. lbs/in²	Equiv. Alt on Air. Ft
45,000	34,000	2.0	S.L.
50,000	37,000	1.5	6,200
55,000	40,000	1.0	14,000

Fig. 11-29
Chart showing the performance of the 1.5-psi pressure suits superimposed on breathing pure oxygen. At 50,000-foot altitude, the suit reduces the effective altitude inside the suit to 37,000 feet. Breathing pure oxygen reduces the effective altitude to about 6,200 feet on air.

and the then-current Italian altitude record holder, Col. Pezzo.

OUR CONCEPT was a suit that provided a small increase in pressure over ambient, say 1.5-psi, for a wearer who was breathing pure oxygen. Hopefully this small differential pressure would allow reasonable movement on the part of the user, minimize elaborate mechanical joints and seals, and be of simple lightweight construction and modest cost. A suit of this general type had been under consideration at Mayo, so we proposed a joint enterprise involving Mayo, Ackerman and Boeing. Boothby and Lovelace suggested the practical approach of first constructing a few prototype tight-fitting rubberized suits tailored to specific individuals, which then could be pressurized to the 1.5-psi differential.

Observations would be made as to where the suits ballooned, and these areas could be "bandaged" down. The hope was that critical joints like the elbows could be developed that had sufficient flexibility to permit movement without substantial air volume changes.

After due negotiation, the venture was formalized. Ackerman acted as project engineer, cooperating closely with Mayo. Reed and I were chosen as the initial subjects. Once the suits were ready, development testing would be done in the Boeing Stratochamber. At the time it seemed like an interesting experiment, but as a subject I was to have some anxious moments.

LET ME FIRST review the theory of the suit. On Figure 11-29 several curves are plotted against true pressure altitude. The first is a curve of standard (NACA) atmospheric pressure. This scale is inverted with 14.7-psi sea-level pressure close to the origin, the pressure falling off as altitude increases. The two other curves are for alveolar oxygen pressure when breathing air and when breathing pure oxygen.

An example of how the suit works is shown on the figure. Suppose the suit is at the external pressure corresponding to 50,000 feet standard atmosphere (Point a). If the suit is pressurized to 1.5-psi differential, the inside suit pressure is that of Point b, which corresponds to 37,000 feet. At this pressure, breathing pure oxygen, the alveolar oxygen pressure happens to be 1.5 psi, which projects to the "breathing air" curve at 6,000 feet. Thus the occupant should feel quite comfortable although he is at the ambient pressure altitude of 50,000 feet.

If the altitude in the pressure chamber, or in flight, is increased to 55,000 feet, the effective altitude experienced by the subject is 14,000 feet. At 45,000 feet the subject is effectively at sea level. Figure 11-30 is a plot of "Equivalent Altitude on Air vs. Pressure Altitude of the Chamber, or Flight."

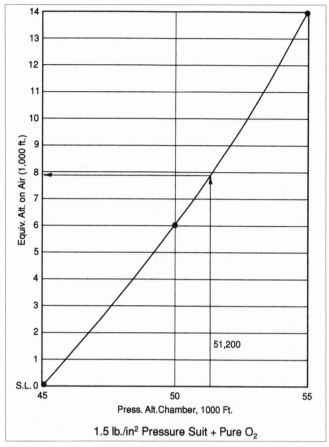

Fig. 11-30
Plot showing effective altitude of about 8,000 feet (on air) when pressure altitude in the chamber is 51,200 feet during my test session.

Three experimental (prototype) suits arrived at Boeing in mid-July of 1942. Two of them were tailored to Al's and my dimensions, and the third to a senior flight test engineer, possibly Blaine or Wersebe. According to one of the contract requirements, "The suit shall be possible to put on and to remove without the help of an assistant." It was to be worn over a suit of warm underwear, and initially was of three pieces: lower and upper body with an airtight joint at the waist, and a helmet.

The following account is based on the Boeing report prepared at the time, and also on a surviving letter I wrote my mother on July 27, 1942. Because the suit experience was confidential I cautioned her to dispose of the letter, but found it in her effects after she died.

While awaiting the arrival of the suits, we engaged in a variety of experiments in our Stratochamber. As I wrote my mother, "Three of us went to a pressure altitude of 46,800 feet in the chamber on pure oxygen alone. That represents the absolute maximum that a human being can go on oxygen alone. At that altitude we were barely conscious and could do no work at all." We were at close to the equivalent of 30,000 feet, breathing air. In essence, we had "climbed" Mt. Everest without any acclimatization, and it is a wonder that we survived at all! I assume we were there only briefly, and have no clue why we engaged in such a hazardous experiment. I'm quite sure it occurred before "pressure breathing," which would have helped.

ON OR ABOUT JULY 25, Boothby, Lovelace, Bulbulian and Ackerman arrived to be present at the initial suit tests. We convened at the

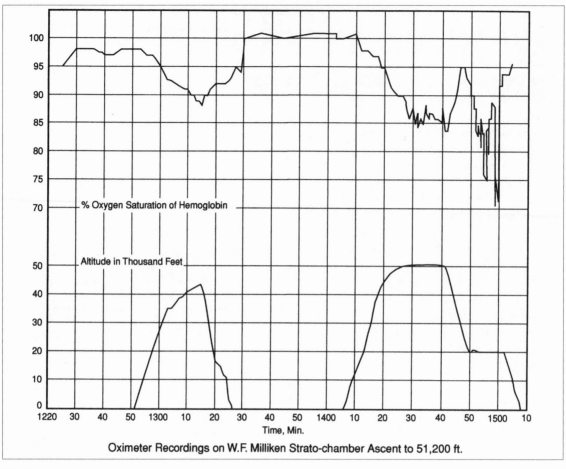

Fig. 11-31
Oximeter recording during my chamber ascent to 51,200 feet.

Stratochamber location in the hanger as Al and I started the process of suiting up. It was impossible to get into these tight-fitting garments without a lot of external help. That took time, and since the air pressure could not be applied until the complete outfit was in place and sealed, the temperature inside became almost unbearably hot. Even more alarming was the sensation of utter helplessness, and the knowledge that one couldn't possibly get out of the suit without help. When the air was finally applied, the suit stiffened up, and the feeling of being in a garment was replaced by that of being confined in a room tailored to one's shape. With sweat pouring out and no ability to scratch a hundred itches, it was terribly uncomfortable, and actually scary if one had the faintest claustrophobic tendency. True, because of the

tight fit there was some mobility, but far less than we had hoped for. Once the helmet was in place any further adjustment of the oxygen mask was impossible, and the space within the helmet was so restricted that only careful head movements were possible for fear of disturbing the fit of the mask.

I never before had been exposed to such a lack of freedom, and survived it only by imposing a high level of discipline on my thinking, without which I easily could have panicked. This was no time for a free-roving imagination. My plight was further exaggerated by the installation of an oximeter, a so-called "oxygen want" indicator, the pickup of which was clamped to one's ear. Dr. G. A. Millikan, son of the famous scientist, had invented this device. Using a small photoelectric cell that sensed the color of the pinched earlobe, it

Fig. 11-32
Eddie Brown operated at Boeing Field, and provided all the parachutes and other services used in the B-17 development testing. Some years before, he and Bob Wark attempted a nonstop flight to Japan in the Rolls-Royce Eagle-engined Fokker shown here. They came to grief in Alaska and abandoned the aircraft. Its remains later were discovered and the aircraft completely restored. The aircraft now is in the Owl's Head museum in Maine. Its engine is the only remaining Eagle still operating. I found Eddie's trans-Pacific flight attempt exceedingly interesting.

could be calibrated in terms of percent oxygen saturation in the blood.

We finally got into the chamber with all of the pressure, oxygen, oximeter and intercom connections. The heavy door was slammed shut and sealed, reinforcing our sense of confinement. At that point our fate was totally dependent upon those outside who were running the test.

In retrospect, we were damned fortunate that Randy Lovelace was involved. An unfeeling experimenter could have taken us to unbearable altitudes or drawn out the test duration. Randy had an uncanny ability to empathize with his subjects and sense what they were enduring, plus the judgment to know when enough is enough.

We later heard that Boothby was all for continuing the test to higher altitudes and duration. We actually reached a pressure altitude of 51,200 feet and stayed there for 15

minutes. During that period we performed some arm exercises from a sitting position, which reduced the blood oxygen saturation by about 30 percent. Recovery was effected by steady deep breathing. The figure shows the oximeter readings on the two ascents, the first to 44,000 feet and the final one to 51,200 feet. We were in the suits nearly three hours.

The Boeing-Mayo-University of Minnesota pressure suit was given one flight test in which I wasn't personally involved. The conclusion that it was not a practical approach to the pressure suit problem was for reasons much the same as we encountered in the chamber—too difficult to use and too uncomfortable. Development was dropped. Modern space suits are much looser, with more elaborate joints; they are much more costly, but much more livable.

Fig. 11-33
The fully developed B-17E at altitude, circa 1942.

My pressure suit experience was traumatic, probably the scariest situation I had ever been in. But having survived I put the incident out of my mind and tried to "forget," which was my method of coping in those days. It would be some years before events forced me to realize that the mind never forgets—that only by being conscious of oneself can one come to terms with the vicissitudes of life and achieve some permanent resolution. As Gurdjieff said, if one does not "remember oneself," then change is impossible.

Writing about my pressure suit episode has been a worthwhile exercise, for even today I experience twinges of emotion when thinking about it. Life is forever creating the unexpected, and we survive by "control." Flying my early unstable aircraft demonstrated that. Control leads to stability, and stability *with* control enables one to face still more difficult challenges.

Avro Lancaster Evaluation

Report by Eddie Allen

Capt. Clyde Pangborn brought a Lancaster Bomber here to Seattle for the inspection by representatives of this Company. Some one hundred-odd engineers had the opportunity of going through the airplane and approximately ten made a flight in the plane lasting approximately one-half hour. I had the privilege of handling the controls for a little while. My impressions of the control and stability of the aircraft are as follows:

The ailerons are reasonably light and quite effective and permit very rapid rolling of the airplane. In this respect, the airplane is approximately equal to the B-17F and is considerably better than the B-17E before the ailerons had been balanced. The elevator of the Lancaster is quite effective and it is reasonably light at normal speeds. In comparing the elevator to that of the B-17, I estimate that the forces and effectiveness are approximately equal. The rudder control of the Lancaster is lighter and more effective than that of the B-17. The yaw stability is not as great as that of the B-17 at small angles of yaw. The damping in yaw on the Lancaster appears to be excellent. In regard to stability, the roll due to yaw is more pronounced on the Lancaster than on the B-17. It is possible to roll up into a vertical bank with no use of the ailerons in a very short time and with no appreciable sideslip. It is quite easy to fly the Lancaster with either the ailerons free or the rudder free. This coordination of lateral stability characteristics is superior to that on the B-17. On takeoff and landing, the *Lancaster* quite apparently has a higher wing loading than the B-17 although we were flying it at a very light gross weight condition. The takeoff and landing speeds appeared to be approximately equal to those of the B-17 with full load. It was noted that the split flaps of the Lancaster go down to 60 degrees which normally gives very difficult handling characteristics with this type of flap. Possibly owing to Captain Pangborn's excellent handling of the airplane, it felt as if it was in complete control during a slow glide and landing.

The pilot's vision seemed to me considerably better than that of the B-17 although the pilot's cockpit was not as convenient since the co-pilot has only a jump seat and emergency controls. It appeared to me that the speed at low altitude is quite a bit higher than that of the B-17 at low altitude. This could be expected from the smaller wing area of the Lancaster. This airplane has one hundred square feet less wing area than the B-17 and therefore, since the overload gross weights are approximately the same, the wing loading at maximum overload is considerably higher on the Lancaster than on the B-17.

The Lancaster crew gave full cooperation to our personnel in obtaining all of the information they had available. We greatly appreciated the opportunity of seeing and flying this airplane.

(signed) E. T. Allen

Pilot's Handbook, B-17E

Flying Characteristics

Introductory Notes
The E model of the B-17 series represents a very material change in tail surface and tail construction which gives greater stability than any of the previous models. The elevator and rudder are directly controlled from the control column, the tabs being added for trim only. The elevator and rudder tabs are more sensitive than before. Changes in trim due to adjustments in cowl flap and power settings will be noted and are as follows:

Increasing the power on the inboard engines causes the airplane to become slightly tail heavy, while a change of power on the outboard engines has an inappreciable effect upon trim. Closing the cowl flaps on the inboard engines causes a similar tail heaviness; cowl flaps on the outboard engines have negligible effect on trim. One of the exceptional characteristics of this airplane is the ability to "go around again" without changes in elevator trim tab setting. With the airplane properly trimmed for a landing with power off and flaps down, if the pilot decides for any reason that he must again circle the field, he can apply power, throw the flap switch into the up position and proceed to take off without any change in trim tab setting. The flaps retract at a satisfactory slow rate. For normal use of ailerons, the rudder force required has been substantially reduced. For this reason the effort in rolling in and out of a turn is small. Due to the inherent directional stability, the airplane will demand a change in pilot techniques for those who are familiar with earlier models.

Takeoff
During the takeoff run, directional control should be maintained with full rudder movement and throttle. When using throttles for directional control, the differential throttling should be with the outboard engines as much as possible. During climb under normal loading, the airplane will require very little elevator trim tab. The elevator control pressures will build up rapidly if climbing speed is reduced below normal. Directional control can be easily maintained with two-engine failure on one side if airspeed is held above 140 mph. With one outboard engine failure, directional control can be maintained at airspeeds over 120 mph.

Level Flight
In handling the B-17E airplane, the pilot will find that turns can be made very smoothly with aileron control only. On instrument flight the pilot should pay special attention to holding the wings level. With one wing down, the strong directional stability gives a noticeable turning tendency. However, care should be taken to avoid the excessive use of ailerons.

Stability
The B-17E is statically and dynamically stable for the usual range of speed with all normal load dispositions. The airplane may appear on the first few flights to be neutrally stable spirally. This is only apparent under turbulent conditions when slight rolling causes accompanying slight turning motion. However, the pilot will find it easy to keep the wings level.

continued on next page

Stalls

The stall characteristics of the B-17E are unusually good. As the airspeed is reduced before the stall, an increase in the control pressure will be noted. Elevator and rudder are quite effective in the stall condition, and can be used to regain level flight. However, as in all airplanes, care should be exercised in the use of ailerons when approaching or in the stall condition. A good stall warning is present several miles per hour above stalling speed with any flap or power condition. The first indication appears with a slight buffeting of the tail. There is very little tendency to roll in the stall for any flap or power condition, unless the ailerons are used.

Landing

During the approach for landing the pilot will have to make very little change in elevator trim. As the flaps are lowered, the ship becomes a little tail heavy. If the airplane is trimmed slightly nose heavy at 147 mph with flaps up, it will be properly trimmed at 120 mph with flaps down.

Warnings

With run-away turbo or propeller, *throttle back first*, then operate prop. control, if necessary. Instantaneous load factors above allowable can be reached very easily with rough elevator control movements. In turbulent air or in combat maneuvering, corrections should be made smoothly.

Watch hydraulic pressure on ground and during flight. In case of pump failure, co-pilot will ascertain that the hydraulic valve is in the normal position and use hand pump to maintain pressure for brakes on landing.

The likelihood of a run-away turbo is small but the danger is great if it occurs during a takeoff. Pilots should be on the alert during takeoff to immediately note and correct with the throttle any excessive manifold pressure.

Table 11-2. Boeing Flight Test Section Personnel 1940–1942

Position	January 1940	January 1942
Pilot	1	4
Co-pilot	1	4
Flight Test Planning Engineer		1
Flight Test Equipment Engineer		1
Flight Test Analysis Engineer		1
Secretary to Flight Test Unit		1
Flight Engineer	1	4
Junior Flight Engineer		24
Instrumentation Engineer	1	4
Junior Instrumentation Engineer		16
Junior Analysis Engineer	1	3
Data Transcriber		4
Clerk and Stenographer		12
Total	*5*	*79*

Chapter 12

Transcontinental Flight

O ne day in February 1940, during a lunch break between
Stratoliner tests, I wandered down the hangar line. Three of
them lined the east side of Boeing Field: the Experimental,
United's Seattle base, and between them the Itinerant Hangar. It was
the last to which I was headed. Because the aircraft in the transient
fleet always were changing, it was fun to see what was there. In one
corner I discovered a Fairchild F-22. It was similar to the one Nancy
and I had wrecked some years earlier, but with an "upright" four-
cylinder Wright Gipsy engine of 90 horsepower instead of an inverted
Menasco. The plane's condition led me to believe it was in for long-
term storage.

Although I was getting plenty of flight time during engineering
flight tests, I also was anxious to log more time as a pilot. An F-22,
with its excellent flying characteristics, modest maintenance and low
operating cost, would be ideal. I found the owner's name and address
on the Airworthiness Certificate in the rear cockpit. I contacted him
and, after the normal amount of dickering, acquired the aircraft for
$2,700.

The log indicated that a major engine overhaul was due, so after
a checkout flight and an hour of solo, I decided to do it and have
some basic maintenance performed on the airframe as well. Willie
Innocenti, United's chief mechanic in Seattle, agreed to do the latter
in his spare time, and recommended that his boss, a former engine
technician and now manager of United's Seattle operation, do the
engine overhaul. He proved agreeable, and his CAA credentials
meant there would be no inspection problems when the engine was
reinstalled in the airplane.

The arrangements with both men were material cost and time, the
latter to be charged at two dollars an hour, a great bargain that produced

On right side of car: WFM, Mama, Lou Averill. On left side of car: Cooper's girl
friend, Cooper, Aunt Clara Waterhouse and cousin, Ruth Waterhouse, 1941.

"Adventure! Adventure! That was the escape, the remedy."

– Richard Halliburton
(*The Royal Road to Romance*)

Fig. 12-1
A good side view of the Fairchild F-22 with Wright Gipsy engine, 1940.

a virtually new airplane by summer. I made the first flight after the overhaul in late June.

My childhood dream of a pioneering oceanic flight had diminished as I became involved in the testing of real aircraft. The impracticality of the idea was apparent, as most of the great oceans had already been flown. Dreams of youth are not easily abandoned, however, and my desire for adventure has been lifelong. This suggested increasing the range and endurance of the F-22.

Boeing had manufactured a P-26 fighter some years before, and I remembered seeing a surplus fuel tank from one in the hangar stockroom. A check revealed a capacity of 55 gallons, with dimensions nearly ideal for fitting into the front cockpit of the F-22 close to the aircraft's CG. The 21-gallon standard tank, plus the additional large tank, would provide a total fuel capacity of 76 gallons, or about 10 hours of flight time and a non-stop range of 800–900 miles.

Fig. 12-2
A ¾ front view of the Fairchild F-22 with Wright Gipsy engine. Note wide-track landing gear, which made for good ground handling.

Seattle to Old Town

The very words "long-range tank" had tremendous appeal—as if somebody had dropped a pair of seven-league boots out of the sky and I had found them. Almost immediately, I came up with the idea of a flight back to my hometown in Maine. There was a hitch. If the big tank was installed the aircraft would receive an X (experimental) license, limiting its operation to the Seattle area. I decided to soft-pedal my plans, and arranged with Willie to work out the installation late in the evenings when no observers were around. This clandestine operation was facilitated by moving the aircraft to a corner of United's hangar, and isolating it with tarps hung from the beams. Once assured the installation was practical, we would remove and store the tank until the flight to Maine was imminent.

On the F-22 the standard tank was located in the fuselage just aft of the engine, immediately ahead of the front cockpit. An engine-driven pump transfers fuel to the carburetor, with a backup wobble pump that was operated by a handle in the rear cockpit. Our installation simply required plumbing the tanks in parallel. A line from the bottom of the big tank tee'd directly into the fuel line from the standard (front) tank, and thence to the engine-driven pump and the carburetor. Shutoff valves on the fuel lines at the bottom of each tank (operable from the cockpit) enabled tank selection. Thus the engine and wobble pumps worked for either tank. One additional line with a shutoff valve allowed me to drain off any condensation that might collect in the sump of the big tank, which would not usually be filled to capacity. There was, to

Fig. 12-3
Standing by F-22 before installation of big tank, 1940.

my knowledge, no similar arrangement for handling condensation in the front tank, but condensation never caused any trouble, perhaps because it was smaller and was topped up more frequently.

In 1928 Burt Hinkler had shown what could be accomplished with a light airplane of about one hundred horsepower. In 15-½ days he established a record from England to Australia (11,000 miles) in a small Avro Avian biplane equipped with large tanks that extended the range to over 1,100 miles. Flying solo and navigating by dead reckoning, he negotiated

249

Fig. 12-4
In rear cockpit of F-22, 1940.

the distance in a series of hops ranging from 400 to nearly 1,000 miles, flying in all kinds of weather and landing on many marginal fields. It was an incredible feat of endurance. Two years later Amy Johnson attempted to lower Hinkler's record in an aircraft of comparable size and performance. Her De Havilland Moth had a tankage of 80 gallons, maximum endurance of about 12 hours, and a range of 1,000 miles. Johnson's attempt was remarkable because of her limited flying experience. She made the trip in 15 flying days, and might have beaten Hinkler's record had she not lost several days due to a landing accident and a delay from an engine malfunction.

I had followed these and other flights with interest through the British publication *The Aeroplane.* What was it like to put in 5–10 hours in the open cockpit of a light airplane day after day? I was hoping to get some perspective on their achievements during my 3,000-mile solo flight from Seattle to Maine.

Although I continued to build up time on the F-22 over the following months, the opportunity for a transcontinental trip wouldn't present itself until August 1941, when I was able to squeeze out a couple of weeks of

vacation. Meanwhile, through Eddie Brown, FBO at Boeing Field, I acquired a few dozen Sectional Aeronautical Charts covering the upper half of the United States. At the time, I was living in a tiny bedroom in a private home on the top of Seattle's First Hill, where the floor space was too limited to lay out the maps and locate a provisional course. Fortunately Mildred Spokely, a young nurse who lived upstairs and was an occasional dance partner, offered her floor. We moved her furniture around and laid out a number of adjacent charts.

I HAD NO INTENTION of becoming involved in instrument flight with just an airspeed indicator, tachometer, altimeter and ball bank—to say nothing of having zero instrument-flight experience. My plan was to use low-level pilotage with visual landmarks on the ground, assisted by dead reckoning with compass and stopwatch. After talking with local pilots, I plotted the route and organized the Sectional Maps sequentially in a couple of evenings in Mildred's apartment. In planning the section through the Cascades and Rockies, I frequently thought of my father. My course to my first checkpoint at Ellensburg would take me about 40 miles south of Stevens Pass, named for the great civil engineer John Stevens, who was my father's friend, and I would reach the route of the transcontinental railroad at Spokane. How I wished my father still was alive to follow my flight over the areas he had surveyed. His was a pioneering era for the railroads, mine for the airplane—a mere 30 years apart.

The Fairchild had a small magnetic compass surrounded by considerable steel in the fuselage and engine, and by the strapping for the big aluminum tank. I decided that a good "compass swing" was needed to determine the deviations. After installing the aluminum tank a couple of weeks before my departure, I

Fig. 12-5
Burt Hinkler's Avro Avian, which first set the light plane record from England to Australia in 15-½ days in 1928.

Fig. 12-6
Amy Johnson's De Havilland Moth, which came close to breaking Hinkler's record in 1930.

Fig. 12-7
Amy Johnson's De Havilland Moth *Jason* about to leave Croydon. She was the first woman to attempt this flight.

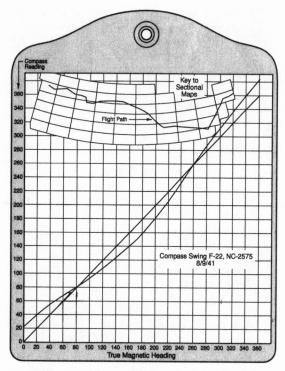

Fig. 12-8
I carried this card on my transcontinental flight in 1941. It has the key to all the sectional maps I used and also the calibration of my compass after the big tank was installed.

did the compass swing on August 9. We used a technique devised for the big Boeing A-314 flying boats, the wing of which originally was designed for the XB-15, a one-of-a-kind large bombardment aircraft for the Air Corps. The wing had built-up truss spars of square steel tubing riveted together, reminiscent of bridge construction. The wing and the hull were built together on launching ways more typical of marine than of later aircraft practice. The combination of the steel structure, the vibration from the riveting and the fixed orientation of the wing in the earth's magnetic field resulted in a highly magnetized wing that because of its huge size could not easily be degaussed. Therefore it was imperative to do an accurate in-flight compass calibration before delivering the aircraft to Pan Am, especially because the deviations could be 50 degrees or more. Essentially, we devised a sundial. A vertical pin about eight inches long was located at the center of a circular protractor that was supported on gimbals to remain horizontal.

Knowing the latitude and longitude of the test location, and the Greenwich Mean Time, and using the Air Almanac, one could calculate the azimuth angle of the sun relative to true north. From the pin's shadow the heading of the aircraft relative to the sun was obtained, and the difference was the angle between true north and the heading of the aircraft. The true magnetic heading—the angle between the heading of the aircraft and the north magnetic pole—then was obtained by applying the magnetic variation (magnetic north from true north) for the location. For the Fairchild, I made a plot of compass reading versus true magnetic heading for the 360 degrees, which I carried in the aircraft. The deviations reached a maximum of about 23 degrees. To obtain my course relative to true north, I would have to apply the local variation as indicated on the Sectional Charts.

It seemed wise to let my boss in on my plans. Eddie Allen proved more than sympathetic, and gave me the bearskin-lined flying suit he had used during his early airmail days when he flew a De Havilland DH-4 on the winter run between Salt Lake and Cheyenne. It turned out to be so warm that I abandoned it the second day out. He also suggested that since I was flying an X-licensed airplane, and was also violating wartime regulations governing private flying, I'd be smart to stick to secondary fields or even hay pastures whenever possible. The portable radio receiver with tower frequency I had invested in obviously would be superfluous, so I was to jettison it as well. The secondhand seat-type pongee parachute I bought from Eddie Brown for $300 would stay with me for the whole trip.

On Saturday, August 23, I made a final check of the airplane, topped up the oil, filled the standard fuel tank and as a general reserve put 15 gallons (a couple of hours of flight time) in the big tank. The engine ran well on 75-octane aviation fuel. The valve oiler—a reservoir and pump in the cockpit—had to be checked and filled; one shot every hour would keep the valve mechanism well lubricated. I then packed my sparse belongings—an extra shirt, underwear and the proverbial toothbrush. The Sectional Maps (except for Seattle), a Weems protractor (for laying-off courses), a five-inch slide rule (for time/distance

Fig. 12-9
L-R: Willie Innocenti, myself, and Bill Talbott after installation of big tank, 1941.

Fig. 12-10
When I found this photo I didn't recognize the attractive lady on the right. It turned out she was Bill Talbott's wife, and Bill had taken the picture.

calculations) and a checklist were stored on board. New batteries were put in two flashlights clipped to a diagonal tube in the cockpit.

Nothing is more compatible with adventure than traveling light. My father had first told me that, and I proved it to myself hitchhiking and reading about Charles Lindbergh's New York–Paris flight. When I returned to my room that Saturday evening I felt relaxed, and confident that things were in good order. All the tools of my trade were conveniently arranged in the rear cockpit. I decided on my wardrobe—ordinary riding britches, a chamois zip-up jacket, leather helmet and goggles—and anticipated with pleasure the hours I would spend in the cozy environment of the F-22.

Fig. 12-11
Standing by the propeller of Fairchild F-22.

All that remained was confirmation of my initial course on the Seattle Sectional. The protractor gave me the true course to Ellensburg as 114 degrees. Magnetic north (the magnetic variation listed on the Sectional Map) was 19.5 degrees east of true north for this leg, giving a magnetic heading of 114–19.5 = 94.5 degrees. From my compass calibration, the compass reading for this heading was 92 degrees. I would fly on this heading until I could observe the wind drift and make a correction to track my true path over the ground. Incidentally, the magnetic variation would change continuously as I crossed the continent, reading some 15 degrees west by the time I reached Maine.

Up and Away

My departure on Sunday, August 24, was a quiet one for obvious reasons. Only Bill Talbott and Willie Innocenti were there to see me off. As a teenager Bill dove off one of Seattle's higher bridges, 80 feet or so to the water. Since then his career had ranged from champion stenotypist to itinerant preacher. You could always count on Bill to be there for anything new and different. As we rolled the airplane out he asked me how far I expected to get that day. My answer: "I'd like to get the Cascades behind me and on past Spokane. That should be an easy start, leaving tomorrow for tackling the Rockies."

In the cockpit I ran through the checklist: front tank on, big tank off, stabilizer set for takeoff, carburetor heat off, mixture rich, prime and wobble up some fuel pressure. Switch off, Willie pulled the prop through a few times. Switch on, with a healthy swing the engine came to life. Willie ran around and looked over my shoulder as I revved up to check the left and the right magnetos. We're set! He slapped me on the helmet and gave a thumbs up as Bill Talbott raised his clasped hands in the pugilist's salute.

Chocks away, I taxied out to the north end of the main runway. It was a gorgeous summer day in Seattle, high cumulus clouds and Mt. Rainier, although 60 miles away, appearing as if it were at the end of the runway. At 11:30 A.M. I was off for Ellensburg. There was a little crosswind, and 94 degrees on the compass seemed to put me on the right ground track.

The realization that I was finally on my way to Maine sank in. It was the same feeling I had when starting a hitchhiking trip from Old Town. Just a few blocks down old Route 1 and I had forgotten all about home. As much as I loved flight testing at Boeing and my life in Seattle, I honestly can say I seldom thought about either until I arrived in Maine. Of course, freedom is more than getting away from the usual; it's being alone and able to make your own decisions. Lindbergh quoted his father in saying, "One boy's a boy, but by the time you get to three boys, there is no boy at all." Alone in the F-22, I'm my own boy in my own airplane with a big tank. I'm looking out over that long nose with the neat fairing that Willie fashioned to cover the front cockpit. Wow!

Once I got over my emotional high and settled into the routine I became aware of two things. The first was the remarkable detail of the Sectional Maps, which correlated exactly with the features on the ground. All the way

Fig. 12-12
Leaving Boeing Field on Sunday, August 24, 1941.

to Maine I found only a few discrepancies. Second was the effectiveness of dead reckoning if one has a good compass calibration and an estimate of the wind, and the air is not rough enough to make the compass oscillate. In general these conditions prevailed throughout my flight, so I could fly the corrected compass heading and watch the landmarks slip by while comparing them with their counterparts on the map on my lap. From an estimate of ground speed I could predict when some prominent feature of the terrain was supposed to turn up, and sure enough it would be there. Like a railroad in the sky, I could almost hear the rhythm of the wheels passing over the joints in the track.

An hour and a half out, at Ellensburg, I made a brief stop to stretch my legs and then headed to Spokane. The Stratoliner test flights had made me fairly familiar with the Moses Lake region, a large plateau whose average elevation above sea level is 2,000–3,000 feet, with north-south and east-west dimensions of roughly 125 miles. The direct distance from Ellensburg to Spokane is only 160 miles. As my ground speed was about 107 miles per hour on this leg, I approached Spokane a little after 3:00 P.M. with the sun still well above the mountains to the west.

SPOKANE FASCINATED ME. My father had talked about Spokane a great deal. It was his base on various occasions, and he and my mother had honeymooned at the famous Davenport Hotel there. Passing over the city at 2,000 feet I could clearly see its main features and the Spokane River off to the east. I followed the river to Coeur d'Alene, Idaho, and on down to Kellogg, Idaho, where I landed at 4:15 P.M. Kellogg lies in a narrow pass, with only a single small runway on the south side, so it seemed a logical place to spend the night before tackling the mountainous regions to the east. The single attendant at the field helped me stake down the aircraft and then drove me to a nearby restaurant and rooming house. Even better, he volunteered to pick me up at around six the next day for an early start. I left the portable radio and Eddie's bearskin suit behind, with the understanding they were his if I didn't contact him in the next week or so. In the half day since leaving Seattle the F-22 had racked up some 360 miles in 4.25 flight hours, at an average ground speed of 84.7 miles per hour, indicating a tailwind of about 10 mph. I went to bed and dreamed about chalking up some real mileage the next day.

At 6:50 A.M. I took off from Kellogg, flying 800 feet or so above the bottom of a canyon whose rocky walls rose to the left and right above me. Overhead was an intermittent, though nearly solid, cloud cover. After a few miles I passed Wallace and, according to the map, the Bitterroot Range to the north and south. Down below, a narrow road wound along a cut in the right-hand side of the canyon's base, with the river close by on the left. Although I felt reasonably comfortable flying down this natural canyon, it obviously was no place for an engine failure. The road seemed so narrow and curvy that I wondered if I could pull off a safe emergency landing on it. The other alternative, pulling up into the cloud base, was equally unattractive because even if I were a capable instrument pilot there were plenty of high peaks to fly into. So I placed my faith in the Gipsy engine.

Following the canyon's meanderings for the next half hour or so at 75 miles per hour took some concentration, and I was not immediately aware that the canyon was narrowing. Quite unconsciously, I had been flying a little higher to maintain a sensible clearance between my wing tips and the sloping walls. Only when I approached the cloud layer did I realize how serious the situation had become. My initial reaction to the narrowing was to turn around and go back, but a 180-degree turn in the space now available was chancy. I'd never make it at 75 miles an hour, and a tight turn at lower speed was a prescription for disaster. By now the walls were a hundred feet off my wing tips as my mind raced through the alternatives. I couldn't go back; it was risky to go down, and even riskier to go up. With no clear way out of this dilemma, I began to feel anxiety and tension building. Although not claustrophobic in the conventional sense, I had an aversion to really tight places like caves and chimneys. I was much too busy in the present moment to be conscious of all this, but the idea of being trapped in this converging tunnel added to the pressure. How the hell did I get into this mess? Why didn't I study the map more closely when it still was safe to do so?

I WAS DETERMINED to maintain flying speed and control, and ride it out as long as possible. The outcome of this crazy ride could not be far off. As the canyon continued to narrow, a zig to the left was followed by a sharp turn

to the right, so sharp in fact that it appeared that the canyon had come to a stop and I was headed for a blank wall. I racked the airplane into a hard tight turn, pulling back on the stick to build up the g's. With the feeling that the canyon width now was less than my wingspan, I whipped into a turn of 100 degrees or more, as I looked down the jagged face of the wall 50 feet off the top of my helmet.

And then suddenly—more suddenly than it had narrowed—the canyon widened. With immense relief I sensed I was in the clear, though I still was charged with adrenaline and yelling to discharge the emotion. As if to celebrate my deliverance, the cloud cover dissolved within the next few minutes and shafts of sunlight poured into the canyon. I wasted no time in studying the map, which indicated there were no more gauntlets to be run. Relaxation came and I found myself humming one of my favorite tunes ("Beyond the Blue Horizon, There's a Beautiful Day") as I landed in Missoula at 8:30 A.M. The trip from Kellogg had been 100 miles as the crow flies, and I still had the best part of the day ahead. Thanks to the meandering path of the canyon, my average ground speed had only been 60 miles per hour.

At Missoula I picked up some gasoline and set off for Helena at 9:00 A.M. I was flying in sunshine over the southern Rockies, where elevations are only several thousand feet above sea level. My true course was 103 degrees, with a variation 17 degrees east, giving a compass heading of 86 degrees, since the deviation happened to be zero. The wind was from directly ahead at about 10 mph, so the 90 miles to Helena was covered at an average ground speed of only 60 miles per hour. At Helena the true course to Billings changed slightly to 107.5 degrees, with a compass heading of 88 degrees. The wind had dropped off considerably and the speed picked up accordingly, averaging 68 miles per hour for the 200-mile Helena-to-Billings run.

Reaching Billings at 2:15 P.M, I realized that the higher mountains were behind me and I was approaching the plains. Without prominent landmarks in this part of Montana, dead reckoning on compass was necessary. My confidence in this form of navigation in smooth air had increased, and it was highly satisfying when my destinations turned up over the nose right on schedule.

I got a bite to eat and then climbed back into the cockpit to consider my alternatives.

Since leaving Kellogg I already had 400 miles behind me, and several hours of daylight were left. If I could run up 600 miles today I would approach the average daily pace of Burt Hinkler and Amy Johnson, and would have been in the air about nine hours—a laudable performance. At Billings the Yellowstone comes in from the northeast in about the direction of Bismarck, North Dakota, the next major city along my route. I pulled out the map and drew a line along the river, 64.5 degrees true, passing north of Miles City. If I left Billings by 3:30 P.M. I guessed that there would be about three hours before sunset, and very conservatively estimated that I could make at least another 150 miles. Laying out that distance along the line, I was surprised to find the symbol of a secondary field close to the 150-mile point. That was fortunate, because once past Miles City there were few towns or cities. Since leaving Seattle I had refueled at airports servicing substantial communities. I hesitated about using this one. Secondary fields are ill-defined; some might better be called emergency landing places. The best can have an elementary hangar, permanent fuel facilities, a windsock and a part-time attendant; the worst might be little more than a hay pasture that occasionally is mowed. The map gave no clue of what to expect, and I wondered why this one was included on the map. I decided to try for it.

For the first 50 miles after leaving Billings at 3:30 P.M., my course followed the Yellowstone River. The countryside was flat and brown, and I flew at 200–500 feet to make life more interesting. Landmarks were few and far between, but at 4:30 the Bighorn, where Custer made his last stand, turned up just as the river swung north. A check of time and distance run showed a headwind of 20 mph and a ground speed for the last hour of only 55 miles per hour. Although the sun still was high, at this speed it would be after 6:00 when I reached the secondary field.

I had enjoyed a long, pleasant summer afternoon in a warm and comfortable cockpit.

Not at all tired, I felt I could go on forever, and was lulled by the thought that in this flat, rolling countryside I could always find a place to put down.

Running Out of Sun

A little after six o'clock my dead reckoning told me I was in the vicinity of the field, and without changing course I started looking for it. The rolling countryside was dotted with farmhouses, irrigation ditches and fields of crops, but in the last hour I had seen no major habitation nor was there any area suggesting a secondary field. There were places into which I probably could sideslip, but since my intention was to land where gas was available, and where the aircraft could safely be tied down for the night, I studied the map again and spotted another secondary field some 25 miles farther on. It was near a town called Terry, at least another 30 minutes away with an ETA of 6:45 P.M.

Behind me the summer cumulus clouds I enjoyed during the afternoon had built up into towering black masses with occasional flashes of lightning. The sky had darkened and the sun, still above the horizon, was gray. Nothing ahead seemed to deter my decision to push on toward Terry, but to have some margin I advanced the throttle beyond normal cruising rpm and got back on compass.

Official sunset on Monday, August 25, 1944, at Terry (46.78 degrees north latitude, 105.22 degrees west longitude) was at 6:54 P.M. I didn't know that at the time, certainly a deficiency in my flight planning, since I was anxious to fully utilize the daylight hours. The air was becoming unsettled, and flashes off to the east said there were thunderstorms ahead as well as behind. The air became progressively rougher. I began to think I never had flown in such turbulent conditions, but that wasn't true. On my trans-Canada flight to Maine the previous Christmas, the "bumps" (accelerations) became so violent I wondered if the structure could take it. Tonight, in the F-22, it was not so much the accelerations as the motions. I was all-out on the controls as the airplane rolled, yawed and pitched like a raft in rapids.

The compass became nearly useless, but enough light was left to line up on some features of the terrain. I hoped I was headed in the right direction. A quick time check indicated that I must be near the field. Minutes later I thought I had found it in a large smooth pasture below, with no noticeable fences or ditches, and something that might be a windsock in one corner. The fringes of the storm had arrived with low clouds and rain. I was down to 600 feet or so, milling around in the turbulence and trying to guess the wind direction for a landing. Making one downwind turn, the airplane suddenly slowed, as if it had stopped in midair. A flash of lighting illuminated the panel and I glimpsed the airspeed needle winding down. I shoved the stick full forward and jammed on full throttle while trying to roll off the turn. It was a defining moment, in which a low-altitude stall was averted by a very narrow margin. After that my only thought was to get down fast—far better to wreck the airplane in a crazy landing than to spin in. In that turbulent air I couldn't figure out the wind direction for a normal landing, so I started down on my existing heading, hoping to maintain a modest rate of descent and still keep the wing flying. It was a juggling act with stick and throttle. Daylight and choices had run out; there was no time for analysis or emotion, only reaction to survival instincts. Aside from my sense of a faint horizon, I was descending into utter darkness with no idea of what was ahead. Down we came—it seemed forever—with the gusts subsiding as we approached the ground. A big swish and we were bumping along in a wheat field with the grass as high as the cockpit. The landing must have been directly into the wind since she couldn't have rolled 50 feet once she hit. In total darkness and with the engine still ticking over, I leaned over the stick and murmured some thanks to all the gods.

For a while I just sat there, wrung out and devoid of a plan. Other than rain blowing into the cockpit I was comfortable enough, and could curl up there for the night and sort things out in the morning. Soon, however, the storm abated and showed evidence of moving on or perhaps exhausting itself. The wind stopped,

the gusts subsided, and the moon showed through scudding clouds. My eyes were getting used to the darkness and I thought I could see the edge of the field. Cautiously taxiing in that direction, I came to a narrow dirt road and started toward the light of a town in the distance. Western towns are built around a wide main street, and the road I was on led into Terry. I taxied slowly down the main street as horses and automobiles conveniently pulled off to the sides. Past a couple of old-time saloons was a rather prominent home with a front yard onto which I taxied. I put on the brakes, revved up the engine, and switched off. The owner of the house came out the front door, walked slowly to the airplane, put both hands on the cowling and said, "I think you'd better come in and have some supper." That was my lifetime "tops" in hospitality.

A marvelous meal and an invitation to stay overnight followed. In conversation that evening I learned that a vice president at Boeing had been born in Terry, and I was delegated to carry best wishes back to the "hometown boy who made good" when I returned to Seattle. Crawling into bed that night and snuggling down under the puff, I remember thinking I had certainly had a day for myself. Over 9-½ hours in the air, 600 miles plus, and a couple of adventures along the way.

The next day we went out to survey where I had landed. The airplane had just missed an irrigation ditch and a substantial fence, and the tracks showed the landing had been very short indeed. The only reasonable place to take off was on the other side of the irrigation ditch. A number of folks got busy with shovels to make an earthen pathway across the ditch. We pushed the airplane across, and after handshakes all around I took off and flew back to Miles City for aviation fuel, which was not available in Terry. Leaving there about noon, I had an uneventful 3-½ hour flight to Bismarck, North Dakota. The mileage that day was only 291, the shortest leg of the entire flight to Maine.

Full Load Takeoff

A major airport with a new long paved runway, Bismarck gave me the opportunity to fill up the big tank so I could run off some real non-stop mileage. Before leaving the airport that evening, I left word that I was planning an early start the next day. Skipping breakfast, I arrived at the airport at 6:30 A.M., a little apprehensive at never having flown the F-22 with a total of 76 gallons of fuel on board. But as Table 12-1 indicates, I had no reason to feel anxious.

By 7:15 A.M. we started the takeoff. The tail came up in a couple of hundred feet, after which the F-22 accelerated rapidly. I held the plane down to an airspeed of 70 before easing off. In my imagination I had envisioned a heavy-load takeoff with the aircraft struggling into the air. In actuality my takeoff technique had been far too conservative. Thanks to the location of the big tank near the CG, there were no noticeable trim or stability problems.

Thus the difference in takeoff and climb performance would hardly be noticeable. It was far from a heavy-load takeoff.

Long Legs

The weather was beautiful, with little wind and hardly a cloud in the sky, as we got on compass for Rochester, Minnesota, 450 miles away. With flat countryside most of the way, I flew at 200 feet checking progress against small towns, roads and railways. A hundred and fifty miles out, the corner of South Dakota was crossed,

and in another 75 miles we entered Minnesota near Ortonville, due south of Fargo, making good time with a ground speed of 75 miles per hour.

How delightful it was to fly at low altitude! The cloud scenery I had experienced at high altitude during the Stratoliner and B-17 flights had its lonely fascination, but at low altitude one is connected with all the warmth of the earth. As a child I had read about the early flights of the big French Farman and Voisin biplanes, and the monoplane *Antoinette*. All these flights were accomplished at little more than treetop height, with the pilot sitting unprotected in the airstream. One children's book, charmingly titled *Over the Sea in a Bleriot Monoplane,* depicted a plane low over the water. Gazing out the grade-school window, I would dream of flying toward Bar Harbor and the Blue Hills, which lay on the horizon near the Maine coast.

In Minnesota I amused myself comparing the shapes of its myriad blue-water lakes with those on the map. When trimmed out, the aircraft held its course with only an occasional nudge on the controls. The F-22 had full-span ailerons that were directly connected to the stick at their inner ends by push-pull tubes that passed through the cowling. By sitting high in the cockpit, I could reach outside the cowl, grasp the ends of the ailerons and move them

Table 12-1. Fairchild F-22 Weight. The standard Fairchild Model 22-C7D with a 90-hp Wright Gipsy engine has a wing area of 170 ft^2, an NACA N-22 airfoil and a gross weight of 1550 lbs., as follows:

Item	Standard	Actual at Bismarck
Weight empty	992 lbs	992 lbs
Big tank (empty weight)		60
Pilot	170	135
One passenger	170	
Parachutes	40	20
Baggage	34	15
Fuel (21 gal.)	126	
Fuel (76 gal.)		456
Oil (2.4 gal.)	18	18
Gross Weight	1550	1696

Landing speed at standard weight is 48 mph. Standard wing loading is 1550/170 = 9.12 lb./ft.^{2}
Wing loading at my Bismarck weight was 1696/170 = 9.98 lb./ft.^{2} The landing speed varies as the square root of the weight, so the landing speed as loaded at Bismarck would be equal to: 48 (1696/1550)$^{1/2}$ = 50 mph.

to control the bank, which I supposed was the closest I ever would come to feeling the air forces as a bird does when twisting its wing to roll into a turn.

At 11:20 A.M. we landed at Rochester for a bite of lunch after a six-hour non-stop flight from Bismarck. Although the longest hop on the transcontinental journey, it also was one of the easiest because of the ideal flying conditions. In retrospect I wished I had flown on for another two hours, to claim a full eight-hour day in a single flight.

Rochester was left at 2:15 P.M. Flying on the same compass course, we entered the northeast corner of Iowa before the hour was out, and in the next half hour met up with the Mississippi River. We followed it south to Dubuque, landing there at 4:10 P.M. By the route flown, the Mississippi is 1,752 miles from Seattle and more than halfway to Maine, exciting news in itself.

Adding seven gallons of fuel to the standard tank, I flew another 80 miles to Dixon, Illinois, 100 miles due west of Chicago. It was 5:15 P.M. and I decided to call it a day after nearly nine hours and 667 miles. By a small margin this was the longest daily mileage of the trip, at a good average ground speed of 73.4 miles per hour. I was beginning to appreciate pilots like Hinkler and Johnson, who flew eight to nine-hour days for nearly two weeks at cruising speeds comparable to the F-22. I really wanted to get an inkling of what these stalwarts had experienced, and decided to put in two more long days on top of the one just completed.

On Thursday, August 28, I got a 6:50 A.M. start out of Dixon and headed for Fort Wayne, Indiana, 250-odd miles away. Sixty miles out, in a little less than an hour, we ran out of fuel in the big tank and made a quick switch back to the standard tank. This provided the opportunity to get a check on fuel consumption. The air was smooth and things were going well, so I got on with some final calculations.

F-22 Fuel Consumption

No fuel had been added to the big tank since it was filled in Bismarck.

When fuel was added to the standard tank, it always was topped off.

Taxi, takeoff, approach and landing always were made on the standard tank; otherwise operation was on the big tank.

From my log, fuel was added to the standard tank as follows:
- 7 gallons at Rochester, Minnesota
- 7 gallons at Dubuque, Iowa
- 4 gallons at Dixon, Illinois

Thus a total of 18 gallons had been used in three takeoffs and three landings to Dixon or 18/6=3 gallons per taxi/takeoff or approach/landing. Leaving Dixon, fuel used from the standard tank was 18+3=21 gallons.

Let's guess that the Gipsy burns 8 gallons/hour, thus: 21 gallons/8=2.63 hours spent on the small tank.

Total flight time from Bismarck to Dixon was, according to the log, 8.73 hours. Since the big tank quit 60 miles out of Dixon (cruising at 65 miles per hour), the tank ran out at 60/65=0.92 hours out of Dixon.

Total time from Bismarck to runout was 8.73+0.92=9.65 hours, and the total time on the big tank was 9.65–2.63=7.02 hours. Since the big tank held 55 gallons, the consumption was 55/7.02=7.83 gallons per hour, close to the assumed 8 gallons per hour.

This was the best I could do in the air; a more accurate analysis on the ground gave 7.9 gallons per hour. (According to the type certificate recently obtained from the EAA Library, the manufacturer claimed 6 gal./hr. for this model F-22, which I never was able to realize.)

My average ground speed from Bismarck to fuel runoff was: (667+60 miles)/(9.65 hours)=727/9.65=75.3 miles per hour giving 75.3/7.9=9.53 miles per gallon, based on winds I had encountered.

For rough estimates I would round this off to 8 gallons per hour and 10 miles per gallon.

Interesting Detour

Other than fuel runout in the big tank the flight went smoothly, with arrival at Fort Wayne at 10:35 A.M. In fact, things were going so well I decided to make a small detour to call on a girl who lived in Hagerstown, Maryland.

A phone call confirmed she was home, so I laid out a course by Wheeling, West Virginia and Chambersburg, Maryland. Nearly four hours away, Wheeling was reached at 3:00 P.M. After seven hours in the air it was time for a break, a fuel-up and a clean-up before pushing on. From the air I could see that Wheeling had a nice long runway, but other than a single hangar it seemed devoid of facilities. More puzzling was the lack of any activity: no parked cars or airplanes in the vicinity of the hangar or in the air as far as I could see.

In those days the Civil Aeronautics Administration (under the U.S. Department of Commerce) published a "Weekly Notice to Airmen" (NOTAM) covering all airport and facility changes that could affect safe use. Runways under repair, inoperative boundary lights and so forth, were called out. Before leaving Seattle I tucked the issue for August 21 in with the maps, and now I consulted it. NOTAMS were tabulated by states, and a quick scan of those for West Virginia revealed nothing. I was tired, the runway was inviting, and although I had a spooky feeling akin to boarding an abandoned ship, I decided to land and investigate.

The runway proved smooth and spacious— brand-new in fact as I later learned, because the airport still was under construction. I rolled to a stop, taxied back and parked near the hangar, and without thinking, switched off the engine. Climbing out, I stretched my legs and in short order concluded that the place was indeed deserted.

There was no alternative except to leave, but to do so I first had to start the engine. The F-22 was not equipped with a self-starter, nor was there any way to lock on the toe brakes. The engine always had been started with the throttle barely off idle, and I didn't remember the aircraft starting to roll at that setting. So again with a minimum of thinking on my part, I decided to get the engine well primed, set the throttle at idle, pull the prop through myself and run around and climb aboard. Of course it didn't work out that way. The engine was well primed all right, starting with a bang probably because the throttle at the carburetor was not quite at idle and the engine was not merely ticking over. As the plane started to move

forward and pick up speed, I ducked under the wing struts and got one hand on the coaming at the edge of the cockpit, first running and then being dragged alongside. By now it was pretty obvious that the throttle was moving still farther forward under the vibration. Somehow I managed to get one foot on the external foot rest on the fuselage and more or less tumbled into the cockpit head first, scrambling around to sort things out before running off the side of the runway. The whole thing was so asinine that it struck me as immensely funny. I laughed at myself for the next half hour.

CHAMBERSBURG WAS REACHED at 5:20 P.M., Hagerstown at 6:00. The day had totaled 10 hours in the air, and 666 miles covered at an average of 68 miles per hour. My friend was at the airport to pick me up. She was cordial enough and her folks were genuinely hospitable, but the elements of a romantic interlude were lacking. I was dead tired, had lived in the same clothes for a week and hadn't had a real bath since leaving Seattle. Perhaps if I had been more famous, I could have gotten away with it. After landing a Sikorsky amphibian at Vought-Sikorsky when I worked there, Howard Hughes had inquired about the way to the summer home of Katherine Hepburn's parents where she was visiting. My attire in Hagerstown was quite an improvement over his, and at least I recently had shaved. Carrying a straggly-looking bouquet, Hughes hiked down the road to a taxi stand. He reappeared the next day in the same outfit (and certainly no cleaner) but by his jaunty appearance I surmised he had made out well with Kate.

Psychological Implications

At 8:30 the next morning I was off on the sixth and last day of my journey. The weather was good, the winds favorable and I averaged some 84 miles per hour for the 575 miles from Hagerstown to Bangor. Having pondered the endurance of Hinkler and Johnson, thinking mainly in physical terms of long hours in cramped cockpits, lack of exercise and irregular meals, I thought I had done pretty well for the five days of my own flight. But now some of the psychological implications of this kind of

Fig. 12-13
First landing (by any airplane) on Old Town's new airfield; F-22, Saturday, August 30, 1941.

flying surfaced. For one thing, although tired, I had not found going to sleep easy because of a free-floating anxiety the minute I hit the sack, followed by anxiety-laden dreams. Sleep deprivation stirs up the subconscious, but while it might amplify my anxieties I felt it could not be the basic cause. Also puzzling was the fact that I seemed to be little bothered during the day when flying, and had reacted well in the several emergency situations. On thinking about it I recognized that occasional moments of anxiety while flying had largely been suppressed by the demands of navigation and the general workload. The incident that revealed the cause of my psychological anxiety occurred upon landing at Lehighton, Pennsylvania, a relatively small airport. My approach should have been on the slow side with a normal stall margin. In fact I felt uncomfortable in slowing down to a reasonable approach speed, and sailed in much too fast, touching down on the main gear. Realizing I couldn't stop, I had to go around again. Once on the ground, a mechanic inquired if I had just soloed the aircraft.

It was all too clear that my problem was a fear of stalling engendered by the incident at Terry, the emotion of which had slipped into my subconscious. Years later, as I learned more about psychology, I agreed with Carl Jung that "whatever isn't brought to consciousness, potentially can get you." Highly emotional material stored like a coiled rattler in the recesses of the subconscious can, when triggered, emerge with frightening effects. Most pilots are aware of the stall and the technique for avoiding and recovering from it, but intellectually I was burdened with a knowledge of the mechanics of the stall and how large components of rolling moment (torque) on the aircraft that are nicely balanced against each other in normal flight suddenly change sign algebraically and add up to an enormous magnitude that rotate the airplane into a spin. Normal control actions are ineffective and the normally huge damping-in-roll is no longer present, allowing amplification of the motion. At MIT I had been fascinated with the physics of the stall as presented in Koppen's course in Stability and Control. Now this knowledge, backed by an active imagination, became a nuisance in practice. I had also been exposed to the catastrophic consequence of tail stall on the XSO2U-1 at Vought, and the stalling behavior of the Stratoliner without tip slots at Boeing.

Coming Home

Leaving Lehighton, I flew on to Pittsfield, near the western border of Massachusetts, then across New Hampshire south of the White Mountains, crossing the Merrimac River and the southern tip of Lake Winnipesaukee. The New England I knew and loved was in glorious array, with scattered cumulus clouds drifting slowly overhead, solid green areas of still virgin forest below and little towns connected by wandering roads that followed the terrain. We were being hurried along with the best tailwind of the entire trip, leaving the miles behind at the rate of 87 miles per hour. After one more stop at Lewiston, Maine, and a phone call home, I got on compass course for Bangor, the last leg. Twenty minutes later Augusta slid by the left wing tip, reminding me of the night landing Nancy and I had made on the muster field in another F-22 some nine years earlier. The field looked much more inviting on this sunny afternoon.

Before leaving Seattle I had wired my mother for information on a landing place near Bangor. The old pasture known as Godfrey's Field had, under wartime impetus, been converted into a major Air Force base, one of the chain used for ferrying aircraft to the European theater. Dow AFB, as it now was known, would become an important postwar air refueling site of the Strategic Air Command. It obviously was no place to land an itinerant X-licensed F-22. My mother had answered my wire three days before I left

Seattle, and I had slipped a copy into the map pocket,

> Examined Doanes Field in South Brewer across the river from Bangor, near Standpipe, River and Eastern Manufacturing Company. Probably best bet with 2 good runways and hangar.
> Signed, Mother

I had visited Bangor frequently since leaving home, but this time it was different. Before, I had traveled to Maine in a hurry. On this occasion, after long hours in the air, I was weary, my resistance was down, and all the old places and events from childhood came flooding into my memory like a kaleidoscope. I was also consumed with that "journey proud" feeling, signaling the end of a dream about to come true.

It started when I saw Dixmont Hills, the site of the old homestead of my mother's ancestors. Approaching Bangor from the southeast brought the Fairgrounds and its half-mile dirt track. At the Eastern Maine State Fair one exciting year, instead of harness racing the track sponsored an auto race, with Fronty-Fords and specials making up the field. The race cars had been garaged in various car dealerships, and naturally Ed and I visited them all. Beyond the Fairgrounds I sighted the Bangor Music Festival's home, a formidable wooden structure where I spent painful hours as a child listening to operatic music with my mother. She was enthralled, but my memory was of hard seats and the chill that pervaded the place. A thousand feet over the city center, I looked straight down on the Freese Department Store, where every year before Christmas my father and I visited the toy department.

BEFORE LANDING AT DOANES FIELD I made a half-circle over the city, spotting the Bangor Library and the former showroom of a dealership that sold Rolls-Royces and Stutz Black Hawks to wealthy summer clients. Looking down at the Penobscot, I could see the power dam and, south of it, the famous salmon pool where the first catch of the year traditionally was sent to the president at the White House. I now was approaching the bridge over the river to Brewer, and saw the corner where Peanut Spruce and I, riding my Excelsior motorcycle, collided with a farm truck delivering eggs.

Doanes Field was easy to locate. I circled once, checked the windsock, and came in on a straight approach at a moderately low speed for the best landing of the day. My mother and brother Cooper were waiting for me. The reunion was a happy one, but as we were all descended from those godawful Puritans, it was more sincere than demonstrative. It would be years before Cooper and I could engage in an honest-to-god hug on such occasions. I could read in my mother's eyes that she was proud of my accomplishment and relieved by my safe arrival. After the plane was hangared with the help of a mechanic, she placed her hand on my arm and said, "You must be tired, William, let's go home. I have a nice supper waiting. You'll want a bath too."

I had been seven hours in the air that day, forty-three hours over the last six days, and was finding it difficult to reorient myself. My mother's simple words brought me back to earth. Where else was I known as William? I was also reminded of my father, the only person in the family who ever called me Bill.

The drive home brought interesting news. Old Town had finally decided to build its own airfield. Although the main gravel runway was graded, no aircraft had yet landed. There the idea immediately suggested itself: why not fly up from Brewer the next day, officially opening the airfield and completing my transcontinental flight in my home town. The occasion would be especially memorable because my father, with his surveying instinct, had been the first to suggest the location for the field. Equally exciting, my brother Cooper had designed the administration building. Earlier he had designed Old Town's town hall.

Only Old Town

As we drove up to 14 Oak Street that night, I gazed at the red geraniums in the upstairs window boxes, the vines of Dutchman's pipe draped over the portico to the kitchen entrance, and the two huge maples shading the bank to the sidewalk—all as they had always been. Conscious of her ancestry, my mother believed in conservation and tradition, cherishing the friends she grew up with and maintaining and saving her worldly goods. Her life was centered on this home on Oak Street.

Fig. 12-14
Greetings by friends and relatives at the new airfield, August 30, 1941. R-L: Rod Averill; cousin Ruth Waterhouse; Susan Pratt; WFM; Mama; cousin Frank Waterhouse; brother Cooper Milliken; Cooper's girl friend, Louise Averill; Lou Averill; a Pratt sister; Judge Averill (behind); Rest—unknown.

Since completing college I'd been away from Old Town for eight years, single and busy and living in rooming houses. Finding home as I had left it lent a sense of continuity to my expanding life.

Supper was among relatives and friends on the canvas-covered deck that looked out over the broad backyard and flower beds. Afterwards I wandered out into the barn chamber to see the M-1. In my bedroom, the sloping walls and ceiling still were covered with clippings of the airplanes and crews of the great pioneering flights.

The next day my brother drove me back to Doanes Field, then returned to Old Town to pick up my mother and cousins and await my arrival at the new airstrip. The sun was brilliant overhead. The F-22 was a spirited aircraft with beautiful lines, and I was proud and anxious to show her off.

I circled the town several times picking up familiar landmarks—the Indian Island Landing, the Old Town Canoe Company with gaily painted canoes weathering on the roof, the rival Helen Hunt and Convent schools, Gray's Mill swimming hole near the site of my father's mill, Bachelor's Field and Blueberry Hill, and of course 14 Oak Street shaded by trees and difficult to spot.

The new field was easy to locate, its gray gravel runway standing out against the lush green of the surrounding forest. I circled once, then made a fast pass over the runway at low altitude, pulled up and let the speed fall off in a 180 and came on in. The wheels touched down and I rolled to a stop near a sizable group of relatives and friends. The Pratt sisters were there on assignment from the *Penobscot Times*. Susan Pratt shot some nice photos of the F-22, and the newspaper story was very flattering, if not wholly accurate, reporting that I had made the entire trip non-stop.

If the big tank had not occupied the front cockpit, this would have been a great occasion to take folks and friends for a flight.

Back to Seattle

A few days later my plans about flying back to Seattle were cut short by a wire from Eddie Allen suggesting I return by conventional air

Fig. 12-15
When Eddie Allen called me back to Seattle I left the airplane at Wiggins Airways, Norwood, Massachusetts. It was flown back to Seattle by Marvin Michael, one of the Boeing pilots. I'm greeting him at Boeing Field, circa 1941.

Fig. 12-16
Eddie Allen presented me with a large pair of dividers with a flexible leg to allow for forced landings and changes in course, 1941.

THE PENOBSCOT TIMES

LOCAL BOY MAKES FIRST LANDING AT OLD TOWN AIRPORT: FLIES NON-STOP ACROSS CONTINENT

Bill Milliken, M. I. T. Grad, Boeing Senior Flight Engineer, Visits Mother; Met By Friends At Unfinished Airport Monday

William F. Milliken, senior flight engineer at the Boeing Aircraft Company's plant in Seattle, Wash., son of Mrs. Abbie Cooper Milliken and the late William F. Milliken, arrived in Old Town Friday night after a transcontinental flight of 3400 miles, for a brief visit with his mother and his brother, Cooper Milliken, 14 Oak Street.

WILLIAM F. MILLIKEN

Mr. Milliken, born with a natural aptitude for mechanics, became interested in aircraft and aviation while a small boy, and that interest grew stronger with the passing years.

While still a schoolboy, he constructed a plane which really flew, but came to grief in landing. His training at M. I. T., from which he was graduated in 1934, was supplemented by vacation study at the Boeing School of Aeronautics during his years at Tech.

During his brief visit to his old home, Mr. Milliken found Monday, Labor Day, the psychological opportunity to make the first landing at Old Town's flying field, now under construction in the section of Old Town in which are included Blueberry Hill and Grass Island.

On that afternoon, he circled above the city and the unfinished airport, made a perfect landing and was greeted and welcomed by the group of friends who knew of his intention, and to whom the sight and sound of his plane overhead was the signal to start for the airport.

It is fitting that the first landing, even if unofficial, should be made by a son of Old Town, who has made good in his chosen calling.

Mr. Milliken spoke in unqualified praise of the layout of this airport in response to the demands of modern transportation; of the character of the work thus far completed.

He made his long flight in his Fairchild 22, converted into a single-seater, and equipped with an auxiliary gas tank.

Fig. 12-17
The article in Old Town's local newspaper, *The Penobscot Times*, reporting on my transcontinental flight. Note that they claimed it was a non-stop flight!

transportation. Things were heating up in the B-17 program, and the XB-29 was in the wings. I flew the F-22 to Boston and left it with Joe Garsides at Wiggins Airways in Norwood. One of our flight engineers, Marvin Michael, flew the plane back to Seattle after a business trip to the East, wiring me his ETA beforehand. I then arranged for Willie Innocenti to help me get the big tank out before a CAA inspector showed up.

When I arrived back at the plant, Eddie Allen presented me a special pair of dividers with a flexible leg, allowing a pilot "to swing suddenly off course for forced landings." A photo of the presentation appeared in the November 1941 issue of *Boeing News*, which led to the following letter from George Haldeman:

> Dear Bill,
> I've just received the November issue of the Boeing News and read with much interest the article in that issue entitled "East by West." Sounds like the little Fairchild-22 is really doing all right, Bill, and I am happy to know that it carried you all the way through to Maine without any trouble.
> I am a little bit put out with you, however, for having passed through Chicago without giving me at least a ring.
> Incidentally, do you have a patent on the pliable dividers and if not please advise me of their flexible construction as I believe I might be able to use one myself on one of my future cross-country flights. Personal regards to you, Bill, please tell the gang "hello" for me.
>
> Yours very truly,
> George W. Haldeman

I HAD LONG WONDERED what it took to set long-distance records in light planes. My transcontinental flight helped to replace imagination and conjecture with experience. My log showed 3,075 miles in six days or 515 miles per day at an average ground speed of 78.8 miles per hour. Burt Hinkler and Amy Johnson had averaged 687.5 and 617.8 miles per day respectively but with average ground speeds of 85 and 80 miles per hour. Since we were flying aircraft of comparable horsepower and performance, one can assume they were benefiting from favorable winds, or were willing to operate their engines at closer to peak power. Although more miles per day were covered, our average time in the air per day was much closer:

Burt Hinkler: 8 hr. 5 min.
Amy Johnson: 7 hr. 43 min.
Bill Milliken: 7 hr. 17 min.

Since hours in the air is, at bottom, a better measure of physical-mental endurance than distance covered, speed is an important factor. A more recent example of this is Clive Canning's circumnavigation of Australia in a Thorp T-18 homebuilt aircraft: nine days, for 7,122 miles at an average speed of 137 miles per hour, which works out to 791 miles per day but only 5 hours 47 minutes of daily air time.

One overall measure of physical-mental endurance may be taken as average air time per day times the number of consecutive days. On this score Hinkler's and Johnson's performance is truly remarkable:

Burt Hinkler: 16 days × 8.01 hours per day = 128.2 hours

Amy Johnson: 16 days × 7.72 hours per day = 123.5 hours

The figure for my transcontinental flight worked out to 43.2 hours. To have approached the Hinkler/Johnson performance, I would have had to turn around, fly back to Seattle and then turn around again and fly to Cleveland. That was well beyond my capability in those days, especially in the psychological department. But by flying one more day, I would have come very close to Canning's performance on the Australian run.

Amy Johnson's England–Australia flight is impressive on another count. Her total solo time prior to her record attempt was only 85 hours, with perhaps 25 hours of cross-

---

g-Level of Lovelace's Parachute Opening

In 2005, my wife Barbara and I drove the Seattle-Missoula leg of my 1941 flight (see page 268). Lovelace's epic jump was one of the powerful memories I encountered, leading me to make this calculation.

Only Reed prophesied that the g-forces (accelerations) would be high; all the rest are loosely basing their opinion on the fact that the air density at 40,000 feet is only a quarter of that at sea level. In the actual event, made with a 30-foot static line, Lovelace blacked out under the deceleration, lost both gloves and nearly ruined his hands from frostbite. He regained consciousness only seconds before landing in the Moses Lake area. I have often wondered why we didn't do a simple analysis of the expected g-forces, since enough data was available. To satisfy my curiosity, consider the following: According to the U.S. Parachute Association, Lovelace must have used a T-4 chute of 28 feet in diameter. In those days the shock absorbing elements, inherent in the material and design of a modern parachute were lacking; thus the opening shock load would be transferred with little attenuation to the jumper. Assume that the B-17 was slowed to 115 mph indicated airspeed at the time of the jump, giving a dynamic air pressure of 31 lbs./ft.² If the chute were to open instantaneously, the decelerating force would be,

$$F = C_D q A$$

- Where, F is the air force on the open canopy of the parachute
- C_D is the drag coefficient of the open chute (1.26)
- q is the dynamic pressure (31 lbs./ft.²)
- A is the cross sectional area of the open chute (616 ft.²)
- F = 1.26 × 31 × 616 = 24,061 lbs.
- and the g force experienced by a 200-lb. man would be g = 24,061 / 200 = 120

In actual fact the chute cannot inflate instantaneously. On the assumption that the projected area of the chute is proportional to the time during opening and assuming one second to full inflation of the canopy, the deceleration is 48g at 0.4 seconds after the ripcord is pulled. This deceleration along the vertical axis of a man is sufficient to cause blackout. The exact indicated airspeed and altitude are not known but the above calculation seems sufficient to account for what happened. The actual airspeed of the airplane for the indicated airspeed of 115, at an altitude of 40,000 feet, is of course much higher, some 230 mph.

country flying in England. I was considerably more experienced, having logged 135 hours solo in light planes before leaving Seattle, some 36 hours of it being cross-country. My transcontinental flight was a great experience, confirming that I had chosen my heroes well. Emulating their performance for even a few days was a challenge that exercised my capabilities to the limit, and added to my confidence and self-esteem.

Looking Back from Ground Level

Shortly after writing this chapter, my wife Barbara and I decided to visit some of my old Boeing friends in Seattle and retrace by car the route of my transcontinental flight from Seattle to Missoula, now Interstate 90. Would I be able to locate that narrowing section of the "canyon" beyond Kellogg where I had to sweat it out some 55 years ago?

Arriving at Sea-Tac (Seattle-Tacoma) Airport, we picked up a car and drove north past the site of old Boeing Field on Marginal Way, exiting from the freeway a block from the Olympic Hotel—now Four Seasons Olympic—where we stayed for several days. The elegant lobby with its dark wood paneling remains unchanged and as distinctive of the Northwest as when I made it my unofficial headquarters during the intensive development period of the B-17 and B-29. The Georgian Room is still one of the great formal dining rooms and while there is no longer a dance floor and a big band, the roast beef and hard-shelled crabmeat cocktail are still unsurpassed. As we walked in for dinner, I swear I saw the shades of Randy Lovelace, the officers from Wright Field, Allen, Reed and Boeing flight test personnel engaged in animated conversation around that table by the door. It could have been the night before Lovelace's pioneering parachute jump from 40,000 feet *(See page 234)*.

During our stay in Seattle we visited with George Schairer and Bill Cook both of whom held prominent engineering positions during the wartime period when I worked at Boeing. As related elsewhere, we were all graduates of MIT who had arrived in Seattle by different routes and were employed in Allen's Flight and Aerodynamics Department George was the head of Aerodynamics and Cook was a sort of freelance engineer who took on various difficult assignments. They made major contributions to the improved Stratoliner, the various B-17 models and the B-29. Their most remarkable achievements, however, came much later in connection with the design and use of Boeing's high-speed wind tunnel and the evolution of the thin, swept-wing (podded-engined) military and commercial jet aircraft.

The most exciting event of our brief stay in Seattle was the opportunity, arranged by Bill Cook, to "fly" the 777 flight simulator at the Boeing Customer Service Training Center located just south of Boeing Field. This full-flight simulator literally produces all of the sensations of flight as one flies in the exact cockpit environment of the real machine. The major airports of the world are stored in the computer, and the computer-generated visual scenes are phenomenally realistic. I was able to take off from Boeing Field, land in Hawaii and fly on to Hong Kong with all of the control feel, motions and visual aspects faithfully reproduced. I tried an approach to "stall" and experienced the warning devices and finally the "stick pusher" that literally inhibits an inadvertent stall. Night landings and operation in the rain were simulated. I tried to catch the facility out by asking for a landing on an icy runway under snow squall conditions such as I've experienced in Buffalo. On came the scene—gusting winds, snow drifting across the runway, visibility down, with the runway lights disappearing in the distance. Having gotten the aircraft onto the runway, I stood on the brakes and the airplane began to skate sideways on the icy surface.

It's amazing how relatively easy it was to fly a modern jet with the stability and control augmentation and instrumentation available. Barbara, who also flew the simulator, and I agreed that it might be harder if there were a couple of hundred people behind one.

To record my impressions on our drive from Seattle to Missoula, we used an Olympus Stylus Zoom DLX camera with color film and a small, hand-held Lanier dictaphone, MS-105. The trip from Seattle to Spokane was uneventful, the scenery much as I remembered it in the F-22. We hoped to spend the night at the old Davenport Hotel, but it was

Fig. 12-18
Recent photo of highway through the Cascades beyond Kellogg. I had to fly at low altitude down the valleys because of a cloud overcast.

Fig. 12-19
Typical weather in the Cascades.

undergoing a major renovation. In locating a motel we passed by the rail yards. One had the impression that Spokane is still a major railhead as in my father's days, but now mostly freight as opposed to passenger traffic.

We got back on Route 90 early the next morning with the sun coming up behind the 5,000-foot Mount Spokane. Ahead of us, clouds began to appear around the peaks in the distance. Cour d'Alene came up in half an hour as the road climbed and descended, sometimes passing through narrow valleys with steep sides flanked with evergreens. Twenty-one miles from Kellogg, the altitude of the highway peaked out at 3,000 feet. The road was so winding, I wondered if I followed it to Kellogg or just stayed on a direct compass course—I suspect the latter. It was still early when we rolled into Kellogg—70 miles by highway from Spokane. We located the site of the old landing strip, which a gas attendant said was long gone; no aircraft had landed there in years.

In many respects the scene on leaving Kellogg was a replica of my F-22 flight. The valley twists and turns and the clouds again were right down on the hilltops. A stream follows the road on the right and occasionally switches over to the left. In constructing the Interstate the foot of the valley was widened from the narrow road I remembered and the sides of the valley have softened with more foliage and less bare rock, but there was little advance notice of which way the canyon would turn or how much.

There was one five-mile stretch some 15 miles beyond Kellogg, between Wallace and Mullen, where we thought we had discovered the location of my episode with the narrowing canyon. It's difficult to be certain but the canyon certainly narrows, the walls are steep and there are sharp turns in the road. Some 15 miles farther on was another five-mile stretch, between Mullen and Saltese, which had much the same characteristics. Without flying the route again I'd be hard put to vouch for the exact location, but this drive was enough to convince me that my memory and account of the incident were by no means exaggerated. I had plenty of reason for working up an honest sweat!

Later that day we drove on to Glacier National Park. One morning during our stay, we drove from East Glacier toward West Glacier on Route 2, which crosses the Continental Divide at Marias Pass. As we approached the pass we observed a statue and stopped to investigate. I was excited to find that it was of none other than John F. Stevens for whom my father had worked. Stevens had "discovered" this pass in the winter of 1889 under sub-zero weather conditions. It is the lowest pass (5,220 feet above sea level) through the Continental Divide in the northern part of the Rockies. Along with Stevens Pass in the Cascades, it enabled the Great Northern Railroad to complete the route to the coast. The sign at the statue indicated that by 1893 the Great Northern "… was running trains over Marias Pass." Lewis and Clark failed in their efforts to locate this route across the Divide for lack of cooperation with the Blackfeet Indians who were well aware of Marias Pass. Stevens, on the other hand, got on well with the Blackfeet. The statue depicts Stevens in winter garb holding the proverbial surveyor's tape in one hand. For me it was one more link to my father's career as a railway locating engineer. A few days later we completed our trip by riding the Amtrak train to Minneapolis and flying on to Buffalo.

Chapter 13 ✣

Triumph and Tragedy

The inaugural flight of the first XB-29 bomber took place in Seattle on September 21, 1942. My last flight in this prototype was December 31 of the same year. What follows is from the perspective of my reactions to events of which I have vivid and indelible memories, with the realization that this personal story is but a small part of the much larger picture involving the place of the B-29 in the overall strategy of winning the war against Japan. Like so many wartime stories, mine was paced by external pressures and exigencies of which I had less than a full understanding at the time.

According to historian Jacob Vander Meulen, the B-29 project was "one of the biggest and most complicated things Americans ever did—at a cost of roughly three billion dollars (1943 dollars), the B-29 made up the most expensive single part of the overall American weapons-building program of World War II."

The first flight of a prototype is a peak event in an aircraft's project history. Like the first ascent of Mt. Everest, when no one was sure what would be found during the final stages of the route, the flight and system characteristics of the XB-29 prototype were not fully predictable or approachable in a reversible step-by-step process. One cannot half-fly an airplane any more than one can be half pregnant.

In both mountain climbing and flight situations, the approach to the peak rests on a tremendous body of previous work that places those striving for the summit in position for the final thrust. Thousands of hours of conceptual thinking, engineering, build and test, as well as planning and decision-making at the highest levels of the military and the government, preceded the first flight of the XB-29. First flights serve to evaluate and confirm the engineering

XB-29 Superfortress.

"I don't know if we should continue flying this aircraft or not."

– Edmund T. Allen
(February 17, 1943, the day
before the accident of the
XB-29, No. 2)

Fig. 13-1
The production B-29 in flight near Mt. Rainier. The clean aerodynamic nose and fuselage shape, high aspect ratio wing, and large vertical tail and dorsal fin are clearly visible.

efforts, and they establish the nature and extent of the development cycle, which in turn paces the production of the service units. This places awesome responsibilities on the test pilot and his crew, particularly since the discharge of these responsibilities takes place in a transient and hazardous environment with the ever-present possibility of loss of aircraft and crew.

With the XB-29 there was one further factor, not normally present, that vastly augmented the flight test burden, namely the importance of this strategic bomber and its overriding military priority and schedule.

At the time of my involvement in the program I was only peripherally aware of the design, engineering and production plans, and knew less about the strategic implication. I was fully occupied in the testing of the B-17 series, and did not move in the circles that would have given me a broader outlook. For first-hand insights into the design of the B-29 I am indebted to Bill Cook and George Schairer. As head of Aerodynamics, Schairer was responsible for the airfoil design and overall aerodynamics as they affected performance,

stability and control. Cook was assistant project engineer on the B-29, and author of the book *The Road to the 707*. For information on the production process, I found Vander Meulen's *Building the B-29* useful, and for the engine design and production, Graham White's *Allied Aircraft Piston Engines of World War II*. Taken together, these three books give an excellent overall account of the problems encountered in producing the B-29 in quantity under wartime conditions.

Origins of the B-29

Strategic bombing as a concept dates back to 1921 and General Guilo Douhet, who theorized in *Command of the Air* that bombing military and industrial targets could seriously impair an enemy's morale and ability to wage war. The more enthusiastic proponents of this philosophy envisioned winning a war by this means. Strategic bombing was promoted in England by Sir Hugh Trenchard, and in America by General William (Billy) Mitchell and subsequently by Generals Henry (Hap)

Arnold, Ira Eaker and Carl Spaatz, among others.

The implementation of strategic bombing hinges, of course, on the development and production of effective long-range bombers. The first American aircraft to meet all requirements of strategic bombing in terms of size, range, speed, altitude, bomb load, etc., was the four-engine Boeing B-17. Developed through a long series of models, it was ultimately used for daylight precision bombing of German targets in World War II. The next American four-engine bomber, which achieved even higher production volume, was the comparably sized Consolidated B-24 Liberator. This aircraft had a greater range and bomb load than the B-17, and these and other advanced design features gave it an advantage for some missions.

Based on the B-17 and B-24 experience and emerging technology, notably more powerful engines, the Air Corps initiated a specification in early 1940 for a four-engine bomber of much larger size and performance. This led to Boeing's B-29 and Consolidated's B-32, but only the former survived to large-scale production. By the end of the war nearly 4,000 B-29s had been delivered to the Air Corps. During that same period more than 32,000 Wright Cyclone R-3350 engines had been supplied, or eight engines per airframe. In effect this was a complete set of replacement engines for each airplane.

Major production facilities for the airframe were located at Boeing-Wichita (Kansas), Boeing-Renton (Washington), Bell-Marietta (Georgia) and Martin-Omaha (Nebraska). The engines were produced at Wright-Woodridge (New Jersey) and Chrysler-Dodge (Chicago). With thousands of subcontractors involved, monumental delays and changes occurred before a steady rate of production was reached.

By late 1942, at the time of the prototype flight, close to 3,500 Boeing engineers were involved in the project, together with hundreds of fabricators and mechanics. This was in addition to the many systems suppliers who produced the remotely controlled gun turrets, electric motors for flaps, gear, bomb-bay doors and other accessories, the self-sealing tanks,

the pressurization, heating, communication, and navigation systems, etc. With full-scale production the number of people involved became staggering. At Boeing-Wichita peak production involved over 21,000 people, the majority of them on the daytime shift, working ten hours per day. At Boeing-Renton an estimated 25,000 people were employed at peak B-29 production in early 1945. Martin-Omaha peaked at nearly 15,000, while Bell-Marietta reached 27,000 workers. Wright Cyclone R-3350 engine production at Woodridge ultimately employed over 13,000 workers, and the Dodge-Unicargo facility had some 16,000 production workers with a total staff of nearly 33,000.

The specialized manpower required for actually fabricating the aircraft and engines could only be met by training a largely unskilled workforce, many of whom were women. The production process was greatly enhanced by Boeing's early decision to build the airframe in a number of self-contained sections that could be joined together in final assembly (the so-called "multi-line"). Thus there were the Forward Pressurized Compartment, the Forward and Aft Bomb-Bays, the Aft Pressurized Compartment, Tail Section and Tail Gunner's Component, Wings, Engine Cells, Landing Gear, etc. Groups of workers could be trained separately to fabricate the various sections. Of course, this is an idealized description, since there were hundreds of sub- and sub-sub assemblies going on more or less simultaneously.

This gigantic production process required the construction of specialized manufacturing plants and equipment. The plants and associated runways, facilities, etc., were financed by the U.S. Defense Plant Corporation, a government entity created to assist private enterprise in expanding its facilities for military production. Plant No. 2 at Wichita boasted the largest and highest unobstructed area under one roof in the United States. Nearly 20,000 construction workers were required to build the Dodge-Chicago engine factory, which was touted as "the largest manufacturing facility in the world."

The planning and coordination required by military and civilian industrial entities, as well as the high-level government and political decision-making, was generally accomplished without violating democratic processes. As pointed out by Vander Meulen, it resulted in "a new partnership between the military and aircraft companies based on mutual support, cooperation, high levels of spending and rapid technological change that still defines the relationship today."

The technical problems encountered in bringing the B-29 project to fruition were of many kinds and sources, but none were more persistent than those associated with the engine. In the past, advances in aircraft design usually were accomplished using well-proven engines. In the case of the B-29 both the aircraft and the engines were pushed into new areas of size and performance simultaneously. The combination of an experimental aircraft and experimental engines, wedded together before either was fully developed, was to prove lethal.

Preparations for Tests

One day in early August 1942, Al Reed walked into my office to say that Eddie was on his way down because "it looks like we'll be testing the '29 in a month or so." This meant that we had to intensify our familiarization with the aircraft's systems and their operation, and begin the flight planning. We drove to Plant 1, the original Boeing factory and the birthplace of a long line of famous fighters, transports and seaplanes. Allen's department had been located there until wartime expansion moved us to Plant 2 near Boeing Field. Whenever I returned to Plant 1 I could feel its history. It seemed appropriate that the prototypes of this advanced bomber were being constructed there.

As we entered the final assembly bay I again was struck by the immense size of the B-29, which seemed twice as big in every dimension as the B-17. I also experienced an emotional reaction that even to this day I find difficult to define. It was the feeling of something sinister about this aircraft, that it would come to no good end. I am certainly not a believer in premonition, but the feeling has persisted.

The B-29 was the most functional design I ever had encountered. In order to meet the stringent performance requirements,

the designers had sought to optimize every feature of its configuration by going to the limit of existing aerodynamic and structural technology. In the past, physical products of the human mind—houses, automobiles, aircraft, etc.—had progressed from pioneering to classical to the purely functional. In the early stages it is a matter of demonstrating feasibility. Once feasibility has been demonstrated, the classical period usually brings a proliferation of approaches by different designers. The purely functional configuration, based on the available scientific knowledge, becomes more stereotyped. Products of the classical stage are more individualistic, bearing the stamp of the designer who, unfettered by the demands of rigorous technology, can introduce humanizing elements of style and beauty.

To me the B-17 is a classic design, beautifully proportioned and laid out with an artist's touch. It has a conventional landing gear, modest wing aspect ratio and, thanks to its long and large tail, "it knows where it's going." Accommodations are compact and cozy, and close enough to each other to promote crew integration. Sitting near the windshield, the pilots enjoy excellent vision. The bombardier's compartment in the nose gives unrestricted viewing, and enough isolation to facilitate uninterrupted concentration. A number of systems remained manual, including the flight controls.

The later B-24 is technically more sophisticated and more functional, but lacking the artist's touch it appears heavy and businesslike. One suspects there will be fewer restorations of this aircraft in the future than of the B-17. The B-29 is high-tech compared with the other bombers. Its external shape, including the long nose, was dictated by aerodynamic performance, and many of the systems such as flight controls and gun turrets used servo actuation. Human intervention was minimized, and the aircraft is attractive only in a functional performance sense.

All three aircraft fit into a single overall design theme, namely: straight wings, four air-cooled piston engines in individual nacelles projecting forward from the wing, and tractor propellers. In that era the only other large American bomber of note, the B-36, employed

Fig. 13-2
Side view of B-29 showing large vertical tail, dorsal fin and tricycle landing gear. The tops of the remotely controlled gun turrets can be seen.

pusher propellers with piston engines, supplemented by podded jets. Only a few hundred were produced. Thus the B-29 stands at the end of the line of a particular design philosophy.

As a matter of interest, the next advances in large bomber aircraft, the B-47 and B-52, pioneered a totally new theme of thin, highly swept wings and podded engines located well outboard along the span. One of the greatest innovative advances in the history of aircraft design, they combined a pioneering design with classical beauty and functional superiority—a remarkable achievement.

According to Bill Cook, the original Air Corps Specification leading to the B-29 called for a top speed of 400 mph, a bomb load of 2,000 pounds and a round-trip mission range of 5,333 miles. The Boeing and Consolidated designs were based on the twin-row, 18-cylinder, Wright Cyclone air-cooled radial engine, initially rated at 2,000 hp and scheduled for large-scale production. The B-29's realized top speed was 360 mph, with long-range cruise about 100 mph less. Weight

empty was about 74,000 pounds. Nominal gross weight was initially about 105,000 pounds, which grew during service to over 140,000 pounds at takeoff. The corresponding wing loadings, based upon a wing area of 1,728 square feet, were 61 and 81 lbs/sq.ft. giving estimated takeoff speeds of over 160 and 180 mph respectively. Operating altitude was between 25,000 and 35,000 feet.

To attain this kind of performance and desired handling, the design incorporated the following features:

- Wingspan of 141 feet; aspect ratio 11.5
- Modified Davis airfoil section (developed by George Schairer)
- Fowler flaps
- Shear web wing spars and stressed-skin construction (butt joints and flush rivets)
- Low location of engine nacelles on wing leading edge
- Pure aerodynamic nose on the fuselage
- Low-profile powered gun turrets, computing gunsights and remote firing stations.

277

- Pressurized cabin maintaining 10,500 feet "altitude" to 35,000 feet; pressurization to be from turbochargers
- Large vertical tail and dorsal fin, similar to B-17E
- Engines dual turbocharged for high-altitude operation
- Self-sealing fuel tanks and crew armor
- Tricycle landing gear
- Electrical operation of flaps, gear and bomb-bay doors (rapid "snap action" operation provided for the latter). Over 125 electric motors were used.

As the initial flight crew, our task was to become familiar with the operation of these various systems and their limitations and, to the extent possible, understand some of the design details of these systems. In addition to crawling all over the aircraft and physically inspecting the systems, we also spent much time in the cockpit area with its controls and instrumentation. In the ensuing weeks, we studied drawings and reports, and consulted with specialists from

Boeing's engineering department. Everything we did was directed toward anticipating what problems might be encountered, and how to cope with them. Gradually, this information was incorporated into the flight plans.

Ground Runs, Taxi Tests and Initial Hops

After Reed, Allen and I approved the plan prepared by Ed Wersebe for testing nosegear shimmy, rudder boost, brake operation, and longitudinal stability and control characteristics, the engine run-ups began on September 9, 1942. They were followed by taxi tests at various speeds. On September 15 we performed the hop tests. The XB-29 No. 1 (Air Force Reg. No. AF41-2) was in a light-gross-weight condition (76,500 pounds). For the initial taxi tests for nosegear shimmy the CG was far forward (14.6 percent MAC or Mean Aerodynamic Chord) to load up the gear, but for the hop tests prior to full-fledged flight the CG was moved aft to 30 percent MAC. A sizable crew was on board for the ground runs,

Fig. 13-3
Cockpit. Pilot station on left, co-pilot station on right. The pilots sit a considerable distance from the glassed-in nose, which is not ideal for visibility.

operating the instrumentation and observing systems performance, while the taxi runs and hops required only a minimum crew of four.

As an example of the engineering effort preceding these first tests, more than 900 engineering change orders purportedly were processed between the spring of 1940 and the fall of 1942. Among these were the installation of a new GE remote-control armament system using .50-caliber guns, and major modification to the electrical system to handle the load associated with specially designed electrical motors. The Ground Run and Taxi Test plan is reproduced at the end of this chapter. (Fig. 13-11).

To THE BEST OF MY MEMORY, the results of the engine ground runs did not suggest any reason for not going ahead with the rest of the plan, although high engine temperatures were encountered at the higher power settings, and poor mixture and head-temperature distributions between the front and rear cylinders were noted from the beginning.

Nose-gear shimmy is a function of a number of variables such as trail, load, speed and damper setting. When encountered it can be a violent phenomenon, causing structural damage. By recording data on successive runs at increasing speed, adequate damping levels can be established. In the case of the XB-29, no problems were encountered in completing this phase of the testing, and we were cleared for the initial hops.

Satisfactory completion of the hops phase of the plan was a prerequisite to attempting full-fledged flight, as it enabled an evaluation of pitch control, stability, trim and other factors. At the time of the XB-29, Eddie Allen, then in his early forties, was at the height of his career, and in 1939 had received the Octave Chanute Award. Because of his interest in safety, he presented a paper that year at the World Automotive Engineering Conference in New York, in which he reviewed the costs of aircraft testing, the need for detailed flight plans, pilot and crew qualifications, and his concept of "least risk." He defined optimum success in flight testing as "never risking more than is absolutely essential at each stage, never taking too large a step into unknown territory." His comments are pertinent to the initial hop testing of the XB-29, which we were about to begin.

This initial flight plan is drawn up in accordance with the principle of least risk as are, too, all later ones, but on the first flight the operation of this principle is most clearly evident. The first flight is an exploration into the unknown territory of the airplane's stability and balance, the operation of engines, propellers, control surfaces and landing gear and, finally, the relationship of the pilot to the airplane. This latter we term 'familiarization.' Technically, it is the task of relegating three new sensori-motor coordinations to the 'automatic' from the 'thinking' stage.

Each new airplane responds entirely differently and, although the basic principles of control are the same, it is doubtful if a pilot whose perfection of technique was confined to one type of airplane could make an initial flight on another, quite different, type without an initial stage of very bad wobbling about. This quality of adaptability from one class and size of aircraft to another can be acquired, and it is one of the distinguishing marks of a test pilot, to whom any airplane, from a glider with featherweight control forces to a 30-ton Clipper ship, is a routine familiarization problem.

Following the principle of least risk, the flight plan of the first flight lays down procedures for engine running and the testing of all engine controls, propeller testing, control surface friction measurement at zero airspeed, brake operation and brake-drum heating, acceleration and deceleration along the runway, stability of the airplane while on the ground, differential brake control, differential engine control on the ground, air control of elevators at gradually increasing speeds, and air control of rudders at higher speeds less than take-off speed. This process of step-by-step exploration is continued until some unsatisfactory condition is found, studied, and remedied.

When a risk is taken which could be preceded by a lesser exploratory risk, the ideal is achieved of never getting the airplane into an attitude from which it cannot be returned safely to an established regime of safety. It may take many hours of this type of testing before the airplane finally soars away from the field but, before that time, almost every element of static stability, controllability and balance will have been explored, in addition to power plant operation and crew coordination.

My own attitude toward the "initial hops" phase and first flight was one of unbounded enthusiasm. I was 31, full of energy and convinced I had the best job in the world. I loved everything about Seattle and the adventurous life I was leading. The idea of being the flight test engineer on the first flight of one of the war's most significant bombers was one more perk for my ego and general feelings of elation.

None of my previous first flights were of prototype aircraft, except for my own M-1—hairy enough but hardly relatable to the XB-29. Because of my great interest in airplane stability and control, I looked forward with fascination to Allen exploring these behaviors on a large, high-performance aircraft. How would he cope

with the unexpected, sneak up on the limits, in short, pull it off without losing it? Eddie was a virtuoso in this kind of situation and I would have a front row seat.

Considering the limitation imposed by the runway length for accelerating up to speed, holding it and then braking to a stop, Eddie suggested some preliminary runs for fixing the cutoff point at which braking would have to be initiated for the 100-mph ground runs. He wanted a recognizable point on the ground. To obtain the maximum time for feeling out the controls, he assigned each of us a task: "Al, you handle the engine/prop controls. Get us up to speed and be ready to back off when I start braking. Bill, you watch for the cutoff point and slap me on the back as we approach it." I was also to observe Allen's control actions and record his impressions after each run. The flight engineer would keep track of engine and brake temperatures. Before taxiing back for each successive run, we had a general discussion, during which I would record all pertinent comments for the log.

Charging down the runway, Allen slowly pulled back on the yoke, sensing the level of the control force and the reaction of the aircraft. Although he had started with the elevator trim tab at three degrees nose down, as recommended by Aerodynamics, several runs were required before he was satisfied with the pitch trim setting. After that he could explore the control levels and "force control" stability. Flight safety

Fig. 13-4
Taken during the initial hop tests at Boeing Field. The airplane is 15-20 ft. in the air with the gear down, and will be landed before the end of the runway. Note barrage balloon in distance.

depended, first of all, on the control forces being well within the pilot's capability. Eddie was unique in his ability to judge a control force. He was said to have "calibrated hands" and on each run would tell me his idea of the maximum force he had experienced. Thanks to his extensive experience with large aircraft, he had a great sense of the acceptable range of force levels for elevator, aileron and rudder years before these levels were rationally established and incorporated in "mil" (military) specs.

Although these tests were mainly for pitch characteristics as critical for takeoff and flight, Allen was able to explore the rudder and aileron feel and responses for small control motions—a preliminary on-center evaluation. This was done on the early runs, when the main gear still was on the ground and the aircraft could be yawed slightly or rocked laterally on the gear. This would be checked further during the hops when the aircraft was in the air.

For the initial hops, Eddie took over the throttles with Al guarding them and handling the other engine and propeller controls. Assuming 0.5g average acceleration, the time to 120 mph is 11 seconds and about 970 feet of runway. If the braking time and distance are comparable, 1,940 feet of a 7,000-foot runway have been used, leaving 5,060 feet (nearly a mile) or about 30 seconds in the air for control evaluation. We spotted a cutoff point for initiating the landing and runout.

The actual hops were as exciting as any flight at low altitude is bound to be. But accelerating behind engines generating over 8,000 hp, and running an intensive test in the next 30 seconds, while sailing along at 120 miles per hour only 15 feet above a rapidly disappearing runway, is not an everyday experience. We made three hops before Allen concluded his familiarization with the flight control system and pronounced it ready for flight. By the time of the hop tests we had become much more conscious of the variety of problems surrounding the R-3350 engines.

First Flight, September 21, 1942

For the first flight, XB-29 No. 1 was stripped down to a gross weight of about 76,000 pounds, with a nominal CG location of 30 percent of the MAC. The minimum crew,

identical to that for the preliminary hop tests, consisted of Eddie Allen and Al Reed as pilot and co-pilot, a flight engineer and me.

We arrived at Boeing Field in mid-morning. The airplane still was being prepped, so we went directly to the hangar for a pre-flight meeting to review the work accomplished in cleaning up "squawks" from the hop tests. Having convinced ourselves that these problems had been taken care of, we walked out onto the ramp toward the airplane. As usual, Allen was calm and casual, as if this were just another routine flight. His demeanor certainly fit his own definition of the ideal test pilot: "one of quiet awareness of the great responsibility of handling a large investment—concern for the lives of all aboard—a pervading attitude of watchful care and a nervous system trained in judgment and motor coordination." Reed seemed tense and serious, caught up with the details and somewhat sharp and edgy. With the least responsibility, and complete confidence in the pilot, I was set to enjoy the ride and the fanfare.

In my memory the day was warm and sunny, with a light breeze and just a few clouds off toward Mt. Rainier. Parked near the taxiway, the sun reflecting from its aluminum surfaces, the B-29 was the center of attention. In addition to mechanics and inspectors engaged in last-minute checks, a sizable number of Boeing executives, engineers, technicians, Air Force personnel and supplier representatives were milling about. I could identify key engineering figures who had participated in the design of the '29, Ed Wells, Well Beall, George Schairer, Maynard Pennell, George Martin, Bill Cook among them. Although not a company holiday, word had passed around and groups of workers lined the field on the opposite side of the runway.

The first flight of a new airplane no longer was a defining moment in the sense of confirming its design success—that would take months of test flying over the operational envelope—but it was a symbolic event for those who had labored with the creation to see the result first take to the air in full flight. An element of risk pervaded the atmosphere. Despite all the engineering and static tests, something might have been overlooked, some component might fail.

As we approached the group, Eddie immediately was monopolized by the high-level Boeing and military brass. While he never exploited his fame, he was so well known and respected that on occasions like this he became a focus of attention. On prototype first flights the CEOs and managers are on the line, knowing full well the implications of success or failure, and physically sweating it out.

Curtiss-Wright, builder of the R-3350, also was on the line. As the only producer of an engine of this power and production status, the company had struggled to meet the B-29 schedule. The engine had experienced a host of development problems traceable to inadequate cooling, and never had been flown and flight tested.

I wandered toward the group of Wright representatives, which included Arthur Nutt, designer of the famous D-12 Curtiss engine, whom I recognized from photos. I was anxious to meet him because he was related to the Robinsons, family friends whose daughter Janet had been one of my regular dance partners during my MIT years. After introducing myself we chatted briefly about his relatives, and then I inquired about the problems plaguing the 3350. When he became quite noncommittal I did not press the issue, figuring that we would find out soon enough.

The mechanics ran up the engines and stood by with fire extinguishers. Eddie Brown appeared with our chutes (mine a backpack) and after a few handshakes, we climbed aboard through the door on the right-hand side. I had a good place to stand behind the pedestal next to the pilot. Reed was in the co-pilot's seat, which in the B-29 is well over to the right, with the flight engineer's station right behind him. Having taxied slowly out to the end of the runway, Eddie ran up the engines one by one again as the pilots went through

Fig. 13-5
Eddie Allen was famous for testing prototypes of large aircraft. Here he is leaning out of a window in the cockpit of the first XB-29. It gives one a feel for man's ability to control the huge devices he has devised.

the extensive checklist. Throttling back, he looked around, "Are we all set?" Cleared by the tower, we started the takeoff run and soon were thundering down the runway toward the southwest. Eddie eased the plane off the ground, dropped back to rated power as the gear went up, and started the climb-out.

My memory of what happened next is vague, but I am sure that by the time Allen had checked out the flight controls and approached a stall, one engine was acting up and had to be shut down, and the propeller feathered. We returned to the field, landing after a flight of a less than an hour. For a first-flight buildup, it was an anticlimactic letdown, to say the least. As we climbed out of the airplane, Allen made his oft-quoted proclamation of "we have an excellent airplane," referring of course to its flight control characteristics, not the engines.

The next day, according to several references, the aircraft was flown by Col. Donald Putt, Project Engineering Officer for the Air Force, who was much impressed by its controls and flight characteristics, notably the light forces and the stall behavior, which confirmed Allen's assessment. This indicated that the engine trouble we experienced had not required an engine replacement.

ON ALL COUNTS Boeing had produced a superior airframe. The heat was on to complete the systems development and explore the operational envelope. This could have been an intensive, highly satisfying activity, but the engines were killing us.

Discouraging Progress

Robert E. Johnson's "Why the Boeing B-29 Bomber and Why the Wright R-3350 Engine?" published in the *Journal of the American Historical Society* (Fall 1988) provides some idea of what we were up against. Sixty-five hand-assembled R-3350 engines had been supplied by the Wright company for three aircraft programs that got underway in late 1942: the Convair XB-32, Boeing XB-29 and Lockheed XB-30. The flight test time of these three programs covered a period of about four months, or 120 days. These tests required 26 engines, and accumulated 365 hours of engine time. As a part of these tests, the XB-29 No. 1 figures are as follows:

Fig. 13-6
First flight of the XB-29 from Boeing Field, on September 21, 1942. The aircraft is in light configuration, gaining altitude rapidly as the gear retracts. A minimum crew of four is aboard. Engine trouble ended the flight early, a portent of what became the overriding theme of the XB-29 flight development program.

Between first flight and December 31st, a period of only 101 days, only 99 engine hours were accumulated, using 17 engines. For a four-engine airplane, this corresponds to 24.8 hours of flight, excluding flight time on dead engines, and was the maximum time a single engine could have accumulated. But none did, the largest accumulated time for any one engine being 19 hours. Thus each engine was changed at least once.

On December 2nd, 72 days after start, and after 18 hours of flight, an altitude of 25,000 feet was reached for the first time. The last flight, No. 22, was made on December 28th. In this 101-day period we had managed to get in 22 flights which, on average, is only one flight about every five days—on the surface not a very intensive effort. However, during that period we had 13 engine changes, each of which would have laid up the airplane for at least 2 days, for a total of 26 days. Assuming perfect weather and no other delays, we were making flights every 3.4 days. However, taking into account Seattle's weather, and giving the maintenance crew an occasional break on Sunday, we were using every possible window for furthering the test program.

Among the engine problems we encountered were: High oil consumption; propeller overspeed on takeoff due to low oil pressure in the dome; moisture in ignition components, ultimately requiring a pressurized harness; three reduction-gear failures in the engine nose cone, due to reduced oil pressure at altitude; exhaust system fires; problems with carburetors prior to installation of pressure carburetors; high engine temperatures; fires in the blower section.

It is difficult to adequately express how demoralizing this period was. We had a great airplane, as well as the backing and incentive to get on with the development flights, but we were stalled at every turn. Company management and the Air Force were relentlessly tracking our every move, while we felt helpless to do more than we were doing. Impatient during engine changes, apprehensive on each takeoff, fearful of some new type of engine failure and devastated by every aborted flight, the three of us reacted differently. More knowledgeable of the B-29 military role and production plans, Eddie Allen exhibited a stoic control. I could detect the pressure he was under, however, by his faster walk, his clipped conversation and his serious demeanor. Because the hazards of the engines were amplified by an active imagination and concern for his own neck, Al Reed was the most vehement in his condemnation of the R-3350s. He strongly maintained that the flights should be curtailed until major improvements had been made. Up to now I had pretty much dismissed the risks of flight testing because of its adventurous and romantic aura, but during the early flights of the XB-29, the seriousness of an engine fire or a power-plant failure on takeoff finally got through to me. I still can feel the terror of being confronted with a major fire in flight. I found myself wondering if we should carry on.

EVEN MORE UNSETTLING, I observed increasing animosity between Allen and Reed, who had always seemed completely compatible. Was the pressure bringing out unresolved differences between them? Even though Eddie was the boss, I began to suspect that, because of his quiet and cooperative attitude, he may have lost arguments to the self-centered and opinionated Reed in the past. We had numerous discussions among ourselves about the engine situation. Reed presented his position in his usual uncompromising way, forcing Allen into a defensive posture. The congenial atmosphere in the cockpit disappeared as their positions hardened.

Matters came to a head at year's end. On December 28, our 22nd flight, two engines failed on No. 1 XB-29. On the initial flight of XB-29 No. 2 on December 30, an engine fire broke out in the blower section of No. 1 nacelle. Without pressure carburetors a backfire could ignite the fuel/air mixture in the blower section, which was a flammable magnesium casting. The onboard equipment completely failed to extinguish the fire, which still was burning when we landed.

Irreconcilable Differences

Eddie called a meeting offsite to review the situation, I believe at his home, on a Sunday. I distinctly remember that George Schairer and others from Engineering were among the participants. No brilliant ideas for improving the engines came out of the discussion, but it was clear that Eddie, from his perspective of the overall B-29 project, believed there was no alternative to continuing the flights. Reed argued that we were heading for disaster, and intimated he wanted no part of it. I felt there was considerable logic to Reed's position but made it clear I was prepared to continue flying if that was the decision.

The following morning I was totally surprised to learn Al Reed had left for California on "vacation." Allen had acted swiftly in answer to Reed's ultimatum, producing the memorandum at the end of the chapter (Fig. 13-12), which suggested that a major break in their relationship had been germinating for some time.

IF THE DISAPPEARANCE OF my boss was not enough of a jolt, this memorandum was. My initial reaction was like that of a man whose home and family had been swept away by a tornado. My sudden demotion and removal from flight status slashed away everything I had worked so hard for and cherished in my job at Boeing. I was stunned, and felt engulfed in a tidal wave of emotion, followed by intense physical reactions. I couldn't sleep, and eating became a struggle as I slipped into a survival mode. I wrote a long letter to my mother—I had to act somehow—and received a wonderfully encouraging letter back. There are times when only love can put one on the right track.

After that I began to take stock of the situation more rationally. I could find no reason for feeling guilty. There had been no real problem in my relationship with either Allen or Reed, both of whom I admired for different reasons. Eddie had hired me and assigned me to Al, to whom I had given my allegiance. If I was guilty of anything, it was my close relationship with Reed. I felt that I was being punished on circumstantial evidence. After agonizing for a few days I decided to stay on and work toward reinstatement, one of the best decisions I ever made.

Allen's position was further clarified in two additional memoranda of January 4 that covered Wersebe's new responsibilities, as well as those of pilots Merrill and Lamson. Schairer was appointed acting director of Flight and Aerodynamics in Allen's absences.

I was in the peculiar situation of being in the same office but officially divorced from the activities of Flight Test, reporting directly to Allen. My close association with Talbott was severed by his relocation in the division reporting to Gulick, the administrative assistant. My full-time secretary, a champion stenotypist named Ermyl Teeter, for whom I had a growing emotional attachment, was relocated in Eddie's office suite. All of my former activities of flight planning, scheduling, reporting, etc., were transferred to Ed Wersebe, our senior flight test engineer, along with responsibility for the flight test engineers, most of whom Al and I had hired.

But my situation wasn't completely hopeless. I still was working and drawing a salary and, best of all, had direct access to Allen. When it became apparent that he was too busy to give me assignments, I decided to make my own. I soon discovered that Wersebe and Blaine were as bewildered by the dramatic increase in their responsibilities as I was with the reduction in mine, so we got together as friends after hours to help each other and keep things moving.

During the day, I turned to my great interest in record flights. With the help of the library I obtained access to the National Aeronautic Association (NAA) listing of all of the categories of national (NAA) and international (FAI) records and the current record holders. As I expected, a host of opportunities existed for record setting with our test B-17s, which involved combinations of load, distance, speed and altitude.

Transcontinental Record Planning

While summarizing this information, I hit on the idea of a spectacular transcontinental record-breaking flight at high altitude. With a tailwind of 75–100 mph, we could break the official transcontinental record of 327 mph that Howard Hughes had set with his specially constructed race plane. Furthermore, we could do it non-stop and with a sizable crew.

Fig. 13-7
My former secretary, Ermyl Teeter, now relocated in Allen's office suite.

Knowledge of the jet stream at high altitude was in its infancy, but Krick Weather Service indicated that on average a wind velocity from west to east of over 75 mph existed at high altitude for at least a few days a year. Krick agreed to supply information on the jet stream as part of its regular reporting. Armed with this information I cranked out a memo to Allen on January 6, 1943, less than a week after my demotion. Another memo followed on the 12th summarizing the record possibilities.

Allen reacted favorably and suggested I proceed to plan for a non-stop flight from Seattle to Washington, D.C. With a 100-mph tail wind at 30,000 feet, our ground speed would be in excess of 375 mph.

On January 16, 1943, we had a planning meeting for a flight using B-17F No. 1, which had been flying since mid-September 1942. A number of features recommended it for such a flight, i.e., higher power at altitude, special propellers, etc. Allen started the meeting by saying, "It is quite possible that weather conditions are going to be favorable for this flight within the next month or maybe even within the next week. Therefore, if we clear up all questionable items we have found we will be all set to go." The discussion among co-pilot Elliott Merrill and engineers Marvin Michael, Chuck Blaine, Vince North and others revolved around fuel transfer, details of the oxygen system including the number of outlets and walk-around bottles, gross weight for takeoff, radio frequencies, navigation (including compass calibration), radio fixes, navigational log, time of departure, extra glycol for heaters, clothing, etc.

"I think we are going to get better weather conditions than the weather bureau predicts," commented Merrill, who independently had been looking into the winds at altitude. "Mr. Smith of the Weather Bureau asked Mr. Carpenter of Krick how often we could expect 75-mph average winds. Carpenter said every three years, but the next morning they had these very conditions while they still were talking about them! They just didn't realize it. We have had these conditions three times since then, and that is only over a matter of two months. It is true that this is exceptional; however, these are the highest winds we have had in a long time. I don't believe the weather bureau ever expected to get winds like this." Allen replied, "I would rather make this flight with a 75-mph wind and clear weather and a straight course than with 120-mph wind under cloud and low ceiling."

After the meeting, preparations proceeded rapidly. One morning, near the end of January, the crew gathered at the hangar for the pre-flight meeting. Allen had relented; because of my involvement in navigational planning, collecting maps, compass calibration and working with the weather people, I was to go back on flight status for this one flight. The prediction indicated a 100-mph trough across the continent at stratospheric heights (35,000–40,000 feet) but with questionable weather at lower altitudes, notably severe icing conditions. We were not well equipped for that, and Allen recognized that neither he nor Merrill were really current for instrument flight. Nevertheless, we were about to go ahead anyway and actually got in the airplane. The final weather summary indicated low ceilings and poor visibility on the Washington, D.C., end, which was sufficient justification for canceling the flight—which Allen wisely did.

The idea of the flight never was officially given up, but it slipped into the background with the intense priority of tests on XB-29 No. 2. Allen was testing with various co-pilots whenever airplane and weather permitted. With his flying and administrative load he had an exhausting schedule. Some months later his wife told me that at the end of each day he would eat a light dinner in bed, and then call it a night.

Grounded

Still grounded, I talked with Eddie on some pretext or other almost every day to try to reinstate my position. Finally, I wrote a letter requesting he sign an "agreement" that at some point in the future I would be returned to my former position and responsibilities. I cited my previous record of accomplishments in hiring and training the flight crews, participating in all of the flight tests on the several major airplane projects, and my activities during the growth of the flight test unit. I also pointed out my familiarity with high-altitude procedures, organizing the data and analysis, etc.

It was a naive gesture on my part, which Allen answered with the following note written during one of his flights east on United.

Eddie never had the opportunity to prepare his statement of the faults of the Flight Test Unit, nor the part that I had played in them, but I suspect the latter was the over-proceduralization that Al had initiated and that I had gone along with. Allen's letter to me follows.

The XB-29 engine problems continued unabated. The record shows that in 27 hours

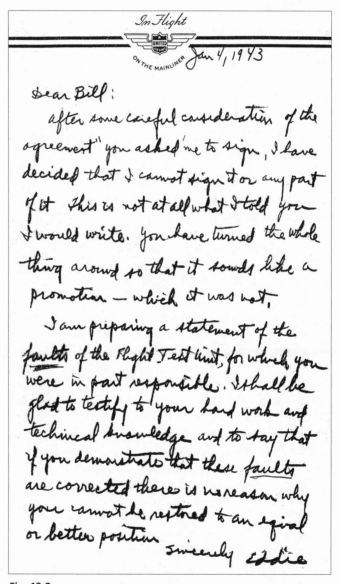

Fig. 13-8
Allen's response to my attempt to be reinstated to my former position and to full-time flight status. I never was to know the faults of the Flight Test Unit to which Allen referred, because of the XB-29 No. 2 accident.

of flight during this period there had been 16 engine changes, 22 carburetor modifications, other engine malfunctions and further blower-section fires. On February 17, 1943, another flight on XB-29 No. 2 ended because of the engines. Allen himself made the remark to a crew member afterward that "I don't know if we should continue flying this aircraft or not." Of the several hundred hours required to finally flight test this airplane, fewer than 50 had been completed as of that date.

Fatal Flight

The next day, when I arrived at my office, I found that a flight on XB-29 No. 2 (AAF41-003) was scheduled for late morning with Allen as first pilot, Bob Dansfield as co-pilot and an engineering crew of nine young engineers. According to reports from our radio station at the hangar, they got off at around 11:00 A.M. heading for the vicinity of Lake Washington. Less than half an hour later, the aircraft reported an engine fire in No. 1 nacelle that, according to one report, was extinguished by the onboard fire equipment.

Reports conflict whether the No. 2 engine then caught on fire or if No. 1 engine re-ignited. Allen was returning to the field for an emergency landing and requested standby crash equipment. The last message from the airplane was an interception of an intercom from the rear compartment to Allen: "A wing is on fire and you better get this thing down in a hurry."

From my office window, I could see across the field in the direction of a normal approach from the north. I cannot remember if I heard the crash but I certainly saw the ensuing flames. The aircraft with left wing down had flown into the meat packing plant of Frye and Co., which was in the flight path a mile or so from the edge of the field. Twenty Frye employees were killed in the fire. Senior flight test engineers Ed Wersebe and Chuck Blaine bailed out of the front compartment seconds before the crash. Both of their chutes opened, although at this low altitude, it was too late. One of them struck the ground, the other, high-tension wires. Neither survived. The entire crew of the plane was lost.

Believing the engines caused the accident, my spontaneous reaction was "My God, we told you so"—as if the accident was a vindication of the position Al Reed and I had taken about further flights with these engines. My summary demotion had been a terrific emotional licking for me, and after the accident all of the suppressed rage and anger came gushing out. My initial irrational reaction was replaced by a shock wave of emotion as I realized the immensity of the personal and professional loss.

Minutes after the accident I visited the site with George Schairer and others. After striking some power lines, the airplane had flown directly into the second story of the plant. Employees on the first floor heard a "blasting impact," and almost simultaneously the entire wooden structure became an inferno. By the time we got there the fire was partially under control. Elements of the tail and tail surfaces projecting from the building were the only recognizable parts of the aircraft. A number of pigs that had escaped from the slaughter room on the second floor roamed around on an undamaged section of the roof—adding to the ghastly appearance of the scene.

With the accident, I became the most senior remaining member of the Flight Test Section, with the first task of producing a notarized statement identifying the aircraft and the crew (Fig. 13-13, end of chapter).

Without Eddie, a Flight and Aerodynamics Department separated from Boeing Engineering no longer was feasible. In Allen's final organization his second-in-command was Schairer, who had already been working closely with Engineering. I had a long talk with Wellwood Beall. Even if an attempt were made to reorganize a Flight and Aerodynamics Department around Schairer, a suitable head for the Flight Section would have to be found. Although I had been viewed as the assistant head of flight test under Reed, I certainly was not qualified to be a replacement, nor did I even consider that possibility.

THE IMMEDIATE CONCERN was for the closest kin of the victims. There can be few more agonizing experiences than having to convey the loss of a loved one. Of the flight engineers, I was closest to Ed Wersebe and Chuck Blaine, 28 and 26 years old respectively, each married and with a young daughter. Ed Wersebe's parents wrote me a beautiful letter, knowing that he and I had worked closely together. Ermyl Teeter and I went to the Memorial Service at her church. Her compassion and practical outlook helped me immensely in coping with my emotional extremes. We became quite close, and one weekend took the train to Spokane to spend a couple of days enjoying the luxury of the Davenport Hotel, a welcome respite from the hectic pace at Boeing. My mother's letters also were a stabilizing influence.

One of the most excruciating phone calls came from Eddie Allen's wife. She said a reporter had told her Eddie was seen to stand up or leave his seat at the last instant, implying an abandonment of his responsibility as pilot; she wanted to know if there was any truth in it. How could anyone have displayed such an appalling lack of sensitivity? I assured her there wasn't a shred of evidence indicating Eddie did anything improper. At the time I could not give her a full explanation of the cause of the accident. We believed fuel had ignited on the leading edge of the wing from which fire spread to the bomb bay, burned through the tunnel and around the nose, and was sucked into the forward cockpit area, producing, in effect, a horizontal furnace. Given these circumstances, is it any wonder that Wersebe and Blaine bailed out or that Eddie might have considered it? I could see no purpose in reviewing these horrifying suppositions with Mrs. Allen.

Al Reed returned from California. Officially he had been on a vacation and still was working for Boeing. Reliable sources told me he wanted to assume Allen's job, but his unpopularity among key people in Engineering preordained a cold reception to that idea. One suspects that Beall dismissed it out-of-hand. By the time I saw Al his employment with Boeing had been terminated. His suggestion we have lunch together, something we never had done in the five years I worked for him, made it obvious he had few friends left at the company.

The general feeling, persisting to this day, is that Reed let Allen down by placing the entire burden of planning and testing the B-29 on Eddie's shoulders. I could sense Al was badly shaken by the accident. Allen had chosen Reed believing he would carry on the "engineer-pilot" tradition Eddie exemplified. Allen's fame had given him a wide choice of candidates. For his age and experience, Reed had been elevated into a position of prominence. I don't see how he could have emotionally survived this accident without feelings of guilt and remorse. Allen was canonized by the accident and Reed became the villain. The Boeing wind tunnel later was named after Eddie.

THE B-29 PROGRAM was put on hold, partly because of the accident and partly because of continuing problems with the R-3350 engines. The first probable cause of the accident that came to my attention, and one that seemed plausible at the time, was that engine vibration had shaken an outboard filler neck loose, allowing fuel to flow into the wing leading edge and down past the bulkheads drilled for instrumentation wiring. The actual cause determined by Boeing Engineering, and confirmed by the formal accident investigation, placed the blame on the design of the fuel filling system. This is described in Graham White's *Allied Aircraft Piston Engines*.

> Because of the critical nature of the B-29 program, a Senate investigating committee was formed, chaired by Senator Harry S. Truman. The conclusion of the committee placed the blame for the XB-29 problems on the R-3350. Cases of poor workmanship and inspection were cited. However, the loss of the XB-29 should not be blamed on the R-3350. The crash investigation determined that the fire started in the leading edge of the wing. An idiosyncrasy of the XB-29 fuel system allowed fuel to be siphoned from the filler cap into the leading edge under certain conditions. The ignition source was thought to have been instrument tubing running through the leading edge that was ignited by contact with the

exhaust system. This then led to a catastrophic fire. A redesign of the fuel-filler system eliminated this problem.

This placed responsibility on Boeing, rather than on Wright Aeronautical, a startling conclusion that confounded those of us who had lived with the R-3350. The engine continued to be the cause of numerous future accidents with production B-29s. In recent communications with Schairer and Cook, I have confirmed that with full outboard tanks the fuel could be siphoned from the filler cap, along the sides of the filler pipe as it passed through the spar into the wing leading edge. The fire had been in the left wing. A new design eliminating that possibility has been widely adopted on other aircraft.

By mid-April the Air Force, under General "Hap" Arnold, had initiated a special project to keep the overall B-29 project moving toward combat use. Col. Jake Harman was assigned to fly the third prototype on its initial flight on May 29. A sizable group of Boeing executives and engineers lined the edge of the field to watch his takeoff. I was among them. Midway on the run, the right wing went down and the airplane slewed around toward the stunned spectators. It was Schairer's impression, and mine, that we were on the run when the aircraft came to a grinding stop. We found out later that the aileron control cables had been crossed on assembly. When Harman attempted to counteract for a minor disturbance in roll, he forced the wing into the ground. That such a mistake could have passed inspection and the normal control check prior to takeoff seemed unbelievable. But it exemplified how a devastating accident can upset routines and contribute to a second accident. One can be sure that rigging procedures at Boeing were tightened after that event.

After five years, the Flight and Aerodynamics Department was disbanded and its remaining personnel were absorbed into Boeing's Engineering Department. As an interim measure N. D. Showalter, a member of the senior group of Boeing engineers, had been given the assignment of pulling together the remnants of the Flight Test Section. He moved into Eddie's old office. For the next month or

Fig. 13-9
Frye and Co. meat packing plant following the XB-29 crash which claimed the lives of Eddie Allen and 10 other members of the Boeing Flight Test Unit. The ensuing fire also claimed the lives of 20 Frye employees.

so I occupied a desk there, and engaged in a variety of miscellaneous assignments. The fact that N. D. was acquainted with the Boeing hierarchy was useful in this reconstruction period. While we got on well together, I found him less direct than my earlier bosses, so when the opportunity came to move into the Preliminary Design group I accepted it.

Looking Past Boeing

Anticipating that the war and the high level of military business could not go on forever,

Preliminary Design was exploring peacetime projects. My assignment was to envision a "roadable helicopter" that Boeing hoped would compete with a segment of the automobile market. After the excitement of flight testing, however, I quickly became disenchanted with this task and made plans to leave Boeing.

This was one of the most conflicting emotional experiences of my life. Full of rage at Allen for what I felt was an unjustifiable demotion, I was having difficulty dealing with the fact that his resistance to putting me back on flight status had saved my life. Thankfully,

Eddie Allen Rated World's Greatest Test Pilot-Scientist

WITH THE DEATH OF EDMUND T. ALLEN in last Thursday's plane crash, the world lost the man who was largely responsible for conquering the stratosphere. In the thin air more than seven miles above the earth, "Eddie" Allen and his crewmen have blazed the trail for tomorrow's aviation.

Other men in his field had conferred on Eddie Allen the unofficial title, "world's greatest test pilot"; but Allen was more than a test pilot. Widely recognized for his ability as an engineer, the Boeing director of flight and aerodynamics declared that the true test pilot is a scientist—and his own record bore him out.

Two months ago, Allen received the highest honor the Institute of Aeronautical Sciences can give, when he was elected to deliver the Wright Brothers anniversary lecture in New York City. In 1940 he was chosen the first recipient of the Chanute Award established that year by the Institute of Aeronautical Sciences. The same year he was appointed to the committee on aerodynamics of the National Advisory Committee for Aeronautics.

His test flying career has carried him, since 1923, to Europe, South America, and all corners of the United States. Probably no man has performed more first flights on new airplane models. His pilot's log book discloses more than 7,000 hours of test flying on famous planes of yesterday, today, and tomorrow.

Best known as a "big ship" pilot, Allen performed the initial tests of most of the large aircraft America has developed. On the imposing list are such world-famous planes as the giant Boeing XB-15 bomber, the Sikorsky "Flying Dreadnaught," the Consolidated PB2Y four-engine patrol bomber, the Boeing Clipper, Boeing Stratoliner, the Curtiss Commando transport, several models of the Boeing Flying Fortress, and the Boeing Sea Ranger. Only last month, he was borrowed by Lockheed to pilot the giant Constellation transport on its maiden flight.

Although Allen is best known for his outstanding achievements in the air, he will be one of aviation's immortals because of his engineering research on the ground as well. Already, in Europe, Africa and Asia, the effects of his research are being felt increasingly in the air war.

The giant planes of the many tomorrows will bear his influence, and incorporate aerodynamic refinement which he and his crew have developed. And when the war is over, peace-time aviation will become a perpetual memorial to Eddie Allen

(Eddie Allen is survived by his wife, Florence, and two young children—a daughter, Florence, and a son, Edmund.)

Fig. 13-10
Eddie Allen's achievements, as published in the *Boeing News* of February 24, 1943, Vol. 2, No. 5.

instead of running away I had stayed on, and had done my best to be reinstated. I never experienced any guilt about not being on the plane that day. But my initial lack of feeling toward the victims of the accident gave me the first clue to defects in my emotional structure that I ultimately had to face, with much professional help. It has taken me years to sort out and understand my thoughts and behavior at that time.

As the years distanced me from those awful weeks in early 1943, I began to see Eddie Allen in quite a different light. He was a great engineering test pilot, not because he was a great engineer but because he approached test flying with the analytical viewpoint of one. His paper on "The Testing of Large Aircraft" explained how the test pilot must think and function in flight in relation to the engineering organization on the ground. He recognized the great responsibilities involved, and the need for devising procedures for safeguarding crews and aircraft. Eddie laid emphasis on quantitative (and when this was impractical, on qualitative) techniques for collecting information of use in design, engineering and service. His overall concept of engineering flight test was that of a "final inspection" of a design, the place where realization of design objectives was confirmed or found to be deficient.

In the air he practiced what he preached, responding to hairy situations in a calm and calculated manner. He was very much "hands-on" and clearly was the dominant figure in the cockpit. He led the crew by example rather than by edict. His sensitivity in feeling out the handling of an aircraft could be interpreted as close to an art form. As co-pilot, Al Reed seldom did the tough and precise flying that emergencies or some tests required.

I never thought of Allen as a great manager or executive. He certainly had none of the brusque and forceful behavior commonly associated with heads of organizations. But when the chips were down, and Reed left him in the lurch, he took fast and positive action and stuck with his decisions. His choice of Reed has to be questioned, but his choice of Schairer proved superb.

After Pearl Harbor, when we were in the war for keeps, Reed and the rest of us worried that the Japanese might attack the Seattle area. Eddie casually remarked, "Not everything is bad about a war." My interpretation was that skilled workers and professionals exempt from the draft could enjoy exciting and profitable work in relatively low-risk occupations during wartime. But this certainly did not apply to the flight testing of aircraft in which Eddie was engaged.

Allen had survived so many desperate situations in flight that one cannot help but ponder the circumstances of the B-29 accident. On several occasions when flight testing '29s No. 1 and No. 2, engine fires were controlled by the onboard fire equipment. As disturbing as they were, these fires did not affect the main aircraft structure. By rapidly returning to the field, Eddie was able to save the aircraft and keep the program moving. On the fatal last flight, the fires in No. 1 and 2 nacelles initially could have been interpreted as recurrences of those earlier fires. By the time it was realized the aircraft itself, not just the engine, was on fire, too much altitude would have been lost. The aircraft was over the populated city center of Seattle, and the field was only seconds away. If this scenario is true, the earlier engine fires had introduced a deceptive element into the decision-making process. From this perspective, the R-3350 bears some responsibility for creating a situation beyond human control.

Apart from these tragic memories, I cherish my Boeing years. What an opportunity it was for a young engineer steeped in aeronautics to fly in those incomparable aircraft with a pilot like Eddie Allen, and to work in the department he had created! Like a first love, nothing in my career can quite come up to those adventurous years and the Seattle I knew.

As for the B-29, the rest of the story is familiar. For all of its problems, sacrificial development and crew training history, the B-29 fully accomplished its major military mission, fire-bombing more than 70 major Japanese cities with multiple raids involving hundreds of aircraft, and finally delivering the atomic bomb to Hiroshima and Nagasaki that ended the war.

FLIGHT & AERODYNAMICS DIVISION

PLAN OF TEST

PILOT E. T. Allen	SCHED. DATE 9-11-42 DAY Friday
Co-PILOT A. C. Reed	CONFERENCE TIME 10:45
ENGINEER W. F. Milliken	Taxi XXXXXX OFF TIME 11:00
G. W.76,500 lbs. C.G.14.6% W.D.	PLACE Boeing Field

CONFIGURATION:

1. Powerplant - All nacelles
   a. Wright R-3350-13 engines.
   b. Carburetors - Ceco 58 CPB-2 fuel injection carburetor.
   c. Turbo superchargers; dual B-11 high-speed turbos, A-11
      regulators with external bleed.
   d. Flame suppression hoods - Dwg. No. 14-3377.
   e. Fuel pumps. Thompson G-9.

2. Propellers - All nacelles
   a. Blade No. 6497A-0 Hydromatic full feathering (Hub. No. 23F60).
   b. Governor model 3G8-A16.
   c. Electric Head - H.S. type 493, Model 5, Style B.
   d. Low-pitch setting 18°.
   e. Positive high angle - stop at full feather - 86° (high-pitch setting).

3. Ignition System
   a. Magnetos - Bendix Scintilla DF18LN-1.
   b. Spark plugs AC LS85-Cap. .012. (cold).
   c. Harness unpressurized.
   d. Distributor pressurized.

4. Airplane in stripped condition per D-3547.

TEST: (W.O. No. 9140-098-04)

PREPARED	ETW 9-11-42	PLAN Ground Run and Taxi Test	MOD. NO. XB-29 1
TYPED	ba 9-11-42		REG. AF 41-2
CHECKED	ACR 9-11-42	Ground Run XXXXXXX 4 TEST NO. 4	D- 3861
APPROVED	ETA 9-11-42	BOEING AIRCRAFT CO. SEATTLE, WASH.	4-1-1

Fig. 13-11a
Test Plan for XB-29 No. 1 (AF41-2) Ground Run and Taxi Tests, including the initial hops. The plan was prepared by Ed Wersebe and approved by Allen, Reed and Milliken. These tests were crucial before first flight because they ensure nose-wheel stability (no shimmy) and that control forces are within the pilot's capability.

Note: The Auxiliary powerplant shall be operating throughout the test.

1. Ground Run, Engines 1 and 2.

    Purpose: To determine the fuel consumption and carburetor characteristics at takeoff power.

    Data: a. Complete cockpit data, including indicated fuel flows.
    b. Photo Recorder, one frame per second.
    c. Conditions:

Cond.	Eng.	RPM	BHP	BMEP	Ind. Torque, psi	Mixture
a	1	2800	2200	185	261	AR
b	2	2800	2200	185	253	AR

2. Ground Run, Engine No. 4.

    Purpose: To determine the effect of warm Outside Air Temperature upon the carburetor compensation.

    Data: a. Complete cockpit data, including fuel flow.
    b. Photo Recorder, one frame per second.

    Note: This item to be run only if atmospheric conditions are suitable warm and dry.

Cond.	RPM	BHP	BMEP	Ind. Torque, psi	Mixture
a	2180	1500	162	219	AR
b	2230	1600	169	229	AR
c	2275	1700	177	238	AR
d	2320	1800	183	247	AR

3. Taxi Tests, Nose Wheel Stability (Test Item 1-1, 1-2)

    Purpose: a. To observe the effect of the shimmy damping at increased setting upon the nose gear stability.
    b. To obtain additional preliminary data on the action of the rudder boost and on the operation of the brakes.

    Data: a. Cockpit data including IAS.
    b. Visual observations by each crew member.
    c. Photographs of nose gear.
    d. Photo-Recorder, one frame per second.
    e. Oscillograph readings on nose gear.

PREPARED KIW 9-11-42	PLAN Ground Run and Taxi Test		XB-29 N° 1	
TYPED ba 9-11-42			REG. # AF 41-2	
CHECKED	Ground Run 4	4	D- 3861	
	FLIGHT NO.	TEST NO.	4-1-2	
APPROVED	BOEING AIRCRAFT CO.	SEATTLE, WASH.		

Conditions: a. Taxi down field on concrete runway at 35 MPH ground speed.
             b. Repeat (a) if necessary.
             c. Repeat at 45 MPH.
             d. Repeat at 55 MPH.
             e. Repeat at 65 MPH.
             f. Repeat at 80 MPH.

4. **Initial Hops.** (Test Item 2-1, 2-4)

Purpose: a. To observe elevator control and determine elevator trim
                 tab position for balance.
          b. To obtain a preliminary indication of longitudinal
                 stability characteristics in takeoffs and landings.

Data: a. Cockpit data.
       b. Pilot Observations.
       c. Photo-recorders, one frame per second.

Note: The following runs shall be performed if Item 1 above has been completed satisfactorily. Before performing these runs, the airplane
shall be loaded to approximately 30% W.D. C.G.

Conditions: Elevator Trim Tab - 3° ND.
             Cowl Flaps - 8°

	IAS	FLAPS	REMARKS
(a)	Accelerate to 100 MPH	Up	Attempt to raise nose wheel at 60, 70, 80, 90 and 100 MPH.
(b)	Accelerate to 100 MPH	20°	Attempt to raise nose wheel at 60, 70, 80, 90 and 100 MPH.
(c)	Accelerate to 120 MPH	Up	A short hop is to be made.*
(d)	Accelerate to 105 MPH	20°	A short hop is to be made.*

$C_L = 1.20$

$C_L = 1.57$

* Apply brakes only after nose wheel contacts ground.

5. **Miscellaneous.**

a. Functional checkout.

Purpose: To obtain a functional check as possible on the ground of the
various airplane systems.

PREPARED BIW	9-11-42	PLAN	Ground Run and Taxi Test		MOD. XB-29	NO. 1
TYPED bd	9-11-42				REG. # AF 41-2	
CHECKED		Ground Run XXXXXXXXX 4		4	D- 3861	
		FLIGHT NO.	TEST NO.		4-1-3	
APPROVED		BOEING AIRCRAFT CO.	SEATTLE, WASH.			

Fig. 13-11c   295

Functional checks shall be performed upon the airplane and the forms provided shall be filled out accordingly.

b. Radio Interference.

Purpose: To obtain a preliminary check of the interference of various airplane systems upon radio reception.

Readings shall be taken as possible of various airplane systems and conductors to determine and eliminate where possible radio interference.

Checked ___W. F. Milliken Jr.___

Checked ___Albert C. Reed___   Approved ___E. T. Allen___

PREPARED	ETW	9-11-42	PLAN	Ground Run and Taxi Test	MOD XB-29	N 1
TYPED	ba	9-11-42			REG. AF # 41-2	
CHECKED			Ground Run XXXXXXXXX FLIGHT NO. 4	TEST NO. 4	D. 3861	
APPROVED			BOEING AIRCRAFT CO.	SEATTLE, WASH.	4-1-4	

December 31, 1942

To: A. C. Reed   E. I. Wersebe
      G. S. Schairer   A. E. Merrill
      V. W. North   R. T. Lamson
      W. F. Milliken   J. D. Gulick
      F. E. Woods   W. P. Talbott
      S. Silber   L. T. Goodmanson

CC: W. E. Beall   R. H. Nelson
      E. C. Wells   G. W. Newton
      L. A. Wood   R. W. Morse
      N. D. Showalter   R. A. Neale
      J. K. Ball   E. R. Perry
      J. C. Sanders   C. W. Tupper
                                           R. W. Boise

SUBJECT: ORGANIZATION CHANGES IN FLIGHT TEST UNIT

The following changes in the organization of the Flight Test Unit are effective immediately.

1.   Mr. A. C. Reed will continue in charge of the Flight Test
     Unit. In the absence of Mr. Reed, the following personnel
     in the Flight Test Unit will report directly to the under-
     signed:

           F. E. Woods   -   Flight Test Equipment
           S. Silber   -   Flight Test Analysis
           E. I. Wersebe   -   XB-29 Flight Test Project
           A. E. Merrill   -   For B-17 Flight Test Projects
           R. T. Lamson   -   For the Test Pilots

2.   In addition to his duties as XB-29 Flight Test Project Engineer,
     Mr. Wersebe is hereby appointed as Acting Group Leader in charge
     of Flight Test Projects and he shall in this connection be res-
     ponsible for Flight Test Planning.

3.   Mr. W. F. Milliken is hereby relieved of his former duties and
     shall report directly to the undersigned for special assignment.

4.   Mr. W. P. Talbott and his stenographic group will now serve the
     entire Division and will come under the supervision of the Admin-
     istrative Assistant, Mr. J. D. Gulick.

                                        E. T. Allen
                                        Director of Flight
                                        and Aerodynamics

Fig. 13-12
This is Allen's memo of December 31, 1942, announcing changes in the organization of the Flight Test group
subsequent to Al Reed's departure for California. I am taken off further flight tests of XB-29s, to my dismay.

I, William F. Milliken, whose position is Flight Test Operations Engineer, of Boeing Aircraft Company, do know of my own knowledge that the following named persons were on test flight No. 5-2 of airplane AAF 41-003 on February 18, 1943, which plane was destroyed in an accident and all persons killed. I further swear that all the persons aboard the airplane were employees of the Boeing Aircraft Company. I have examined the flight and crew record and I am personally acquainted with the signature of E. T. Allen, who approved the crew record prior to the take-off and the signature appearing on the crew record is that of E. T. Allen.

> E. T. Allen
> R. L. Basel
> C. E. Blaine
> R. R. Dansfield
> J. Henshaw
> T. Lankford
> R. W. Maxfield
> F. Mohn
> V. W. North
> E. I. Wersebe
> H. Ralston

W. F. Milliken

STATE OF WASHINGTON)
　　　　　　　　　　　) SS.
County of King　　　)

Before me personally appeared Mr. W. F. Milliken, to me known to be the individual who acknowledged that he executed the above instrument of his own free will and accord.

Donald C. Husted
Notary Public in and for the State of Washington, residing at Seattle

Fig. 13-13
My notarized memo of the composition of the crew of XB-29 No. 2, which was destroyed in a tragic accident February 18, 1943.

Transition
to Research
1944–1947

Chapter 14

Secret Wing

> ## "Against all odds, mission impossible."
>
> ### – Anonymous

In the aftermath of the XB-29 accident, I entered a period of instability in both my personal and professional lives. I was quite infatuated with my former secretary, Ermyl Teeter. Even if she had fully reciprocated it would have gone nowhere, because we had such diverse views on religion. Soon thereafter I became engaged to an heiress, Elizabeth Phillips (nicknamed "Phil"), whom I would marry in Seattle, some months after I left Boeing. Phil was a radio operator in our Flight Hangar at Boeing, and an ardent skier and mountain climber. At the time, my position at Boeing was becoming more and more uncomfortable. Having been transferred to the Preliminary Design Group, I found designing a "roadable helicopter" tedious stuff after the thrill and intellectual satisfaction of flight testing.

At this difficult time an unexpected telegram from Al Reed arrived, which I read with great interest. He had secured a job as Chief of Flight Test and Aerodynamics at Avion (a Northrop Aircraft subsidiary), and offered me a position as his assistant. My mood improved the moment I made the decision to leave Seattle for southern California. I resolved to make a non-stop drive to Los Angeles with only occasional catnaps. It was great fun to cruise down the coastal highway; coursing through the ghostly redwoods at night was like threading a trail past giants in a fairy tale.

As I progressed south, the temperature rose in my old Chevrolet. By the time I reached Kings Canyon I was pretty uncomfortable, so I parked and walked down a trail alongside a stream. The water was inviting, and since no one was around I stripped off my clothes and dove in, only to be confronted by a huge water snake swimming rapidly toward me. I quickly decided this was his territory, not mine.

The YB-49 jet-propelled flying wing bomber. Note the addition of fins.

Fig. 14-1
Avion's logo. The arrow symbolizes Northrop's interest in swept-back tailless aircraft.

Located on East 50th Street in Los Angeles south of Pasadena, Avion Inc. was a small two-story plant with an administrative lobby, manufacturing machine shop and fabrication area on the first floor, and engineering on the second. I had no idea of what I would be working on or what the job would entail. The company was involved in a secret project for the Air Force, the nature of which would not be divulged until my security clearance had been confirmed and I had officially been hired. This necessary formality was accomplished by the administrative types in the lobby area, after which I was escorted upstairs. Al introduced me to Avion President Dick Palmer, well known as the principal designer of Howard Hughes' transcontinental record race plane, and to Chief Engineer W. C. Rockefeller, a student of von Karman at Caltech who had made a name for himself in developing performance methods. To me, Rockefeller was typical of the very smart and mathematically sophisticated PhD graduates of Caltech's Aeronautical Engineering Department. The university was largely responsible for the stature of the southern California aircraft industry. Unlike their MIT counterparts, Caltechers dressed casually and were relaxed and informal, except for the stoic Al Reed. At Avion only Dick Palmer had an office; the engineering department of approximately 30 people shared quarters in an open area. They encompassed all of the specialties required to

design and develop a small aircraft.

Avion's secret project was the design and construction of the XP-79, a small flying-wing interceptor fighter in which the pilot controlled the aircraft from a prone position by means of a handlebar. It was believed that lying prone would enable the pilot to survive high normal (i.e., 90 degrees to the plane of the wing) accelerations. As originally conceived, the aircraft was to be powered by an early version of an Aerojet rocket engine located at the pilot's feet. Fuel for the rocket engine consisted of nitric acid (the oxidizer) in the left wing and aniline in the right wing, both of which were fed through two-inch pipes to the engine. The entire structure was welded magnesium, over two inches thick at the wing leading edge and decreasing in thickness toward the trailing edge.

The aircraft's mission was to intercept and destroy high-altitude bombers, not only by firepower but also by literally ramming their vulnerable tail surfaces. High subsonic speeds on a steep flight path with short range and endurance was the aim. In some respects the XP-79 was similar to Germany's last-ditch attempts to produce jet- and rocket-propelled fighters that could get to altitude in a hurry and harass the B-17 bombers whose raids over Berlin were devastating the city.

A "Pure" Flying Wing

The original concept for the XP-79 belonged to Jack Northrop, the flying wing proponent and legendary father of the California aircraft industry. A man of extraordinary talent, Northrop's aviation resume included Glenn Martin (where he began his career), Douglas World Cruisers, the Lockheed Vega, Orion, Sirius, Air Express, et al., plus the all-metal monocoques in the Northrop Alpha, Beta and Gamma series. He also pioneered the

Fig. 14-2
This photo is of the XP-79 Model B, with two vertical tails and a "bellows rudder." It was powered by twin Westinghouse 19V turbojet engines. The XP-79 with which I was involved with used a single Aerojet rocket engine and no vertical tails or rudder. We desperately wanted to install some fins and rudders to improve lateral and yaw damping and directional control but were prohibited by Northrop's purist attitude at the time.

multiple-spar stressed-skin wing and the early use of wing flaps. After conceiving the XP-79 as another one of his flying wings, Northrop is believed to have personally convinced General Arnold to support it.

Northrop's main plant in Hawthorne was producing large flying-wing bombers (the XB-35 experimental propeller version and the production turbojet version, the YB-49). The company had a long history of experimental "flying wings" including the N1M, N9M and XP-56. Jack Northrop was a purist, intent on avoiding drag-producing control elements such as fins and tail surfaces.

From the beginning it was made clear that Al and I had final responsibility for the flying characteristics of the XP-79. We learned that Northrop had constructed a full-scale plywood replica, MX-334, for preliminary assessment of stability and control. Harry Crosby, a well-known racing and stunt pilot, was at the controls when this non-powered glider was towed to altitude at the Muroc Air Force Base,

first to low altitude by car and subsequently by a Lockheed P-38 fighter. The latter test did not go well. In releasing the tow cable, Crosby also accidentally pulled the latch on the escape hatch on which he was lying. As he accelerated downward, his automatic reaction was to push the nose of the glider down, creating centrifugal force to keep him from falling out. Whether it tumbled about its pitch axis or gyrated in roll is not known, but the glider ended inverted, where it was trimmed and reasonably stable. Harry stayed with it for a while before parachuting down.

The rebuilt MX-334 was fitted with an early Aerojet rocket engine, according to Irv Ashkenas of Northrup, and again towed to altitude with Harry Crosby at the controls. When the rocket was fired, a short but successful flight followed. The stall was investigated briefly at some point, and seemed to be "relatively benign" according to Northrup's chief aerodynamicist Bill Sears. Although the MX-334 was not a dynamically

Fig. 14-3
The N9M, one of Northrop's early flying wing prototypes. This low-speed machine had no vertical surfaces and used ailerons for pitch and roll control. Some years later we measured the dynamic derivatives on an N9M at Flight Research, Cornell Aeronautical Laboratory.

scaled model of the projected XP-79, this flight was encouraging as an indicator of the probable flying qualities of the latter.

Al and I also were briefed on other flying wing activities at Northrop, and became acquainted with Sears and Ashkenas, both of whom had been involved in flying wing developments from the beginning. Although impressed by the progress Northrop had made with this novel aircraft configuration, we were skeptical about the possibilities of producing good handling characteristics in a maneuverable fighter like the XP-79. Not until after our stint at Avion, it should be noted, did stability augmentation and automatic control techniques became common, which vastly reduced the limitations of the purely aerodynamic approach and dominated aircraft control systems ever after.

Because of my training under Otto Koppen, I thought in terms of the equations of motion and their various force and moment derivatives. A preliminary examination of the flying wing dynamics indicated that the yaw damping, lateral damping, pitch damping and drag damping were small compared with conventional aircraft. This helped explain the reported behavior of the prototype wings and their lack of stall recovery by conventional control use. Experience with fighter designs had shown that optimum maneuverability resulted from minimum stability, heavy damping and large amounts of control—not easy to achieve in a purely aerodynamic flying wing design. Koppen laid great stress on adequate directional stability and yaw damping, the importance of which had been reinforced by the experience at Boeing, when large vertical tails had improved the flight and stall characteristics of the Stratoliner and B-17. Koppen's comprehensive approach to aircraft stability and control was unique; no other university in the United States had anything comparable.

Our Approach

The approach Al and I hoped to pursue in discharging our responsibilities for XP-79 handling was to calculate flight dynamics for alternative design configurations. This required numerical data from wind tunnel tests supplemented, where necessary, by theoretical estimates. The static derivatives were measurable by conventional wind tunnel tests, but the rotary derivatives required specialized balance systems that were not generally available. At the time it seemed reasonable to assume that for a simple, modestly swept wing the rotary derivatives could reliably be calculated.

Thus, as a starter, we initiated scale-model wind tunnel test programs. Since some of them involved government tunnels (NACA), the Aerodynamic Branch at Wright Field approved and financed them (presumably on the aircraft contract). My records are incomplete, but notes indicate we performed two series of tests in the 10-foot GALCIT tunnel in Pasadena, and another two series with the same $^1/_5$-scale model in the 7 × 10-foot NACA tunnel at Moffitt Field. These tests were primarily directed at evaluating low-speed control and stability. We investigated a variety of devices such as slots, spoilers, fixed fins and movable surfaces. In my MIT days I had been impressed with the "slot and interceptor" control developed by the British, in which a small spoiler moving in conjunction with the ailerons closed off a fixed slot on one wing tip. This was among the configurations we explored that never had been used by Northrop. I also remember a test program at Langley Field during the summer months.

Since the XP-79 was to fly at high subsonic speeds, a $^5/_8$-scale model was tested in the 16-foot high-speed NACA tunnel at Moffitt Field. I particularly remember this program for the cooperation I received from Carl Tusch who was in charge of the Air Force liaison office, Manley Hood, who headed the high-speed facility, and test engineer Ed Laitone. As liaison for all these tests, I spent months away from Avion that year.

Between tests Al and I struggled to make sense out of the tunnel data and use it in meaningful calculations. Without the flight experience available at Northrop from the various prototype "wings," we had no standards with which to compare. Convinced that the magnitude of non-dimensional derivatives for an acceptable flying wing were quite different from those of a conventional airplane, we had a strong feeling that more directional stability

was desirable, and certainly more yaw damping. The low damping of the Dutch roll had proven acceptable in the small prototypes, but we questioned if it would be satisfactory at really high speeds. Finally, experience with the big wings (XB-35 and YB-49 bombers) did not seem at all applicable to a small high-speed interceptor.

I remember Jack Northrop's first visit. Appearing unannounced, his suit jacket slung over his shoulder, he impressed me with his quiet approach and informality. I think Al and I felt somewhat abashed in his presence. Northrop listened intently to our concerns about adequate damping and directional stability, the need for large fins and so forth. Without taking direct issue, he gave the impression that our apprehension was unwarranted and the basic configuration of the XP-79 would prove satisfactory. This remained his attitude on all subsequent visits. We were talking in different languages—Northrop from his vision of the concept and his prototype wing experience, the two of us from considerations of theoretical stability, control technology and our knowledge of more conventional aircraft behavior.

The construction of a welded all-magnesium wing was an original development in itself. The basic wing, as I remember it, was a thick symmetrical airfoil section that for fabrication purposes was split along the center plane. The top and bottom halves were produced in a heavy metal jig. The magnesium strips were machined to shape (very thick at the leading edge) and were bolted down in the jig prior to welding. Because of the internal stresses created by the welding, a great "bong" (audible to us in engineering) sounded when the bolts were removed and the section twisted into some unintended shape. It is my impression that considerable experimentation was necessary before two halves conforming to design specifications could be welded together to make a wing. Magnesium chips and filings were a potential fire hazard, so every Friday afternoon the shop was carefully swept, and all magnesium bits and pieces were piled up in an open area out back to be burned. Most of the employees attended the "bonfire." I was told that five pounds of magnesium burned on the

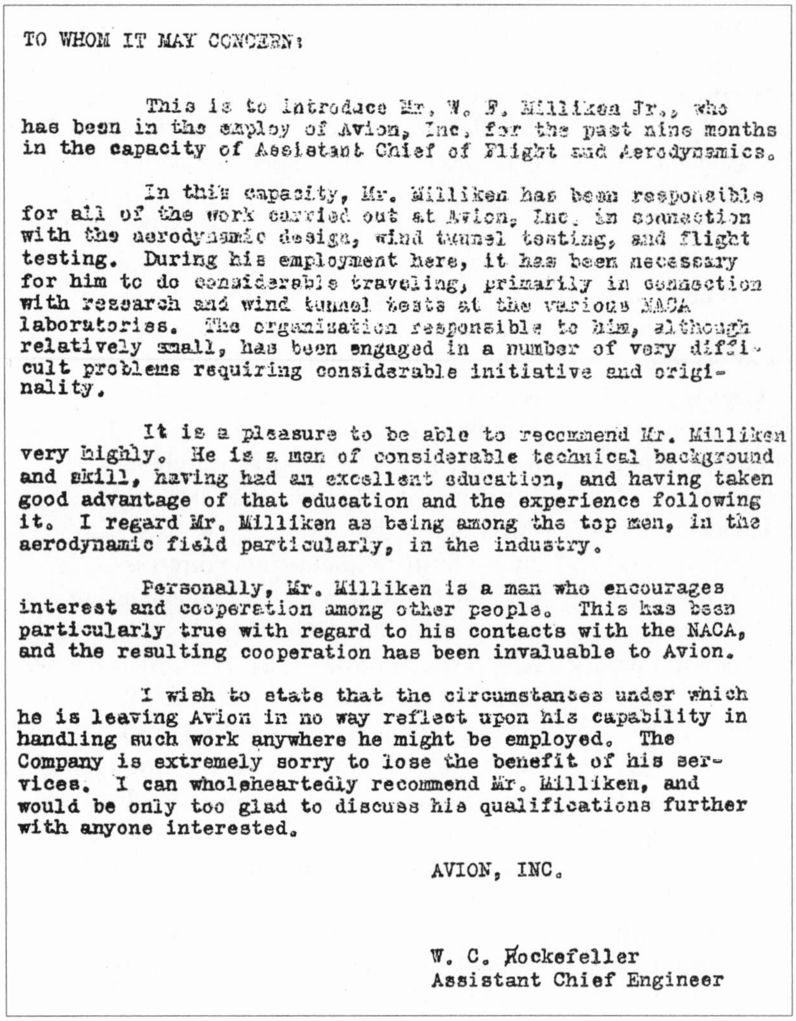

TO WHOM IT MAY CONCERN:

This is to introduce Mr. W. F. Milliken Jr., who has been in the employ of Avion, Inc. for the past nine months in the capacity of Assistant Chief of Flight and Aerodynamics.

In this capacity, Mr. Milliken has been responsible for all of the work carried out at Avion, Inc. in connection with the aerodynamic design, wind tunnel testing, and flight testing. During his employment here, it has been necessary for him to do considerable traveling, primarily in connection with research and wind tunnel tests at the various NACA laboratories. The organization responsible to him, although relatively small, has been engaged in a number of very difficult problems requiring considerable initiative and originality.

It is a pleasure to be able to recommend Mr. Milliken very highly. He is a man of considerable technical background and skill, having had an excellent education, and having taken good advantage of that education and the experience following it. I regard Mr. Milliken as being among the top men, in the aerodynamic field particularly, in the industry.

Personally, Mr. Milliken is a man who encourages interest and cooperation among other people. This has been particularly true with regard to his contacts with the NACA, and the resulting cooperation has been invaluable to Avion.

I wish to state that the circumstances under which he is leaving Avion in no way reflect upon his capability in handling such work anywhere he might be employed. The Company is extremely sorry to lose the benefit of his services. I can wholeheartedly recommend Mr. Milliken, and would be only too glad to discuss his qualifications further with anyone interested.

AVION, INC.

W. C. Rockefeller
Assistant Chief Engineer

Fig. 14-4
W. C. Rockefeller's letter of recommendation, which certainly helped me relocate after leaving Avion.

moon would be visible to the human eye on earth. I could well believe it.

Al was the logical pilot for the first flight of the prototype XP-79, and as time passed it became apparent he wasn't happy about it. Nothing we had learned from our tunnel tests was very encouraging, and our analyses of XP-79 flight dynamics still were incomplete. I knew Al was discussing his "first flight" reservations with Palmer and Rockefeller.

STILL, I WAS SHOCKED when we were separately called into Dick Palmer's office one day and informed that we no longer were employed by Avion. I could only conclude that Reed had flatly refused to fly the aircraft.

Because of our negative view of its probable flying characteristics, there was little point in continuing our employment. Palmer and Rockefeller were very considerate in presenting my severance notice, the latter providing me with a written recommendation. The experience had been an interesting one, and Avion and I parted with no ill feelings.

After Al and I left, the XP-79 prototype was taken to Northrop. At some stage, two 1,000-pound-thrust Westinghouse 19V turbojets were installed side-by-side in the tail, along with two vertical tail fins (Model B). Northrop added a so-called "bellows rudder" for directional control. Harry Crosby was the pilot for the first and only flight from Muroc. Little agreement exists between the written and verbal accounts of what happened. After a dramatic takeoff, Harry made several passes over the group of Air Force and Northrop personnel. In one account he flew by at low speed as if approaching the stall; in another he had gained considerable altitude and was exploring maneuverability. Whatever the case, the airplane got into a roll. Crosby exited from the escape panel and released his chute. Whether he was struck by the aircraft or his chute tangled with it is not known. He was killed and the plane was demolished. Avion went out of business.

The cause of the accident remains obscure. I still believe that achieving adequate directional damping and benign stall/spin characteristics in this high-performance, maneuverable fighter was difficult or impossible without active augmentation. There is no irrefutable evidence

Fig. 14-5
The XB-35 propeller-driven prototype flying wing bomber. The huge size of this aircraft is apparent in this photo.

that handling qualities did him in. The pilot may have attempted unreasonable maneuvers after too brief a period of familiarization. Harry Crosby was fearless, but not noted for a slow and systematic approach.

Seeing a New Dimension

The demise of the XP-79 should not overshadow the achievements of the Northrop period of flying wing development. By any standard it was a memorable chapter in the history of airplane design—one that relied almost solely on Jack Northrop's creative talents, reputation and persistence. Only Northrop could have inspired the support within his own company to pursue such a radical configuration. Only he could have

acquired the military sponsorship to continue its development, from his early prototypes to such phenomenal aircraft as the XB-35 and the YB-49.

A spectacular plane, nothing of its era compares to the YB-49. It had a wingspan of nearly 80 feet, a wing area of 4,000 square feet, and 8 GE J35 turbojet engines totaling 16 tons of thrust. This gigantic wing sailed through the air with invisible means for control and stability, at a cruising speed of 450 mph and a range of 5,000 miles. Numerous technical features lay behind the YB-49, among them a full hydraulic (irreversible) control system with artificial feel-augmentation in the form of the first yaw damper, and a variety of aerodynamic features that included the ailerons, drag rudder, tip slots (with closure doors), trim flaps, etc.

Fig. 14-6
A dramatic illustration of the YB-49 on takeoff. Col. Glen Edwards was killed in a stall-spin accident in this aircraft. For all of the pioneering effort in aerodynamic and servo control by the engineering group at Northrop, this aircraft never reached service use.

The basic innovations were of course the distribution of load along the span, which decreased the structural weight and improved the range, and the low aerodynamic drag of an extremely clean wing.

Many of the features of modern military and commercial aircraft were pioneered in these flying wing developments, notably fully powered control and feel systems, and artificial damping. Liberal use of augmentation now makes it possible to create good handling characteristics in a wide variety of aerodynamic configurations, including tailless designs, and in controlling the flight of stalled aircraft at very high angles of attack. Studies performed by Northrop showed that with appropriate pitch augmentation, a flying wing of statically unstable aerodynamic configuration would yield a substantially improved range.

For my own part, the experience at Avion generated a great curiosity for understanding more about aircraft dynamics.

Once over the shock of my sudden unemployment, I reacted rapidly. I didn't want to be out of work for long. Al was extremely helpful, and in addition to giving me a strong letter of recommendation he suggested that I contact a Caltech associate, Dr. Norton Moore, who was working at Curtiss-Wright Research Laboratory in Buffalo, New York. Moving back East had some appeal because I was becoming bored with the consistently good weather in southern California. As a New Englander, I harbored the feeling there was something "artificial" about all those palm trees and the fresh orange juice on every corner. Life seemed too easy. I needed the challenge of real weather. But before I decided on Curtiss-Wright, Al and I explored an idea he had for our continuing to work together in California.

At Boeing we had organized a flight test operation of some note under Eddie Allen. Because our high-altitude experience and general test techniques were recognized throughout the industry, Al had the notion that we had something to offer as consultants. He arranged an interview with A. E. Raymond of Douglas Aircraft, proposing that we independently fly and appraise the handling of Douglas prototypes. Raymond reacted in no uncertain terms, telling Al that "if I wanted such an appraisal, you are the last one I would turn to." I was less surprised at the turn-down than the vehemence with which it was given. Reed's persona non grata status now included Boeing, Avion and Douglas. Having satisfactorily worked with Al for a number of years, accepting him as an individual and admiring his engineering abilities, I couldn't help but wonder what lay behind these rebuffs, and the effect they must be having on him. I concluded that for understandable reasons, and their consequences, he had a tragic life. His life and struggles should not pass unnoticed. (Al's story appears in Appendix III.)

THE AVION XP-79 EXPERIENCE triggered a fundamental change in my career that led to pioneering research in flight dynamics at Cornell Aero Laboratory. This, in turn, resulted in the increased adoption of the equations of motion by other research organizations and by industry. This was followed by the translation of aeronautical technology to ground vehicles, and the complete theory of automobile stability and control. These are the accomplishments of my associates and myself that justify this memoir as a technical autobiography. Prior to Avion I had been acquiring the interests, focus, education and experience from which to launch these creative years, beginning in 1946 and continuing to the present.

Chapter 15 🦅

Flight Dynamics

D r. Norton Moore, an old friend of Al Reed's, was in charge of
an aerodynamic department in the Curtiss-Wright Research
Laboratory Division in Buffalo, New York. One of those
smart analytical types from Caltech, he was informal in dress and
speech, highly energetic and a chain smoker. His ideas about the
direction the laboratory should take conflicted with those of Dr. C.
C. Furnas, the laboratory director, but at the time I met them the two
men were still on reasonable terms. During my two-day visit I met
most of the department heads and reviewed the types of projects in
which they were involved. Although Moore had a slot for me in his
aerodynamics department, another possibility seemed much more
exciting.

When the SB2C Helldiver ran into longitudinal instability
problems in high-speed dives and high-g pullouts, Curtiss-Wright
Airplane Division (the parent company) assigned the task of
resolution to the Aero-Mechanics Department of its Research
Laboratory. Because the lab had no flight test department, an ad hoc
group of test pilots, aero and instrumentation engineers, technicians
and mechanics operated out of a base in Van Nuys, California, where
the weather was more predictable than in Buffalo. Among the several
pilots involved were Vance Breeze, Lloyd Child (who had dived a
P-40 into the high subsonic range) and understudy John Seal, who
in time would surpass them both. Also in the group was Ira Ross, a
very competent electronics instrumentation engineer with a physics
background and good managerial skills.

So successful was this *ad hoc* group that plans were being made
for a full-fledged Flight Research Department at the Buffalo airport
adjacent to the C-W Airplane Division. With my background in flight
testing I figured I was a logical candidate to head up this department,

Measuring the moments of inertia on the P-80A by the pendulum method.

"In your attempt to obtain the derivatives from flight test using automatic control, you might focus on a frequency response as used in electrical engineering."

– Ira G. Ross, Head of CAL Flight Research, 1947

(That led to the first-ever frequency response of an airplane in flight)

and decided to toss my hat into the ring. More than logic motivated me. Sheer ambition was involved, of course, plus the opportunity to increase my piloting experience and also engage in some test flying. But far deeper incentives made this opportunity attractive. My Avion experience had crystallized my lifelong curiosity about vehicle control and stability. Consumed with the idea of developing test techniques for assessing aircraft dynamics, I had no clear idea how to go about it, but sensed that some form of automatic control based on autopilot experience offered the best chance for success. I also felt certain that with my enthusiasm I could find sponsorship for such research among my friends in the Air Force Flight Division at Wright Field.

Negotiations with Dr. Furnas led to a job offer placing me on salary, and providing a two-month leave of absence so I could obtain a commercial pilot's license before officially starting work. A visit to Van Nuys also was arranged because the nucleus of the new department would come from that group, and we should become acquainted. It was agreed that I would be considered as a candidate

for manager of the new department, but the decision would be deferred until the work at Van Nuys was finished.

Commercial Pilot's License

For flight training I chose a flight school in Lone Pine, California, which lay west of Death Valley and east of Sequoia, in a flat valley area with the Sierra Nevada range rising to the west. In early May of 1944 I checked into a motel near the airfield and met instructor William Barris. A typical Western cowboy type, relaxed and easygoing, Bill diligently drilled me in S-turns, rectangular courses, series of eights, series of stalls, pylon eights, spirals, overhead approaches, emergency procedures, accuracy spins and precision landing, plus chandelles and lazy eights. After a workout we would adjourn to the local steak house to discuss what I should continue to practice solo. My solo flights for the cross-country requirement were to Silver Lake, Las Vegas, Boulder Dam, Olameka and Independence. After the high-tension work at Boeing and Avion, Lone Pine was a welcome break. There was no rigorous

Fig. 15-1
Lone Pine (California) Airport lies in the Owens Valley, 3,600 feet above sea level and about 170 miles slightly east of north of Los Angeles. It enjoys a spectacular view of Mt. Whitney, in the Sierra Nevada range, whose summit is 14,445 feet above sea level. Mt Whitney is the highest mountain in the continental USA.

schedule to be met and no external pressures, just a strong internal urge to obtain the commercial pilot rating.

Before arriving at Lone Pine I had accumulated nearly 200 hours of solo flight time on a variety of light planes, and some co-piloting on military aircraft at Boeing, but I never had been exposed to the kind of precision flying required to pass a commercial pilot's license test. My attitude toward flying had been one of adventure and experimentation. Just as I had rebelled at practicing the piano, I disliked the repetitious activity required to perfect routine flight maneuvers. It would be years before I could accept the drudgery necessary for perfection in certain physical and mental tasks.

Bill sensed this, and accepted it as part of his personal challenge of getting me a license. His task was twofold: first, to convince himself that I had enough skill, judgment and experience to justify a commercial pilot's license; second, to teach me to fly well enough to convince the official examination pilot. From the beginning we agreed to no time limit, that we would continue until he thought I was ready. His judgment of my qualifications went beyond specific piloting performance, to my aeronautical education and overall experience. I suspect he imparted this to his old friend John Adams, a CAA examiner operating out of Reno, whom he selected to conduct my official flight test. In one month under Bill's tutelage I put in over 77 hours of air time (38 dual instruction, 39 solo; 28 local, 11 cross-country). I averaged about three hours a day in the air, and spent the rest of the time studying for the written exams.

On May 23, 1944, Bill and I flew to Reno in the Taylorcraft with Lycoming 65 engine on which I had done all my training. Adams was thorough; we went through every maneuver in the books while he plied me with all kinds of questions. He seemed as interested in my understanding of the purpose of the maneuvers as my performance of them. At the conclusion of the tests I felt I had done a fair job, although my maneuvers were far from sharp and accurate. Nevertheless, I passed and could take some satisfaction in going directly from a private license to a commercial, bypassing the limited commercial category. After the test, Barris and I took Adams to dinner and stopped by a casino where I managed to lose 50 dollars.

Back at Lone Pine, Bill and I celebrated our success by renting and flying every light plane on the base, including a Porterfield, Aeronca, Luscombe, Piper and Waco YKC. After that we decided to fly over Mt. Whitney. On a glorious day in the desert country we climbed steadily and topped out at about 14,500 feet, which must have been close to the T-Craft's service ceiling at the existing temperature. After briefly circling the ridges we descended to base.

A couple of days later I left Lone Pine and moved to Buffalo, New York, leaving behind Bill Barris as one of the special people in my life.

Fig. 15-2
Taken on a flight over Mt. Whitney (14,491 ft.) in a Taylorcraft in celebration of passing the test to earn my commercial pilot's license.

Phil had been with me in Lone Pine and we moved to Buffalo together. We proved to be incompatible, officially separated and then divorced amicably in 1952. She came into her fortune soon afterward when her mother and aunt died. Phil traveled to Europe, climbed the Matterhorn, married a ski instructor and had a daughter. She visited me once at the Cornell Lab with her husband and on another occasion visited my family in Maine. We remained friends.

Flight Research Department

Shortly after my arrival, Dr. Furnas made his decision. Ira Ross was chosen to head up the new department. I was offered the position of assistant head. I accepted the decision but resented Ross, and questioned Furnas's judgment. It seemed to me that with my qualifications I should have been awarded the position. I had been assistant head of operations at Boeing and Avion, and had more flight experience, a commercial license, and an aeronautical engineering background. A few years my senior, Ross had been a physics major, was relatively new to flight testing, but had a background in the management of research organizations.

In hindsight, I am confident Furnas made the right decision. In addition to his organizational skills, Ross was more mature and emotionally stable, had demonstrated his ability to work with the main laboratory and was a known quantity. Furthermore, he had a strong background in electronics and instrumentation, new technologies that were becoming vitally necessary in flight testing. I was consumed with creative ideas and the energy to drive them through. The compromises required for good managerial practice in dealing with contracts and administrative people were factors I never thought about, and I had little concern for good fiscal performance.

Although our relationship had its rocky aspects, Ross and I proved to be an unbeatable team. Although I initially took out my dissatisfaction on him, he never reacted negatively. After a couple of years I realized how nasty I had been, and had enough sense to apologize. During his subsequent career at the laboratory he consistently backed the exploration (and exploitation) of my ideas.

Before moving into a hangar on the other side of the airport, we spent a couple of months at the main laboratory putting together the nucleus of the department. This comprised the hangar group mechanics, an instrumentation group, data and engineering analysis, technicians, pilots and the necessary administrative and support personnel. Some of the staff came from Van Nuys and some from the C-W plant; still others came from various sources and contacts Ira and I had. The hangar and instrumentation sections were built up first, while the engineering staff expanded slowly as projects came on line.

For chief of the Hangar Group we chose Len Gifford, who had run C-W's experimental hangar during the war and knew the best mechanics and technicians in Curtiss-Wright. His choice of mechanics included Frankie Babchek, Shorty Miller, Art Mandale and Casey Jaworski, as well as Bill Wilcox, who had started out as a fabricator on the P-40 line. A self-educated engineer, Bill proved a tremendous asset to the organization, and ultimately headed up the Hangar Group when Gifford retired. Giff also brought in Johnny Eichorn, an outstanding sheet-metal fabricator, and Carl Oddo, an experienced painter, in addition to Henry Sonnen and Bill Frey to operate the hangar machine shop. Henry and Bill were mechanical artists who could make anything from a simple sketch, rather like the men who worked for Ettore Bugatti. Later additions included Bill Rouzer, who was to carve out a career as an engine rep. It would be

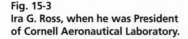

Fig. 15-3
Ira G. Ross, when he was President of Cornell Aeronautical Laboratory.

Fig. 15-4
Henry Sonnen (left) and Bill Frey, who operated the machine shop in Flight Research. Thanks to their level of skill and experience, test installations could be fabricated rapidly with a minimum of formal design layout.

hard to imagine a more skilled, ingenious and dedicated group.

Of the initial aircraft mechanics group, none was more colorful than Casey Jaworski. During the Lindbergh era he had entertained weekend visitors at Buffalo Airfield with parachute jumps. His special stunt was to free-fall a thousand feet while manhandling his chute out of a homemade bag. The crowd loved it. With the onset of World War II Casey was permanently employed on the P-40 final assembly line. More than 19,000 of these fighter aircraft would be produced. Rapid changes in the aircraft necessitated the creation of a Modification Center on the other side of the airport, and it became Casey's task to taxi hundreds of production aircraft there from the end of the line. Although not a pilot, Casey managed to get several of the planes off the ground en route. Our group was located in the "Mod Center," which consisted of eight consecutive hangar bays. We were assigned the bay closest to Cayuga Road, along the west side of the airport. Full access to each hangar

was provided by a door that was hinged at the top and swung outward and upward. On the day we moved in, Casey could hardly wait to "ride" the door as it opened. We left him up there—40 feet off the tarmac—to cool off for a bit. Early on we learned that one of his more bizarre stunts was to break up wine glasses with his teeth before returning them to a bartender. A continual source of entertainment in the old hangar, Casey proved to be an excellent mechanic.

We also were fortunate in the selection of personnel for the instrumentation group. Walt Hirtreiter was a self-trained electronic technician whose background was ham radio, and who at one time had operated one of the most powerful stations in New York State. Other early instrumentation personnel were Jack Beilman, developer of the low-range airspeed indicator (LORAS), Earl Edighoffer, Art Pulley, and Ed Skelly. With Ross's formal training in electronics and the practical experience of this group, the department was well equipped to instrument high-performance military aircraft. In addition to pilots, we had to build up our engineering group of project engineers and analysts, data handling and administrative/secretarial personnel.

During this formative period I met Lloyd Child, Curtiss-Wright's most senior and famous test pilot, who casually inquired if I would like a flight in a P-40. Since it was a single-seat fighter I expressed surprise, but he said one airplane had been rigged with another seat behind the standard cockpit. Since I assumed we were going for a joy ride, I was doubly surprised when, at the head of the runway, he suggested I do the takeoff. There was a duplicate set of controls but the forward vision was near zero from my seat. Although I had never flown a high-performance single-engine airplane, I knew it took a lot of right rudder to counteract the slipstream effect on the vertical tail. So I opened the throttle slowly and pushed the right rudder as hard as I could. Still, without more rudder trim the aircraft slowly swung left. My impression was that the plane took off in a turn, and I remember asking Lloyd afterward why he didn't help me out. He replied, "Oh, a P-40 always gets off no matter what you do." In the air we did some maneuvers and stalls, after which I did a successful takeoff by using some trim and adjusting the seat so I could get some real force on the rudder pedal. My final surprise was his memo afterward, indicating that this flight was a formal check of my ability to fly this fighter without any sort of transition familiarization!

The memo (reproduced at the end of this chapter) reflects the easygoing attitude that prevailed at C-W at that time. However, I can't disagree with Lloyd's conclusions.

Flight Dynamics Project

In late 1944 I began promoting a project to measure aircraft dynamic behavior in flight (see Figure 15-35). It was greeted with little enthusiasm, to put it mildly; in fact, strong opposition was generated by members of the Aero-Mechanics Department. From his academic background in chemistry at Yale, Dr. Furnas was not versed in aircraft handling. Because internal support was nil, I decided to tackle the Air Force directly, an action Ross

supported. My initial contacts were with the Flight Test Division at Wright Field. In those days we traveled to Dayton by rail. The train left Buffalo close to midnight, but before the cars were positioned a passenger could find the one to which he was assigned and go to bed. The porter then awakened you at Springfield, Ohio, just in time for a quick shave and a toothbrush before pulling into Dayton at around 7:30 A.M. for breakfast at the Biltmore or Miami Hotel. On those occasions when the train was late we could enjoy an extra hour of sleep. (Once Dick Koegler and I boarded and were lulled to sleep by the usual shaking and rattling as the train was being made up. Upon being awakened, we stepped off into a chilly Buffalo! Because of a huge snowstorm the train never had left the station).

In Dayton I started talking up my ideas with the test pilots who routinely lounged around in the offices between flights and always had time for "hangar flying." The favorable reaction I received still amazes me. In reality the only thing I had to sell was a general notion of using automatic control, but I had lots of enthusiasm, which is about all one can have in the early stage of an idea. The test pilots certainly had encountered inexplicable aircraft behavior, and any promising research technique had great appeal. My experiences at Vought, Boeing and Avion had much in common with their own, and I became good friends with many of the group. Conveniently, the Flight Division had unassigned funds that could be used for "technique development."

With sponsorship in sight, it was necessary to become more specific. "Automatic control" implied the use of a standard or modified autopilot. Orin Johnston, a former member of Boeing's Flight Instrumentation Group and a good friend, had moved to Minneapolis Honeywell, the producer of a well-known autopilot. An appeal to him was successful. M-H would lend us an autopilot if our project was sponsored by the Air Force.

The next problem was obtaining a plane. The only aircraft available to the Curtiss-Wright Research Laboratory were unsuitable or otherwise involved. The SB2C was tied up with a continuing program of dive testing. The Brewster Buffalo, never a popular aircraft, was out of favor with the Air Force. Following another trip to Dayton, the Air Force agreed to lend us a North American B-25 twin-engine bomber (a type made famous by Doolittle's Tokyo raid). Since our only pilot, John Seal, was fully occupied with the SB2C, the Air Force finally lent us a pilot too. After returning from two years of combat flying in the North African campaign, Glen Edwards had been assigned to the Bomber Test Branch of the Flight Test Division at Wright Field. This was an elite group of pilots responsible for performing acceptance tests on all military aircraft types and for working with the manufacturers to enhance their performance and handling. Taking prototype aircraft to their limits not only was a hazardous task, but also one requiring a nice blend of practical engineering judgment and responsibility. When I met Glen Edwards he was a trim 27-year-old, modest, sociable and enthusiastic.

WE NOW HAD AN AIRPLANE, an autopilot and a pilot. The next step was to work out a detailed approach. With his electrical engineering background, Ira Ross suggested a frequency response of the longitudinal motion. This fundamentally sound approach was novel to those of us trained as aeronautical engineers. Hirtreiter modified the autopilot to give us the elevator control we needed, and we were ready to start the program.

Flying as co-pilot with Edwards, we made our first flight on the afternoon of June 12. Having reached a safe altitude, we turned on the autopilot and soon were oscillating in pitch at various frequencies and amplitudes. We recorded the responses of the aircraft on an oscillograph in terms of pitch angle, normal acceleration and control force. For years, of course, test pilots had studied longitudinal control and stability by applying random control inputs and subjectively noting the aircraft's responses. By using an autopilot we could obtain consistent response data over the full range of frequencies and amplitudes, making possible a more fundamental analysis of the longitudinal dynamics. Glen and I

Fig. 15-5
North American B-25, used on the frequency response project. L-R: Bill Rouzer, Bill Milliken, Lee Maefs, Bill Wilcox, Capt. Glen Edwards, Paul Kase and Sam Liebfeld.

immediately recognized this. He glanced at me with a boyish grin, "I think we've got something, Bill!"

Since the days of Bryan and the equations of motion, it had been known that an aircraft had two natural longitudinal frequencies, the so-called "short" period and the "phugoid." In our test we were operating in the short-period frequency range (essentially constant speed with changes in angle of attack and normal acceleration), the mode that defines normal aircraft maneuvering.

The results were reduced by Ed Laitone, one of the first analytical engineers we hired for the department, whom I had met at the 16-foot tunnel at Ames during my Avion days. Ed not only plotted the original data but also analyzed it with a graphical electrical engineering tool called the Circle Diagram to yield a measure of the effective spring and damping constants for this two-degree-of-freedom system. He was able to extend the analysis to evaluate the aerodynamics derivatives in the classical equations of motion and to examine the possibility of other forcing functions such as step inputs.

In January 1947 I presented a comprehensive paper on these results at the Fifteenth Annual Meeting of the Institute of the Aeronautical Sciences, "Progress in Dynamic Stability and Control Research," which became the feature article of the *Journal* for September 1947. With the help of a number of other engineers who had joined our staff, notably W. O. Breuhaus, G. F. Campbell and R. C. Kidder, this paper also summarized previous dynamic research and forecast further developments.

Daniel Ford's book *Glen Edwards, The Diary of a Bomber Pilot*, contains the dates on which we flew the B-25 on the dynamic stability project and Glen's view of the project. Six flights were made between June

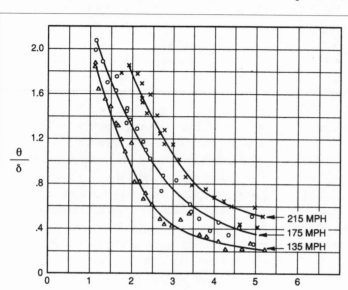

ω_F , Radians per Second

Experimental variation of pitch angle amplitude with frequency of elevator oscillation for the B-25J airplane.

Fig. 15-6
Pitch angle amplitude measured during frequency response tests.

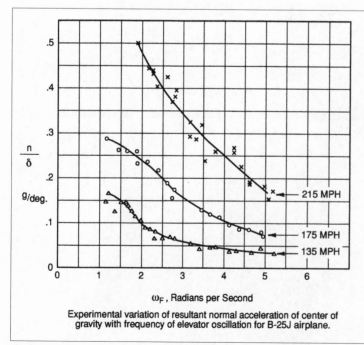

ω_F , Radians per Second

Experimental variation of resultant normal acceleration of center of gravity with frequency of elevator oscillation for B-25J airplane.

Fig. 15-7
Normal acceleration measured during frequency response tests.

Copyright, 1947, by the Institute of the Aeronautical Sciences and reprinted by permission of the copyright owner

JOURNAL OF THE
AERONAUTICAL SCIENCES

VOLUME 14 SEPTEMBER, 1947 NUMBER 9

Progress in Dynamic Stability and Control Research

WILLIAM F. MILLIKEN, JR.*
Cornell Aeronautical Laboratory

Fig. 15-8
Lead article in *Journal of the Aeronautical Sciences*, which documents our pioneering frequency response research and the historical background of aircraft dynamic stability and control.

11 and July 5, 1945. Before the first flight Glen noted "tests on a B-25 equipped with autopilot, which is set up so that calculation and obtaining the results for longitudinal stability are greatly simplified and made more concrete over the old methods—we hope."

By June 14, he was more confident: "Believe we are going to have some success in this experiment." The following day Glen, Col. Horner (Flight Test chief at Wright Field) and I reviewed the results to date. After completing the flights on July 5, Glen noted, "We are on the verge of something really great—a positive, quantitative measure of airplane stability. Once perfected, we can design planes to fly as we want them to—not design them by a guess and by-god basis as so many of them are built today."

What we actually had accomplished was the first in-flight frequency response, obtaining a measure of the aircraft's dynamic maneuvering behavior. This scarcely met Glen's desire for a tool that would enable the rational design of aircraft, but it put our Flight Research Department into the business of flight dynamics. In the next half-century, Flight would play a major role in developing handling specifications for military aircraft, using Variable Stability Aircraft (VSA) that utilized automatic control techniques. This certainly contributed to the more rational design of stability and control, partially fulfilling our early hopes and predictions.

Glen Edwards and I almost became involved in another project together. During the war, pilots who flew the "hump" into Burma frequently reported a mountain that, based upon altimeter readings, appeared higher than Mt. Everest. I thought it would be fun to fly over that region in a B-17 on oxygen, with suitable aerial mapping equipment. A mountain higher than Everest would have been a sensational discovery. So during my visits to Wright Field, I spent time with the aerial mapping and navigation folks. Through them I had access to all the existing maps of the Himalayas and found that large areas, especially near China, never had been mapped. Some simply were marked "unexplored." Edwards was fascinated with the idea, and whenever we met he would bring it up and we would discuss the question of sponsorship. For various reasons, however, we never seriously pursued it. With the arrival of satellites the Himalayan area was surveyed, and one very high mountain, Minyi Konka, was located in western China. It has since been climbed, and is considerably lower than Everest.

Heroic Test Pilots

Glen Edwards's diary is a reminder of the remarkable collection of test pilots in the early postwar Flight Test Division. Dick Horner,

Bob Cardenas, Fred Ascani, Ken Chilstron, Bob Hoover, Chuck Yeager, Guy Townsend, Pete Warden and Pat Kelly come to mind. They lived an intense life, comparable to combat flying. Accidents were common, and some fatalities also occurred. When not engaged in testing they were making frequent cross-country flights between Wright Field and Muroc, or to aircraft companies in southern California and Seattle. Glen once mentioned to me how exhausted he was after a period at Muroc and the long flight home.

My impression was that test pilots loved to fly almost anything that had wings. Some had an engineering education, others had specialized training sponsored by the Air Force (especially at Princeton University under Courtland Perkins). All of them exhibited a practical interest in engineering in general and aerodynamics in particular. Thus they represented an early generation of engineering-test pilots.

Col. Albert Boyd, head of the Flight Test Division since 1945, was a tough but highly respected disciplinarian. He saw to administration during the week and personally flew the various prototypes on weekends. His strong convictions, and his participation in the flight tests, including such far-out aircraft as the X-1, contributed greatly to the high morale of the division.

Test pilots worked hard, and they also played hard. They loved to party. After a group of them flew into Buffalo, only to be snowed in for several days, we put them up at the downtown Statler. When not dancing or at the bar, the pilots were wrestling or playing leapfrog down the hall by their rooms. The hotel management finally moved them to a floor of their own. Amidst all of this, I was surprised to find they also were studying aerodynamics together and swapping related flight experiences. What a crew!

On one occasion, when I was in Los Angeles for a meeting of the NACA Stability and Control Subcommittee, I bumped into a couple of pilots who were ferrying an A-26 back to Dayton, and they offered me a lift. A

Fig. 15-9
The B-25 used for the lateral frequency test program. Contributors included (from L-R): Paul Kase, Bill Wilcox, unidentified, Bill Milliken, Lee Maefs, Casey Jaworski, Bill Frey, Cleve Mott, Len Gifford and the Wright Field delivery pilot.

few hours out the heater quit while we were flying above icing conditions at around 14,000 feet. There was no warm gear in the airplane, but I had half a dozen dirty shirts and some underwear from my stay in L.A. By the time we got weathered in at St. Louis, I had layered all of them on.

Glen Edwards had always expressed an interest in flying one of Northrop's big wings. During the three years following our frequency-response tests he had flown about everything in the Air Force bomber inventory, as well as the N9M, Northrop's small-scale version of the big wing. He became one of the most experienced pilots in the group, with a reputation for special expertise in stability and control. With this background and Bob Cardenas's recommendation to Col. Boyd, Glen was assigned to the YB-49 program on May 21, 1948, having made his first flight in this aircraft with Cardenas the day before. Earlier, in a hair-raising experience, Cardenas had stalled the big wing at some 30,000 feet, finally regaining control at low altitude after a series of gyrations. He had recommended to Boyd that the aircraft should be placarded against further stalling.

But on May 27 two flights were made, and on one of them Edwards performed a stall. On June 3 he ran a series of stalls in various configurations. He admitted the aircraft was "quite uncontrollable at times" and he had little control during stall recovery. "Damnedest airplane I ever tried to do anything with" was his conclusion. On the same day, Boyd flew with Edwards and they agreed it was a "possible airplane for ideal conditions only."

On June 5, with a crew of five, Edwards was flying as co-pilot and Danny Forbes as pilot when the airplane was stalled at 15,000 feet. In the course of the recovery effort the aircraft came apart, probably in a high-g maneuver. All of the crew were lost. Glen was 30 years old. Subsequently, Muroc Air Force Base was renamed after him.

From my XP-79 experience I was not totally surprised at this outcome, but was greatly saddened. During our brief acquaintance Glen and I had developed a genuine rapport, based upon mutual interests from airplane stability to ballroom dancing.

Progress in aircraft design depends on innovation, so in the big picture one hardly can fault Northrop's efforts in flying wing development. But it does seem inexcusable that no provisions were made to give the crew a fighting chance to bail out of the big flying wing, which was known to have such marginal stall characteristics.

Other Projects

The projects in which Ira Ross was deeply involved, and that contributed greatly to establishing the department's reputation, were the continuation of the SB2C dive tests of the Van Nuys period and a flight flutter project involving the Vought F4U-5 inverted gullwing fighter. The former occurred in 1944–45, the latter in 1946.

The SB2C was a short-coupled dive bomber for Navy carrier-based operations. In high-speed dive pullouts it proved longitudinally unstable, subjecting the aircraft and pilot to excessive g's. It was necessary to fully explore this behavior to establish safe operational limits and procedures and, of course, to have the aircraft accepted by the Navy. After Van Nuys, John Seal did most of the flying.

The aircraft was instrumented with an oscillograph whose elements had been dynamically balanced to handle the high g's. The procedure was to increase the dive speed and the pullout g's on successive flights, hopefully working up to limits that a service pilot could live with, and also avoiding aircraft structural damage. The instrumentation was subjected to the buffeting of the aircraft, and separating "noise" from valid data was marginal at best. When the instability occurred the elevator control forces could reverse, and Seal would have to apply a large "push" force to the control, occasionally to more than 100 pounds. Seal's subjective judgment, and Ross's analysis of the data, resulted in improvements in the aircraft and completion of the program.

There were some exciting moments. On one of the few flights made at the C-W Columbus facility, when returning from Van Nuys, half the elevator surface was lost by structural failure. The aircraft became marginally controllable, to the point where Seal could justifiably have bailed out. Realizing that loss of the aircraft also meant loss of the instrumentation and months of work, Seal took the plane to altitude and practiced simulated landings with various combinations of flaps, power and trim. He finally found a combination that enabled him to make what he called "not a good landing but a barely survivable one."

One of the members of the original staff at Van Nuys was Hans Weichel, later an early member of the Flight Research Department. Now a retired senior vice president of Bell Helicopter Division in Fort Worth, Hans revealed some interesting history of the SB2C Helldiver test program, among them that seven pilots were killed trying to qualify it for zero-lift dives. The basic problem was the relatively thick wing airfoil. When airflow over the wing reached critical Mach number (MN = 1.0), shock waves were created—a phenomenon little understood at the time. In a dive one wing could reach critical MN and induce a yawing oscillation. The original vertical fin was marginally strong enough to withstand these oscillations, and the rudder was ineffective. The aircraft almost was lost, but by instrumenting it so the pilot could reference zero yaw, and by installing a rudder with a blunt trailing edge, the investigation could continue. The

longitudinal stability problems finally were worked out in Buffalo. Three demonstrations, one at Van Nuys and two at Curtiss plants, finally met the Navy's dive requirements.

In addition to John Seal, Vance Breeze flew the aircraft at Van Nuys. Breeze encountered the critical Mach number first and could see the shock waves shimmering off the wing, a scary and unknown phenomenon as far as he was concerned. On landing he reported, "I am not a religious man but I have had a disturbing experience and will not continue the program." Reportedly, Vance never was very happy with instrumentation, which he viewed as "a mechanical stool pigeon."

THE F4U-5 CORSAIR flutter program proved to be equally hairy. Early in 1946 the Marine Corps decided to acquire some Navy F4U-5s. "External stores" were added, and it was suspected that they would reduce the wing flutter speed. Sam Loring, Chance Vought's expert on wing flutter calculations, had predicted the original airplane was good to some 400 knots, and the airplane had been dived to that speed with no problem. He now repeated his calculations with the external stores, and concluded that flutter would be encountered at considerably less than 400 knots, which put the whole transaction on hold.

Fig. 15-10
Curtiss-Wright Helldiver, SB2C-3. In order to fit on the carrier elevator the aircraft is very "short coupled," i.e., has a short tail length.

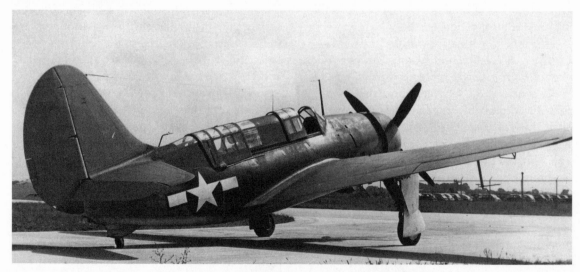

This looked like a real opportunity, so Ross approached the Marine Corps with the idea of a flight flutter test program. The Vought company took a dim view, standing behind Loring's estimate. Nevertheless we were given a contract to go ahead, and an F4U-5 was flown to Buffalo where a large "shaker" was installed in the fuselage. This unbalanced mass could be swept through a range of frequencies to excite the structural modes, and the wing response was measured by a number of accelerometer pickups installed in the structure. The idea was to start at a conservative speed, progressing to higher speeds while shaking the aircraft and noting the response. A reduction in the damping of the oscillatory response would indicate an approach to flutter speed.

John Seal took the airplane to altitude, throttled back to idle, dove to the initial speed and ran through the shaker sweep while recording, after which he made a normal landing. An examination of the records showed they were useless. The hash resulting from the windmilling propeller and engine masked the accelerometer recordings, so that no clear indication of the wing damping could be obtained. Tests at higher speeds yielded the same results.

In this challenging situation Seal suggested shutting down the engine and feathering the propeller before making the dive/flutter test, after which the propeller would be unfeathered and the engine restarted. To consistently make dead-stick landings on the relatively short main runway was not viewed as an option, and accomplishing the sequence Seal suggested in the available altitude also was marginal. To ensure there was enough battery power available to unfeather the propeller and restart the engine, Ross proposed hanging a wind-driven generator from the bottom of the fuselage. When developed this unit was less than a foot in diameter, with a smooth air entrance to a ducted fan connected directly to the generator. Before the initiation of the flutter program its effectiveness was tested in flight.

Giving us the go-ahead, and recognizing the hazards involved, the Navy offered to pay John Seal a bonus of $1,000 per flight. Everybody was happy, except Vought. Ross started the program at a dive speed of around 250 knots, increasing it on each successive dive in increments of 10 knots—up to 300 knots, after which smaller increments were used. Nothing showed up. All the accelerometers in the wing indicated well-damped responses.

Fig. 15-11
F4U-5 Vought Corsair with external stores proposed for marine use.

Fig. 15-12
F4U-5 with external stores. Note the wind-driven generator attached to the belly of the fuselage, which kept the aircraft battery charged up in a dead-stick dive.

Tension mounted as the speed approached 400 knots, the calculated flutter speed of the *original* aircraft without external stores, but still there was no problem. By that time we had a lot of respect for the aeroelastic characteristics of the airplane, and decided to go five knots above the original flutter speed for good measure. The Marine Corps was delighted to have an airplane without extra dive limitations, and we had established a reputation for doing a tough job. The program also said something about the reliability of flight flutter calculations. John Seal had increased his salary for the year by some $30,000 and moved his living quarters to the swanky downtown Saturn Club. The successful completion of the difficult SB2C and F4U-5 programs was the start of a reputation that led him to win the Chanute Award in 1952.

Cornell Aeronautical Laboratory

On January 1, 1946, the Curtiss-Wright Research Laboratory became the Cornell Aeronautical Laboratory. C-W had decided to abandon the airplane business, erasing from the ranks of aircraft manufacturers the two most famous names in aviation. Financial types took over, and C-W became a holding company for patents. I remember walking through the

design offices and drafting rooms, barren of any postwar designs on the boards.

Dr. Furnas believed we could become an independent, self-supporting, not-for-profit research laboratory. Since the tax situation was favorable, C-W agreed to give the lab to Cornell University. The gift was accepted under the proviso that the university contribute nothing to the transaction except its name. Furnas acquired the necessary working capital from East Coast aircraft firms. Again, the tax situation was favorable and a total of $650,000 was raised. The laboratory was in the process of installing a large, high-speed pressurized wind tunnel that could be used for testing proprietary aircraft designs, and it was thought that other capability at the laboratory would be useful to the East Coast industry as well.

When the decision was made to go non-profit under Cornell's name, Dr. Furnas called a meeting of all department and assistant department heads and stated emphatically that survival depended on our ability to generate contractual work. This was mainly a matter of dreaming up ideas and finding sponsors to pursue them. Competitive bid requests would be relatively few.

Having conceived and promoted the B-25 project, it made sense for me to pursue sponsors. Better suited to administration, Ira ran the department. For the next two years, I was the principal salesman conceiving the projects, writing the proposals and finding the sponsors. The contracts I brought in formed the core of our flight dynamics work.

The formation of the laboratory as an independent not-for-profit entity had a major effect on my piloting ambitions. After Boeing, the idea of test flying had a lot of appeal. I missed the excitement of that wartime period and wondered if I ever again would experience an adrenaline high. Although I might have made the grade as an engineering pilot, I lacked the tough attitude toward aircraft that characterized most of the top test pilots I had known.

ONE OF OUR FIRST JOBS in flight dynamics came as somewhat of a surprise. In the fall of 1946 the Stark Draper Instrumentation Laboratory at MIT was involved in a project sponsored by the Flight Control Laboratory at Wright Field for the development of an automatic flight control system. The goal was to accurately position the aircraft orientation for weapons launching, thus reducing the burden on the human pilot. This system went beyond the demands placed on conventional autopilots of that era, and utilized servo-control analysis techniques that had been under development in World War II. Specifically, the project consisted of devising an automatic tracking control for an A-26 twin-engine bomber, including a flight demonstration.

One element required for the overall systems analysis was dynamic response data for the A-26. Although we had not completed our frequency response tests on the B-25 or published all of our results, our work must have come to the attention

Fig. 15-13
Dr. Theodore Paul ("Ted") Wright, who was director of research at Cornell University and to whom Dr. C. C. Furnas, President of Cornell Aeuronautical Laboratory, reported. Ted Wright held numerous important positions in industry, government and education, including chief engineer of the Curtiss Airplane and Motor plant in Garden City and the Air Production Board during the war. He was a real asset and supporter of CAL.

of the MIT project (probably through our contacts with the Flight Test Branch at Wright Field), and we were approached to make A-26 response measurements. Some time prior to November the test airplane was flown from Hanscom Field in Bedford, Massachusetts, to Buffalo, probably by Tip Collins, project pilot for the Instrumentation Laboratory.

Upon arrival in Buffalo, Walt Breuhaus, who formerly had worked for Vought-Sikorsky in much the same position I had held before the war, was assigned the analysis of the B-25 frequency response data. Because he also had been involved in aircraft stability and control at Vought-Sikorsky, he was the logical engineer to take along when we received a call to visit MIT to discuss our part of the A-26 program.

Arriving at MIT we were greeted by the overall project engineer, Bob Seamans, and taken to lunch with a number of other project participants. We didn't realize we were expected to tell them about our approach to the response measurements at a large meeting afterwards. Although I certainly could talk in generalities about our B-25 work, I felt that Breuhaus was far more qualified to make the presentation. More than half a century later, Walt recalls how difficult it was to "gin up" the presentation on such short notice. My impression was that he did a fine job. We were cleared to go ahead.

We used step inputs and converted the results to frequency response data. MIT provided a liaison to assist and monitor our work. Cliff Muzzey was an outstanding engineer with a very broad engineering background. He arrived in the summer of 1947 and followed the tests to completion. To our good fortune he fell in love with Betty Yaeger, who worked in Flight Research. They were married in 1948, and Cliff joined our department as a permanent member the following year.

Still in the throes of developing the instrumentation and analysis group, the A-26 project failed to move at a pace that satisfied Bob Seamans, who paid us at least one visit to hasten things along. We finally completed the job, and at the completion of the overall automatic flight control system we were invited to attend a dinner in Boston. Later Seamans was to play a major part in NASA at the time of the moon shot, and the MIT Instrumentation Laboratory was responsible for the navigation system.

In late 1946 lateral response tests were made on the B-25J, using a Sperry autopilot. This work was sponsored by the Aircraft Laboratory Aerodynamics Branch, and was reported in AF Technical Report 5735 by Whitcomb and Campbell. Dynamics work initiated in the Flight Division now had been transferred to the Aircraft Laboratory, whose principals were Court Perkins, Mel Shorr and Charles Westbrook.

John Seal was the pilot on this program, and I went along as co-pilot on some of the flights. Sometime that fall, while checking out a problem, we got caught in one of Buffalo's sudden snow squalls. Touching down, Seal locked up the brakes, which sent us skating down the runway. To add to the fun the aircraft had picked up a large yaw angle. Seal's whole attitude in flying performance aircraft was "I'm the boss," and he talked to the plane as if he were taming a lion, pouring full throttle on one engine to combat the yaw. When the end of the runway approached he blasted the other engine, and we took off for the first of a number of go-rounds. I witnessed a masterful display of piloting as John, all-out on the controls, wrestled with the airplane. Charged with adrenaline, cursing and swearing, he gave the impression of having the aircraft by the throat. Finally, he got things right and we slid to a stop a few feet from the end of the runway. I remember thinking what an asset we had in a pilot like Seal.

The large high-subsonic wind tunnel (later to be converted to a transsonic tunnel) was about to come on line in late 1946. It could be pressurized or evacuated to give some independent control of RN and MN, and would be a major asset for use by aircraft firms.

Dr. Furnas had the task of appointing a head of the new Wind Tunnel Department,

Fig. 15-14
One of many large meetings in CAL Flight Research in which we presented progress reports of our flight dynamics research. L-R in front row: Elmer Sperry, Jr., Preston Bassett, Harry Goett (NACA), Bill Milliken and Bob Seaman (Draper Lab, MIT). Seaman later became chief engineer of NASA at the time of the first moon landing. In the second row, behind Goett and Milliken, is Jerome Hunsacker, one of the great pioneers of dynamic research and education at MIT.

which he discussed individually with each of the existing department heads and their assistants. I made a strong pitch that Ira Ross was the logical candidate because of his managerial abilities and his electronic instrumentation background. Presumably others made the same suggestion because Ross was given the position and, as predicted, made a great success of the tunnel. It became the largest source of profit for the laboratory, and at one time was the busiest tunnel in the United States, with two- and three-shift operation.

If Ross went to the tunnel, I was in line for his job, which had not escaped my notice. This posed a problem for Furnas, however, who was far from certain that I would make a good department head for Flight. While recognizing that I was bringing in Air Force contracts and Flight Research was currently running a good fiscal show, Furnas lacked the knowledge of flight dynamics that would give him assurance about the future of our activities. Further, several

**Fig. 15-15
My Taylorcraft.**

problems existed between us. Based on my sales, technical and piloting qualifications, I had been hitting him up for a raise. I was not popular with the laboratory contracts people and was impatient with many of the administrative details. In truth, I harbored the notion that I could run a flight organization quite nicely without affiliation with the Laboratory at all, a short-lived dream in which I overlooked such details as to how to pay the hangar rent. In my enthusiasm for the dynamics work I had reacted as I did in high school, when I became frustrated with the sports programs and proposed to substitute motorcycle racing.

FURNAS WAS STRAIGHTFORWARD. He said to me, "We have fundamental disagreements. I propose to bring in a third party, namely, the

dean of Engineering at the University, to help us resolve them. I'll make a date for you to talk with him. Tell him how you'd run Flight, what your plans and ambitions are and we'll get his reaction." So I went to Ithaca.

Although winter was approaching I decided to fly down in my Taylorcraft. According to the map Ithaca had a small landing strip near the lake shore. Arriving over its northern end, I started down. The day had been overcast and the weather deteriorated as the ceiling came down. Then, with little warning, visibility dropped to nearly zero as I flew into a whiteout. At low altitude I clung to the shoreline, when suddenly out of the mist a water tower passed by a few feet off my right wingtip. Somewhat shaken, I flew well on the lake side until the landing strip showed up.

I still was cold and upset when I got to my appointment. But the dean was friendly and we spent most of the hour discussing high-speed flight problems and the opportunities for research. My enthusiasm must have been contagious because he failed to press for my views on administration. Furnas went along with his recommendation. I got the job and a modest raise and took over Ira's old office when he left for the wind tunnel in April of 1947.

My first and best decision was to appoint Walt Breuhaus as my assistant. A graduate of Carnegie Tech, Walt had worked for my old boss, Paul Baker, at Vought on the F4U-5 as well as the XF5U-1 and XF7U-1, both unconventional shipboard fighters. Thus, he had an extensive background in the solution of flight control problems, as well as more recent experience with the B-25J and A-26 projects at the Laboratory. Our common approach to aircraft stability and control was based on a knowledge of Bryan's Equations of Motion, aircraft statics derived from wind tunnel tests, and a burgeoning interest in servo-control techniques.

THERE WERE TWO FUNDAMENTAL responsibilities in managing a department at CAL: bringing in the work, and then accomplishing it. I had considerable confidence in playing the major role in the former, and recognized the necessity for ensuring the latter. Breuhaus would be a major contributor in building the department's reputation for meeting its contractual obligations.

Quite apart from his obvious technical qualifications, Walt was a man of impeccable honesty, openness, objectivity, thoroughness and dependability. I was well aware of the demoralizing effects of internal politics and had complete confidence that we were in agreement on its avoidance. I also felt that we respected each other's position in the organization. On the

operating level, Walt and I had a horizontal, project-type arrangement, combined with specialist grouping for technique development. Our goal was an organization that worked without excessive formality and was based upon the people we had. I knew Walt got on well with the rest of the laboratory and would initiate reasonable administrative procedures. We stressed quality and competence in the technical staff and expected that this would be built up as time and opportunity permitted.

Without saying it, we assumed that Flight would go on indefinitely, and we had an obligation to ensure job security for the people we hired. Many of them had pulled up roots to join us, had bought homes and were raising families. Finally, I knew that no matter what my tenure, Walt Breuhaus was the logical successor. With those basics behind us, we went to work.

Progress in Flight Dynamics, 1947–1956

For the next nine years, through 1956, most of my professional efforts were devoted to Flight Research. During that period I conceived and sold, and our department performed, a series of advanced flight dynamics projects evolving from the B-25J parameter measurement work.

The first of these, sponsored by the Air Force Aircraft Laboratory, involved a Lockheed turbojet P-80A (later called F-80) in a parameter study to higher speeds and Mach numbers. The first phase was longitudinal, measuring the response to sinusoidal and step inputs. The purpose was to "prove the practical equivalence of the transient and steady-state oscillation method to high subsonic speeds, and to show the feasibility of testing under these conditions." Tests were performed to Mach 0.7 at altitudes of 10,000 and 20,000 feet, with good agreement obtained between transient and steady-state responses, as well as with

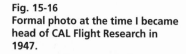
Fig. 15-16
Formal photo at the time I became head of CAL Flight Research in 1947.

Fig. 15-17
Lockheed P-80A Shooting Star used on the AF project to take the frequency response technique to higher speeds and Mach numbers, a highly successful program.

calculations based on wind tunnel data. The longitudinal derivatives were reduced from the responses. The longitudinal phase was followed by a lateral program, in which responses to rudder and aileron oscillations were measured. Lateral derivatives also were deduced from the responses and compared to calculated derivatives based on wind tunnel data. Measured and calculated trends were similar. The overall conclusion was that the response measurement techniques pioneered on the B-25J were applicable to much higher performance aircraft.

A critical aside to this project, that I had to resolve, was a large (nearly 100 percent or $100,000) cost overrun, in part chargeable to amplifier development. Although our control of expenditures improved over the years, I was learning that overruns in a research organization were not uncommon, especially with technically enthusiastic project engineers. In this case I went to Wright Field and made a clean breast of it to Mel Shorr, AF technical liaison, and his administrator, Harvey Anderson (with whom I had developed a good rapport). I felt absolutely certain the accomplishment of this difficult project was a major technical

step forward, and to this they agreed. Thus, the recovery funds finally were found, and a phone call back to Buffalo led to a celebration in the dining area with a cake entitled "Remember the F-80."

Early in 1947 the AF Aircraft Laboratory funded a study project of stalled-flight dynamics, leading to the automatic control of a stalled aircraft. Because of my fascination with the stall, I was determined to initiate a project for Flight Research. Without a formal proposal, I jotted down the elements of a sales pitch on the back of the menu during breakfast at the Dayton Biltmore. More nervous than usual, I caught up with Harvey Anderson at lunch time. It has been my experience that promoting an idea and convincing someone to sponsor it is a balance between logic and emotion. If you are over-prepared and the emotional zest is absent, or if it's all smoke and mirrors, failure is assured. In this case I had years of contemplating the stall to draw on, I was not bogged down with a fixed agenda and I was emotionally cranked up. I don't know what I said, but it was enough to convince Anderson. We were asked to submit a formal proposal, from which we obtained a contract.

Fig. 15-18
Instrumentation installation in the ammunition compartment of the P-80A. Tremendous improvements in the size and capability of instrumentation occurred as progress went from vacuum tubes and oscillographs to modern computers and digital recording.

Fig. 15-19
Corradi Harmonic Analyzer, an early tool for treating dynamic response records.

Fig. 15-20
PT-26 primary trainer used in the stalled flight project. An angle of attack vane was installed on the vertical boom for making measurement outside the propeller slip stream and, we hoped, independent of the wing downwash.

Because there was no point in compounding the difficulties of stall research by using a high-performance military aircraft (at least at this stage), the program was built around a Fairchild PT-26, a two-place low-wing primary trainer powered by a Ranger

Fig. 15-21
About to leave on a PT-26 stalled flight test.

C-5 aircooled engine. The airplane arrived in Buffalo in July of 1947. I decided to pilot the first phase of this program myself. According to my log book, Seal checked me out on the aircraft on July 28.

The first task was to establish the lift curve into the stall regime. To do this, increasing the stabilizer adjustment was necessary so the airplane could be trimmed to these high angles of attack. With much practice I found that to control the normal roll-off (primarily by use of rudder), the aircraft could be flown in reasonably steady glides at angles of attack in the stall region. During June and July I made 23 flights totaling about 40 hours, and developed the basic lift curve from 4- to 28-degree angles of attack. Since stall occurred at 15.5 degrees, we were 12.5 degrees into the stall regime. The flights were performed with a range of CG locations from 21.8 percent to 29.8 percent of the wing chord. The maximum lift coefficient was 1.28, falling off quite rapidly to 0.94 at the highest angle of attack. A long boom was attached to the wing with an angle of attack vane, and recording equipment was installed in the aircraft. Dave Whitcomb went along during shakedown and flight calibrations. In addition to sneaking up on the trimmed stalled conditions in smooth air, we tried elevator step functions of different magnitudes, but without success.   331

Fig. 15-22
Ted Wright (left) took great interest in our stall project. On stalled glides most of these tufts would be pointing forward. Phil Reynolds, right.

In late 1948 the program was turned over to Project Engineer Graham Campbell, with Giff Bull as test pilot. It continued into 1951. In addition to investigating and analyzing lateral motions under stalled conditions, they devised an automatic control system for stabilizing the aircraft in stalled flight. The system was extremely flexible, permitting rudder and/or aileron movement proportional to bank angle, rolling velocity, rolling acceleration and rudder motion (for counteracting adverse aileron yaw). Stalled glides were performed in which the normal roll-off of stalled flight was completely eliminated.

I flew one flight with this automatic stall control. The aircraft had a calibrated angle of attack vane on a long boom with an indicator in the cockpit, and the wing was tufted. Upon approaching the stall, the tufts oscillated wildly and considerable buffeting occurred as the wing wake impinged upon the horizontal tail. When well into the stalled region, the buffeting

subsided as the wake moved above the tail, and the tufts were either standing straight up or pointing *forward*. The fuselage remained close to horizontal but the flight path was steeply downward as the lift decreased. Flying an aircraft in which the wing flow had largely separated, the buffeting had ceased and we were descending at the speed of an elevator produced an uncanny feeling.

Campbell and Bull produced six comprehensive reports showing the boundaries for stable stalled operation and the character of the modes. They performed analog calculations using average "effective" derivatives from wind tunnel data. These compared favorably with the experimental results when a constant time lag was introduced for those derivatives that were dependent upon wing lift.

At the time, we conjectured about the practical use of stalled flight. One possibility was that of a steep descent for carrier aircraft operation. Calculations indicated that a stalled

F4U-5 Corsair descending from altitude could be flared for landing by the application of full power. None of our conservative Navy friends was interested in pursuing this idea.

Although the PT-26 project has largely been forgotten, it is interesting to note that the subject of stalled flight is back on the military research agenda. Using jet thrust control, aircraft have been flown to nearly 80-degree angle of attack, and the potential of stalled flight for fighter operations is being seriously considered.

IN ADDITION TO FINDING SPONSORS, I had to sell top management on the importance of our technical program to ensure receiving our fair share of working capital for sales effort and internal research. Because communication with Dr. Furnas about flight dynamics was severely limited, we needed a "bridge" to receive his full and continuing support. This came about as follows.

CAL's need for operating capital had been resolved by East Coast aircraft manufacturers. In exchange, an advisory committee of representatives from these firms was established, giving them a mechanism for influencing the research direction at the laboratory, or at least being informed of its programs. The committee met monthly in Furnas' office, and technical department heads were called upon for presentations on their research.

Finally, it became my turn. Waiting in the outer office, I had a good dose of stage fright. I'd been giving all kinds of presentations to technical groups for the Air Force and Navy, but facing a group of such high-level executives as Larry Bell, Leroy Grumman, George Page, Burdette Wright, etc., got to me. If I couldn't explain to Furnas what we were doing, I imagined it would be still tougher to make our work intelligible to this committee. Dr. Norton Moore's efforts to turn our "aeronautical" laboratory from a name into an actuality had failed, and it still was organized along academic lines with departments like physics, chemistry and materials. I had no way of knowing that much of what had been presented in previous meetings was of peripheral interest to the aircraft types on the committee. So when I started to talk about flight dynamics a surge

Fig. 15-23
Madame Jacqueline Auriol, France's most distinguished aviatrix. In 1962 she set a speed record of over 1,100 mph and was a Harman Trophy winner. During her visit to CAL and Flight Research we discussed our stalled flight work and its implications. Giff Bull, in the background, did most of the flying on the project after my initial flights.

of interest followed. I obviously was in their ballpark, and they reacted with a variety of questions and suggestions. What had seemed a fearful event turned into an exciting exchange of experiences. Best of all, Furnas became convinced that we were doing worthwhile research, and we were assured of his future support.

AS A RESULT OF our in-flight response measurements, I was invited to become a member of the NACA Subcommittee on Stability and Control, chaired by Captain Walter S. Diehl (USN, ret.). Diehl had been head of the Aerodynamics Group in the Navy's Bureau of Aeronautics (BuAer) and was the author of *Engineering Aerodynamics*, first published in 1928. I had acquired a copy when I was designing the M-1. Diehl's book presented a large amount of empirical aircraft design data based on wind tunnel tests of a variety of naval aircraft, much of it measured at low Reynolds numbers and uncorrected for scale effects. As Shats Ober pointed out, Diehl's design plots and derived constants were based upon the aircraft data he had available but had not been generalized by use of theory. Therefore his book had to be used with some discretion.

Diehl seemed to be a very practical engineer, with strong leanings toward the empirical. Despite his avoidance of sea duty he had some of the brusqueness of a sea captain, somewhat tempered by a devastating sense of humor. As the newest member of the committee, with a New England accent and a research interest in the esoteric subject of

aircraft dynamics, I frequently was his target. There is no question he held the record for practical jokes, one of which is worth retelling.

Among BuAer's tasks was the making of quick estimates of proposed aircraft performance. A young BuAer engineer came up with an elaborate graph for this purpose that proved so useful Diehl kept a carefully inked copy in his desk. Whenever the admirals called, the chart facilitated quick answers to their questions. On a weekend when the originator of the chart was not present, an exact duplicate was made on which some India ink was spilled, and it replaced the original in Diehl's desk. Following a briefing, the reigning admiral placed an urgent call to Diehl, who rushed down to the admiral's office. Shortly thereafter Diehl called for the author of the chart to bring it down. One can imagine his reaction when he unrolled it on the admiral's desk.

The Equations of Motion

The title of this book stems from George Hartley Bryan's linearized equations of motion which were published in *Stability in Aviation : An Introduction to Dynamical Stability as Applied to the Motions of Aeroplanes* (London, Macmillan, 1911). They enable the calculation of the dynamic stability and control of aircraft. Adopted widely in British research circles, they were introduced and taught in this country solely by Professor Otto Koppen in his airplane stability and control course at MIT. No other university in the USA presented such a comprehensive treatment of aircraft dynamics.

These equations were a core element in the flight dynamics program which I initiated at the CAL Flight Research Department in 1944, continuing to this day. The program started by measuring the stability derivatives in flight using an automatic pilot, followed by augmentation of the derivatives and on to variable stability aircraft and development of an autopilot for stalled flight. We then made a major conceptual step in the use of variable stability for rationalizing flying qualities specifications by quantifying pilot opinion data in specific tasks. Our major contribution, however, was the use of "closed-loop system dynamics," implemented by high-frequency hydraulic servos. This eliminated the constraints of "fixed surface dynamics" and led to unlimited design possibilities which we predicted in 1950.

Our flight dynamics activity at CAL Flight Research was largely responsible for creating an interest in flight dynamics in US research and industry circles.

In this book, I am interested in understanding, in an historical sense, *why* things happened, as well as *what* happened. I never sat down and dreamed up a research program in flight dynamics; rather, a sequence of events and circumstances in my life led to it. Without Lindbergh's flight, without my homebuilt airplane's impossible flight characteristics, without Koppen's MIT course and my Avion XP-79 experience, I doubt if CAL would have ever been involved in flight dynamics. So much for the "dream," if you will. The activity was a tremendous, group effort as recounted in this chapter.

Fig. 15-24
B-26 variable-stability project aircraft undergoing inertia measurements.

The subcommittee, composed of representatives from NACA, the Navy, the Air Force, aircraft firms and academia, many of whom I knew, like Mel Shorr, Court Perkins, Bob Seamans, Gerry Kayten and Stu Krieger, proved to be a valuable venue for new acquaintances, and a nationwide forum for what was going on in airplane stability and control. We met in Washington, at Langley Field, Moffett Field, etc. The initial reaction to our B-25J frequency-response work was one of skepticism, but by the time I left the committee in the late 1950s aircraft dynamics had risen to the top of the agenda, and NACA had initiated substantial research. For many years I had liaisoned industry research between both the East and West Coast NACA laboratories and Vought, Sikorsky, Boeing and Avion, but it was not until I served on the S & C Subcommittee that I realized how strong the "not invented here" syndrome was at these government

laboratories. I am a great admirer of NACA and its research staff, but the truth is that no one organization can cover all the bases or have a corner on all the ideas and talent.

Another Air Force project, closely related to the B-25J and P-80A parameter studies, was to make response measurements on Northrup's N9MB, a small flying wing with twin conventional engines that had served as a proof-of-concept aircraft prior to the XB-35 and YB-49 large bombardment aircraft. Glen Edwards was killed in the YB-49 on June 5, 1948. I believe I approached the Air Force for the N9MB job prior to this accident, but in any event there was a lot of interest in Northrop's aircraft and it was an easy sell. Our project started in 1948 and continued into 1950, when the first reports were delivered.

John Seal was the pilot, and the tests were performed at Muroc. Step functions were manually applied to the elevator, ailerons,

Fig. 15-25
Seminar on Vehicle Dynamics. Dr. Furnas about to introduce me. B-26 in background.

and rudder, and response-time histories were obtained. In addition, a frequency-response plot of the longitudinal motion was deduced from the step data, and both the longitudinal and lateral derivatives were calculated from the test results. To check the validity of our method of arriving at them, the derivatives were used to recreate the original time histories. The results showed that a set of derivatives in the linearized equations accurately characterized the motions of the aircraft.

The lateral response tests were performed at 100-mph indicated air speed at 2,000-foot altitude. The responses in sideslip, roll, yaw and side acceleration were highly oscillatory, with periods of 6–8 seconds and very low damping—requiring several cycles to reach half amplitude. The lateral derivatives showed large variation with lift coefficient. One can see why the flying wing was an early candidate for stability augmentation.

Muroc was inundated by a heavy snowstorm during the program. To keep the base operating, plows had cleared the runways, piling the snow in banks along the sides. On one takeoff, the N9MB drifted to the edge of the runway and slewed into the snow bank, so that the engine's air intake on that side was blocked.

The engine cut out, and with it the boost for the flight controls. Somehow Seal managed to continue the takeoff. He later reported that during the engine-out period, he had the now unboosted control stick all over the cockpit. We later calculated that he must have experienced forces of over 100 lbs. With the adrenaline flowing, he had no memory of this, but he was lame for a couple of weeks. Bill Wilcox, our head mechanic, witnessed the event and had a dramatic story to tell of how the aircraft staggered into the air with one wing down and snow flying. Once again, Seal had demonstrated his ability to get out of a tight spot.

Pioneering Variable Stability

In our earliest research, we had used automatic control technology as a tool for obtaining response data during parameter identification measurements. In the PT-26 stall project we had a very convincing demonstration of the effectiveness of automatic control for inducing "artificial stability" in an unstable flight regime. By late 1948 we had become a pioneer in *variable-stability aircraft* (VSA), a still more generalized application of automatic control. Our overall research objective, however, remained one of understanding and improving the dynamic flight characteristics of aircraft.

Inasmuch as variable stability became the stock-in-trade of Flight Research, it is desirable to place this application of automatic control technology in the general evolution of aircraft flight control. Let's start with conventional aircraft prior to the application of any form of power to the control system.

In these airplanes the aerodynamic control surfaces (elevator, aileron and rudder) were mechanically connected to the cockpit controls. The forces and motions the pilot experienced in flying the aircraft were the result of the aerodynamic hinge moments of the surfaces, and the leverage ratio and friction of the system. Response behavior could be predicted from the aerodynamic stability and control derivatives in the applicable equations of motion. "Fixed surface aerodynamic airplane" is an appropriate title for this control system.

As airplane size and performance increased, various aerodynamic and static (non-powered) devices were used to modify aircraft response, and the power and motion of the pilot's control. These included aerodynamic balances on the surfaces, control tabs of various types, down springs, springy tabs, inertia devices, etc.—all with no direct application of power. Some of these were effective in the position-control mode, others in the free-control mode (when the pilot relaxes his control force input).

THE FIRST APPLICATION of external power was control "boost." In large and/or high-speed aircraft, the control forces exceeded the pilot's capability and some form of "power steering" was needed, usually implemented hydraulically or pneumatically. While this changed the control forces, it normally did not change the aircraft motion derivatives.

The idea of completely eliminating the human pilot and flying the aircraft with an "automatic pilot" occurred early in the history of the airplane. The aircraft could be made aerodynamically stable with "guidance" provided by an automatic device, or the autopilot could both stabilize and navigate the aircraft based upon sensor signals. In our PT-26 we had used a specialized autopilot for stabilizing the aircraft in stalled flight. When

Wiley Post decided to fly around the world alone (after his record-setting flight with Harold Gatty in 1931), a reasonably good autopilot was installed in the *Winnie Mae* that kept the aircraft on course and provided some stabilization. Although not entirely satisfactory, Post was able to get some sleep and lower his earlier record.

A more limited use of power, that leaves the human pilot in the control loop, *stability and control augmentation* appears to have first been used in Germany, with other applications in England and in the US shortly thereafter. In this scheme the aerodynamic control surfaces are moved independently of the human pilot in order to make "effective" changes in particular derivatives, thus modifying the response characteristics of the aircraft while the human pilot still can superimpose his control actions. The principle of augmentation is confusing, because in practice the motions of the aerodynamic control surfaces are the combined result of the automatic control input for augmentation and the manual pilot input for the overall guidance task. A simple example in which the two functions are separated is instructive: Suppose one has an automobile with two steering wheels, one connected normally to the front wheels and the other to a steering linkage at the rear wheels. Assume that the driver controlling the front wheels is unaware of another driver steering the rear wheels. If the rear steer is inactive, i.e., no augmentation, the vehicle responds to front steer in the normal fashion. On the other hand, the driver of the rear steer can increase or decrease (augment) the response of the car by adding or subtracting to the front steer effect. Unaware of what's going on at the rear, the front-steer driver only knows that the response of the vehicle has changed. The vehicle can be made to oversteer or understeer its normal front-steer response, i.e., the directional stability can effectively be changed, which is equivalent to changing a derivative in the equations of motion. The aeronautical parallel to this automotive example is the case where separate control surfaces (like a split aileron) have been provided for augmentation and for pilot control.

The earliest applications of augmentation were aimed at changing particular derivatives, such as the pitch damping (M_q), where an elevator was moved as a function of pitch velocity, q, or the yaw damping (N_r), where a rudder was moved as a function of yaw velocity, r. Toward the end of World War II, yaw dampers were provided to improve the directional characteristics of Northrop's large flying wing, the jet-powered YB-49, and the Boeing XB-47. Other examples occurred in Europe.

The concept of *variable stability and control* follows from that of augmentation. In essence, a variable-stability aircraft is one with in-flight *adjustable* augmentation, so that simulation of various configurations of "fixed surface aerodynamic airplanes" can be accomplished. It is an in-flight simulator and has the great virtue (over the fixed-base ground simulator) that the visual scene and the maneuvering accelerations are real.

The most extensive review of the history of variable-stability aircraft is by Walt Breuhaus ("The Variable Stability Airplane from an Historical Perspective," published February 26, 1990, in the *American Aviation Historical Society Journal*.) Walt was associated with the development of nine variable-stability aircraft worldwide prior to 1989. Since CAL produced more VSAs than any other single organization, his experience is unique and authoritative. I am heavily indebted to him for piecing together the variable-stability activity that occurred in Flight Research when I was there.

The first two variable-stability aircraft[1] were developed independently by two different research groups—NACA Ames Laboratory and the Cornell Aeronautical Laboratory—at about the same time. The NACA F6F-3 Hellcat flew shortly before the CAL F4U-5 Corsair, although the two projects overlapped. The objectives and implementation were quite different for the two aircraft.

Conceived by William (Bill) Kauffman, the purpose of the F6F-3 project was to modify the rolling moment due to sideslip (the derivative L_β, called the dihedral effect). This was accomplished by using an electric servomotor

that sensed the output of a sideslip vane to extend or retract the conventional aileron pushrods from their pilot-controlled position. Thus the aileron positions were the sum of the pilot and servo inputs. The additional aileron aerodynamic hinge moments due to the servo operation were canceled by tabs on the ailerons, so that the forces at the pilot's stick were approximately those due to the deflection of the ailerons only. Later systems included artificial changes to the yawing moment due to sideslip (N_β, the static directional stability derivative), yawing moment due to yawing (N_r, the yaw damping derivative) and yawing moment due to rolling velocity (N_p, the coupling derivative between rolling and yawing). As in the case of the ailerons, the rudder hinge moments due to the servo control were canceled out by a tab on the rudder. The aircraft was successfully used for a number of research projects.

THE FOLLOWING EVENTS led to the F4U-5 variable-stability aircraft at CAL. As previously noted, my main responsibility was to keep the place in business. To this end I was forever imagining new project areas as well as new sponsors, and found it useful to generalize and extrapolate from work already in-house. In the flight dynamics area, the military offered by far the greatest opportunity. Since we were well established with the Air Force, the next logical customer was the Navy, to whom I sent a letter entitled "Dynamic Stability and Control Research" that reviewed our research and included a four-page long-range research plan listing a variety of project ideas. Ultimately the letter reached the desk of Gerry Kayten of the Bureau of Aeronautics. The soft sell was left for the end: "If the Navy should decide to take an active part in this program, the contractor would be glad to supply further information and specific proposals." Discussions with Kayten ultimately focused on a carrier landing problem for fighters with poor damping of the Dutch roll mode.

Of the several trips I made to Washington negotiating a contract, the final one with Dave Whitcomb was the most memorable. The Navy's Aeronautic Department was located in an old World War I temporary building on Constitution Avenue. During our afternoon

---

[1] *Kauffman, Breuhaus and I received the Laura Tabor Barbour Air Safety Award for 1967 for the invention of the variable-stability aircraft (VSA).*

meeting in Kayten's office, an agreement was reached on the content of the proposal, and we said we'd be back with the cost estimate the next day. After dinner Dave and I returned to the Statler Hotel. In the lobby was a large group of high school students on a field trip to the Capitol, all smartly dressed for the occasion. Pushing through the crowd we took the elevator to the 14th floor and proceeded to produce the detailed cost estimate, a considerable task in the era before calculators. We just had finished it when the fire alarm went off. Running down the stairwell, we reached the 13th floor landing before Dave remembered our cost estimate. "Fire or no fire, I'm going back," he exclaimed, "I'm damned if I'll do that estimate again!" We ran back for it and then took the stairs to the lobby. All the high school students were there too, half dressed and in the most amusing collections of sleep and underwear. One of the students had pulled the alarm as a prank.

THE F4U-5 PROJECT WAS EXCITING. For the first time, we had an airplane with the pilot in the standard control loop. By using augmentation to modify a number of the lateral derivatives, we could simulate an airplane of different flight characteristics. Furthermore, the augmentation was adjustable, so the aircraft could truly be categorized as "variable stability."

In order to investigate the Dutch roll damping for various roll/yaw ratios, and the spiral divergence, it ultimately was necessary to augment not only the directional derivatives, N_β (the directional stability) and N_r (the yaw damping) but also the roll derivatives: L_p (the damping in roll), L_β (the effective dihedral) and L_r (the rolling moment due to yawing velocity). The Goodyear F2G-2 version of the F4U-5 carried a small separate rudder below the standard fin, a rudder that could be used for yaw augmentation. Roll augmentation was accomplished by converting the wing flap between the inboard end of the aileron and the wing-fold hinge line into a plain flap that could move up as well as down. This left the normal flight controls untouched, so pilot control forces (except for some slight aerodynamic crosstalk between the auxiliary control surfaces and the standard control surfaces) were completely standard. A modified Sperry A-12

autopilot was used to move the augmentation surfaces.

The program, which was started in 1948, was successively headed by Dave Whitcomb and Dunstan Graham. Twenty pilots (Navy, AF, NACA and CAL) flew the aircraft to a total of 160 hours. The program, which continued into 1950, accomplished its objectives and stands as our earliest demonstration of the successful use of variable stability.

Specifying Stability and Control

Our next major program in variable stability involved two aircraft, and started with a memorandum I produced on August 23, 1950, with the rather grandiose title, "Research Leading to the More Fundamental Application of Artificial Stability and Control in Improving the Military Usefulness of Aircraft." As I read this memo today I am impressed by the number of advanced ideas presented, but am unimpressed by the long sentences and circuitous English. As the principal salesman for the department, I had been wrestling with the next logical step after the F4U-5 project. Walking home one evening I distinctly remember the moment when I got the idea of using variable-stability aircraft for *rationalizing flying qualities specifications*. Although not new, the idea of specifying flying qualities had been approached only on a sporadic basis as opportunities presented themselves with specific aircraft and particular problems. Using variable stability, a systematic approach could be taken and over time a comprehensive military specification could be developed. My memo discusses such items as:

- The difficulty of discerning stability and control deficiencies because skillful pilots can hide them or have them interpreted as "pilot error."
- The potential of augmentation for alleviating undesirable design compromises.
- The development of minimum acceptable performance boundaries for the airframe alone.
- The development of optimum flying qualities boundaries, rather than the current "satisfactory boundaries" that merely

represented the current state-of-the-art for fixed-surface aerodynamic aircraft.

• The necessity for advancing the use of augmentation by designers, i.e., to provide incentives to produce aircraft of improved mission capabilities.

• The recognition that "fixed-surface aerodynamic aircraft" may ultimately be seen as a special case of a more generalized class of flying devices making extensive use of (requiring) augmentation. (I found this concept one of the most exciting prospects in aeronautics, although it has taken over 50 years to fully realize it.)

• The possibilities of non-linear control augmentation, which can be accomplished with electronic systems.

The memo then states the necessity of making the control forces and gearing (as presented to the pilot), as well as the aircraft responses, fully adjustable. The use of pilot opinion and comments, rating scales, etc., were included, the most significant being a study of bandwidth and phase shift when simulation of aerodynamic derivatives was sought. One of the features of CAL's variable stability work was the high bandwidth achieved. Finalized late in the year, the actual proposal focused on the longitudinal dynamics, that is, on the short-period maneuvering mode, and to a lesser extent on the phugoid.

According to Walt Breuhaus, a number of flight experiences and studies suggested that longitudinal dynamics worth investigating included pilot-induced oscillation (PIO) in high-speed dives, the behavior of aircraft in turbulence, and predicted behavior at transonic speeds. All maneuvering involved the "short period" which, since it *was* short and the damping normally high, would not usually command the attention of a pilot. Breuhaus recently conjectured that the widespread recognition of the importance of these longitudinal modes on flying qualities might be due to these systematic studies using variable stability.

We obtained a contract involving research on a B-26 (representative bomber) and an F-94 Starfire (representative fighter) from the Office of Air Research. The variable-stability systems

were such that the short period and phugoid frequencies and damping could be varied, along with stick forces and position gradients. A standardized pilot-rating scale was used, and pilot comments were thoroughly analyzed. Both airplanes were well instrumented. By fixing certain variables and varying others it was possible to obtain boundaries of various levels of "satisfactory-ness," that is, from very poor to nearly optimum performance in specified maneuvers. The techniques developed in this program were further developed over the years, in the pursuit of rational handling standards.

The standard "Handling Qualities Rating Scale" (Fig 15-26) was jointly developed by George Cooper of NASA Ames and Bob Harper of Flight Research, Calspan. Using this rating scale, test pilots could consistently characterize their opinion of aircraft behavior in a particular task.

To develop a numerical "Handling Standard Specification," significant design parameters were changed on a VSA (variable stability aircraft) and evaluated in flight using this rating scale.

The problems presented by short-period dynamics required a different graphical analysis. In Figure 15-27, "Pilot Objections to Various Short-Period Dynamics," the frequency and damping of the short period were evaluated over wide ranges, and the boundaries of these changes in flight dynamics were characterized as being "satisfactory," "warrants improvement," "requires improvement," or "mandatory improvement." Further, the behavior on different parts of the boundaries is indicated. Optimum behavior is at point A at a frequency of 0.47 and damping ratio 0.7.

R.A.S. – I.A.S. Conference

In September 1951, while the B-26 and F-94 projects still were ongoing, I was invited to present a paper at the Third International Joint Conference of the RAS–IAS (Royal Aeronautical Society–Institute of the Aeronautical Sciences) in Brighton, England. The paper, entitled "Dynamic Stability and Control Research," summarized overall developments and recent progress in the United States. Extensive research was

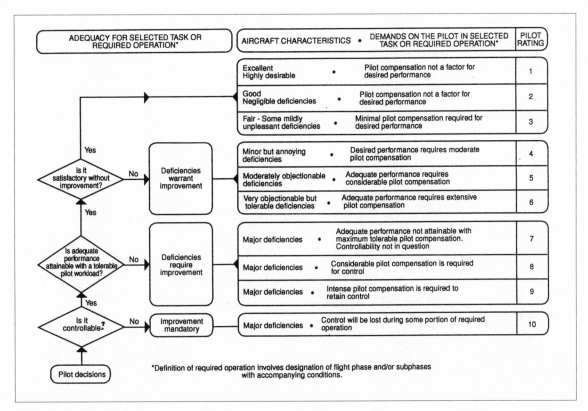

Fig. 15-26
Handling Qualities Rating Scale (Cooper-Harper).

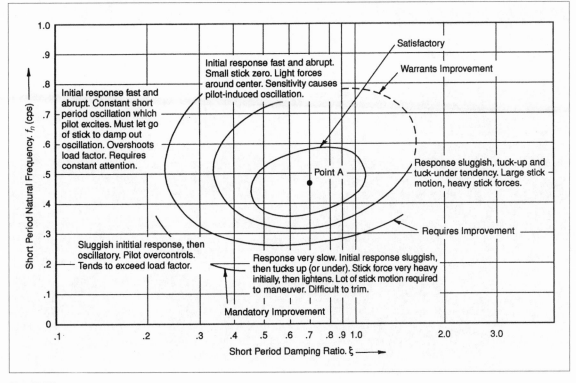

Fig. 15-27
Pilot Objections to Various Short-Period Dynamics.

involved, including a trip to West Coast aircraft firms, NASA Ames, *et al.*, and review of more than 100 reports and papers. When I sat down to organize this massive amount of information and find a coherent theme, I experienced a monumental case of writer's block. After struggling for a month, I finally divided the mass into ten sections and began to make some headway. Fortunately, I was backed by Flight Research and could solicit

the help of a number of engineers to plot test results in the several areas. Once I got down to the specifics good progress was made, but I only really enjoyed writing the sections on dynamics of the stall, artificial stability and the rational specification determination.

When I presented the paper orally at the conference I emphasized the section on artificial stability as the trend of the future. I had convinced myself that at least for high-

Fig. 15-28
T-33A variable-stability aircraft.

Fig. 15-29
CAL Flight Hangar, Full-Scale Division.

performance applications, "fixed surface aerodynamic aircraft" would be replaced by heavily augmented machines of more generalized flight characteristics. Now we have aircraft with fly-by-wire controls and synthetic feel, with response characteristics produced by electro-hydraulic servos. An exerpt from the published paper is on page 346 ("Artificial Stability Possibilities").

The B-26 and F-94 program continued through 1952. The F-94 was used to simulate the longitudinal control of Convair's XB-58 Hustler. Both the B-26 and F-94 aircraft were ultimately donated to CAL. The B-26 found a new use in the training of test pilots at the Navy and Air Force schools, and the F-94 was replaced by a T-33 three-axis variable-stability airplane that had a long career in developing handling qualities specifications—40 years, 5,200 flights, and 8,000 flight hours at CAL/ Calspan, the longest life of any research aircraft.

Full-Scale Division

By 1952 my interest began to shift from aircraft to automotive dynamics, and while I remained the head of Flight Research it is only fair to say that Breuhaus was acting head during the several years I was building up to a Vehicle Dynamics Department. In 1956 the Laboratory management agreed to the creation of the Full-Scale Division, comprising two departments: Flight Research and Vehicle Dynamics. Breuhaus became head of Flight Research and I wore two hats, heading Full-Scale and Vehicle Dynamics.

The real justification for a new division was to transfer aeronautical know-how and technology to the automobile. We reasoned that the government had spent millions of dollars on stability and control research for aircraft, so why not make further use of it? I had enjoyed a terrific period of innovation in Flight, and was about to embark upon an equally creative period for a different vehicle.

Flight Research History

Before initiating the Full-Scale Division, I produced a summary of the history and progress of the Flight Research Department. To my mind, this department had all the elements of a great organization: well-defined objectives, the technical disciplines for accomplishing them and a horizontal project organization with vertical specialty groups. Management genuinely believed that innovative ideas and advanced research required considerable latitude, informality and friendly working conditions. A technician's input could be as valuable as that of the most highly educated analyst.

The facilities were functional, communication was natural and open, growth was modest, personnel turnover was nil. In the years I ran Flight we never let a single person go for lack of work. Even today, people who worked there look back and say it was the best job they ever had. We opened up the hangar on weekends for members of the department to bring in their cars, boats, motorcycles, or whatever, and use the shop facilities to work on them. As a Flight Research operation many of our projects were hazardous, and we shared the responsibility for maximizing pilot and crew safety.

From 32 people in 1946, our staff had increased slowly to 79 by 1955. The total contract value, including internal research, was about $250,000 in 1946 and had approached $900,000 by 1955. At that point our backlog was more than two million dollars. We had built up our capital assets progressively in terms of hangar equipment, instrumentation and data handling, including a Corradi Harmonic Analyzer. Most important, we had developed major customers for flight dynamics in both the Air Force and the Navy, contacts that kept the department going for the next four decades. Flight's reputation in variable stability was second to none, based on its specialized servo-control technology.

During the 1946–1955 period more than 50 different types of military aircraft were flown. We logged some 1,600 flights by John Seal, Nello Infanti and Giff Bull, with some help from loaned Air Force pilots and John Olmsted, Leif Larson and Bob Watts. Only one major flight accident was due to structural failure (Leif Larson was killed), and there was one fatality in a collision on the ramp. Considering the nature of our projects, that was a good safety record. In variable stability and dynamic instrumentation we had many technological firsts, and our output in terms

Fig. 15-30
Typical flight instrumentation.

of technical reports, papers, and permanent internal reports was well above average.

We also had our fair share of the excitement—good and bad—that adds to Flight's heritage. One warm day Casey Jaworski dove fully clothed into the reservoir near the hangar, to the delight of the data-processing girls eating their lunch outside. That same summer, Casey got wet for another reason. The sprinkler system in the hangar let go and flooded the area. With 550 volts in the hangar electrical service it was a close call for everyone working on the airplanes. On another day, unaware that a B-26 was being jacked up to exercise the retractable gear, chief inspector Lee Maefs started to inspect its nose gear and was caught inside as the wheel came up. Casey heard the shriek and reversed the gear.

Upon receiving funding from the Navy to pursue the concept of air-supported buildings, we set one up on our ramp and left it there all winter to test its utility in arctic conditions.

The building survived handsomely. Dr. Furnas invited the admirals to come up for a dedication, to which department heads were invited. We crowded into the building along with the celebrities. Furnas had just started his speech when the lights went out. A few seconds later, the building collapsed, providing the most intimate encounter I ever had with an admiral.

Somehow in Flight we combined all the delights of immaturity with the responsibility to do our basic job well and professionally.

Contributions to Aircraft Stability and Control Technology

Flight Research was started in 1946. I was assistant manager at the time and two years later became manager, a position I held for ten years. This was followed by seven years as director of the Full-Scale Division.

They were tremendously creative years, with many outstanding accomplishments.

We did the first in-flight frequency response analysis, pioneered parameter measurements, were an inventor of the variable-stability airplane and were the first to use it to determine specifications for rational handling qualities and test pilot training, developed an automatic stabilization system for a stalled aircraft, and a whole variety of other projects related to these advances.

The team behind these accomplishments was equally remarkable. Our analytical capability, expertise in dynamic recording and systems design, aircraft maintenance and installation, piloting, flight operations and data analysis were second to none. They were the nucleus of the department's reputation and longevity. Because we had a solid background in the dynamic equations of motion, and a willingness to tackle the tough and risky jobs, we were able to build a solid customer base that would go on for years.

During my tenure, I was the department's principal salesman and idea man, while Walt Breuhaus was the in-house manager, responsible for project accomplishment. We worked in an open, effective and friendly organization, and had complete confidence in each other.

When Walt became manager he conceived and promoted a generalization of variable stability in the Total In-Flight Simulator (TIFS). This used model-following (the TIFS vehicle follows a computer model of a particular aircraft) and created a variety of exciting projects related to the space shuttle, the military SST, the B-1, the B-2 and the Concorde. Test pilot training also was expanded with the development of specialized variable-stability aircraft and became a regular part of our work. The X-22, Bell's ducted-fan VTOL aircraft project, proved to be challenging but successful!

Fig. 15-31
Flight Research personnel circa 1948–49.

Flight, under Breuhaus, lost none of its integrity and survived the disruption created by Cornell University's board of trustees and president. By early 2000, Flight Research had moved into its 60th year.

In 2005, the present manager, Lewis Knotts, and associates bought the department and other transportation elements from their owner, General Dynamics. This buyout brings back local ownership, and ensures the operation of Flight into the future.

I can bask in the remembered sunshine and excitement of those early years. We believed we were creating an unbeatable venture, and so it proved.

Artificial Stability Possibilities

Exerpted from a report entitled "Dynamic Stability and Control Research" by William F. Milliken, Jr., Cornell Aeronautical Laboratories, presented at the Third International Joint Conference of the Royal Aeronautical Society – Institute of Aeronautical Sciences (RAS – IAS), Brighton, England, September 3–14, 1951.

Only the briefest outline has been given above of a few actual and proposed artificial stability schemes; nevertheless it is perhaps indicative of the enthusiasm for this subject which is rapidly being generated on our side of the Atlantic. A more complete statement of the potentialities of these devices has been given by the present author in an unpublished paper wherein an attempt was made to show the extent to which established ideas of stability may be displaced by developments stemming directly from artificial applications. The remarks below are, in part, quoted from this paper:

The primary design conception of airplane stability and control, and hence flying qualities, has been associated with fixed stabilizing fins, and manually movable surfaces for control. This is the commonly held conception of the airplane, and is the direct result of the fact that aircraft early attained their primary stability and control in this manner. The mind should be open to the possibility, however, that the conventional scheme for stabilizing and controlling aircraft may be neither the most basic nor general; that it may in fact be in the nature of a special case of broader and more far-reaching means.

For the conventional airplane whose stability and control is fixed by design geometry, a supplementary and interesting trend may be observed. This trend, detectable from the very beginning of flight, but heavily on the upswing during the last decade, is the use of "mechanical" adjuncts to modify and enhance the stability and control inherent in the basic configuration. A surprisingly large number of these so-called gadgets have appeared, and many, including such items as irreversible control systems, power boost, down springs, slats, slots, trim tabs, boost tabs, de-boost tabs, etc., conventional autopilots, rate dampers, Ch_x balances, Ch_δ balances, etc., are still in regular use. We are wont to think of these devices as independent entities, unrelated equipment applied to the airplane as afterthoughts to fortify characteristics not easily handled in the initial compromises necessary in the design. In the aggregate, however, they are all part of a general family of artificial stability and control devices, and it is the opinion of the writer that this class of equipment is more fundamental than is frequently conceded.

There has always been a natural reluctance on the part of flying personnel and others to the incorporation of the above devices in aircraft, and this has undoubtedly increased as dependence has been placed upon electronic actuation as opposed to mechanical, hydraulic or aerodynamic. The question of reliability, however, should be considered as transient, and not allowed to overshadow the potentialities of this equipment in furthering the beneficial evolution of the stability and control picture. No practical airplane today can get along without items of this type, and it is safe to say that the high-performance aircraft of the future will be far less immune. The complex and oftentimes conflicting requirements imposed upon the aircraft

continued next page

by service usage now preclude the possibility of really satisfactory stability and control through aerodynamic means alone.

It is somewhat surprising that, while we do make partial allowance in our handling qualities specifications for the effects of these devices, we hardly do so in a manner aimed at encouraging their full and potential use.

Consider for a moment the class of conventional "fixed surface-aerodynamic" aircraft, which may be represented by a set of linear differential equations with constant coefficients. It is readily seen that any aircraft falling within this class is defined by a set of values of the real non-dimensional derivatives. Moreover, all conventional aircraft defined by the above equations are severely restricted in their stability and control performance by practical limitations which arise in the geometry of the fixed surfaces and the basic dimensions of the airplane such as tail length. These limitations also exert an indirect but powerful effect upon the drag and hence performance. How great an imposition is placed upon the stability and control may be illustrated by representative figures on the range of damping-in-yaw values obtainable with a reasonable-sized fixed vertical tail. Presented below are values of the percent critical damping for a conventional fighter-type aircraft; for comparison, information is also given on the damping which may readily be obtained through application of moderate, fail safe, artificial control:

Condition	% Critical Damping[1]	Pilot's Opinion
Test aircraft at 40,000 ft	7.32	Unsatisfactory
Marginal boundary from test	8.0	Marginal
Test aircraft at 10,000 ft	12.6	Relatively satisfactory
Test aircraft[2] with maximum available artificial damping	29.5	Relatively excellent
With increased, but reasonable, additional area for use with artificial control. (Total vertical tail area constant.)	30–60	Expected optimum range

[1] *The percent critical damping equals the ratio of damping coefficient to critical damping coefficient, and frequently runs to 70% or better for mechanical dynamic systems having optimum response characteristics.*
[2] *The amount of artificial damping available on this aircraft was severely limited by the small auxiliary rudder surface, although it was ample for the particular research program.*

The comparison indicates that increases in the critical damping ratio of 20%–50% are readily achievable and furthermore worthwhile. This in itself is significant, but the figures also emphasize the excessively low damping available in the conventional airplane about the yaw axis. To fail to recognize the deficiency of the present day "fixed surface-aerodynamic" airplane in this respect is to bar the mind to possible progress. Because pilots have become used to a minimum of damping seems hardly sufficient reason for accepting it as satisfactory, or for continuing to promulgate less than a more nearly optimum amount. The low damping about the yaw axis seems never to have been sufficiently recognized and appropriate comparisons have only recently been made with what is considered adequate in other well-known dynamic systems. The airplane as a precise military weapon may hardly be considered satisfactory when the available damping permits several cycles of oscillation.

As a further example of the design restrictions that are imposed by fixed surfaces, a chart has been prepared, and presented in Figure 15-32, which shows the maximum numerical

continued next page

variation of the derivatives practical to attain "aerodynamically." (While these data are presented for the lateral case, a comparable situation exists for the longitudinal derivatives.) This figure also gives the approximate increase in the range of each derivative when a reasonable amount of supplementary artificial control is used. It appears that with the "fixed surface-aerodynamic" airplane, one is both confined to constant derivatives and severely limited in the practical range of values of these derivatives. Furthermore, in a conventional airplane it is impossible to modify the derivatives independently; the obvious illustration in the lateral case being the dependence of

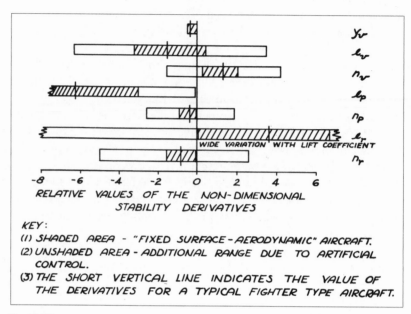

Fig. 15-32
Estimated increased range of lateral derivatives with artificial control.

both the static directional stability and the damping in yaw upon the vertical tail area. These interdependencies and others hardly simplify rational design.

A wider range of choice of the individual derivatives gives the designer a degree of latitude in the final motion of the airplane which has never before been possible. Studies made by NACA and McDonnell Aircraft indicate that feasible artificial derivative changes may completely modify the character of the motion. Thus Figure 15-33 has been calculated to illustrate the effect of large artificial changes in n_p, a lateral derivative normally not under the control of the designer. For the standard aircraft, a lightly damped "Dutch roll" exists, with an approximately zero real root for the "spiral" mode, plus the heavy "damping-in-roll." Within the range of artificial stability application (as shown in the figure) it is possible to produce either an unstable Dutch roll or a real unstable roll root. While neither of these extremes is desirable, a moderate positive increment in n_p producing a more heavily damped Dutch roll and smaller damping-in-roll root might be advantageous. The great power of artificial stability, as illustrated here, should be readily comprehensible to those who fly, since moderate use of the controls normally overshadows the inherent stability tendencies.

The use of artificial control enables effective changes in the stability characteristics while in flight. Conceivably these may be accomplished between missions, or flight conditions, and, should it be desirable, might be effected automatically by appropriate sensing equipment.

Without artificial control, it is essentially impossible to add new and additional derivatives over and above those normally contained in the stability and control equations; there is no choice in what may be "sensed" with a fixed aerodynamic configuration. In the application of servomechanisms, on the other hand, utilization may be made of the output of many

348

continued next page

different types of sensing devices and even combinations and functions of them. Possibilities here seem limitless; by appropriate angle sensing it is practical to achieve space orientation unpossessed by the basic aerodynamic airplane; by sensing angular acceleration it is possible to effect equivalent mass and inertia changes, different along different axes; it is also conceivable to utilize angular acceleration sensing and phase shifting in the provision of damping. In a resume of this length it is impossible to go into these ramifications in detail, but the fact remains that once artificial means are used to supply entirely new derivatives in the equations governing stability and control, a departure of no mean significance has been made from the conception of the aircraft as we know it.

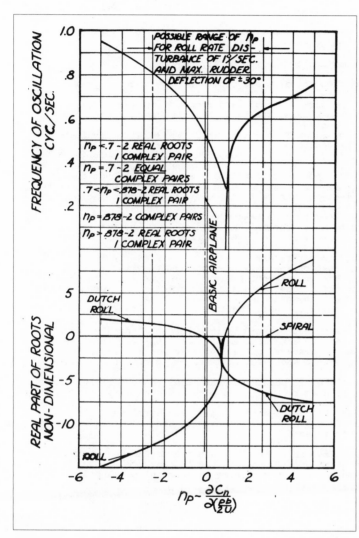

Fig. 15-33
Effect of large changes of the derivative, n_p, on lateral motion of an airplane.

The equations of motion normally used in describing the airplane are linearized, and experience has shown that for reasonable motions the "fixed surface-aerodynamic" airplane is described rather accurately by these equations. There is, however, no reason to suppose that the most useful airplane is one whose motions can be closely represented by linearized equations. To the contrary, there is reason to believe that certain non-linearities in the design may enhance the characteristics. Analogy may be had to the automobile in which some of the more desirable characteristics of its stability and control are obtained through non-linear design elements such as non-linear springs, shock absorbers, and steering. An even more pertinent analogy is the situation which exists in electronic equipment design where great advantage is taken of the non-linear characteristics of the components. With the application of electronics to airplanes via the medium of artificial stability it is entirely practical to integrate non-linearities into the aircraft. An experimental and analog investigation of artificial non-linear "spring" and "damping" elements on the yaw axis is now being completed by CAL for the Office of Air Research.

June 28, 1944

Mr. Paul E. Hovgard   Buffalo, NY

Piloting Check William Milliken

On June 26 I gave William Milliken a check flight in a two place P-40 Airplane from our Modification Center.

This consisted of 1 hour and 10 minutes of flying time.

A. Mr. Milliken flew the airplane from the rear seat in straight flight and figure eight turns.

B. Mr. Milliken performed a stall and recovery satisfactorily after I had demonstrated stalls in the flap neutral and flap extended positions.

C. I performed three landings during which Mr. Milliken followed through on the controls.

D. During the flight Mr. Milliken coordinated his controls satisfactorily. He kept the bubble in the middle very well. Mr. Milliken was not able to maintain a steady attitude during steep turns. He was always gaining or losing altitude at the rate of 400 feet per minute. This would not be satisfactory for passing a CAA test.

E. Mr. Milliken attempted two take-offs. On his first take-off the airplane swung to the left and would have gone completely off the runway; so I had to take over the controls and complete the take-off. Mr. Milliken did not open the throttle nearly enough during his first take-off.

F. On his second take-off Mr. Milliken started down the runway and performed the entire take-off himself. He held the nose down much too long which caused the airplane to have its wheels on the ground at a high speed and to be skidding sideways when he should have been in the air. Neither of his take-offs were satisfactory.

G. No landings were made by Mr. Milliken because I considered that he was not ready to attempt them. As this was the first flight of the first two-place airplane, our time was limited. It was necessary for me to spend some time checking out the airplane.

In fairness to Mr. Milliken it should be noted that the visibility from the rear cockpit is not as good as that of a two place advanced training type airplane. There is excessive distortion in the cabin glass. Mr. Milliken realizes that he is not ready to "check out" on this type airplane. I think that he should have another 6 or 8 hours of practice in the two place P-40 before he will be able to fly it solo.

Although Mr. Milliken does not fly well enough "to be checked out" I believe that his being a test pilot will benefit the company eventually. Therefore, I believe he should be given more time in a two place airplane.

H. Lloyd Child

HLC:mdk-54
cc: Dr. Furnas
      Mr. Milliken

Fig. 15-34
Lloyd Child's memo to his boss at Curtiss-Wright, re my "piloting check" on a P-40.

Research Laboratory

September 9, 1944

TO:

SUBJECT: Automatic Pilot in Flight Test

          Attached is a discussion and proposal for the
investigation of the electronic automatic pilot for flight testing
purposes. The Research Laboratory is considering a program along the
lines discussed herein and would appreciate having your comments and
suggestions.

          The possibilities of the use of an automatic pilot
for flight test are generally conceded and have been considered by
many people. The purpose of the proposed flight program would be to
evaluate these possibilities fairly and without preconceived contentions.
While the program as outlined is ambitious, it would be possible to cut
any unprofitable phases or concentrate attention on any phases that appeared to be particularly promising.

          It seems inevitably true that, as time goes on,
both commercial and military aircraft will spend an increasing percentage
of their lifetime on automatic pilot, even to blind landings and takeoffs.
This being the case, it is only logical that airplane characteristics on
automatic pilot will become more significant and that flight testing will
have to be performed with the automatic pilot in operation.

          The understanding and the technique of flight test-
ing on automatic pilot is something that test pilots and personnel will
be called upon to know in the future. Like every other mechanical device which increases productivity, the position of those understanding
and using it will be enhanced.

          The many avenues of development, such as radio con-
trol, which tie in closely with the automatic pilot should widen the
scope of flight testing as an agency for the provision of design information.

                                        W. F. Milliken, Jr.
                                        Assistant Manager
                                        Flight Research

WFM:rf
Enc.

Fig. 15-35
Title page of memo, "Automatic Pilot in Flight Test." The idea was not enthusiastically received at CAL, but I found sponsorship through the US Air Force.

Fig. 15-36
F-86 Sabre with non-linear yaw damper. In the front row are (L-R): John Seal, Jack Beilman, Irv Statler. Behind (L-R): Lee Maefs, Vince Hinds, Shorty Miller.

Irving Statler

Our early response research covered in the RAS–IAS paper (see page 346) assumed that the derivatives in the equations of motion were constant. The question was raised that at higher subsonic, transsonic and supersonic velocities, the derivatives might be time dependent, i.e., subjected to unsteady aerodynamic flow effects.

In Flight Research was a young engineer, Irving Statler, a native of Buffalo, who had graduated from the University of Michigan with a degree in mathematics and aeronautics. His stint in the Compressibility Unit at Wright Field provided the analytical ability to tackle the problem of nonstationery flow effect on the derivatives under compressible subsonic flow conditions. In the 1949–50 period in Flight Research Irv produced three papers, the last of which, entitled "Dynamic Stability at High Speed from Unsteady Flow Theory" was published in the Journal of Aeronautical Sciences (Vol. 17, No. 4., April 1950). He further surveyed the availability of theoretical estimates of the derivatives for various wing planform shapes at supersonic speeds. One conclusion from his work was that in the longitudinal case, the derivative m_w had a significant effect on the phasing of the wing downwash on the pitching moment arising from the horizontal tail (predicted earlier).

Irv has numerous other distinctions; to my knowledge he was the only Flight Research engineer in those early years who had a Ph.D, which he acquired at Caltech during a leave of absence from CAL. He returned to Flight Research to become the project engineer on an F-86 project involving a nonlinear yaw damper, then transferred to CAL's aeromechanics department. Subsequently, he had an illustrious career as director of the Army Aeromechanics Laboratory co-located with NACA Ames Research Center. He remained in this position until he left for Paris to become head of AGARD (The Advisory Group for Aerospace Research and Development of NATO).

Automobile Racing 1947–1956

Chapter 16

Entrée Bugatti

"Peak Revs—A record run in America's one classic hill climb. Louis Unser in the 3-litre Maserati at Fourteen Mile Corner on the ascent that set the present record."

– *Autocar* magazine (British)
September 1946
(An inspiring illustration that led to our Type 35 Bugatti entry at Pikes Peak 1947, the first competition by an SCCA member)

On a business trip to New York in 1946, I stepped out of the Lexington Hotel after breakfast to sample the June weather and enjoy the sights. Parked at the curb was an MG sports car with its top down, a polished black paint job with British racing green upholstery, chromed radiator and wire wheels. For years I had read about MGs but had never seen one. I waited until the owner came back. Would he sell the car? Yes. And for how much? $1,500. I wired my mother, who always had ready cash. While awaiting her response, I learned that the car was a model TB, a fairly recent import. The deal was closed, and I drove up the Hudson, planning to stay overnight at Ed Waterhouse's home in Albany.

Driving the MG was a revelation. The secondhand Chevrolet that had been serving my transportation needs was little more exciting to maneuver than a grocery cart. Now, quite suddenly, I found myself in a machine that turned on all my senses and made driving a delightful experience. At first I tried to analyze why, and thought of all the old clichés: the driver being in the control loop, the challenge of a stick shift, the car as an extension of the driver, etc. But then I just relaxed and let the sun and the wind take over. My childhood euphoria of driving had returned, and I was to never lose it.

During my stay at the Waterhouses, Ed suggested I join a new sports car club in New England, and gave me George Boardman's phone number in Hartford, Connecticut. Back home, I called and made a date for a visit. On the appointed weekend I flew my Taylorcraft from Buffalo to Hartford. I was met at the airport by George, driving his Standard Swallow SS-1, and Russ Sceli, then the president of the Sports Car Club of America. It proved to be a

The AAA regulation for Pikes Peak called for a minimum wheelbase of 98.5 inches, so we increased the Bug's wheelbase by about five inches by moving the front axle forward.

Fig. 16-1
My MGTB acquired in New York City quite by chance, 1946.

memorable weekend. I was briefed on SCCA history, became the second member from the Buffalo area (John Oshei was the first) and received a full set of back issues of *Sports Car*. We also visited the Sceli home and attached garage. Russ was in the process of turning his hobby of tuning and restoring sports/race cars into a business. Every wrench and spanner known to me, US, British and metric, was neatly hung up on one wall.

Type 35A Bugatti

A few weeks later I received a postcard announcing a Sunday afternoon club get-together at Paul Ceresole's home in Concord, Massachusetts. I drove the MG up to Boston (450 miles) to meet SCCA founders Ted Robertson, George Weaver, Col. George Felton, and George Boardman, among others, and to view some interesting machinery. In particular, Russ had a Type 35A Bugatti (chassis No. 4906) that formerly belonged to McClure Halley, and originally to George Rand who, so the story went, bought it from the Malcolm Campbell Bugatti agency in London. The car

had been raced in several Automobile Racing Club of America (ARCA) races before the war. Following a crash, Sceli had done an excellent job of restoration.

Fascinated by the MG, I was completely bowled over by the Type 35. It was my first encounter with a Bugatti, although I had some familiarity with its racing history. My right brain was in high gear that day, and I asked Russ his terms for selling it. His immediate answer: $2,000 plus the MG TB. We shook hands and agreed that I would pick up the car at his home in Connecticut in the fall, as I currently was short of cash.

During the summer my wife Phil and I drove the MG to Maine to visit my folks. When we reached Old Orchard Beach, where I had flown my M-1, I thought it would be fun to take one last run down the sand to see how fast the car really could go. Unfortunately the tide was coming in. When we ran into a soft spot and got stuck, we needed help in a hurry. A local wrecker broke the main leaf in one of the springs, leaving the car drivable but lopsided. Generously, Russ agreed to accept the car in that condition.

In late October I finally got around to collecting the Bugatti. Aware of the unpredictable weather, I loaded up the MG with a flying suit, leather helmet, warm gloves, winter underwear and sweaters. The trip to Hartford proved uneventful. Arriving in midmorning, Russ and I worked out the details of the transaction, after which he gave me a tutorial on the maintenance and operation of the Bugatti. Among other things, I learned that Hudsonite, a proprietary mixture of light motor oil and kerosene, worked well in the wet clutch, that leakage from the clutch was normal, the appropriate fluids for the engine, transmission and rear end, the preferred fuel, spark plug ratings, etc., and, of course, the starting procedure.

We then took the Bug out for a spin on some back roads. Starting proved simple, attesting to Sceli's engine tuning. After pumping up some fuel pressure, setting the magneto to retard, giving it a shot of prime, cracking the hand throttle on the dash, and cranking a half turn, the straight-eight engine purred into a fast idle. Other than in exceptionally cold weather, I don't remember having any starting problems in all the years I owned her.

Getting used to the gearbox was more of a challenge. Since the clutch always dragged, a determined yank was necessary to engage first gear. Any concern I had was dissipated by the width of the gears, a little worn on one side but with plenty of width to go. Double-clutching for downshifting was unnecessary in most circumstances. The engine revved up so fast, all you had to do was to load up the throttle, hit the clutch and bang the shift lever through. With a little practice the revs for the lower gear would be right-on and the shift would be noiseless.

I left Russ in late afternoon, intending to drive straight through to Buffalo. Around 10:00 P.M., well into New York State on Route 20, snow showers began. Visibility and temperature started to drop. As the snow increased and the road became more slippery, traffic moved more slowly. I was the last car in a line of perhaps ten approaching a steep hill. Traction became so marginal that the lead car couldn't make the top, and the whole line came to a standstill. I sat there wondering what to do next when, with no provocation at all, the Bug slowly started to rotate about the rear wheels until the car was pointing downhill. Obviously I had acquired a very intelligent vehicle, so I accepted its

Fig. 16-2
My Type 35A Bugatti (Chassis No. 4906) bought from Russ Sceli, who had restored it. It now is viewed, according to Sandy Leith, registrar of the American Bugatti Club, as "quite possibly the most significant GP Bugatti in US amateur racing history" because of its prewar and postwar racing record. This is my arrival at CAL Hangar from Hartford, Connecticut (Sceli's home).

decision, coasted down the hill and put up for the night at a nearby motel.

The next morning, with the temperature below zero, the motel owner gave me a stack of newspapers that I stuffed inside the flying suit. Donning my leather helmet, hood, goggles and face mask, I completed the drive to Buffalo, pulling up on the apron in front of our hangar. John Oshei filmed my arrival.

The Bugatti would be kept in the hangar, where the aircraft mechanics could maintain it. Although management looked the other way, I was somewhat concerned because of regular visits from the Air Force and Navy. One day a unique solution occurred. One of our instrumentation engineers needed a wooden box with dimensions of 12 by 6 by 4 inches for an electronic installation, and sent a request to the shop in Lab 1. Soon a truck appeared with a box 12 feet long, 6 feet wide and 4 feet high, which promptly was shoved into one corner of the hangar to become the Bug's garage.

By AMERICAN STANDARDS everything about a Bugatti was novel and unconventional, and this created great interest and curiosity among our engineering staff and mechanics. The latter in particular were astounded by the clutch mechanism, the brake cable equalizer, the low-pressure engine lubrication system, the narrow (but deep) radiator, and the double breathers on the crankcase with no internal baffle between them. At first, big Bill Wilcox and his crew found the Type 35 difficult to work on, but ultimately became very proficient at it.

My own knowledge of Bugattis would be improved by extensive reading, a visit to Prescott, three trips to Molsheim, membership in the American Bugatti Club, and great conversation with French racing champion René Dreyfus at his restaurant, Le Chanteclair. I learned that a Bugatti gets to you in subtle

Fig. 16-3
My great friend René Dreyfus in a Type 35 Bugatti.

ways. On Saturdays I found it pleasing just to look at it, or to sit in the cockpit and view the narrow radiator and double curvature of the hood. Living with the car was a great experience. As my only means of personal transportation I drove it everywhere, summer and winter.

Early SCCA

On January 18, 1947, the SCCA had its annual meeting in New York City at the Henry Hudson Hotel. Russ Sceli presided at the business meeting, attended by perhaps 35 members. Recognizing that I had traveled the farthest to get there, he appointed me director of a new region called Western New York, comprising all of the state except New York City. That's how informal things were. Everyone applauded, and I went home as the R.E. (regional executive) of one, if not the first, of the club's regions.[1]

Back home I called our first meeting at Bill Reid's home in Williamsville, which was attended by John Oshei, Dave Whitcomb, Bill Close, and one or two others from Flight Research. The meeting began at 8:30 P.M., ended at 2:30 A.M. and included showing a number of movies including a sound version of the 1946 Indianapolis 500.

At the annual meeting, although not on the planned agenda, a strong undercurrent of interest in competition was evident. A number of former members of the Automobile Racing Club of America (ARCA) had joined the SCCA and brought great tales of prewar road racing.

The interest in competition was furthered when Al Garthwaite announced the Garthwaite Trophy for a speed trial on the Pennsylvania Turnpike over a specified and

---

[1]*As the club expanded, New York State was divided into several regions, but one still is centered in western New York.*

easily identifiable 15-mile stretch. During the "qualifying period" (January 1 to August 15, 1947), any club member could self-time runs in up to six trials for publication in *Sports Car*. The "finals" would be run off by the two fastest qualifiers in the Unlimited Displacement class and in the 1,500-cc-and-under class. Qualifying runs could be made in either direction.

I came away from the annual meeting with the strong conviction that I wanted to race, and the Garthwaite Trophy run looked like a good way to start. So early in June I made my qualifying attempt, and sent the time and a brief story to the editor of *Sports Car* (published in the July–August issue and reprinted at the end of this chapter). My run had averaged 90 mph.

Later, Al Garthwaite averaged 95 mph in his Type 43A, 2.3-liter supercharged Bugatti, but he finally was topped by Virgil Exner at 105 mph in his ex-Indianapolis 5.5-liter Studebaker. These were the three best runs, but only Garthwaite and Exner made the finals in the Unlimited Category.

Before the finals could be run off, however, the police became suspicious of all these "weird" sports/racing cars making

Fig. 16-4
Repairing the Bug during the Garthwaite Trophy weekend.

multiple runs over the same stretch of road at speeds greatly in excess of the speed limit. Al Garthwaite had to formally announce the "cessation of hostilities."

Fig. 16-5
Louis Unser in the record-setting 8CTF Maserati *monoposto* broadslides around the 14-Mile corner. This photograph in *Autocar* magazine inspired me to take my Type 35A Bugatti to "The Hill" in 1947.

Pikes Peak, 1947

Early in 1947, Phil suggested entering the Bug in the Pikes Peak Hill Climb. "It's a combination of a Continental road race, the Shelsley Walsh Hill Climb and the old Vanderbilt all wrapped into one," she said.

Phil made a good start on convincing me, but it was the photograph in *Autocar* of Louis Unser in the Maserati 8CTF *monoposto* broadsliding the 14-Mile corner that finally clinched it. This single photo, taken during Unser's 1946 record run, best portrays "The Hill" and the spirit that has kept the event alive

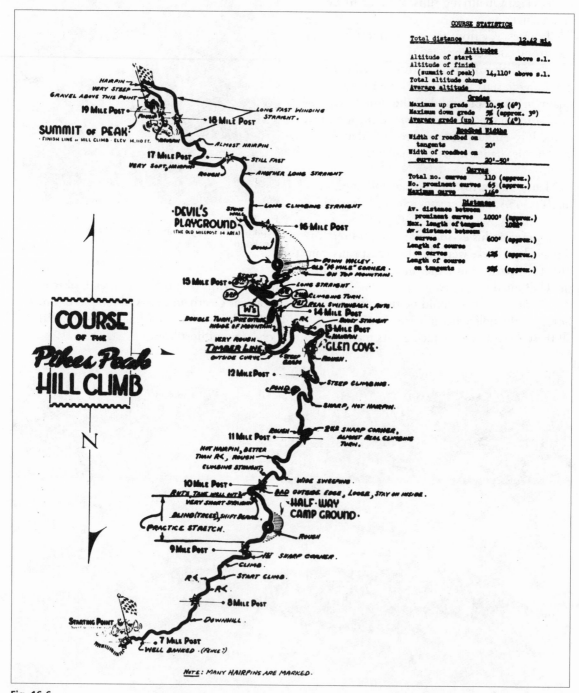

Fig. 16-6
A map of the course up Pike's Peak, along with some notes I used to try to learn it. The course proved too hazardous to depend upon memory.

since its inception in 1916. On that occasion the "Old Man of the Mountain" made the climb in 15 min. 28.7 sec. at an average speed of 48.3 mph. And if you don't think that's fast, consider the narrow tires, rear drive and over 100 hairpin turns. Inspired, I made an immediate decision to enter the Bugatti in the 1947 Labor Day event on September 1.

The first order of business was to contact the AAA Contest Board for the regulations governing the event, make a formal entry and acquire an AAA driver's license. I did this on a business trip to Washington, where I met Contest Board secretary Jim Lamb. Through correspondence, phone calls and meetings, we established a good relationship during the summer's preparations.

Pikes Peak rises out of the Colorado Plateau to a height of 14,110 feet, where water boils at a temperature 28°F lower than at sea level (185°F), and where the air has but 65 percent of its sea-level density. Weaving back and forth, seemingly always on the edge of nothing, the famous Pikes Peak Highway is an all-dirt road 19 miles in total length, and in many places less than 20 feet wide. The race starts at the 7-Mile post, where the elevation is 7,415 feet, giving a total driving distance for the course of approximately 12 miles with a vertical rise of 6,695 feet. The average altitude (for which carburetor settings, etc., must be made) works out close to 11,000 feet.

But statistics do not adequately describe this road course. While I had entertained ideas of memorizing a cutoff point for each turn, a few minutes on the hill convinced me of the utter hopelessness of that. With more than 100 turns, a large majority in the near-hairpin class, a beginner's only hope was to visualize the course in general. As Louis Unser contended, planning one's attack on the corners too carefully in advance was hazardous, because the road surface and weather conditions are so variable. To quote "Uncle" Louis: "One year I followed the snow plow to the top."

The course starts with a hard right corner 50 feet from the green flag and traverses the lower levels, called the "flats," in a series of irregular bends. Here the speeds are high, better than 100 mph for a car in the Maserati class. Then the road swings into a series of "climbing turns,"

difficult to drive and deadly on the revs, since the grade becomes noticeably steeper at the apex of the corners. In low gear and full throttle, 4,500 to 5,000 rpm, clutching the Bug several times to hold the rpm up was necessary. Coming out of the last set of these turns, near 12-Mile post, the road takes a short straight through Glen Cove, the halfway point and a popular congregating place for the crowds. This brief respite is followed by a really terrific right-hand corner leading into the "W's." From these, one strikes the switchbacks, through 14-Mile corner, and on to the faster stretches leading along the ridges to the top. The race finishes in a spectacular right-angled corner. If you have reached this point, you are dead tired but supremely happy.

All in all, Pikes Peak is a course that is so hazardous it's safe. There are few places at the higher levels where it would be worth looking for a car that ran off. But the corners are well banked, and a few runs convince you it wouldn't be worthwhile to leave the road.

PREPARATIONS FOR THE LABOR DAY EVENT necessarily centered around cooling and carburetion requirements. Time did not permit supercharging the Bug, and we were forced to content ourselves with less than 61 percent of the full-throttle sea-level horsepower when we reached the top. As an AAA Championship event, a wheelbase of 98.5 inches was the minimum, necessitating a five-inch increase for the Bug.

Preliminary planning began in May, and by July first decisions on the major features of our enterprise had been reached. The car would be prepared in Buffalo, personally taken to Detroit by boat and shipped to Denver via Western Auto Transport, the only through auto-trucking service between those two points. From Detroit, a business trip would take me to Seattle and San Francisco, after which my vacation leave started. The plan was to fly to Denver and drive the Bug to Colorado Springs in time for a week of prerace practice. Concurrently, Phil would drive our old car out from Buffalo. It all sounded simple, but by the middle of July it became necessary to set up a rigid day-by-day schedule and adhere to it.

No one would have guessed, watching the smooth operation of the Flight Research

Department at Buffalo Airfield during the day, that at 4:30 sharp the place was transformed into an intense and frenetic racing stable. Under the high overhead lights, fortified with good humor and an occasional beer, Bill Wilcox, Shorty Miller and Johnny Eichorn performed nightly miracles as the Bug was tuned and modified. As time grew shorter, Bill Frey, Hank Sonnen, Carl Oddo and others joined the team, making it possible to complete the work, which included painting the numbers, by Thursday, August 14, the day we left for Detroit. The extensive mechanical changes described below were accomplished in the amazing space of three weeks.

Major Modifications

The Type 35's wheelbase was increased to comply with event regulations by providing frame extension blocks of 4130 heat-treated steel bolted inside the channels, the frame having been cut at a point almost directly above the front axle. These blocks were hand-fitted, and attached with large, ream-fitted bolts. A stress analysis also was prepared. The shock absorbers were moved forward on the frame, and as a precautionary measure the aluminum hangers for the rear of the front springs were replaced with redesigned steel ones. All steering parts were removed, and a new unit-rim-and-spider stainless steel wheel, steering post, drag link and cross link were made up, while the remaining parts were Magnafluxed. Through the generosity of L. P. Saunders of Harrison Radiator, calculations were performed to determine the cooling demands, and it became obvious that the original radiator, beautiful as it was, wasn't up to the job. A special Harrison radiator of about 2.1 sq. ft. frontal area was provided with a #10 pressure cap. The latter was an effective means of combating the low boiling point of water at high altitude, giving us an internal pressure of approximately 18 psi (14.7 psi for sea level) and a boiling point of 223°F at 14,000 feet. In addition, the radiator surface was made especially effective by the provision of a tunnel-type shell.[1]

Once the new radiator was installed on the lengthened chassis, a suitable hood was constructed, the whole assembly giving the front end of the car a truly formidable appearance. To the uninitiated, that hood could have contained a 400-horse engine, which led to the rumor when we first arrived that the Bugatti undoubtedly had as much soup as the Maserati (the Federal Engineering Special that Russ Snowberger drove at Indianapolis that year). For a day or two the local oddsmakers had us taking second place.

The problem of carburetion had been tackled by Walt Breuhaus, who concluded after a session with mass flows, orifice coefficients and pressure drops that we had better take two extra sets of jets along, successively smaller than the standard sea-level set. The original jet had an orifice diameter of .061 inch (1.55 mm); our medium jet had a diameter of .0595 inch, while the small jet was .055 inch. On the hill we found that the mixture became so rich with the original jets, and the engine ran so rough, it was impossible to reach the top. With the medium-sized jets the top could be attained, and the acceleration at lower altitudes was good. With the smallest jets we had a maximum of "stomp" above Glen Cove, with a small sacrifice in power below that point. The race finally was run with this size, although only the night before did we finally conclude that this was our best compromise.

A new electric tachometer was installed, and lights removed; the rear end, brakes, transmission, engine, wheels and all other components were carefully gone over. The SCCA emblem then was bolted down in a prominent location, and the car rolled out for a trial run. The paramount question now was whether the steering qualities had been affected by the various changes. Great care had been taken to maintain the original geometry, and we were greatly relieved that none of the original characteristics had been lost. The steering forces, if anything, had been somewhat reduced. The wheelbase now was

[1] *The calculations were borne out in practice. On race day, after running the entire hill in low and second gear, and never at less than 4,000 rpm, not a particle of water had boiled off. This was in sharp contrast to two unfortunate machines whose cooling systems literally blew up during the event. One interesting car, the Shanahan Special ('46 V-8 Ford) carried no less than three full-sized radiators for the climb.*

Fig. 16-7
Ready to leave for Pikes Peak, with the mandated longer wheel base and a special Harrison radiator and cowling necessary for engine cooling at altitude.

98-¾ inches (a quarter-inch longer than the minimum required), and the machine gave a noticeably better ride. Incidentally, the most desirable wheelbase for Pikes Peak seems to be a compromise between shortness for cornering and length for traction and ride; Snowberger's estimate of 100 inches as optimum seems pretty accurate.

At the Foot of Pikes Peak

Preparations complete, the Bug made the trip as planned and pulled up in front of the Chamber of Commerce on Pikes Peak Avenue in Colorado Springs on Monday, August 25. One had to see the sponsoring Auto Hill Climb Association's work to appreciate its effectiveness. A scant two hours after our arrival in town, we were comfortably installed in a motel, the Bug had passed inspection, and we knew where our special tires, plugs, gas, oil, etc., were coming

from. We also received free dinner reservations for the week, and were lined up for our first practice runs the following morning.

By mutual agreement, the drivers congregated in the vicinity of 10-Mile post at an ungodly early hour. Practice from seven to eleven in the morning meant getting out of bed at five. Here the carburetor settings were made (around 10,000 feet altitude). Because of the sweep of the road, the cars could be seen and timed by a man standing at the top of the stretch. The first three cars to arrive were Unser on the Maserati, Snowberger on the dual overhead McDowell and, as I remember it, George Hammond on a four-cylinder Offy. I already had dropped down one jet size in the carburetor, and soon joined the group.

After making a series of runs with the Bug, all distressingly slow, Unser came over and asked how much air I was carrying in the tires. "About 28 to 30 pounds," I replied. Pulling a tire gauge out of his pocket, he successively gauged a front and rear tire of each of the other cars, showing they all ran around 20 to 22 pounds. This was the first in a long series of kindnesses shown to us by the other drivers, and that put the show on a fine sporting basis.

DURING THESE PRACTICE SESSIONS I soon discovered how little I knew. Back in Buffalo we had ideas about getting up into third and fourth gear occasionally, but it soon became evident that all sharp corners had to be taken in low, so fourth never would be used, and third only rarely. We had set 4,100 rpm as the continuous maximum on the basis of the Turnpike run, since we knew the engine would take it indefinitely. Soon we decided to gamble on a limit of 4,500, which reflected well on Russ Sceli, who rebuilt the engine that had not been touched inside since. Unfortunately we had no extra rear-end gears; a ratio somewhere between first and second would have helped a great deal. That first morning we also drove to the top, establishing that the ignition, carburetion and cooling at least were in the ballpark. The gearbox ran too hot to touch, but everything held, and I finally got used to the noise.

Coming off The Hill after that first four-hour session, I fell into the shower feeling like I'd jousted windmills. The dust encountered on the way down, from the sightseeing buses coming up, always topped off these daily practices. A shower was the greatest event of the day.

The Madman

The following morning, immediately after the first of our fuel line breakages, the Madman arrived. Walt Friel was a local used car dealer ("Wheel and Deal with Madman Friel") and owner of a garage that housed, among other things, the Madman's beloved hot rod "Betsy." A genuine addict of cut-down flywheels and shaved-down heads, Walt was on the hill with his mechanic Glen Gieseke. When our line let go they supplied tools and ideas; the line was repaired and practice continued. We moved the car over to the Friel garage, and that entire establishment got behind the Bug and me in a way that was perhaps the biggest factor in such success as we enjoyed at the Peak. While

we argued over the fuel mixture, the carburetor jets and the spark advance, the Madman's firsthand experience with racing at those altitudes nearly always was correct. The spark, for example, was advanced 30 degrees, with a definite improvement in altitude performance that might be hard to account for by theoretical reasoning alone.

Since it was permissible in practice, the Madman rode along in the mechanic's seat. His experience in driving hot rods on dirt tracks made him an ideal tutor, and in the ensuing days he drove home point after point in driving technique. Generous in praise, he righteously hit the ceiling when he found out that I had bounced off the rocks on the inside of one of the turns during the time trials. "Shoey" Shoemaker, an oldtimer who drove sightseeing buses up the hill for 20 years before starting his racing career, remarked, "My God, Bill, you sure hit rock No. 9 on turn No. 46 a terrific wallop today."

During practice we were dogged with unforeseen mechanical troubles. Six fuel-line breakages drove us to a completely flexible line system, while two distributor and fuel pump failures took away valuable practice time. It is hard to describe the terrible beating a car takes when practicing hour after hour on a course like this.

TIME TRIALS TOOK PLACE on Thursday. Eight cars were to decide who would get the starting flag first on Labor Day, an advantage since the weather is almost always good early but may change rapidly as the morning progresses. (This is the theory, although throughout our entire stay there was nothing but a cloudless sky.) The lineup consisted of Shoemaker (Miller), Desch (Chevy 6), Sankey (McDowell), Snowberger, (McDowell), Unser, (Maserati), Rogers (Offy), Killinger (Miller) and the Bug.

The real rivals at Pikes Peak were Unser and Rogers, both of whom lived locally. Rogers drove an Offenhauser Special this year, built up in town by Joe Coniff, and obviously designed with the single purpose of trimming Unser if humanly possible.

The time trials belonged completely to Rogers, who had undisputed FTD (Fastest

Time of the Day). Unser never made the first turn. Snaking away for a flying start, he got up into third and a speed of close to 100 as he took the green flag before the corner. Above the screaming, Russ yelled, "He'll never make it," and he didn't. He went straight off the six-foot embankment into the bushes. Some strenuous day and night work was required to rebuild the Maserati's front end in time for race day. The Bug didn't get to the finish line either (more ignition trouble) so we shared the doubtful honor of drawing with Unser for a position after those taken by the qualifying machines. He got ninth and the Bug tenth.

Ready, Set...

By Friday we finally were convinced that our car was right and nothing could keep her out of the race. Our elation was short-lived, however, for by noon Saturday our chances of even starting seemed slim indeed. Late Friday afternoon, after filling the tank with a new and untried fuel mixture, we had gone out for a short check run. With an overconfidence born from days of practice on the hill, we came screeching around the bends on the way to the practice area, with the inside front wheel just lifting and that wonderful "on the edge" feeling. But we hit one turn at far too high a speed, sheer misjudgment, and there was nothing to do but go straight on in: a 50-foot slide from 70 mph, a shallow ditch, and finally a grass embankment. Our confidence was back where it should be, but there were anxious moments about the car.

No sooner had we removed the machine from this scrape, with the engine still running, when serious ignition trouble began. Due to vibration, the distributor cap had started to disintegrate. A handful of Bakelite chips fell out when the cap was removed, and the engine was hitting irregularly on four to five cylinders. We tore back to the motel for the spare distributor that had been air expressed from Detroit for just such an emergency. The Madman ripped open the package, and with a groan handed me a distributor for a six-cylinder engine! (The Bugatti, of course, had eight).

Our friends made an all-out effort to locate an eight-cylinder distributor. Colorado Springs was scoured, and a contingent consisting of Ethyl Corporation representatives and my wife

Fig. 16-8
"Madman" Friel working on the carburetors. Harry Hartz observing as an AAA rep.

left for Denver. In desperation we put more than 40 dollars into a pay telephone, and finally late on Saturday located an official of the distributor manufacturer in Detroit. What he went through to get the parts out of stock that night, and onto a plane, can well be imagined. They reached us late Sunday. We were back in the race.

Walt Breuhaus and Dave Whitcomb flew their Ercoupe out to see the fun, arriving about the same time as the distributor. After ten hours of flying and without so much as supper, they took over where the Bug's exhausted crew had left off, and worked into the early hours of race day to ensure that everything that *could* be done *was* done. When the tachometer acted up during an engine run, they completely overhauled it without so much as a single bona-fide instrument tool, and with nothing but a droplight for examining the intricate mechanism.

If all of the above were not sufficient to entertain us that weekend, I should add that the Madman's wife was due to have a baby "any minute," an event fortunately postponed until after race day so the services of her husband were available to the Bugatti team.

The Buffalo contingent also took in one of the races at the local hot rod track. "Betsy," with Glenn Gieseke at the wheel, was the favorite, while the Madman drove the Queen of the event slowly by the stands in his big Buick before the heats got underway. To those of us who never had seen closed-course hot rod racing, the events had a singular fascination.

Betsy did not run right that evening, except for one brief occasion when she came on with a sudden burst of power, throwing the machine into a skid and into the guard rail. Standing with us at the opposite turn, the Madman ran toward the oval to signal Glenn in, but he was stopped in his tracks when a hub cap that resulted from a smash between two other cars sizzled by his head. A tragicomic scene ensued, in which the Madman continually tried to reach the edge of the track only to be stopped on each attempt by the flying products of the collision. To our amusement, he finally threw up his hands and beat a hasty retreat after the manner of a World War I "over-the-top" scene.

Start

Leaping out of bed on race day, I threw up the shades. A glorious morning was in the making as the first rays of sun fell on the Peak, which stood out clear and challenging. After a hasty breakfast we gathered at the Madman's. The Bug was out being fueled, washed and polished.

Crowds still were on their way up, though many spent the night at Glen Cove and the 14-Mile corner (at which altitude one drink is equivalent to *three*). Phil and a group of friends were among those who stayed up there all night. Killinger roared by the garage in the Indianapolis Miller, and we soon joined the traffic going up. The general public was allowed on the road until 9:30, after which it was cleared for the scheduled start at 10:00 A.M.

The cars lined up diagonally alongside the road. Crowded about them were mechanics, drivers, officials, friends and photographers. Clamping a crash helmet on an unsuspecting individual usually was good for a news photo. Truckloads of soldiers, who were to be stationed at the corners to secure the course, rolled by while the state police prodded the traffic, and Jeeps with cans of water for boiling radiators tore up and down the line of pleasure cars. Telephone communication, and walkie-talkies by the dozens, would maintain contact between all crucial points. Harry Hartz pulled up in the official Studebaker, followed by Jim Lamb of the Contest Board.

Finally the road was cleared, and the cars placed in qualified positions, to start at five-minute intervals. Rogers was off first and didn't spare the Offy, taking the green flag on the first try and disappearing from view. Hammond made a clean getaway, then Snowberger. We anxiously scanned the hill, and followed the cars as the clouds of dust rose above the trees. Rogers was reported to have reached the top, but we couldn't obtain the time. Hammond had spun out. With a great smile, Shoey left the line in veteran style, dressed in a white coat with necktie. The Shanahan, draped in radiators, was next. Killinger experienced difficulty, couldn't take the flag and was relegated to tenth starting place. The Bug moved up to ninth. Finally, with Desch and Mauro away, it was Unser's turn. Seven times a winner, he was the day's defending champion. On the first try he passed up the flag. The engine wasn't hitting, and he backed for another run. This time he got away with a terrible roar, followed by a gigantic dust plume.

We finished the job of changing to hard plugs and waited for the flag. Five minutes was eternity. With the smallest displacement car in the race, we hardly could hope for much, and I was almost praying out loud for the Bug to make the summit. I reflected on the effort so many people had put in to get the Bug to this place at this time. The Madman gave me a big handshake, and mercifully the signal finally came.

THE BUG SETTLED DOWN to the job and sounded fine, but as we wound through the flats it wasn't revving. Perhaps it was slightly cold; a change in spark setting helped. Perhaps it was just the compromise in carburetor jets. At any rate, it got better as we got higher. Somehow Turn 46 was negotiated and never

under 4,000 rpm again. What a relief. The straight through Glen Cove was lined with people, like a human tunnel. I realized that half the hill was down below.

To the Peak!

Now the Bug ran right and felt right: 5,000 rpm and better for full throttle. Forgotten were the limits, nothing pierced the consciousness but the job at hand and the desire to get there; 14 miles and the altitude and corners were beginning to tell. From there I remember little but the mounting urge to reach the top. "Come on, you Bug!" Then the checkered flag, and the whole adventure became a glorious memory. Dead tired, I appreciated the drink that was half coffee and half whiskey that one of the officials offered me. At 14,000 feet this was a knockout relaxant. Unser won (16 min. 34.89 sec.) by a fraction over second-place Rogers, who slid into the rocks at the finish line. We came in sisth and were completely

Fig. 16-9
Waiting for the start of the climb.

Fig. 16-10
Cornering above Glen Cove—one switchback after another.

Fig. 16-11
At the finish line, 14,110 feet above sea level. We came in sixth place.

happy to have run the hill and carried away a portion of the prize ($250 plus $80 for using Champion spark plugs). Our time was 21 min. 3 sec. Perhaps the Bug received the greatest satisfaction of all by having shown a younger generation what a 20-year-old product of the marque could do. Ed Waterhouse followed with a note (Fig. 16-12) that made the venture still more worthwhile.

We came away from Pikes Peak with the belief that traction is the key to performance. We hoped to locate a four-wheel-drive machine and go back for another attempt in 1948.

Side Trip to the Salt Flats

After shipping the Bug back to Detroit, we decided to take a side trip to the Bonneville Salt Flats to watch John Cobb's attempt to raise the land speed record in the Railton Mobil Special. Driving in from Salt Lake City we arrived in the vicinity about an hour before dusk. Following directions indicating a route to

the trials area, we drove out onto the flats. No sooner had we approached the yellow markers indicating the start of the measured mile when Cobb and the Railton roared by.

This was his first run after a two-week lay-up waiting for camshaft parts from England. As Cobb told us the next day over Cokes at the State Line Cafe in Wendover, he had reached a speed approaching 300 mph but was dissatisfied with the right-hand engine, which ran excessively rich and spouted black smoke. This prevented the rapid acceleration required to hit maximum speed before the beginning of the measured mile. He was shooting for close to the 400 mark.

We spent the next day examining the Railton, and talking with Cobb and the Dunlop tire representative. The course had been made usable by dragging it with railway rails. Even so, one end before the measured mile still was rough, resulting in a high-frequency vibration when traversed. Cobb rode without a safety belt, and the cockpit was equipped

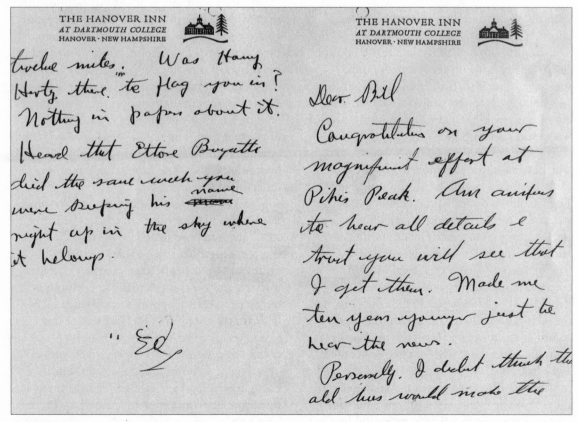

Fig. 16-12
Ed Waterhouse letter of congratulations.

Fig. 16-13
My associates in CAL Flight Research commemorate the Pikes Peak event with a nice plaque. Dave Whitcomb on left.

in England and on the Continent. Considerable advance planning apparently was required to get Cobb's car here on time.

We met Ken Taylor and Reid Railton, but only briefly because they both were working on the machine. Some interesting facts relative to the car's design were mentioned: wind tunnel tests had been run by Railton at the National Physical Laboratory, and the body was designed so there was no tendency to lift or pitch. Railton spent two years designing around the only engines available at the time, ex-Schneider Cup Napier W (three bank) units, of approximately 1,300 horsepower. The engines operated at about 50 inches Hg manifold pressure, low compared with about 90 inches Hg maximum for the Novi. The 400-pound body was beautifully constructed of aluminum alloy, but not flush riveted. No attempt was ever made to use ram air for the engines. Apparently the problem of carbon monoxide in the cockpit was not critical for the short duration of the runs and with the degree of compartmentalization around the driver. An ice tank for cooling water and for cooling the transmission was located to the rear of the rear axle. The rear suspension was by coil springs, with both friction and conventional hydraulic shocks. The front wheels were independently suspended.

The wheels were made in two halves, since no possibility existed for stretching the heavy steel-enclosed bead necessary for handling the centrifugal loads. Tire thickness varied uniformly from the bead to the top, where it was exceedingly thin. Actually, the tread was only a rubber strip approximately three inches wide on the top of the tire. The rest of the casing was painted to simulate rubber. The tires were designed with appropriate factors of safety for 420 mph. Some 48 of them were brought over, and several had made as many as three practice runs. How they stood up on the hard crusty surface of the flats was a source of wonder.

with the bare minimum of instruments and controls. He mentioned that during the 2-½-to-3-minute run he had his hands full holding to the line painted on the salt beds, and seldom got more than a fleeting glance at the two huge rev counters (one per engine). The American-truck-like flat position of the steering wheel was, as I suspected, dictated by space considerations and not by control force levels. The gearing of the steering was about that of conventional racing cars ("about like your Bug," Cobb said) and at the higher speeds the steering forces were proportionally high. The freewheeling arrangement made shifting easy, and conventional in operation.

We found Cobb a congenial conversationalist. He gave little hope of Brooklands or Donington Park being reopened for racing, and said he felt certain that his lap record at the former track in the big Napier-Railton (146 mph+) was "one they can't take away from me." When quizzed about the possibilities of getting Raymond Mays over for Pikes Peak, he emphasized the cost and time involved, and the fact that Mays would lose out on participation in several important events

370

Fig. 16-14
John Cobb's Railton Mobil Special at the Salt Flats. He was the first to reach 400 mph on a one-way run.

Wendover consisted of several gas stations, a railway junction point, the Army's Wendover Field and barracks, plus some second-rate overnight camps and one good (but small) hotel. The Railton was housed in one of the service station garages, visitors being kept at a respectful distance by a chicken wire screen. Cobb took us in through the side door, and we viewed the "works" at close quarters. Cobb made no pretense of being an engineer. "That's Railton's job," he said. When I asked why there were no tail fins on the Railton, Cobb pointed out that if the machine was reasonably well in hand you didn't need one; if the vehicle began skidding to the point where one was needed, you already were in deep trouble. A fin might make it worse in crosswinds. Presumably, the record runs would be made when crosswinds were light.

Back home, I reflected on the obvious but golden rule the Pikes Peak experience had taught me: the shortest time on a straight occurs when maximum acceleration and maximum braking are utilized. That is, you exit a corner accelerating as fast as you can down the straight, applying the brakes to the max entering the next corner. If it can be avoided, you never should drive at a constant speed in competition. Racing is a tough and relentless sport, demanding concentration and continuous effort.

Bug on Ice

After Pikes Peak life was somewhat colorless. The Bug began collecting dust. Cursorily checked over after our return, the press of other work relegated the car to her far corner of the hangar, temporarily lost among the wings and propellers. But when the snows came the urge to make a winter run was upon me like some recurrent, incurable malady, and preparations soon were in full swing.

On her maiden trip to Buffalo, I had faced a long cross-country winter jaunt, and although we had made it the margin had been slight. At the time I felt less victor than vanquished. This time a more careful plan would be laid, with no detail overlooked, in order to sally forth on even odds with whatever the weather might bring. A red mark was placed on the calendar for a Friday two weeks hence; the 300-mile "course" from Buffalo to Albany would be run at night.

Hardly had the schedule been set than reports came in advising that New York City was experiencing the worst blizzard in years, Albany and eastern New York were impassable, and the snow was continuing. Our worthy competitor had lost little time making the first move. We responded by adding a set of full chains and a trench shovel.

Soon satisfactory attire for the expedition evolved. From a base of long woolies, the garments went on for several layers, ending in a flying suit and full face mask. Only one sequence for getting into so much clothing would prevent becoming hopelessly entangled. The mere detail of sliding in behind the wheel required attention and was solved by removing the back cushion. New headlights were hung, the clutch was overhauled and adjusted, and Phil turned a neat trick in the food department, designing a lunch that could be eaten through the face mask flap with a heavily gloved hand.

By Friday we had been visited with local ice storms, and snow was falling. "Route 20 is entirely unplowed, 5 is a possibility, but what kind of a car are you driving?" the girl on the phone at the local AAA inquired. "A Bugatti Type 35," I replied. "It's an open job, and I *could* squeeze in a passenger." Silence. At noon the mechanics installed the chains; departure was 5:00 P.M.

As Ed Waterhouse remarked the next day in Albany, "I'll bet that's a record for a Bug with chains." On for the entire trip, places along the route would have been quite impassable without them. On the random patches of hard-packed snow or ice , it was another story, however, and the skittish Bug was a handful.

Surprisingly enough, the ten-hour run passed without incident, our careful preparations leaving just enough reserve to meet the changing conditions. But if we were lacking in extraordinary thrills, there was much to compensate. After several hours, and with that mass of clothing, I reached the state where physical existence separate from the machine all but ceased. This happy state gave rise to a mental detachment that allowed me

Fig. 16-15
My Type 35A Bugatti leaving for an all-night winter run to Albany (approximately 300 miles). We had chains on the rear wheels and needed them. Note flying suit and all the fixings.

to observe not only the car's behavior but also my own, as if my mind were viewing the whole proceedings from another vehicle. Driving was reduced to an impersonal affair, and when the car slid, the necessary corrections I made with less concern than if I were turning the pages of a book.

From time to time other details absorbed my attention, like the sheer delight of watching the chains as the cross links rose high above the tires and then carried over and down into the road beneath. I wondered at the play of forces when the flying links met and bit the surface, urging the car on through the swirling snow. In the fascinating action of the front suspension, the springs fought to hold the wheels to every indentation in the road, and the gleaming tubular axle beam vibrated in the backwash of the headlights, presenting a pretty sight not soon forgotten.

Arriving in Albany with so little effort, and after a thoroughly enjoyable experience to boot, I decided to push on to Greenwich, Connecticut, the following day. The next ten hours were far from uneventful.

An ice storm during the night left trees and wires glistening in the sun. It was as beautiful a winter sight as one ever was likely to behold, and having paid my respects I went to the garage to examine the Bug. The evening's run had left fantastic patterns of snow and frost on the wheels and exposed chassis parts, and the sides of the tail had a solid coating slung up from the wheels. Otherwise the car appeared anxious to be off. I decided to run the 125-odd miles from Albany to Greenwich the next morning, and return to Albany by evening. I was anxious to examine the Pauley-Ford that had performed so well at the Fairfield Hill Climb as a possible machine for next year's Pikes Peak.

Roaring south down a two-lane secondary road smooth with hard-packed snow, I got a full measure of living fast and well. While there are many who would baby a 20-year-old automobile, there was something ageless about the Bug that said it should be well maintained, but that it also should be used. On this particular morning the Bug had its head completely, and since traffic was light we engaged in the new sport of rolling up onto the snow banks lining the road as corners were negotiated. After the ice storm the banks were substantial enough for the purpose, and relatively smooth for a few feet up. The road was like a long toboggan chute.

Despite the sun beating down, it was cold that morning, so several stops were made to add cardboard to the radiator. Finally an area approximately four inches square was found sufficient to hold 160-degree water temperature. This was the same radiator used at the Peak, and the comparison was interesting, for in Colorado all the radiator area was required. I reflected that in the course of six months and 2,000 miles, the radiator had been tested to the extremes of its performance.

What happened from the time of our arrival in Greenwich until 7:00 P.M., when we finally left, was a story of wrong telephone numbers and missed connections, a slide into a snow bank, and a minor collision that bent several spokes in the left rear wheel. These were behind us when we finally settled down to the job of getting back to Albany as expeditiously as possible, with the pleasant prospect of a hot, though late, meal.

Hard Ride Home

It was not without concern that the return was started so late. The generator had been acting up intermittently all day, and the battery could be down from the previous night's ten-hour run. Nevertheless the car started easily, the lights appeared normal, and the inaccessibility of the generator on the forward end of the crankshaft prompted me to push on.

An hour or so later the situation changed rapidly for the worse as the generator cut out completely, and the lights started a gradual sickly yellow fade. I stopped by the roadside and dug beneath the seat for a flashlight. Proceeding at a snail's pace, in second gear, I drove on for another few miles, careful to conserve the flashlight and praying for a moon. The cold crept in around the seat, and the misery of the whole business came home. Then as the battery teetered between life and death, the engine missed and backfired, and

Fig. 16-16
My sketch of the Buffalo–Albany run. There was no Thruway then, and I used Routes 5 and 20, the historic stagecoach routes.

progress was possible only in low. The car came to a halt within sight of the lights of a small town.

My impulse was to hike to town for help, but the snow prevented my getting the Bug well off the road, and although no cars had passed in an hour it seemed hazardous to leave the machine. While debating this, the battery underwent self-rejuvenation, and I found it possible to restart the engine and reach town.

No gas stations were open, but the local bus company had its own garage and its facilities were offered. I worked with a droplight as huge shadows were cast on the walls, and the atmosphere seemed to suggest secret work going on at the bottom of a pit. An interference with the radiator required its removal before the generator housing could be reached, a major operation. Finally its mysteries were explored and an adjustment was made to the third brush. But this labor was for naught. An engine run at 2:00 A.M. proved the defect was beyond repair with the facilities available. The faithful bus mechanic left for home, and I crawled up into a bus labeled "Rural Schools," pulled my flying togs around me and slept.

In the morning, quick-charge equipment was located and a fresh start made. By this time it was discovered that two cells of the battery barely could hold a charge. Procuring a 12-volt battery in a small town on Sunday being out of the question, the strategy was to obtain at least one more charge before reaching Albany. Sunday is a day of rest for many people, and once again we were caught between towns. The car came to rest in front of a huge stone mansion, whose owner not only phoned for a tow car but served a welcome breakfast.

By noon prospects seemed propitious, with only 30 miles to go and a fresh charge completed. The contrast with the last 20 hours roused me to a burst of speed, and I was able to laugh at obstacles overcome. Alas, I laughed too soon! A loud banging from behind, and we slowed down to find that the long exhaust pipe had come adrift. The steady vibration from the chains on the run from Buffalo had been too much for the rigid fittings. Slung up in place with the tow rope, the exhaust pipe, along with the Bug and its occupant, finally reached Albany.

Later that fall, driving down country roads in the early evening to visit some friends, a typical snow squall came up. The visibility went down and I switched on the lights, proceeding with caution. As I made a sharp turn to the right, a Red Label Bentley suddenly came toward me and disappeared into the mists. I had never seen a Bentley before and suspected there only were a few in the entire country. Later, at the annual meeting of the SCCA in Washington, D.C., I was conversing with a member from that region. Having inquired where I came from, he said, "I had an experience up your way that you *won't believe*. I got caught in a snowstorm and a Type 35 Bugatti came out of the mist and passed me." I looked at him and said, "It's a really great story but who the hell would believe it."

Later we exchanged the truth.

MY "TURNPIKE" WEEK-END

By Bill Milliken

After spending the better part of Saturday in preparing for the 300-mile run from Buffalo to the Turnpike, I finally left here late in the afternoon. The trip down turned out to be a succession of rough roads, detours, fairly deep ruts, rain and fog. Though I had hoped to arrive at the Pike in time for an early morning run, I finally reached the Bedford entrance about 8:30 a.m. Sunday morning, after an all-night run.

At this point I changed to Champion R-7 plugs, since the hotter, commercial ones give bad pre-ignition at over 80 m.p.h., and after considerable starting difficulty, made a first attempted run. This run was terminated in a hurry when the water temperature gauge was observed to exceed 220°F. It was found that one of the water hose clamps had failed, and all the water had run out of the system!

By the time the car had been towed to a service station, water system repaired, engine started and warmed up, it was 11 a.m. The Turnpike was crowded with Sunday traffic, but a second run was made--this time successful. It was my impression it must be something over 15 miles, since the calibrated speedometer never dropped below 90 for the entire run, and speeds of better than a hundred were reached on several occasions. It was an extremely hot day, and both the water and oil temperatures ran 25° higher than at normal cruising. Also it was apparent that the hasty wheel balancing job which had been done in Buffalo was inadequate, as violent "wheel tramp" was encountered during the entire run. Needless to say, there were some interesting brushes with the other traffic!

After crossing the finish line I received a terrific surprise when removing my foot from the accelerator the car continued with no let-up in speed. The hand throttle had crept up to the position of the foot throttle, and a few bad moments were experienced before getting the car under control in the traffic which converged to one line at the entrance to the tunnel.

Driving back up the Turnpike it was discovered that one head light had vibrated loose, and then to top off the performance, the fuel line to the front carburetor let go and fuel sprayed up through the louvres under the fuel pump pressure. The afternoon was spent in towing the machine back to a service station and making repairs. I left the vicinity of the Turnpike at 5:00 p.m., and after another all-night run enlivened by heavy thunderstorms, I arrived in Buffalo at 7:00 a.m., thoroughly soaked, with less than half an hour's sleep in 48 hours.

Fig. 16-17
Story in *Sports Car* of my Garthwaite Trophy run in Type 35A Bugatti.

Chapter 17

Four-Wheel Drive

As long as the wheel speeds are approximately equal on all four wheels, the car should behave as a "four-wheel drive" and handle satisfactorily. Locking out the center differential should do it.

– Bill Wilcox
Crew Chief, FWD Special, 1948

Traction was the key to performance on the loose gravel road at Pikes Peak. After a typical dirt track slide, rear-drive cars engaged in "digging" (a local term) to return to speed on a grade after a hairpin turn. Despite the spectacular plume of gravel this left, acceleration was slow. Braking before a corner was not seen as necessary because of the high drag induced by the slide, and the use of more than two gears was infrequent. Clearing the engine after the slower corners by hitting the throttle usually resulted in wheel spin, i.e., "digging."

Thus I assumed that four-wheel drive (FWD) could be a real advantage, and certainly more suited for the amateur driver. This should not imply a lack of appreciation for the dirt track slide, one of the most exciting features of oval track racing. On the contrary, I greatly admired drivers who had mastered the art of cornering at large slip angles on low coefficient of friction surfaces, controlling the path and attitude by the use of power. But I felt sure I would be more competitive at Pikes Peak with a four-wheel drive machine.

In those days FWD race cars were a rarity. I wasn't even sure one that met AAA regulations existed, so on a trip to Washington I set about inquiring. Smith Hempstone Oliver, automotive curator at the Smithsonian, had the answer. Over lunch, Hemp said the Four Wheel Drive Auto Co. of Clintonville, Wisconsin, had entered a FWD-Miller at Indy that Mauri Rose drove to 4th place in 1936. Returning home, I sent off a letter to the Four Wheel Drive company (at the end of this chapter).

Preparing the car at CAL Flight Research. L-R Breuhaus, Babchek, WFM, Wilcox, Rouzer, Oddo.

Fig. 17-1
Letter from FWD.

The letter reads:

THE Four Wheel Drive Auto Co.
FWD
MFRS. OF TRUCKS
CLINTONVILLE, WIS.

December 17, 1947.

OFFICE OF THE PRESIDENT

Mr. W. F. Milliken, Jr.,
Cornell Aeronautical Laboratory
Cornell Research Foundation, Inc.,
4455 Genesee St.,
Buffalo 5, New York.

My dear Mr. Milliken:

Replying to your letter of December 10th addressed to our Mr. R.L. Koehler, our racing car is here at Clintonville and is in good condition and we are interested in having someone put it to use in the racing field.

We would suggest that you come here and go over the matter with us.

Yours very truly,
THE FOUR WHEEL DRIVE AUTO CO.

Walter A.Olen
ELV
President.

The answer arrived a week later, and was dated December 17, the anniversary of the Wright brothers' first flight. I took this to be a lucky omen. After some additional correspondence, I arranged my trip to Clintonville, Wisconsin.

In late January I arrived in Clintonville on the night train from Chicago. Deep packed snow was on the ground, and the thermometer registered fifteen below zero. I wasted no time taking a cab to the FWD plant.

Four-Wheel Drive Pioneers

The Four Wheel Drive Auto Company was a family business. It had been created by Clintonville attorney Walter A. Olen to produce vehicles invented and patented by local machinists Otto Zachow and his brother-in-law, William Besserdich. A major supplier to the military during World War I, the company survived the postwar depression by branching into specialty 4WDs for logging and oil field use, and for fire trucks. When I visited, Walter Olen was in his eighties and still serving as president. His elder son Robert was general manager, and his younger son Don was director of engineering. Straightforward integrity characterized the entire operation.

Tremendously enthusiastic about the four-wheel drive principle, the Olen family had financed research conducted by Professor Archie Easton at the University of Wisconsin to demonstrate its superiority on low coefficient of friction surfaces like ice.

The Olens got into the race car business following the Indianapolis race in 1931, when Harry Miller and Harry Hartz visited Clintonville to propose building a four-wheel drive race car to explore (and exploit) the FWD principle at high speeds. Walter Olen was sold on the idea. The racing car I was about to see was one of the two machines resulting from this unlikely collaboration.

Reminiscent of Bugatti's Molsheim facility in possessing most of the elements of a much larger car company, the Four Wheel Drive plant was self-contained. In addition to a machine shop that boasted Gleason gear-cutting machines, there also was sheet metal fabrication, an assembly bay, component test equipment, a toolroom and an experimental model shop that, incidentally, had machined and assembled the Miller-Offy engine for the race car.

The main office building facade fronting the manufacturing units was reminiscent of Pierce-Arrow in Buffalo and Stutz in Indianapolis. It was an unadorned, functional design of vertical elements spaced by windows, with horizontal strips defining the various floors. Walking up a series of stone steps to the first floor, I entered a small lobby and was shown to Walter Olen's office, where I was met by Bob Olen and Herman Larson, head of the experimental shop. They reviewed company history, their Indianapolis racing experience and the four-wheel drive race car, about which I asked detailed questions. I told them of my interest in motor sports and my Pikes Peak experience, as well as my affiliation with Cornell Aero Laboratory. It was a good exchange, after which we went to see the car at the plant and at the small proving ground out back.

The Last Great Miller

The car was in good shape. It was a two-seater Indianapolis car powered by a 255-cubic-inch four-cylinder Miller-Offy engine. The FWD-Miller was designed as Harry Miller was leaving the company and Fred Offenhauser taking over. Thus, the engine was the pioneer Offenhauser unit that, with various improvements, would dominate Indianapolis racing for years.

Power from the engine was carried through a multi-plate clutch to a straight-cut three-speed manual transmission, and then to side, forward and rearward driveshafts via a center differential and a lateral transfer unit that used herringbone gears. The side shafts were connected to differentials at the front and rear wheels. Since both front and rear suspensions were de Dion, the differentials were mounted on the frame, and power was delivered to the wheels via sliding half-shafts and universal joints.

A feature of the center differential unit was a two-position control that in one position left the center diff operating and in the other *locked* it out. In the latter case, the average speed of the front wheels and the rear wheels was the same. Since wheel spin was prohibited, the locked center diff provided maximum traction on slippery surfaces. We were *strongly warned* by FWD, however, to operate with the open center differential, because that had proven desirable at Indy.

Using de Dion suspension was an advanced feature of the design, but the dead axles were very stiffly sprung through quarter elliptic springs. Later, we measured the suspension's natural frequency with shocks disconnected, and found it to be 230 cycles/minute, very stiff indeed.

The car's empty weight was about 2,620 pounds, and the loaded center of gravity was close to the wheelbase center point. Since the same tire sizes were used front and rear, and the drive was to both ends, the car was very symmetrical fore and aft and close to neutral steer by design.

Competing again at Indianapolis was mentioned, but I felt the car was outdated for another try at the 500. I also was certain that my racing experience was far from the Indy league. By the end of the day the decision for a go at Pikes Peak had been made. I agreed to summarize our discussion in a letter, and they offered to propose a contract, subject to Walter

Fig. 17-2
The FWD Miller as raced in Indianapolis in 1932 with Bob McDonogh. The car is in the FWD Co. plant in 1948.

Olen's approval. Seeing the car, I realized its overall gearing was not suitable, and was assured FWD would provide suitable ratios. If the steering proved too slow we could go directly to Ross Gear, the maker of the gearbox and drop arm. The transmission was a three-speed crash box, which meant I would have to become proficient at double-clutching. Further problems included high-altitude cooling and carburetion, neither of which seemed insuperable. I was cranked up; here was a car suitable for the Peak and I didn't want to miss the chance of working with the folks at FWD. The plans were finalized in a letter and lease agreement.

Preparing the Miller

Once the car arrived in Buffalo I decided to familiarize myself with it before the teardown for race preparation. A large paved ramp in front of the Flight Research hangar was convenient for running circular skid pad tests and other stylized maneuvers. In addition, we laid out a handling circuit on the airport made up of various taxiways and part of a little-used runway that we could use under tower control.

An exciting car to drive, the Miller had more punch than any other machine I had experienced. Because of the stiff suspension it didn't pitch, roll or dive to any extent, and felt like a large go-kart. Four-wheel drive tended to make the car go where it was pointed and gave the impression of running on a track. But when the throttle was dropped from a high-g turn, the machine "ducked in," i.e., tightened the turn (or even spun out) unless corrective steering immediately was applied. This behavior, now known as "trailing throttle oversteer," was not well understood at the time, nor were we able to improve it by changes in tire pressure, weight distribution, etc. Although more pronounced on front- and four-wheel drives, all cars exhibit this behavior to some extent. It was a handling characteristic I learned to cope with, but I nearly got caught out on a couple of occasions.

The caster of the steering was low and hence the control forces. Maximum steering lock was limited by the universal joints, which would be something of a problem at Pikes Peak with its hairpin turns. Finally, the whole car was very much "alive" (i.e., prominent

Fig. 17-3
The FWD Miller arriving at Flight Research by FWD truck, 1948. I revved it up in second gear on our ramp, so
everyone could hear the "big banger," four-cylinder Offy at 5,000 rpm.

vibration) because the engine and everything else was solidly bolted to the frame.

After a couple of days of playing around on the ramp, we got down to serious preparation. After the teardown, we prepared a list of work to be accomplished, work that had to be completed by August 19, a few short months away, if the car was to reach Colorado Springs in time for practice and time trials.

Major items included changing the ring and pinion gears on front and rear to an overall top-gear ratio of 4.30 (vs. the 3.16 used at Indianapolis). This would provide 100 mph at a conservative 5,200 rpm in third gear (a piston speed of 3,900 ft./min.), and over 80 mph in second because of the close spacing between second and third gears. These speeds would be adequate for Pikes Peak, and also gave us lots of acceleration (see gear ratio chart Figure 17-9). Because we thought a cooling problem would exist at altitude, a special radiator was acquired from Harrison.

A peculiar noise from the gearbox noted during practice on the ramp was traced to failure of the forward ball bearing on the countershaft. A thrust bearing had been installed *backward*. Changing it required removing the box from the engine and disassembling it.

Following the complete check of engine and chassis, the steering parts were Magnafluxed. After weighing the pros and cons we installed a seat belt, concluding I would be in better control and less liable to run off the road. All preparations were performed on evenings, weekends and holidays by members of the Flight Research Department, who put in more than 300 hours at the agreed-upon rate of $1.50 an hour. Big Bill Wilcox, crew chief and head mechanic, put in another 50 hours in Colorado Springs.

Fig. 17-4
We checked the understeer characteristic by plotting steering wheel position versus lateral acceleration (ball bank) on a circle. It was close to neutral steer position control.

Fig. 17-5
Test with forward center of gravity, to reduce the "trailing throttle oversteer." It was unsuccessful.

As the specialists who make it all possible, mechanics are the true heroes of motor racing. In addition to some of the smartest engineers in the business, Flight Research had autonomous groups of fabricators, mechanics and instrumentation specialists. Henry Sonnen had apprenticed in Germany, where he worked

Fig. 17-6
Changing the final drive to 4.3:1, at CAL Flight Research. Note the deDion suspension and quarter elliptic springs.

Fig. 17-7
Straight-cut, three-speed gear box. Note gear wear.

for a licensee of Bugatti. Give him a sketch and he could produce a work of art in metal. His colleague, Bill Frey, came up through the experimental shop at Curtiss-Wright. If our facilities did not suffice we could turn to the main Lab 1 shop on Genesee Street under Joe Muncey, who had come to Cornell from Curtiss in Garden City.

All our mechanics were hand-picked, several from the P-40 assembly line. Charlie Mummert

was only one generation removed from Glenn Curtiss' Hammondsport plant, where his father Harvey Mummert had been chief engineer. In Johnny Eichorn we had a top "tin knocker" who could fashion sheet metal into intricate shapes with a sandbag and an assortment of hammers. Shorty Miller, Frankie Babchek and Bill Rouzer had aircraft and engine licenses and military aircraft experience. We had our own Magnaflux equipment and a stock room full of A-N hardware.

For years, crew chief Bill Wilcox and I went to the races together. I might not have had the most modern or competitive equipment, but the quality of preparation was second to none. When Wilcox gave the thumbs up, I knew we were ready to race.

Furthermore, we had a terrific "big boss" in Doc Furnas. If he discovered us working on the race car during working hours, as occasionally happened, he graciously left the hangar. He knew that what we were learning from racing ultimately would find its way into research projects for the lab.

Sports Car Spring

The spring and summer of '48 was one of the busiest I ever remember. In addition to preparing for Pikes Peak, I was to help organize the first postwar road race at Watkins Glen, which came about as follows:

In May SCCA president Russ Sceli had organized a rally to the Indianapolis 500. Speedway management agreed to give our group parking on the inside of the first turn, and local members arranged a Time Trial Event for Saturday the 29th on a strip of road outside the city. My wife and I left Buffalo in the Type 35 early the day before, driving down the shore of Lake Erie to Cleveland, and then on to Columbus and into Indiana. Stopping for gas, the question often was the same: "Can you open up the hood so we can see the engine?"

APPROACHING INDIANAPOLIS, we spotted a red MG up ahead, with Cam Argetsinger and his wife Jean aboard. Although I never had met the Argetsingers, I had read Cam's article in *Sports Car* about establishing record times from Watkins Glen to surrounding towns with his Packard Darrin during his summer vacation. He noted that "in all the years I owned the car, nobody had ever passed me." In Indianapolis we both stayed at the famous Claypool Hotel, a center of activity during race week and frequently mentioned in the *Indianapolis Star*, to which Eddie and I had subscribed in Old Town.

The next day Cam joined me in the Bug for one run of the time trials against Mike Vaughn's Lagonda. Cam remembers that Mike, who might have had one too many for lunch, nearly collided with us. Later Cam ran against Denny Cornett, also in an MG, and won.

That evening all of us attended a cocktail party hosted by the Indianapolis SCCA, during which Cam announced his plan for a road race at Watkins Glen in the fall of '48. These many years later it is difficult to articulate the impact of this announcement, which led to the U.S. Grand Prix at Watkins and the resurgence of amateur racing in America.

Racing would become the backbone of SCCA. Cam made it possible. The germination of his idea, the choice of the original circuit and his success in persuading the village fathers to agree is classic stuff. It changed the lives of many people, not the least mine.

Fig. 17-8
The three-speed transmission and transfer case to side driveshaft, also input shaft from 255 cu. in. Miller Offy engine. The lever (upper right) enables locking the center differential.

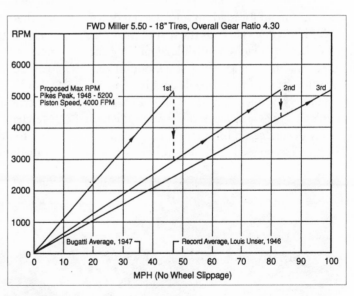

Fig. 17-9
Gear ratio chart, MPH vs engine RPM. Note wide spacing between 1st and 2nd. Max speed at 5,000 RPM is close to 100 MPH at a conservative piston speed.

After the finish of the 500, as the sports car group drove from the infield at the first turn, I turned the Bug onto the track and made one lap of the 2-½-mile oval before being flagged in by a track official. This was the closest I ever came to racing at Indy.

Fig. 17-10
Indianapolis Time Trial, Type 35A Bugatti. Other contestants were Charles Addams, Ken Hill, Cam Argetsinger, James Melton, Bill Spear, Denny Cornett, Russ Sceli, and George Boardman.

Grand Prix Groundwork

Back in Buffalo I wasted no time driving down to Watkins Glen. This was the first of many such trips I became involved in while organizing the race as chairman of the Technical Committee. My impression of the 6.6-mile circuit Cam had under consideration was that by European standards it was a classic in every respect: length, variety of surfaces, turns, grades and hazards. With no escape roads and obviously very fast,

Big Bend was a real challenge. We looked at another possibility Cam had turned up, but found it too prosaic. Stirling Moss would later refer to Cam's first choice as a circuit with qualities of "greatness by any standards."

On June 10, 1948, I was invited to attend the crucial meeting at the Manufacturers & Merchants Club in Montour Falls, the town next to Watkins Glen. Dave Whitcomb and Walt Breuhaus from CAL Flight Research came with me. The village was represented by Mayor A. D. Erway, Don Brubaker and Art Richards (chairman and secretary, respectively, of the Chamber of Commerce), Village Race Committee chairman Leon Grosjean, Nick Faboni, and Sam and Ann Cobean. Representing the Sports Car Club were activities chairman Alec Ulmann and treasurer Nils Michelson, with Dave Whitcomb and me as technical advisers. Also on hand were the Argetsingers, as well as Cam's parents. After convincing speeches

Fig. 17-11
My Type 35A Bugatti.

by Alec, Nils and Cam the deal was done, with October 2 set for the race date.

Sharing responsibility for the formal announcement package to the SCCA membership, Cam and I used Indy and Pikes Peak entry blanks as models, but expanded the supplementary information. For the first time (to my knowledge) we mandated the use of seat belts in racing. This was Cam's idea, one I endorsed wholeheartedly from my knowledge of Ed Dye's automobile safety research at CAL. It would save my neck on at least two occasions at the Glen. Based on our time trial experience at Indy, we outlawed drinking on the day of the race. I remember writing the regulations on a train trip to Dayton. We reviewed and finalized these when Cam and Jean came to Buffalo.

I also made a sketch of the circuit. The Herculean effort of getting all this material typed, mimeographed, collated and mailed out to the membership was accomplished by my secretary, Florence Shanahan. At the same time Florence also was handling a raft of correspondence relative to Pikes Peak and the routine paperwork of a CAL department head. Walt Breuhaus put together a group of about 20 engineers and technicians to take on timing and scoring. Stopwatches from all over the lab were commandeered, and the same master chronometers that officially timed Lindbergh's New York to Paris flight were loaned by Longines.

Because this first race at Watkins Glen was a landmark in the history of American road racing, a complete copy of the information and entry material sent to the SCCA membership is reproduced in Appendix II. It includes SCCA's first race regulations. Cam's August 24 letter to me at Colorado Springs (at the end of this chapter), where I had arrived for practice the week before the 1948 Pikes Peak event, illustrates the prodigious amount of work we accomplished in putting this show on the road. Pioneering events don't just happen.

Fig. 17-12
My secretary, Florence Shanahan, in Flight Research. She typed and mailed the entry blank for Watkins Glen, 1948 (see Appendix II).

As the summer progressed I saw a great deal of the Argetsinger family. Cam truly is a one-off. His interests largely centered on two subjects: automobiles and women. He seldom wasted time on anything else. Even more intriguing, he talked only about automobiles up to midnight, after which, almost like clockwork, he switched to women. The researcher in me was curious about when he switched back from women to automobiles. Invited to stay overnight at his Seneca Lake cottage, I rose early and discovered that the switch occurred just after breakfast.

One of Cam's idols was Napoleon, about whom he read widely. Perhaps this was the source of his discipline. But there also was a soft and delightful side to his nature. A friend in England usually finishes his Christmas greetings to me with "I hope you haven't done anything silly this year." But when the situation is right, Cam and I both can get back into our "child" and have a good laugh. In a way our wives were saddled with raising us along with our children.

On August 19 I left with the Miller on the overnight boat to Detroit. It would be transported to Denver by Western Auto Transport, while I made the trip by train.

I used the trip west to study. After boarding the train on the 21st, I spent the next three days trying to familiarize myself with the road up Pikes Peak, using the map and notes developed during our 1947 Bugatti attempt. (See Chapter 16.) I also mentally practiced double-clutching, since we already had concluded that most of the hill would be run in first or second gear.

I sat on the train imagining my left foot on the clutch, my right foot on the throttle, my right hand on the shift lever. The procedure: hit the clutch while backing off on the throttle, shift to neutral, let the clutch out, rev up, hit the clutch again, shift to first (if a downshift), step on the throttle. The idea

385

was to accomplish this sequence as fast and naturally as possible, while trying to imagine the sound of the engine "blipping" up. I must say this practice worked well. I don't remember missing a downshift at the Peak, and there were times when double-clutching was helpful on an upshift.

Arriving in Colorado Springs on Friday, August 28, I headquartered at Strang's Garage, which was centrally located and the best-equipped establishment in town. It was open 24 hours a day, and the only drawback was its distance from the Peak. Using a rental car, I spent the weekend re-familiarizing myself with the course. Bill Wilcox and Herman Larson arrived on Monday the 30th. On Tuesday we began practicing in earnest.

On our first day out we started with 6.50 × 18 Firestone cross-grooved tires, the Harrison radiator and the center differential *unlocked* (as recommended by FWD). Handling was nearly impossible. Two violent spins occurred, and on one occasion we plowed out of a turn. Excessive cooling meant we couldn't bring the engine up to reasonable operating temperatures, so the special radiator was taken off that evening. Its removal restored the longitudinal balance of the car, which had become nose heavy with the radiator installed. We also dropped down to 5.50 × 18 Firestone cross-grooved tires. The next day handling improved slightly. We got to the summit and concluded we could live with the cooling of the standard Miller radiator.

The third day out, when I was pushing for a good time during trials, the car spun to a stop twice. Adding ballast in the right-hand seat, and experimenting with the driving technique, did nothing to improve the situation.

In the hindsight of present-day knowledge, it seems amazing we didn't try locking out the center differential sooner, particularly since the vehicle spins were preceded by spinning of the rear wheels, and vehicle plow by spinning of the front. We were influenced by FWD's insistence (reinforced by Larson) that Indianapolis experience on a high-coefficient surface was applicable on the loose gravel at Pikes Peak.

Fig. 17-13
The FWD Miller at Pikes Peak, 1948. All smiles at having a competitive machine!

Four-wheel drive racing experience in 1948 was very limited.

Wilcox's analysis, from observation of the car from the roadside, and also from the right-hand seat, was remarkably correct in light of subsequent experience with the locked center differential. As he put it, "So long as the speed is actually distributed approximately equally among all four wheels, that is, as long as the car is behaving and acting as a true four-wheel drive, its handling characteristics were satisfactory. The minute that, for any reason, the speed is unequally distributed between the front and rear ends, the car is no longer a true four-wheel drive, nor does it behave like one, and the stability and control characteristics degenerate rapidly." We concluded locking the center differential would be a worthwhile experiment, and without informing Larson got up early on Saturday and snuck up to our practice area to try it.

The results were profound. No other single change had such a favorable effect on the handling characteristics. The car felt like an entirely different machine, one in which the safe margin of operation had been extended in all directions. It no longer was necessary to use the throttle with extreme care, and the general skid-resistance characteristics of the car were enhanced beyond all expectation. To obtain some quantitative check on our impressions, two runs were made over the practice mile. On the first, made in 60 seconds and driven very conservatively, the car tended to wander at the higher speeds but this was not alarming. The second run was made in 56 seconds, equaling our previous best time, still without pushing the car. Further runs unquestionably would have improved our times, but we chose to push on up into the W's (the series of pronounced hairpins connected by short straights) and then to the summit, to obtain a final check on engine operation at the higher altitudes. The four wheel drift of the car on high-speed turns was noted as interesting and desirable.

Locking the center diff changed the car from the worst-handling machine on the hill to

Fig. 17-14
FWD cornering during the Time Trials.

quite likely the best, "a baby carriage," as I said to Bill Wilcox. We were elated, of course, but careful not to enlighten the competition. In due time we convinced Larson. With the car now handling well, we confirmed that the steering was too slow and ordered a longer drop arm from Ross Gear.

I developed a driving technique better suited to an amateur, that consisted of approaching hairpin turns on the inside, and then applying power to initiate a four-wheel drift toward the outside. This made it easy to adjust the power as the turn progressed, so the machine used the full width of the road. It was far less spectacular than the dirt track slides of the rear drives, but avoided digging and high drag.

As part of my bargain with FWD, I agreed to write a detailed report of our Pikes Peak attempt. The one I wrote that winter ran 190 pages. The following table summarizes our week of practice.

With all this behind us, we approached Labor Day with high hopes.

Up Pikes in the Miller

Before the start, the atmosphere in the pit area was charged with expectation and excitement. The pits were on a semicircular side road built through a grove of birches, with individual stalls cut back at intervals. This natural enclosure, carpeted with green and backed with the blue of the sky and the sun shining down, provided a setting of unsurpassed beauty. Since all the drivers and crews were on the friendliest terms, the tension prevailing at other races of this magnitude happily was not present.

Since no rain had fallen the preceding week, we suspected the road up to Glen Cove would be loose and treacherous. I made up my mind to start conservatively and take a quick calibration on the surface during the first quarter mile or so, since it is very easy to misjudge this in the early stages of a run. Because we wanted the information for future situations, special pains were taken to note that the outside air temperature at the starting line

SUMMARY OF FWD ACTIVITY ON THE "HILL"
DURING THE WEEK PRECEDING THE RACE

DAY & DATE	CONFIGURATION: Tires	Tire Press	Radiator	Fuel (3)	Carb. adj.	Spark adv.	Windshield	Center Diff.	Steering Arm (4)	Ballast	Spark Plug /Gap	Location on "Hill"	Timed Runs (2)	REMARKS
Monday Aug. 30	Servicing and Preparing Car for First Practice.												-	- - -
Tuesday Aug. 31	6.50 x 18 (7)	25# front & rear.	Special	100 oct. aviation	Main jets 12 notches down, accel. jet off.	35°	Small	unlocked	medium	none	R-7/.025	Half-Way Camp Ground	66 sec.	With this configuration handling very poor: two bad spins experienced. Excessive cooling. Decided to remove special radiator and drop down tire size. (1)
Wednesday Sept. 1	5.50 x 18 (7)	25# front 23# rear	Original	Special		"	None	"	"	"	4M/.025	Half-Way Camp Ground: & summit.	56 sec. (55-56 Unser) (54 Rogers)	Marked improvement in handling: no spins but tendency still existed. Engine operation satisfactory at "start" and "summit." Cooling marginal but passable. Steering too slow.
Thursday Sept. 2	"	"	"	"	"	"	"	"	"	"	"	Start to Glen Cove	8 min. 27.04 sec. (7 min. 5.07 sec. Rogers "pole" position)	TIME TRIALS - Handling still unsatisfactory: car spun twice to stop. Obtained 9th position in race starting lineup of 15 cars. Engine operation excellent.
Friday Sept. 3	"	"	"	"	"	37°	"	(5) "	"	75# in r/h seat	R-13/.025	Typical corner below Half-Way Camp Grd.	-	Photos early in a.m. with FWD truck on Peak road. Spent rest of practice trying to improve cornering characteristics & eliminate spinning tendency. Tried "brake & power" technique(6). Rear wheels always break traction before spin.
Saturday Sept. 4	"	"	"	"	"	37° & wired in place	"	Locked (wired)	"	"	"	Half-Way Camp Grd. (also up on W's & summit.)	60 sec. 56 sec.	Tremendous improvement in handling during accel., braking & cornering. Could have improved two Practice Stretch with more driving practice. Steering still slow. Movietone News shots and stills while practicing on "W's".
Sunday Sept. 5	"	"	"	"	"	"	"	"	LONG	[illegible]# shot r/h seat	"	-		Completely serviced, checked & cleaned car. Installed "long" steering arm which had just arrived. Radiator flushed, magneto checked etc.

Fig. 17-15
This chart is a day-by-day account of our activity at Pikes Peak prior to the race.

was 65°F and the radiator water temperature was about 190°F.

Five minutes after George Hammond in the Kurtis-Kraft-Offy, I was ready to leave in the FWD. Difficulties with the timing apparatus the previous year led us to take no chances, and we installed a calibrated stopwatch mounted in sponge rubber on the instrument panel. I clicked this as the starting line was passed. Because of the possibility of fouling a plug before the engine was thoroughly warmed up, we had decided to cross the starting line in top gear, thus ensuring we would not exceed 3,000 rpm in the first quarter-mile or so. After that any rpm was acceptable, because by then the engine was sufficiently warm insofar as oil was concerned. The engine behaved perfectly throughout the entire run, never once failing to take the throttle, and sometimes going up to the rev limit in an alarming manner.

That the road surface was slippery was discovered immediately, but no appreciable slides were encountered. It was apparent the overall configuration was excellent. The first sharp turn just below the 9-Mile post, where one of the spins had occurred during the trials, was negotiated with caution and the run continued over the practice stretch at Half-Way Camp Ground. Unfortunately no time was obtained for this stretch; the machine was running beautifully and the rpm reached in top gear indicated that the true speed on this straight portion of the stretch was about 90 mph. One of the fastest stretches on the entire course, speeds of 100 mph or better based upon tachometer readings were reported by some entrants, but considering the wheel spin of two-wheel drive machines, they probably were no more than an honest 90. Wheel spin on the FWD at this speed with locked center differential must have been small.

Among the more difficult corners between the start and Glen Cove is the right-hand hairpin at the end of the practice stretch, where we had observed digging and loss of acceleration by the two-wheel drives in practice. During the race I intentionally took the normally well-rutted corner wide. Slight slide was experienced, but the moment the accelerator was pushed down hard the car took off in low and accelerated rapidly up the

grade, momentarily exceeding 5,800 rpm. Shifted into second, it held on to the wide sweeping outside turn that followed. But on the prevailing grade, with the horsepower available, the car would not continue to accelerate in second, and although I realized the rpm might become excessive, I shifted back into low. The corner was negotiated with slight acceleration, the rpm holding at about 6,000 for possibly five seconds.

Since it was impossible to take my eyes from the road to check engine behavior, other than a hasty glance at the tach, I was not certain how the fuel pressure was holding. Whenever the road was momentarily straight, I reached over and got in a few stokes on the hand fuel pump as a precautionary measure. No loss in fuel pressure seemed to have been experienced. Because the hand pump was a minor source of irritation, I made a mental note that it could be eliminated for future occasions.

Up and Out of the Race

Shortly before Glen Cove, snow flurries were encountered, illustrative of the weather changes that can occur at Pikes Peak between the time the first and eighth car leave the starting line. Passing through Glen Cove, I took the left-hand hairpin and the right and left bends that followed leading into Shoey Straight. The grade becomes fairly steep here. The FWD was running in low gear. Suddenly, with no noise other than the engine, rpm momentarily soared up to 6,000+. At first I thought the machine had slipped out of gear, which frequently happened on the Bugatti when running in low, but rarely with the FWD. Immediately hitting the clutch, I hauled the lever back toward low only to find it already was there. I thought the gear had been stripped. Putting the lever in second and third brought the car to a stop, and a check was made in reverse. By then the FWD was not moving at all and I rolled back against the embankment at the side of the road. My next thought was clutch failure but a hasty examination revealed that wasn't the case. After looking around in the cockpit and then under the hood, and still finding nothing untoward, I restarted the engine and went through the gears, again with no success. We were out of the race.

Fig. 17-16
FWD cornering on one of the wider hairpins. Note complete absence of guard rails (characteristic of Pikes Peak).

A few minutes later, when the rest of the team arrived at the spot, we discovered the transfer case had split and separated the big herringbone gears. The sustained high torque in low gear when I momentarily exceeded 5,800 rpm could have been a contributing factor. At the time, however, mechanical failure was the last thing I expected, and it seemed a good idea to take advantage of the car's excellent handling characteristics to cut the time by a few seconds.

Unfortunately the stopwatch on the dashboard was not shut off as soon as the car stopped. Upon returning to Glen Cove we checked with a number of people who had unofficially timed the cars from the start to that point. From Bill Wilcox, who had remained at the starting line, we also were able to get a rough idea of the time made during the first portion of the run. With no official time at Glen Cove, the exact performance of the FWD never will be known. Our best estimate, which we reported to the Front Wheel Drive Company, was that we were well up in the money, possibly not more than five seconds behind Al Rogers's time up to Glen Cove. The gross weight of the FWD was almost twice that of his Coniff-Offenhauser Special, while both cars had similar engines of about the same horsepower. This confirmed the importance of traction, and the potential of four-wheel drive for the Peak.

It was not possible to repair the transfer case (an aluminum casting) before the Watkins Glen event on October 2, 1948, so we scratched the FWD entry and focused on running my Type 35. It was not until 1949 that we were able to race the FWD at Watkins. Before leaving Colorado Springs, I received another letter from Cam indicating that the Grand Prix would indeed take place.

Fig. 17-17
Cover of our extensive report to FWD on their car at Pikes Peak, as required by the lease agreement.

10 December 1947

The Four Wheel Drive Auto Co.
Clintonville, Wisconsin

    Attn: Mr. R. L. Koshler, Sales Director

Dear Sir:

    It has recently come to my attention that you had a Four Wheel Drive, Miller engined race car entered in one of the late pre-war Indianapolis races and that this machine is still in your possession.

    This year, driving a small 122 Cu. in. unsupercharged Bugatti, rebuilt by a group in our flight research department, I was able to finish in sixth place in the annual Pike's Peak Hill Climb, a championship event under the jurisdiction of the AAA. It is my desire to enter next year a car more suitable for the event, and it occurred to me that you might be interested in entering into negotiation relative to the use of the above mentioned machine. Since I am primarily concerned with the sporting aspects of the event, I would be willing to assume a large portion, if not all of the cost associated with the preparation, entry, and running of this machine, and in addition would be willing to accept any reasonable and equitable manner of dispensing the winnings. Based on our experience this year, and on the imminent suitability of a Four Wheel Drive machine for this event, I honestly believe that the machine could be placed well up in the money. Since this is now a national championship event, I presume much good fortune might be worthwhile from an advertising standpoint.

    I am planning a trip to Boston in the near future, where I am informed your machine is stored. Would it be possible for me to examine it at that time?

    Should you desire references in connection with negotiations of the type outlined above, I would suggest you contact Mr. James Lamb, Secretary of the AAA Contest Board, Pennsylvania Avenue at 17th Street, Washington 6, D.C.

                  Yours very truly,

                  W.F. Milliken, Jr., Manager
                  Flight Research Department

WFM:fas

Fig. 17-18
My inquiry to the Four Wheel Drive Auto Company regarding their FWD Miller.

2 January 1948

Mr. Walter A. Olen
Four Wheel Drive Auto Co.
Clintonville, Wisconsin

Dear Mr. Olen:

    Thank you very much for your recent letter and invitation to visit Clintonville for the purpose of discussing the use of your four wheel drive racing car.

    I am planning to make such a trip, but it will be a few weeks before it can be worked into my schedule. Under any circumstances, I will let you know in advance of my arrival.

    On a more detailed examination of the Indianapolis statistics, I find that a four wheel drive racing machine ran each year from 1932 to 1937 inclusive. The records seem to indicate it was the same machine which ran each year, and I wondered if this is the machine which you have in your possession.

              Yours very truly,

              W. F. Milliken, Jr.,
              Manager,
              Flight Research.

WFM:fas

Fig. 17-19
Letter to FWD.

THE
Four Wheel Drive
FWD AUTO Co.
MFRS. OF FWD TRUCKS

CLINTONVILLE, WIS.

OFFICE OF THE PRESIDENT

January 7, 1948.

Mr. W. F. Milliken, Jr.,
Cornell Aeronautical Laboratory,
Cornell Research Foundation, Inc.,
4455 Genesee St.,
Buffalo 21, New York.

My dear Mr. Milliken:

Replying to your letter of January 2nd,
the race car that we have was one of the last
cars built by Harry Miller of Los Angeles. It
represented his very latest design incorporating
the principles of a four wheel drive.

It had an eight-cylinder motor, an
entirely new design by Miller at the time the car
was built and during the first two years the car
was raced we tried to use this motor but it was
a failure and the motor was removed and we built
in our own plant a motor of the Harry Miller design
that had been so successful in other cars. The
car has won between $10,000 and $12,000 in the
few races it has participated in. The four wheel
drive principle has worked very satisfactorily
but the motor and other parts of the car have been
subject to the same failures as other cars in
races. We believe that if these matters can be
straightened out that the four wheel drive should
be able to out-perform any car now in the racing
game. The car is in good condition and could
very easily be put into shape to enter the next
Indianapolis race.

Our interest is to see the car used to
bring out the advantages of a four wheel drive
in high speed work.

Harry Miller was permitted to build two
additional cars - a duplicate of ours. One of
these was converted into a pleasure car and sold
to a man by the name of Burden who toured
Europe with it on a pleasure trip. I do not know
what became of it.

The other car was taken by Peter DePaolo
who toured Europe with it and one of his spectacular
races with it was when Hitler was sitting in the
stand and came very near being injured. The story
will be found in the book "The Wall Smacker" by
Peter DePaolo. The car was finally brought back
to Los Angeles but what became of it from then on
I do not know.

One of the difficulties we have had in
using this car for racing purposes is that a four
wheel drive is distinctly different in its construction and in its action on the track and should be
driven as a four wheel drive but the only drivers
that we have been able to secure were those who
were trained and formed habits in driving rear drive
cars, so that our Four Wheel Drive, we feel, was
never driven as it should have been. The year
that Mauri Rose won his national medal it was, in
part, a result of driving our car in the Indianapolis
race.

Yours very truly,
THE FOUR WHEEL DRIVE AUTO CO.

Walter A. Olen   President.
ELV

Fig. 17-20
Letter from FWD.

393

<u>L E A S E</u>

THIS AGREEMENT entered into this 1st day of May, A. D., 1948, by and between The Four Wheel Drive Auto Company, a Wisconsin Corporation, with its principal office at Clintonville, Wisconsin, hereinafter referred to as the lessor and W. F. Milliken, Jr. of Buffalo, New York, hereinafter referred to as the lessee:

WITNESSETH:

The lessor hereby leases to said lessee and lessee hereby agrees to rent from lessor, one Racing Car, described and known as the "Four Wheel Drive Special," owned by The Four Wheel Drive Auto Company; said lease term to commence on the 1st day of May 1948, and end on the 1st day of November 1948, a period of 6 months.

It is expressly agreed and understood that said racing car may be driven by the lessee in the Pikes Peak Hill Climb and two or three amateur Hill Climb events of the Sports Car Club of America; said lessee to bear the expense of entry fee and to furnish all necessary money for gasoline, oils, and repair parts while racing said car and transportation to and from said racing events and to assume and pay all expenses incident to the tuning and repairing of said car for the same.

Lessee further agrees to return said car to the lessor at the end of said term in substantially the same condition as when leased, reasonable use, alterations approved by the lessor, and damage, other than damage caused through the fault or negligence of the lessee, or his agents, servants and employees, excepted: it being understood that participation in any racing event as aforesaid shall not, in itself, be construed as negligence.

Lessee agrees, during the time that the car is in his care, to carry proper insurance insuring the vehicle against loss or damage caused by fire, by theft, and by damage due to collision when towing the car between events.

Lessee further agrees in consideration of this lease to inform the lessor of the results of all races or other trial runs, contests, or experiences with the race car, including information concerning the mechanical result of any technical engineering or other information.

It is mutually agreed by the parties hereto that in the event that spare parts for said race car are unavailable from any other source, that the lessor will furnish said spare parts to the lessee and the lessee will pay cost price therefor.

Fig. 17-21a
Lease agreement. In actual operation some variations from the Lease agreement occurred. The period was extended by several years, and to numerous other events. The announcement of the first Watkins Glen Grand Prix happened after the signing of the lease, so I immediately entered the Miller for that event as well as for Pikes Peak. FWD took care of the insurance and arranged to deliver the car via truck to our Flight Research Hangar in Buffalo.

Lessor agrees to deliver said car to the lessee on or before the 1st day of May,1948, at the City of Clintonville, State of Wisconsin, and lessee agrees to re-deliver said car to the lessor on or about the 1st day of November, 1948, at the City of Clintonville, State of Wisconsin.

It is further agreed that the lessor shall not be liable to said lessee for damages of any kind, or from any cause whatever to the persons or property of lessee, or any outside parties who make claim, and lessee agrees to defend at his own expense all damage suits which may be brought upon claims relating to said race car or the use thereof by the lessee.

The loan of said race car by the lessor to the lessee is on a non-rental basis, with such prizes and awards as may be won by the lessee during the lease period remaining his property.

It is further agreed that this Indenture is not transferable without the consent of both Lessor and Lessee in writing.

IN WITNESS WHEREOF, the parties hereto have hereunto set their hands and seals the day and year first above written.

IN THE PRESENCE OF: THE FOUR WHEEL DRIVE AUTO CO.

___Edythe Vaughan___ /s/   By:____Walter A. Olen___ /s/
                                                Lessor

                                        _____W. F. Milliken, Jr.___ /s/
                                                Lessee

STATE OF OHIO   )
COUNTY OF MONTGOMERY) ss:

Before me, a Notary Public in and for said county and state, personally appeared W. F. Milliken, Jr., this 4th day of May, 1948, who did sign in my presence and of his own free will.

                        Clara Jean Tasker ___ /s/
        SEAL   CLARA JEAN TASKER, Notary Public
                        In and for Montgomery County, Ohio
                        My Commission Expires Sept. 9, 1949.

Fig. 17-21b
Miller FWD lease agreement (continued).

CAMERON R. ARGETSINGER
246 BROADWAY
YOUNGSTOWN 4, OHIO

August 31, 1948

Mr. William F. Milliken, Jr.
419 E. Platte Street
Colorado Springs, Colo.

Dear General Pike:

Thanks for your letter, and telegram. The miners shack
has arrived, but is a little narrow in the eaves. Am having
alterations made. *Western Union sure made a mess of TAZIO!*

We are all hoping that the FWD is in shape by now and that
you have the sort of weather desired for the big day. More power,
and the nine Argetsingers at Seneca Lake all know you are the
one to do the trick this year.

Glad you are agreed about the name Grand Prix. Would be
a shame to change now.

Oliveau's letter was very interesting. We will have the
road at the foot of the hillpen for an escape, though it makes
a damned poor one. We'll have to emphasize at the Driver's
Meeting the importance of extreme caution on that long down grade.
Actually, the MG comes around at over 5000 RPM (indicating 80 plus)
and I only hold her down because of the possibility of uneducated
traffic. Gears and common sense should make that hill safe.

There are only two entries for the Veteran G. P., and that
event is out, I'm quite certain. I'm not sorry, though the two
who entered will be disappointed. Have sent lists of the entries
to Bud Miller, and to Nils. Have sent the stack of blanks and pix
to Alec.

WG has tossed the program back into the lap of the SCCA. WG
does not want to have anything to do with compiling or printing, and
I think they are right in that Ulmann will do a better job. Phoned
Nils about it, and he griped a bit, but agreed it could be done, and
really seemed not too upset about the SCCA doing it.

Nils will send out a card requesting members & subs. to make
their reservations direct with Art Richards. Your own rooms are
taken care of, but the card will also ask about the Banquet, Breakfast,
and Box Lunch at the Paddock. *All contestant's reservations are OK.
now — From entry blanks*

Official approval is expected momentarily by the local people,
and should surely be here in couple of days. Jean and I are now
planning to drive to New York tomorrow returning here Fri or Sat.
Will see Ulmann and Nils. Want them to meet here with WG officials
in next couple of weeks. You won't be back, I suppose.

I am going to Youngstown the 19th of Sep, returning here the
25th or so. Hope yu can get here a few days ahead of the race.

Have written the Montreal Sports Car people, and Nils will keep

them posted re reservations. Don Brubaker will make special
rates at the Lodge for large parties - eight or more, or so.

Bill, I believe we can race all the cars so far entered at
one time. My own thoughts on the Program of Events have changed
since seeing the entries, and are as follows:

Run only one race, the eight lap Grand Prix. Utilize the
time originally scheduled for Events 1 & 2 and have time trials
for each car. Then assign starting positions according to best
times made. The time for time trials would of course be part of
the time the course is policed.

I believe we should still have the four classes, though
smaller displ. cars may get very favorable starting positions.

Nils M. said for you and me to decide this. Will of course
discuss it all thoroughly with Nils and Alec, but what do you think?
We always thought time trials the best way, did we not, but thought
we did not have enough time?

That Healy of Ferguson's is out, so Nils said. The fellow
is a dealer, and they don't like him, evidently. That is none of
my affair, thank God. I am sorry to have the Healey miss out, but
membership et al is out of my bailiwick.

Dad went back to the hospital for ten days, and is now home,
feeling much restored, and we believe on the right road. His
doctors talk of him returning to full work in a few months. He
and Mother of course send their best to you and Phil, as we all do.

There are countless details I could write about, but will not.
My fingers wear out. *And you have the Peak to think about — not the G.P.*

Again thanks for all the wonderful work you have done. Looking
forward to seeing you soon, and do hope you'll be here several days
before race day.

We are all thinking of you, and will be urging you on next
Monday. Best of luck, take care of yourself.

Sincerely,

Cam

Cameron R. Argetsinger

Box 48 WG NY

Fig. 17-22
Letter from Cam Argetsinger.

Chapter 18 Milliken's Corner

> I was always thinking of eventually bringing all the European teams and champions to Watkins Glen . . . for a Formula One Grand Prix.
>
> – Cameron Argetsinger, 1948

To my knowledge, few of the people who have written about this first postwar road race were actual competitors. I not only was there but also was in the thick of the fray. This is my story of this historic event, the start of SCCA racing, exactly as I remember it.

The transfer case failure of the FWD at Pikes Peak was a double whammy, not only ruining our hopes there, but for Watkins Glen too. We thought the Miller with its 255-cubic-inch Offy engine and the overall transmission ratio of 4.3 in top gear had the speed and acceleration to be highly competitive at the Glen. But it was not to be. Arriving back in Buffalo we focused on the preparation of our alternative entry, the Type 35 Bugatti. Wilcox was not available, so Shorty Miller agreed to take on the job. Earlier we had increased the compression ratio with a new set of pistons, and we hoped to do well in class. I left for the Glen on the last day of September, with spares and personal effects in the left-hand seat. Some friends from the department were on the ramp to see me off.

East from Buffalo, Old Route 20 is smooth and rolling, passing through some of the most beautiful farming and dairy country in western New York. Bales of hay dotted the fields as farmers prepared for winter. I drove without helmet or goggles, enjoying the engine's note as we slowed for each small hamlet, then accelerated out. Near Canandaigua was wine country, with Geneva at the northern end of Lake Seneca, the deepest of the Finger Lakes. Past Geneva was a smooth, fast stretch of road ideally suited for checking out the setup for top-end operation. I would use it for this purpose for years, with many brushes with the constabulary and not a few

The Type 35A crossing the bridge on Franklin Street right after the Glen entrance and approaching the first corner.

Fig. 18-1
Cockpit of my Type 35A Bugatti, Chassis No. 4906. According to Sandy Leith, a director of the American Bugatti Club, this car "may quite possibly be the most significant GP Bugatti in US amateur racing history." It was owned and raced by several prominent drivers in ARCA events prior to the war and, as related here, we campaigned it postwar. It now resides in France.

George Weaver, George Boardman, Paul Ceresole, Mike Vaughn, Col. George Felton, and Russ Sceli were among the familiar faces at the registration table.

We were a motley group insofar as racing experience was concerned. Some had raced in ARCA and had a number of races under their belts; others had no experience at all, but followed the sport and wanted to get in on the fun. A few drivers like me had a modicum of experience. With a couple of genuine hill climbs behind me, and lots of cross country in the Bug, I imagined myself among the professionals.

The same diversity was seen in the machinery, from an out-and-out Grand Prix car to a variety of sports cars and a special or two. Nearly a dozen MGs were in the field. Some participants could barely afford to be there; others were members of the moneyed elite. Over the years the distinctions would become apparent, but at this first event the atmosphere was egalitarian. "Wow, we've finally got a place to race."

Following registration I drove to Smalley's Garage. Tremendous supporters of the event, Les and Flossey Smalley accepted no fees for garage space or mechanical help during my 15 years of racing. I always figured Amoco, with its high benzol content (which they carried), was the best fuel in town.

PRACTICE WAS INFORMAL. During the summer I had driven around the circuit and walked a good part of it, but decided to take a couple of laps as a refresher. The increase in traffic provided no opportunity for anything approaching racing speeds. Large farm wagons were unloading hay bales for the outside of turns and in front of trees and ditches. Signs had been prepared indicating distances before corners and warnings of significant features

tickets.[1] No member of law enforcement was around on this occasion, so I opened up the Bug and accelerated cleanly to about a hundred.

Approaching the long hill that descends into Watkins, I noted an increase in traffic and a number of foreign makes. Race headquarters was the old Jefferson Hotel on Franklin Street—my first stop. Alec and Mary Ulmann were holding court on the porch as I entered; inside Miles Collier was setting up a bulletin board of photos from prewar ARCA events.

[1] *As Watkins Glen became more speed conscious there was some relief from this nuisance for race regulars. Any ticket within 30 miles of the circuit would be vacated. In those early, glorious days of racing, I would just call up Henry Valent, lawyer and chairman of the Grand Prix board, who would laugh and say, "Well, how fast was it this time?" Then I would drop off the particulars at his office and forgot about it.*

Fig. 18-2
Before leaving for the Glen. L-R: Dave Whitcomb, John Eichorn, Bill Milliken, Carl Oddo and Bill Wilcox on the ramp at Flight Research.

Fig. 18-3
Engine compartment, Bugatti Type 35A, Chassis No. 4906.

like the plunge down to Stone Bridge from School House. Progressing around the circuit, I was reminded of the appropriateness of the corner names (some of them coined by Cam) starting from old Corning Road: Seneca Lodge Corner, Ess Bend, The Back Stretch, Railway Underpass, School House, Stone Bridge, Hidden Valley, Archie Smith's, Railway Straight (after Brooklands), the Grade Crossing, Friar's Turn, Big Bend, Thrill Corner, then back into Franklin Street.

Fig. 18-4
L-R: Cam Argetsinger, Les Smalley, Florence Smalley (seated) and Don Brubaker, all prominent in the early Glen races.

Archie Smith, who had been critical of the race, changed his mind when the parking fees for his property rolled in. The New York Central agreed to stop the trains at the Grade Crossing, and also to bring spectators in on an excursion special. A telephone crew was working under Dewey Alter as I motored down Railway Straight, which was very close to the steep drop-off from the road down into the actual Glen. The circuit had a variety of road surfaces—blacktop, cement, gravel, smooth, rough—and was highly cambered in places, all of which contributed to its charm and challenge.

My next stop was to check into my cabin at Seneca Lodge. Proprietor Don Brubaker was an Altoona, Pennsylvania, lawyer who had been widowed with five young children. Gravitating to Watkins Glen, he decided to raise his family in this more rural setting and acquired a large tract of land where he built the first all-wood lodge in the midst of an old cabin colony. Following a fire a year or two later, the community rallied to his support and a new lodge rose from the ashes. As chairman of the Chamber of Commerce, Don was one of Cam's early supporters for the race.[2]

On Franklin Street everyone was in a gala frame of mind, parading up and down and making and renewing acquaintances. All shops and stands were open and decorated with flags and bunting. Strang's Garage served as the inspection station, and was where Dave Whitcomb painted the numbers on each car with removable paint. The garage was packed with spectators, crews and officials, all leaning over and rubbing against the cars, which messed up the numbers almost as fast as they were painted on. Patiently, Dave went around repainting them. Our Bugatti was No. 21B in the 1½- to 3-liter class.

1948 Watkins Glen Grand Prix

Race day was clear and a little chilly. Leaving the Bug at Smalleys', I walked up to the Court House where a crowd had collected. Painters were putting the start/finish line on the street, while others installed tables for timers and scorers, public address system, etc. Everyone of note was there including Mayor Erway in his wheelchair, the Ulmanns, Charlie Lytle, Nils Michelson with his flags, Smith Hempstone

[2]*Donald Brubaker and his Seneca Lodge exemplified the local support for the races. Many of the planning meetings took place in front of his great stone fireplace, and the banquet after the first race, chaired by Alec Ulmann, was in the lower level. Most of the drivers and crews stayed in the cabin colony, and the bar and restaurant were popular with officials and racers. A homespun philosopher, Don also promoted his pioneering ideas about organic food and exercise to all his racing clients, changing the lives of many of them.*

Fig. 18-5
Lining up for the start, Dud Wilson's Stutz in the foreground. Wilson was president of the SCCA at that time.

Fig. 18-6
Our Bugatti in starting position. We were in Class B, 1½- to 3-liter category. Leaning is Ray Miller of CAL Flight Research, who prepared the car.

Oliver and, of course, Cam and Jean and part of their family, race physician Dr. Fritz Landsberg, and Walt Breuhaus and his T&S team.

The first race, the Junior Prix to determine starting positions for the Grand Prix, was scheduled for 12:30 P.M., preceded by a concours d'elegance where I marveled at the Phantom Corsair that Rust Heinz (of the condiment family) had built and that was years ahead of its time in aero styling. A parade, with neighboring town bands led by baton twirlers in miniskirts, further livened the proceedings. A number of people spoke at the Drivers' Meeting, including Dud Wilson and Russ Sceli, the current and past presidents of the SCCA. As Race Technical Chairman, I was called on to say a few words, and I believe Michelson reviewed the flags.

The 23-car field lined up with larger displacement cars in front followed by progressively smaller displacement classes. The diversity of vehicles led Philippe Defechereux to call the four-lap (or 26.2-mile) event a "local formula libre." Some of the more interesting entries were Frank Griswold's Alfa Romeo 8C 2900, Briggs Cunningham's BuMerc Special,

George Weaver's Maserati V8R1 ("Poison Lil"), Col. Felton's Vauxhall OE 30/98 ("Quick Silver"), Ken Hill's Merlin Special ("The Flying Banana") and Haig Ksayian's supercharged MG TC (owned by Cunningham). MGs were driven by Cam, the Collier brothers and Denny Cornett, among others. There were two Bugattis in addition to mine.

My starting position was on the outside fairly far back in the field, alongside Sam Collier's MG TC. At the starter's signal, the whole snarling pack rushed down Franklin Street and into the first bend. With a good start, the Bug was screaming along in second gear for this relatively slow turn.

Although my experience was limited, I had one attribute of a genuine race driver: I desperately wanted to win or, at the very least, do well. I felt extremely competitive, as if nothing else mattered, and was fearless in the sense of not realizing the risks. It never occurred to me that I might get hurt. At Boeing I had survived so many close ones that risk-taking was normal to me. Subconsciously I wanted to join the band of heroes who had peopled my dreams and given direction to my life.

Fig. 18-7
At the start. Hands in air signifies that our engines are running and we are set to go.

Going up Old Corning Hill, I passed both Colliers, which surprised and elated me, since I was aware of the brothers' prewar race experience and reputation. Afterward Miles admitted being surprised too, since they recognized my Bugatti from ARCA events, where it never had done particularly well. I'm sure I was pushing hard, because movies show the tail breaking loose on a number of corners. An even better indication was the lifting of the inside front wheel at School House as I turned to plunge down to Stone Bridge and Hidden Valley. On a Type 35 Bugatti most of the "roll couple" is taken by the stiff front suspension. If the inside front wheel lifts, you can be assured you really are cornering. I also have the impression that the car momentarily left the road at School House and landed on the left-hand side of the road as it pitched down. In short, I was racing all right but probably over my head.

Fig. 18-8
Entering the first turn off Franklin Street at start of the fourth lap.

Fig. 18-9
Approaching School House corner that leads down to Stone Bridge. I've started the turn as indicated by the right front wheel off the ground. A large percentage of the lateral weight transfer is reacted by the very stiff front suspension on the Bugatti. When a front wheel comes off the ground, you can be certain you are really racing!

At Stone Bridge I got far over on the left and cut hard to the right by the hay bales, then on to the sweeper through the valley and up the winding hill at the end, holding as close to a straight line as possible with the car light at the left-hander on top. Near this crest was a huge tree on the right which, in a later race, Ken Hill would slide into in a borrowed Jaguar, breaking the car neatly in two, while "Indestructible" Hill just walked away.

A slight bank at Archie Smith's corner assisted in accelerating around and onto Railway Straight, which was unpaved but smooth and one of the fastest sections on the circuit. Faster cars literally flew over the banked Grade Crossing in a ski-jump effect. Friar's Bend (so named by Cam because of the old monastery nearby) led down to Big Bend. I don't know how fast I negotiated the latter but the steering forces were so high I had both hands on one side of the wheel pulling as hard as I could!

I must have passed a lot of cars in the field, because by the fourth lap I was in fourth position, and then passed Haig Ksayian to move into third. Haig maintains the pass occurred after the Grade Crossing but I have

a distinct recollection it was near the end of Big Bend as the circuit straightened out before Thrill Corner at the bottom (an excellent viewing place opposite the unique Flat Iron Building). Earlier in the race George Felton got his Vauxhall into this turn too fast and spun down the escape road near the barbershop. Steeped in the lore of European road racing, "Fearless" Felton slammed it into reverse gear and was back in the race.

Discovering Milliken's Corner

My own experience was somewhat different. Approaching the corner much too quickly, I stood on the brakes as hard as I could with my left foot. Not enough. The problem was the small drum brakes on the 35A (non self-energizing) and the high-standing brake pedal that made it difficult to get my right foot onto it in a hurry. My line on the corner was good but the speed was too high and the tail let go. The car spun around and then proceeded backward into the hay, swung around again and rolled over. The Bugatti was so solidly built the noise was more of a thud than a clang. Thanks to the seat belt and the cut-down side

Fig. 18-10
Last lap of the first race. I've passed Haig Ksayian in Cunningham's supercharged MG and moved into third place, but am about to lose it on Thrill Corner, which I entered far too fast. In this photo the car is about to break on the rear and spin out.

Fig. 18-11
An instant later the car strikes the hay bales and is on its way over.

Fig. 18-12
After I emerged from under the car, Haig Ksayian's MG came to a screeching stop in front of me. That was as scary as the rollover.

Fig. 18-13
Surveying the damage. Thanks to the cutdown sides of the cockpit, the seat belt and the helmet, I received only a slight scratch on one elbow. I owe a lot to Cam, who proposed requiring seat belts in the regulations (a first in auto racing). Shorty Miller, left.

of the cockpit, I was only rotated sideways as my helmet struck the pavement on the way over. I ripped off the belt and stood up just as Haig came to a sudden stop in front of me. Had he run over me, safety experts probably would have referred to it as the second collision. At the time it was somewhat unnerving. Haig went on to finish the race in third place behind Griswold and Cunningham, and for some reason spun out after passing the finish line.

The spot officially has been known as "Milliken's Corner" ever since. Some years later I found out this amuses good friend John Fitch, who points out that despite his victories on the old circuit, and his back-to-back SCCA National Championships, no corner ever was named for him, while all I did was lose it and became immortalized. The morning after the races the Argetsingers hosted a breakfast for everyone involved at the Point near their cottage. I remember it as socially warm but physically chilly.

The old Jefferson Hotel has long since disappeared, as has the headquarters building on the corner where Cam had his office and organized the early races. But the famous Flat Iron Building still is there. The barbershop where the Bug came to rest now is the site of the most risqué bar in town!

The old circuit has survived much as it was on October 2, 1948, so one can experience how it was and relive the glamour of the early street racing. The Argetsingers now are engaged in creating the International Motor Racing Research Center in Watkins Glen. And New York State recently placed the old circuit on the list of historic places, so it will forever remain unchanged.

Fig. 18-14
New name for the corner!

Fig. 18-15
Frank Griswold's Alfa Romeo, the outright winner of the Watkins Glen Grand Prix, October 2, 1948. Griswold occupied the cabin next to ours at Seneca Lodge, and this beautiful machine was parked outside.

Fig. 18-16
George Weaver's Maserati V8R1 moving into its starting position in the field.

Fig. 18-17
The "Phantom Corsair," in the concours d'elegance, with its low-drag aerodynamic body. Owned by Rust Heinz.

Fig. 18-18
The winner, Griswold on the Alfa Romeo, about to turn onto Franklin Street.

Fig. 18-19
Years later, artist Bob Gillespie, shown here, depicts "Milliken's Corner" with this mural on the side of a building off Franklin Street.

Chapter 19

Racing Takes Off

Other circuits and other events followed the reintroduction of road racing at Watkins Glen in 1948. Within two years, seven road races and hill climbs were held, and I competed in all of them. Four of them are summarized here. This growth was accomplished amidst numerous factions, incentives and objectives. The correspondence involved in my various SCCA activities as chairman of the Competition Board, vice-president, governor for Area 11, and head of the Western New York Region, was voluminous. Florence Shanahan typed it all from Dictaphone belts during her spare moments during the workday.

Bridgehampton, June 11, 1949

Immediately upon hearing about the Bridgehampton race, Florence sent in the entry forms and my Flight Research crew began preparing the Type 35. Fenders were required in our class, so "tin knocker" Johnny Eichorn made up a very professional-looking set that we attached to the brake backing plates. We failed to reckon with the high acceleration on the stiff suspension of the Bug, however, and by the time I reached Albany on the drive to Long Island all of the fender supports had fractured. So I packed the fenders into the left-hand seat to be jury-rigged to the chassis before the race.

Compared with the classic seriousness of Watkins Glen, the Bridgehampton circuit was simple. I thoroughly enjoyed the race until I lost it at Clubhouse Corner—driver error in a big way—and wound up with the Bug's front wheels on top of the hay bales. But mine was not the only humorous moment in the event. On the backstretch at the corner leading to Humpback Bridge the organizers had installed a

Lineup for Watkins Glen, 1949. On pole, an Alfa, outside front row, Ken Hill's Flying Banana. We are in FWD Miller, second row, outside.

Personally I walked with gods for weeks after.

– S.C.H. (Sammy) Davis
(*Motor Racing*, 1932)

Fig. 19-1
Driving to the starting line at Bridgehampton, 1949. Note the front fenders jury-rigged to the frame and no longer attached to the brake backing plates.

Fig. 19-2
Bridgehampton, 1949, on the back stretch. Note the larger tires on the rear.

Fig. 19-3
Bridgehampton, 1949. Lost it on Country Club Corner. Bent steering tie rod and forced to retire.

huge pile of hay bales on the outside. An MG entrant wearing a football helmet perched high on his head wound up on top of this pile, with his rear wheels hanging out and still spinning. Surprised and not sure what to do, the driver sat there until spectators rushed out and lifted the car off the bales. He was back in the race—still wondering, I suspect, what to do next.

Bridgehampton had been a busy few days. I don't ever remember being so tired as on the drive back to Buffalo.

Watkins Glen, September 17, 1949

A new transfer case had been made for the FWD Miller by the Four Wheel Drive Company, which we installed in Buffalo. We believed the car would be pretty competitive. Pikes Peak had been a good learning experience, and there was time to check out the handling on the hard surface of our test loop at Buffalo Airfield. All we had to do was notify the tower to give us a red light when air traffic was approaching. During the testing we decided to operate with the center differential locked. I had a lot of practice coping with trailing-throttle oversteer which, although we tried various configurations, never was eliminated.

Enthusiastic about running the machine at Watkins Glen, the FWD Company sent senior design engineer Jack Fabian and a top mechanic, together with Professor Archie Easton of the University of Wisconsin. I liaisoned directly with Donald Olen, director of engineering at FWD. Bill Wilcox headed our crew, with Art Mondale, Frankie Babchek, Casey Jaworski and Len Gifford brought in for prep work.

We decided to run 6.50 × 18 tires. With an absolute limit of 6,000 rpm, 120 mph was possible and the acceleration seemed close to ideal for the Glen circuit. The FWD would run on 100-octane aviation fuel, so a 50-gallon drum was taken along. We even put an extension on the gearshift lever to make shifting easier. The FWD-Miller was entered in Class D, 122 cubic inches and up. I still was Chairman of the SCCA Technical Committee; Cam's title was General Race Chairman. As in the previous year, Alec Ulmann was Chief Steward, Nils Michelson the Starter, and Les Smalley Pit Steward. Indy great Wilbur Shaw agreed to be Honorary Starter, and the famous singer James Melton came on board as toastmaster for the Victory Banquet. Peter Helck did the cover illustration for the program as he had in '48, and I got stuck with writing a story about the first Watkins Glen race.

As before, Walt Breuhaus and crew organized the timing and scoring, with

Fig. 19-4
FWD Miller in the pits, Watkins Glen, 1949. L to R behind car: FWD mechanic, Jack Fabian (FWD engineer), Bill Wilcox, Phil Milliken, Dunstan Graham.

Fig. 19-5
Cam Argetsinger picking up the Type 35A to drive in Watkins Glen, 1949.

Longines providing the master chronometer. As the entry list expanded and competitors wanted more details (like times on each lap), this task became increasingly difficult. Walt began developing a "photo box" for 1950, financed by the SCCA, that was the first attempt to improve the accuracy of timing and scoring before electronics came into the picture.

On a handshake deal, Cam borrowed my Type 35A Bugatti to enter in Class C, and picked up the car in Buffalo a couple of weeks earlier. A few days before the event our entourage once again settled in at Smalley's Garage and Seneca Lodge. I remember two incidents before race day. First, while pondering how we were going to get the several-hundred-pound drum of aviation fuel off the high platform of the truck, a sturdy lad related to Cam stepped up and wrestled it to the ground with no other help. The other incident was a little more involved.

Cam had tried operating the Bug on various brands of pump gas. But we had raised the compression ratio, so Cam decided to drain the tank and refill it with our 100-octane fuel. Les offered a section of an old rubber-covered hose for siphoning. The transfer was going well until a sizable piece of the rubber covering fell into the tank. Cam and I exchanged glances. With the time left, removing and flushing the tank was out of the question, so we assumed the screen on the exit line to the carburetors would do the job. During the race, when I saw the Bug parked on the side of the road near the underpass, I had no illusion as to what had happened.

STARTING IN THE SECOND ROW on the outside, I got into the first turn off Franklin Street with most of the snarling pack behind and held position in second gear as we charged up Old Corning Road Hill.

Negotiating Seneca Lodge Corner on a good line, I remember the rough ride up the hill and an even rougher one down the back straight. The FWD Miller was designed for Indy, and the suspension was stiff by any standards. The backstretch under the railroad overpass was far from smooth in those days, and I was much too busy in top gear to know how fast we were going. As usual, we left the ground momentarily on the plunge down to Stone Bridge. The Miller was running fourth at the end of the first lap, and moved into 3rthurdd behind Cunningham's BuMerc and Huntoon's Alfa at the end of the second. For the next half-dozen laps I managed to hold onto fifth place while experiencing distributor malfunction, but finally had to pit. Bill Wilcox did what he could and I still was running at the finish of the fifteen laps, but way back.

Photographers from Cornell Lab had been stationed around the circuit, shooting reels of movie film that engineer Cliff Muzzey pieced together and added captions. The film remains one of the best records of the early Glen races. A great scene was caught just after Stone Bridge. As the race progressed, the dozens of hay bales on the outside of the turn gradually turned into a large pile of loose hay. One competitor drove into the hay and disappeared.

Fig. 19-6
Concentrating in FWD Miller before start of Watkins Glen, 1949.

Fig. 19-7
FWD Miller finishing at Watkins Glen, 1949. We had done well in early stages until the distributor started to fail due to the rough circuit and an overly stiff suspension.

An instant later he reappeared and rejoined the race. Later we asked him, "What was it like in there?" His answer: "It was dark as hell."

Palm Beach Shores, January 3, 1950

Some time after Watkins Glen, Alec Ulmann introduced me to Sam Scher, the well-known Park Avenue plastic surgeon. Doc Scher had a substantial collection of classic race cars and wanted to see them in competition. The first event in which I drove for him was Palm Beach Shores. This locally sponsored SCCA event was officially titled "Round the Houses Road Race of the Palm Beaches, Florida." Miles Collier was chairman of the organizing committee.

Although uncertain of what car I might drive, I applied early and was taken to task by Miles, who mildly accused me of sliding in "at half-fee without having an entry," a practice Rudi Caracciola had gotten away with for awhile in the Mille Miglia. Doc Scher decided

to run his 2.3-liter supercharged Type 51 Bugatti which, in my view, was almost ideal for the 1.98-mile circuit. Having spent so much time in the Type 35, I felt completely at home in the 51 with its greater power and performance.

While visiting the Doc at his home in Mamaroneck, we prepared a work list, since there was no time to get the car to Buffalo. We also came up with the logistics for transporting the machine to Florida. Bill Wilcox would drive my new step-down Hudson to Mamaroneck to meet Cam's mechanic, Tony Weinberg, and the two of them would trailer the machine down while the rest of us made the trip by train.

Initially, Miles Collier was concerned about having enough cars and drivers for the event, and on the 25th of November wrote me, "The situation of drivers is desperate. The Florida region has the following highly powered experienced chauffeurs, all unemployed: George S. Rand, Sam C. Collier, George G. Huntoon,

Fig. 19-8
Bill Milliken in Dr. Samuel Scher's Type 51 Bugatti in the Palm Beach Shores "Round the Houses" race, 1950.

George Roberts. [Each of the four] is assuming that he is going to drive one of Cunningham's cars, but Cunningham has already written me that he has five drivers and twelve cars (not counting any of the above). What this country needs is a few good cars without drivers, we are sure all our *good* drivers are dismounted at present."

Ultimately things got sorted out. Rand drove Cunningham's Ferrari Inter, Sam Collier a supercharged MG; Miles Collier piloted his Ford-Riley, and Briggs entered a Jaguar, a Cadillac-engined Healey Silverstone, and a Cad-Allard, according to the last listing I received. George Roberts wound up with an MG.

During practice the Doc and I had some serious discussion about the rev limit to be used in the race. Although in excellent condition, the Type 51 was a 1930s machine. According to our gear ratio chart, 5,000 rpm would give 115 mph in top, which seemed a reasonable limit to me. Scher was adamant we could go over that figure and not worry about it, because in European road races the cars had exceeded 5,000 rpm on plenty of occasions.

The circuit was a delight to drive and I felt confident that I really was racing without going over my head. From a 16th position start we had worked up to 4th by lap 21. My best lap was at 56 mph, just one mile an hour slower than the best of the faster cars. Most satisfying was staying with George Rand in the Ferrari Inter as we entered the main straight.

Around the 30th lap it began to rain, and I got into the long sweeping bend too fast. When I backed off on the throttle, the car started drifting toward the hay bales. For some reason I eased back into the throttle, which changed the path of the car to a few inches parallel to the hay bales, and we went around the corner in spectacular fashion. I couldn't have repeated it in a hundred tries, but I never forgot what a neat experience it was.

On Lap 33, running behind Rand's Ferrari, I revved up to perhaps 5,500. A terrific explosion followed and what appeared to be a ball of fire came up through the firewall and flew over my shoulder. Pulling off the course, I got out and opened the right-side hood. Nothing appeared wrong. The

419

engine still was running, so I drove on to the pits. As Doc Scher yelled "get back in the race," Bill Wilcox took a look on the left-hand side and reported a "picture window" in the block where the con rod had come out. That was the end of a great run. That night at the banquet, the Doc offered to sell me the 51, as is, for $750. Today I wonder how I could have turned him down.

That a plastic surgeon was at Palm Beach proved a lucky break for Perry Fina. Before practice, officials had forgotten to remove a wire strung across a run-off road to keep spectators from wandering onto the course. Using the run-off, Perry Fina was severely cut on his cheeks and mouth, and the Doc went to the hospital with him to minimize the damage and disfiguration. Perry was lucky on another count; had the wire been slightly higher or lower the accident could have been fatal.

Mt. Equinox Hill Climb, May 22, 1950

Mt. Equinox was a vindication of all our expectations for the FWD Miller. We won and set a record. The event was best described in my

letter to Don Olen, as transcribed in full, which also relates my hope that FWD would finance a more suitable transmission and brakes for road racing. Our success in this hill climb seemed to confirm the potential of four-wheel drive under traction-limiting conditions.

29 May 1950

Mr. Donald B. Olen
Director of Engineering
The Four Wheel Drive Auto Co.
Clintonville, Wisconsin

Subject: Resumé of Mt. Equinox Hill Climb
May 21, 1950 (the first Mt. Equinox event)

Dear Mr. Olen:

Needless to say, it is with considerable pleasure that the following report on our experiences with the FWD at Mt. Equinox is presented. The success in this hill climb would seem to culminate one phase of a mutual endeavor whose objective has been to demonstrate that the FWD Special in

Fig. 19-9
Bill Milliken on FWD Miller winning the first Mt. Equinox Hill Climb in record time, 1950. Far left, Dave Whitcomb.
Our time was 6 min., 59.4 sec. (54.2 mph average).

its present form, and without appreciable modification for hill climbing, or road racing, is still by virtue of its four-wheel drive superior to the conventional rear-drive cars. While the performance times speak for themselves, I would like to emphasize, in addition, that the basically excellent handling characteristics of the Four Wheel Drive were markedly demonstrated in the present event.

For some time the Sports Car Club of America has been attempting to obtain the use of a hill climb site in the east which would be in many respects comparable to Pikes Peak. All postwar attempts at obtaining the use of the Mt. Washington Toll Road had failed, and attention was focused on the relatively new Equinox Sky Line Drive which ascends Mt. Equinox, located at Manchester, Vermont. This venue turns out to be superior to Mt. Washington, and now is the outstanding speed hill climb site in the east. While the total distance run is about one-half of that at Pikes Peak, the *average* grade and the *maximum* grade encountered are approximately *30%* greater than that of Pikes Peak. The number of turns per mile, and types of turns, are very similar to Pikes Peak, and the road surface and road width are comparable. In general the "hill" comprises two peaks, namely Little Equinox, which is 2,720 ft. above the base, and Big Equinox, the summit, which is some 496 ft. in elevation above Little Equinox. There are two pronounced groups of switchbacks and hairpin turns, one of which occurs below the summit of Little Equinox, and the other relatively short of the summit of Big Equinox. The initial portion of the road between the two peaks runs along an exposed ridge and has a pronounced dip in it. From the driver's point of view, the most hazardous point on the course is that section just at the top of Little Equinox and down onto the ridge. The approach to the summit of Little Equinox is steep, but fast, and since the trees

stop just short of the summit, there is no way of judging the exact direction of the road as one comes up, over and down onto the exposed ridge.

Table 19-1 compares Mt. Equinox with Pikes Peak.

On the day of the climb, the weather was beautiful and the road surface was dry. No work had been done on the surface since the winter, but with the exception of the section along the ridge, it was quite smooth.

The Event—On the day preceding the hill climb, some time trials were run on a very rough backwoods road circuit of about five miles in circumference. These preliminaries gave a further opportunity for tuning the car.

The Mt. Equinox Climb was organized in the following manner: Three climbs, if desired, were permitted each entrant—the first climb being purely for practice, and was untimed. A standing start at the Toll House was used throughout, the driver being given two warning counts, and then the flag. Timing was accomplished by two-way radio between the Start and Finish. As will be noted in the summary of results, the entrants were divided into the standard SCCA categories and displacement classes. In addition, the Fastest-Time-of-the-Day, irrespective of category and class, was recognized as the record for this ascent.

As will be noted, the FWD competed in the Unrestricted Category, operating without full road equipment as required by the Sports Category. It so happened that the first three finishers in the Unrestricted Category were also all in Class C (which is defined by engine displacement limits, whether the car is supercharged or not).

It was, however, apparent from previous experience that the primary competition was to be expected from Weaver in his Grand Prix type Maserati. This machine is similar in many

Table 19-1. Comparison: Mt. Equinox, Vermont, and Pikes Peak, Colorado

	Mt. Equinox	Pikes Peak
Distance	6.25 miles (33,000 ft.)	12.42 miles (65,800 ft.)
Vertical rise, base to summit	3,216 ft.	4, 960 ft.
Gradient (average)	9.75%	7.38%
Max (steepest) gradient	14.0%	10.5%

respects to the car in which Unser currently holds the Pikes Peak record. Table 19-2 compares the FWD and the Maserati.

An examination of the table serves to show that *with the exception of drive type, the Maserati has everything in its favor, including a 50% higher power/weight ratio.* In addition the car is equipped with a single-seat body with excellent vision of the front wheels so desirable in hill climbing, and has a much more suitable transmission, brakes and suspension, for this type of work. The Maserati was designed for road racing and is newer than the FWD Special. It will be remembered that this Maserati driven by George Weaver won the Seneca Cup Race at Watkins Glen last year, and though dogged with mechanical trouble, is one of the outstanding machines in the Club.

The FWD was selected by draw as the first car to make a timed ascent. Without any previous mark to shoot for, and in an essentially conservative manner, this run was made in *7 min. 24 sec.* or an average of nearly 52 mph. This run was normal in all respects, except that with the relatively high tire pressures (25# all around) it was noted that it was possible to spin all four wheels on the softer corners, when operating in low gear. It was, however, felt that the technique used on the hairpin turns was not correct, and that the car had been allowed to drift too far to the outside. A different and more satisfactory technique was tried on the subsequent runs.

After several other cars had completed the climb, including the two Jaguars, Weaver made his ascent, and recorded a time of *7 min. 8 sec.* or some 6 sec. faster than the FWD. This was a

well-executed run and, as Weaver later described, his main problem was that of minimizing wheel spin, particularly on the hairpin turns. His statement of the rear-drive performance on the loose hairpin turns coincided exactly with our observations of the high-powered rear drives at Pike' Peak, namely that the cars lose momentum and nearly come to a stop as the wheels dig in. In this respect both the Jaguar drivers (Spear and Cunningham) and Weaver stated that it was better to operate in a higher gear (thus losing the high power associated with more RPM) and avoid wheelspin as much as possible. Incidentally, Weaver was operating with 19–20 lbs. rear tire pressure, and hence was probably achieving optimum traction. There was never any question on the Maserati of power limitation, so the increased rolling resistance of the tires at low pressure could not have been influential.

Before making our second run with the FWD, tire pressures were reduced as previously indicated, and a new set of tires installed on the rear wheels. Since this run did not take place till some time after the one described, it was necessary to carefully warm up the engine before proceeding to the starting line.

With the four-wheel drive and the FWD's power there is very little problem in making a clean getaway from a standing start. On this final run it was decided to take full advantage of everything the four-wheel drive has to offer, and the engine was revved up to about 5,000 RPM before letting the clutch out; as the clutch was engaged, the throttle was pushed hard down, and for an instant there was momentary wheel spin after which the machine literally

Table 19-2. Comparison of FWD Miller and Maserati

Item	FWD Miller	Maserati
Weight, lbs.	2,817	1,950
Maximum BHP	225	255
Ratio: lbs./BHP	11.7	7.7
Ratio: BHP/ton	172	260
Body Type	2 seater	1 seater
Transmission	3-speed (crash type)	4-speed (synchromesh)
Brakes	cable	hydraulic
Suspension	Stiff, de Dion	Soft, independent
Drive type	Four wheel	Two wheel (rear)

"took off." Wilcox, who was standing aft of the machine, described the start as spectacular in the extreme, and further noted *that the machine accelerated in a perfectly straight line with no apparent fish-tailing.* The rev limit in low gear was reached very shortly and the car was shifted into second before the first turn, through which it continued to accelerate. Because of the lower tire pressures, and also because of the lower pressure in the rear tires in relation to the front, the car did not have as nice a feel as during the first run. Nevertheless, it was perfectly controllable and the traction was improved.

The technique used on the hairpins on this run—an improvement over that of the preceding run—was as follows: The car was brought into the turn well on the outside and then rather sharply cut directly across the inside of the apex of the turn in an almost straight line, and thence to the outside of the road at the exit from the turn. It had the disadvantage of going through the middle of the loose dirt on the inside of the turn, but had the great advantage that there was never any question of sliding off the outside or having to decelerate in the middle of the corner. The impression was gained that the car was either accelerating slightly or maintaining a constant speed on all corners.

One especially bad slide was experienced when the car was brought into the sharp corner preceeding the first set of switchbacks. The approach to the corner had been made much too fast, and heavy braking was resorted to, which with the left rear locking up, threw the car into an incipient spin. A substantial burst of power straightened the machine out. (On a rear drive it would have been necessary to remove power, and hence lose time.)

Anticipating the fast stretch along the ridge, the summit of Little Equinox was approached in high gear at 70-odd miles per hour. Needless to say, the sensation of coming up over this rise and out onto the ridge with nothing but blue sky ahead is one that will not soon be forgotten! Along the ridge the speed was limited entirely by the characteristics of the suspension. This ridge is the roughest section of the course and with the FWD's suspension, the driving problem reduced itself to maintaining the car within the boundaries of the road.

Before reaching the last set of switchbacks and hairpins, a shift to second gear was made, and as on all down-shifts, double clutching was used. On this occasion, the moment the lever was placed in second position a terrific chatter set up and the car did not appear to respond to the throttle. It was apparent that something drastic had happened to the second gear, and that it was probably stripped. The writer had no impression of encountering any difficulty in throwing the lever into second, or any impression that the box was being maltreated; however, it is entirely possible that the fault may lie with the driver. The lever was immediately placed in third gear and an attempt made to accelerate. The lever was then placed in first gear and the remainder of the climb made in this ratio. Fortunately, because of the hairpins and the relatively sort distance beyond them to the top, this was not too adverse a handicap, but it is believed that it must have lost us several seconds. In the final run to the finish line, the engine RPM momentarily hit 6,800, which is a speed of some 65 mph. This calculates to a piston speed of about 5,000 ft./min. which is extremely high for even a short burst. If the engine power curve continued linearly, this RPM would represent a BHP output of some 260.

To complete the story of the climb it should be mentioned that the safety belt had become unfastened just over the summit of Little Equinox and whenever second gear was used (on all climbs) it was necessary to hold the lever in place with one hand, which means that at least one-half of each climb was made with only one hand on the wheel.

Table 19-3 presents the Mt. Equinox Hill Climb results. Handicapped though it may be, the FWD has fairly beaten the rear drives under circumstances where everything was in their favor.

If any further evidence of the superiority of this drive type is needed, a comparison between the FWD's performance at Mt. Equinox with other famous hill climb records is in order. The four climbs which have been prominent in this country at different times are: Pikes Peak, Mt. Washington, Grand Junction, and now Mt. Equinox. A summary of these climbs is given in Table 19-4.

Table 19-3. Final Results

Driver	Car	SCCA Category	Eng. Class*	Superchd.	Time Min:Sec.	Remarks
Milliken	FWD	Unrestr.	C	No	6:59.4	Record, irrespective of class
Weaver	Maserati	Unrestr.	C	Yes	7:08	
Pfund	FordSpl.	Unrestr.	C	No	10:04	
Spear	Jaguar XK-120	Sports	C	No	7:53	Class winner, larger sports cars
Cunningham	Jaguar XK-120	Sports	C	No	7:53.3	

Class C is 3.0 to 5.0 liters displacement, unsupercharged or 2.0 to 3.0 liters displacement, supercharged

Table 19-4. Comparative Record Averages in Prominent American Speed Hill Climbs

(Unlimited Class; standing start unless otherwise noted.)

Venue	Avg. Speed	Distance	Car
Pikes Peak	48.3 mph*	12.42 miles	8CTL Maserati
Mt. Washington	29.1 mph	8.0 miles	Ford Special, Old Gray Mare
Mt. Equinox	54.2 mph	6.25 miles	FWD Special

Grand Junction—Known to be lower average than Pikes Peak; no other data.
*Flying start permitted

It will be seen that the average achieved on Mt. Equinox is the highest yet attained in a prominent American speed hill climb. It is also interesting to note that the speed is comparable to those obtained in very short speed hill climbs held in Great Britain. The present record for the 0.75-mile Shelsley Walsh, which has only one moderate S-turn and a couple of gentle bends, is approximately 53.0 mph, while at Craigantlet, Raymond Mays's record average is 49.2 mph. While none of these records are strictly comparable, the figures show that the FWD put up an outstanding show by any standards.

Sincerely,

W. F. Milliken, Jr.

Fig. 19-10
The start at Bridgehampton, 1949. Type 35A Bugatti.

Fig. 19-11
Bridgehampton, 1949. Entering the back straight.

Fig. 19-12
Braking for the corner at the "Bridge," 1949. Type 35A Bugatti.

Fig. 19-13
Bridgehampton, 1949. Entering the main straight, having passed Humpback Bridge.

Fig. 19-14
Start-Finish line before start of Watkins Glen, 1949. To the left (behind the banner) is the Timing and Scoring Group from CAL Flight Research under Walt Breuhaus. At the line are Nils Mickelson (chief starter) talking to James Melton (banquet speaker) and Wilbur Shaw from Indianapolis. On right in white shirt is Charles Lytle.

Fig. 19-15
Cam Argetsinger picking up the Type 35A to drive in Watkins Glen, 1949, with crew that prepared the car. L-R: Dave Whitcomb, Art Mandale, Cam, Frankie Babchek, WFM, and welder from Lab 1.

Chapter 20

The Big Bug at the Bridge

This chapter was edited from an article written in the fall of 1950 and published in the December 1981 issue of Road & Track.

by Bill Milliken

The day of the Bugatti as a competitive road racing car is long gone. In all probability the Type 54 "Big Bug" will remain one of the last of these famous machines to make a really competitive bid in a major (non-historic) road racing event in this country.

This is the story of the 1950 Bridgehampton race, the first of three events in which I drove the Type 54 Bug for Sam Scher. The other two were the Watkins Glen Grand Prix in 1950 and the Giant's Despair Hill Climb in 1951.

The Doc had approached me early in 1950 with the offer: "Bill, would you like to drive my Type 54 at Bridgehampton? She's reputed to be Varzi's car and boy, is she terrific." I knew about its short and mysterious racing career, her reputation as a killer, her fabulous win at Avus at 128 mph, the unexplained, nose-heavy tendency when she aviated on rough circuits, and the elusive rumor that nobody ever had mastered her. When I quizzed René Dreyfus about the car, he replied, "Yes, she was different from other Bugattis, with that big, slow-turning engine and difficult handling . . ."

The Big Bug never won a road race in this country, at least not in the conventional sense. But those who knew her those many months may think differently. Like a great tired old race horse matching skills with a younger generation, she could give unexpected bursts, putting her into second or even first, pushing the leaders, forcing the pace and shaking off the dust of the decade when she literally was buried underground during the occupation of France. She conceded nothing and demanded the respect of all who knew her.

Bridgehampton: Turning onto the back straight.

The Type 54 gained very quickly the reputation, justified, of being delicate to handle and frankly unstable.

– Pierre Dumont, 1975
Thorougbreds from Molsheim

After the Doc bought her, the Big Bug was dropped some 40 feet onto the dock during the loading process at Le Havre, an inauspicious beginning. The cracked wheel, bent front axle and other damage were handled at Plisson's restoration shop in St. Cloud. Two new wheels with drums were ordered directly from Molsheim and instructions given to install full road equipment while the repairs were being made.

Days ran into months. The blizzards had begun to wane in Buffalo and spring could not be far behind. An inquiry about progress brought this reply from France: "The road equipment is fabricated, the front axle straightened but the wheels are not in and the car will be shipped *Queen Mary* as is." Remarks included a description of "a new paint job, the authentic Bugatti blue, a huge mahogany-covered steering wheel, and an engine so large, really huge."

Our plan was to truck the Bug to Buffalo to survey the repairs, check everything thoroughly, familiarize ourselves with her handling on the airport circuit and do a tune-up. We clung to this hope until the fortnight before race day. During the waiting period, I had reviewed the Bug's specifications: 86 by 107 mm bore/stroke ratio, 4,840 cc displacement, nine engine bearings, magneto ignition and twin Zenith carburetors. Dimensions were 274.3 cm wheelbase, 124.5 cm track, 965 kg weight, 13×74 cm tires. The rear axle ratio was 45/13 or 3.46:1; first gear 8.60:1, second gear 4.80:1, third gear 3.46:1 (direct). Further sources told me the Type 54 was supercharged, the gearbox was integral with the rear end, upward of 300 bhp could be expected from the engine and the top speed was more than 145 mph.

On May 26 the car arrived. A week later it still was in customs. Apparently the accident at Le Havre had muddled formalities and papers were lacking. Monumental struggles in road racing can occur long before the starting flag is dropped. Omitted from the record are battles with people who are but remotely interested in the race, and yet may be the most influential in its outcome. While no fan of motor racing, Sam Scher's wife was a lawyer with years of brilliant practice, and she assumed a key position in our fortunes. Customs officials used to the red tape of regulations soon found themselves spinning in their own web as it was deftly unwound, and in just two more days the Bug was cleared.

All thought of work in Buffalo was abandoned, and a new plan based on expediency was formulated. The following Tuesday I flew to New York and the car was taken to mechanic Dick Simonak in Paterson, New Jersey. Early the next morning the Doc and I arrived there, and we all agreed Dick should do what he could in the next thirty-odd hours, at which time our regular crew would get the machine to Bridgehampton for inspection and practice on Friday. This gave us a couple of days in New Jersey to learn the mechanical intricacies of the Type 54.

On examining my notes, I am surprised we were not more amazed at what we found. Across the page summarizing anticipated gear ratios and speeds is a note in red: "This doesn't hold for Scher's Bug." Instead of a rear-end ratio of 3.46:1, we discovered the fantastically high ratio of 42/16 or 2.63. The gearbox was not integral with the rear axle but more conventionally located just aft of the clutch, the latter dry and not wet as we might well have expected. Nor were the box ratios similar to our published material.

The gearbox itself was an aluminum casting integral with a webbed cross-bracing member that was bolted rigidly to the frame (which was an exceptionally deep channel at this point). Torsional loading on the chassis by a large up-load on one wheel would subject the gearbox-cum-crossmember to combined stresses in the thin wall sections at the front and rear faces. (Such a loading could have occurred when the car was dropped, since only one wheel had been damaged.) Particular attention was directed to the gearbox, and a crack was found at the top of the rear face extending halfway down to the driveshaft bearing housing. Drilling a hole to stop further development of the crack would have caused leakage, but welding would require a major disassembly. Nothing could be done. Still, optimism prevailed and we agreed that if no further crack growth could be detected after practice we would go ahead.

We now were confronted with overall ratios of 4.90:1, 3.60:1 and 2.63:1 giving 18.9

Fig. 20-1
Bridgehampton at the start: Dave Whitcomb standing left. Bill Rouzer holding carburetor jets (floats) down because we are using gasoline instead of alcohol.

mph at 1,000 rpm in first gear, 25.6 in second and 35.2 in third. If you don't think these are high, imagine yourself rolling along at 90 mph with the engine ticking over at 2500 rpm, or consider the problem of rounding Country Club Corner in the mad scramble after the start with the car in low and the engine running at 500 rpm, which as it turned out was below idle.

Of interest also was the compression ratio, since the race regulations required a pump fuel. Several checks revealed the delightfully low value of 5.3:1. Although we had no knowledge of the manifold pressure on the output side of the supercharger, we assumed (and subsequently confirmed) that we were safe, especially when running rich. The latter was easily accomplished (in fact, inevitable) as the twin Zenith carburetors had fixed alcohol jets of about twice the size of corresponding gasoline types. We left the original jets intact, put up with the black smoke and roughness of low speeds, and found that the car cleaned out admirably at racing speeds. Our worries

about fouling at the start were eliminated with the suggestion that the pins on top of the carburetor bowls be held down until the last minute, thus lowering the float level and leaning out the mixture. The new wheel did not arrive, but the damaged wheel proved usable. One had to look carefully to find the bent flange, and the crack, which had been stopped, was in an inconsequential position.

As Thursday evening approached, the Big Bug seemed in good shape for the job ahead. We spent no time looking backward as we hitched up its tow rope to the Hudson and headed through the Lincoln Tunnel across Manhattan to Long Island during rush hour. "You can't drive that car through this city with nothing but a beat-up international license plate," a cop roared at me as we waited for a light at Third Avenue. Before I could point out the tow rope to him, I heard the policeman in the intersection make a disparaging remark about how gingerly the Hudson was getting away, and the Bug slid majestically by the infuriated cop.

Fig. 20-2
Bridgehampton: In the pits before start of race. On front, Bill Rouzer, behind him left are Dr. Sam Scher and wife (in broad-rimmed hat). Far left: Walt and Sally Breuhaus, who were timer and scorer.

By the time we reached Bridgehampton we were tired, hungry and happy. Cutting the Bug loose on the Island, she had demonstrated her prowess in no uncertain fashion. Tearing along the deserted roads, the way lighted by the dim yellowish glow of French headlights and a nearly full moon, was indescribably delightful. In some respects the Type 54 is like a scaled-up Type 51. Pushing the accelerator down from 40 mph in top gives a momentary delay as the blower winds up, which is followed by a great sense of acceleration and much engine and transmission noise. This reaches a peak in the high 70s. At which point all gives way to a moderately pitched shriek, a disappearance of incidental vibration and an unsurpassed sensation of speed. At the century mark there seemed to be power to spare, and any sensation that the power plant was a reciprocating machine was replaced by one of "solid iron."

A white house about two centuries old on Sagaponack Road, which formed the back leg of the Bridgehampton circuit, was our headquarters on all visits to Bridgehampton. An enormous oak stood at the entrance to the narrow gravel driveway leading to the stable that housed the car and provided storage for the equipment and a place to do our work. The day preceding the race brought inspection, practice, chasing down needed items and hasty, unsatisfying renewals of acquaintances. Traffic was frightful, and the delays in clearing the course for practice monumental.

A set of outdoor hay scales two houses down placed the Type 54's center of gravity at 63 percent of the wheelbase back from the front axle, which upset the rumor that the machine was nose-heavy, at least in a static sense. On the contrary, the location was comparable to the 60–65 percent of load on the rear wheels of other high-powered machines of its era. Still, in practice the car did exhibit an undeniable nose-heaviness, a phenomenon we would not understand for many months. Worse behavior could have been exhibited had the friction shocks on the front been operative, but they were locked solid, a fact we would discover later.

The Big Bug hardly was a car of just one vice. Toward the end of practice, when I was enjoying her sparkling performance, light steering forces at speed and the typical Bugatti brakes that absolutely never fade, I was taking the 90-degree turn onto the main straight. With the rear end drifting comfortably out under power, reasonable control forces and a feeling of security, I was unprepared when the car suddenly and violently let go. The wheel was jerked completely out of my hands and the tail swung around, with the nose stopping as rapidly as it had begun at about 90 degrees off-course. Silence. I had been completely unhorsed. Other cars I have driven would have required 360 degrees of spin to have achieved such a resounding victory. Technically, this behavior, like nose-heaviness, can be traced to the distribution of masses and spring stiffness that produce unconventional dynamic effects while giving normal static balance. The large and sudden increase in vehicle slip angle had resulted in a reversal in steering torque.

"TIME TO GET UP" was the call on race day morning, and a roar from the vicinity of the stable told me our crew was working on the carburetion. Half awake, I chuckled about the towing process necessary to start the Big Bug. You don't just crank a Type 54—at least no one I ever knew was willing to tackle it. Granted, there is a crank impossibly located behind a crossbar and nearly colliding with the front axle, but it might have been one of Ettore Bugatti's mechanical jests.

As I dressed I kept listening to the machine. To a firm believer it is more thrilling to awake to the sound of a Bugatti than to die to the note of a Bentley. I listened carefully to each blurp, wondering what gave rise to such a distinctive and satisfying noise. Analytically speaking, the gnashing din issuing from a Bugatti power plant must be traceable to combustion chamber shape, inlet and exhaust pipes and passages, the supercharger drive, the straight-cut gears and other details of the ensemble, but how does one contrive to get the same orchestration in a variety of different keys? The Big Bug was a slowed-down, bass version of the treble 35. A more fundamental composition of elemental mechanical sounds is hard to imagine.

Fig. 20-3
Turning out of the tree-lined chute leading to the main straight.

Fig. 20-4
The fast bend on the first leg of the circuit.

Like no other course in this country, Bridgehampton provides a light, stylish holiday atmosphere. A small and simple circuit, it's pure fun compared with the classic seriousness of Watkins. There always are several events, and none of them stands out as the heavy feature. If you have an eye for something besides automobiles you will see attractive women, beautifully dressed, congregating near the country club, and even the men's costumes reflect the good weather that always prevails. It's a Continental atmosphere, a bit of a lark, and a Bugatti must feel at ease here.

Arriving at the starting line, people appeared from nowhere to push the Bug, with its water temperature climbing, to its position in the third row. Tired is the foot that holds in a Bugatti clutch pedal for long, so it was a minor relief when we were off. The start was noisy and jammed and very slow. I accelerated past a couple of slower cars but was well bottled in by the first turn.

Driving the original Cadillac-Allard, Tommy Cole was the man in this race. From a starting position in the second row, he was out in front—way out—by the second lap, and his lead would increase to half a lap over the number two car by the finish. I never saw the Allard until Tommy gave me an opportunity to drive her the next day. Private battles were waged farther back in the field, however.

For the first three laps, the Big Bug held a comfortable fifth. The car was a handful, especially on the wavy back stretch that exaggerated the oversteer. She followed the camber with disconcerting exactitude. I tried the bridge at a good 70—once. The sensation was that of cartwheeling over the front axle. She crashed heavily on the front wheels, swerved, came back under control and was braked heavily for the bend and the sharp turn that followed. Seventy was unsafe for the bridge.

The gearbox also was proving rough. Conceivably, an experienced professional could have clicked up and down through the gears without a miss, and maybe without even using the clutch. But I couldn't. The three speeds, with abnormally spaced second and top, made consistently good downshifting impossible.

But the car still was running well, and on the fourth lap, at 80 mph, I moved into third. From the pits, the signal "hold" was replaced by "faster." An inveterate enthusiast, the Doc wanted nothing less than the limit. When the Bug squeezed by a Meyer on the main stretch and took second behind the fleeing Cole, his cup was full.

From the cockpit, the time seemed interminable for the radiator of the Meyer to slide backward behind our scuttle, and I was past my cutoff point. With no time for shifting down, and with all the force I could muster

Fig. 20-5
Cornering.

in my leg, I hit the brakes. Oh, those lovely brakes. Like an animal with four legs extended, crouched and sure, the Big Bug came down to the low 30s around Club Corner with only a trace of tail slide. Back up to speed, I headed for the fast right-hander that was one of the finest on the circuit. A very slight downgrade on the approach and a clear view across the corner itself, with moderately favorable camber on the inside, combine to whet the appetite of contestant and spectator alike. At that exact moment, crouching low on the inside exit, Cam Argetsinger panned a shot of the Bug coming through in nosed-in attitude. The photo gave the impression the car was drifting slightly (bear in mind that the development of slip angle at the rear tires affects attitude of the car). To this day, the photo brings back an assortment of emotions, for it was on this lap that the last of the oil drained out through the crack in the transmission case. Heat, pressure and distortion took over, and it became impossible to shift out of second. The Big Bug froze solid, and I rolled to a stop. "What would you ask of

me when you drop me 40 feet at Le Havre," she murmured in her last and most appealing speech of the day.

WITH ME AT BRIDGEHAMPTON was Barbara Roesch, whom I met early in 1950 in Buffalo when she visited her sister Arline, the wife of CAL project engineer Dunstan Graham. Barbara lived in Long Island and worked as secretary to an account executive at Compton Advertising. Over the next couple of years we continued to meet there, and were married in 1953 in Forest Hills. After acquiring five acres of an old orchard that was a 15-minute drive from CAL we commissioned my brother Cooper to design a house. He was to introduce us to modern architecture, especially Frank Lloyd Wright's work, which we visited between Buffalo and Chicago as well as Taliesin East in Wisconsin. The modern house Cooper designed for us remains our home and base of operation. Our first son Douglas arrived in 1954, Peter in 1960 and our daughter Ann in 1963. Marrying Barbara was the best decision I ever made.

Chapter 21

Dynaflow Epic

> "I reckon that as a racer one should go for it, as fast as possible . . . I like to have a dice, a real old tear-up . . . to me that's the name of the game."
>
> – Stirling Moss
> (*My Cars, My Career,* with Doug Nye, 1987)

A s Philippe Defechereux points out in his history of the early years of Watkins Glen, 1950 was "the year of the Big Bang" in American road racing, a theme also expressed earlier in an article by Brock Yates entitled "The Last of the Gentlemen Drivers."

I sensed it was a watershed year. Those of us who had been drawn to the sport by its romantic, adventurous aspects, and had raced as amateurs, were being overtaken by those with more professional and international interests driving more modern machinery. The stage was set for "The Great Controversy."

The main race of the SCCA's 1950 "International Sports Car Grand Prix of Watkins Glen, N.Y." was organized under "general AAA sanction in conformity with FIA (Fédération Internationale de l'Automobile) regulations." A competition license and insurance from AAA (the American representative of FIA) was required, this being seen as an initial step toward a fully FIA-sanctioned race. Cam was general race chairman, and Alec Ulmann chief steward. As chairman of the SCCA Contest Board, I wrote an article for the program about the Sports and Unrestricted categories, explaining the reason for the latter and pointing out that "to encourage foreign amateur competition in our events and parallel competition by our members in the great foreign classics," the definition of the former had been made to conform to that of the FIA.

The day after Bridgehampton 1950, Tommy Cole had given me the chance to take a couple of laps in his Cadillac Allard. Convinced that this was a car that could win races, I suggested to the Doc that he acquire one, but he turned me down. In a sense I agreed with him. Although each of us wanted to win races, we both had fallen under the spell of the Type 54. The urge to have another go with it was irresistible. So the Big Bug was brought to Buffalo, with instructions

Start of 1950 Watkins Glen Grand Prix. Behind are (L to R) Bruce Stevenson, Meyer Special, and Fred Wacker, Cad-Allard.

from Doc Scher to find a suitable transmission for the Glen. Entering the Type 54 in the 1950 main event also implied a considerable effort to ensure it met the FIA Sports Category requirements.

Since the main event was to be run under international sanction, Cam felt that it should be open to other than SCCA members. SCCA President Cam Peck led a faction of the SCCA that considered it to be a closed "gentlemen's" organization. He tried unsuccessfully to pressure Cam Argetsinger to confine the event to SCCA members only. Cam Argetsinger invited the New York Motorsports Club of America to submit three entries who had appropriate international credentials, as well as three MG Car Club members. Tough qualification standards were imposed on these non-SCCA members: A high finish in the Seneca Cup race earned a back-grid starting spot for the Grand Prix.

The NYMSCA proposed Erwin Goldschmidt, Bob Grier and Larry Kulok.

Fig. 21-1
Stripped-down chassis of Type 54 Bug. Note bulkhead at rear of engine to which the Dynaflow was attached. The FIA sports car regulations required a spare wheel, which we mounted under the tail of the car.

Goldschmidt had a rough manner which put off some people. I had met him over breakfast at Bridgehampton, where he shared with me some excellent advice on tires. In that race, I gained great respect for his driving ability and sportsmanship. Hearing of Goldschmidt and Grier's potential participation, I heartily approved of Cam's decision to invite non-SCCA members to race.

First Installation of Torque Converter in a Race Car

When the Big Bug arrived in Buffalo on June 22 we began a complete teardown of the chassis and engine, and tried to locate an appropriate gearbox. We assumed the Bugatti's power plant developed an honest 300 brake horsepower and a max torque of approximately 400 lb. ft. With little experience in overstressing standard transmissions of Ford, Mercury, Cadillac, etc., we dismissed them as possibilities. Instead, our thoughts turned to foreign boxes such as Wilson, Cotal, Alvis and even an ex-Maserati. Later we searched for something of appropriate size from suppliers to the American truck market like Spicer, Warner, Allison and Twin Coach. The Doc had already assured us there was no hope of acquiring a replacement from the Bugatti factory. Thus we lived, without progress, in a world of synchromesh, critical shaft sizes, epicyclics and overdrives.

One noon on his way to lunch, our administrative assistant Dave Loughborough stopped by the office and suggested I try out his new Buick Century with Dynaflow, the hydraulic torque converter transmission introduced in 1948 by Buick. Initially I didn't think of the Bugatti, I just took the opportunity to experience a new type of drive. But comparing its acceleration with that of my manual-shift Hudson changed my mind. A longitudinal accelerometer mounted in each car showed the significant time lost in manual shifting. If the overall ratio was appropriate, the "Lo" range might be useful as a retarder, supplementing the brakes. Aware that the efficiency of a hydraulic drive was less than a direct mechanical one, we thought this might not be critical in a high-powered machine, and decided to take a serious look at the Dynaflow as a replacement for the defunct Bugatti box.

On July 13 the calendar pad stared at me as I nervously tapped the desktop waiting for the operator to complete the call. "This is Charles Chayne speaking, Buick Motor Division," the voice said. After introducing myself I told him about the Type 54 Bugatti, with which I suspected he was familiar, and asked if the Dynaflow could be adapted to this car. When I commented that its engine put out 300 hp and perhaps 400 lb.ft of torque, Chayne came back clearly, "I'm familiar with this machine but I don't think it runs that high on power or torque." We discussed at length the possibility of a modified Dynaflow installation. Chayne seemed enthusiastic: "Let me talk it over with my transmission boys and I'll call you back."

Later that day he phoned to say the installation definitely was a possibility. The combination of the relatively low rpm of the 54's engine, and a comparison of the weight and rear-end ratios of the Bugatti and the Buick, added plausibility. He had his own estimates of the actual power and torque we could expect from the Type 54: max power of 200 bhp at 4,000 rpm with 263 lb.ft torque, and 171 bhp at 3,000 rpm with 300 lb.ft torque. He said he would send a set of prints and a mockup converter.

This was action. I knew of Chayne's interests in Bugattis and had seen his Royale in the Ford Museum in Dearborn. A few days went by before the mockup unit arrived but the prints, which were numerous and complicated, came overnight. Bill Wilcox and I studied them after work, wondering how an installation could be made. "It's apparent

the Dynaflow is a unit installation with the Buick power plant, thus eliminating a front bearing," Bill said. "It looks to me like a tough alignment problem." Wilcox looked up from the assembly drawing as Cliff Muzzey, hat in hand, stopped by on his way home. Cliff's interest in mechanics, which I never had realized before, became apparent in the next hour. He had been working in Flight Research as a project engineer from MIT, and was versed in instrumentation and aerodynamics. As the two of them became absorbed in the drawings I started taking notes, jotting down questions and comments for further discussion with Buick engineering.

When Muzzey returned the next morning with the handful of prints he had taken home, things began to look up for our Watkins Glen entry. At lunch Cliff gave us a clear explanation of how the Dynaflow worked, and preliminary ideas on its installation. There was never any official agreement that he was "chief engineer" in charge of the torque converter installation, it just became obvious. Muzzey worked well with Wilcox, and the two of them should receive the major credit for the success of the project.

Our next long conversation was with a staff engineer named Coughtry in GM's

Fig. 21-2
This shows the bulkhead in more detail. It is a substantial plate attached to both the engine crankcase and the frame rails.

Transmission Division, whom we peppered with questions:

- We can see our way clear on installing the unit as far as size and weight go, but we have concerns about a suitable mounting. How much flexibility is introduced by the plate that carries the ring gear?
- Is that flexibility intentional, and how much angularity between the crankshaft and the converter will this plate permit?
- You mentioned a rag joint, but won't this require another bearing?
- Why can't we tie the unit down tight?
- We don't plan to use the Buick starter, so we need a bell housing with the starter bump removed.
- About the cooling: our radiator runs about 190°F and is pressurized. How does the converter cooling system work and what are the critical conditions?
- Regarding the rear-end situation: we plan to use your universal and adapt your Buick driveshaft. The Bug, you know, has a design for handling the rear axle

reactions. Please reiterate the structural limitations of the unit, torque and rpm limits and what "lets go" first.
- Could you provide a speedometer drive gear set that would work with our final drive ratio of 2.625 and 19 × 650 tires? If you can get close we can calibrate out the remaining errors. We need more info on the oil pumps.

I left Cliff on the phone to argue out the finer points of the installation, and went back to our overall schedule.

My initial schedule for the Bug was dated June 26, which gave us 89 days to the Watkins Glen Grand Prix. Seventeen days had been irretrievably lost before our first conversation with Chayne, and another week went by before we were committed to engineering the Dynaflow installation. The actual order for the Dynaflow and associated components was placed on August 11.

Dismantling had begun immediately upon the Bug's arrival. With no time to do a proper inspection before its first race at Bridgehampton, the detailed condition of the engine and chassis

Fig. 21-3
The rear suspension of the Type 54 remained standard, but the driveshaft for the Dynaflow replaced that of the Bugatti.

was still largely unknown. The work list at this point included removal of the front axle and spring assembly, to be followed by Magnafluxing the axle, spindles, steering arms, tie rods, king pins, etc. Houdaille would supply hydraulic shocks to replace the Bugatti's, which had galled and locked the axle solid (we had run Bridgehampton with no spring movement at all). A new steering arm had to be fabricated for a slower ratio. The radiator required reworking to accommodate installation of an aircraft starter on the nose of the crankshaft. All traces of castor oil were removed and replaced with mineral oil during the teardown.

THE FIA's SPORTS CATEGORY required a starter, a spare wheel, a regulation door and the widening of the body to 33 inches. We were not satisfied with the electrical wiring, and the fuel system needed new lines, filters and a standby pump in the form of an electrical booster. The starter required a substantial battery, and rearrangement of pedals, brackets and seat was necessary to accommodate the Dynaflow transmission. Growing daily, the final work list is shown below.

During engine disassembly we found fatigue cracks in the con rods. They had been roughly machined, and definitely were

---

Bugatti Type 54 Race Preparations

1. Complete disassembly of car. Strip chassis, remove engine, axles and all steering components.
2. Magnaflux front axle and all steering parts.
3. Fabricate new steering arm.
4. Acquire and install Houdaille shocks.
5. Free up sleeve on front axle and fabricate new sleeve with Alemite [grease] fittings.
6. Install Fairchild aircraft starter on nose of crankshaft, and modify radiator to suit.
7. Design and fabricate mount for spare wheel under tail of car.
8. Install a regulation door and widen body to 33 inches (regulations).
9. Redo all electrical wiring.
10. Install 24-volt battery.
11. Install electrical fuel boost pump (standby pump).
12. Install all new fuel lines, filters, etc.
13. Tear down engine. Replace castor oil with mineral oil.
    a. Locate and replace con rods from Erie Richardson after stress calculation and rework.
    b. Reassemble engine.
14. Engineer Dynaflow installation, including bulkhead at engine, forward arms to support bulkhead, cross-chassis support, crankshaft to Dynaflow shaft alignment, drive shaft mods to joints, accessories including oil coolers, assemble Dynaflow and engine.
15. Calculate Dynaflow performance.
16. Design and fabricate Lo-Hi range Dynaflow lever.
17. Install speedometer and tachometer.
18. Fabricate and install new underpan.
19. Modify brake pedal.
20. Modify seat and seat belt installation.
21. Install new tires, balance all wheels (incl. spares).
22. Paint car (including numbers).
23. Weight and balance calculations and final weighing.
24. Tests on chassis dynamometer.
25. N.Y. State registration (for driving on road).
26. Progress photographs.
27. Design and install parallelogram mechanism to eliminate brake tramp that occurred on test
28. Complete all paperwork, including correspondence with General Motors, Doc Scher, and race organizers.

Name	Hours Charged	Work Description
Wilcox Chief Mechanic	83.0	Powerplant, Dynaflow installation, general supervision, tuning, etc.
Muzzey Chief Engineer	35.0	All engineering for Dynaflow installation including performance estimates and dynamometer tests. Also, axle tramp mechanism.
Mandale Mechanic	63.0	Powerplant, Dynaflow installation, torsional damper
Babcheck Mechanic	50.0	Miscellaneous mechanical work, mostly on front axle
Rouzer Mechanic	38.0	Starter installation, shock absorber and radiator mods
Grass Machinist	44.0	Machine work on Dynaflow mounting plates and coupling
Sonnen Sheet Metal	20.0	All body work--door, spare wheel, mount, etc.
Oddo Painter	8.0	All finishing and painting
Seckel Engineer	5.0	Analysis of shock settings and other calculations
Strosewiski Welder	3.0	Miscellaneous welding
	349.0	Total hours not including those of WFM

Fig. 21-4
Summary of labor of Dynaflow installation. This work was done "after-hours," and I paid for it at an agreed rate.

not Bugatti quality. We never did find an explanation for this. Cam Peck, I believe, got the word around, and we received a phone call from Major Erie Richardson of San Mateo, California, who offered his set of Type 50 con rods that we could later return (or pay for another set that he would order from Molsheim). The offer indicated the interest among Bugatti enthusiasts in seeing the Big Bug run at the Glen. We took him up on it.

As the photos and sketches show, the Muzzey-designed installation of the Dynaflow was unique and successful. A large bulkhead was attached to the rear of the engine and to the two chassis side rails. Since the front end of the Dynaflow was attached to it, the bulkhead was stiffened by triangular girders built up of aluminum plates and angles that ran forward to the front engine mounts. It could deflect a bit to accommodate any slight misalignment of the engine crankshaft and the shaft in the Dynaflow. To carry the weight at the rear, a substantial cross-member was attached to the frame rails. With no forward bearing,

Fig. 21-5
Showing the installation of an aircraft engine (Fairchild) starter to the forward end of the Bugatti crankshaft.

the Dynaflow unit relied on the rear bearing of the engine crankshaft. We shortened the Buick driveshaft to suit. A lot of measurement and jigging was required to closely align the Dynaflow shaft and engine crankshaft.

The major problem of cooling the Dynaflow unit was resolved with help from General Motors and Harrison, who made the two cooling units. To accomplish this work we had to build up our team. Doc Scher agreed to pay for this labor at the rate of two dollars an hour, but most of the crew put in more hours than charged.

Dynaflow Performance

Predicting the Big Bug's performance with Dynaflow was among the most interesting aspects of the project. Basically this consisted of estimating the *thrust available* and the *thrust required* over the speed range. Muzzey calculated the former at full throttle using Chayne's estimate of 200 bhp at 4,000 rpm with a peak torque of 300 lb.ft at 3,000 rpm, and the characteristics of the converter. The final drive ratio was 2.625, and the rear tires were 19 × 6.50, i.e., a rolling radius of 1.3 ft. The calculation was performed in the high or drive range of the converter.

Using an aerodynamic drag coefficient (C_d) of 0.76 and a frontal area (A) of 14.2 ft.^{2}, plus an estimate of the rolling resistance, I estimated the thrust required. Our dynamometer tests indicated these figures were too high, and the adjusted values were C_d = 0.70 and A = 12.27, I also calculated the thrust required for a four degree hill. The curves are shown on Figure 21-10.

Fig. 21-6
View of cockpit of Type 54 with the Dynaflow installation. Note the "low-high reverse" shift level attached to the Dynaflow. To get into reverse one had to pull up the pin on the side of lever. In addition to the large standard tachometer (right), we installed a speedometer (upper left). The left-foot brake pedal (high-standing) was required because of space limitation with Dynaflow installed. The typical Bugatti throttle pedal with ball bearing is to right of brake pedal. I always wore narrow shoes when driving this car.

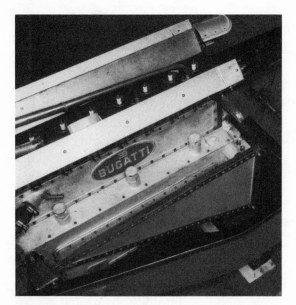

Fig. 21-7
This figure shows the built-up side bulkheads (triangular) that run forward to the front engine mount and brace the bulkhead for the Dynaflow at rear of engine. They stiffen the Dynaflow support structure.

The actual points measured on a chassis dynamometer are shown, and the thrust available curve is adjusted to them. The test results showed that 120 mph was top speed (V_{max}) in the drive range of the converter, using full throttle. This occurred at 3,600 engine rpm, and indicated we could achieve 93 mph full throttle on the four-degree hill.

The *thrust available* at zero speed corresponds to "stall" of the converter, somewhat comparable to static thrust on an airplane propeller. At the high speed point on this curve, the torque converter's slip is low, the operation is close to lockup, and the efficiency is maximum.

The point where *thrust available* equals *thrust required* is the steady-state 120-mph maximum speed, as noted. The acceleration at any speed is a function of the excess thrust (difference between available thrust and

required thrust), the percent load on the rear wheels and the weight of the vehicle.

We calculated the initial acceleration (at zero speed) for the low range and high range of the converter as thrust available, high range = 1,100 lbs., thrust available, low range = 2,000 lbs., where the low range thrust equals the high-range thrust times the low-range ratio (1.82:1).

Using these values, we calculated the load transfer to the rear (driving) wheels, which adds to the static weight, to yield the total rear wheel loads under acceleration.

This calculation was based on vehicle gross weight, 3,000 lbs, center of gravity location, 57.5%, rear wheelbase, 9 ft. and center of gravity height, 1.5 ft.

This says that if the tire/road coefficient of friction is less than 0.58 the rear wheels will spin in the high range; if the coefficient is less than 0.97 they will spin in the low range, both under zero-speed conditions.

If the friction coefficient is 0.58, the thrust in the high range is 0.58 × 1908 = 1,107 lbs. and the vehicle acceleration is 1,107/3,000 = 0.37 g. If the tire/road coefficient is less than 0.58 one might as well start in the high range.

If the coefficient was higher than 0.58, starting in the low range was suggested, even with wheel spin, because with 1950-vintage tires the peak tire-force coefficient was probably much less affected by spin than are modern tire compounds. For example, at a coefficient of 0.7, even with wheel spin in low range, the thrust probably equals 0.7 × 2059 = 1,441 lbs., giving a vehicle acceleration of 1,441/3,000 = 0.480 g, and, at 0.8 the thrust equals 0.8 × 2059 = 1647, with a vehicle acceleration of 1,647/3,000 = 0.55 g. This suggests starting in low range and shifting to high range at perhaps 60 mph if the tire/road coefficient is above 0.58.

In reviewing my prerace plans I found a note suggesting we use low range at the standing start of the race and at slow corners.

Table 21-1. Bugatti Type 54 Dynaflow Thrust Calculations

Converter Range	Static Load Rear Wheels, Lbs.	Load Transfer Lbs.	Total Load Rear Wheel, Lbs.	Ratio: Thrust/ Weight (rear)
High	1725	183	1908	0.58
Low	1725	334	2059	0.97

Fig. 21-8
Mechanics Frank Babchek (left) and Art Mandale working on the installation. The Dynaflow unit is in place.

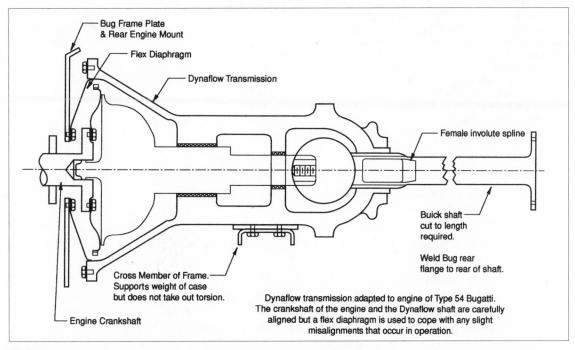

Bug Frame Plate
& Rear Engine Mount

Flex Diaphragm

Dynaflow Transmission

Female involute spline

Buick shaft
cut to length
required.

Weld Bug rear
flange to rear of shaft.

Cross Member of Frame.
Supports weight of case
but does not take out torsion.

Engine Crankshaft

Dynaflow transmission adapted to engine of Type 54 Bugatti.
The crankshaft of the engine and the Dynaflow shaft are carefully
aligned but a flex diaphragm is used to cope with any slight
misalignments that occur in operation.

Fig. 21-9
Muzzey's general layout of Dynaflow installation. The forward end of Dynaflow housing was attached to the bulkhead at rear of engine by a flex diaphragm. The rotor of the Dynaflow was located in the engine crankshaft with some flexibility fore and aft. A frame cross-member was added to help take the Dynaflow weight.

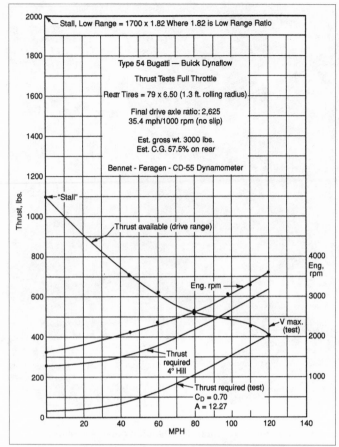

Graph labels:
Thrust, lbs. (vertical axis, 0 to 2000)
Eng. rpm (right axis, 1000 to 4000)
MPH (horizontal axis, 20 to 140)

Stall, Low Range = 1700 x 1.82 Where 1.82 is Low Range Ratio

Type 54 Bugatti — Buick Dynaflow

Thrust Tests Full Throttle

Rear Tires = 79 x 6.50 (1.3 ft. rolling radius)

Final drive axle ratio: 2,625
35.4 mph/1000 rpm (no slip)

Est. gross wt. 3000 lbs.
Est. C.G. 57.5% on rear

Bennet - Feragen - CD-55 Dynamometer

"Stall"

Thrust available (drive range)

Eng. rpm

V max. (test)

Thrust required 4° Hill

Thrust required (test)
C_D = 0.70
A = 12.27

Fig. 21-10
Performance curves for the Dynaflow installation, as measured
on a chassis dynamometer. The test was run in drive range only.
Knowing the ratio between drive and low ranges, we could
estimate the low-range performance. The thrust at the rear wheels
versus speed is plotted. The *thrust required* curves are calculated
from tire rolling resistance and aerodynamic resistance. Top speed
occurs when *thrust available* equals *thrust required*, in this case 120
mph in high range. The acceleration at any speed can be calculated
from the "excess" thrust.

I don't remember that I did this. On the day
of the race the weather was overcast and the
road was damp. Conceivably, we assumed the
coefficient was less than 0.58 and used high
range from the beginning. Unfortunately we
did not repeat the dyno test in the low range, so
there is some conjecture as to its performance.

General Motors assured us we were safe
in using the converter as a retarder and could
poke it into the low range at any speed below
70 mph. Once during the race, approaching
Milliken's Corner too fast, I shoved it into
the low range at about this speed and felt I
had thrown out an anchor. The car not only
slowed down but its directional stability

improved since the rear wheels could
not lock up—a really great feeling
under the circumstances.

The Bennet-Feragen D-55
chassis dynamometer, consisting of
a drum upon which the rear wheels
of the Bugatti were set, was located
in a downtown Buffalo facility. The
drum torque was measured on a 63-
inch arm and read on a calibrated
torque gauge. The test, performed on
September 20, was run with various
indicated velocities (engine rpm),
and thrust computed, up to about
120 mph. Despite safety claims, it
was scary sitting in the cockpit at an
indicated 120. As noted, we had no
time to run in the low range of the
converter or at part-throttle points,
which would be indicated by manifold
pressure.

As far as we know, this was the
first successful installation of a torque
converter in a race car. Jim Hall ran
his first race with the "automatic" in
the Chaparral in May of 1964. Hall's
transmission was a torque converter
plus a single forward gear, and initially
relied on converter slippage to take
the place of multiple speeds.

Hall's transmission was excellently
described by David Kimble in
"Chaparral's Mystery Automatic,"
published in *Road & Track* in
September 2001. Both his and our
applications used the torque converter slippage
as traction control. The Kimble article is quoted
in what follows.

In the Big Bug, we had two forward ranges,
which were adequate for Watkins Glen in
1950. Fourteen years later a single forward gear
was inadequate for the speed range, so second
and third gears were added to the Chaparral
installation, plus a couple of alternative final
drive ratios. In Hall's case the additional gears
were engaged by dog clutches of a special
design for easy engagement. Interestingly, by
the late 1960s tires had improved to the point
where the amount of power being lost through
converter slippage was no longer being offset

by increased flexibility, and a converter lock-up clutch was added. With his transmission, Hall could shift gears merely by lifting off the throttle, so one suspects that he also could use his transmission as a retarder. The procedure for starting off the line described by Phil Hill in the referenced article was exactly the one we used on the Bug: "hold the car with left foot on the brake . . . release the brake and drive off, the accelerator being on the right."

Weight and Balance

Over the years, the Type 54 Bugatti had acquired a bad reputation. In an article entitled "Sorting out the Bugatti Types" in the British *Motor Sport* of May 1949, J. Lemon Burton, states, "Ettore's next production was the racing Type 54 . . . but it proved a killer, only Varzi and Froy being able to hold it and then only up to 130 or so mph. *The weight again was too far forward* [emphasis mine]." Other references also suggest a forward weight distribution.

I do not believe the Type 54's handling problems were the result of this. The following table is largely based upon our own weight and balance measurements, and indicates a center of gravity well aft on both the Types 54 and 35. Furthermore, such data as we have seen indicates aft CGs for the 1938–'39 Mercedes and Auto Unions, and other high-powered rear-drive cars.

The nose-heavy reputation of the Type 54 stems from its behavior on a bump taken at high speed. I experienced this at Watkins Glen in 1950, when I tried the railway grade crossing at 75–80 mph. The car aviated with nose down and tail high, and landed heavily on the front wheels. Fortunately, the wheels were pointing straight ahead.

This behavior was the result of the very stiff front springing (compared to rear spring stiffness) that was typical of axle cars of that period. The natural ride frequency on front is very high, so the front wheels rebound before the rear wheels strike the same bump, which tosses the tail up into the air. This general behavior also is experienced to a lesser degree

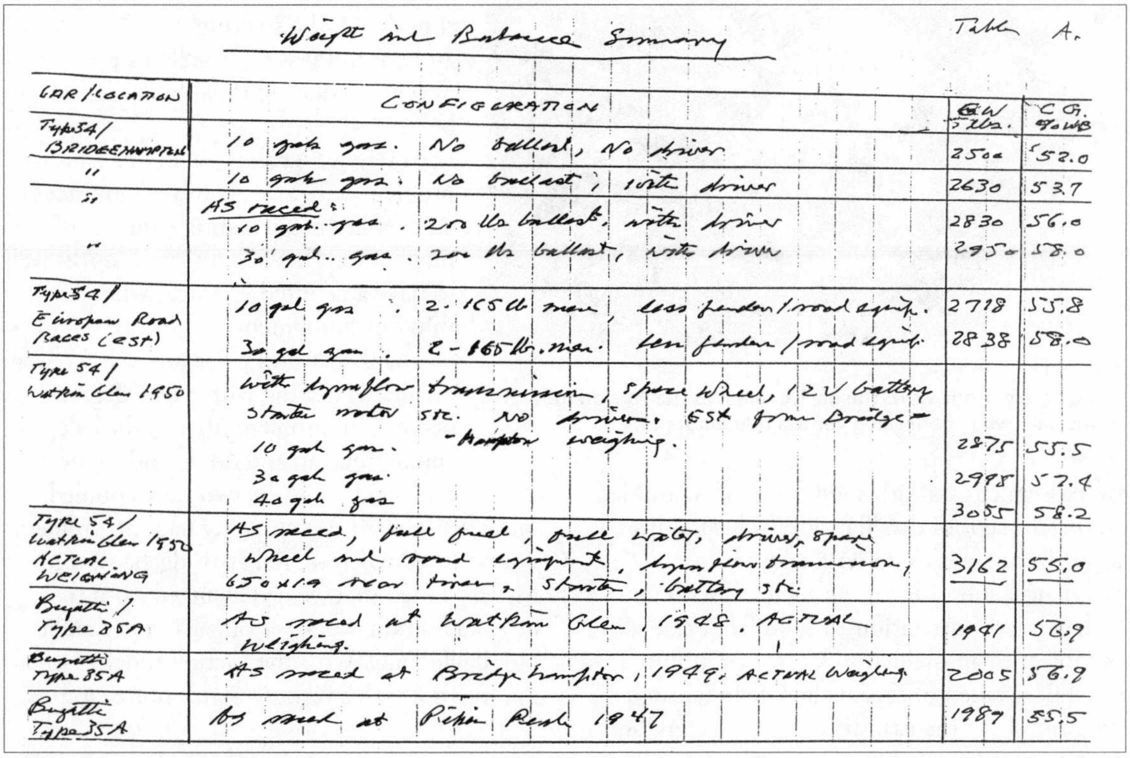

Weight and Balance Summary — Table A.

CAR/LOCATION	CONFIGURATION	GW lbs.	C.G. % WB
Type 54/ Bridgehampton	10 gals gas. No ballast, No driver	2500	52.0
"	10 gals gas. No ballast; with driver	2630	53.7
"	As raced: 10 gal. gas. 200 lbs ballast, with driver	2830	56.0
"	30 gal. gas. 200 lbs ballast, with driver	2950	58.0
Type 54/ European Road Races (est)	10 gal gas. 2-165 lb men, less fender/road equip.	2718	55.8
	30 gal gas. 2-165 lb. men. less fender/road equip.	2838	58.0
Type 54/ Watkins Glen 1950	With dynaflow transmission, spare wheel, 12V battery starter motor etc. No driver. EST from Bridgehampton weighing. 10 gal gas.	2875	55.5
	30 gal gas.	2998	57.4
	40 gal gas	3055	58.2
Type 54/ Watkins Glen 1950 ACTUAL WEIGHING	As raced, full fuel, full water, driver, spare wheel and road equipment, dynaflow transmission, 650x19 rear tires, starter, battery etc.	3162	55.0
Bugatti/ Type 35A	As raced at Watkins Glen, 1948. Actual weighing.	1941	56.9
Bugatti Type 35A	As raced at Bridgehampton, 1949. Actual weighing.	2005	56.9
Bugatti Type 35A	As raced at Pikes Peak 1947	1989	55.5

Fig. 21-11

Weight and Balance Summary—It seemed desirable to produce this summary from our measurements because so much confusion exists re. the CG location of the Type 54.

Fig. 21-12
Our device for eliminating brake tramp (rear view).

Fig. 21-13
Same device, front view. The device removes the torsion motion of the axle while permitting vertical ride motion.

on passenger cars with solid front axles, and led to the concept of the "flat ride." This requires a soft front suspension with a low natural frequency, and only can be achieved with an independent suspension. A solid front axle also is subject to an oscillation known as "tramp."

Films taken of cars at the Glen's railroad crossing show the vast difference in behavior, for example, of the Inter Ferrari (independent suspension on front) and the Vauxhall (Col. Felton's "Quick Silver") with its solid front

axle. I have always believed that the accident experienced by John Fitch in the Cunningham at Rheims in 1953 was due to tramp of the solid front axle. As long as the shocks were tight enough, and no disturbance was large enough to trigger the tramp, Fitch got away with it.

At a lower speed, a large disturbance could result in the Big Bug's front end leaving the ground while the rear stayed on the track. This occurred at Giant's Despair in 1951. On one bump halfway up I felt I had lost all steering control. A photo taken by a spectator showed the front wheels nearly a foot off the ground. Current solid front axle cars are still subject to this phenomenon.

On Friday, September 15, before the dynamometer test, we had the car running on the ramp with the Dynaflow installed. I decided to give the brakes a good check and jammed them on hard from about 60 mph. The front axle went into a violent case of brake tramp, the whole front end shook and shuddered, the steering wheel oscillated and control was essentially lost. I had never experienced this phenomenon before.[1]

Here we were, with an unsuspected problem only a week away from race date, after an exhausting summer of preparation. In such a situation it is well to have a talented engineer who can think in fundamental terms.

Muzzey reasoned as follows: We were essentially dealing with a two-degree-of-freedom problem; that is, the axle could move up and down and rotate torsionally, and the two were coupled into a self-excited system. Why had the problem not occurred when we ran at Bridgehampton? Muzzey noted that we had changed from the original friction shocks of Bugatti to hydraulic Houdaille units. With the friction shocks locked up, the front axle's vertical degree of freedom

---

[1] *Years later I would find it fully explained by Maurice Olley. (See Chassis Design by Milliken and Milliken, SAE 2002, Section 6.8.)*

was nonexistent and the system had only a single degree of freedom. Since we did want some ride motion, the answer lay in controlling this torsional motion of the axle.

Over the weekend of September 16–17, Muzzey sketched a parallelogram mechanism and machined it out of aluminum bar stock in our Flight Research shop. It permitted the axle to move up and down but not rotate, and completely eliminated the brake tramp (which never recurred during testing or in the race).

There was to be an amusing sequel. Some years later the Type 54 appeared in an exhibit of sports cars at the Ford Museum in Dearborn, which I happened to attend. I had wondered what happened to the car after it left Doc Scher's stable. The parallelogram frame was still installed, and our other changes appeared intact. Two gentlemen near me were discussing the car, one a self-styled Bugatti expert. He said to his friend, "You know, Bugatti always had brake tramp and controlled it with that mechanism you see attached to the front axle."

Three days before the race the whole crew posed with the Big Bug, now resplendent in a new paint job and race number, after which I drove it to Watkins Glen. On the stretch of Route 20 along Seneca lakefront south of Geneva I opened up and topped out at 120 mph, as predicted. When I phoned Cliff later he was pleased but not astonished.

A large contingent from Flight Research arrived the next day, including those who had worked on the car plus another 15 or so in the Timing and Scoring Group under the direction of Walt Breuhaus. For the 1950 race a photographic box was installed at the start-finish line. It was sponsored by SCCA, and designed and built at Flight by Jack Beilman, Bill Close and Gene Skelley, under Walt's direction. A timer pressed the button for each car as it crossed the line, the appropriate light went on, and the camera took a single-frame photo showing the light and the timer. Thus it was possible to track every car in the race and compute its position and lap time. Each

Fig. 21-14
The completed Dynaflow installation and preparation for Watkins Glen Grand Prix, 1950. This is part of the crew that did it. (Left to right) Len Gifford, hangar chief; Big Bill Wilcox, assistant hangar chief; Carl Oddo, painter; Dave Whitcomb, section head flight res.; Unidentified; Cliff Muzzey, designer of Dynaflow installation, WFM; Unidentified; Ed Seckel, engineer, Flight Research; Henry Sonnen, machine shop; Bill Frey, machine shop; Bill Rouzer, mechanic (installation of self-starter). Several mechanics, Art Mandale and Frankie Babchek failed to get in this photo.

Fig. 21-15
Cliff Muzzey at the wheel.

member of the T & S group was assigned two cars in the field.

After arrangements were made at Smalley's Garage, I drove out on the circuit for some practice. Completing my first lap, I saw Doc Scher by the first turn off Franklin Street. Each time I had offered to give him a ride in the Big Bug, he had declined. On this occasion I pulled up, yelled "get in" and, without thinking, he did. The Doc had always raved about the car's performance, so I assumed he wanted a lively ride. By the time we reached Stone Bridge he was shouting, "Slow down," but I pretended not to hear. After negotiating the railroad grade crossing with only a modest flight, he cupped his hands and yelled directly into my ear, "Slow down, I'm a valuable man." I could hardly disagree with that, and slowed down by my own volition.

Working with Scher that summer had been a novel and pleasant experience. He couldn't understand why anyone would want to drive a race car. I knew

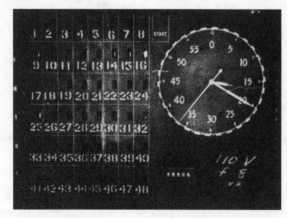

Fig. 21-16
Typical photo from T & S.

nothing about plastic surgery. On one visit to his Park Avenue office, when I commented on the mounting bills, he jocularly replied: "I'll have to get another movie actress job to keep up with you guys." When I asked what he did for these gals, he showed me rows of "before and after" celebrity pictures, and I began to appreciate that his profession was not at all boring.

The Big Bug attracted lots of attention in front of Smalley's. Some of the Bugatti purists felt installing a Dynaflow was a desecration, but others were more liberal. Sam Collier dropped by, studied the installation and asked intelligent questions. He seemed intrigued with the two-pedal operation, commenting that "this sort of innovation is good for the sport." By that time our crew had arrived and were enjoying the fanfare.

The starting positions in the Grand Prix were drawn by classes, the larger displacement cars up front. We were in the front row, next to Tommy Cole's Allard on the pole. That evening, having attended all the festivities, I went back to the Lodge hopeful of our summer's labors and race preparation.

Race day was overcast and somewhat threatening. I sensed I was in for a rough ride, so after a shower I wrapped a bath towel around my waist under my driving uniform, figuring I'd have Wilcox cinch the seatbelt up as tight as possible. The Seneca Cup and Queen Catharine Cup preceded the Grand Prix, so there was plenty of time to build up one's emotional commitment. Having walked down the pit lane, I wound up at Paradiso's Cafe, a cozy dining place near the entrance to the main straight on Franklin Street, and a good place to wait it out. On

Fig. 21-17
Walt Hirtreiter, Head of Instrumentation Section of CAL Flight Research.

one wall was a large autographed photo of George Weaver's Maserati, "Poison Lil," one of the more potent machines of the early Glen races. George is standing on the far side of the cockpit, talking to someone whose back is to the viewer. I had seen this photo many times before I recognized my old raincoat – I was the one conversing with George!

As I waited my anxiety built up, despite efforts to control it. We were no longer racing for fun, we were out to win. The best machinery and drivers were there. In the Big Bug I had a seriously competitive machine, but it also was the heaviest car in the race. It had a very stiff suspension and was a handful to drive, to say nothing of having a novel transmission with which I had little

Fig. 21-18
Big Bug being fueled at Les Smalley's Amoco station. Photo shows Les and Bill Milliken.

Fig. 21-19
Seneca Cup, pacing the field at Stone Bridge. Cam Argetsinger drove Briggs Cunningham's Cadillac-based
Le Monster, the pace car for the Seneca Cup.

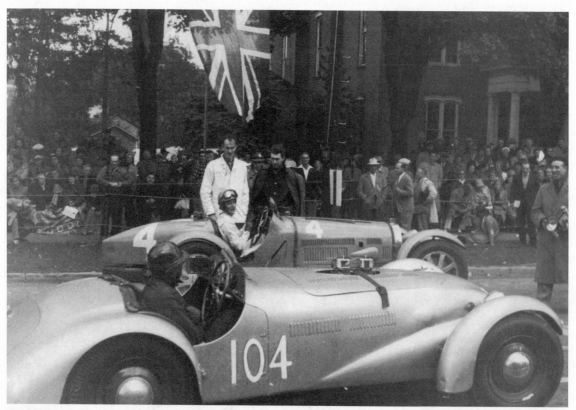

Fig. 21-20
Front row of the Watkins Glen Grand Prix 1950. Tommy Cole's Cad-Allard and the Big Bug with Bill Wilcox and Bill
Milliken.

experience. I felt a responsibility I had never experienced in a competition event, and was approaching the stage-fright level when our race was called. Once I climbed into the car all fear disappeared as if by magic. With commitment came a complete change. Here I was in the front row of the main event, in an historic machine of no mean performance. How lucky could I be? Behind Tommy Cole and me was a choice field of Ferraris, Allards, Jaguars, Healeys, etc. The whole experience reinforced my theory that if you can't accept some anxiety you miss out on the fun.

The crowd was huge. Every available spot was taken down to the edge of the street, and the crowd of spectators extended to porches and even rooftops. Mechanics and well-wishers hovered around their entries as far down the street as one could see.

Bill Wilcox stood by the cockpit, calm and unmoved by all this fanfare. Together we ran through a mental checklist, then Bill cinched up the seat belt. I had absolute confidence in him as crew chief, a tremendous asset for a driver.

The Race

As starter Nils Michelson raised the flag, I held the car with the left-foot brake and revved up to converter stall with the throttle. Since the weather was overcast and the road was damp, the transmission was probably in the drive range. After a clean start, Cole and I led at the first corner and went up Old Corning Hill in tight formation. Mistaking the road to Seneca Lodge for the course, Cole started that way, suddenly turning back when he realized his mistake. We nearly collided in a T-bone accident that was saved by my left-foot braking.

Continuing up the road to the top, I hit the rough back straight, gained speed and began to realize what I was up against. Bridgehampton was a relatively smooth circuit, and practicing at Watkins in normal road traffic I had never reached racing speeds. While I could stay with Cole, the Bug with its stiff suspension was leaping all over the road, and to make matters worse I felt as if I was connected to the car by a spring. Handling had deteriorated along with the ride, so it was a matter of staying "between the fences." Cole was undoubtedly having problems of his own with his front swing axles and the road camber changes.

We are accustomed to thinking of a race car as an extension of the driver's physical and mental capabilities, as a marriage of compatibility. But my relation to the Big Bug on a rough and cambering road was more like an unhappy dysfunctional couple. The best I could do was exercise some overall guidance and allow the Bug to work out its own dynamics.

Fig. 21-21
The first turn off Franklin Street. Cole in lead followed by Big Bug, Stevenson and Wacker.

Fig. 21-22
Up the hill toward Seneca Lodge.

The first lap had been taken at close to a 70-mph average, and Cole was still leading by a couple of car lengths as we swept out of town. It was my impression that he took a questionable line entering Townsend Road Corner near Seneca Lodge. In any event he lost the benefit of the road camber, went into a slide and plunged off the road on the outside, winding up in the trees and bushes.

That put me in the lead, closely pursued by Cunningham's Inter Ferrari driven by Sam Collier, who ultimately passed me onto the back straight. Rushing down toward the railway underpass, we typified the extremes of race cars in that 1950 event: the Ferrari the most modern import in the country, and the 20-year-old Bugatti with a torque converter transmission. Except for the rough ride I had no problem staying with Collier through the underpass. We then approached the first bend to the right. Having walked the course during the summer, I knew there was fresh gravel on the inside and took it wide. Collier, without benefit of much practice, chose a more conventional line, got onto the gravel and went into a broad slide. As the Ferrari slid down the road, it created a curtain of dust and gravel through which I dimly saw Sam leave the road and career into an old apple orchard. A large rock as big as my fist landed in

Fig. 21-23
Big Bug followed by Wacker's Cad-Allard, Watkins Glen 1950, third lap.

the cockpit beside me. At the time it didn't occur to me that this was a serious accident. My only reaction was I was back in the lead.

By the beginning of the third lap Erwin Goldschmidt had taken the lead with Wacker second, both in Cad-Allards, while I was running a close third. All of us were lapping at over 70 mph, and Goldschmidt was about to set a lap record of 73.49 mph. On the next lap the first three positions remained unchanged, while Cunningham in a Cad-Healey moved into fourth.

Fig. 21-24
Fifth lap with Wacker on Big Bend. I retook second place.

One observation I made at the railway grade crossing concerned a large and formidable tree on the right near the landing point of the aviating cars. On our first lap, I could see a photographer standing in front of the tree; on the second lap he was standing beside the tree; on the third lap, except for his arm and camera, he had disappeared behind the tree. Protection of spectators was a tenuous thing in those early races.

Too Much Thrust

On the fifth lap I moved back into second place behind Goldschmidt, with a 72.96 mph lap. I am quite sure I used the Dynaflow as a "retarder" on this lap, poking it into the low range at the foot of Big Bend.

I was in no mood to let up as we approached Townsend Road Corner, which was characterized by camber changes across the road width and also along the path of travel. This was a tricky turn that, with the proper line, could be taken quite fast. Taking it too tight puts one on a short radius with less than optimum speed; taking it too wide results in loss of favorable camber. I had studied this corner during my summer visits to the Glen and certainly thought I knew it. My impression was that earlier in the race Cole had got outside the line too soon and lost the camber effect,

leaving the road on the outside. I got into it too fast to hold the line and lost the camber effect later. At any rate the tail started to come around when I was in the middle of the road. I got in enough reverse lock (even with our slow steering ratio) to hold the attitude, but needed tractive thrust to maintain the path in a typical dirt-track cornering maneuver. Instinctively, I poured on the power and, with the tires spinning and scrabbling at the pavement, got more than enough thrust to hold the path, so much so that it drove the machine toward the inside of the road. Had I been Phil Walters, with his years of driving midgets on dirt tracks, I could have adjusted the power and taken the turn in spectacular fashion. As it was, the front wheels hooked into the ditch, the tail whipped around, and the car rolled upside down facing back down the course.

A small fire started in the engine compartment as I tried to unbuckle my belt, an aircraft type that could be opened in only one direction. Approaching the panic stage, I distinctly remember saying to myself: "You're going to have to look at that damned buckle and figure it out." Of course I had been working the buckle in the wrong direction. Once released, I fell down into a few inches of water and crawled out. When the Bug landed upside down, it had produced the same audible "thud" the Type 35 had on my previous rollover. I still thought it should be more of a

Fig. 21-25
Sixth lap. My accident at Townsend Road Corner.

"clang." Once clear of the car I told myself I didn't want any emotional reaction from this incident. And I never did.

Erwin Goldschmidt won fair and square, a victory that annoyed those in the SCCA who viewed the club as a closed gentlemen's amateur activity. As required to qualify for the Grand Prix, he had finished 2nd in the Seneca Cup to earn a last-place starting position for the Grand Prix, which made his victory even more impressive

A sense of gloom pervaded the finish, not because of Goldschmidt's victory but because of Sam Collier's death. This first fatality at Watkins Glen was especially tragic because Sam's brother Miles was a strong proponent of improved safety for both spectators and contestants. That evening, when I arrived at Cam's cottage, Miles also was there. Having been involved with road racing since before the war, and with a realistic outlook on its hazards, Miles appeared to have a tight control on his emotions. Or was he still in shock? The failure of the seat belt anchorage had killed Sam. I found it hard to accept that anyone could fail to

install a seat belt properly. Miles and I discussed Townsend Road Corner and agreed on the most desirable line. We also agreed that I had failed to find it on lap six.

My Best Race Ever

The 1950 Watkins Glen Grand Prix remains a high-water mark in my racing career. I never drove a more exciting car than the Dynaflow Bugatti, nor was I ever involved in a more intense competition. Design and installation of the first successful torque converter in a race car was an engineering feat that illustrated the high level of competence of Flight Research personnel. Consistently lapping that original Watkins Glen circuit at over 70 mph with that demanding car and novel transmission is something I look back on with genuine satisfaction.

The day after the race we made arrangements to truck the damaged machine to Buffalo. Doc Scher wanted it repaired and available for further competition, but first we saw to the financial settlement for installation

Fig. 21-26
The winner, Erwin Goldschmidt on Cad-Allard at Stone Bridge on victory lap. Watkins Glen Grand Prix, 1950.

of the Dynaflow and preparing the car for the Glen. Thanks to Charles Chayne, there was no charge for the Dynaflow unit, such accessories as the driveshaft, or for the mockup unit, drawings and the consulting help (which also included modification to the casting). GM invoiced us only for the speedometer, cable and adapter ($358). The oil coolers for the Dynaflow were supplied at no cost by Harrison Radiator. I billed Doc Scher $2,172.76 for the labor and expenses at Flight Research that summer. It's still difficult to believe that this complicated engineering and development task was accomplished at that figure, even in 1950 dollars. If no help had been received from GM and Harrison, and they had charged at their normal rate, the cost for this effort would have been $4,907, so I felt Scher got good value for his money while we had the fun of doing a pioneer installation.

The cost of repairing the car to race condition after the accident was $578. The story of the Type 54 Dynaflow Bug at Watkins Glen concluded with a nice letter from Charles Chayne.

Giants' Despair Hill Climb, Saturday, May 12, 1951

Claimed to be the oldest event of its type in the US, this Wilkes-Barre, Pennsylvania, hill climb dated back to 1906 but had last been run in 1916. The road racing resurgence prompted several local groups to join with the SCCA in sponsoring a revival (or "renewal," as it was phrased on the entry blank). Ken Hill of "Flying Banana" fame was general race chairman, Walt Breuhaus was the chief timer and scorer.

With the restoration of the Big Bug completed, we thought about running it in the Unrestricted Category. Doc Scher indicated some reluctance.

The Doc's subsequent letter made clear I was to be responsible for any damage. Convinced I would not bend the car, and enthusiastic about the chance of driving it again, I accepted his conditions.

At Watkins Glen we had run alcohol but were still uncertain about the best fuel, so I wrote to Hal Ullrich, who had driven a Type 55 at the Glen. The mixture he used was 29

Fig. 21-27
Giant's Despair, 1951. The Big Bug is second in the lineup to tackle the hill. One car goes up at a time. Typical run times are a little over a minute. Big Bill Wilcox stands beside our car.

Fig. 21-28
Giant's Despair, 1951. At the starting line with two XK-120s behind us.

percent alcohol, 30 percent benzol, 40 percent gasoline and 1 percent castor oil. The gasoline was 91 octane. With his Bugatti carburetor (38-mm venturi, 2-1/8-inch throttle opening), he used 150 main jet (fixed size): "Depending upon atmospheric conditions and temperature, may have to go as high as 240 on the main jet. If too rich add more alcohol to fuel, decreasing gasoline and benzol content. Solex jets will fit." I relayed this information to Bill Wilcox

who came back that "it looks like a matter of adjusting the alcohol content to jet size. Some fun." I am not sure what Bill did, but the engine ran great with little smoke at Giants' Despair.

The day before practice I drove the car to Wilkes-Barre on an absolutely gorgeous spring day. No car was finer for a cross-country drive than the Dynaflow Bug. It had plenty of punch and the less-than-smooth road was a delightful

Fig. 21-29
In the "esses" at Giant's Despair, 1951. The road was very rough. Steering felt marginal.

Fig. 21-30
Giant's Despair, 1951. At the beginning of the first pitch up the hill.

challenge. I could imagine how Jean Bugatti must have felt on his Molsheim-to-Paris runs in the Type 55. In East Aurora I sighted a local cop parked by the roadside. The Bug was a magnetic attraction to local law enforcement types, so to discourage a chase I poured on the speed, assuming he would not appear in my life again.

Giants' Despair is a measured mile, beginning with a steep pitch, leveling off a bit at a pronounced S turn, and continuing

another pitch for the finish. Shortly after the top the road plunges down by a cemetery on its return to the start. In my memory, the initial part of the hill was smooth, with bumps through the S turn.

Back in 1910 the record for the hill had been made by Ralph De Palma at 1 min. 28 sec. In 1951 records fell rapidly, Del Lee driving a Cad-Allard with the best time of the day at 1:07.5, followed by Bruce Stevenson in the

Fig. 21-31
Giant's Despair, 1951. Accelerating away at the start. Since the hill is so short a good start is imperative for a good time.

Meyer Special at 1:10.0 and Gordon Lipe at 1:11.6. All of those cars were in the big Sports Category.

We managed fourth fastest at 1:12.0 overall and fastest in the Unrestricted Category, this on my second run, which was eight seconds better than the first. My most interesting impression was of the "s" turn, when I hit one bump and seemed to lose steering completely. Someone shot a photo showing the front wheels inches off the ground. Since my average speed from a standing start was about 50 mph, the reaction of the car was quite different from taking the railroad tracks at Watkins Glen at high speed.

The other impression I had was of the hairy finish. At the Giant you received the

Figure 21-32
In the Big Bug at Wilson, 1951.

checkered flag close to the top of the hill, and had to be on the brakes immediately as you plunged down the other side.

In my several times there I always had my left foot on the brake, but was careful not to upset the balance and go into a slide.

At the banquet that evening, Doc Scher was delighted with our Unrestricted win. The winning trophy was a charming statue of a race car carved from anthracite coal. Since our agreement was that I pay all expenses and receive all awards, it never occurred to me that the Doc would have the least interest in this prize, but at five the next morning I was awakened by his phone call. Sounding terribly upset, he said he had arranged with the sculptor to make a duplicate statue, but would I lend him mine to take home? In our four events together, this was the first time we had any obvious success. I lent him the statue and never saw it again. It was still a good bargain; the opportunity to compete with that classic machine was reward enough for me.

On the way home I spent a lot of time with a gas station owner answering questions about the car, raising the hood so he could see the engine, and giving him a complete rundown on its recent history. In a happy mood afterward, I opened up on one of Pennsylvania's back roads and got nailed at perhaps 80 mph. The trooper insisted on taking me to the local justice of the peace who, it turned out, was the owner of the gas station I had just left! After the details of my offense were recited, the J.P. ruled that the young man sitting before him, driving such a valuable vehicle, could not possibly have exceeded the speed limit. In the heated exchange that followed, I was treated to the extraordinary scene of the judge defending my position so vigorously that the trooper finally stormed out. The ticket was torn up and its remains deposited in the wastebasket. The J.P. looked up at me and we both started laughing. We shook hands, and I was on my way.

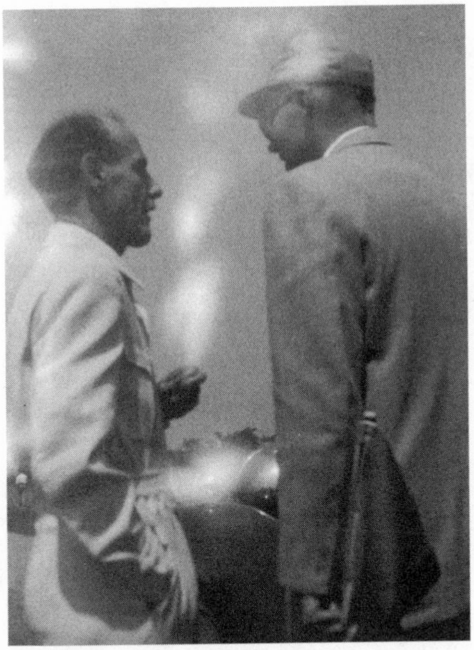

Passing through East Aurora on my return, I was nailed by the cop who recognized the car from our earlier encounter, and was fined $25. Justice will be served.

My last event in the Big Bug occurred shortly after Giant's Despair: a quarter-mile time trial in Wilson, New York, that we won with a

Fig. 21-33
Bill Milliken and Dave Whitcomb at the Wilson time trial.

modest 15.6-sec. run. After that the Doc and I worked out a financial settlement and the Type 54 passed on to other hands. The Dynaflow transmission was eventually replaced with a Bugatti crash box by Ray Jones, who sent me the low-range shifter quadrant and lever we had installed. Some years later Phil Hill, while driving the Big Bug in vintage races on the West Coast, phoned to discuss some handling modifications and the success he was having. It was great to hear that the competition career of this extraordinary vehicle was by no means finished.

First Sebring Six-Hour Event, Sunday, December 31, 1950

The last event in the 1950 season was the brainchild of Alec Ulmann. Reginald S. Smith was the very dynamic secretary of the SCCA Activities Committee, and carried much of the organizational load. In a phone call in

Fig. 21-34
Phil Hill driving the Type 54 (Big Bug) in an historic race in California. The car's handling had been improved by Jan Voboril of Fine Restorations, who "stiffened the front shocks, softened the rear spring, and positively located rear end sidewise." He also appears to have used larger tires in the rear. I had nice letters from both Jan and Phil; the car's handling was definitely improved in terms of directional stability.

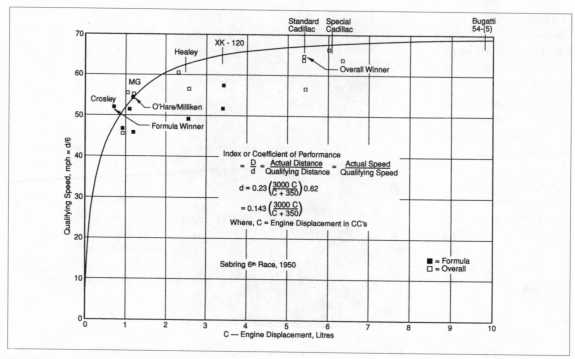

Fig. 21-35
Plot of formula for Sebring six-hour event, December 1950. This shows that the formula is biased toward the smaller-displacement cars. The formula (i.e., handicap race) was won by a Crosley, whereas the overall winner, a Cadillac, fell short of its formula requirement. O'Hare and I in a standard MG were right on formula.

early November, Alec had told me about the proposed six-hour endurance race at Sebring, which would be patterned on the famous 24 Hours of Le Mans. He had discovered the Florida circuit through his surplus aircraft business. Alec described the 3-½-mile course as "partly on flat paved roads and on airport runways with two 0.9-mile straights."

"The Sam Collier Memorial Grand Prix of Endurance," sponsored by the Sebring Firemen Inc. and the SCCA, was scheduled for 3:00 P.M. to 9:00 P.M. on New Year's Eve. General race chairman was Phil Stiles. Alec was chief steward.

The race was to be confined to the SCCA Sports Category conforming to the "*Code Sportif* of the FIA for January 1948," with "SCCA registered sports cars that complied with FIA rules" to be entered in ten displacement classes. Overall winner would be determined by a formula producing a "Coefficient of Performance" defined by D/d (D the total miles covered in the six hours, d a prescribed qualifying distance). The latter was a function of the displacement of the car by the Le Mans

formula, adjusted by the factor .23 because the Sebring race was one quarter the time of the French contest. The 0.62 converted kilometers to miles. The C in the formula was the engine displacement in cubic centimeters. For supercharged cars the displacement was doubled.

$$d = 0.23\ (3{,}000C\ /\ C{+}350)\ 0.62\ \text{miles}$$

In his follow-up letter, Alec described the above formula and asked that "your engineers take a look at it, and do you agree?"

To this end we first made a plot of the "qualifying distance (or speed)" versus engine displacement (see plot). We then spotted a few known cars on this curve, i.e., MG, Healey, XK-120, the Big Bugatti Type 54, etc.

Certainly the curve gave the proper trend, i.e., the smaller displacement cars have a shorter qualifying distance (or lower speed) than the larger displacement machines. To get some feel of the sensitivity of the "Coefficient of Performance" to an increase in distance (or speed) over that of qualifying distance, we compared the MG with the Type 54 Bugatti.

First we assumed a five-mph speed increase for both cars. The increase in "Coefficient of Performance" was 9.1 percent for the MG and 7.2 percent for the Type 54. It seemed apparent that increases in speed over qualifying would be easier to accomplish on the smaller displacement cars—thus the formula tended to favor those machines. The larger displacement cars would also cover more racing miles (at higher average speeds) than the smaller-engine cars.

Although perhaps not ideal, the "Coefficient of Performance" formula seemed reasonable, and I so informed Alec.

Shortly after the announcement of the race, MG owner Frank O'Hare of Rochester, New York, called to ask if I would be his co-driver. He had lost his sight in one eye, so he suggested that he drive the first three daylight hours and I do the last three. The MG would run in Class F displacement. I was delighted with the invitation.

The race attracted a large entry of nearly 40 cars. Although held under FIA regulations, the race was sanctioned by the SCCA, so few seemed concerned that emphasis was shifting from amateur to international, which certainly was one of Alec's objectives. Everyone wanted to race and Sebring was another good opportunity.

No map of the circuit was published in the race program, but I remember some fairly slow and tricky turns before the access road connected with a long runway that were poorly lit at night. One contestant missed an oil barrel marker and got lost out on the wide runway expanse. Based on Piero Taruffi's book, *The Technique of Motor Racing* (available from BentleyPublishers.com), I tried with some success to move the clipping point beyond the apex on the slower corners.

The field included a number of top drivers, among them Luigi Chinetti, Briggs Cunningham, George Rand, John Fitch, Phil Walters, Bill Spear, Jim Kimberly, Fred Wacker and Erwin Goldschmidt. Formula winners were Koster and Dashon, driving the Crosley Hot Shot (724 cc displacement), who completed 89 laps (Coefficient of Performance = 1.0854). We finished sixth on formula, completing 94 laps with a Coefficient of Performance of .9894, and were second in class. Overall winners were Wacker and Burrell on a Cad-Allard, at 111 laps with a Coefficient of Performance of .9653.

Plotting the actual performance of all the cars completing the race indicates that only the smaller displacement cars could reach or exceed the "qualifying distance." Of the large displacement cars, only the overall winner approached the handicapped speed and many fell far short of the formula.

The first Sebring race was quite a success, and it was increased to 12 hours, and I competed on a number of occasions. More details of these events are given in the next chapter.

Leaving Buffalo's winter in March was always great fun. Barbara and I stayed with Dr. and Mrs. Eberly, a gracious retired couple who turned their master bedroom over to us and who had their own grapefruit tree in the backyard. The many "thank-you-ma'ams" made driving from town to the airport always interesting.

The O'Hare MG we raced in the first Sebring turned up 51 years later at the Watkins Glen race anniversary in 2001. It was owned by David Kyle of Holland, Ohio, and still in race condition.

The Great Controversy, 1951

The complex issues of this SCCA controversy are well presented in the Philippe Defechereux history of Watkins Glen 1948–1952. Leading to it were the following issues:

- Bitterness surrounding non-SCCA entries in the 1950 Watkins Glen event.
- The "controlling" interests of SCCA President Cam Peck and others.
- Briggs Cunningham's entry in the Le Mans 24-hour race.
- Alec Ulmann's organization of the Sebring Grand Prix of Endurance conforming to the *Code Sportif* of the FIA.
- Ulmann's dismissal as chairman of the SCCA Activities Committee and expulsion from the club.
- The representation of the FIA in the United States by the AAA Contest Board and the associated Peck/Herrington correspondence.
- Sam Collier's death in the 1950 Watkins Glen Grand Prix.

Fig. 21-36
The O'Hare MG still is in existence and appeared at Watkins Glen a few years ago.

Last, but not least, was Cam Argetsinger's dream and commitment to fully FIA-sanctioned international races at the Glen.

The controversy came to a head in the sanctioning of the 1951 Grand Prix. Would the race be run as an SCCA event under its rules, or as a fully FIA-sanctioned event with its international regulations? The decision was to be made by the Watkins Glen Grand Prix board of directors at a June 1951 meeting.

Supported by Miles Collier and Ken Purdy, Cam Argetsinger made the presentation on behalf of the "internationalists." The board split and failed to reach a decision. As SCCA Contest Board chairman I was asked to attend a second meeting, presumably to present the virtues of continuing under SCCA sanction for the immediate future. George Weaver was also present. I provided a number of arguments reflecting the position of the Contest Board and the conservative members of the club. The Grand Prix board voted to go along with this position for 1951.

The decision had a devastating effect on my relationship with Cam. Although aware of it, I doubt if I fully appreciated the depth of his commitment at the time to FIA sanction. Because we had worked so well together, I took

our breakup very seriously indeed. It would not be mended for some time.

Although I was a strong supporter of SCCA, I did not endorse all the policies and politics of Cam Peck's administration. No one could say I was in favor of an "exclusive country club" organization. On Goldschmidt's participation in the 1950 Watkins Glen event, I fully agreed with Cam Argetsinger, and was appalled at Alec Ulmann's expulsion.

Fundamentally, I was an internationalist, having been lured into racing by a knowledge of European road competition, which was demonstrated by my participation in the 1950 Watkins Glen GP in a car conforming to the FIA Sports category. Furthermore, I had competed in the first Sebring, again conforming to FIA *Code Sportif*. During a 1951 European trip I went out of my way to attend the Grand Prix race at Monza.

Although my position in the controversy may sound inconsistent and self-serving, it aligned with my attitude toward competition. Above all I wanted to race, and I was desperately anxious to do well. Without the resources of those in the club who could acquire expensive modern machinery, my best hope lay in the SCCA Unrestricted Category, which led me to potent, though far from reliable, vehicles. What I had going for me was a great team able to tackle complex vehicle modifications. My racing always had an engineering component and a fascination with car handling. Furthermore, I was certainly inclined toward the free formulas that had produced the Mercedes-Benzes and Auto Unions of the 1934–39 period. In that it allowed me to do something I loved and to be competitive at it, the SCCA Unrestricted Category meant a great deal to me.

I am glad that Cam Argetsinger and I again worked closely together on the permanent circuit at the Glen through many Formula Libre and F-1 events at the track.

Watkins Glen Permanent Circuit, Formula Libre and U.S. Grand Prix

In 1953, to avoid the legislation against racing on New York State public highways, the Grand Prix moved to "the town circuit," which enabled the series to continue. Far less interesting, the new course had a wavy downhill straight that, in my opinion, was especially dangerous.

I can't claim to have originated the idea of a "permanent" circuit, but the action I took in 1955 brought the matter to a head. After preparing a slide show of famous circuits around the world, I invested $25.00 in an artist's rendering of an idealized circuit for the Glen. My concept also included business enterprises that I believed could become associated with the Glen for testing and research. At the time I was not a member of the WGGP board (this occurred in 1957) but I had good rapport with chairman Henry Valent. He readily agreed to my making a presentation before the full board. At its conclusion, I was amazed to hear Henry announce they would "go ahead and do it." I was even more astonished when he called a couple of weeks later with the news that 550 acres of farmland had been acquired, with a plan for financing construction of a track already in the works.

During the winter of 1955–56, Henry, Cam Argetsinger and I tramped around the proposed site in the snow, visualizing the proposed circuit. Cam insisted it should enable a 100-mph lap with existing Grand Prix machinery, thus making it the fastest road course in the country. I made contact with the Civil Engineering Department at Cornell University, where the necessary survey and plan layouts were made. Contracts were let and the 2.3-mile circuit was built in the summer of 1956. A couple of years later, in the first of the Formula Libre races, Jo Bonnier negotiated a lap in less than 85 seconds, for an average of approximately 103 mph.

Meanwhile Alec Ulmann organized two FIA-sanctioned U.S. Grand Prix events, one at Sebring and the other at Riverside (1960) on the West Coast. By 1958 Cam had initiated the first of three Formula Libre races on the new circuit, required to qualify for FIA U.S. Grand Prix events. Cam was executive director of the WGGP Corporation and general race chairman, and I was chief steward.

I well remember the first of the series. Because of the rain we slogged through mud to get to the course. The drivers had congregated at Seneca Lodge bar, with no interest in practicing. I got them together and announced "no practice, no race." Nobody moved until Dan Gurney stood up and said, "Let's go." They all followed. Jo Bonnier won the race driving a 250F Maserati, a genuine GP car. It was an entry that Cam had arranged, effectively sponsored by the WGGP Corporation. In the 1959 Formula Libre, Stirling Moss, who drove an F1 Cooper Climax, noted this was his first experience winning a race in a snowstorm.

The first FIA-sanctioned Formula 1 United States Grand Prix took place at Watkins Glen in 1961. For the next ten years Cam and I worked together, he as general race director, I as chief steward. These were heady years.[2]

---

[2] *The reader is referred to* Watkins Glen: Fifty Years of Competition at the Home of American Road Racing *by Bill Green and J. J. O'Malley, which supplements Defechereux's account and carries on into the late 1990s. Currently historian of the International Motor Racing Research Center at Watkins Glen, Bill Green has followed racing at the Glen from the beginning, has a house full of memorabilia, and an unbelievable memory of the events, the personalities and the statistics. He helped me reconstruct some of my racing activity at Watkins.*

Watkins Glen was certainly a big part of my life. In a decade and a half I raced on all three circuits, and served in various official capacities over the years. I had three notable crashes on the old circuit, and my own named corner.

But most important of all were the wonderful friends I made in Watkins Glen. Our three children were born in a local hospital, and we own a large piece of wilderness property near the permanent circuit.

U.S. Grand Prix Memories

- High point of the festivities were the parties at the Argetsinger home in Burdette. All contestants and organizers were there in an atmosphere of pure fun and excitement, bolstered by great conversation, good food and dozens of magnums of champagne from the local vineyards. The homespun hospitality led to permanent friendships and was never forgotten by the drivers and teams.

- I will never forget the emotional high I experienced at the first U.S. Grand Prix in 1961 when our national anthem was played. I looked down the line of cars to Cam. By bringing an international event to a tiny village, he had accomplished the impossible and was about to see the realization of his dream. How fortunate we were to live in a country where such a thing can happen.

- As chief steward, I experienced both woe and satisfaction. It was my responsibility to collect the drivers, make sense out of the Drivers' Meeting and start the race on time (not always successfully). This became something of a hassle. GP drivers are a tough and independent lot, so I tried to focus on the few essentials.

- Cam and I agreed the pits are no place for the police, so we controlled that area ourselves, working closely with the teams.

- Red-flagging a race was a serious matter. The injured had to be taken to the hospital as quickly as possible, so it was far better to continue the race than to release the crowds and block the highway. Cam and I agreed that the red flag would never be thrown without our mutual agreement. Fred German's Race Communications Association course workers, who might well be at an accident site, did not always agree. The subject came up every year. Recognizing the tremendous contribution the RCA made to the conduct of a race, we met with Fred and Joe Cerrino at the Depot Restaurant in Pittsford every year to coordinate the flags and other issues.

- Community and business support for the races was a remarkable feature of Watkins Glen. No one made greater contributions than Watkins Glen Grand Prix Corporation President Henry Valent and Executive Director Malcolm Currie. Totally devoted to the cause of racing, and in the forefront of its organization, they suffered financial and health losses in the battle to keep up with the requirements of FIA Grand Prix events.

- Timing and scoring for the Grand Prix was handled by Bill and Ginny Close, whose team was so effective that Cam and I never had to give their work a thought. But the Closes always had problems with Colin Chapman. Getting the fastest times during qualifying was important to getting the best positions on the grid. Colin was timing his own entries and claimed his faster figures were correct, so Bill, a solid Scotsman, put two clocks on Lotus cars. When electronic timing arrived, Chapman had no leg to stand on.

- The Lytles were great friends of the Argetsingers and always on deck at the races. Well known as a race historian and photographer, Charlie was very competent and could be called upon to help in any emergency. When Stirling Moss came over for the Formula Libre race, Charlie volunteered to pick him up at the Elmira airport, and suggested Moss create a sensation at Registration by walking up to the girl at the desk and giving her a big hug and a kiss. Moss thought this a reasonable suggestion and followed through. The girl nearly collapsed but it made her day.

- Because we talked the same engineering language, I always made it a point after the Grand Prix to talk with Bruce McLaren, who knew of my interest and was very open. I felt a deep personal loss when he was killed testing one of his cars.

- Track announcer John Duvall of Syracuse stayed at the old Jefferson Hotel where we frequently met for breakfast. A delightful and knowledgeable acquaintance, John was also involved in the AAA event at the Syracuse fairground.

- The first hat trick at the Glen was accomplished by Graham Hill driving for BRM. I got to know some of the drivers and crew members, Hill as well as Tony Rudd, BRM's chief designer and team manager. Whenever Graham was on the grid and I was within eyesight, he would look over and give me "the wink," acknowledging that chief stewards perform a necessary, if sometimes painful, task in motor racing events.

- BRM was a small part of the Rubery Owen empire headed by Sir Alfred Owen and owned by the two Owen brothers and their sister Jean. Jean and her husband Louis Stanley closely followed BRM racing activity and regularly appeared at the U.S. Grand Prix. They added prestige and style to the event, became great supporters of Watkins Glen and made friends with the officials. Everything the Stanleys did was first class, and their banquets after BRM wins, which I attended on several occasions, were memorable affairs. Big Lou, as he affectionately was known, was an author of note and produced a series of insightful volumes on motor racing. Apt at character study, he recognized genuine personalities and ruthlessly exposed phony ones, introduced medical facilities at the tracks in Europe and handled difficult negotiations adroitly.

- The Grand Prix circuit was not without horseplay, which I had to deal with as chief steward. Our room at the Jefferson was not far from John Cooper's, and on more than one occasion in the middle of the night he banged on our door insisting we were in his room.

- The Watkins Glen events depended on many individuals who volunteered a variety of services. Among those not yet mentioned were Tex Hopkins, the colorful starter in the purple suit; Smith Hempstone Oliver, announcer; Dewey Alter, who installed the telephone communication on the original circuit; Jim Berry, who met the Grand Prix cars on arrival in New York City and arranged their transportation to Watkins Glen; and Peter Helck, who did the program covers.

- In 1971, when the permanent circuit was extended to 3.4 miles, Mal Currie engaged the Transportation Research Department at Calspan to develop a computer simulation program predicting lap-time performance of a Formula 1 car of that era. This was performed by R. Douglas Roland and Carl Thelin, and ranks as one of the early lap-time simulations in this country and a predecessor of MRA's current program.

Chapter 22

Butterball Saga

My usual participation in Watkins Glen in 1951 was replaced by a trip to England to present a paper entitled "Dynamic Stability and Control Research" at the Third International Joint Conference, sponsored by the Royal Aeronautical Society and the Institute of Aeronautical Sciences. A number of British attendees introduced me to the motor racing scene. At the Bugatti Owners Club headquarters, while attending a Prescott hill climb, I met Sydney Allard, Dennis Poore, Archie Butterworth, Mrs. Kay Petre, and S. C. H. "Sammy" Davis, whose great Bentley drives and "never give up" racing philosophy had impressed me as a youngster when I read *Motor Racing*. At the end of the day, Kay Petre offered me a ride back to London. In the 1930s this quiet, sophisticated woman had established herself as an outstanding driver on the Austin factory team.

Dennis Poore was well known as the owner/driver of a former Nuvolari monoposto Alfa Romeo. Upon learning that I was flying down to Monza for the Italian Grand Prix, and low on cash, he offered to lend me a thousand pounds on a handshake. Such accommodations among reputable Englishmen were common, I was told. The Monza Grand Prix was an experience to remember. Farina on a 159 Alfa drove a beautiful race, making fastest lap at over 120 mph before experiencing engine problems. Ascari won, piloting a 375 Ferrari at a race average of 115 mph. Some of the other great names in that event were Fangio, Gonzalez, Villoresi, Taruffi, Chiron, Bonetto and Stuck. Naturally, on my return to New York, I hastened to repay the loan.

Butterball near the top of Mt. Equinox, 1956.

Calculated Risk.

– Anonymous

Fig. 22-1
Bill Milliken and Sydney Allard discussing Allard's record-breaking Steyr-powered car.

The Butterball

Sydney Allard had extensively modified an air-cooled Austrian Steyr tank engine to produce a light single-seat car of perhaps 270 horsepower that proved to be a successful hill climb racer. When I expressed interest, he told me about Archie Butterworth's four-wheel drive car that also used a Steyr tank engine, and had a number of unique features that made it seem a logical replacement for the FWD Miller.

The Four Wheel Drive Company agreed to my proposal to buy the machine, but Archie was hesitant because he still was competing, and was enjoying some success. Following my return home, however, I received a letter with the return address of a British hospital near Shelsley Walsh. After taking Crossing Bend 10 mph too fast, Archie and the car had crossed the ditch separately. He had collided with the safety bar and broken his ribs. Archie thought there must be a laugh in that.

He now agreed to sell the car in its wrecked condition, and FWD agreed to support our efforts at Flight Research to repair, develop and compete with it. After the big crate arrived at our hangar in February of 1952, Dave Whitcomb described the car as having been "wrapped up in a ball" and christened it the "Butterball."

Miller's Last Stand

While work on the Butterball proceeded, we ran the FWD Miller in several events. The most successful was in Canada at the 1952 Edenvale Airport race, for which the Miller was ideally geared. We won the first event, defeating a Cad-Allard J-2X, but after making fastest lap we finished second in the main event thanks to brake fade. Considering that the Miller was heavier and less powerful than the Allard, we attributed our success to less shifting and minimal wheel spin.

No less important to the drivers than track condition were the restroom facilities! At most early circuits these facilities were poor at best, but Edenvale topped (or bottomed) them all.

The single wooden outhouse was located on high ground in the center of the track and could be reached only by marching through water several inches deep. Water also covered the floor of the facility, and once inside a hopeful, if not urgent, user found no way to lock the door, which persisted in flapping open.

After Edenvale we rushed off to Mt. Equinox and broke the record three times during the weekend, finally finishing second fastest. Less than a month later, in Vermont for the Burke Mountain Hill Climb with its smooth, paved winding road seemingly a cinch for the Miller, we got off to a terrific start but suddenly lost power after a mile when an exhaust valve broke and exited through the tailpipe. After pulling off to the side, a young man rushed up holding it in a handkerchief and exclaiming, "Hey, mister, you lost something and it's pretty hot." The valve head was beat up but I took it home to add to my collection of broken bits. Some 20 years later, while having lunch in the General Motors Research dining room, the conversation turned to motor sport, and one of the engineers commented, "I don't know much about racing but I did retrieve a valve head once to give it back to the driver at a hill climb near my home town." Small world.

Fig. 22-2
FWD Miller at Mt. Equinox on June 15, 1952. We broke the record three times on the weekend, but finished a close second to Weaver's Maserati *Poison Lil*. Barbara in background.

AFTER BURKE MOUNTAIN, all of our efforts were channeled to the Butterworth car.

My racing career had focused thus far on two products of genius: the Bugattis, unique, beautiful and elegant, and the FWD Miller

Fig. 22-3
L-R: Butterball with dual rear tires, FWD Miller, F1 Lago Talbot on loan, in front of Flight Research Hangar at Cornell Lab, 1953. Dual rear tires on Butterball as used at Edenvale in 1955.

from the unbeatable triumvirate of Harry Miller, Leo Goossen and Fred Offenhauser, functionally conceived, and masterfully engineered and built. With the arrival of S.2, as Butterworth designated the car, I was confronted with quite a different machine of ingenious and advanced features, the result of one man's dream and produced on a shoestring.

A Pioneering "Special"

Like Colin Chapman, John Cooper and Eric Broadley, Archie was one of that band of talented and creative individuals who, with limited resources and despite great obstacles, laid the foundations for Great Britain's later supremacy in race car engineering. Butterworth

Fig. 22-4
Special components of Steyr engine: cylinder head, aluminum alloy con rod, Alfin barrel and 14:1 domed piston.

Fig. 22-5
Steyr engine with Alfin barrels, 14:1 compression ratio and eight Amal carbs.

was an inventor of note, a first-class mechanical designer and draftsman, a hands-on machine shop operator, and a man grounded in engineering fundamentals and materials. Above all, he was absolutely honest, straightforward and open, and we became great friends.

After sending the car from England, Archie wrote two letters describing its critical design features and providing tuning information as well as his race setups and handling experience. These technically and analytically enlightening letters are included in Appendix VI. Acknowledging that he still was learning the S.2 when it crashed, Archie assumed we would continue the learning process. Although never focusing on race driving as a career, he seems to have had all the attributes of an outstanding engineering test driver.

Essentially, S.2 began during WWII when several captured Austrian Steyr-powered German tanks, with spare engines, were brought into the armored vehicle research establishment at which Butterworth worked. These V-8 air-cooled units of 3.07 by 3.62 inches (bore and stroke) were rated at perhaps 100 bhp. Someone must have recognized that increasing the bore to 3.44 inches, raising the compression ratio to 14:1 via Alfin cylinders and domed pistons, and using alcohol-based fuel, would make the Steyr a lightweight racing engine of more than 250 bhp. I never asked Archie how he acquired his engine or the additional components he later supplied, of which there were many. The engine came with eight Amal motorcycle carburetors. The engine's crankcase and bottom end remained close to the original Steyr design.

The four-wheel drive S.2 had three differentials, the center one lockable. The rear axle was solid, the front a swing-axle independent derived from Jeep components. It featured a Rzeppa joint, with the differential on one of the swing axle elements and a sliding joint on the driveshaft. The clutch was conventional, but the transmission followed motorcycle practice as a manual five-speed progressive of Butterworth's own patentable design. He was years ahead of the hydraulically controlled Moog valve shift of current Grand Prix practice that rattles through like a Gatling gun. In the Butterworth unit all gears were in

Fig. 22-6
Butterball in final form, 1956. This shows the front swing axle and revised steering setup and Cadillac brakes.

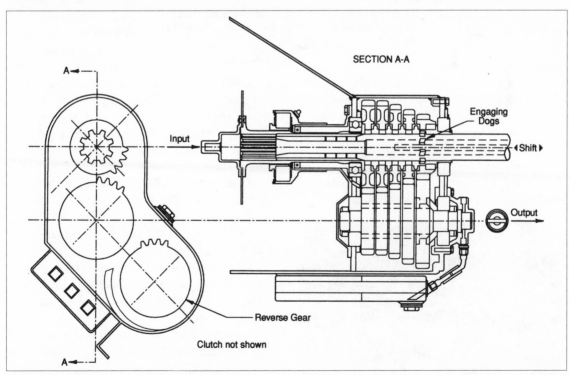

Fig. 22-7
Butterworth designed and built a five-speed progressive transmission, believed to be the first progressive transmission installed in a race car. The input shaft from the clutch is shown on the left, supported by a roller bearing. This shaft is enclosed in a sliding tube that is keyed to the input shaft, and hence turns at the same speed. Attached to this tube is a set of "dogs" that can selectively engage the free-floating gears, which mesh with the gear cluster on the output shaft. Since the cluster gears rotate as a unit, all of the gears on the input shaft are made to rotate when the dogs engage any gear on the input shaft. This facilitated shifting because the five speeds are closely ratioed. The driver's shift mechanism merely moves the shift tube in and out.

mesh and rotating, but engagement occurred only when dogs on the sliding driveshaft locked onto a free gear. Neutral occurred when the dog fell between two of the free gears. The gears were closely spaced in number of teeth, which facilitated shifting. Archie considered various modes of gearbox operation, including two-pedal, up and down.

While we were racing the Butterball, Archie Butterworth was involved in some interesting developments. The first was a flat four-cylinder engine with swing valves. The valve face was attached to an arm, so that upon opening there was no obstruction of the port by the valve stem. Using a Strobotac he was able to solve problems of valve dynamics and develop a lightweight engine of high specific output. Unfortunately this system never went into production. Archie also was negotiating with Lotus to use his progressive gearbox, a deal that for various reasons fell

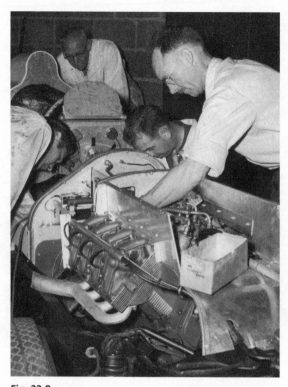

Fig. 22-8
Butterball rebuild, 1952. Bill Close, designer, works on Steyr engine. Frankie Babchek on left. Airbox for engine cooling.

through, although Lotus later used a similar design in one of its cars.

Butterworth also was involved in a GP car design using FWD and a patented suspension with hydraulically controlled differentials. Powered by his 2-½ litre flat-four engine, the entire car weighed just 700 pounds. Another of his ideas was the "Sidler," a unique device for parking a car sideways.[2]

Like so many creative inventors, Archie had difficulty patenting his ideas, defending them and getting them into production.

Originally built in 1948, the subsequently modified AJB Special S.2 competed in 25 hill climbs, speed trials and road races in England. On six occasions the car made fastest time of the day. The best efforts from a standing start were at speed trials in 1951: a quarter mile of 12.69 seconds at Gosport and a kilometer in 26.63 seconds at Brighton in heavy rain. S.2 also held course records at the Blandford Hill Climb (30.15 seconds) and the Bornham Speed Trials (25.12).

Bill Close took a great interest in the Butterball. What successes we had in competition largely were due to his efforts. Our first objective was to design a new rear suspension, steering system, cockpit area and engine cooling airbox in time for Watkins Glen, which required a complete teardown of the engine and chassis. Bill designed a straightforward solid-axle rear suspension with parallel forward links and a Panhard

Fig. 22-9
Butterball engine/transmission and original steering system, Cornell Lab, 1952.

[2]*MRA attempted to interest major car companies in the U.S. in this product.*

Fig. 22-10
Butterball final assembly, at Cornell Lab, 1952. Bill Close third from right, Bill Milliken back to camera with work list.

rod, the slope of the links determining the oversteer/understeer characteristics. Archie had mentioned Sydney Allard's idea of running the steering post through the engine's V with the steering box in front, a system we devised. We also thought we might improve engine cooling by developing some cowling around it. Neither of these elements worked out in practice.

Back to Milliken's Corner

We got Butterball to the Glen in time for practice for the 1952 Grand Prix. It was the first time I drove the car. We followed Butterworth's recommended fuel mix of methanol, benzol and avgas, and his jet sizes, etc. The engine had a healthy but peculiar staccato sound, probably due to its 14:1 compression ratio. Spectators told me they always could tell when the Butterball was approaching. The car showed phenomenal acceleration

and plenty of top speed, and I had no trouble staying with Weaver's Maserati Poison Lil. But the handling was difficult to impossible, reminding me of Maurice Olley's famous comment about "steering a car through a fish pole." Our modifications to the steering

Fig. 22-11
First corner on start of Seneca Cup, 1952. Butterball following Weaver's Maserati Poison Lil.

475

Fig. 22-12
In the paddock at Watkins Glen, 1952. The Butterball is surrounded by (L to R): Jack Fabian, FWD, Cam Argetsinger, J. C. Argetsinger, Big Bill Wilcox. WFM is in the cockpit talking with Bruce Stevenson, who initiated the Bridgehampton races.

system had resulted in a very flexible system, so compliant that when I held the steering wheel fixed, Bill Wilcox could turn the front wheels several degrees by hand.

Fig. 22-13
Bare chassis of Butterball during rebuild at Cornell Lab in 1952. Note the Close-designed parallel-link rear suspension with Panhard rod.

Since practice on the street circuit was minimal, contestants were given several preliminary laps before the start. On the second one, I lost Butterball in Milliken's Corner (history repeating itself). Although pavement tracks showed the car seemingly parallel to the hay bales after the corner, the car suddenly spun to the left, the tail (at the rear axle) crashing into a steel telephone pole set in concrete. I was held in by the belt, but remember thinking, "My God, I must have gotten a dozen g's." A film made by a spectator from the third floor of the adjacent building was shown at the annual meeting of the SCCA. In it my head, arm and upper body stretched out toward the pole a foot or so before snapping back. This verified my impression, and validated Sir Henry Royce's dictum that "in the last analysis, every material (including the human) is rubber." The base cause of the accident was the compliance in the steering system. We went back to Buffalo determined to eliminate the problems found at Watkins Glen, as well as improve the appearance of the car, and its performance, which had not even approached its true potential.

Fig. 22-14
Butterball accident at Milliken's Corner due to flexible steering system.

Fig. 22-15
WFM and Bill Wilcox with Butterball at Glen Cove, Pikes Peak, 1953.

Butterball Progress

Over the next five years we raced the Butterball in ten events, continuing to develop the machine as time and resources permitted. Table 22-1 at the end of the chapter summarizes our efforts and results.

I've always believed Butterworth and Allard did a remarkable job getting so much power out of the Steyr engine despite its bottom-end limitation and setting a safe rev limit of 4,800 rpm. Unlike the Miller, which could be over-revved and seemed almost indestructible, the modified Steyr had to be treated carefully. Once, upon removing the pan, we found the webs supporting the crankshaft severely cracked, and endured a year's delay getting another crankcase from Butterworth.

A few remarks on our Butterball experiences follow:

Pikes Peak, 1953

Prior to taking the car to Pikes Peak in 1953, in addition to developing a new minimum-compliance steering system, we also developed a "double ratchet" shift mechanism (a spring-centered lever that shifted up when pulled back and down when pushed forward). Together with the engine tachometer on the engine hood, this allowed me to shift up or down while keeping the revs within limits without taking my eyes off the road. Unfortunately this shift lever broke off, leaving the car in third gear just before the completion of the qualifying run. I should have stopped and asked for another attempt. Instead, we were disqualified from the competition. I felt I had let FWD down and experienced the roughest moments in my racing career. All the summer's labor, and the long trailer tow to Pikes Peak and back, had come to naught. At the 1953 Watkins Glen which followed, the cracked crankcase webs were discovered.

Edenvale, 1955

By 1955, we were back in business with a new crankcase and entered the Edenvale Airport event in Canada. Tests on our ramp proved the car had a bad case of "trailing

Fig. 22-16
WFM and Bill Wilcox with Butterball at Pikes Peak, 1953. Note dual rear tires (tried in practice but not used in the event).

throttle oversteer" (see Chapter 17), difficult to cope with in a race but livable in a hill climb. Installing dual rear tires could just about eliminate the problem, so that was the configuration we used at Edenvale. While running first or second and feeling great, I suddenly lost all "fixity" at the rear, the rear axle slid over and the tire hit my elbow. The Panhard rod anchorage had failed. Talk about oversteer!! Upon turning the wheel, the axle moved to the other side and the other tire banged my other elbow, offering demonstrable proof that rear wheels (like the vertical tail on an airplane) provide the directional stability of an automobile.

At Edenvale I had a chance to do a standing quarter mile on the airport drag strip. My experience in "dragging" was about zero. When I let out the clutch at 4,900 rpm, it felt like someone had given me a swift kick in the tail end. We did the quarter mile in about 11 seconds and topped out at about 130 mph—not a bad performance for a road racing car of that era.

Fig. 22-17
Steyr block and engine components, Bill Wilcox and Bill Milliken, 1952.

but were so sensitive I had to think before every application. Cutting back to only a fraction of the original lining cured the problem. The potential of the Butterball was shown that year at the Glen, but clutch failure put us out of the race.

Watkin's Glen (second circuit), 1955

Later in 1955 we installed some huge (12-inch-diameter) Cadillac drum brakes for the first event on the second Watkins Glen country-road circuit. The course was roughly rectangular, with one downhill leg ending alongside an apple orchard at a slow corner with no escape road. The hill had several long waves in vertical curvature, so the car was either on the down stops or floating with little load on the suspension, with the front swing axles hanging down at positive camber. I was running first and second, lapping at over 80 mph and hitting about 125 mph in fifth gear on this downhill leg, which was really scary. The plan was to touch the brake pedal halfway down to make sure I had brakes. If I had lost them, I would start downshifting, one gear after another, and hope for the best. The huge Cadillac brakes had plenty of stopping power

Watkin's Glen (permanent circuit), 1956

After doing well at Giant's Despair with a record in the rain, we entered the Butterball for the first event at Watkins Glen's third and permanent circuit in 1956. Two-minute practice laps at an average of 68.5 mph boded well for the race. The brakes finally were right, and the steering and shift mechanisms were working as advertised. The car's development seemed to be complete until a rock knocked the sump plug off the transmission, and all the oil ran out of the box. Assessing the damage at Smalley's, we discovered a ruined ball bearing on the main shaft and a bronze bushing on a lay shaft scored beyond use. We worked outside the garage, surrounded by a group of spectators. The remains of the ball bearing indicated French manufacture. Chance of replacement seemed nil but Les produced a box of used ball bearings and I found an identical

Fig. 22-18
Butterball at Giant's Despair, 1955.

unit. The possibility of replacing the bronze bushing seemed even less likely, until a shop instructor at the local high school stepped forward saying he could turn one out if he had the bronze. A second spectator, who worked in the stockroom at Corning Glass, replied that he knew how to sneak in the back door and get some. As if by magic, a third spectator offered to drive us to Corning. Off we went. Turning a sizable hunk of bronze on a high school lathe seemed an impossible task to me but the instructor reappeared in the early hours on race day with the finished part. I left to get a few hours of sleep while the crew reassembled the transmission and had the car back at the track for the Seneca Cup. We shot out from the front row at the start, but gearshift trouble developed, we lost ground on missed shifts, and finished 3rd in class and 15th overall. But it was a great try.

The final configuration of the Butterball is on page 490. Not noted on the list was our installation of a push switch on top of the spring-loaded gearshift lever that cut out the ignition, allowing shifts without use of the clutch. One pressed the switch and banged the lever into the next gear, up or down.

For all the problems of reliability, the Butterball was an experience I wouldn't have missed. How exciting it was to come out of a corner and see that right-hand front wheel leap off the ground from the torque reaction of the offset differential as you accelerated away at a phenomenal rate. When the shift mechanism was working perfectly it was a thrill to bang your way up or down through those five speeds. The handling always was a challenge, especially if one was balked and had to back off. We may not always have finished events, but we always rocketed into the lead on a standing start with the pack howling behind us.

After the Butterball

As I approached my 50th birthday, I still was racing with whatever machinery was available: Sebring three times with an Elva and twice with an Alfa Veloce. On a fourth occasion I became part of the 1957 SS Corvette team after Zora Arkus-Duntov asked me to set up a timing and scoring system for the car. It was one thing to run a lap chart for overall race position, but knowing where his car stood on Formula, which he required, was quite another matter. So I arranged for several folks from Flight Research with timing and scoring experience to be available for practice and the race.

There were great hopes for the SS. Piero Taruffi was flown over from Italy to share driving with John Fitch. During practice Fangio was invited to try the car and made two very consistent laps at near-record speed. Stirling Moss followed, again very consistently but a second slower than Fangio.

On race day I still had qualms about supplying accurate and timely information, so when Harley Earl showed up and asked to watch the race from the second story of the pits, I shoved a stopwatch in his hands. But the real lifesaver was Charlie Lytle, who appeared with John Wyer and a friend. I knew that if anyone could keep track of the SS Wyer could, so I asked him to run a separate lap chart, and installed him with his friend in a favorable corner of the roof. The SS went out early but John Wyer continued to maintain his chart, which proved invaluable later in the race when questions arose in the adjacent pit about the positions of the standard Corvettes.

I concluded from this experience that while race driving has its problems, timing and scoring is an art of its own. Later we were to see it mastered and perfected by Bill and Virginia Close during the Formula One races at the Glen.

In 1959 Millard Ripley, who had worked out a deal with Colin Chapman to drive a Lotus XI at Sebring, invited me along as co-driver, an exciting opportunity. But after each of us had one lap in practice, Chapman reneged on the deal after locating better drivers. This was my only encounter with Chapman on a business level.

The advent of racing at Watkins Glen released a pent-up desire for speed in many motoring souls. Every drive to the Glen was an opportunity to lower elapsed times. Speeding tickets naturally followed, my record being two on one weekend. Some were justified but others were a quick and convenient way to extract a toll for support of surrounding villages, and were akin to highway robbery. I got sufficiently cranked up to write an article on the subject for the Grand Prix program that resulted in a number of congratulatory letters, one of which said my thinking was the "best thing since the Magna Carta."

On September 25, 1959, with four-year-old son Doug, I left Buffalo in the early hours to drive Les Smalley's XK-120 MC to Watkins. Completely barren of traffic, the New York State Thruway offered a great place to check out wheel balance and general setup. We were nailed at 115-plus mph by a patrolman who appeared out of the woods. Before he said a word, I let go: "Why do you have to ruin my day? For Christ's sake, why don't you get yourself a decent job instead of frustrating the hell out of everyone?" He just stood there, speechless, finally signaling me to go on. I was probably as surprised as he was by my outburst. Sometimes an expression of true feeling, despite the risk, is better than playing games.

In March of 1960 Cam and I co-drove a Veloce at Sebring, finishing fourth in class and enjoying every moment of it. It was our first race together, the last formal race for both of us and a poignant way to wrap up our active competition. But in a sense we never left racing. I pursued the technical side. Cam went on to join Jim Hall's operations, directed SCCA and, with Jean, created the International Motor Racing Research Center. His dream of a postwar road race has had a profound effect on the lives and activities of so many people.

Table 22-1. Butterball Competition History

Event/Car No.	Date	Configuration	Results
Watkins Glen Seneca Cup No. 24	Sept. 20 1952	• Close rear suspension • Steering very flexible • Brakes poor • Airbox around engine • Tach on front	• Used Butterworth's fuel mix • Started in pole position (car fast) • Lost control after Milliken's Corner • **DNF** (due to flex in steering)
Pike's Peak No. 46	Sept. 7 1953	• Improved steering • Double ratchet shift • Airbox • Improved brakes	• 46.2 mph average (unofficial) • Shift lever broke • **Failed to qualify**
Watkins Glen (second circuit) No. 1	Sept. 19 1953	• Same as Pike's Peak	• Cranckcase webs cracked • **Did not start**
Edenvale No. 22	June 18 1955	• Dual rear wheels • Installed new crankcase • Still Jeep wheels	• Ran first and second • Panhard rod failed • **DNF** (standing 1/4-mile: 11.0 sec.)
Giant's Despair No. 111	July 22 1955	• Same as Edenvale, but with single wheels	• **3rd overall**, (63.771 sec.)
Watkins Glen Seneca Cup Race (second circuit) No. 47	Sept. 17 1955	• Cadillac brakes • Original wheels • Airbox • Dunlop tires 6.00×16	• Towed car to start • Ran first and second • Lapped 80 mph+ (downhill 125+) • Clutch failure 3/4 way • **DNF**
Mt. Equinox No. 15	June 17 1956	• No airbox • Perforated side panels	• Handling poor • Gearshift trouble • **Off'l time 5:30.02** (Weaver 5:12)
Giant's Despair No. 57	July 20 1956	• Installed Halibrand wheels • Cadillac brakes very sensitive • New steering box	• Dry: Shelby Ferrari 0:58 sec. (all-time record) • Wet: AJB 1:06; Shelby 1:06.1 • **2nd in Unrestricted class**

Watkins Glen (permanent circuit; 2.3 miles) No. 2	Sept. 15 1956	• Installed oil cooler
		• Brakes sensitive
		  Shoes adj. to make
		  concentric
			• Practice lap 2:01 min. (68.5 mph)
			• Rock punctured sump (fixed)
			• Car wouldn't stay in gear in race
			• **3rd in class, 15th overall**

Holland Hill Climb No. 76	Aug. 25 1957	• Same as W.G. 1956	• **Time: 0.8672 min.** • Set all-time record
Watkins Glen 10th Annual Sports Car GP (Last Unrestricted Event) No. 90	Sept. 21 1957	• Tire differential 31/40 • Brake linings cut back • New oil cooler • Locked center differential	• Best lap 74.4 mph • Pushrod broke • **5th in Unrestricted, 7th overall**

Autumn, 1957: Car shipped to FWD Museum in Clintonville, Wisconsin.

Fig. 22-19
Left-hand view of Butterball during rework at Cornell Lab, 1952.

Fig. 22-20
Butterball engine overhaul. L-R: Bill Milliken, Al Schwartz, Henry Sonnen, Bill Wilcox and Frankie Babchek.

Fig. 22-21
Butterball in Watkins Glen paddock, 1955. L-R: Casey Jaworski (with badge), Bill Close, Bill Milliken and Charlie Lytle.

Fig. 22-22
Butterball, preparation crew for Watkins Glen Seneca Cup (last unrestricted event) on permanent circuit (1957).
L-R: Chuck Hutchinson, Henry Sonnen, Bill Close, Lee Maefs, Bill Milliken, Frankie Babchek, Bill Wilcox, Jack Fabian, Dick Koegler, Carl Oddo and Al Schwartz.

Fig. 22-24
Sebring, with special Corvette team, 1957.
Milliken with Piero Taruffi.

Fig. 22-23
Butterball setting all-time record and winning permanent trophy
at Holland Hill Climb, 1957.

Fig. 22-25
Sebring, with special Corvette team, 1957.
Betty Skelton and Bill Milliken.

Fig. 22-26
Watkins Glen, Seneca Cup, 1958. Ripley's Ferrari with Doug Milliken.

Fig. 22-27
Sebring, 1958. Bill Milliken in Ripley's Elva passing Abarth 750GT.

Fig. 22-28
Watkins Glen, 2nd Annual Glen Classic, 1958. XK120M (owned by Les Smalley) on permanent circuit.

Fig. 22-29
Sebring, 1958 (with Ripley's Elva). L-R: Cam Argetsinger, Bill Case, Virginia Close, Barbara Milliken, Jean Argetsinger.

Fig. 22-30
Sebring, 1958 (with Ripley's Elva). L-R: Cameron's mother, Jean Argetsinger, Barbara Milliken, Mrs. Ripley—in the pits.

Fig. 22-31
Sebring, 1958 with Ripley's Elva. L-R: Bill Milliken, Millard Ripley, Cam Argetsinger.

Fig. 22-32
Sebring, 1958. Ripley's Elva, me driving.

Fig. 22-33
Sebring 12 Hour with Alfa Veloce (owned by Cam Argetsinger), 1960.

Fig. 22-34
Sebring 12 Hour, 1960. L-R: Bill Milliken, Cam Argetsinger, Barbara Milliken.

Fig. 22-35
Sebring 12 Hour, 1960. Barbara Milliken and Jean Argetsinger.

"BUTTERBALL"

FOUR-WHEEL DRIVE, A.J.B. SPRINT CAR

Owned by The Four-Wheel Drive Auto Co.
Driven by Bill Milliken

This car was originally built in England by A. J. Butterworth in 1948. It was wrecked at Shelsley Walsh in September 1951, and imported to the U. S. A. early in 1952. It has since been extensively redesigned with longer wheelbase, new rear suspension, improved steering, brakes, chassis and body. This work was performed in the Flight Research and Vehicle Dynamics Departments of Cornell Aeronautical Laboratory under the direction of William Close.

TECHNICAL DATA

Powerplant - 90° V-8 modified Steyr (Austrian)
Displacement, 4425^{cc}
Compression ratio, 14 to 1
Alfin cyclinder barrels
8 Amal carburetors
Fuel, mixture of methanol, benzol and unleaded gasoline
Harrison oil cooler
BHP, approximately 280 at 4900 rpm

Transmission - 11" Borg and Beck clutch driving special Butterworth 5 speed constant mesh gearbox with incorporated transfer drive. A separate reverse gear is provided and inter-axle differential which can be locked or un-locked.

Positive stop "progressive" gear shift with spring loaded return to mid-position. Gear shift position indicator on cowl aft of engine.

Suspensions - Swing axle front.
Conventional rear
Coil springs with special
Houdaille piston-type shocks

Wheels and Brakes -
Halibrand wide base magnesium wheels with modified Cadillac brakes. Dunlop racing tires.

Weight -   In sprint configuration with fuel and driver, 1975 lbs.

Weight/Power Ratio - 7 lbs/HP

PERFORMANCE

Alternate axle ratios available. With present ratio the following road speeds are achieved at 4900 rpm:

1st gear - 55 mph
2nd gear - 76 mph
3rd gear - 99 mph
4th gear - 122 mph
5th gear - 138 mph

Standing 1/4 mile in approximately 12 seconds, or over 130 mph at end of quarter.

Top speed with an alternate ratio approximately 160 mph.

WFM:ecj
1/3/58

Fig. 22-36
Butterball final configuration.

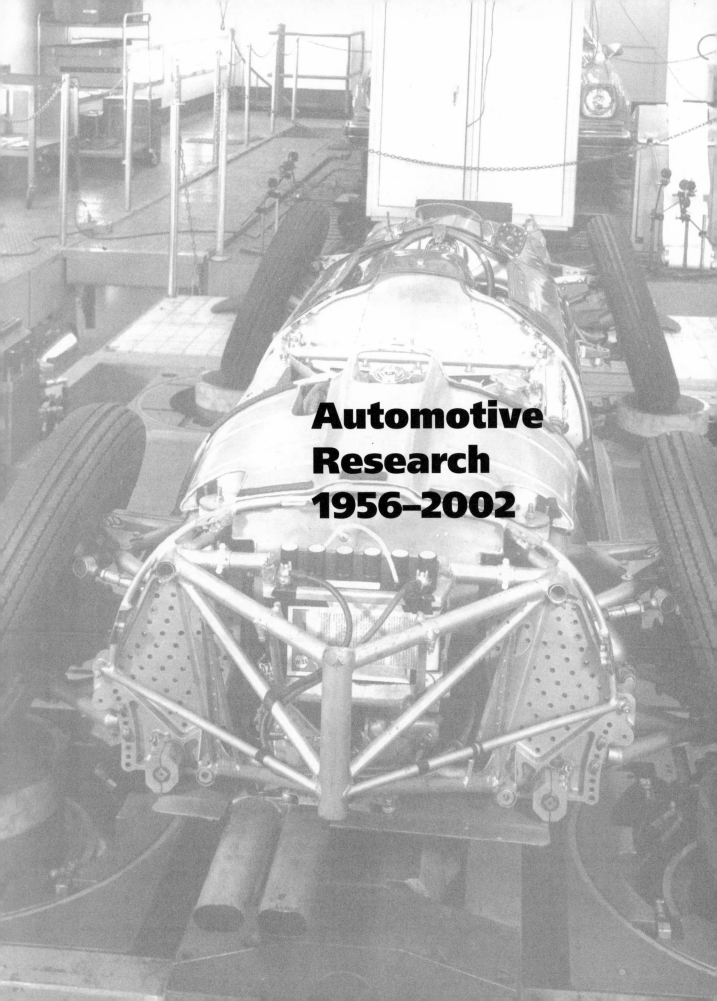

Automotive
Research
1956–2002

Chapter 23

Camber Galore

> "A moment's insight is sometimes worth a life's experience."
>
> – Oliver Wendell Holmes

The idea had been rattling around in my subconscious for a long time. During a vacation in Watkins Glen in 1960 it finally surfaced, and with enough conviction that I had to take action. I wanted to build a car.

For nearly ten years we had been analyzing the fundamentals of automobile handling with considerable success, but in analysis one can abstract a problem and avoid many of the nuances and subtleties of the real thing. This was brought home to me during lunch with Colin Chapman and Lawrence Pomeroy at the Racing Drivers Club in London. Colin was wrestling with the desirable location of the center of gravity (CG) for a racing car. As we talked, it became apparent that a wide variety of design factors affect the control and stability of a vehicle, of which the longitudinal location of the CG is but one.

The desirable combination of variables for a given vehicle design was not addressed with our mathematics. We had given the analytical designer a bag of quantitative tricks, but with no real clues how to use them. Consider the design compromises of the successful Grand Prix Bugattis. All these rear-drive machines, from the Type 35 to the 59, had CGs located well aft at 60–65 percent of the wheelbase. This made for good traction and brake balance but failed to facilitate neutral steer at the limit. To achieve that, Bugatti took a large percentage of the lateral load transfer on the front track and cambered the front wheels in a positive sense, i.e., leaning outward. The camber thrust, a strong function of load transfer, was in the understeer direction. There were other effects (i.e., compliances at the rear suspension) but overall the car was close to neutral steer.

The compromise of this configuration was poor ride/pitch behavior, with a tendency to fly nose-down on big bumps. On small-scale roughness the nose was forever bobbing up and down, giving a great impression of liveliness that I found enjoyable. High control

MX-1 at Chevrolet Vehicle Handling Facility, their kinematic and compliance machine.

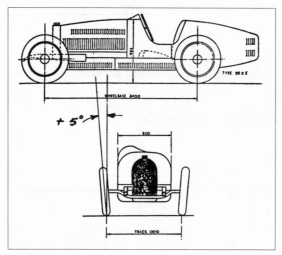

Fig. 23-1
The very popular and successful Type 35 Bugatti. Note positive camber on the front wheels, which contributed to its directional stability.

forces and inside front wheel lift during hard cornering were other results of the Bugatti configuration.

The lunch with Pomeroy and Chapman made me realize the *challenge of design*, which influenced my subsequent vehicle dynamics activity. It finally led to the Moment Method, based on my previous aircraft research, that is a powerful technique for compromising vehicle performance over its full operational range. This became a strong incentive to design and build an experimental car.

A further incentive was my exposure to the creative process in general. Thanks to racing, I was continually experiencing, examining and studying design arrangements, and trying to understand how they came about. Major breakthroughs can change the course of design for years. Certainly the use of aerodynamic downforce by the Winchell/Hall Chaparral group was one of these. Lesser breakthroughs are characterized by their fundamental nature, their effect on the core equations governing the process. I wanted my involvement in an experimental vehicle design to have an innovative theme.

This team effort would be one in which I could have personal engineering input. Cornell Lab was a great place to work, but for the last 15 years my professional life had been focused on administration and sales. In 1966 the National

Traffic and Motor Vehicle Safety Act led to the formation of the Transportation Division at the Laboratory, and my promotion to head it. The MX-1 project[1] would be superimposed on my other responsibilities at the Lab.

Since I had no machine shop, parts would have to be farmed out to local facilities for fabrication. Overall, we produced nearly 150 drawings, both major layouts (with details) and smaller detail drawings. Because it was a major educational activity for me, every design element was analyzed as we proceeded. We built up a design file of more than 150 folders. Inexperience in automobile design restricted us to fundamentals.

In 1949, a dozen years before the MX-1 project, I conceived what I believed to be a new way to use tires, namely in a heavily negatively cambered configuration with all four wheels leaning inward. By 1955, after making a plasticine model of an enclosed car with high camber and studying the arrangement, I made a patent disclosure to the Laboratory's Patent Committee. At the time I was thinking in terms of a race car application. The committee regarded the idea as too far out and of questionable utility, and never pursued it.

Other virtues of negatively cambered wheels came to light later, and since I still was enamored with the idea it became the *innovative theme* of MX-1. The entire vehicle design evolved around it. Because there were so many unknowns in achieving satisfactory steering and handling on a −25° camber car, we designed large ranges of adjustment into the steering and suspension systems. As a result, the MX-1 became one of the most mechanically adjustable variable-stability vehicles ever constructed.

In summary, the MX-1 project met all of my basic objectives. It was a chance to do some personal creative engineering and provided an education in the design process. It was a natural extension to my vehicle dynamics research and racing interests. It satisfied my curiosity

[1] *The MX-1 was strictly a personal project. Many of the team members were CAL employees who worked for me on weekends or after hours. I paid them an agreed hourly rate, and I paid for all outside machine shop time. After 1975 the MX-1 became a capital asset of Milliken Research Associates, Inc.*

Camber Car Patent Disclosure

INVENTOR(S): Full Name RESIDENCE: Street Address TOWN COUNTY STATE

William Franklin Milliken, Jr. 293 S. Union Road, Williamsville, Erie, New York

SKETCH AND DESCRIPTION: IF SUITABLE SKETCH AND/OR DESCRIPTION HAS BEEN MADE, ATTACH TO THIS SHEET IN PLACE OF SKETCH OR DESCRIPTION HEREON.

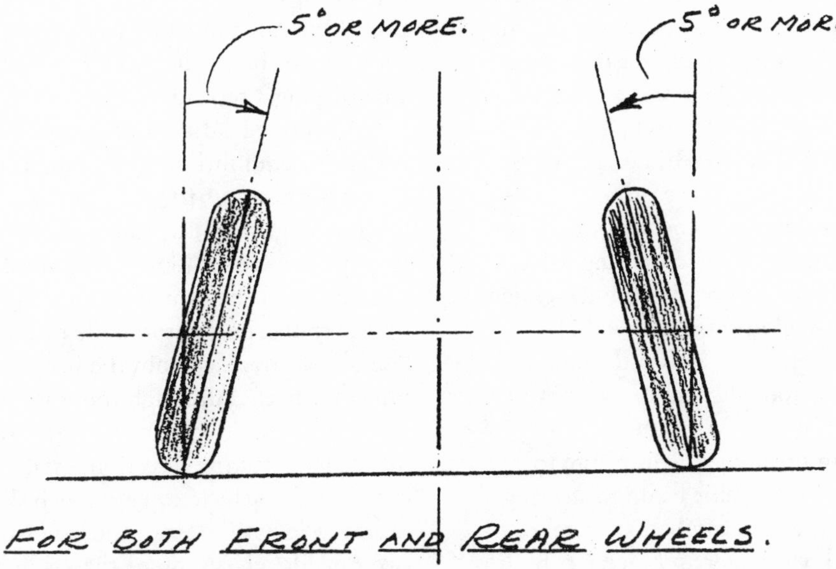

THE FOLLOWING DATA MUST BE COMPLETELY AND ACCURATELY FILLED IN:

1. CONCEIVED BY William Franklin Milliken, Jr. ON January 1949.
   ON ______ 19__

2. (a) FIRST SKETCH OR DRAWING MADE ON January 1949.
   (b) WHERE IS THE ORIGINAL SKETCH FILED? W. F. Milliken's personal file.
   (c) SKETCH OR DRAWING WITNESSED BY David Whitcomb.

3. (a) FIRST WRITTEN DESCRIPTION MADE ON 11/4/55 1955 BY W. F. Milliken, Jr.
   (b) WHERE IS THE FIRST DESCRIPTION FILED? W. F. Milliken's personal file, Flight Research

4. INVENTION WAS FIRST DISCLOSED TO
   (1) (SIGNED) David Whitcomb David Whitcomb WITNESS, ON January, 1949
   (2) (SIGNED) ______ WITNESS, ON ______ 19__

5. RECITE OTHER ACTS PROVING CONCEPTION, SUCH AS PREPARING PRELIMINARY CALCULATIONS, PREPARATION OF SHOP ORDER FOR MODEL, etc., GIVING DATES, AND STATE WHERE SUCH DATA ARE FILED: Plasticene model of proposed vehicle made in 1949 and still extant (W. F. Milliken's clamp)

6. (a) FIRST WORKING MODEL (REGARDLESS OF MATERIAL) COMPLETED ON May, 1949.
   (b) WHERE IS MODEL OR PROOF OF ITS FABRICATION AND SUCCESSFUL OPERATION TO BE FOUND? Model no longer available but rough sketch available.

7. THIS SHEET PREPARED November 4, 1955 (SIGNED) William Franklin Milliken Jr.

8. AUTHORIZED BY DEPARTMENTAL PATENT REP. ______ 19__

9. CONCEIVED WHILE WORKING ON WORK AUTHORIZATION NO. Conceived at home...

Fig. 23-2
Patent Disclosure: Competition vehicle utilizing front and rear wheels inwardly cambered (tilted negatively) to angles in excess of –5°, November 1955. Such a vehicle would have lower frontal area and aerodynamic drag for a given track, plus other virtues.

regarding camber. Finally, the MX-1 project stretched my self-discipline and stick-to-it-iveness to the limit.

Camber Experience

A good place to start thinking about the automobile in fundamental terms is with the tires, which produce all lateral forces for cornering, control and stability. Lateral forces from a loaded tire are developed in the "print" on the roadway by two distinct modes of operation: (a) when the tire is yawed, i.e., moving at an angle to the wheel plane and (b) when the tire is cambered, i.e., the wheel plane is tilted relative to the road.

In a conventional passenger car the yaw mode provides most of the cornering force, although incidental camber from independent suspension is useful in providing stability. For example, the positive outward camber on independent front suspension contributes to understeer. On race cars some negative camber is common and can contribute to the max lateral of the vehicle and to steering effectiveness. However, camber is severely limited on both passenger and race cars by modern wide tires. Thus, one can conclude that in current passenger and race car design, camber is not a primary variable but useful in the sense of trim or augmentation.

In another class of vehicles, camber plays a larger role, i.e., single-track machines like bicycles and motorcycles. In the latter, cornering is not possible without banking the vehicle and developing the camber thrust. Calspan tests indicated that with the small print sizes of bicycle tires, yaw as well as camber contribute to the lateral force; certainly both camber and yaw effects are present in achieving the maximum cornering forces from motorcycle tires. One can conclude that on single-track vehicles camber is the primary variable, with yaw playing a secondary role.

A unique feature of the single-track vehicle is that for equilibrium the resultant force on the tires must pass through the CG, and thus roughly align with the tilt of the machine. Because the CG is above the ground, the lateral tire force and the centrifugal force of cornering on the four-wheel automobile produce a lateral load transfer from the inside to the outside wheels. Although there are reasons for minimizing this load transfer (except as a means for affecting directional stability), when it occurs the vehicle can approach that of the motorcycle with most of the load carried on the two outside wheels. Since these wheels are near vertical, the force balance of the motorcycle is no longer possible and potential rollover exists. This certainly suggests that a "leaning" vehicle in which *all* wheels lean inward would closely eliminate the phenomenon of load transfer.

The concept of leaning vehicles ("tilters") is not new, and there is extensive literature on the subject. My first encounter occurred when Al Fonda, one of our most creative engineers, produced a double bicycle, followed by a three-wheeled banking go-kart (two wheels in front, one on rear) with a clever control system that he later patented. When the steering control was turned to the right for a turn in that direction, the front wheels actually turned to the left, thus promoting the centrifugal force to bank the machine. As the

Fig. 23-3
Fonda three-wheel banking vehicle (two wheels in front and one in rear), cornering at close to 52° bank. The feet of the rider actually are about 14" ahead of the front wheels. The wheel base is about 40", track 28", and overall length 64". The static weight is distributed equally to the three wheels, and in steady-state cornering there is no lateral weight transfer.

machine banked to the right, a mechanical follow-up that sensed bank angle removed the left steer and produced appropriate right steer. In principle the control followed that of the bicycle in which some "reverse" steer is initially required to create the bank.

This kart on a dry surface attained 52° of bank at 1.2g steady-state cornering. I found it very impressive on a big circle. However, if one ran over an ice patch (or reduced coefficient surface) the machine compensated by going to a higher bank angle—as Al says, "lies down"—but when it hit the dry surface again the recovery was so rapid it tended to eject the driver in a "high side" maneuver. I concluded that camber had great potential but the success of banking vehicles would depend upon a thorough understanding of their *transient dynamics*.

The conventional automobile is contrary to nature and other vehicles, all of which lean inward on cornering:

Human beings	Horses and other animals
Bicycles	Motorcycles
Birds	Airplanes
Sleds	Ships and speedboats
Hydrofoil boats	Skiers, etc.

Only in the conventional automobile do we accept the heavily loaded (outside) wheels remaining vertical or leaning outward. I began looking for exceptions, and found them in the rear suspensions of several successful racing cars. The Kieft 500-cc car of 1951–52 utilized a swing "run-around" rear suspension that could be trimmed to give some negative camber on the rear wheels. This innovation, among other desirable design features, led Stirling Moss to call the Kieft "the biggest step forward which I have ever experienced." Earlier, the Teutonically named, but completely British-Freikaiserwagen, which established a number of English hill climb records between 1936 and 1948, had utilized the same general

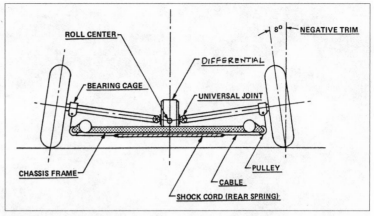

Fig. 23-4
Example of an early competition car negative camber rear suspension setup. This simple swing-axle suspension produced the desirable negative camber. For the Kieft and Freikaiserwagen it also facilitated low jacking and low roll stiffness—effects independent of the negative camber, which can be obtained by other means such as A-frame adjustments, as on MX-1.

type of rear suspension. Around 1950, Roger Penske drove a racing Porsche with a rear swing axle at Watkins Glen with the rear wheels trimmed to nearly eight degrees of negative camber.

Load transfer on a pair of vertical or positively cambered wheels results in loss of total lateral track force due to the non-linearity of the lateral force versus load curve for the tire. This factor is used with anti-roll bars to adjust the over/understeer characteristics by reducing the lateral force on the track on which the bar is installed. Load transfer on a pair of negatively cambered wheels can actually increase the total lateral track force.

From the beginning we realized that we could not analytically produce a good-handling vehicle with such a radical configuration as –20 degrees camber on all four wheels. Our only hope was to have a highly adjustable experimental vehicle to work with. The following final specifications result from the design goals dictated by the adjustability we anticipated we would need in suspension geometry, in the springing and damping and in the steering and braking systems.

MX-1 Specifications

A single-seat, rear-drive, rear-engine research vehicle with numerous mechanically adjustable features as illustrated in Figures 23-5 and 23-6.

Fig. 23-5
MX-1 with Goodyear Eagle motorcycle tires, with author at the wheel, late 1960s.

General

Wheelbase	95.5 in.
Track	51.0 in.
Overall length	154.5 in.
Overall height	30 in. to the top of roll bar at 4.5 in. ride height
Empty weight	1,272 lb. (no fuel or driver), CG 56.2%
Gross weight	1,460 lb. (full fuel and driver), CG 56.8%
Suspension	Independent front and rear via double A-frames

Suspension—Geometry and Kinematics

Camber	0, –5, –10, –15, –20, –25 deg. leaning in (all four wheels)
Swing arm length	Variable front and rear
Roll center height	Variable front and rear
Toe	Adjustable on each wheel, in or out
Caster trail (front)	Adjustable

Suspension—Springing, Ride and Roll

Basic ride	Square torsion bars with adjustable length and helper springs for individual wheels; wide frequency range
Ride height (trim)	Adjustable at each wheel and for the car as a whole
Bump stops	Adjustable against "material with a memory" for each wheel
Rebound stops	Adjustable by cable for each wheel
Shock absorbers	Armstrong adjustable for each wheel
Antiroll bars	Adjustable front and rear by variable size bars

Steering System

Rack and pinion	With long drag links (2) to isolate the steering system from suspension adjustments
Ratio	Discrete adjustment over a small range. Chain drive adjustment over a large range, approximately 3:1 to 40:1

Type	Adjustable to Ackermann, reverse Ackermann and parallel steer
Roll steer	On front, adjustable
Steering damper	To control wheelfight with certain suspension configurations

Brake System

Saab drum brakes	Two master cylinders, adjustable front and rear by balance bar; adjustable force level

Engine and Transmission Installation

Engine	Mercury outboard 800 (1961 model): 6 cylinder, 2 cycle, 76 cu. in. (1.25L), laid flat, carburetors relocated
Horsepower	Nominal 80 hp
Cooling system	Special radiator with nose air entrance and fixed cowl flap, special water pump driven by a timing belt
Starter and battery	Provided
Transmission	Four-speed VW Beetle manual shift
Clutch	Originally used Porsche, later shifted to VW Beetle manual

Wheels and Tires

Wheels	Saab, to which a 3-in. dropped-center motorcycle rim was adapted
Original tires	Goodyear Eagle, 5.00-16 notched ribbed tread (5.00-16 slick also was tested at TIRF, but not used on car)
Current tires	Dunlop K591 motorcycle rear, Sports Performance, 150/80 VB16TL, directional tread. Normally used on 3.5-in. rim, tubeless (but used with tubes). Max. load rating 761 lb. at 42 psi. Operated at 20–30 psi on MX-1.

Chassis and Body

Chassis	Welded steel tube triangulated frame with steel firewall in front of engine and structural bulkhead at instrument panel, steel underpan
Body	Fiberglass nose cone and tail fairing, removable aluminum panels via Dzus fasteners on the rest of the car
Seat	Molded fiberglass, leather upholstery

Control and Instruments

Steering wheel, clutch pedal, brake pedal, throttle designed for heel-and-toe, spark control, choke, gear shift with lockout for reverse, tachometer, lateral accelerometer (on turntable), step input steering device, space for dynamic recorder above engine, rear-view mirrors.

Design/Build Approach

I've often wondered if the MX-1 could have been designed without the help of the powerhouse of experts in materials, structures, aerodynamics, mechanics and tires that existed at CAL. Although I never imagined it to be a one-man job, in hindsight I'm amazed at the size of the team required to produce this

Fig. 23-6
Front view of MX-1.

complicated car. They worked for me after hours and I paid them at a normal hourly rate.

The first major design task was to adapt the engine, clutch, transmission, differential, driveshafts and high-angle universal joints to the rear-drive wheels. Early on we had decided to use a two-cycle Mercury outboard engine for its compact size and smooth power flow, a VW Beetle four-speed gearbox and a Porsche clutch. High-angle "OR"-size Dana Rzeppa disc universal joints were used at the differential housing, with a simple universal at the wheel end.

Bill Close was responsible for the entire design, assisted by Sheridan Smith, who had joined CAL in 1946 and performed design work on missiles, the propeller dynamometer for the wind tunnel and the automobile crash facility and crusher, as well as the variable-stability aircraft.

Drive system drawings were used by the Trottnow machine shop in Niagara Falls to produce the parts, and the assembly was accomplished by Bill Wilcox and other technicians in Flight Research's Hangar Group on weekends, doing their usual professional job.

In general the design progressed from the engine-transmission bay, worked forward into the cockpit section, and finally reached the nose section.

The next major task was the arrangement of the rear suspension, with suspension plates for setting camber and swing arm/roll center height, and an adjustable torsion bar suspension scheme with height trim adjustment. A number of ideas were considered for the "continuous" adjustment of camber, but Bill Close's proposal for fixing camber at five-degree intervals from zero to twenty-five degrees was adopted as the best structural arrangement, suitable for investigating the use of high negative camber. The basic steel-tube chassis design was produced at this time.

By December of 1963 some 40 layouts and detailed drawings by Close and Smith established the basic design parameters of the car. Remaining were the complete steering system layout, and the brake system, front suspension, radiator, cooling system and body lines. From August 1961 through December 1963 Bill put in 259 hours on MX-1 design,

at which point his services on variable-stability aircraft in Flight Research demanded that he withdraw from the project (although he remained available to consult and assist on a more informal basis). Sheridan Smith continued to do design work and, according to my records, put in more than 400 hours by October 1965.

At this point I took on design responsibility for completing the car, and it proved to be the most difficult engineering challenge I ever faced. At the University of Maine, some three decades earlier, I had taken an elementary course in mechanical design involving simple drafting problems, followed by Koppen's course at MIT on overall aircraft layouts. But on MX-1 I had the task of conceiving, designing and drafting complex mechanical assemblies so they could be made and would work.

CAL president Ira G. Ross, who had taken an interest in the project, realized I was out of cash at a critical stage and offered $1,000 worth of free machine-shop time. Joe Muncey, whose aeronautical career began with the early wind tunnel at Curtiss in Garden City, headed the Laboratory's outstanding model shop. He had gathered together a group of experienced machinists, welders and fabricators, many of German descent, who could build anything from an experimental aircraft to wind tunnel models. I wasted no time getting together with Joe, who was enthusiastic about the MX-1 but stressed the necessity for *complete* and *legible* drawings and material specifications. He offered the services of Carl Roose and Elmer Wik, a top machinist/fabricator and welder.

At home I set up design operations on the dining room table, then moved to the garage, and finally upstairs to an office in our new addition. Right from the start I bought the best tools of the trade, including a number of special items such as proportional dividers, a planimeter, families of curve and ellipse templates, an electric eraser and templates for nuts and bolts. Close and Sheridan worked in decimal inches and my friends at GM contributed a tape measure in hundredths of an inch, great for measuring long distances accurately. In time I was to build up a library of A/N Standards, material specifications, conversion factors, surface roughness scales, catalogues of ball bearings, cables, fittings, sheet and tube suppliers, design texts, handbooks, samples of commonly used hardware and even Luxo lights to illuminate the board.

Having established a workplace and surrounded myself with all the accoutrements, I found myself absolutely baffled about how to proceed, like a non-swimmer tossed into water. What I had going for me, in addition to a terrific incentive and a commitment to the high-angle camber idea, was a great respect for vehicle designers and an overwhelming desire to join that exclusive clan.

First, I decided to tackle the steering system layout, knowing I would have to think through every step of the design procedure. Having survived this, I went on to the nose section of the car.

In total, Close, Smith and I spent more than 1,000 hours in design time. Many others contributed to the MX-1 project, listed at the end of this chapter.

Finally, my son Peter Milliken provided miscellaneous help with mockups and my son Doug Milliken provided work on suspension and steering mockups, all road equipment installation, development testing and great support throughout.

When the project began, Doug was only six. He grew up with race cars and MX-1. On weekends I brought Doug to my office, where the walls were painted in the international Grand Prix colors of green (England), red (Italy), blue (France) and white (Germany).

Fig. 23-8
My two sons Doug and Peter participated in the MX-1 project from the beginning.

After I taught him to drive the airplane tractor tug around on the ramps, he invited his first-grade class to visit the hanger and see the airplanes. The teacher went wild when Doug jumped into the tug and drove it out of the hangar. When I started MX-1, Doug helped calibrate various arrangements on our suspension board and mockups. When he was 12 he saw a minibike at Indy, came home and built one with very little help from me.

Brief Description of MX-1 Systems

1. Suspension— Geometry and Kinematics

The suspension plate shown in Figure 23-7 enabled the suspension A-frames to be set for discrete cambers (0 to 25 degrees in 5-degree increments) and for various swing-arm lengths and roll center heights (zero body roll). The plates were cast in aluminum, with holes drilled from an accurate steel template. Figure 23-9 is a layout of these holes indicating their number system (for example, J15S, where the upper A frame is denoted by J15 and the lower by S).

Figure 23-10 is a sketch of the suspension board, made full size in three sections and metal covered. Wooden A-frames, and a two-dimensional wheel-tire template and strings, enabled the location of the swing center and roll center heights. In effect this was a

Fig. 23-7
Suspension plates for adjusting the A-frames for different cambers, swing-arm lengths and roll center heights.

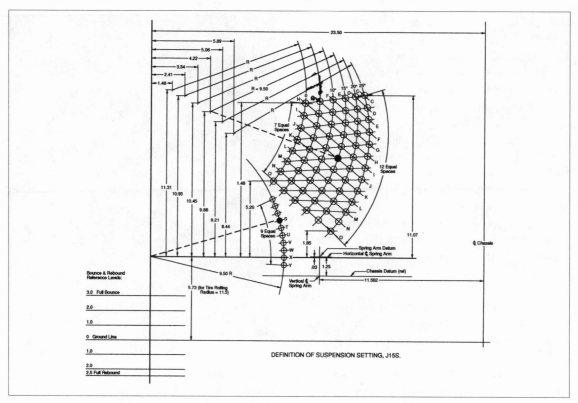

Fig. 23-9
Drawing showing the definition of the suspension settings on MX-1. The camber is basically adjustable in 5-degree increments (0°–25°). Further adjustments in the locations of the inner ends of the A-frames enable the swing-arm length and roll center height to be varied (over wide ranges). The example shown is J15S, where 15 refers to 15 degrees of camber and J and S locate the upper and lower A-frames.

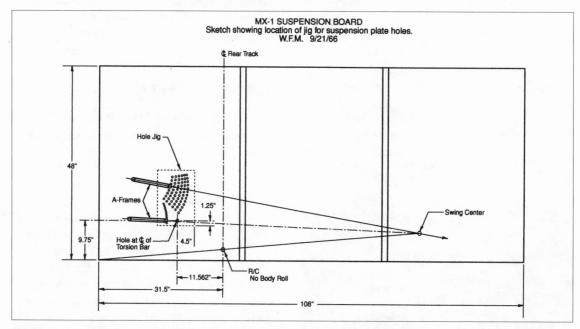

Fig. 23-10
A two-dimensional suspension board (full scale) was used to obtain the swing-arm lengths and roll center heights (for no body roll) for many combinations of A-frame settings. One-dimensional wooden A-frames were used; strings projected the angles of the A-frames to the swing center. An accurate jig and dowels located the A-frame positions. (This "string computer" is very common; see *Competition Car Suspension* by Allan Staniforth (Haynes, 1999).

geometric calculator in those pre-computer days! Figures 23-11 and 23-12 further illustrate the suspension board.

Doug and I obtained swing-arm lengths and roll center heights for a large number of settings of the A-frames. (See Figure 23-13) These data were then plotted, one graph for each camber angle (see Figures 23-14 and 23-15). Figure 23-16 is a plot of roll center height versus swing-arm length for a number of then-current race cars for which we had data. Six MX-1 A-frame locations were plotted on this diagram for orientation purposes.

Figure 23-17 shows the full-scale three-dimensional wooden mockup that was used for developing the suspension and steering geometry and kinematics.

2. Suspension—Ride and Roll Springing

Torsion-bar springs were used front and rear, one bar for each wheel. The springs were anchored in a sliding fixture, enabling changes in the natural frequency. A trim mechanism was incorporated in the fixture for adjusting ride height. The other end of the torsion bar was anchored in a tube to which was welded a "spring arm" that was attached to the outboard end of the lower A-frame (hence to the wheel). An arm for the shock absorber was also welded to this tube. Because of space constraints the torsion bars for the front track were doubled back, the two sections being connected by a link. Figure 23-18 shows the rear tube carrying the torsion bar, the "spring arm" attached to the lower A-frame, and the sliding fixture anchoring the forward end of the torsion bar.

3. Steering System

Since this was the first system for which I had full design responsibility, I will outline my approach to it in some detail.

Available components:

–A steering wheel and shaft, located relative to the seat.

–A small rack-and-pinion box or unit, 20.5 in. overall length, i.e., short enough to fit into the cockpit area. This box was used in England in a Humber-Hillman Imp and produced by Engineering Productions. With the help of Richard Hodkin, who headed Long-Term

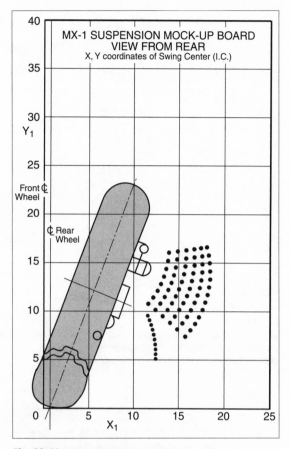

Fig. 23-11
This is a drawing of the simulated tire/wheel on the mockup board, and the holes in the suspension plate.

Fig. 23-12
Bill Close (right) and the author working with the suspension mockup board.

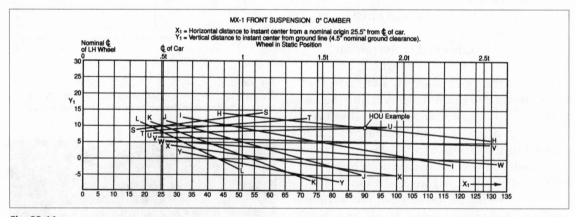

FRONT SUSPENSION CONFIGURATIONS
NEW LARGE, 2-DIMEN. MOCKUP BOARD. FINAL SUSP. CONFIG. TESTED.
SUSPENSION AT STATIC HEIGHT
ALL QUANTITIES DEFINED ON P@, FOLDER 121, SUSP. REAPPRAISAL - II   1-28-67   DM&NFM.

0° CAMBER

CONFIG	X₁	Y₁	Xₗₜ	"R/C"
HoS	54.50	13.00	52.00	6.30
JoS	30.26	10.40	30.76	8.75
LoS	21.60	9.32	22.10	11.10
1oT	44.76	10.13	45.16	5.70
RoT	27.90	8.80	28.10	8.13
HoU	90.12	9.49	90.32	2.65
10U	55.37	8.31	55.57	3.80
LoU	25.70	7.51	25.87	7.43
HoV	—			
10V	73.50	5.06	73.70	1.74
JoV	47.80	5.75	48.04	3.00
1oW	103.10	0.20	103.15	0.03
JoW	60.16	2.70	60.36	1.10
KoW	41.30	4.10	41.40	2.55
LoW	31.82	4.81	31.82	3.84
10X				
JoX	79.27	-2.82	79.27	-1.00
LoX	36.85	2.60	36.85	1.75
KoY	64.80	-4.20	64.70	-1.65
LoY	43.24	-0.34	43.14	-0.25

5° CAMBER

CONFIG	X₁	Y₁	Xₗₜ	"R/C"
HSS	41.53	12.40	42.2	7.70
JSS	27.2	10.3	27.9	9.75
LSS	20.3	9.35	21.1	11.7
1ST	38.1	10.2	38.7	6.85
KST	25.5	8.95	26.2	8.95
HSU	64.7	9.65	65.3	3.85
1SU	44.8	8.65	45.3	4.95
LSU	23.9	7.7	24.4	8.25
HSV	92.95	6.15	92.95	1.70
1SV	55.0	6.65	55.5	3.10
JSV	39.7	6.65	40.2	4.30
1SW	71.5	3.30	72.0	1.20
JSW	47.42	4.35	47.92	2.35
KSW	35.9	4.9	36.4	3.5
LSW	28.85	5.3	29.35	4.67
1SX	103.2	-3.5	103.7	-.85
JSX	60.2	0.75	60.7	.30
LSX	32.4	3.65	32.9	2.85
KSY	50.35	-0.65	50.65	-0.35
LSY	37.0	1.37	37.3	0.97
GSS	58.25	14.85	58.95	6.65
GST	78.9	14.25	79.5	4.67
GSU	124.15	124	124.75	2.55

15° CAMBER

CONFIG	X₁	Y₁	Xₗₜ	"R/C"
E1SS	94.25	24.65	95.55	6.85
F1SS	54.5	16.65	55.8	7.88
G1SS	39.8	13.7	41.2	8.93
H1SS	51.4	12.0	52.7	9.80
I1SS	26.6	11.05	27.9	10.58
J1SS	23.13	10.33	24.43	11.43
K1SS	20.68	9.80	21.98	12.10
L1SS	18.65	9.45	19.85	12.78
M1SS	17.10	9.15	18.40	13.60
N1SS	15.67	8.83	16.87	14.16
O1SS	14.40	8.60	15.60	14.60
F1ST	75.7	17.1	77.0	5.92
G1SU	61.6	12.28	62.9	5.21
G1SV	88.4	10.37	89.5	3.06
H1SV	54.12	8.15	55.31	4.20
I1SV	40.08	8.03	41.28	5.20
J1SV	31.85	7.67	33.15	6.22
K1SV	26.90	7.35	28.10	6.98
L1SV	23.23	7.20	24.43	7.96
M1SV	20.48	7.02	21.68	8.75
N1SV	18.32	6.92	19.52	9.58
O1SV	16.60	6.80	17.80	10.42
L1ST	19.95	8.75	21.15	11.68
F1SH				
L1SU	21.50	8.10	22.70	9.62
H1SW	70.83	6.25	72.03	2.30
K1SW	29.68	6.20	30.88	5.31
H1SX	103.90	1.18	105.10	0.25
K1SX	33.50	4.65	34.50	3.50
I1SY	81.33	-1.82	82.63	-0.63
L1SY	31.18	3.22	32.38	2.68

25° CAMBER

CONFIG	X₁	Y₁	Xₗₜ	"R/C"
E1SS	53.95	19.02	55.65	9.28
F1SS	37.68	14.8	39.38	10.17
G1SS	30.27	12.9	31.87	10.95
H1SS	25.65	11.68	27.25	11.60
I1SS	22.67	10.87	24.17	12.23
J1SS	20.5	10.30	22.20	12.74
K1SS	18.7	9.82	20.30	13.26
L1SS	17.3	9.47	18.90	13.67
M1SU	18.0	8.05	19.50	11.17
N1SU	16.67	7.82	18.17	11.68
O1SY	15.92	4.83	20.32	6.40
E1ST	82.50	32.15	83.90	7.10
F1SU	65.10	15.58	66.70	6.35
G1SV	56.65	11.57	58.15	5.30
H1SV	46.32	9.68	41.82	6.27
I1SV	32.20	8.80	33.90	7.10
J1SV	27.24	8.30	28.94	7.76
K1SV	23.74	7.85	25.34	8.45
L1SV	21.14	7.55	22.84	9.07
M1SV	19.21	7.36	20.91	9.65
N1SU	17.60	7.17	19.10	10.20
O1SV	16.28	7.08	17.78	10.78
F1SV	102.30	16.43	104.00	4.25
H1ST	29.30	11.16	30.70	9.80
H1SU	33.85	10.58	35.25	8.08
J1SU	24.50	9.10	26.20	9.53
G1SW	81.20	10.35	82.90	3.45
J1SW	30.68	7.28	32.38	6.10
H1SX	66.68	6.33	68.38	2.55
K1SX	29.00	5.78	30.70	5.10
H1SY	101.0	1.90	102.5	0.47
L1SY	27.55	4.55	29.15	4.23

X₁, Y₁, coords of swing center
Xₗₜ, swing arm length
"R/C" Zero Roll Center Height

Fig. 23-13
This tabulation is an example of some of the suspension settings for the front suspension tested on the suspension mockup board. For each configuration we recorded the coordinates of the swing center, swing-arm length and roll center height for static ride position.

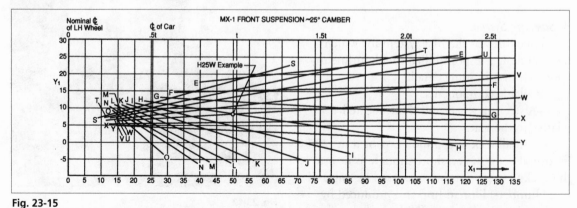

Fig. 23-14
0° camber. These curves are plotted from data such as Fig. 23-13 and show the changes in suspension characteristics with different A-frame locations, useful for setting up the car.

Fig. 23-15
−25° camber. These curves are plotted from data such as Fig. 23-13 and show the changes in suspension characteristics with different A-frame locations, useful for setting up the car.

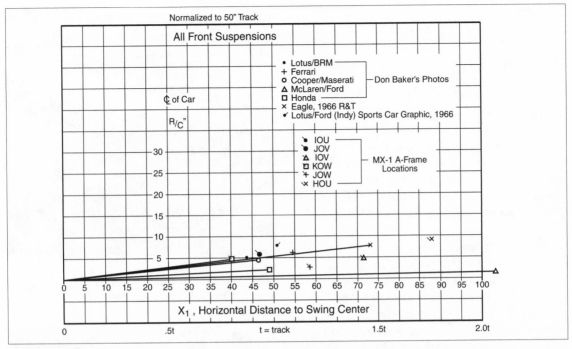

Fig. 23-16
Front suspension characteristics for contemporary race cars and comparable MX-1 suspension settings.

Fig. 23-17a,b,c,d
Because of the complexity of the front suspension on MX-1, the author built up a three-dimensional mockup which includes the castor (trail) adjustment (see d), the steering drag link and steer angle scale (see c) and the suspension plates and A-frames (see a and b). The actual wheels and tires are located in their proper position (see a). This mockup was completed before the design layouts, and greatly facilitated them.

Development at Humber, I had acquired a unit plus complete drawings and test results.

Design Requirements:

a. Range of steering ratio changes.

b. Ackermann, reverse Ackermann and parallel steering.

c. Adjustable front roll steer.

d. A stiff system with minimum friction.

e. A steering system that would permit suspension adjustments of swing-arm length and roll center height (i.e., separation of steering and suspension adjustments).

Steering Conception

To come up with a layout meeting the system specifications was the creative part necessitating numerous freehand sketches. To meet requirement 3e, long drag links had to be used on both sides of the car. Requirement 3c was met by height adjustments of the aft ends of these drag links. Ball bearings facilitated 3d, while discrete hole locations in bell cranks in the system handled 3a and 3b. Large changes of steering ratio were made by changing sprockets in the chain drive system.

Figure 23-19 shows the steering column going down to an enclosed chain drive to a side countershaft along the floor, and to the rack-and-pinion box located just in front of the seat.

Figure 23-20 shows the countershaft, the rack-and-pinion box driving two links from the center of the box to bell cranks actuating the long side drag links. This linkage is better shown in Figure 23-21.

Figure 23-22 shows the bell crank with a series of holes for setting Ackermann, reverse Ackermann and parallel steer, and the long drag link to the steering arm at a front wheel with vertical adjustment of the rear end of the drag link for front roll steer.

Several layouts of the steering system were developed, with considerable effort expended to determine the best views to facilitate fabrication and assembly, the material specifications, the use of antifriction bearings, etc.

When the parts cranked out by Roose were assembled I was immensely pleased. Nothing can be overlooked in mechanical design: dimensions, fits, finishes, materials, stresses, stiffness, etc., must all be addressed, requiring patience to

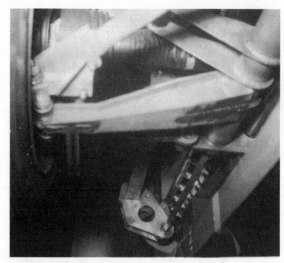

Fig. 23-18
Rear swing arm attached to outboard end of A-frame. Double arms above connect to shock absorbers.

Fig. 23-19
Steering column and enclosed chain drive. This turns the side countershaft, which ends at the rack-and-pinion box located under front of seat.

Fig. 23-20
Steering system showing column, countershaft, rack-and-pinion box and lateral link to the quadrant that operates the arm at the aft end of the drag link to the wheel. See also the two following figures.

Fig. 23-21
Steering system components: the rack-and-pinion box and links to quadrants. These quadrants have holes that enable parallel, Ackermann or reverse Ackermann steering.

organize one's thinking. Presenting the results in legible and clear drawings is an art in itself.

In my era technical schools emphasized the analytical approach to engineering, almost to the exclusion of mechanical drawing. Today the drafting board largely has been replaced by

CAD (computer-aided design) systems. Still, Alex Moulton in England, and some primary designers of Grand Prix cars, feel that nothing compares with pencil and paper for the creative process.

4. Brake System

The brake system (Figure 23-22) was relatively simple. Two Girling master cylinders, one each for the front and rear, were located side-by-side on a mounting plate on the tube structure behind the cockpit bulkhead. A sliding balance-bar actuating the two master cylinders was connected to the brake pedal arm, where a series of holes permitted brake force adjustment. The system had a return spring on the balance bar, and its cable attachment could be adjusted laterally to change the balance between front and rear brakes.

5. Engine and Transmission Installation

Figure 23-23 shows the adaptor plate and bearing assembly that fits on the Mercury 800 engine. Figure 23-24 shows the transmission, and Figures 23-25 through 23-27 show the installation of the engine/transmission unit in the rear frame.

Fig. 23-22
Center section of MX-1, showing the brake actuation system located behind the center bulkhead and near the top. A slider is located on a supporting plate and connected to the two brake master cylinders (for front and rear). The system is cable operated from the foot pedal. The proportioning between front and rear brake is adjustable, as is the pedal force and motion.

6. Chassis and Body Lines

The chassis was a welded-steel tube structure in three sections: the engine bay, the cockpit and the nose section. The three sections are shown in Figure 23-28, with the wheels sketched in a vertical orientation.

The engine bay was completed first. Figure 23-26 indicates that for stiffness the frame completely surrounded the engine and transmission, which were supported on a built-up bulkhead near the engine-transmission CG as well as at the front of the frame.

Fig. 23-23
The six-cylinder Mercury 800 two-cycle engine with the adaption bulkhead (left) and relocated carburetors.

Fig. 23-24
VW four-speed transmission with driveshaft, ready to be mated to the engine at the adaption bulkhead.

Fig. 23-25, 23-26, 23-27
To increase the chassis torsional stiffness the engine/transmission unit is fully enclosed in a welded-steel tube frame. The engine is supported on a bulkhead (left) and a single forward LORD mount support on top (top right, also bottom right).

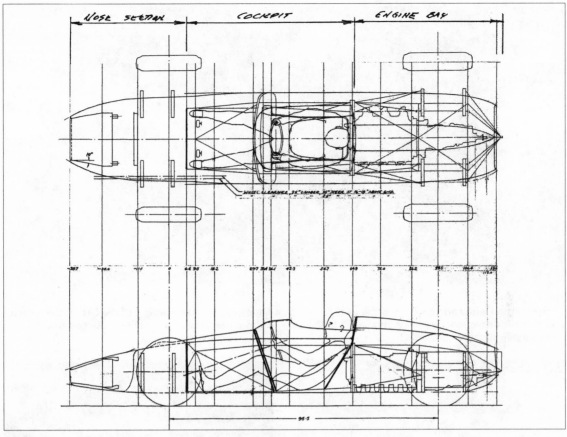

Fig. 23-28
This is the general chassis layout showing the rear, middle (cockpit) and nose sections. The heavy bulkhead just forward of the steering wheel is also shown. A permanent underpan is installed in the cockpit section and a removable pan under the engine section. Wheels are illustrated in vertical orientation for simplicity.

For assembly the engine was inserted into the frame, which was then bolted to the rear of the cockpit frame at the steel firewall locations.

The center cockpit frame in Figures 23-29 through 23-31 shows the nose frame attachment, the firewall at the front of the engine and the removable aluminum panels attached with Dzus fasteners.

Figures 23-32 and 23-33 show how the body lines were developed on the drafting board. Solid wooden bucks were made from these drawings, and those in turn were used to make the fiberglass nose cone and rear body. See also Figure 23-34.

7. Seat
The wooden mockups for developing the fiberglass seat design are shown in Figures 23-35 and 23-36. The seat shape was approximated with three boards that could be adjusted between the side boards to give roughly the desired shape, and the mockup could be tilted to simulate lateral acceleration in cornering.

MX-1 Related Contract Research

My connection as a consultant to Frank Winchell, Vice President of GM Engineering Staff, enabled us to obtain some contract research at CAL relating to MX-1.

Chevrolet Kinematics and Compliance Tests
The first program involved testing MX-1 suspension kinematics and compliances at the Chevrolet Vehicle Handling Facility. These tests were performed during the weeks of October 7–12 and November 11–14, 1974. All tests

Fig. 23-29
Cockpit section with Carl Roose, right, the chief fabricator, a highly experienced member of the CAL machine shop, and Dominic Angrisano. Carl was a great asset to the project. This center section was built on a large surface plate and carefully jigged for accuracy.

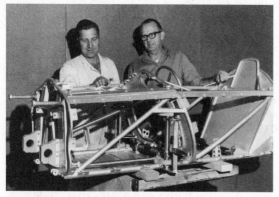

Fig. 23-30
Cockpit section with Elmer Wik (left), who did all the welding, and Ross Holmes. Wik's experience was essentially with aircraft. He could weld aluminum and steel with equal facility. All welding was carefully jigged and heat treated when necessary. The caster frame pivoted on the hefty frame extentions at the front.

Fig. 23-31
The cockpit section with aluminum panels Dzus'd to the frame. Joe Muncey, head of the CAL model shop, facilitated the use of his group and was a great supporter of the project. He insisted on accurate, carefully detailed drawings of all components.

used suspension configuration H20V on the front and G20U on the rear (long swing-arm lengths), which was our original high-camber setup. Gross weight was 1,437 lb., CG at 56.2 percent wheelbase, and the tires were Goodyear Eagle motorcycle tires. On average the static camber was –23 degrees and the swing arm length was 53.8 in. on both front and rear, with roll centers 2.10 in. on front and 3.5 in. on the rear. Suspension frequency was 87 cpm on front and 95 cpm on the rear. All of the standard tests for steer effects, ride effects, roll effects, compliance, weight transfer effects and driving/braking effects were performed, and the testing was very complete. Figure 23-37 and the chapter opening image show the machine on Chevrolet's K&C rig.

Tire Tests at Calspan Tire Research Facility, Sponsored by GM

These tests were performed in 1975 on a standard, treaded, bias-ply Goodyear Eagle

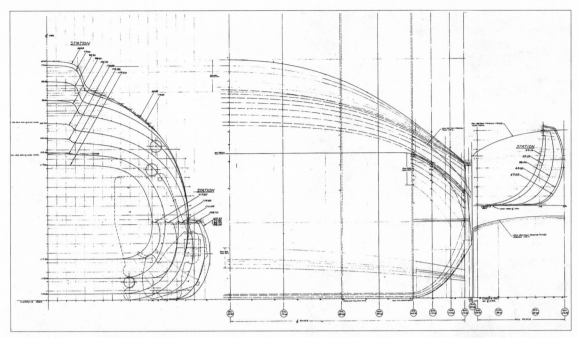

Fig. 23-32
Lines for the rear body buck. Using the body side and top views, I was able to develop the cross-sectional lines shown here. With slight adjustments they were used to produce the male body buck for the fiberglass rear body.

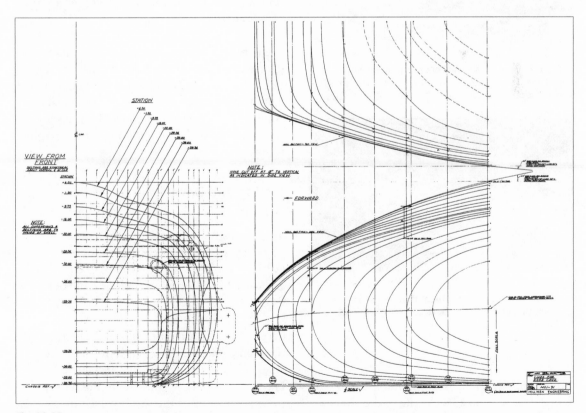

Fig. 23-33
By a similar procedure, I produced the lines for the nose cone, shown here. The cross-sections were used to produce the male buck. In both the tail body and nose cone, the fiberglass parts were well contoured, smooth and professionally appearing, beyond my expectations.

511

Fig. 23-34
Rear body buck. This buck was fabricated by Al Bajorek, a master technician and close friend.

Fig. 23-35
Cockpit mockup. It was tiltable to simulate the centrifugal force of cornering. It is shown here in the 0.5g position.

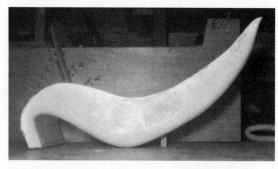

Fig. 23-36
Fiberglass seat tailored to the author. We used a mockup, plasticine and elaborate testing to simulate different operating conditions.

motorcycle tire (5.00 × 16) of notched-ribbed design, and also on a "slick" tire of the same size. The tests, which were free rolling and at 12 and 18 psi pressure, were run at 0, 10, 20, 30, 40 and 50 degrees of camber, and at

each camber in a complete range of loads and slip angles. Thus these were perhaps the most comprehensive tests ever run on a motorcycle tire. My report on the program, entitled "High Camber Tire Tests on Calspan Tire Research Facility," included all original data and numerous cross-plots and analyses.

Moment Method Analysis of a Vehicle with Highly Cambered Wheels Using a Computer Simulation

This study, performed by Dennis T. Kunkel at Calspan and published as Report No. ZM-5591.V-1, October 1975, utilized the aforementioned K&C and tire test data in a Moment Method computer simulation. The program was useful in showing how the handling changed with alterations in speed, camber, toe (front and rear), antiroll bars, and changes in CG and various compliances. An optimized combination was developed, giving a large performance area and excellent limit behavior.

Analysis of High Camber Tire Data for a Pair of Wheels on a Single Track

A pair analysis based on the Calspan cambered tire tests, this report was performed for General Motors Engineering staff in August 1980. It illustrates a technique for calculating pair analysis of lateral force with particular emphasis on negatively cambered wheels up to –40 degrees. Rolling resistance and kingpin torque also were studied.

Testing and Development

This phase of the MX-1 project happened in eight distinct stages over a period of 13 years using Calspan's Vehicle Research Facility (VERF), on-highway with full road equipment and on a 100-foot paved circle at Milliken Research.

My son Doug played a major role as development driver and engineer. He installed the road equipment and put in most of the labor in creating our 100-foot test circle. Having followed the construction of MX-1 from the beginning, he was involved in the various mockup tests and contributed to numerous aspects of the design, test planning, adjustments and calibrations.

Fig. 23-37
Rear view of MX-1 with high negative camber on the Chevrolet K&C machine. We tested various configurations over a two-week period, which far exceeds the normal K&C testing for a prototype passenger car.

Doug is a natural development engineer with a great physical sense and intuition, both invaluable traits in solving vehicle dynamics handling problems. His inputs in Stage 6, the on-road tests where we solved the major handling problems associated with high negative camber, were absolutely essential.

Following is a summary of the various stages of tests and development. Note that Goodyear Eagle 5.00-16 bias-ply motorcycle tires, with notched ribbed tread, were used throughout. Test speeds were approximately 30–60 mph.

Stage 1

This was performed at Calspan VERF. I did the driving.
Configuration:
• 0 degrees camber, long swing arms.
• Front I0U, Rear H0T. Note: For an explanation of this nomenclature see Figure 23-9.
• See also Figures 23-38 and 23-39.
Duration:
• Initial shakedown 9/21/68, concluded 4/17/71.

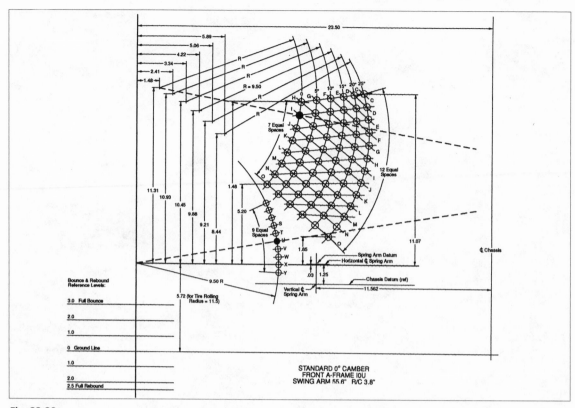

Fig. 23-38
A-frame settings used in development testing of the complete car. This illustrates the front suspension setting for the standard 0° camber case.

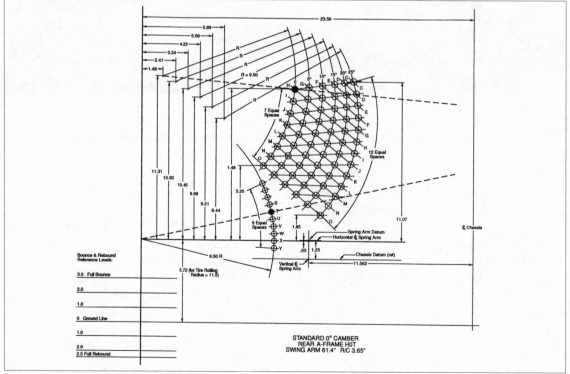

Fig. 23-39
Rear suspension setting for the standard 0° camber case.

Coverage:

• Engine cooling development.

• Adjustment and improvement of controls.

• Front engine mount failure—installed LORD mount.

• Standard SAE steady-state tests. Control force 11 lb./g. Max. lateral 1.04g.

• Other SAE tests: transients, lane changes, serpentines, trim changes, etc.

Stage 2

This was performed at Calspan VERF. Doug and I drove.

Configuration:

• –22 deg. camber, long swing arm.

• Front H20V, Rear G20U.

• Shown on Figures 23-40 and 23-41.

• 5 deg. caster, 0 deg. toe.

• Steering ratio 15.4:1.

• 20 psi rear, 14 psi front.

Duration:

• 8/22/71 to 11/14/71.

Coverage:

• Fixed control, over/understeer on 200-ft. circle.

• Left rear wheel came loose—made permanent fix.

• Tried various loadings, tire pressures and antiroll bars. Got to 1.0g. No sudden breakaway.

• The "stub shaft" connecting the engine crankshaft and clutch sheared off.

Stage 3

Repair of flywheel shaft failure accomplished in our garage. Required disconnecting rear and middle frames.

Duration:

• 11/14/71 to summer 1973.

Coverage:

• New part made of VASCOMAX 250 maraging steel, ultimate tensile strength 260,000 psi, C-48.

• Installed VW Beetle clutch, replacing Porsche.

Note:

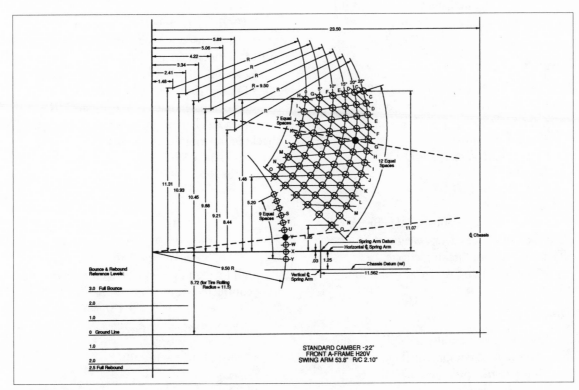

STANDARD CAMBER -22°
FRONT A-FRAME H20V
SWING ARM 53.8" R/C 2.10"

Fig. 23-40
Standard –22° camber case used on front suspension.

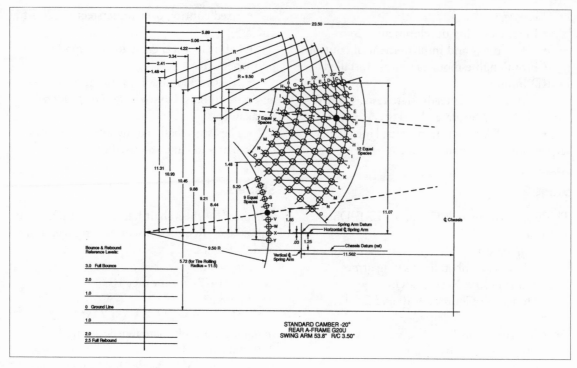

Fig. 23-41
Standard –22° camber case used on rear suspension.

• Big job accomplished by Doug Milliken, home from MIT for the summer.

Stage 4

Kinematics and compliance tests at Chevrolet, which I liaisoned with Dennis Kunkel.
Configuration (same as Stage 2):
• –22 deg. camber.
• Front H20V, rear G20U.
Duration:
• 10/7/74 to 11/14/74.
Coverage:
• Complete steer effects, ride effects, roll effects, compliance effects, weight transfer effects and driving/braking effects.
• CG height and weight distribution.

Stage 5

Could no longer use Calspan VERF. Doug installed the road equipment (Figure 23-54).
Configuration (same as Stage 2):
• –22 deg. camber.
• Front H20V, rear G20U.

Duration:
• 10/26/77 to 5/13/78.
• Car licensed for road use with lights, mirrors, fenders, etc., 9/79.
Coverage:
• During 10/79 ran rolling resistance pull tests and compared data with Calspan TIRF tests.
• Heard "chatter" in transmission when checking out engine. Removed engine again and had VASCOMAX part plated. Reassembled by 10/79.

Stage 6

Doug and I started road development program (Brompton, Sheridan and Brompton Circle) with full road equipment. Sixteen test sessions were completed from 10/13/79 to 7/18/80.
a. Test sessions 1–6, 10/13/79 to 1/13/80.
Configuration (same as Stage 2):
• –22 deg. camber.
• Front H20V, rear G20U.
Coverage:
• "Wander problem"—car darts off in either direction.

• Tried more caster, 0 deg. toe, used Heim joint to get 21.2 deg. caster (4.5 in. trail).

• Went to 2 deg. toe-out in stages. This cured wander.

• Study explained cause of wander.

• Once wander was cured, car ran straight.

• Reduced caster to 7.8 deg (1.75 in. trail) and still okay. Some toe-out per wheel.

• Wander reduced by higher tire pressure. Devised way of measuring toe with high camber.

Notes:

• Cowl flap no help to engine cooling at these low speeds.

• Changed universal joint on steering column to remove slop.

b. Test sessions 7–8, 1/19/80 to 7/1/80.

Configuration:

• As before.

Coverage:

• To check out cooling—can live with temperature levels.

• Steering ratio—prefer faster but don't want force increase.

c. Test sessions 9 (7/2/80), 10 (7/10/80), 11 (7/12/80) and 12 (7/13/80).

Configuration:

• –15 deg. camber.

• Front and rear O15V.

• Shown in Figure 23-42. This is a *very short swing arm* with huge camber change and high roll center.

Coverage:

• Car remains flat, no roll at all.

• Car pitches on acceleration or braking.

• Some jacking but less than expected.

• Don't like big camber change on reversing.

• Gyroscopic kicks in steering.

d. Test session 13, 7/15/80, on wet surface.

Configuration:

• As before, i.e., short swing arm.

Coverage:

• No noticeable effect of going to low coefficient surface.

e. Test session 14, checked out front bump steer (roll understeer).

Configuration:

• As before, i.e., short swing arm.

Coverage:

• Car rose to limit and camber approached zero. Front definitely is unstable with roll understeer.

f. Test sessions 15 (7/18/80) and 16 (7/18/80), rebound travel reduced, steering damper installed, ran on rough surface.

Configuration:

• As before, i.e., short swing arm.

Coverage:

• Gyroscopic effect in steering eliminated.

• Amazed at how well the car handles even with this short swing arm and high roll center, but far from optimum, with considerable jacking.

Stage 7

Constructed our own circular skid pad (paved), 110 ft. diameter, 7/18/80 to 10/18/80. Seven test sessions were completed as summarized below.

a. Test session 17, 10/17/80.

Configuration:

• As before, i.e., short swing arm.

Coverage:

• Installed two cooling fans in nose cone—improved cooling.

• Considerable jacking.

• High steering rim forces (22 lb./g).

b. Test session 18, 10/23/80.

Configuration:

• –20 deg. camber, *medium swing arm* length approximately corresponding to swing axles.

• Front L20X, rear L20X.

• Shown in Figure 23-43.

• Used 10.8 deg. caster (2.58 in. trail).

• Tires 35 psi front and rear.

Coverage:

• A very good configuration. Less roll. Control force 7.8 lb./g. No noticeable jacking. Doug went to 0.93g.

• In every respect, seems a desirable configuration.

c. Test session 19, 11/16/80.

Configuration:

• Same as above with 2 deg. toe-out at front, 1 deg. toe-out at rear.

• Used Brush recorder (from Calspan for transient measurements).

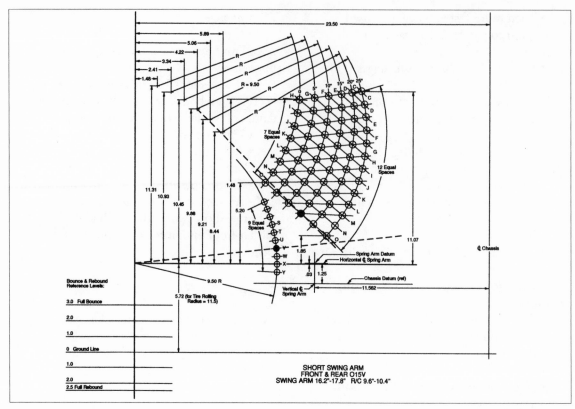

Fig. 23-42
Short swing-arm configuration used on both front and rear suspensions.

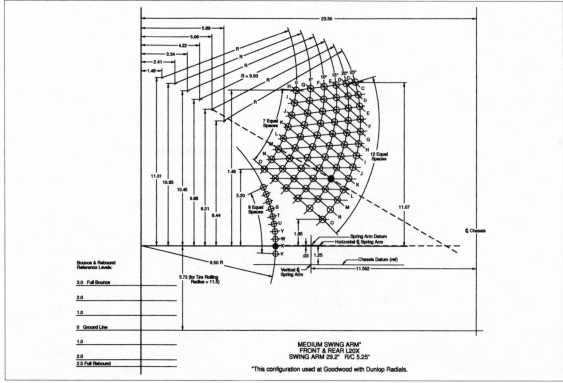

Fig. 23-43
Medium swing-arm configuration used on both front and rear suspensions.

- Used 20 oz. oil/4.5 gal. fuel. Engine ran better, but still some smoke.

Coverage:

- Ran steering step-input transient at 33–50 mph. Average lateral response time to 90% steady-state is 0.18 seconds.
- Also did a manual frequency response test.
- Car runs straight and centers well.
- Small tail raise on reverse (not serious).

d. Test session 20, 4/19/80.

Configuration:

- *Medium swing arm* L20X front and rear.
- 2 deg toe-out front, 1 deg. toe-out rear, 10.3 deg caster, 35 psi inflation front and rear
- Big antiroll bar on rear.

Coverage:

- Steady-state test on circle.
- Very close to neutral steer—within 1 deg/g at steering wheel (0.06 deg./g at front wheels) right out to 0.8g. Close to neutral steer at the limit.

e. Test session 21, 6/19/81.

Configuration:

- Same as test 20, but with big antiroll bar on the front, forked bar used during Chevy K&C tests.

Coverage:

- Over/understeer remained same when the antiroll bar was shifted rear to front.

Conclusion:

- Car seemed unaffected by roll couple distribution within limits tested. Test run in both directions to 0.7g.

Notes:

- Above analyzed in April 1981, "Effect of Roll Couple Distribution on Cambered Wheels," and confirmed.
- Suggests use of bar on front to control roll and swing run-around on rear for maximum traction (on a future car).

f. Test session 22, 6/27/81.

Configuration:

- Same as test 21.

Coverage:

- Check run 21 to confirm—no effect of shifting roll bar from rear to front
- Car remained close to neutral steer to 0.8g.

g. Test session 23 (same day).

Configuration:

- Same as tests 21 and 22, except added 100 lb. 21 in. aft of rear axle line.
- Brush recording.
- I drove.

Coverage:

- Car remained near neutral steer.
- One run (counterclockwise) went to 0.90g and held for 15 seconds.
- On next run (clockwise) went up to 0.96g with peaks of 1.04g. Held 0.86g for 60 seconds. Tail broke twice around 0.96g and driver corrected.
- *Lost it.* Car ran wide under some braking. No evidence of spin. Probably driver error.
- One conclusion—extra weight on rear increases rear camber and car remains neutral steer.

Stage 8

VERF tests using Brush recorder on 200-ft. diameter circle with full road equipment. Tests directed at *max. lateral* and *limit behavior*.

Configuration:

- −22 deg. camber, *medium* swing arm.
- L20X on front and rear.

Test Sessions:

- Total of 28 runs (14 driven by Doug and 14 by myself) from 7/9/81 to 8/31/81.

Parameters Varied:

- Tire pressures.
- Longitudinal CG by moving ballast.
- Antiroll bars (front and rear).
- Water on track.
- Traction/braking effort.
- Repeat of run 23 from our paved circle.

Measurements:

- Brush recorder time histories of steer angle versus lateral acceleration.
- Subjective evaluation and comments.

Analyses:

Extensive analysis was made of these data.

Results:

Of the 28 runs, we pick No. 24 (Doug Milliken) as the optimum configuration (highest total lateral acceleration and best limit behavior) to report, based on both Brush recording and subjective opinion. This configuration is given in detail below:

- Suspension L20X front and rear, swing arm length 29.2 in., roll center height 5.25 in.

• 2 deg. toe-out on front, 1 deg. toe-out on rear.

• Caster 10.3 deg. (2.58 in. trail).

• Static camber as measured: –23.18 deg. front, –23.25 deg. rear.

• Goodyear Eagle 5.00-16 bias-ply motorcycle tires, notched ribbed tread.

• Pressures 27/32 psi front/rear hot, 25/30 cold.

• CG at 52.09% wheelbase.

• Gross weight 1,555 lb.

• Measured lateral acceleration response time to 90% steady-state = 0.182 sec.

• Steering ratio 15:1.

An analysis of this run shows that at 1.0g on the circle the understeer gradient was 0.11 deg./g. That is, the vehicle was very close to neutral steer at the limit. Driver subjective opinion was:

1. Car felt very slight "push" at steady-state road load.

2. If additional power was added the car felt slightly loose.

3. Dropped throttle, no change from No. 2 above (two-cycle engine).

4. Response time near max. lateral, short and desirable.

5. It took some juggling of the control to hold max. lateral.

6. Since driver could hold 1g for some time and he can control some excursions from it, the breakaway probably is occurring at the rear. He is not losing enough control to "plow off."

7. Car felt close to neutral steer.

8. Car runs straight, steering centers okay.

General conclusion is that Brush recorder data and driver opinion agree, and this configuration is outstandingly good and can be achieved by simple swing axles.[1]

Figure 23-44 summarizes the suspension settings tested.

High Negative Camber Technology

Already noted have been the problems of leaning machines and tilters, and how we

[1]Recent MX-1 developments are discussed in Chapter 27, Full Circle.

SUMMARY OF SUSPENSION SETTINGS TESTED:		
CONDITION	S/L (in.) SWING ARM	R/C (in.) ROLL CENTER
Standard 0° Camber		
Front I0U	55.47	3.80
Rear H0T	61.40	3.65
Standard -20° Camber		
Front H20V	53.8	2.10
Rear G20U	53.8	3.50
Short Swing Arm		
Front O15V	16.2-17.8	9.6-10.4
Rear O15V		
*Medium Swing Arm		
Front L20X	29.2	5.25
Rear L20X		
*(This configuration used at Goodwood with Dunlop Radials).		

Steering Ratio   14 to 1 - 15 to 1   Track = 51.0"
   Parallel Steer
      S.W. Shaft Sprocket   15
      Counter Shaft   12

Fig. 23-44
Summary of development suspension configuration settings tested. Settings are illustrated at the end of this chapter.

arrived at the concept of high negative camber, which retained the highly desirable *direct yaw mode control* of the conventional automobile.

The MX-1 was constructed in 1960–67 before wide, low aspect ratio tires, "sticky" rubber compounds and aerodynamic downforce had appeared. Negative camber enhances performance due to sticky compounds and downforce. The effect of the introduction of wide, low-aspect-ratio tires on a negatively cambered configuration is far less obvious. On the MX-1 we used narrow, round tread tires that followed general motorcycle practice. For the Mercedes-Benz F400 Carving active camber car, a wide, asymmetric tire was developed that can be actively cambered in one direction and still retain some of the believed advantages of the modern low-aspect-ratio tire. A technical appraisal of the virtues of high negative camber thus becomes involved with the issue of wide versus narrow tires in general.

We believe that high negative camber is a niche concept most applicable to performance and competition vehicles, recognizing that high camber places a restriction on interior volume and tends to limit its use in passenger cars.

Slip, Camber and Print Shape

There are two ways to develop lateral force on a loaded tire, i.e., by slip (yaw or steer) and by camber angle. On rounded, relatively high-aspect-ratio motorcycle tires, the print shape with slip angle is approximately triangular, with the greatest lateral stress near the rear of the print where the load is falling off. With either positive or negative camber angle, the print shape is approximately semicircular, with the greatest lateral stress near the center of the print where the load is highest. Therefore this type of print tends to produce progressive, mild breakaway.

On MX-1, we actually utilized both slip and camber to generate maximum lateral force on the heavily loaded outside wheels in a turn. Figures 23-45 and 23-46, based on tests of the original Goodyear Eagles used on MX-1, are plots of lateral force versus camber angle for various yaw (steer) angles (the negative of slip angle). The curves correspond to the outside wheel in a right-hand turn, with camber to the right and yaw (steer) also to the right. Two load conditions are presented. Note that with zero slip angle the camber thrust increases up to more than 40 degrees of camber. At 30 degrees,

for example, the camber thrust is increasing 14 percent faster than the load ratio. At any camber angle, additional and progressive lateral force due to slip angle (from 0 to about 6 degrees) is available. At the higher load the contributions of camber and slip angle are roughly equal. At the saturation limit the slip angle curves are close together, suggesting mild limiting conditions.

The high lateral acceleration of MX-1 (1.0g with the bias-ply Eagles and 1.3g with the recent Dunlop radials) is due to using *both camber and slip angle*. The M-B F400 Carving also achieves about 1.3g with comparable camber and slip. Both cars gain 20–25 percent in maximum lateral acceleration by use of negative camber, regardless of the exact tire configuration.

Because the print shape of modern low aspect-ratio tires is wide and short, they tend to break away suddenly. Furthermore, these tires are not amenable to the use of camber, producing excessive edge wear and erratic

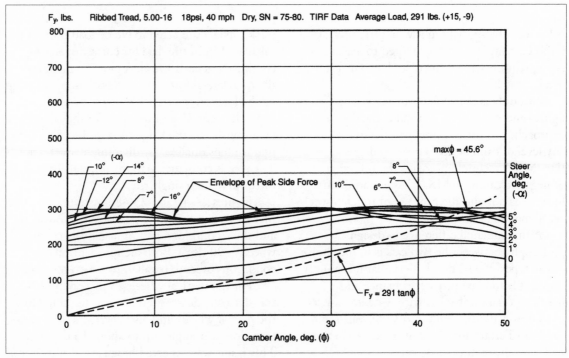

Fig. 23-45
Plot of lateral tire force vs. camber angle for various slip angles, for Goodyear Eagle motorcycle tires as used on MX-1. The data were taken at Calspan TIRF as part of a comprehensive tire test program at camber angles up to 50° and slip angles to over 15°, with large load changes. This figure is for 291 lbs. load, and the next figure is for 492 lbs. load. At the time this was one of the most complete tests of a motorcycle tire available anywhere. It enabled us to analyze the behavior at high camber on MX-1. The zero-slip-angle line represents the contribution to lateral force of the camber alone. At 25° camber the addition of slip angle roughly trebles the available lateral force of the tire. The outside tires on MX-1 approach the peak side force envelope.

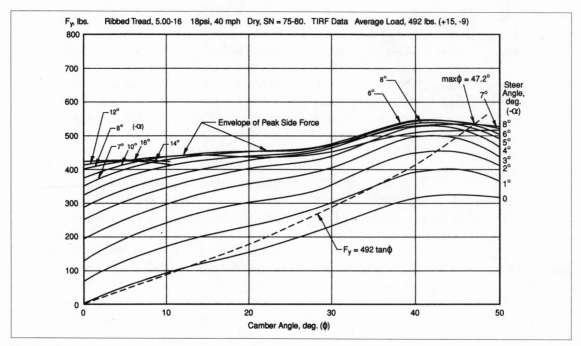

Fig. 23-46
This figure is similar to that of Fig 23-45 but at a higher load. These basic tire data are analyzed for pairs of tires on a single track with various levels of lateral load transfer (see next figures).

behavior. The specialized asymmetric tires of F400 Carving, which are tailored to *one* camber angle, require active control and are far from ideal at the limit.

Not only is the MX-1 passive system lighter and much simpler than the active approach, its rounded tires are effective at any level of camber up to over 40 degrees (i.e., MX-1 technology covers the full range of negative camber). MX-1 has extraordinary limit behavior and the promise of much lower aerodynamic drag.

A fundamental difference in design philosophy between the two cars is in the choice of tire types. We tend to believe that it is almost impossible to maximize performance and handling on a camber car with wide low-aspect-ratio tires. Parenthetically, Corvette, Viper and the latest Ferrari use wide low-aspect-ratio tires, and they all are near –1.0g cars.

Lateral Load Transfer
A powerful analytical technique for understanding the high negative camber concept is *pair analysis*. In this technique the lateral force from a pair of wheels on a single

track ("axle") subjected to lateral load transfer is calculated from tire data for correct operating conditions at each wheel. A plot is created for the total lateral force (or acceleration, by dividing by the load on the track) versus the steer (yaw) angle. It is convenient to represent the lateral load transfer by the height of a fictitious CG (h), non-dimensionalized by dividing by the track (t). The plot is comparable to the normal cornering force curve for a single tire.

Figures 23-47 and 23-48 illustrate this. The first set of curves is for a pair of vertical wheels, and the second for a pair of negatively cambered wheels (–20 deg.). Both are for identical conditions of load, parallel steer, zero toe, etc.

For the vertical wheels an increase in load transfer (h/t) decreases the cornering slope for the pair of wheels and also decreases peak lateral force for steer angles up to about 15 degrees. This result was expected because the addition of an antiroll bar, which increases load transfer, is a recognized way for decreasing the lateral track force.

On Figure 23-48 the –20 deg. camber case, *increasing* the load transfer (h/t) *increases* the cornering slope and the peak lateral force for

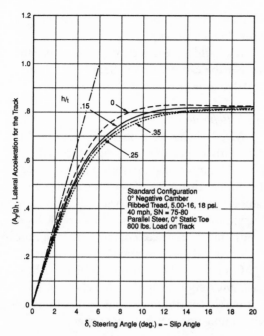

Fig. 23-47
This figure is a plot of normalized lateral force for a pair of vertical wheels on a single track vs. steer angle (or, slip angle). It is the cornering force curve for a pair of wheels with various lateral load transfers, as represented by *h/t* (see text). It shows that with vertical wheels (no camber), the lateral force for the wheel pair decreases both the cornering stiffness and peak force. This is well known and accounts for the use of an antiroll bar for adjusting the over/understeer characteristic.

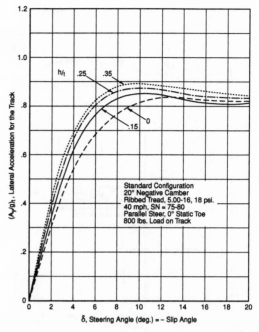

Fig. 23-48
This plot is similar to that of Fig. 23-47 except for a pair of negatively cambered wheels (–20° camber). It will be noted that the cornering stiffness and lateral force increase with lateral load transfer. This remarkable result is the only configuration we know of where lateral weight transfer is desirable. It accounts for the high lateral accelerations (over 1g) of MX-1 and its exceptional limit behavior.

steer angles up to 18 degrees, *a remarkable result attributable to the increase in the inward camber thrust on the outside, heavily loaded wheel.* The camber thrust increases roughly in proportion to the load, and is explained by an increased "bending" of the curved print shape of a narrow, cambered tire.

We have run dozens of pair analyses for various combinations of tires, pressures, types of steer, toe, load, etc. Our camber technology allows us to tailor the cornering slope and the magnitude and nature of the peak. Negatively cambered wheels *like* lateral load transfer, and is the only configuration we know of that does. In the course of this work, we have developed a useful method for performing pair analysis.

Figure 23-49 illustrates an extreme case of what can be done with high negative camber and load transfer.

On the MX-1, an antiroll bar on the rear promotes understeer by *building up* the rear lateral force, rather than by *tearing it down*

through use of an anti-roll bar on the front of a car with vertical wheels.

Wide, low-aspect-ratio tires with their typical print shapes not only dislike high camber but do not respond to load transfer in a way that controls cornering slope and peak.

Suspension Geometry

On the MX-1, in addition to changing the static camber one can vary the swing-arm length and the roll center height of the suspensions.

At Goodwood we ran L20X with a 29-inch swing arm (which approximates a half-track swing axle) and a 5-inch roll center height on both the front and rear. We also had a small steering damper. With this rather extreme suspension setup and –22 degrees of static camber, no noticeable jacking or steering kicks were experienced. We reached 115 mph on the hill and the car handled well throughout. The setup was close to neutral with extraordinary behavior at the limit.

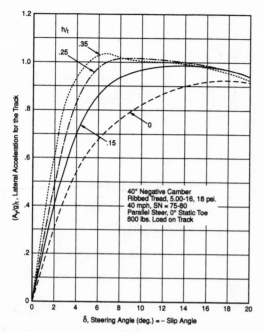

Fig. 23-49
An extreme example of the cornering force curves for very high negative camber.

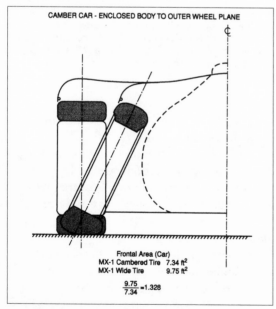

Fig. 23-50
This figure illustrates the reduction in frontal area (hence aerodynamic drag) for a camber car with narrow tires, compared with the use of vertical wide tires. Same track for both vehicles.

The aforementioned configuration would be very poor with upright or positively cambered wheels. Cars with short swing-arm lengths (front and rear), like the Corvair and

J2 Allard, have marginal steering, handling and limit characteristics.

It should be noted that with high negative camber the camber never changes sign from negative to positive with suspension travel.

Limit Behavior

MX-1's behavior is phenomenal at the limit. It is nearly impossible to break the rear end loose. The more load is transferred, the higher the camber thrust (i.e., lateral force due to camber) builds up in the correct direction on the outside wheels. This is in addition to the high steady-state lateral acceleration. Thus the car can be dramatically maneuvered near the limit.

On MX-1, the steering sensitivity is high, transient response rapid with well-damped, reasonable control forces and returnability, all with a non-powered steering system.

Aerodynamic Drag

Mickey Thompson introduced wide, flat, low-aspect-ratio tires in 1963 at Indianapolis. By keeping the overall diameter small, his intent was to *reduce* aero drag. Stylists and tire companies extended the idea of wide low-aspect ratio-tires to large diameters so that they now are the *major source of air drag* on race and passenger cars, increasing frontal area and the drag coefficient. They also inhibit low-drag three-dimensional aircraft shapes with the reduction in negative base pressure. As noted earlier, these tires also inhibit the use of camber as an important variable in tire performance, have short print lengths and sudden breakaway, and are poor in wet and hydroplaning conditions. They adversely affect suspension and steering design, and interfere with underbody downforce airflow on race cars.

Design layouts indicate a 30 percent increase in frontal area (and hence drag) for an enclosed body shape using vertical low-aspect-ratio tires over the use of narrow motorcycle tires cambered to –20 degrees, as sketched in Figure 23-50. The drag coefficient on the cambered car can be as much as 40 percent less than on the wide-tired machine.

The sloping sides of a camber car reduce crosswind disturbances.

The futuristic styling adopted for the M-B F-400 Carving indicates a total lack of

Fig. 23-51
Illustration of the Mercedes-Benz F400 Carving of 2001, a show car with active camber on outside wheels and wide, asymmetrical tires. This complex vehicle failed to equal MX-1's cornering performance and aerodynamic drag reduction.

understanding of the potential of high negative camber for reducing aerodynamic drag (Figure 23-51.

Aerodynamic Downforce

Because aerodynamic downforce can enhance the camber thrust on the outside, heavily loaded wheel of a camber car, a favorable interaction exists. Other desirable effects are present.

On a camber car with narrow tires, the underbottom area available for downforce generation is larger. The narrow tires also minimize interference with underbody airflow. A major problem associated with developing downforce from the underbottom is that of

achieving a favorable location of the center of pressure near the car's CG (for cars without wings). Peter Wright believes the condition on the bottom of a narrow-tired camber car is favorable to bottom shaping for both high downforce and center of pressure location.

Le Mans Car Comparison

A rough comparison was made between the recent Cadillac Le Mans car (for which data was available) and a proposed camber car of the same top speed (205 mph) on the Mulsanne Straight with chicanes. The camber car with a frontal area of 54 percent of the "boxy" Cadillac with wide tires and a drag coefficient of (conservatively) 58 percent of the Cadillac requires only about one third of the horsepower of the Cadillac. Figure 23-52 lists the virtues of the cambered car with its narrower tires.

In discussions of the virtues of narrow tires with high negative camber, the question of tire availability frequently comes up. There is really no problem. Current radial motorcycle tires speed-rated to 160 mph are on the market in a range of sizes. If there were an interest in other sizes, or even higher speeds, companies like Dunlop (Goodyear) would be delighted to produce them, and they have the technology to do so well in hand.

A tabulation of the problems of wide low-aspect-ratio tires follows.

Camber Car - LeMans Car Comparison

	Cadillac LMP 2000	Proposed Camber Car
Frontal Area, ft²	18.38	10.00
Drag Coefficient	0.513	0.30
Vmax, mph	205	205
Drag at Vmax, lbs.	1018	324
BHP	556	177

Virtues of Camber Car, narrow tires:
- Small reliable engine
- Better fuel economy
- Fewer, faster pit stops
- Much lighter car, braking & drive trains less critical
  - Easier car to drive:
  - Remarkable maneuvering ability
  - Less noise, better vision
  - Better in wet, better in cross winds
- Avoids unreliable electronics and hydraulics

Fig. 23-52
A Le Mans car comparison of a conventional wide tire design vs. a camber car with narrow tires, assuming same top speed. The camber car not only has less frontal area, but also a lower drag coefficient.

Camber Car - Problems with the Wide Low Aspect Ratio Tire

- The camber approach is an **alternative** to the **wide, low aspect ratio tire.**
- Mickey Thompson introduced the low aspect ratio tires (with small diameter) at Indy in 1963 to **reduce** aero drag, now they are the **largest** drag producing element on open and closed wheel race cars. Huge frontal area and high Cd's.
- They inhibit use of camber, an important variable.
- Have a poor print shape, sudden breakaway (require stability systems).
- Interfere with underbody downforce airflow.
- Are poor in wet and hydroplaning.
- Are poor in cross winds.
- Critically affect suspension and steering designs.
- Adverse effect on overall race car design. Make for "boxy" (brick) designs with high power requirements.

Fig. 23-53
Our contention is that for a car where interior volume is not important, the wide, low aspect ratio tire is a poor solution. This list summarizes why, and suggests that high negative camber is better.

MX-1 Contributors

Records and memory indicate the following people also contributed to the MX-1 project:

Dr. Hugo Radt analyzed cambered tire forces and moments, and consulted throughout the project.

Frank Winchell and staff at Chevrolet Research arranged for kinematic and compliance tests on Chevrolet K&C machine, and supported motorcycle tire tests at Calspan TIRF and the analysis thereof.

Mechanics in CAL Flight Research, including Casey Jorworski, Art Mandale, Gerry Ewers, Frankie Babchek, Al Schwartz, Ray Miller, Everitt Ross, George Dalton, and Bill Wilcox.

Walt Metcalf conducted 400x7 tire tests on small drum at 0, 15, 33.5 and 45 degrees of camber, and developed a method for analyzing the track forces.

Neil Mizen manufactured the components of the torsion bar trim mechanisms, pedals and footrest, torsion bar clamps, etc.

Bill Moran and Wally Gerstung liaisoned on radiator development at Harrison.

Bob Green of Eaton Corp., torsion bars.

Richard Hodkin performed chassis stress analysis for a variety of loading conditions.

Irv Osofsky performed calculations regarding the engine cooling system.

Joe Muncey, head of the CAL Model Shop

Carl Roose, chief fabricator (CAL Model Shop).

Elmer Wik, chief welder (CAL Model Shop).

Al Bajorek manufactured the wooden body bucks for fiberglass body parts.

Ignaty Gusakov and George Tapia conducted motorcycle tire tests at Calspan TIRF.

Ray McHenry performed suspension analysis for torsion bars and helper springs.

Ralph Jones, for the photographic record.

George Duryea consulted on high-strength materials.

Dennis Kunkel conducted the Moment Method analysis and report on MX-1.

Eugene Warner fabricated the gearshift mechanism.

Tony Mills and Steve Yanacek of Dunlop Tire Company, for new radial tires.

Dick Critofen, designer/draftsman.

Joe Ellman of Precision Patterns for suspension plate castings.

Grassel Fiberglass Boats for plastic body work.

John Cerra of Niagara Gear splined the half shafts.

Earl Ray of E. B. Trottnow machine shop for all drivetrain machined parts, and for engine mods.

Ron Gerstner, for body painting.

Strang (Chief Engineer) of Mercury Outboard Company for engine procurement and modifications.

Henry Sonnen and Bill Frey at CAL Flight Research shop for miscellaneous machine shop and fabrication work.

Fig. 23-54
MX-1 with full road equipment and licensed for road use. We did this in 1979 when we no longer had access to the Calspan VERF. My son Doug did the entire job on his summer vacation. It was fun to watch spectator reaction around Buffalo!

Folio of MX-1 Design Drawings

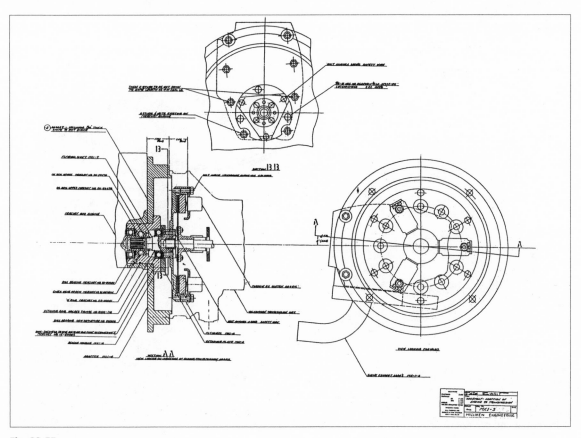

Fig. 23-55
Engine-transmission adaptor.

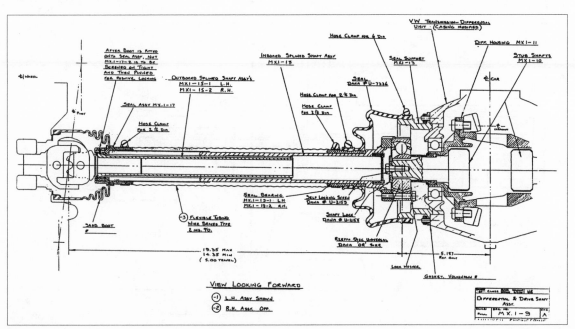

Fig. 23-56
Differential and driveshaft assembly.

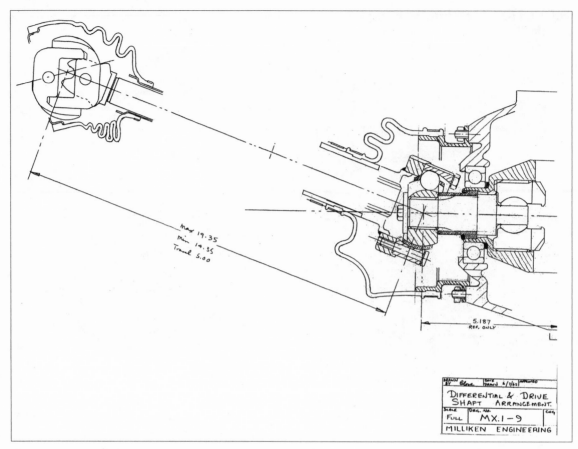

Fig. 23-57
Differential and driveshaft arrangement.

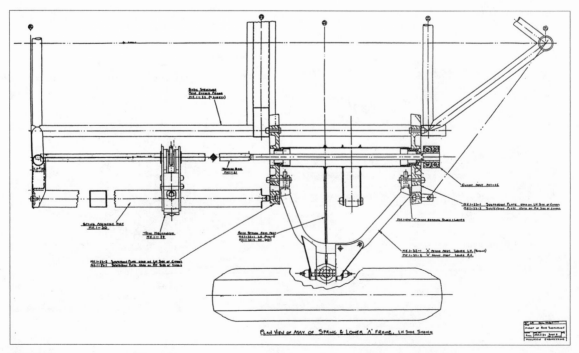

Fig. 23-58
Arrangement of rear suspension.

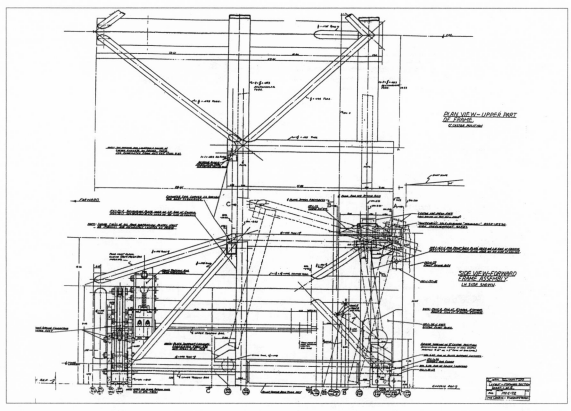

Fig. 23-59
Layout—forward section 1.

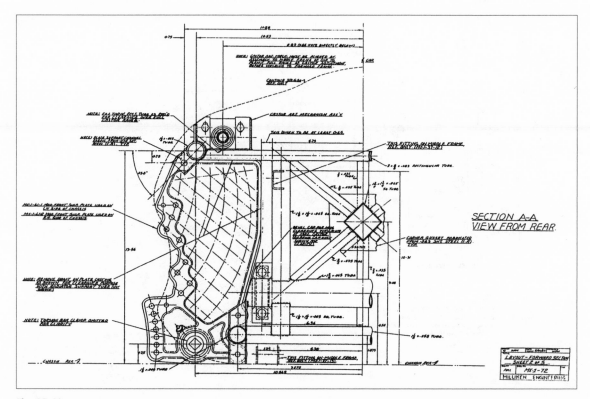

Fig. 23-60
Layout—forward section 2.

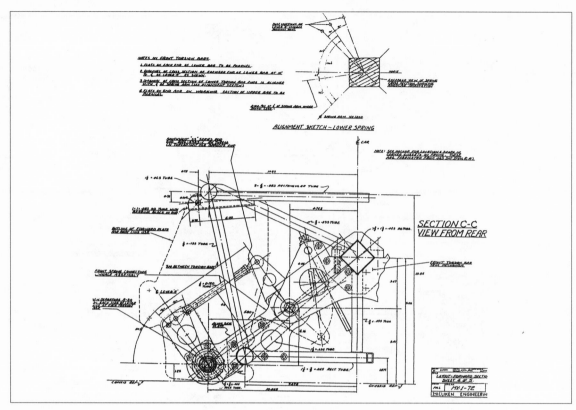

Fig. 23-61
Layout—forward section 4.

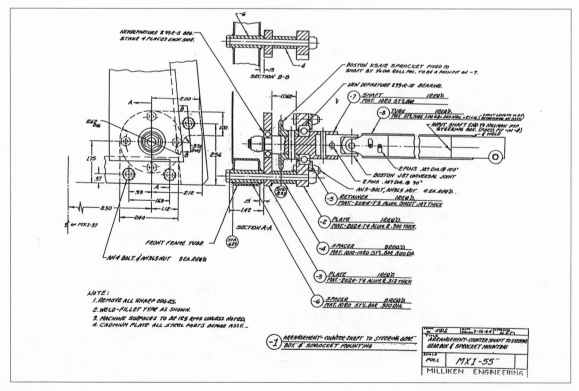

Fig. 23-62
Countershaft to steering arrangement.

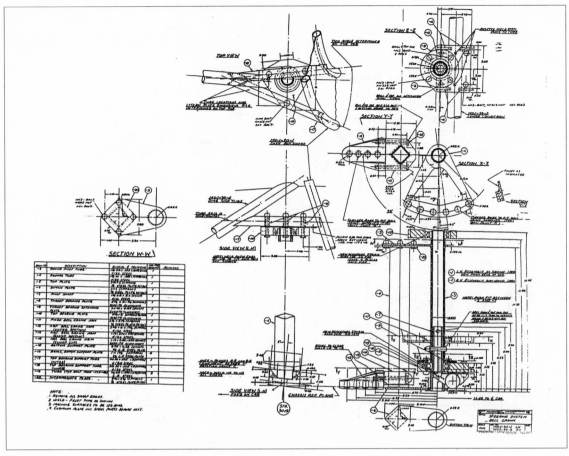

Fig. 23-63
MX-1 steering system bell crank.

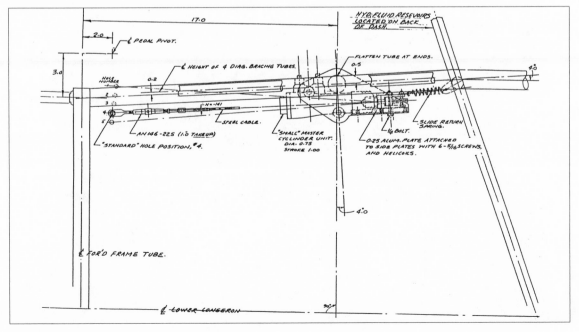

Fig. 23-64
Braking system.

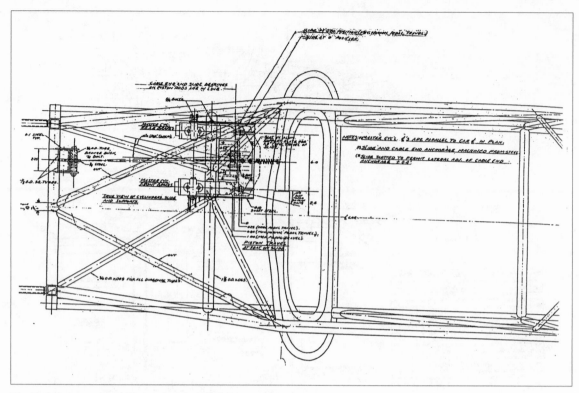

Fig. 23-65
Bulkhead and control layout.

Chapter 24

Vehicle Dynamics

"Fortune favors the prepared mind."

– Louis Pasteur

Following the end of World War II Curtiss-Wright Corporation effectively went out of the aircraft manufacturing business. Its Research Laboratory, located at the Buffalo Municipal Airfield, was given to Cornell University and started operation as the Cornell Aeronautical Laboratory (CAL), a not-for-profit corporation. As a Curtiss-Wright employee, I had been assistant head of the Flight Research Department since 1944 and became its head in 1946. Our base of operation was an old hangar off Cayuga Road on the northwest side of the airport.

Under President C. C. Furnas, CAL was a remarkably free-wheeling enterprise. Its largely independent departments were responsible for developing their own research programs with military or commercial customers. CAL had no salesmen *per se*; the engineers peddled their own ideas. Some internal research funds were available for exploring new areas, but after that one hit the road. As recounted in Chapter 15, I had introduced an advanced program in aircraft dynamic stability and control that led to pioneering frequency-response research, followed by variable stability using automatic control, and finally to flying qualities specifications (mostly sponsored by the Air Force and the Navy). This research was to go on for nearly 50 years.

Although Dr. Furnas had always looked the other way at my racing activity, my New England conscience began to bother me about the Lab time being spent on what basically was my hobby. Meanwhile Dave Whitcomb and I had become interested in race car handling. We occasionally would stage a lunchtime race around our hangar block, Dave driving his MG TC.

Demonstrating the value of good handling characteristics to National Highway Traffic Safety Administration personnel, 1966, Watkins Glen (GT40).

535

You can't drive a race car without becoming involved in its handling, especially if your profession is aircraft dynamics. Aeronautical textbooks provided the basics of stability and control, though not in the frequency domain in which we were conducting research. Dave and I presumed that since the automobile had been around longer than the airplane, there must be an equivalent text on car control. But other than a single reference to a technical paper by Maurice Olley,[1] we had no luck finding one. Frustrated, in 1952 we decided to visit Detroit automobile companies. Having participated in winter driving tests of the National Safety Council Committee, we had contacts and made arrangements to visit Chrysler, Kaiser-Fraser and General Motors.

We Should Do It!

Arriving at GM Proving Ground, we were surprised to find a sizable group awaiting us in a conference room. Among them was Tom Carmichael (our contact), Bob Schilling, Ken Stonex, Von Pohlemus and Maurice Olley, whose "Road Manners" we had tried to read in microfiche with a magnifying glass the previous night. We had no idea that the GM engineers at the table were responsible for most of the early work on car control. Since we had called the meeting, I was asked to "start talking" and began describing our current research in the dynamics, or transient response, of aircraft. Olley suddenly got up and shouted, "We should do it." I soon learned this meant they should hire us to apply our aircraft dynamics technology to the automobile. At the time GM had a reasonable understanding of steady-state maneuvering, but only a qualitative idea of transient turn-in and exit during cornering. That evening, together with Schilling, we

Fig. 24-1
Maurice Olley, head, Chevrolet Research and Development, GM, 1952.

went to Olley's apartment and had our first tutorial on the state of the art of car control. The next day found us with an initial $25,000 contract from Schilling's Mechanical Engineering Department of the GM Research Laboratory Division—something we had never expected.

This initial meeting opened the door to both the continuation of Olley's pioneering work and to finding a new approach to automobile stability and control based on a transfer of technology from the aircraft field. As Tom Bundorf was to point out later, the modern vehicle dynamics era began right then, and in the next 50 years would result in the body of technology that is the basis of our understanding of car control. This involved a complete career change for me.

Dave Whitcomb and I were elated. We hadn't found the book on car control, but we sensed that we were destined to write it. In addition to the financial sponsorship by the world's largest car company, we also had access to its pioneering developments as well to the people who had made them. There also was a huge body of aircraft control technology,

Fig. 24-2
Bob Schilling (left), head of Mechanical Engineering Dept., GM Research Laboratory, 1952. Joe Bidwell (right) head of Mechanical Engineering Dept., GM Research Laboratory, 1955.

[1]*Maurice Olley,* "Road Manners of the Modern Car," *Proceedings of The Institution of Automobile Engineers, Vol. XLI (1947).*

accumulated over a half-century of government and military support, and our own pioneering research in aircraft dynamics. Further, CAL Flight Research offered analytical talent, first-class capability in automatic systems and instrumentation, and design and experimental expertise. Finally, GM defined our contract work as "fundamental and non-proprietary," thus allowing us to publish it whenever we saw fit. Dave had an ideal background for technically directing the program, while my experience fit into the liaison role with GM and our continuing sales effort.

Fig. 24-3
Leonard Segel, project engineer on GM automobile stability and control research at CAL, 1952.

In short, we felt we had it made. All we had to do was a first-class job, keep the sponsorship going and continue to inject advanced ideas into the activity.

For project manager we picked Leonard Segel. Employed by Flight Research since 1947 after he received his aeronautical degree from the University of Cincinnati, Len worked on military projects involving the dynamic equations of motion and their use in analyzing flight tests. With the strong analytical capability required for laying down a lasting theoretical foundation, he had a solid academic and professional outlook on engineering mechanics and was undistracted by any emotional attachment to racing or automobiles. Len would remain project engineer to the end of GM sponsorship in 1963.

The first phase of the GM program was accomplished in Flight Research and extended from late 1952 into 1956, during which time Dave built up the staff to Section size. GM increased its sponsorship to about $100,000 a year. The six major accomplishments of this period are summarized below.

1. Equations of Motion
Segel developed a mathematical model of the so-called lateral motions (yaw, roll, sideslip) encountered by a driver in maneuvering a

car on the road. By assuming small deviations from a desired path, he was able to use the linear "derivative" approach. The equations enabled the prediction of the car's motion from driver movements of the steering wheel. Calculations from the model were then substantiated by instrumenting a 1953 Buick and running a comprehensive test program that involved steady turning maneuvers and the transient maneuvers that occur on turn entry and recovery. Unlike the airplane, which can be treated as a single mass, the automobile has a "sprung mass" and also has "unsprung masses" that consist of the wheels and suspension components. These two mass categories are connected at a roll axis that can be sloped to the horizontal. The roll axis is a line connecting the roll centers of the front and rear suspensions. It is the axis about which the body rolls when disturbed. Correctly sorting out the inertia coupling terms of this system proved difficult. Once the correlation between theory and experiment had been accomplished, Segel was able to identify the modes of motion and fully

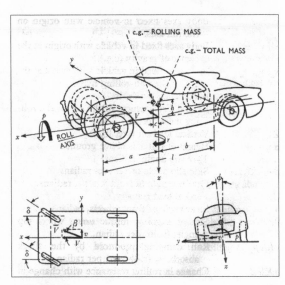

Fig. 24-4
Definition of axis system and control and stability parameters.

explain the steady-state and transient responses of the "fixed-control automobile" for the first time. Whitcomb, using a simplified two-degree-of-freedom model, enabled us to obtain a more physical feel for the primary design elements. As a matter of research policy we laid great emphasis on physical as well as mathematical understanding.

Fig. 24-5
The Air Force/Cornell on-road tire tester. Development started in 1952, and it became operational in 1954. This machine pioneered flat-surface testing. It had a pneumatic loading system, used a six-component measuring system and was capable of large amplitudes of slip and camber angles and a wide load range.

Fig. 24-6
Test tire at a high camber setting. We wanted to be able to test motorcycle tires to high camber. The trailing wheel off to right measures the slip angle. Test programs on the machine measured tire data for GM stability and control research at CAL. They were sponsored by GM and other car companies, and by tire companies.

2. Tire Tester

Very early on we were aware of our need for comprehensive data on pneumatic tire forces and torques. A summary was available in a British report by Hadekel (1952) that was helpful but did not apply to specific tire designs. Basic tire theory was very incomplete. At Maurice Olley's request, Goodyear and U.S. Rubber had acquired some force/moment tire data obtained by running the tires against steel drums. The Air Force also had an interest in nose-gear tires in connection with shimmy problems.

Early in 1952, through our Air Force connections, I was able to obtain a contract from the Mechanical Equipment Branch of the Aircraft Laboratory at Wright Air Development Center (Dayton, Ohio) to design and construct an on-road tire tester with advanced features. The basis of the system was an M-45 dual rear axle military truck, appropriately ballasted and capable of 50-mph highway speeds. The test wheel/tire was supported on an adjustable frame attached to the truck, which enabled the tire to be set at slip and camber angles over a +/− 30° range. Load was applied by a pneumatic cylinder (up to 3,000 lbs.) that maintained a constant force between the tire and the road. The force and moment measurement system was designed into the test tire axle support using a strain-gauge balance that was adapted from a successful design used in the CAL high-speed wind tunnel.

This machine was a major advance over previous tire testers, enabling accurate measurements of the six force and moment components over large slip, camber and load ranges under actual road and speed conditions. Braking effort could also be varied. After completing a test program on nose-gear tires, the AF gave us a long-term loan of the machine and we acquired tire data for our vehicle programs. We also began contract testing for a variety of tire companies, thus building up our business base and reputation in the automotive field.

3. Variable Steering System Vehicle

Bob Schilling of GM Research, a contemporary of Maurice Olley and a man who had made major contributions to car control in its earliest pioneering days, recognized that "steering feel," the forces that the driver senses in the steering wheel, is an important element in the man-machine performance. During one of our frequent dinners together in Detroit I gave him a rundown on the artificial feel servo system (utilizing Moog valve hydraulics) in our variable-stability airplanes, and suggested producing a variable-feel and free-control car. Manually controlled vehicles operate somewhere between position (or fixed) control and force (or free) control depending on the situation and the driver. Segel's initial modeling assumed position control; a variable-feel car would let us examine the other extremes of force and free control. Schilling was particularly interested in artificially introducing torque into the steering system that was a function of lateral acceleration and yaw velocity, hoping, among other things, to assist the driver in maneuvering at high speed and in the approach to skidding.

Two engineers with experience in servo control analysis were added to our automotive staff: Cliff Muzzey, who had worked with Stark Draper at MIT, and Bill Thayer, who later became a vice president of Moog Inc., the servo valve manufacturer. Together they performed a comprehensive analysis of the steering system, including tire aligning torques, compliances, inertias and steering boost, to modify the basic Saginaw power steering system. The analysis could also simulate free control by setting driver hand torque at the steering wheel to zero. The installation was made in a 1954 Buick and checked out late that year. Performance curves were calculated for steering wheel torque/path curvature

vs. speed, with variable boost as function of yaw rate and lateral acceleration. Before the car was delivered to GM, a limited handling evaluation was performed in which five drivers subjectively evaluated the vehicle in two tasks. Driver opinion indicated that the typical passenger automobile would be significantly improved by the addition of steering torques not normally present, plus additional damping in the steering system.

In 1955 Bob Schilling organized a large conference at the GM Proving Ground to update GM engineering personnel on our progress. Five of us from CAL Flight Research put on a full day of presentations. Cliff Muzzey performed the briefing on the Artificial Feel and Force Control Car (1954 Buick). The description that follows is from Muzzy's talk.

A major program was the development of a "Variable Feel and Free-Control Automobile" for GM. The idea was to utilize servo control to change the force level at the steering wheel (i.e., making it proportional to such variables as lateral acceleration and yaw rate). Normally the steering force is primarily due to aligning torque from the front wheels. On the block diagram (Fig. 24-7), the reader can trace the lateral acceleration and yaw-rate signals that are summed with the steering boost gain as input to the "feel servo" and thence to the steering system through the front wheel inertia (I_{FW}) to yield steering angle (δ_{FW}). The vehicle responds to this steer angle to produce motion feedback in terms of β (vehicle slip angle), p (roll velocity), r (yaw velocity) and a_y (lateral acceleration). Tests with this vehicle indicated that vehicle control could be improved by lateral acceleration gain and more yaw-rate damping. Especially when the steering wheel torque (T_{sw}) was reduced to zero (the free control case), control was much improved by more damping. Drivers drive by a combination of position control and force (or free) control.

Fig. 24-8 relates steady-state subjective driver impressions such as "sloppy," "touchy," "heavy" and "ineffective" steering to measurable steering wheel motion and steering wheel force (torque). It shows the effect of speed, the possible force variation with power steering (boost) and the large range of force variation

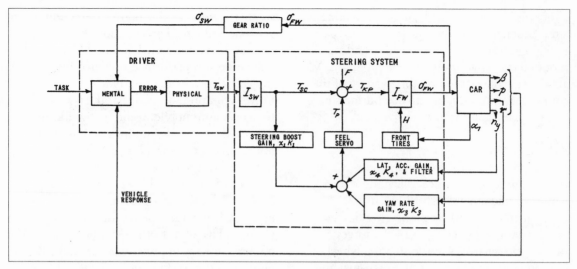

Fig. 24-7
Block diagram describing variable feel and free-control automobile signal path.

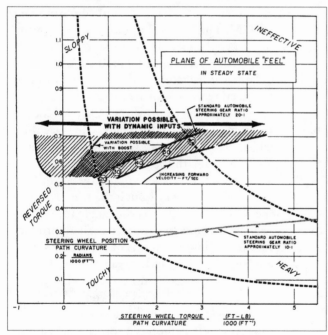

Fig. 24-8
Steady-state driver impressions.

4. Long-Range Automotive Stability and Control Research Program

As early as 1952, based on the history of aircraft stability and control research, I realized it should be possible to outline a comparable long-term research program for the automobile. Both are vehicles normally controlled by humans. The maneuvering forces are aerodynamic in origin for aircraft and can be measured in a wind tunnel; for the automobile they come from the tire/road interaction and can be obtained from a tire tester. Both vehicles have control elements that produce steady and transient turning capability and inherent stability characteristics. Furthermore, both vehicles have maneuvering limits based upon the available external forces from wings and tires that, when exceeded, result in dramatic changes in control and stability (i.e., stalling and skidding). Many other analogous features of vehicle dynamics and analytical techniques exist between the aircraft and the automobile.

Over a weekend I produced a 20-page document outlining such a program for the automobile; it would serve as a guide for our research activity for the next 50 years. This does not represent a stroke of genius on my part, but rather an example of the scientific method

with dynamic servo control. The change in steering gear ratio moves any point along a hyperbola as shown by the example, which translates the normal car from a 20:1 to a 10:1 ratio. This type of plot shows the steady-state behavior of the car and the variations possible with the 1954 Artificial Feel Car. Muzzey also discussed how best to use this vehicle for steering research.

Fig. 24-9
A conference on automobile stability and control was held at Cornell Lab in 1954. L-R are Dr. W. Kamm, WFM, Bob Schilling, Ed Dye, Dave Whitcomb, W. Cyrus, Cliff Nuthall, Len Segel, Bill Close, Ernie de Fusco and Al Fonda.

applied to analogous situations. Some of the objectives of the program were:

- Devise prediction methods at various levels of sophistication.
- Experimentally validate these prediction methods.
- Provide the facilities and techniques for acquiring input data (for tires, chassis compliances, aerodynamics, mass and inertia properties, etc.).
- Devise methods for evaluating handling qualities.
- Develop specifications of desirable handling.
- Investigate the use of automatic control for augmentation, etc.
- Explore design and development of a yaw damper for improving breakaway, overall laboratory simulators for full-scale cars and advanced tire design.
- Write a textbook on car control.
- Develop a variety of computer programs for passenger car design and race car use.

Many of these objectives have since been met by ourselves and others.

5. Creating a Vehicle Dynamics Department
The first four years of our work were intense and exciting. I was personally involved in

the project activities, bringing more staff on-line, liaisoning with GM, and promoting new sponsors. But most rewarding for me were the pioneering advances we made in our understanding of car control, satisfying our curiosity about why cars "do what they do."

Our staff had increased to 15, 12 of them experienced engineers. On the analytical side we had Segel, Radt and Reece. Fabian, Fonda and Metcalf were involved with the tire activity, while Clark, Muzzey and Thayer were the servo specialists on the 1954 Buick steering system. In addition, Close, Hutchinson and Metcalf specialized in mechanical design and test and were also using resources from the instrumentation and mechanics sections of Flight Research.

I envisioned a separate department for automotive projects. After much discussion and negotiation, CAL top management agreed to the establishment of a full-scale division in the Lab (the first division). It would comprise the Flight Research and Vehicle Dynamics departments. I wore two hats as division manager and manager of the Vehicle Dynamics department; Breuhaus moved up to head of Flight Research; Whitcomb would be next in line to take over Vehicle Dynamics. These organizational changes were completed by the end of 1956.

6. *The IME Papers*

Once we realized that an independent Vehicle Dynamics Department was in the offing, Dave Whitcomb and I were anxious to exploit its birth in a technically sound but noteworthy fashion. Because Segel's work and our tire testing were major breakthroughs, a series of technical contributions at a prominent SAE meeting seemed an ideal way to establish our reputation in automotive circles. We decided on five related papers: A general introduction to vehicle dynamics; Segel's prediction and experimental substantiation of the response to steering control; a description of the on-road tire tester development; some tire tests and interpretation; and the design implications of automotive stability and control theory based upon a simplified model for physical understanding.

SAE turned the papers down, as they were too mathematical and of academic value only.

Maurice Olley then sprang into action. Soon an invitation arrived from the Automobile Division of the Institution of Mechanical Engineers for a presentation in an exclusive session at its headquarters at 1 Birdcage Walk in London. We could only assume the invitation was an expression of respect for Olley, since our credentials in the automotive world were still largely unknown. And we were slightly amazed, but thoroughly delighted, as the IME made extensive arrangements for our trip to England.

Our contact was Reginald Main, secretary of the Automobile Division and assistant secretary of IME. Upon receiving our final drafts in August, Reg assigned Dorothy Cridland as full-time editor. She exhaustively proofed the text, checked every reference and later incorporated all discussions and author's replies into a bound monograph of 150 pages for sale and for the archive. That's how seriously the IME viewed our papers. It amused us that she also converted our American English into British English.

Soon we learned that our papers were also to be given in Luton (Vauxhall) and Coventry, and that plans had been made for us to visit Rolls-Royce, Jaguar, Hillman, Dunlop Research, Rover, MIRA, Avon Tire and Butterworth Engineering. Two companies made cars available for our transportation. All hotel reservations were placed. Miss Cridland was to travel with us to ease the "navigation" problem, and to ensure a few breaks in the routine by side trips to Blenheim Palace and a Shakespeare play. Special tours were planned for our wives.

Our technical team consisted of Dave Whitcomb, Len Segel, Bill Close, Al Fonda and me. With our wives we converged on London on November 11

AUTOMOBILE DIVISION

THE INSTITUTION OF MECHANICAL ENGINEERS

INCORPORATING THE INSTITUTION OF AUTOMOBILE ENGINEERS

RESEARCH IN AUTOMOBILE STABILITY AND CONTROL AND IN TYRE PERFORMANCE

GENERAL INTRODUCTION TO A PROGRAMME OF DYNAMIC RESEARCH
By William F. Milliken, jun., S.B., and David W. Whitcomb, B.A., S.B., S.M.

THEORETICAL PREDICTION AND EXPERIMENTAL SUBSTANTIATION OF THE RESPONSE OF THE AUTOMOBILE TO STEERING CONTROL
By Leonard Segel, M.S., B.S.

A DEVICE FOR MEASURING MECHANICAL CHARACTERISTICS OF TYRES ON THE ROAD
By William Close, and Clifford L. Muzzey, S.B.

TYRE TESTS AND INTERPRETATION OF EXPERIMENTAL DATA
By Albert G. Fonda, B.M.E., M.S.

DESIGN IMPLICATIONS OF A GENERAL THEORY OF AUTOMOBILE STABILITY AND CONTROL
By David W. Whitcomb, B.A., S.B., S.M., and William F. Milliken, jun., S.B.

Fig. 24-10
List of the IME papers and authors, 1956.

and met at IME the next day for a dry run. The London meeting on November 13 began with a reception at 4:30 P.M. with IME officers and staff. IME president A. G. Booth chaired the technical presentation, and a tea break preceded the remarks of these engineers:

- Donald Bastow – Coventry-Climax (assistant chief engineer)
- Eric Gough – Dunlop Research
- G. Grimes – Road Research Laboratory
- David Hodkins – (ERA chief engineer)
- J. A. Channer – ERA
- Donald Turner – Avon Tyre
- Maurice Olley – excerpts of letter read by Main
- Harry Grylls – Rolls-Royce, Crewe (chief engineer)
- R. A. Wilson-Jones – Royal Enfield
- M. Ronayne – Ford, Dagenham
- C. G. Giles – Road Research Laboratory

The audience, which also participated, included such luminaries as Dr. R. Hadekel, Professor Murphy (principal of Cranfield College of Aeronautics), Peter Wilson (chief test pilot of the Empire School), Dr. Albert Fogg (director of MIRA) and Colin Chapman (Lotus). Written versions of the discussion were later made available for our detailed replies prior to publication. After the session we were taken to the Royal Automobile Club for dinner and toasts.

About 90 representatives of the British automobile and tire companies attended the presentations in London. In our travels we met with chief engineers and with executives in board rooms. In short, we were exposed to a large number of key figures in the British automotive industry under extraordinarily friendly and open conditions, which was both an education and a huge shot in the arm for our new department. Lasting contacts at technical and future business levels were made. To top it off, the IME awarded Len Segel the Crompton-Lanchester Medal for his paper, the first time this prestigious honor had been awarded outside of Britain.

This classical paper contained the Linearized Equation of Motion for the automobile. For the first time it was possible to analyze the dynamics of the automobile in both steady-state and transient modes. This included the role of understeer and oversteer, the damping terms and modes of motion and conditions for complete stability. It set the stage for the modern approach to automobile stability and control analysis.

In writing this book I pondered why the IME would have given us such a royal reception. Did it happen only because of Maurice Olley? To find out, I called Reg Main, who had clear memories of the circumstances

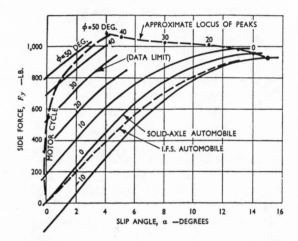

Fig. 24-11
From Fonda's IME paper "Tire Test and Interpretation of Experimental Data," showing typical motorcycle operation as well as automobile solid axle and independent suspension.

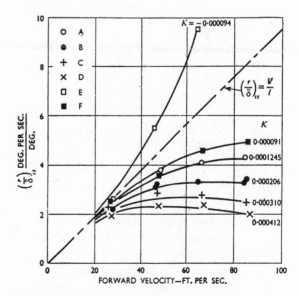

Fig. 24-12
Experimental and theoretical steady-state response comparison from "Response to Steering Control" presented by Len Segel, 1956.

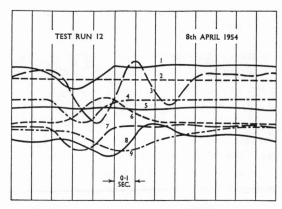

1. Steering wheel position, δ_{sw}.
2. Forward velocity, V.
3. Lateral acceleration, n_y.
4. Left front wheel, δ_L.
5. Pitch attitude, θ.
6. Yaw rate, r.
7. Right front wheel, δ_R.
8. Roll rate, p.
9. Roll angle, ϕ.

Fig. 24-13
Transient response to pulse input of front-wheel angle (from "Response to Steering Control").

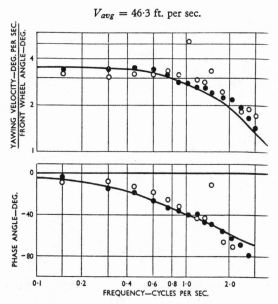

$V_{avg} = 46\cdot3$ ft. per sec.

Fig. 24-14
Calculated and experimental frequency response yawing velocity (from "Response to Steering Control").

of more than five decades past. With the inauguration of a system of motorways, speeds in Britain increased and, in his words, "vehicles were drifting all over the place" with consequent accidents. Instead of promoting speed limits, which would have destroyed the very purpose of fast point-to-point travel, the IME concluded the problem lay in the "cut and try" method of car design. A more *scientific* approach to the design of car handling

was indicated, and our work pointed in that direction. Thus the IME went out of its way to ensure that British car and tire industries were made aware of our application of aeronautical technology to the automobile.

Vehicle Dynamics Department, 1956–1966

Our return from England brought the realization that except for some funds left on our GM program we had little backlog. Preparing the papers and the expenses of our travel had exhausted our overhead allowance, and our sales efforts had languished in the meantime.

I temporarily transferred or loaned out Muzzey, Koegler, McKibben and Thayer, all high-salaried personnel, and started an intense sales effort. Our labor utilization remained low for the entire year, but Lab management gambled that we were worth saving. The next blow came in October of '57 when an Air Force contract we had picked up on adaptive servo development was cancelled.

While involved in these struggles, General Motors completed the reorganization of its internal Vehicle Dynamics activity that had begun with assigning Joe Bidwell to head Engineering Mechanics. Having closely followed these developments, I initiated an eight-month sales effort directed toward a continuation of our work for GM. My efforts were successful, and in 1958 resulted in a five-year $500,000 contract carrying a 15 percent fee with no disallowances, the largest commercial contract received by CAL to that date. The fee was higher than normal for government contracts, and the boilerplate paperwork was far simpler than for the military. In 2004 dollars we had $3.2 million in hand, which not only gave us a great year in 1958 but a sustaining core program while we built up a reasonable backlog of work. I am still amazed that General Motors had the foresight to finance such fundamental research with so little hope of any immediate return. It was reminiscent of "Boss" (Charles F.) Kettering's reaction (". . . we can't afford not to do it.") to the "flat ride" demonstration on Olley's K^2 rig in 1932 that led to independent front suspension.

During the history of the Vehicle Dynamics Department we acquired contracts and worked in a number of categories:

1. GM Research in Directional Stability and Control

My complete file of documents indicates thirty-three detailed program reports, of which Segel produced sixteen as the sole or principal author. Of the seven major summary reports, Segel was first author for five and a contributor to the two remaining.

Two of the reports (See items 4. YC-857-F-17 and 6. YC-857-F-24) refer to the very *first* variable-stability automobile in which stability and control were modified by an electro-hydraulic servo system for the *front* wheels, and with independent servo control of the motion and forces at the *steering wheel*.

Fig. 24-15
WFM at time of the IME papers.

In the course of the program there were, as Segel points out, a large number of "subsidiary experimental and theoretical investigations . . . to implement the attainment of the overall project objective." These included measurement of moments and products of inertia, instrumentation developments, tethered skid-pad tests, rollover measurement, specific force/moment tire tests, simulated chassis shake tests and development tests of servo controlled system.

Despite the pioneering work by Olley and associates (much of it design oriented) and substantial contributions by the Bidwell group at GM, it is my belief that Len Segel is largely responsible for the theoretical foundation for understanding the directional stability and

---

GM Research Reports

These are the major research reports we prepared on behalf of General Motors Research Laboratory Division.

1. Segel, L.: *Theoretical Prediction and Experimental Measurement of the Automobile's Response to Steering Control.* CAL Report No. YC-857-F-9, May 1955.

2. Segel, L.: *Driver Evaluation of Varying Force-Feel and Free-Control Dynamics in a Variable-Feel and Free-Control Automobile.* CAL Report No. YC-857-F-18, December 1956.

3. Segel, L., and Reece, J. W.: *The Lateral Response Characteristics for the Automobile Traversing a Rolling Road.* CAL Report No. YC-857-F-20, September 1957.

4. Segel, L., and Thayer, W. J.: *Design of a Variable Stability Automobile—Objectives, Requirements and Description of the System.* CAL Report No. YC-857-F-17, October 1956.

5. Segel, L.: *Theory and Measurement of the Directional Response and Stability of the Free-Control Automobile* (force control), CAL Report No. YC-857-F-31, November 1960.

6. Radt, H. S.: *Analysis of 1956 Buick Variable Stability Automobile Response Characteristics.* CAL Report No. YC-857-F-24, October 1958.

7. Pacejka, H., and Comeau, R.: *Study of the Lateral Behavior of an Automobile Moving Upon a Flat, Level Road and of an Analog Method of Solving the Problem.* CAL Report No. YC-857-F-23, December 1958.

Note: Radt and Pacejka reported to Segel during this period.

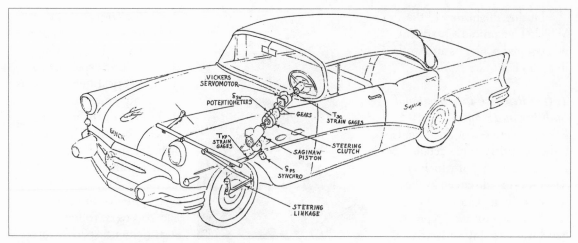

Fig. 24-16
1956 Buick variable-stability automobile developed under our General Motors contract. In operation, the front wheels were disconnected from the steering wheel by a clutch that could be reconnected if system failure occurred. The stability system and artificial "feel" systems were electro-hydraulic with Moog valves, sensing a variety of motion signals. The system was limited only by the moments and forces derived from the steering motion of the front wheels.

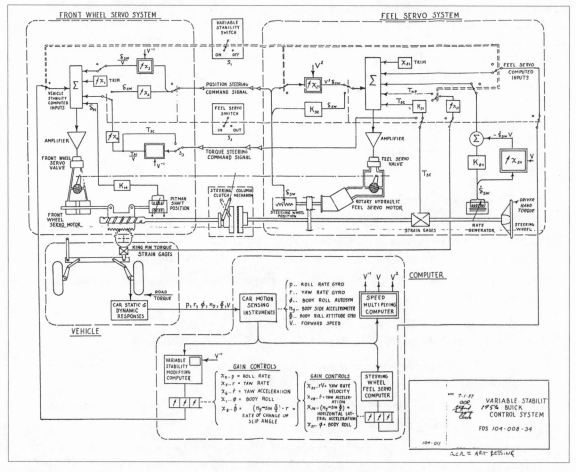

Fig. 24-17
An illustrated schematic of the actual variable-stability system of the 1956 Buick that provides artificial force and position control stability. The motion variables from the car (i.e., yaw rate, roll angle, lateral acceleration and angular acceleration) are sensed and fed to the "feel" servo and to the front wheel position servo. The effective steering ratio also is adjustable.

Fig. 24-18
Control panel, variable stability car (1956 Buick).

control of the automobile. He approached this task with a high level of professional competence in the use of engineering mathematics, and a facility for technical writing. His last report, *Response and Stability of the Free-Control Automobile,* is a classic example of this. Len's accomplishments certainly are part of the permanent legacy of our Vehicle Dynamics Department. Although much of his work has reached the open literature, it has never been put into book form, which is unfortunate. It would still be an outstanding text on the fundamentals of car control.

2. Tire Research

The Air Force/CAL on-road tire tester was a superior machine, measuring all six components of force and moment for high load and large slip and camber angles. Following the completion of nose-gear tire tests for the Air Force, we had no trouble acquiring test programs on automobile tires from Dunlop, Firestone, Goodrich, Goodyear and DuPont (the cord manufacturer). We recorded the strain-gauge data in different fashions, finally using a Brush chart recorder to plot the most interesting data directly. Jack Fabian had left FWD in Wisconsin and we hired him. Having been involved in ice tests of tires for the National Safety Council, he was a natural project engineer for tire tests. Al Fonda also ran several test programs on the machine and directed and analyzed tests on three round, treadless tires of different sizes. The several Buicks used in the GM project also required tire data.

Another aspect of tire testing was the determination of road surface friction, which is measured on a so-called "skid tester." For the Portland Cement Company, we designed and built a two-wheeled trailer with adequate brakes for locking up the wheels and a pump for water delivery (25 gals./min.) for wet-surface tests. Provision was made for a standard load of 925 lbs./tire (on specified 6.70 × 15 tires) and a means for accurately recording the *horizontal* force as the wheels were locked up. The suspension and towing arrangement was worked out by our designer Bill Close, who also used the machine in a road survey test covering a

Fig. 24-19
The Portland Cement skid tester.

number of states. This work was reported at the First International Skid Prevention Conference at the University of Virginia in August 1959. Fabian and I also presented a paper on "Dynamic Aspects of Driver and Vehicle Behavior" based upon our racing experience and our knowledge of aircraft behavior.

One day, quite unannounced, a large Lincoln car appeared in the driveway outside my office. Its driver was Walter Lee, head of the Tire Development Section at Goodyear. This dapper, soft-spoken gentleman had an interesting story to tell. Plagued with two dynamic tire phenomena called "thump" and "roughness" that affected tire noise and life, Goodyear had been trying for some time to understand and eliminate these problems with changes in tire design and production techniques. The many modifications made were to no avail. Our progress in force and moment testing had come to Lee's attention, and he asked if we would be willing to take on a contract of perhaps $100,000 to get to the bottom of these problems. That was the easiest sell in our history and led to a business relationship with Goodyear that was to go on for more than 40 years.

Hugo Radt was made project engineer. An understudy of Len Segel and an aeronautical graduate from MIT with experience in wind tunnel testing, Hugo possessed an extraordinary analytical ability. His approach involved the measurements of tire radial force runout, sound recordings and subjective ratings. Radial force runout measurements were only satisfactory when made on a drum of large diameter. Both thump and roughness were noticeable to an observer within a car as sound variations due to amplitude modulations of the sound. For thump, one modulation occurs per wheel revolution, for roughness one to two modulations per wheel revolution. The final conclusion of the three-year program was that thump and roughness could only be reduced by an improvement in tire uniformity. Prior to the CAL project all effort had been directed to specific aspects of tire construction.

As a result of this project Goodyear gave us a contract to develop a machine for measuring radial force runout under laboratory conditions. The subject of uniformity ultimately became so important that machines for measuring runout under production conditions were developed, notably by Jacques Bajer.

Research in tire dynamics had been initiated under our GM contracts. The need for analyzing the development of time lags of tire forces with changes in slip and camber angles and load had long been known.[1]

[1] Lippman, S. A., "Car Stability and Transient Tire Forces", SAE National Passenger Car Body and Materials Meeting, March 1954 (probably the earliest tire transient measurements).

Using "running board" theory, Segel derived side force and aligning torque frequency responses of a tire "experiencing lateral oscillation of the tire's center plane, yawing oscillation (with no lateral motion) and combined lateral and yawing oscillations so phased that the tire center plane aligned with the direction of motion." The responses were a function of the half-print length and the relaxation length, a measure of the distance rolled by the tire to return to some fraction of steadystate.

In addition to this original theoretical analysis, tire dynamics tests directed by Walter Metcalf were performed on a 4 foot diameter drum with a half-sized (4.00 × 7) tire. The relaxation lengths were determined for steer, camber and load changes. Of particular interest was the effect of a time-varying load on the side forces (with slip angle constant), which corresponds to traversing a rough road.

Hugo Radt frequently dropped into my office at lunchtime, and among our favorite subjects of discussion was that of automobile behavior under limit cornering conditions such as encountered in racing. Hugo suggested a small analog computer study using a bicycle model with a non-linear representation of the cornering force curve and the effect of traction/braking with a friction circle. Starting with the Fiala Tire model, he came up with a scheme for non-dimensionalizing the cornering force curve so that all the load data fell on a single curve. The simple model that resulted demonstrated the effects of driving thrust at the limit of rear and front-drive cars. The study was expanded

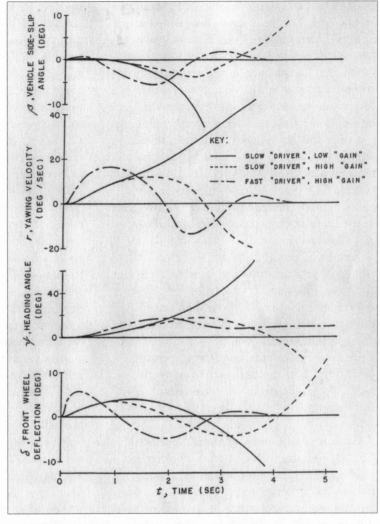

Fig. 24-20
In our paper "Motions of Skidding Automobiles" (SAE 600133), Radt and I introduced a simple driver model with adjustable response time and variable "gain." We initiated a "spin" by reducing the lateral forces on the rear wheels to zero and then calculated the spin "recovery" with three different drivers. The one with slow response and low gain never recovered from a rapid divergence. If only his gain was increased he went into a divergent oscillation. But if his control response was fast with high gain, he recovered in a decreasing oscillation. This seemed to confirm the old racing adage, "Keep fighting it, son, you may make it yet!"

by a simple driver model that responded to heading angle with a closed-loop proportional steering control. To this was added a first-order lag time due to perception and neuromuscular delays. All kinds of interesting time histories were developed for drivers with various lag times and gains, which seemed to correlate with experience.

A paper entitled "Motions of Skidding Automobiles" followed in 1960 (SAE Paper No.

600133 by H. S. Radt, Jr., and W. F. Milliken, Jr. of CAL). The study led to the general idea of non-dimensionalizing tire data, which we later were to pursue with major support from Goodyear. The pneumatic tire is an extremely complicated device. For years aerodynamic forces and moment had been expressed as non-dimensional coefficients, greatly reducing test time and generalizing the results. Radt's approach, based on Fiala and other theory, reduced data taken at different loads to single curves. We worked on many aspects of partial and complete "lumped parameter" models, one of the more extensive sponsored by DuPont and General Motors. The virtues include not only reduced testing costs but also improved and consistent data and ease of inserting it into computer programs. It yields a better physical understanding of tire behavior than empirically fitted test data. Using advanced finite-element and computer techniques, the performance of a tire can be calculated for specific operating conditions, but empirical tire testing is still used. We were to make important advances in this discipline.

3. Stability and Control of Other Vehicles

An acquaintance with Col. M. G. Bekker led to contract research on track-tread vehicles. Bekker was a pioneer in off-road vehicle technology, much of which he developed during World War II while working for the Defense Department, the National Research Council and the U.S. Ordinance Corps in Canada. After the war he became affiliated with Stevens Institute, where he taught a graduate course in land locomotion and produced his textbook *Theory of Land Locomotion* in 1956. We met Bekker in the early 1960s when he had started a Land Locomotion Research Laboratory (LLRL) at the U.S. Army Detroit Automotive Command.

Our work for LLRL was in the area of improved stability, controllability and mobility, including various means for steering articulated vehicles and multi-element "land trains" that operate on a variety of soils. To facilitate full-scale and model testing, a system of characterizing soil properties had been devised. Soils of particular properties were used in "soil bins" for research testing. We acquired a major

contract for the design and construction of a circular soil bin, and measurement equipment for testing models under maneuvering (turning) conditions. This was an original idea with us and had its counterpart in the conventional circular skid pad testing of automobiles. We were also involved in active suspensions for tracked vehicles operating on rough terrain.

Submarine research followed after winning a competition with Electric Boat on information flow in submarine control systems (SUBIC). Compared with that of the human pilot, a submarine's control responses are slow enough to pose problems in dives to critical structural depths. We proposed augmented systems based upon variable-stability aircraft technology. To assist in our sales efforts we simulated a submarine's control response on our GM variable-stability car, and found it totally undesirable except for trained submarine operators, and even they had difficulty with control precision. We later hired an ex-submarine commander, Ted Haselton, and did a series of projects for the Navy's Office of Naval Research (ONR) on a "tandem propeller" control system. Despite the slow vessel responsiveness, submarine research was not boring. On one occasion a project engineer visiting Electric Boat was asked if he would like a brief sail on a sub, and was surprised and shaken when the test run involved 30 hours of submerged operation.

Our aircraft artificial (servo) control experience led to research for the Navy on rough-water seaplane control augmentation. During takeoff and landing, a water-based aircraft becomes a hybrid vehicle experiencing large hydrodynamic and aerodynamic forces, marginal control and structural loads on the hull that may exceed design limits.

In addition to contract research, two original vehicles were created. Al Fonda, who became interested in "banking" vehicles, i.e., machines in which all four wheels tilt or camber into a turn, combined two bicycles to tilt in parallel when cornering, and followed up with a machine from go-kart components for which he devised a unique steering system. Steady-state cornering was remarkable with the go-kart. Bank angles of more than 50° were achieved, with lateral accelerations well in excess of 1g on standard go-kart tires. I was impressed when I drove it. However, once the go-kart reached the limit of adhesion on wet surface, it tended to bank suddenly in the opposite direction, i.e., "high side," when a dry surface was encountered, a dynamic problem not easily overcome.

Fonda's efforts inspired me to develop the MX-l, as recounted in a previous chapter.

4. *Vehicle Parameter Measurements*

In addition to measuring most of the significant parameters of an automotive chassis under the GM contracts, Vehicle Dynamics also conducted a long-term investigation into experimental methods for measuring the moments and products of inertia of full-scale aircraft. This included the design of a permanent facility capable of handling all types of operational aircraft, including large bombers. Hutchinson and Close performed this multi-year contract.

For the GM Proving Ground we also designed a crosswind simulator that used a hydrogen peroxide rocket to apply a lateral force to the vehicle under test.

5. *Human Factors*

Studies of the human transfer function, already a part of Flight Research's experience, were continued with relevance to the automobile. Especially interesting was the evaluation of a variable-ratio steering system to determine whether the driver could achieve higher proficiency of control. Specific interest was also directed toward objective measures of driver ability that could be utilized to rate driving skill.

All the experience of the Vehicle Dynamics Department, combined with optics capability in the Applied Physics Department and CAL's Human Factors Department, were brought to bear on a feasibility study of a driving simulator. This program was sponsored by the U.S. Public Health Service's Accident Prevention Program, and examined the engineering feasibility of constructing a simulator for use in research

Fig. 24-21
General Motors acknowledged our research for them by giving CAL a Corvette. The ceremony took place in our Flight Hangar. GM was represented by Walter McKenzie of GM Racing (left) and John Fitch, who drove a Corvette at Sebring for GM (in the car). The CAL recipient of the registration was Al Flax, CAL vice president. Dave Whitcomb on the right.

on driver behavior in near-accident situations. A full-sized demonstrator was constructed that used a unique optical system to give a 360° simulation of the visual scene and the proper feedback to an arbitrary driver path. Incidentally, this contract was won by Vehicle Dynamics against heavy competition.

A member of our Human Factors staff, Grady Eakin, conceived and patented the idea of a "man-amplifier," an exoskeleton suit of rigid elements and joints that moved with the wearer but was powered by servos to increase the force capability of the human. To demonstrate the idea we first built an "arm amplifier" with a powered rotational actuator at the elbow. With the elbow resting on a table it was possible to lift several hundred pounds at the hand! The idea was extended to a full suit where force amplifiers were located at all the major joints. Among the uses envisioned were to assist a stevedore confronted with lifting heavy cargo, or a servo-soldier with an Atlas-like ability to carry heavy armament and armor. Considerable sponsorship was obtained from the Army Quartermaster Corps. Although the

general idea never reached practice, the current miniaturization of components might make it useful in specific application (e.g., surgery) where very small and well-damped movements under human control are required. Recently, the idea of a man-amplifier has again surfaced, this time in Japan.

6. Road Mechanics

The life of a road pavement is dependent on many factors, especially the loads imposed by vehicles. Vehicle Dynamics studied this problem from two points of view: the dynamic load applied by the vehicle and its relation to the vehicle's suspension design, and the response of the road to these transient loadings. The applied dynamic loads were found to be critically dependent on the damping of the suspension system; in some cases the load magnitude could be several times higher than the static load. Development of the road equations followed under project manager Dan Clark.

Devising an experimental method to ascertain the condition of the foundation below

Fig. 24-22
CAL became involved with many aspects of car safety, including crash injury, highway guard rails, crash helmets and seat belts. This shows the participants in one of the several safety conferences at CAL. Norris Shoemaker, who worked with Ed Dye to develop the New York State continuous-beam, small-post highway barrier, is at the left front. Dr. John States, a prominent safety researcher, is seventh from the left. Chris Kennedy, who headed Chrysler's safety coordination with the government, is eighth from left, John Fitch, ninth, and WFM, tenth. We have been unable to positively identify the other participants.

Fig. 24-23
In 2000, SAE International held a Conference on Dynamics and Stability in Troy, Michigan. A number of prominent individuals in automotive stability and control were there. In this figure, L to R: Thomas Gillespie, Tom Bundorf, WFM, Marion Pottinger, Dr. Pacejka, Len Segel.

a paved road was the objective of this research for the Bureau of Public Roads. With a theory of road/foundation response to an applied vertical force, a "thumper" could be applied at the road surface and the foundation condition obtained.

7. Highway Safety

Although our program in car stability and control had safety implications, a number of specific safety research projects, some originating elsewhere in the laboratory, were participated in by Vehicle Dynamics. These included deceleration zones and barrier designs (for highways and race circuits), evaluation of brake safety devices, membership in National Safety Council winter driving tests, highway painting for night visibility, and crash testing.

Working with John Fitch, we were able to contribute to barrier and circuit designs for Lime Rock Park. Fitch invented the inertial barrel, the ubiquitous yellow barrels that guard dangerous highway obstructions throughout the United States and played an important role in Lime Rock raceway.

8. Automatic Control Systems

Vehicle Dynamics had a basic capability in the design and development of electro-hydraulic control systems utilizing Moog valves, which we were able to use for a variety of applications. This stemmed from the artificial variable-stability systems of Flight Research and from our own variable-stability and control cars.

Based on our development for GM, Whitcomb and I acquired a basic patent on stability augmentation, variable stability and variable force feel for automobiles, which was assigned to GM. Two of our top system designers, Dan Clark and Bill Thayer, were ultimately hired by Moog and became vice presidents, a recognition of the kind of talent in our department.

By the early 1960s, as Vehicle Dynamics became well known, we had many prominent visitors. Olley, Schilling and Bidwell dropped by on short notice. Olley's informal tutorials and stories of the early days of motoring made him a favorite; word would go out when he arrived and our key engineers would converge on my office to get in on the fun.

One rainy day, I received a phone call from a Lawrence Pomeroy who said he was in Buffalo and asked to come out for a visit. Why the famous author of *The Grand Prix Car* would be in Buffalo I could not imagine. But I played it straight, thinking it was a prank by my friend John Oshei of Trico, who could fake an English accent and was well-known as a practical joker. Sure enough, Pomeroy showed up wearing his famous purple vest. His father, while consulting for Hudson, had married an American woman and was currently living in Buffalo. We knocked off work and spent an entertaining afternoon discussing European racing.

Other notable visitors were Reg Main and Dorothy Cridland from IME, Eric Gough of Dunlop Research (England), Donald Campbell, Goldie Gardner, John Hollings of

553

Rolls-Royce, Bill Haynes of Jaguar, Mauri Rose, Ken Davidson of Stevens Institute and Dr. Wunibald Kamm, the German aerodynamacist.

To keep track of the variety of Vehicle Dynamics projects, the department comprised two sections. One, under Segel, was strongly analytical and had responsibility for the General Motors work, tire thump and roughness, tire research, seaplane load alleviation, articulated all-terrain vehicles and submarine control. The other section, under Charles (Chuck) Hutchinson, dealt with more experimental work and mechanical design, including such projects as the moment of inertia equipment, the tire tester design, road loading mechanics, the soil bin test device, simulators, the man-amplifier and the Portland Cement road friction measurements. Within each section we had at least two young talented engineers in each of the various engineering specialties such as mechanics, servos, aerodynamics, tires, design and engineering mathematics, all available under a project type of operation.

For me, these were intense years with much traveling, notable successes and a running crisis with CAL headquarters. The technical aspects were so interesting that I never could focus for long on administration, with the result that we always were on a slippery business slope. When things became dicey we would dream up a new idea and I would charge off to a potential customer.

Although Whitcomb and I could take credit for envisioning the Vehicle Dynamics Department and the sources of sponsorship, the technical advances were the result of the team we had put together and the free-wheeling organization in which it functioned.

Chapter 25

Transportation Research Division

"Out of bounds"

– Anonymous

Vehicle Dynamics' five-year core contract with GM ended in 1963. Because of this and other problems we began losing a number of key engineers. Dave Whitcomb had contracted a permanent illness, Len Segel decided to transfer to the main laboratory, Dan Clark and Bill Thayer accepted positions with Moog Inc. and Hugo Radt, Bill Close and Jack Fabian were on loan or transfer for lack of work in their respective specialties. Although we tried various reorganizations and an enhanced sales effort, our profit margin continued to fall. I had become involved with MX-1, which probably didn't help. We reached a critical point when an event occurred that markedly changed our prospects.

In 1966 Ralph Nader's book *Unsafe at Any Speed,* among other influences, led to passage of the National Traffic and Motor Vehicle Safety Act and the creation of the National Highway Traffic Safety Administration. Through the efforts of Edward Dye, Cornell Aero Lab had been engaged in some of the earliest crash research, ranging from football helmets to full-scale cars, the safety car concept and highway barriers. Dye was an ingenious and inventive hands-on mechanical engineer who had the backing of Dr. Furnas but was less popular with some of the highly analytical types in the laboratory.

When I became manager of Flight Research in 1947 my former boss, Ira Ross, was given the task of completing the large transonic wind tunnel. His success led to his appointment as CAL president when Dr. Furnas left to become chancellor of the University of Buffalo in 1958. Ira held a well-balanced view of experiment and analysis, and recognized the potential of contract research sponsored by the new NHTSA in both crash and precrash vehicle dynamics. To this end he proposed setting up a Transportation Research Division covering the full

Opening lap of the thrill show in the Astrodome before the fun started. I am in the right seat but unaware of the routine.

spectrum of automobile safety. I was offered the position of director. After the early days of Flight Research, Ira and I had worked out a good relationship and I had every reason to believe he would give the new division his full support.

All activity for every type of vehicle except aircraft would be centralized in the new division at CAL (and to an extent in the Cornell family), broadly including:

1. Continuation of precrash vehicle dynamics, including tire research,

2. Crash mechanics as pioneered by Ed Dye, which was of great interest to the new National Highway Traffic Safety Administration,

3. Occupant behavior in accidents, accident reconstruction, highway barriers, seatbelt performance, etc., and

4. Accident statistics as developed by the Accident Crash Injury Research (ACIR) which had started at the Cornell Medical School in New York City.

To sustain such a comprehensive research activity, Ira envisioned a customer sponsorship base of:

1. NHTSA.

2. Bureau of Public Roads.

3. Office of Naval Research and other military centers.

4. Manufacturers of ground vehicles (cars, motorcycles, bicycles, etc.).

5. Rubber Manufacturers Association.

6. Motor Vehicle Manufacturers Association.

7. Component and equipment manufacturers.

8. State agencies (highway departments) and

9. Racing organizations.

Most of these customers materialized.[1]

The division consisted of two departments: Transportation Research and Vehicle Research,

Fig. 25-1
Bill Milliken (circa 1963) about to start ten years of creative research under sponsorship from GM, Goodyear, NHTSA and other sources.

in addition to Accident Crash Injury Research (which relocated to Buffalo). Naturally, the transfer of a number of key individuals from other parts of the Laboratory was required to form the core of our technical expertise.

Home for the division would be Lab One on Genesee Street opposite the Buffalo Municipal Airfield. Personally, I regretted leaving the informality of the old flight hangar with its aircraft and race cars, paved ramps and taxiways. For some years Ira had been enticing me to move to Lab One, but I had resisted with one excuse or another. With the offer of the Transportation Research Division directorship I couldn't justify holding out any longer. But before accepting I waited for a staff meeting in Ross's office. When the subject of the new division came up I turned to Ira and said, "Isn't it about time you invited me to move to Lab One?" For the first time I saw Ira momentarily lose his composure. Afterward I thought that perhaps it was time for me to grow up.

I made the switch, although I never quite fit in. Too many opportunities to "pull the elephant's tail" presented themselves, like screeching around that nice bend into the parking lot and incurring the wrath of comptroller Henry Moffitt.

TRANSPORTATION RESEARCH was headed by Bob Wolf, who had an extensive aeronautical background dating back to the early years of Bell Aircraft helicopters and was recognized as an excellent manager. This department was responsible for crash tests, crash mechanics, occupant dynamics analysis, accident reconstruction, barriers, seatbelts and traffic studies in general.

Assistant to Wolf was Ed Kidd, a former Air Force captain. He had worked at Wright Field in the Aircraft Laboratory before joining CAL Flight Research as a project engineer

---

[1] *There was never a shortage of first-time projects and even today, more than thirty-five years later, transportation research continues under current laboratory ownership.*

on variable-stability aircraft. He was a solid engineer and leader.

Vehicle Research was set up under King Bird. He had joined the Lab in 1951, and was successively responsible for the large wind tunnel and the Applied Hypersonic Research Department. Bird brought much managerial experience to the new division.

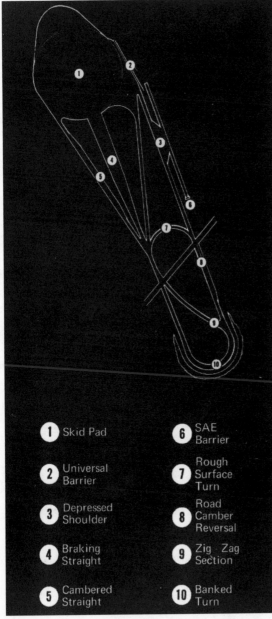

1 Skid Pad

2 Universal Barrier

3 Depressed Shoulder

4 Braking Straight

5 Cambered Straight

6 SAE Barrier

7 Rough Surface Turn

8 Road Camber Reversal

9 Zig - Zag Section

10 Banked Turn

Fig. 25-2
The Vehicle Experimental Research Facility (VERF) located behind CAL/Calspan main laboratory, the scene of specialized crash research and handling dynamics tests. For a university-owned facility it was outstanding.

Assistant department head Fred Dell'Amico, best known for his servo-control experience as applied to missiles and variable stability aircraft, was an outstanding analyst in general and had experience in project direction. Vehicle Research was responsible for land and water-borne vehicle projects.

Unlike the Flight Research and Vehicle Dynamics departments, where I was able to make substantial technical contributions, my relationship with Transportation Research was more administrative and less hands-on. My new duties entailed staff meetings, financial reviews and organizational and planning sessions. I occasionally managed to inject or initiate worthwhile ideas or engage in significant promotional activity, but I generally depended on the department managers to develop and sell their own programs.

I felt less comfortable in my new role. In a small way, my situation was analogous to Frank Winchell's. Ideally suited to head up Chevrolet's Research and Development Group, where he established the Chaparral connection and took on the Corvair litigation, he seldom enjoyed or excelled at being chairman of the corporation's Technical Committee and other administrative duties as he rose to the vice presidency of GM's engineering staff.

Transportation Research Department

Developing a proving ground was an early priority. An interesting tract of land with varying terrain was available about 30 miles from Buffalo, but the issue of convenience won out and an area behind the main lab was chosen. Ed Kidd had primary responsibility for the design of the Vehicle Experimental Research Facility (VERF). It covered 33 acres and included a 400-foot skid pad, a 100-foot-radius high-banked turn that was very rough with poor entry but still served to build up the speed required by some tests, and a complex of approaches and test lanes featuring specialized road geometry and various friction coefficients. Seven possible uses for VERF were considered in its design:

- Handling
- Vehicle crashworthiness

- Component performance
- Driver performance
- Vehicle performance
- Vehicle ride
- Vehicle stability and control

A permanent automobile crash facility for towing vehicles into a collision barrier at various attitudes was installed as part of VERF. Powered by two Chrysler Hemi engines with appropriate speed controls for meeting crash standards, the barrier could also be used to hold simulated roadside obstacles such as utility poles and signs. There was a separate area for testing roadside and bridge guardrails, using automatic vehicle guidance.

With VERF it was possible to obtain long-term contract support from NHTSA for a program in crashworthiness to study driver protection from engine intrusion, underride guards for trucks, the development of crash testing technology, etc. Pat Miller, a member of Transportation Research since 1968, was the project engineer, assisted by Norris Shoemaker, who had formerly worked with Ed Dye doing early crash research. Jim Greene and Dave Romeo were also involved. The towing test facility was designed by Carl Thelin and the instrumentation by Rudi Arendt, both transfers from Flight Research.[2]

The crash work for NHTSA attracted a great deal of attention. Leaving the parking lot in the morning, I usually walked through the high bay area where the cars were being prepped for their demise. One might observe a shiny new Corvette covered with tape and decals in the morning and its remains after a 30-mph frontal crash in the evening. All the

Fig. 25-3
Raymond McHenry, pioneer of comprehensive computer models for crashworthiness and vehicle handling. An early user of computer graphics, he was famous for his conception and execution of the spiral jump.

crashed vehicles were impounded for later analysis by the government.

This was serious business, but once in a while humor intervened. On one occasion NHTSA members arrived to witness some crashes, presumably to observe the progress being made in reducing the effect of a head-on collision. To enliven the proceedings, an old rusted-out Chevrolet was to be put into the barrier at 50 mph instead of 30. Anticipating something interesting, King Bird and I were there as spectators. It was an incredible crash. The car crumpled in accordion fashion into a Toonerville Trolley with the steering wheel projected through the rear window. Much to the chagrin of our visitors, King and I burst into laughter.

Before finite-element analysis (FEA) computer programs had been developed there was need for force-deflection data for use with simple crash models. Under Pat Miller's direction a large static crusher was built in which a full-sized car could slowly be crushed.

Roughly coincident with the full-scale crash research programs, Transportation Research had acquired an analytical project in crash mechanics from the Bureau of Public Roads that was to have far-reaching consequences. Carrying the impressive name of Highway Vehicle Object Simulation Model (HVOSM), the project, whose original objective was to model single-vehicle accidents, continued with multiple contracts for more than seven years. The model itself had 15 degrees of freedom: 6 degrees rigid body sprung mass, 4 degrees suspension deflections, 1 degree steer and 4 degrees wheel rotations. It was fully nonlinear and large amplitude, had detailed terrain representation and had an associated driver model. HVOSM set the stage for large, comprehensive models that simulate real vehicle behavior and crashes to a high level of accuracy.

The project engineer and principal author of this development was Ray McHenry,

[2]*Miller, Greene and Arendt later teamed up to start their own company, MGA, a major spin-off from CAL. With facilities in Akron, New York, the former American Motors Proving Ground in Wisconsin and three laboratories in Michigan, they operate three test-sled facilities and five machines for seat testing, and also sell test equipment to automotive customers.*

an extraordinary results-oriented engineer who combined a solid understanding of the mathematical foundations of vehicle dynamics with the empirical approach of the practical engineer and designer. He utilized closed-form theory when available but was never stopped by its limitations, pressing on with the incorporation of experimental data from a variety of sources to a good engineering result. Highly competitive, armed with a good sense of humor and anxious to tackle the tough problems, Ray pioneered a variety of models in crash simulation and general vehicle dynamics.

Major contributions to HVOSM were also made by Dave Segal, who joined CAL in 1966, and Norm Deleys, who arrived somewhat later. As a result of this team effort, Ray McHenry received the Crompton-Lanchester Medal and Safety Award in Mechanical Engineering from the British IME in 1969.

Spiral Jump

A dramatic follow-on to the project enlivened our routine for months, climaxing in an unforgettable weekend at the Houston Astrodome. McHenry was forever looking for ways to demonstrate HVOSM's ability to simulate difficult situations. When an automobile thrill show appeared in town, Ray arranged to analytically recreate some of its most extreme maneuvers, including a jump in which the vehicle took off from a ramp, flew through the air and landed on another ramp. The simulation was astonishingly successful and inspired Ray to dream up a still more unlikely task: the vehicle taking off from a spiral ramp and doing a complete barrel roll in the air before landing on a reverse spiral, effectively unwinding itself. Using HVOSM, Ray came up with convincing proof of feasibility. Jay Milligan, a local thrill show operator, was

interested, and a takeoff ramp was constructed for test on VERF. After a number of junked cars were towed over the ramp confirming reasonable landing attitude, a landing ramp was constructed and driverless cars using wire-following and speed control were tested. The whole exercise proceeded in a most scientific fashion. For example, the American Motors Javelin was fully tested on Chevrolet's K&C machine and inertia rig, yielding data for Ray's calculations. Anticipating a human driver, the driver's seat was relocated to the center of the car with full harness and a NASCAR roll cage.

Chick Galliano, a professional parachute jumper, stunt man and friend of Jay Milligan's, voiced an interest in becoming the driver for the spiral jump. The jump speed was only about 45 mph, so none of us viewed the situation as very hazardous, but issues of liability and insurance were mentioned. A further problem arose when a religious group in the Lab proposed a prayer session and a period of silence before the first manned jump. With tongue in cheek, Ross called me in to assess the risks, and I suggested that the Lab finance a few

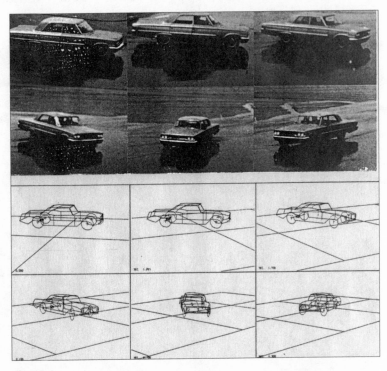

Fig. 25-4
Early demonstration of HVOSM predicting the motions of a skidding automobile.

Fig. 25-5
The spiral jump design team. L to R - WFM, R. McHenry and J. Milligan, president of J.M. Productions—the thrill show operator.

more computer runs before we fastened Chick into the machine.

Chick's final instructions were to maintain the specified speed and try not to second-guess the straight run-in line (easy to do if you looked at the odd ramp shape). The first jump was a pretty good validation of Ray's calculations, although a somewhat rocky landing. Chick's reaction was, "What the hell happened?" Other jumps followed, one a never-to-be-repeated

event. The machine crashed down onto the landing ramp, jumped up and did *another* complete roll (in the opposite direction) before coming to a stop.

Jay had arranged the first public showing at the Astrodome as the finale to his thrill show that included a female demolition derby and a motorcycle jump over 12 cars. Ray, a contract rep and I flew to Houston and were fitted out in JM Productions uniforms as part of the crew. At the Astrodome we were greeted warmly and, in effect, offered the keys to the city. For those so inclined, attractive young women were available as live-in female companions for the weekend. One of the conservative members of the CAL group, who was also somewhat deaf, found himself shackled to a blazing redhead.

Getting down to business, we discovered that the necessary run-up and stopping distances could not be obtained in the confines of the Astrodome floor that was below ground level. Chick would have to start his run in

Fig. 25-6
Unloading the spiral jump Javelin at the Houston Astrodome for its premiere public performance. WFM on left.

the parking lot, plunge down a ramp into the lighted Astrodome, make the jump and quickly stop to avoid endangering the spectators.

The Astrodome was packed. I was standing near the entrance gate when Jay invited me to ride along with him at the thrill show opening. I jumped in and fastened the belt. At Jay's signal each car broke off from the parade, headed for the stands and spun to a stop 30 feet away from the spectators, the driver jumping out and taking a bow. Unaware of this procedure, when Jay stopped and yelled "get out," I gave a great heave with my belt still fastened. By the time I got it unbuckled and fell out I barely had time to fall back in before we were off, running at high speed over single-wheel bumps. Without a seat belt, I was performing my own show in the front seat.

The next act, a single-car jump through a ring of fire, was being set up in the middle of the Astrodome. Seeing a problem, Jay drove over to the ring, jumped out and told me to drive back to the garage. I was suddenly in the show, a novice on the loose. With nothing to lose, I did a couple of half-assed gangster getaways, spun out a couple of times and worked my way back to the garage. Afterward Jay said something to the effect that "I had the spirit but not the finesse."

Before Chick started his act he was told how to adjust the speed control we had installed, and to cancel the run if not on speed and try again. On his first run he aborted. On the next run he aborted again. The crowd accepted all this as part of the buildup but, after six aborts in a row, assumed something was phony and began to boo. We conferred with Chick in the parking lot and found he had been adjusting the speed controller in the wrong direction!

On the next run the speed looked close and Chick went for the jump. We held our breath as the car sailed through the air—would it make the landing ramp or crash into it? As a precaution, McHenry had designed a "coward's lip," a sloping lip at the forward end of the landing ramp. The car hit it, bounced up and careered onto the main ramp to a very rough landing. For the crowd it was enough. Everybody stood up, cheering and clapping, as Chick crawled out and took a bow.

As a sequel to the Astrodome show, the jump was used as part of a chase scene filmed in Thailand for the James Bond movie *The Man with the Golden Gun*. The ramps were built of teakwood to our drawings, the takeoff ramp disguised as a broken-down twisted bridge and the landing ramp as the sloping side of a roof. The movie stunt man did a superb job, probably the best spiral jump ever completed. The jump car is still in Jay's possession, at JM Production headquarters in Buffalo.

An early user of computer graphics during his spiral jump development, Ray McHenry went on to develop highly successful computer models of vehicles and occupants in crashes (CRASH and SMAC) that were for specific accident analyses. As an expert witness he won some spectacular litigation cases and finally set up his own company.

Defending the Corvair

Early in 1965 I was invited to become a consultant to Chevrolet for the Corvair litigation defense. Setting up this consulting arrangement was far from easy. I would be doing business with GM and with NHTSA, the government agency responsible for safety regulation of the automotive industry. The Corvair litigation was a very controversial issue. Matters were further complicated by the relationship between Jim Hall's Chaparral Cars and Chevrolet R & D, and although perfectly legal this seemed to belie GM's official position of having nothing to do with auto racing. Legal types in the Lab did not share Ira Ross's view of the advantages of working with all parties while keeping confidential material in its proper slots. He approved my accepting a consulting contract with GM, a decision that ultimately was to work to the benefit of everyone. I would be consulting with Frank Winchell until his retirement from GM in 1982.

Frank Winchell was chosen to head GM's defense team in the Corvair litigation. He was the logical choice. Because of his Chaparral work, Frank was in the forefront of knowledge on car handling, particularly near the limit of adhesion where many accidents occur. Having worked closely with Schilling and Olley, and aware of the evolution of the Corvair's design,

Fig. 25-7
The spiral jump in the James Bond movie *Man with the Golden Gun*. Performed in Thailand, it was a perfect jump.

Frank tackled this assignment as if it were a personal vendetta. His defense was broadly based, involving exhaustive testing of the Corvair, the training of the legal teams, the use of knowledgeable expert witnesses, and so on.

Given a Corvair to drive for a couple of months in case I was called upon as an expert witness, I got used to the car's handling and liked it. Confidently, I took out my two young sons and did rapid lane changes at 60 mph. The Corvair was equal to or better than the VW Beetle, which had sold in record volume in every country in the world and had a good safety record by then-current standards.

Thinking a famous race driver's opinion of the Corvair would be useful, Frank invited Juan Fangio from Argentina for a spin on the Proving Ground. One of the great stories is how Frank Winchell and Fangio, unable to converse in a common language, arrived at the handling loop where Fangio took over and made two record laps, drifting and sliding the corners while shouting his approval, "Magnifico, Magnifico!" Any tendency for the car to roll over certainly did not show up in this performance.

To train the lawyers, Winchell produced several films and a number of models explaining the basics of car handling. These were first-order tools that provided the fundamental essence without confusing the picture with excessive details.

After a struggle that lasted several years, the allegation that the Corvair suffered from a defective design was demonstrated to be untrue and the vehicle was exonerated. Of the 294 Corvair lawsuits, 10 were tried to a verdict, 8 of which were in GM's favor.

Frank Winchell

I first met Frank Winchell in the fall of 1964 when he was in charge of R & D at Chevrolet. "You've got to see how Frank builds experimental cars and what he is learning," Maurice Olley had told me. So he and I talked a lot about race cars, especially Chaparral, with whom he was already involved. At lunch we got into an argument about 4WD cars. I thought they were the race car of the future, Winchell thought otherwise. This was the first of a number of stormy encounters, some via correspondence, that led to a profound and enduring friendship. When I met with Frank a couple of months later, he had built up a 4WD car and tested it himself.

One of the most creative and independent thinkers I ever met in my professional career, Frank was extremely tough, competitive, forceful, direct and literally scared off some people. To my good fortune, I recognized that he had a brand of fundamental engineering thinking that was worth cultivating. I also found it a relief to know someone with absolutely no hidden agenda, who said exactly what he believed. For financial reasons Frank had never completed college, so he was largely self-taught and his approach to engineering problems was strongly experimental. One of his earlier jobs was at GM's tank plant in Indianapolis, where on one occasion the tank line was stopped when the rotating turret hung up for no obvious reason. Frank crawled into the tank and emerged some 20 hours later with the solution. Transferred to Detroit, he played a prominent role in developing the original automatic transmission.

**Figure 25-8
Frank Winchell, at the time
he was vice president of GM
engineering staff.**

Early in his career Frank had experienced something close to a nervous breakdown, which forced him to analyze his thought processes. He discovered Korzybski's *Science and Sanity*, a book that examines the effects of language, abstractions, imagination, etc., on our nervous system's attempt to sense reality. Korzybski came up with the concept of a "structural differential" that could be represented physically by a mechanical model. Such a model was on Winchell's desk when I first met him. I don't wish to pose as knowledgeable about Korzybski's work, but I do know that Frank had a monumental effect on my own thinking.

At this time, I was going through some emotional problems, had been exposed to psychoanalysis and was dabbling in such parapsychological areas as ESP and hypnosis. Winchell made a strong point that highly educated engineers frequently confuse abstractions of a phenomenon with the real thing. I had observed this in our Stratoliner certification at Boeing, when my academic knowledge of stability and control theory was useful but did not get to the real problem.

Frank also pointed out how the name of a phenomenon can semantically take on a mysterious life of its own. The term over/understeer still has a variety of meanings depending on context and the background of the user. For years auto racing literature was confused by the term "four-wheel drift." In one of his letters, Frank took up the subject of being aware of what one doesn't know:

"Awareness is a condition that should occupy all of us. I believe man's intolerance to a state of not knowing is his greatest fault. We boast of our technological achievements, yet there is nothing on this earth now that was not here thousands of years ago. Why, then, has it taken so long to assemble these basic elements into today's technology? I think it's because of what we 'knew' we knew, not what we didn't know. Regrettably, the process of unlearning seems far more formidable than learning. In fact, to most, unlearning is impossible. They hold with what they want to believe, with the word of their chosen source of truth; civilization's own kind of painted, chanting dancers; all the priests, most of the politicians and too many academicians."

Chaparral

As a consultant to Winchell, I had a firsthand opportunity to see the Chevrolet-Chaparral collaboration in operation. To me it was a near-perfect amalgamation of the complementary talents of a number of very smart people motivated by the single goal of winning by learning. With a solid team behind them, Winchell, Hall, Jim Musser and Hap Sharp built complete race cars and tested them on an instrumented track in Midland, Texas.[3]

There was one turn on Rattlesnake Raceway in Texas that Hall initially had been taking at something over 100 mph. In the course of development he could take it at 140 mph. Chaparrals, of course, radically changed the Can-Am series.

During this exciting period, in which Chaparral and the Corvair litigation were moving along on intersecting tracks, NHTSA had broached the idea of developing handling standards to be imposed on the industry. One of the approaches was of "task performance" (as opposed to any form of design standards) which led Winchell to devise some unique tasks. One involved a two-lane road section, either lane of which could be barred by a sliding curtain triggered by the car approaching from a highway entrance ramp. The driver had to choose the open lane, which required a rapid decision and maneuver. Winchell thought this task would be useful in acquiring a quantitative number on the effect of blood alcohol on a driver's performance, the measure being the run-in speed at which the driver could accomplish the task.

Jim Hall, Hap Sharp and I were invited to participate in a drinking and driving test to

**Fig. 25-9
Jim Hall, Chaparral Cars.**

**Fig. 25-10
Jim Musser, Winchell's assistant at Chevrolet Research and Development.**

take place at the Proving Ground on a Sunday. The idea of getting drunk for science had an amusing appeal. We anticipated some interesting results, since Frank, Jim and Hap were fairly regular drinkers and I was a very irregular social drinker. Further, there were large weight differences among us for which no compensation was planned.

We arrived at the Proving Ground on empty stomachs and in high spirits, to make several familiarization and baseline runs with zero alcohol before getting down to business. Jim Hall, his wife Sandy and I sat in one car while awaiting our turn; Frank and Hap occupied another. The test vehicle had certain onboard recording equipment, with additional instrumentation on the ground between the two exit lanes.

The initial shot of alcohol removed any inhibitions and the trap speeds were higher. As our alcohol content increased, all of us started down but my rate was faster than the more regular drinkers. During the day, the participants routinely wandered out into a wooded area to take a leak. With more alcohol, we performed this task alongside the car. I remember saying to Jim Hall, who was sitting by Sandy's side, "Jim, you have a remarkably attractive wife," to which he replied, "Oh, I dunno." Once, as the nurse was taking a blood sample out of my arm, Hap Sharp grabbed the syringe and squirted it all over my white shirt. Hap was one of the most intelligent persons I have ever met and a real asset to Chaparral. He was also a great joker and labeled me "Boston Bill."

As we were staggering around I remember saying, "If you guys can put me in the car, I'll drive it." Once there, I closed the door and passed out. When I came to, I started the engine and passed out again. Coming to, I made half a dozen runs and passed out for

[3] They had a tire tester, an instrumented track, aerodynamic facilities, etc., and were the first to use aerodynamic downforce and an early automatic transmission.

good. Hap made the next run but couldn't decide whether to go left or right, so charged straight ahead, ruining the instrumentation and ending the program.

Arriving back at the Winchells, Frank's wife Marguerite greeted the crew on the doorstep. I was told that as they carried me in she saw the blood on my shirt and exclaimed, "Oh my God, they killed him." They dropped me onto a spare bed with my hat still on my head. I woke up in the middle of the night and made a snakelike trip to the bathroom 30 feet away. The plotted results indicated all of us reached the same low level of performance but at different rates.

Early in their association, Winchell, Hall and Musser developed their own analysis of car control and stability, which was summarized in a confidential report. Upon joining the team I attended a week-long session in which Frank, at the blackboard and with models, ran through their complete line of thinking. Using free-body diagrams, fundamental mechanics and tire data measured with their own machine, they had worked out the major features of the successful Chaparral design. It avoided the higher-order derivative concept we had used in our 1956 IME papers, and lacked a number of detailed effects, but it provided a real physical sense of what car control was all about. I found it most impressive. It was an eye-opener for someone like me, who had been educated in the full dynamic (mathematical) approach.

The Winchell-Hall folks, who ran their own trimmed circular skid pad tests at Midland and used that low-speed data to help set up the cars, had also acquired race data from instrumentation in the cars themselves. Their experience, and the fundamental theory

based on steady-state conditions, had proven adequate in solving problems they encountered. In their view the ideal race car was one with negligible transients, that went directly from one steady-state to another. Nevertheless, they recognized that transient states must exist, and were curious about them.

I suggested that a training session on one of Cornell's variable-stability aircraft would give them a sense of transient behavior, i.e., the effects of frequencies and damping, and how they influence pilot control. So we arranged a week-long program in Buffalo on the aircraft used at the Air Force test pilots' school, flown by Giff Bull, our top instructor. Jim Hall was a pilot himself and Winchell was enthusiastic. It was an enlightening experience that confirmed the belief that on smooth circuits the best

Fig. 25-11
Chevrolet R & D adjustable test vehicle, shown with front and rear wings. This led to the concept of aerodynamic downforce now used in all high-performance race cars.

Fig. 25-12
Taken at Watkins Glen after another victory for Chaparral in the Can-Am series. L to R: WFM, Frank Winchell, Hap Sharp and Jim Hall.

Fig. 25-13
Don Gates, formerly with Chevrolet R & D, explains the features of the Antares Indy car to me in Gasoline Alley, 1972. Gates was well known for his advances in vehicle instrumentation.

tactics were to ease the car into a turn and avoid any noticeable transients. On rough circuits transient behavior is a significant problem. Experience at Indy was that the smoothest drivers were the fastest.

Formulating the Moment Method

There is a middle course between steady-state trimmed (or equilibrium) analysis and the full dynamic treatment that is related to wind tunnel testing and is referred to as aircraft statics. In a wind tunnel no attempt is made to run tests that compare with trimmed steady-state flight conditions. Rather, one measures the forces and moments over the full range of such operating variables as wing angle of attack. The forces and moment that do *not* correspond to a particular trim are the ones that create the transient. These are the unbalanced forces and

moments that show the tendency for stability or instability, and hence are very useful in themselves. Thus "static stability" indicates that the aircraft will return to a trimmed attitude if disturbed. In reasonably well-damped systems it can be a sufficient measure of stability.

Aircraft are designed largely by wind tunnel tests and static data. Great designers like George Schairer of Boeing can interpret wind tunnel data and produce satisfactory flying characteristics in aircraft like the 707. Going back to the early 1950s when we started working on automobile control for General Motors, I had been interested in analyzing an automobile's statics. But because their interest lay in transients, and because analytical engineers like Len Segel were "hot-shot" dynamicists, we never took a good look at statics.

By 1969, in parallel with my wind tunnel aircraft experience, I had come up with a preliminary statement on the importance of static directional stability for automobiles. Both were constrained tests but the six-degree-of-freedom constraint for aircraft models was not usable for automobiles, which are subjected to tire forces. For the first time, a suitable constraint system for automobiles was proposed in which the vertical, pitching and rolling motions that together determine the vertical tire forces are unconstrained. The fore and aft constraint corresponds to a d'Alembert, or reversed, effective inertia force that keeps the vehicle in force equilibrium under simulated acceleration. Similarly, the lateral constraint corresponds to lateral acceleration. The yaw (turning) moment is the independent constraint in the system.

In 1968, on my consulting contract with GM, I embarked upon an attempt to calculate the static stability and control of an automobile. The Chaparral 2G of 1967 had a successful racing season and was one of the first race cars to use aerodynamic downforce with a movable wing on the back and a small aero surface in the front duct. At the end of the racing season complete documentation of its final configuration had been obtained, including full-scale tests on the tires, aero data from pressure measurements on the car and wings, weight and inertia, and so on. By using this data for my calculations I could compare the results with the skid-pad measurements on the car and those made under track racing conditions, as well as driver opinion.

This proved to be a major analytical effort. I started by plotting all the available data on the car and tires. For this first statics analysis I felt it desirable to develop a hand-calculation procedure that avoided the iteration normally used in computer solutions. I hoped that this would give me more insight into automobile statics.

I first specified an aerodynamic configuration, a speed and a steady longitudinal acceleration (if traction or braking was involved). A roll couple distribution was also specified. The key to the calculation was to assume a lateral force and a yawing moment applied by the tires, and then work through the system to calculate the corresponding output, namely the front and rear slip angles, the chassis attitude, and the steer angle, δ. The spreadsheet to perform this calculation was eight pages long. Using a slide rule, one pass took about four hours—a labor-intensive operation by any standards. I worked out some 12 solution points in the course of a month.

At that point I turned my spread sheet over to Doug Roland, who produced the first computer program for what we termed the Milliken Moment Method. My calculated points fell on his more complete curves. For the first time we were able to come up with a characteristic Moment diagram, in this case yawing moment vs. lateral acceleration for sets of steer angle and vehicle-slip angle lines. Such plots, and others developed later, give a portrait of the vehicle's stability and control over its full operating range, including

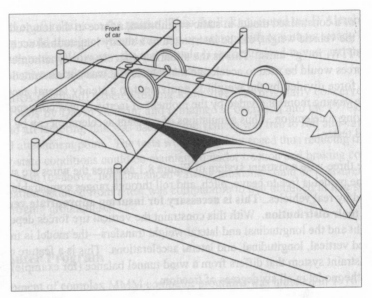

Fig. 25-14
Concept of the Moment Method Constraint System that enables the wheels to experience the proper vertical forces and hence correct tire forces. The constraints are the fore and aft and lateral forces, and yawing moments (torque).

numerical measures of limit and skidding behavior.

In the next few years a great deal of talent was brought to bear on the Moment Method technology by such outstanding engineers as Roy Rice, Fred Dell'Amico, Doug Roland, Dennis Kunkel and others, who broadened the concept, introduced other types of diagrams, and expanded the interpretation. By 1972 we submitted a comprehensive proposal to General Motors—specifically to Joe Bidwell and Frank Winchell—that was accepted and led to major financial support.

In 1973 Vehicle Research became involved in the analysis of a large test facility (Constrained Vehicle Tester) for measuring Moment Method type data on full-scale cars. The original intent was to install this fixture in the GM full-size wind tunnel that was coming on-line. Ultimately, the CVT concept formed the basis of the MTS Flat-Trac Roadway Simulator.

Fig. 25-15
Doug Roland. He developed an early computer model of the Moment Method and was responsible for DK-4 and a number of other major projects.

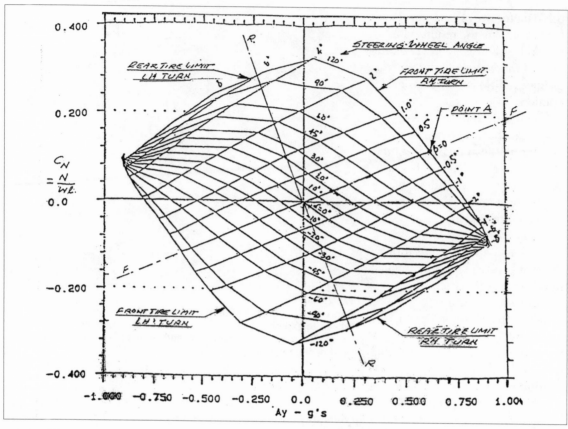

Fig. 25-16
Typical Moment Method diagram (C_n vs. A_y). This is basically a plot of yawing acceleration vs. lateral acceleration, hence it is a maneuvering diagram. The maneuvering area is fixed by the limitations of the front and rear tires. The internal curves are for steering angle and vehicle yaw, which determine the tire slip angles. Most of the stability and control parameters can be obtained from this diagram, including the vehicle behavior at the limit. Thus we view the diagram as a "portrait" of the vehicle stability and control.

Vehicle Research Department

Under King Bird a wide variety of exciting projects and activities were performed. Following are summaries of a number of them.

1. DK-4 Computer Program

A major project was the development of a comprehensive non-linear, large amplitude computer model for vehicle stability and control. The DK-4 project was a result of my relationship with Frank Winchell, but was contracted through Chevrolet Engineering, whose project engineer was Ernie deFusco. The idea was to utilize the experience of HVOSM but emphasize vehicle handling.

As the CAL project engineer we chose Doug Roland. Exposed to Den Hartog's course in vibration analysis and computer programming

at MIT, he was familiar with Euler's equations, moving axes, numerical integration, etc. At CAL he had worked on a steering and suspension degradation project for NHTSA, a good prerequisite to tackling DK-4.

Doug did a superb job developing the basic core equations in great detail. His report on the mathematics still serves as a reference after nearly 30 years. DK-4 also benefited from inputs by section head Roy Rice, Ray McHenry and Ernie deFusco, who checked every aspect. The program was parameter-based and capable of predicting limit behavior and drastic maneuvers such as rollover.

2. Tire Research Facility (TIRF)

The Air Force/Cornell six-component on-road machine of 1954 pioneered the modern approach to tire force/moment testing. Since then it has been copied, and Porsche has produced its large inside-drum tester enabling tests on wet surfaces.

Early on, well aware that nearly every aspect of automobile performance depends on the tires, we concluded that a greatly advanced tire testing facility would attract automotive and tire

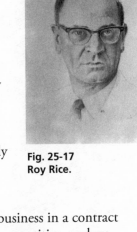

Fig. 25-17
Roy Rice.

Fig. 25-18
Fred Dell'Amico.

customers. Staying in business in a contract research laboratory is competitive, and we intended to use every fair means to stay out front in the area of vehicle dynamics. First, we defined broad performance objectives and specifications for such a machine: an indoor location, flat surface (not drum), six components, large amplitude of the independent variables, high load capacity, very high speed, traction and braking, wet surface, large range of tire sizes (motorcycle to truck) and computer control. We were thinking in terms of 200 mph and up to 14,000 lb. load, the ability to lock up a wheel or spin it up, various dry friction coefficients and adjustable water depths. For slip angle we sought 360 degrees, and camber (with offsetting) up to 50 degrees to 60 degrees. All this was a very tall order, since the concept of a flat-surface machine of this magnitude had yet to be developed. But setting challenging goals can pay off, and this one did.

Late in 1967, it occurred to me that one way to get the project off the ground was to survey tire research facilities in Europe. Ira Ross agreed and King Bird made the trip that December. On his return we thrashed over alternative approaches and by February of '68 made the decision to use a rotating belt for the roadway surface. I had leaned toward a large rotating disk supported locally at the test tire location, with the use of camber to cancel out the curvature effect, but I now am sure the approach chosen was the right one.

The eventual specification was for a steel belt 30 inches wide running on 67-inch-diameter steel drums (an industry standard that yielded 300 revolutions/mile), the belt coated with various surface materials to provide desired friction coefficients. Under the test tire the belt was to be supported by an air or fluid bearing. This configuration, which proved desirable, offered some difficult technical problems. How would the belt be restrained laterally under several thousand pounds of side force from the test tire? Could a bearing be developed that would maintain the belt essentially flat under the test tire and still support high normal loads? Could a scheme be devised for putting a water film of controlled thickness on the belt for wet tests?

All these problems were ultimately solved and, in part, were demonstrated on a quarter-scale model of the drum/belt assembly that was completed in 1968. The lateral force requirement was solved by first analyzing why belts tend to ride on the high part of crowned drums. The mechanism proved to be related to the way tires develop lateral force from slip

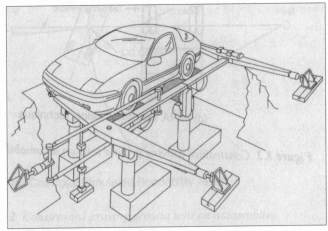

Fig. 25-19
The theory behind the MTS Flat-Trac Roadway Simulator is the Moment Method. In principle the constraint system is similar to that of Fig. 25-14.

571

Fig. 25-20
The Air Force/Cornell on-road tire tester measured all components of forces and moment and defined the tire axis system. Al Fonda is at the control and recording station.

and camber angles. The solution we adopted permits one drum to tilt (against a stiff spring) about an axis perpendicular to the drum axis, under the lateral force from the test tire. George Duryea, grandson of pioneer automaker J. Frank Duryea,[4] made major technical inputs to the basic design of the facility.

The equally difficult problem of financial sponsorship for this phase was solved by a feasibility and design study in which the following companies contributed $10,000 each: GM, Goodyear, Dunlop (USA), Ford,

Goodrich, Armstrong, AMC, Uniroyal, General Tire, Chrysler and Calspan.

The second phase was financed equally by the Motor Vehicle Manufacturers Association and the Rubber Manufacturers Association, plus a $100,000 sole-source contract from NHTSA for shakedown of the facility. Forty meetings outside of town were required to bring in the sponsorship. To avoid any problem with antitrust regulations the contributions, totaling some $670,000 from MVMA and RMA, were made as gifts.

The TIRF facility, which became operational in January 1973, has been in continuous operation ever since. After its shakedown period, an experimental validation was performed against other test facilities located at Firestone, Ford, General Motors,

---

[4] *J. Frank Duryea was the winner of the first automobile race in America in 1895 and, with his brother Charles, organized the first company in the United States to manufacture a gasoline car. (See Carriages Without Horses, Scharchburg, SAE R-127, 1993).*

General Tire, Goodrich, Goodyear, Uniroyal, and the University of Michigan (HSRI). There was a considerable spread in the data, the largest for the on-road machines. Data from TIRF fell close to the mean data from the other machines and the report concluded that ". . . within the evaluated performance range, TIRF was indeed a valid test facility."

Setting a new standard in tire testing, TIRF pioneered flat-belt technology and high-speed testing. Among widely copied features of the machine were the belt tracking principle and the air and water bearings (we used an air bearing but also produced the earliest design of a water bearing). Using the basic features of TIRF, MTS Systems Corporation developed a production tire test facility, the Flat-Trac, which has been widely sold and has increased the availability of reliable tire force and moment data.

Full credit for the major sales effort and construction of TIRF should go to King Bird, his project engineer Jim Martin, George Duryea and their team.

Because the machine created considerable interest in the technical community, we had several visits from Japanese groups. One of them arrived at New York's LaGuardia Airport in the dead of winter and completed the trip to Buffalo by taxicab. Their first question was, "How do you keep the belt on the drums under large side forces?" Until we had an opportunity to publish we were reluctant to give this secret away, so we answered by citing the slight crowning of the drum surface. Our visitors left shaking their heads.

Once the machine was up and operating, I made a six-week

Fig. 25-21
TIRF showing the flat belt supported on an air bearing under the tire. The tire is shown at some camber and slip angle.

Fig. 25-22
King Bird. He was responsible for TIRF development and for acquiring the sponsorship from RMA and MVMA. He also set up the operation teams for the facility.

sales trip to Europe to visit every major tire and automobile company on the continent, which resulted in some contracts and useful future contacts.

Following Ignaty Gusakov and Dr. Dieter Schuring as technical analyst, TIRF's operation was placed under George Tapia. Just about every kind of tire has been tested on the machine, including military vehicle tires and race tires, the latter to over 180 mph. Multiple shift operation continues to this day.

3. Lap Time Simulation (LTS)
One of the nation's earliest lap-time simulation computer programs was developed on a contract from the Watkins Glen Grand Prix Corporation in 1971. (An earlier study had been performed in the 1954–56 period for John Fitch on behalf of the Lime Rock circuit.) The

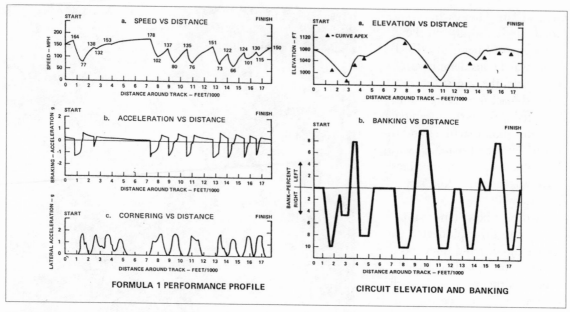

Fig. 25-23
Typical results from a lap-time simulation program.

program was developed by Doug Roland and Carl Thelin using a "point mass" vehicle with assumed "g-g" diagrams for cars of that era.[5]

4. "g-g" Diagram

An extremely useful device that quantifies the maneuvering envelope of the vehicle and its tires, the "g-g" diagram can be used to assess the task performance of different drivers in a particular maneuver or determine the maneuvering area of a driver/vehicle in a comprehensive series of tasks such as laps on a race course. By comparing the latter with the maneuvering envelope, one obtains a measure of the driver's ability to utilize the stability and control characteristics inherent in the car.

The friction circle or ellipse for a given tire is a measure of its lateral plus longitudinal performance for various slip angles and traction/braking levels. When the performance of the four tires is totaled and expressed in "g" units, one has the "g-g" diagram. According to the best information, CAL played a major

part in pioneering "g-g" development. In 1957 Al Fonda deduced friction circle/ellipses from test data by Joy and Hartley of Avon Tire Ltd. A year later he installed a two-axis recorder in a Corvette and obtained what is probably the earliest "g-g" diagram for a vehicle. In 1960 Dr. Hugo Radt used the friction circle in our paper "Motions of Skidding Automobiles."

That year, too, Stirling Moss used a cornering technique that exploited most of the area of the "g-g" diagram of the Lotus

Fig. 25-24
A "g-g" plot of a maneuver. Lateral "g" is plotted versus longitudinal "g."

[5]*Some years later, Peter Milliken developed an LTS which used two friction circles, one for the front track (two tires combined) and another for the rear. Currently, MRA licenses a very detailed LTS, which is used by NASCAR and other race teams.*

race car he was campaigning. This remarkable achievement revolutionized the technique of race car driving.

Many further advances and applications of "g-g" were made in Vehicle Research. The work of Roy Rice, who published two SAE papers (1970 and 1973) formalizing the "g-g" concept, should be particularly noted.

5. Bicycle Dynamics

The National Traffic and Motor Vehicle Safety Act of 1966 brought an expanded interest in safety in all aspects of our industrial society. Schwinn, anticipating the possibility of federal safety regulations of its product, decided to sponsor some fundamental analysis of bicycle mechanics and approached CAL. With Doug Roland as project engineer, a long-term contract was set up.

The object soon became one of modeling the bicycle and its rider so that computer studies could be made of bicycle handling in specific maneuvers. With a comprehensive model, changes in the vehicle configuration could be studied. Accomplishing this objective required development of a bicycle tire force/moment tester, measurement of the inertial properties of the moving and non-moving parts of the machine, development of realistic control algorithms for the rider and, finally, programming a dynamic maneuvering model. The proof of model validity would be to calculate the path and attitude of the bicycle/rider in a particular maneuver and compare it to real bicycle/rider performance of the same task. A visual check also could be made via computer graphics and movies.

The analytical model proved to be extremely complex but gave results that compared closely with real life. The tire tests themselves were enlightening. The general

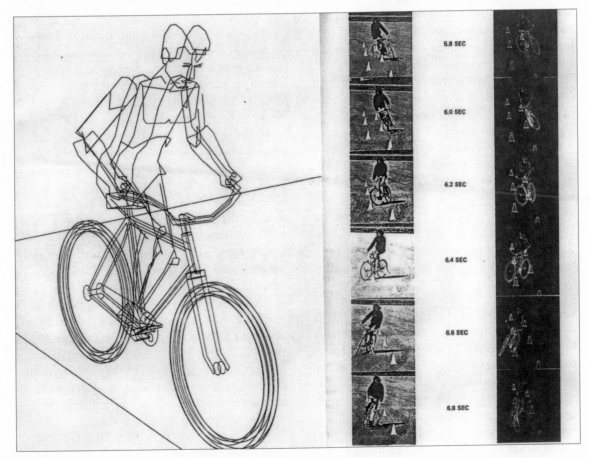

Fig. 25-25
A slalom maneuver on a bicycle. On the left is an actual rider going through the cone course and on the right a computer simulation of a bicycle and rider. The two compare well.

assumption that most of the lateral force on a bicycle tire comes from camber was not substantiated. Slip angle effects are also important in lateral force development on these narrow, high-pressure tires that have such a tiny footprint on the road.

Needless to say, the Schwinn people were exceedingly happy with the program and what they had learned about their product.

6. Tandem Propeller Submarine

Commander Ted Haselton of Vehicle Research was responsible for this novel project performed for the Navy. A former submariner, he was the inventor of the tandem propeller concept that used two variable-pitch propellers, one on each end of a submarine. By varying the propeller collective and cyclic pitch like a helicopter rotor, force components could be obtained for controlling the motion of the sub in six degrees of freedom, even at low or zero forward velocity, obviously impossible with conventional submarine control surfaces. The tandem propeller concept offered great promise for rescue vehicles and for other tasks requiring accurate maneuvering.

The CAL project consisted of developing a closed-loop remote control system for a tandem propeller model and demonstrating it in the David Taylor Model Basin. A unique aspect was the operator control stick, which could be moved in three linear and three rotational modes. Haselton was assisted in this project by Dave Romeo.

7. Monocycle

As a fun project of their own, Doug Roland and Ted Haselton built a powered monocycle consisting of a large outer loop of steel tubing to which a tire tread was laced and within which an inner loop of tubing ran on a series of small rollers. The small gasoline engine and the rider were carried on the inner loop. In theory, the control force was the camber thrust developed by leaning into the turn.

There is some question how the operator was chosen for the initial trial, but the evidence suggests that Haselton was more than happy to relinquish this honor to Roland. The test was made on the ramp in front of our old hangar. Roland started off bravely enough but soon found the high inertia of the heavy rim made turning almost impossible. In his desperation to avoid running into an old dump site, he leaned over so far that the small rollers fell out and the machine disassembled itself beneath its rider!

8. Mailster Post Office Vehicle

About the same time, I had a little fun of my own. Because its small, boxy three-wheeled Mailster had a propensity to roll over, the U.S. Post Office feared the vehicle might fall on a child during a mailman's delivery route. A contract was given to A. D. Little of Cambridge, Massachusetts, to survey the Mailster's behavior, but the consulting firm's analytical approach did not determine what inputs initiated the rollover and how severe it was. A subcontract to Calspan (as CAL was renamed in 1972) to instrument the vehicle and perform an experimental test program was assigned to Vehicle Research.

With no rush of volunteers for test driving, and my history of rolling two Bugattis, I was viewed as the logical candidate. Intentionally rolling over a vehicle was far less attractive than doing it in the heat of battle, but I finally decided the best way to get over my qualms was to do it. So we took the Mailster to the ramp at Flight Research. I put on my crash helmet, buckled up the harness, started a straight full-throttle run, put in the biggest steering step I could muster, whipped the Mailster over on its side and slid along the tarmac. When the flat side hit the ground, I experienced a few g's but nothing as severe as I had imagined, and I did several more rollovers in each direction. In the ensuing days we mapped out the maneuvers and inputs required to put it over, and the resultant g's.

Finally we decided to make a movie. By that time I could whip the Mailster up onto two wheels and slam it down in a spectacular fashion. With a speed of less than 30 mph, the chances of getting hurt were nil. Because the rollover tendency could not be reduced, the vehicle was phased out of service.

9. Gangster Getaway

From the age of ten my history had been one of fast driving. In the absence of driving schools

I honed my skills by driving fast on the highway, making it to Watkins Glen from Buffalo on old Route 20 in two hours. The byproduct was a rash of speeding tickets at every hamlet *en route*. So you can imagine my reaction the day Ira Ross phoned to say the head of the Police Training Academy of New York State was visiting the Laboratory, and would I show him VERF? Here was an opportunity for payback without fear of a speeding ticket. I started off by charging toward the high banked turn at the highest possible entry speed, sweeping around it two feet from the top, scaring myself as well as my passenger. On heavy, front-engine American cars, we had found that full steering lock at high speed resulted only in a plow straight ahead as the front tires peaked out. But most people, including my passenger, did not know that. Charging down VERF, I yelled that I was going to put in full steering, and before the chief could respond we were screeching to a stop with front tires smoking.

In our spare time several of us had been practicing "gangster getaways," a maneuver used during Prohibition when rum runners parked at a speakeasy were discovered by the "revenuers." Those unaware of the maneuver would find it rather startling—so I tried it next. With the car in reverse, I sped up to about 40 mph, then suddenly put in full steering, and as the car swung around, snatched the transmission into a forward gear. If you have the

Fig. 25-26
WFM sitting in the bow of the raft as we approach the rapids below Niagara Falls.

timing right, the car accelerates smoothly away after completing a 180° turn. For once in my life, I executed a perfect getaway, and my passenger was mightily impressed, exclaiming, "My God, this is a fantastic maneuver. You've got to teach it to my officer trainees." I looked at him and replied, "I'm sorry but damned if I will—the driving public has to have some defense against you bears."

10. Niagara Raft Ride

Some executives of the Carborundum Company of Niagara Falls, New York, came up with the idea of organizing raft rides down the Niagara Gorge, a narrow channel about a mile from the foot of the falls where the 30-mph flow velocity is highly turbulent because of the rough bottom and relatively shallow water. Indeed, it is now believed to be the roughest

Fig. 25-27
A number of CAL crew members on the raft. L to R - Jim Davis, Doug Roland, Dave Segal, Roy Rice and Dave Romeo. Everyone wore a life jacket; seat belt use was optional.

inland waterway in the world. From the Gorge Walk one can see the so-called "haystacks" where the waves build up to over 30 feet above the general surface of the river.

An experienced raft pilot, asked to rate the severity, estimated 7.5 to 8.0 on a 10-point scale. Piloting an experimental trip through the rapids, he revised his estimate to 12. Nevertheless, Carborundum began a passenger service, assigning all passengers life jackets. On an early run, they struck a haystack and the raft rolled over. Fortunately all passengers were rescued, but the Coast Guard stopped the operation.

The promoters of the raft ride then approached Calspan to see if a roll-resistant raft design could be created, and were referred to the Transportation Division. Developing one had appeal, but we had little to go on. My suggestion of making an experimental run through the rapids to obtain some firsthand experience brought a dozen volunteers. The Coast Guard proved agreeable. A life jacket was mandatory; a seatbelt was optional, and most preferred to be unattached in case of a rollover. We installed a couple of accelerometers and King Bird took along a Dictaphone to record his impressions.

Our jovial crew met at the *Maid of the Mist* embarkation point. The raft pilot sat in the rear to control a small outboard motor and provide some steering to the raft. King Bird and I sat opposite to each other in the bow. A helicopter would photograph the run. Friends and relatives observed from the Gorge Walk on the opposite cliffs. In brilliant sunshine we sailed smoothly down the river under the railway bridge toward the gorge entrance. When we hit the narrows, King's last Dictaphone recording was "Jesus K-rist!" At times we were down in a hole surrounded by a wall of water; other times we were balancing on the peak of a haystack. Passing King Bird's wife on the Gorge Walk, we were out of sight and she exclaimed, "My God, they've sunk!"

When we struck a huge haystack at an angle, the raft rolled to what seemed like 90°, where it hesitated, poised between completing the roll or recovering. I happened to be on the high side—and exchanged glances with King. Finally, the raft rolled back and we completed the run without further incident. The measured

accelerations were small but the attitude changes were tremendous. The movie showed the raft pitching, rolling and using the full width of the channel.

Based on that experience, a raft was designed with outriggers like those used by South Sea islanders, with a prototype built by a firm in France. Several experimental trips were made, all them successful. In deference to our design expertise, the raft operator invited Calspan personnel to a complimentary ride. I was in New York City on a business trip, but Dave Segal, Dennis Kunkel, Dave Romeo with his sixteen-year-old son, and Jim Davis were among those who accepted the invitation. Twenty-nine people were on board. In the course of the run, the raft plowed into a haystack that lifted the nose of the raft and flipped it over onto its back. Some of the crew were thrown clear, but Dave Segal came up under the raft, then dove down and came up clear of it. It was impossible to swim to shore but he hung on until the calmer waters of the Whirlpool were reached. Two men and one woman drowned. The outriggers apparently were successful in keeping the raft from rolling over, but were of little benefit in resisting a half-loop. The raft service was terminated by the Coast Guard.

11. Man-off-the-Street Driving Study

For years questions regarding average driver performance had been raised. How much lateral acceleration would the average driver use in an emergency, how did he behave in an inadvertent skid, how would he recover if he ran over a curb and off the road, and what was his behavior after a tire blowout? The answers had a bearing on car design, safety legislation and advanced driver training.

With a contract from Joe Bidwell, then in GM Research, we were to try to find some of these answers. Project manager Roy Rice designed a course on VERF that incorporated a series of "surprise" tasks, and performance measures for them. Advertising for 100 subject drivers brought volunteers who were screened for their accident record, age and sex. The final group was believed to be representative of so-called "average drivers off the street." Two ordinary passenger cars that appeared identical were used, but one was set up with a performance suspension (i.e., stiffer springs, heavier shocks and less understeer).

More than 30 tasks were involved, and a tremendous amount of data was collected—so much in fact that much of it was never analyzed. Some of the conclusions were:

- The average driver seldom exceeds 0.3g, even when it would help him avoid an accident.
- Large performance differences occur in the driver population.
- Drivers accommodate rapidly to different vehicle characteristics.
- Performance differences can be quantified with different tasks.
- When the test was given to a local sports car competition driver, he performed much better on all tasks, suggesting that advanced driver training is worthwhile.

12. GM Saginaw Steering Simulation

Another contract from Joe Bidwell was for an experimentally validated mathematical model of the Saginaw power steering system (typical of the boost systems of the 1966–68 period). Simplifications of the completed model could be used to study the steering-force control dynamics of an automobile by combining the steering system model with existing position-control car characterization.

Project engineer was Ewald Schroeder, who had substantial assistance from Roy Rice and Fred Dell'Amico. Staff members provided additional assistance by performing the experimental tests and programming the model on a hybrid analog-digital computer. This is believed to be the first mathematical model of a complete automobile power-steering system, including all the significant non-linearities. Detailed mathematical models of all the major system components were required, including the open-center valve, the rack and actuator, and the vane pump. Fluid compliance and inertia effects were included, as well as fluid friction and Coulomb friction, flow reaction forces, etc. To measure the characteristics of the overall system and components a complete dynamic test rig was developed.

A simplified model that could be used for vehicle steering-force control studies was proposed, based on valve symmetry, zero fluid compliance, zero flow reaction torque, negligible viscosity effects and constant valve flow. The final report was more than 230 pages long and is a classic of technical literature. Saginaw Division finally acquired the model and hired Schroeder as well.

13. Minibikes and Bicycle Safety

In 1968 a consumer products safety entity gave Calspan a contract to evaluate minibikes and bicycles from the standpoint of ride, handling and general defects. The experimental project, under Roy Rice, was well suited to various tests that could be performed on VERF with external and perhaps some onboard instrumentation.

Rice's two sons, Peter and Steve, were avid bicyclists and agreed to act as test riders for the bicycle part of the contract. Our oldest son, Doug, was a logical candidate for the remainder of the testing because of his daily use of the half-mile dirt track we had built on our property for go-kart and minibike racing. In 1966, at the age of 12, Doug had built his first minibike, and two years later was a competent rider.

The minibike craze began in California, and the early examples were well-engineered. As the craze caught on, however, many copies were produced that fell short of the original standards. On one bike tested the foot peg failed; on another, the rear suspension had long undamped travel, resulting in a violent pitch when excited by a road bump. Doug remembers that this nearly threw him off the bike.

A variety of tests were performed including circle, slalom, braking, acceleration and rough roads. Subjective opinion was recorded as well as quantitative measurements. A final test used a model rocket engine to disturb the bike laterally as if by a wind gust.

All in all it was an interesting project that revealed several design and construction deficiencies.

14. Handling Standards

Within a year following establishment of the NHTSA in 1966, procurement requests were issued for planning studies for initial safe-handling standards for automobiles and long-term research to update initial standards. The importance of handling to automobile safety comes in the precrash or avoidance phase of an accident. Our Vehicle Research Department received planning contracts for both initial and updated standards.

Unlike crash standards, which can be couched in objective criteria with standardized repeatable tests, the specification of "handling" is far more difficult. Handling, by definition, involves both the vehicle dynamics and the driver responses as a system. The former is complex, whether based on design details or response parameters, and the latter is nearly impossible to describe if one thinks of the vast variations in the driving population. Thus we were working for both government and industry in a highly controversial area.

The mere thought of handling standards met with a violent reaction from industry. It obviously is very difficult to separate the contributions of the driver and the vehicle to a preaccident situation. Further, the "personality" of a vehicle and its competitive position in the market is wrapped up in its handling behavior, which is usually subjectively assessed by expert drivers working for the car companies. The tight performance feel of many German cars differed markedly from the heavy understeering of American automobiles of that period. Handling generally is a closed-loop system operation with many possible solutions and nuances.

The idea of developing a handling standard led to a sizable number of technical investigations and papers over the next ten years. Before attempting to write this section, I pulled some twenty of the more important papers from our files, including contributions from GM, Ford, Mercedes-Benz, Volkswagen, Pirelli, HSRI, System Dynamics, Cranfield and British car companies.

Our own engagement at CAL was substantial. I was a member of the Presidential Task Force on Highway Safety that had been implemented by SAE, and wrote an analysis entitled "Highway Accident Reduction—Handling and Roadability" in which I tried to sort out the fundamental factors influencing handling standards. This was followed by a paper presented by Fred

Dell'Amico at the Joint Symposium on Vehicle and Road Design for Safety at the College of Aeronautics, Cranfield, England, entitled "Standards for Safe Handling Characteristics of Automobiles." To facilitate communication between government and industry, we hosted (and I led) a Handling Survey Trip for four key individuals from NHTSA to General Motors, Ford and Chrysler in Detroit. We also spent a day at CAL and Watkins Glen, the latter to demonstrate the extraordinary handling of a Ford GT-40 at speeds up to 130 mph. The concern the industry had over the possibility of the government legislating even *minimum* handling standards was illustrated by a contract we received from Daimler-Benz to keep that company abreast of actions by NHTSA related to handling standards. With our numerous contacts in industry and government, the German firm felt we were in a position to sort out the trend of events. To retain credibility we made our position with D-B an open secret.

There were a number of possible approaches to handling standards methodology, including:

1. Vehicle design parameters,
2. Vehicle response parameters,
3. Task performance,
4. Mission performance,
5. Subjective evaluation.

Most investigators concluded that if standards were warranted, the task performance approach was the most viable. The decision about what safety-related tasks to include, the measure of performance, and what driver to use in the test remained. In evaluating task performance, one is at least working with handling, i.e., the driver and the car. Furthermore, there are tasks that appear safety-related, like an avoidance maneuver, responding to a tire blowout, a sudden change in tire/road friction coefficient, etc. Numerical measures of performance could be defined. For consistency, using the most experienced test driver made some sense. But many nagging questions remained. We concluded that barring a catastrophic situation, a responsible, alert and unimpaired driver probably is safe in any reasonable vehicle. On the other hand there are drivers who are unsafe in vehicles of refined stability and control qualities. The fact is that the driver was the only intelligent entity in the system and was responsible for guidance, i.e., maintaining the desired path, while the vehicle characteristics can only influence the driver's decisions. The difficulties of imposing rational handling standards and their value has subsided over the years. There is a huge number of constraints and deterrents such as the size of the task structure, the realization that the driver is much more of the problem than the vehicle, the necessity of limiting the government's role in vehicle design and so forth. The industry has accepted crashworthiness legislation, the use of belts, interior redesign and even active front and side airbags. Furthermore, antilock brakes, traction control and active stability systems have come about in the natural course of competition.

Taking into account the size of the highway system, the variation in driving capability, the endless variety of road, weather and traffic situations, the mix of trucks and passenger cars and so on, the highway is still a remarkably safe system in relation to its immense utility role in our society.

In reviewing the literature of the "handling standards era," I came across two interesting technical papers. Both consider cases in which a solid correlation was established between driver subjective opinion and measured performance data. The first, by Volkswagen, analyzed step inputs and measured yaw velocity and sideslip response; a short yaw velocity time response and a minimum developed sideslip were shown to be desirable. The second, by Bergman of Ford, correlated driver feel with sideslip acceleration in the second phase of a lane-change maneuver. It concluded that most drivers want to minimize transient effects and are most happy if the vehicle goes where it is pointing.

15. Motor Trend Car of the Year

In 1972 I was invited to be on Motor Trend's Car of the Year panel along with Phil Hill, Karl Ludvigsen and others. We convened with

Figure 25-28
Karl Ludvigsen and I were two members of the panel that selected the 1972 Motor Trend Car of the Year. Other members included Phil Hill.

our wives in Los Angeles and then drove to Borrego Springs in the desert. Here we could drive the cars without concern for speeding tickets, and as Eric Dahlquist said, "[I'd take] any excuse to race on a public road." Each evening we gathered at a nice restaurant with great conversation. I particularly remember Phil Hill's tales of working with Ferrari.

End of One Career

Cornell Aeronautical Laboratory was a great place to work. It offered a creative individual full opportunity to pursue and develop his particular interests. I would have stayed there indefinitely but, as in so many organizations, when you turned 65 you had to leave. I always felt that an arbitrary retirement policy was a dumb idea, ruining the lives of creative individuals and divesting companies of vast amounts of hard-won experience. I once gave a talk at SAE on the subject and applauded Bob Lutz when he went to work at General Motors after normal retirement age.

In 1976 I was given a nice retirement party with the usual roasting and a fine artist rendition of the 4WD Miller at Pikes Peak. But, of course, I had no intention of retiring.

Chapter 26

Milliken Research Associates, Inc.

"On into the twenty-first century."

– Anonymous

As mandatory retirement approached I began planning my post-CAL career. Two things were clear: I wanted a company of my own and I wanted to continue the automotive dynamics work we had pioneered in the Vehicle Research Department and Transportation Research Division. Retirement benefits would support the family while I was getting started. Through my consulting for General Motors and sales contacts for CAL, I could envision a customer base for this new enterprise.

But things never go totally according to plan. With the gift of Curtiss-Wright's Research Laboratory Division in 1946, CAL began operating as a not-for-profit, tax-exempt corporation. Although Cornell University owned the stock of the Laboratory, it had never put a nickel into it. CAL's working capital came from gifts from East Coast aircraft companies who hoped to benefit from its use. The relationship between the university and the Laboratory had been cordial. CAL supported a couple of chairs, the university sent professors to the Lab as guest speakers and supported the vice president, Dr. T. P. (Ted) Wright, to whom Dr. Furnas reported.

CAL lifted itself by its own bootstraps, became nationally known as a Defense Department contractor and as an innovator, and the fees earned went back into unique facilities and the exploration of new ideas. Dr. Furnas and his successor, Ira Ross, encouraged entrepreneurs to set up independent business enterprises based on patents that the laboratory assigned to them on a no-cost basis. Twenty-five or more companies in western New York are spin-offs of this kind, Moog Inc. maker of precision aerospace and industrial controls, is a notable example.

An early and unusual project, to develop a slide for Kissing Bridge ski resort. Doug has just completed a prototype section of the track, which Barbara and I are sampling. The alignment of the sled to the track is under operator control, and the sled can be made to be oversteer or understeer.

Thus the university's proposal in 1972 to convert CAL into a commercial, for-profit organization, and to sell the shares to a commercial buyer, was a shock of the first magnitude. Student-body protests about the Lab's classified government work in this Vietnam War era was the justification given, but grabbing a quick $25,000,000 to make up for a university cash shortfall was the real reason. The willingness of the university president and board chairman to allow the destruction of a great research laboratory remains unbelievable.

What followed was a long, sad story and two court cases. The technical staff at the Lab organized behind Ira Ross. The quick sale for $25,000,000 failed to materialize. The University turned down a local offer of $16,000,000 (the actual net worth of the Lab), fired Ross and set up a "housekeeping" operation. In 1972 CAL became Calspan and the Lab was finally sold to Arvin Industries some years later for $9,000,000.

All this posed major problems for department and division directors like me. A number resigned. As long as Ross remained at the Lab I played a prominent part in the battle with the university. Together he and I visited Board Chairman Purcell at his office in Rockefeller Center. We also visited with GM President Ed Cole to see what help he might offer, and I put in a rough morning under cross-examination on the stand during the first court case. After Ross was fired, a number of the staff hurriedly left in sympathy. While I understood their moral indignation, I stayed put because

Fig. 26-1
Doug Milliken, who now is vice president and operating manager. He first brought computers into MRA. He is an outstanding vehicle dynamicist with a strong physical sense.

Fig. 26-2
Peter Milliken graduated in three years from Cornell University with a degree in electronics. He briefly worked for Moog Inc. and then became a member of MRA, where he developed early Lap Time Simulation and Path Optimizer programs. He also participated in Moog vehicles development.

my future plans necessitated retiring with full benefits. Without becoming involved in the "housekeeping," I continued as director of the Transportation Division until I retired on April 30, 1976. The next day I started Milliken Research Associates, Inc.

A lawyer and an accountant were engaged. We incorporated as a subchapter S corporation. Barbara learned how to keep the books. I set up shop in our second-floor addition and installed a vehicle dynamics library of technical papers and references collected over the years. We were entirely self-financed. Upon graduation from MIT and Cornell respectively, our two sons began to work for the company, Doug in 1977 and Peter in 1982. Consulting got us underway, but we soon found that we could acquire specific research contracts. To accomplish this we subcontracted back to Calspan to take advantage of our association with Roy Rice. Shortly thereafter we began to take on associates, some short term, others longer, all as independent contractors to simplify bookkeeping. With some exceptions we have worked for industry to avoid the complexity of bidding on government contracts. Most of our workload has come from promoting and selling our own ideas. To survive as a small company we have been involved in a huge variety of projects and types of activities, and at last count we have had more than 50 customers.

Starting my own company was an exciting experience. As president I was beholden to no one, had no bosses to placate, and was on my own to sink or swim. The challenge of winning swept aside all doubt, and I went to work with a newfound joy. I wanted to create an enterprise endowed with integrity that would not be judged by size, magnitude and bottom line.

**Fig. 26-3
MRA Logo.**

An appropriate logo, one that would express the spirit of our enterprise, had long been on my mind. My background was both aeronautical and automotive. Why not a race car with wings? When I got to the wheels, I set them at positive camber to represent all the fun I had derived from racing Bugattis.

Getting Started

Some of our work derived from projects in which I was involved at CAL/Calspan, notably in 4 areas.

1. Moment Method Technology

By the time Milliken Research Associates was reality, Moment Method had reached a level of general application. We obtained contracts from Goodyear, Rolls-Royce, Chevrolet, Bridgestone, Ford, Nissan, Fiat and Cadillac among others, a number of which were performed by Roy Rice. Major advance was to be made by Dave Segal, who converted the original program from mainframe to IBM PC and added post-processing, which immensely improved the utility of the program. Doug Milliken also played a part in this. The program originally ran under DOS, but now runs under Windows.

A crowning achievement for all who participated in it, Moment Method technology is the one technique that provides a visual portrait of a car's stability and control over the full operating range. No other method gives one such a concise numerical measure of what goes on at the limit. Post-processing makes all the indices of stability and control available, and with the "friction circles" the operating conditions at each wheel can be obtained for any point on the diagram, trimmed or untrimmed.

This feature is a tremendous learning tool in itself.

More than 30 years was required for the MRA Moment Method (MMM) to reach its current state of development. Although we are still finding new uses at MRA, it has not been widely adopted, apparently because automotive engineers tied to the concept of over/understeer cannot easily comprehend a method based on the overall forces and moments that act on the automobile. Even the idea of yaw damping is catching on very slowly. In the racing field, MMM has much to offer in terms of car setup and in sorting out stability and control effects. Perhaps as the Moment Method is introduced in university courses we may expect a new generation of race engineers to become familiar with it.[1]

2. Lap Time Simulation

MRA has continually improved Lap Time Simulation, notably by using more complete vehicle models. The current LTS is a very complex four-wheel-vehicle, non-linear representation, using real car tire and aerodynamic data. The track representation has been greatly improved and now includes variations in local friction coefficient and other details. This can be seen on www.millikenresearch.com.

The simulation can be used for race car setup. Since the program output lists more than 200 variables at each track location, a very complete understanding of performance around the circuit can be obtained.

Any lap-time simulation requires a knowledge of the path followed by the car. A reasonable line generally can be drawn based on experience or measured data. Goodyear requested that a "path optimizer" program be developed; it was programmed by Peter Milliken in 1984 and is still being used.

---

[1] *Our associate, Edward Kasprzak, published a two-part article on MMM in* Racecar Engineering, *December 2003–January 2004.*

3. The "g-g" Diagram

In developing the "g-g" diagram, the first attempt to calculate the maneuvering envelope for real vehicles taking into account traction limitations, load transfer effects, suspension effects, brake balance and limiting stability balance was accomplished by Dave Segal, using the comprehensive model of the Moment Method. With all these design detail effects incorporated, the "g-g" diagram only approximates a circle or ellipse.

4. Vehicle Dynamic Simulation (VDS)

At MRA the DK-4 computer program was reprogrammed on an IBM PC by Dave Segal and still is for sale as VDS (Vehicle Dynamics Simulation). It continues to rank as one of the classic vehicle dynamics programs.

BECAUSE OF THE DIVERSITY of MRA's activities, it is difficult to produce a comprehensive description of its long history. I'll begin with an overview.

Categories of Work

- Consulting (engineering and business)
- Design and research projects
- Lectures and workshops
- Proprietary computer program sales
- Commissions for promotional sales
- Royalties from technology licensing
- Royalties from book sales

In addition to contacts with Goodyear and General Motors dating back to CAL Flight Research, I also had access to the Nissan USA facility in New Jersey via Teruo Maeda, son of Nissan's chief engineer, who had worked in Vehicle Dynamics during a summer at Princeton. Through tire research channels, an introduction to Bridgestone Research also was available. A combination of consulting and small studies with these sources served to get MRA off the ground, and led to substantial projects later.

The following is based on an analysis of the number of formal project technical reports we have produced for various customers over the years, and is one measure of the magnitude of our project work. Among our customers,

Goodyear, General Motors and Nissan were staples during the first 15 years, and Chrysler has been a strong supporter during the next 15.

Client Educational Lectures and Workshops

Vehicle Dynamics Lecture Series:
   Goodyear
   Chrysler
   MTS Systems
Lectures on Specific Subjects:
   TRW
   Ford
   General Motors
   Gleason-Torsen and Zexel-Gleason
   Hyundai
   Rockwell
   New Venture Gears
   Eaton
   Honda TRC
   Firestone
Subjects Covered:
   Elementary Automobile Dynamics
   Tires (Steady State)
   Steady-State Linear Model (2 Degrees of
      Freedom)
   Transient Linear Model (2 DOF)
   Linear Model with Roll (3 DOF)
   Comprehensive Non-Linear Models,
      HVOSM, DK-4, VDS
   Wheel Loads
   Vehicle Suspensions
   Steering Systems
   Tire Dynamics
   Parameter Measurement (Suspensions)
   Instrumented Vehicle Testing
   MRA Moment Method
   Active Suspensions
   Aerodynamic Fundamentals
   Pair Analysis
   Non-Dimensional Tire Data
   Ride and Roll Rates
   Camber

MRA Computer Programs

To promote physical understanding, MRA computer programs are based on "lumped parameter" models. They run on PCs, usually are delivered with a single-user license for the compiled version, along with user's and interpretation manuals, familiarization training and follow-up servicing. More detail is available on our website, www.millikenresearch.com, and in our book *Race Car Vehicle Dynamics*. Brief descriptions of proprietary MRA software follow.

MRA Moment Method (MMM)

An original approach to analysis of automobile stability and control based on the overall forces and moments on the vehicle (described earlier).

Vehicle Dynamics Simulation (VDS)

A comprehensive dynamic model suitable for generating time histories for a wide range of maneuvers over varying terrain (offshoot of DK-4, described earlier).

Lap Time Simulation (LTS)

A very complex non-linear representation using real car tires, aerodynamic data and track representation including variations in local friction coefficient.

Vehicle Dynamics Matlab/Simulink® (VDMS)

The current version of this model shares equations of motion and other core code with VDS and MMM, and allows users to work in the popular Matlab and Simulink environment. VDMS was developed and used on the NHTSA Vehicle Dynamics Test Vehicle (VDTV) and is an excellent tool for adding active control elements such as controlled differentials and active antiroll bars.

Path Optimizer (Pathopt)

Using a point-mass representation of the vehicle and a survey of the left and right edges of the roadway to compute an "optimum" path (minimum lap time) around a track, Pathopt is particularly useful for new street circuits where no established line exists. Developed by Peter Milliken in 1984, it has been extensively used by Goodyear.

Tire Data Assistant (TDA)

This program was developed to assist the user in nondimensionalizing tire data. This method enables the representation of lateral force and aligning torque for a variety of loads on a single curve. It also enables data for slip and camber to be combined into a single effective slip/camber variable, and also combines slip ratio with slip and camber angles into a single resultant slip variable. Reduced test times are possible in which a small amount of data is normalized and then expanded to the full range of loads. The data are more consistent than if all loads were tested.

Milliken Research Associates Books

Race Car Vehicle Dynamics (RCVD)

Authors: William F. Milliken, Douglas L. Milliken.
SAE, 890 pages
Started on contract in 1986 to expand the *Chevrolet Powerbook* for General Motors. GM had the first draft of "Vehicle Dynamics for Race Cars" until 1992, when copyright was given to MRA. An eight-year effort, RCVD was published by SAE. The book was introduced at the first Motor Sports Engineering Conference in December 1994, and has been a steady best-seller—over 20,000 copies have been sold.

Race Car Vehicle Dynamics Workbook

Authors: Dr. L. Daniel Metz, William F. Milliken, Douglas L. Milliken
SAE, 1998. 63 pages
Includes problems and experiments for each chapter in RCVD, plus supplemental material and bibliographies. Sold separately and also as a package with RCVD. Photocopied answer guide distributed to faculty only.

Chassis Design—Principles and Analysis (Olley)

Authors: William F. Milliken, Douglas L. Milliken
SAE, 2002. 637 pages
Based on previously unpublished technical notes by Maurice Olley. Permission to publish was obtained from GM in 1996, with a publishing contract from SAE the following year. A five-year effort in which Olley's material was rearranged and edited, with

all symbols converted to those used in RCVD.

Race Car Vehicle Dynamics: Problems, Answers and Experiments (PAE)
Authors: Douglas L. Milliken, Edward M. Kasprzak, L. Daniel Metz, William F. Milliken
SAE, 2003. 280 pages
Includes problems, answers and experiments for each chapter of RCVD, and also a vehicle dynamics program suite by Edward M. Kasprzak on CD. A companion to RCVD that is used as a textbook in university courses.

Associates

Since 1985, Dave Segal, and more recently Edward Kasprzak, have been heavily involved in MRA projects. Five of our associates have passed on. Our roster of scientific and technical associates indicates the breadth of expertise that we have used. We generally were able to find these resources locally.

Roy Rice	Bill Close
Hugo Radt	Dave Segal
Dave Kennedy	Tom Podgorsky
Fred Dell'Amico	John Hague
Nancy Robinson	Max Behensky
Phil Henderson	Jim Scandale
Dan Clark	Gus Gusakov
Tony Best	Terry Satchell
Len Segal	Joe Bidwell
Frank Winchell	Ray McHenry
Steve Radt	Edward Kasprzak
Phil Reynolds	Jim Dittenhauser
Ralph Siracuse	

Goodyear

Our largest and most consistent customer has been Goodyear, a great American firm dedicated to the quality of its products, peopled by outstanding engineers, and absolutely straightforward in dealing with its subcontractors.

While working with Maurice Olley in the 1950s, I met Goodyear's Cap Evans, who had performed the earliest force/moments tire tests in the United States. I had met Walter Lee, Goodyear's director of tire development, during the thump and roughness research in CAL's Vehicle Dynamics Department, but our long-term relationship really began during the planning of the Tire Research Facility (TIRF), for which we sought Goodyear's participation. At that time I met Walt Curtiss, subsequently director of New Tire Technology, who realized that to stay on top a tire company had to understand the relationship between the tire and the vehicle. As he commented in a 1991 letter to me: "I also recall our first joint Goodyear/Calspan project involving a seminar by you and your colleagues to begin to educate us on vehicle handling and dynamics. This activity was the beginning of what I feel has been the development of a world class tire/vehicle engineering technology group at Goodyear. It was also the start of a relationship between yourself and Goodyear which has profited our company immensely."

The Goodyear Tire/Vehicle Engineering group was headed by Dave Glemming, with whom we worked as he developed its staffing, programs and direction. What began as consulting agreement turned into literally dozens of projects, frequently contracted annually on an open-funding basis. On several occasions we received ten-year open contracts to cover specific subjects and proposals as they came up.

Over the years, Goodyear acquired copies of all our computer programs. Two were developed by Peter Milliken, namely RCsim (originally on an Apple II) and a Path Optimizer (VAX and IBM mainframe). Peter had long hair and wore what might charitably be termed as casual clothing. We went to Goodyear together; as a member of the old school it was a lesson to me how unimportant appearances are. No one could have appreciated Peter's work more than the Goodyear engineers. RCsim (now renamed LTS) has continued through a long series of improvements, mostly accomplished by Dave Segal, and is now used by a number of NASCAR teams, among others. The Line Optimizer still is in use by Goodyear.

Martin Johns, who became Goodyear Tire/Vehicle Engineering Technology chief

Fig. 26-4
Dave Glemming headed Tire/Vehicle Engineering at Goodyear for many years. He is shown here with their Anthony Best Dynamics (ABD) kinematic and compliance machine. MRA represents ABD in the USA, and this is the first machine sold in the USA (three more followed). The machine features electromechanical actuation, as opposed to hydraulics.

engineer, made original extensions to our Moment Method program and more recently acquired our VDMS. He was also responsible for Goodyear's acquisition of an Anthony Best Dynamics SPMM, a British kinematics and compliance measurement machine that MRA represents in the United States Goodyear had earlier acquired a Lotus Active research vehicle via our connection with Lotus.

Some of our assignments from Goodyear proved amusing, if not hazardous. Goodyear tires used on vehicles in a gypsum mine in New Hampshire were experiencing excessive wear, so Hugo Radt and I were dispatched to investigate. Driven by Jeep into the mine, which we were informed was 1,200 feet below ground level, we branched off into side tunnels with rough rocky surfaces, easily accounting for

the tire wear. Neither Hugo nor I were entirely happy being a quarter of a mile beneath the earth's surface, but we were assured that an emergency exit existed: a wooden ladder in the three-foot-diameter hole drilled in the middle of the spiral road down into the mine. Hardly a comforting thought.

Automobile manufacturers annually take their new models to a proving ground with hundreds of sample tire designs for testing and evaluation. The results determine which tires are ordered for the production cars. On Goodyear's behalf, I attended one of these sessions, rode with the test drivers and observed their rating procedures. The ability to predict the results would be a huge advantage in reducing the number of samples the tire companies had to provide. This was a

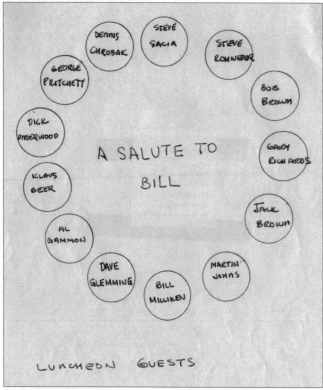

Fig. 26-5
The luncheon guests at the Goodyear "salute" to our 30 years of working together. Dave Glemming and a number of his associates in Tire/Vehicle Engineering at Goodyear were present. This occurred in 1991 when I was 80 years of age but still far from retiring.

bewildering assignment. Each test driver chose his own evaluation tasks, rated the tire set subjectively on a 1 to 10 scale and frequently tested several sets before recording the results on paper. The tests were supposed to evaluate overall tire suitability in ride, handling, noise, etc. I never questioned the experience or sincerity of the test drivers but concluded there must be a more rational approach to tire selection.

In the late 1970s Doug Milliken built up a fully instrumented car suitable for handling tests for Goodyear. He also was involved in motorcycle tests of the transient behavior of various tire designs.

BILL'S "MOMENT"
A NEW METHOD

Fig. 26-6
"Take-off" on Milliken Moment Method plus an ultralight flight incident described in Chapter 27.

Inducing the motorcycle weave and wobble oscillation modes (sometimes riding hands-off) proved a memorable experience with large motion excursions, but safe if you knew what to expect.

In 1960 Hugo Radt and I published an early investigation entitled "Motions of Skidding Automobiles." Beginning with Fiala's theory, Hugo had conceived a way of non-dimensionalizing the expressions for lateral force and aligning torque that was analogous to airfoil coefficients. This technique compressed data into a single curve for a range of loads, and had many virtues, including the possibility of reducing expensive tire test time. As early as 1985 Goodyear began supporting a research program projected by Radt to generalize the normalization approach. By 1993 Radt and Glemming published "Normalization of Tire Force and Moment Data" in *Tire Science and Technology*'s April–June 1985 issue.

A small niche company like MRA can survive on a few original, fundamental ideas, if properly developed and promoted. Hugo's idea of non-dimensionalizing tire data was one of these. Based on theory, it is fundamentally sound and not merely a process of curve fitting. Compressing measured data at different loads on different test samples into a single curve is a realistic way of compensating for tire variability, tire wear and varying test conditions. Mathematical expansion back to specific loads creates a consistent set of data desirable for application in computer programs. The non-dimensional approach has been extended from the free-rolling case to cover traction/braking, combined cornering, addition of speed, camber, etc. The most general case for all the operating conditions, as well as force and moment components, is being addressed in a doctoral thesis by our associate Edward Kasprzak. Because MRA is small and does not have a large internal research fund, it takes time to bring a good idea to fruition.

In late November of 1991, the Tire/Vehicle Engineering group at Goodyear honored me with a luncheon to acknowledge the 30-odd years we had worked together. Lured to Akron by Dave Glemming, I was completely surprised when I walked into a private dining room to be greeted by my 12 closest Goodyear colleagues. An amusing program had been prepared, and I was given a crash helmet[2] emblazoned with their signatures and a diploma for Doctor of Imagineering. Certainly working with Goodyear has been a high point in my professional life.

Nissan

A good example of projects undertaken for Nissan occurred in 1987. During development testing of the 300ZX prototype, the company had compared its handling to that of a marketplace competitor, the European-spec Mercedes-Benz 190E 2.3-16.

Fig. 26-7
Walt Curtiss was the originator of the Tire/Vehicle Engineering group to whom we consulted.

Nissan test drivers felt the Mercedes' critical controllability or limit handling was superior, and we were asked to explain in technical terms the basis for their opinion. This seemed an ideal application of our Moment Method.

With Nissan's help we collected all the necessary input data and went to work. The conclusion from our study, which was performed by Dave Segal, was that the trim changes due to alterations in longitudinal acceleration were considerably greater for the Nissan than for the Mercedes-Benz. We looked at this in two ways: first, the change in lateral acceleration with a fixed steering wheel angle when the vehicle is accelerated or braked ("Lateral Acceleration Trim Sensitivity"); second, the change in steering wheel angle required to maintain the original lateral acceleration trim as the vehicle is accelerated or braked, ("Trim Control Sensitivity"). In either case, the driver has to accept a trim change or counteract it with steering, which gives the

---

[2] Used when I drove the MX-1 at Goodwood in 2002, it elicited many comments.

feeling the vehicle is not stable near the limit. This accounted for the test drivers' opinion.

Trim change is common in aircraft when speed, power, altitude, etc., are changed and trim tabs on the control surfaces are used to compensate for it. Trim is a less common term in automotive circles because there are no separate trim controls, and the steering wheel serves as both a control and a trim device. But as we all know, trim changes do occur (when driving in a crosswind, for example) when a constant small force on the steering wheel is required to maintain the path on the road. This project illustrated the virtues of applying aircraft stability and control concepts to the automobile.

Moog Vehicles

I didn't know Bill Moog when we were both CAL employees in the late 1940s, although his servo valves[3] were used in our variable-stability aircraft. When he left in 1951 to begin his own company, and hired away two of our most talented engineers, I became well aware of him. Bill and I finally met in 1978 under interesting circumstances. Among his inventive ideas dating back to high-school days was a two-wheel, roll-stabilized automobile that would stay upright while parked and lean appropriately on turns. After exploring various unsuccessful schemes for accomplishing this, including gyros, he hit on the idea of generating a roll torque by accelerating an inertia wheel mounted on a fore-and-aft axis in the vehicle. He also visualized a pendulum sensor acting through a Moog valve to control a hydraulic motor for accelerating the inertia wheel. The patent for this arrangement also included a transverse movable weight to correct for any static imbalance.

A Porsche and Ferrari owner, Bill was an enthusiastic sports car driver as well as a motorcyclist. Traveling in Germany, he approached Porsche about building a prototype with his patented roll control system. Familiar with MRA, Porsche engineers told Bill to contact us, since we were "in his backyard." Wayne Hawk, Bill's right-hand man, phoned and the result was three prototypes incorporating Bill's ideas of a roll-stabilized vehicle.

The first approach, with mechanical design by Bill Close, consisted of converting a golf cart to two wheels, installing an inertia wheel of several hundred pounds, a control system consisting of an hydraulic torque servo mechanism, a sensing mechanism in the form of his compound pendulum and a movable lateral-trim weight controlled by a servomechanism. The vehicle was treated as an inverted pendulum with its pivot slightly below ground level. The sensing element was supported on flexures with a very small distance between their support and the center of gravity (about 0.03 inch), which gave the pendulum a very long period. The system was analyzed by Hugo Radt and Dan Clark of Moog, and Doug and Peter were also extensively involved.

In the initial tests the tires were replaced by knife edges; Moog supplied a portable hydraulic supply unit. The result was dramatic. Once trimmed, the vehicle sat balanced with the inertia wheel and lateral trim weight completely still. If the vehicle was disturbed in roll by dropping a laterally-disposed weight on it, the inertia wheel accelerated, counterbalancing the disturbing roll moment, while the lateral weight moved to establish a new trim. When the vehicle was placed on its tires with their additional degrees of freedom, however, it no longer could be stabilized.

Observing that an experienced motorcyclist could balance his bike at zero speed by appropriate steering motion of the handle bars, Bill Moog proposed a second stabilization scheme. The large steering trail on most motorcycles caused the steering to move the weight on the front wheel laterally. To test this approach, we built up the equivalent of a minibike with a large amount of trail and, to amplify the control rolling moment, installed a lateral beam approximately at the vehicle CG, like the balance pole used by tightrope walkers. Weights were hung at the end of this beam and a cable drive with pulleys was attached to the steering fork to add a direct inertial moment in roll to the trail effect. While an

---

[3]*Like a synapse in the nervous system, the servo valve uses small electrical signals to control the flow of high-pressure oil to an actuator. It is essential to missile and aircraft flight controls, with many industrial applications.*

Fig. 26-8
The Moog outrigger machine, which uses an auxiliary power plant to operate the hydraulics, the Moog pendulum and servo control of outriggers. L-R in upper figure: Doug Milliken, Bill Milliken, Dan Clark, president of Moog Industrial Division, and Peter Milliken.

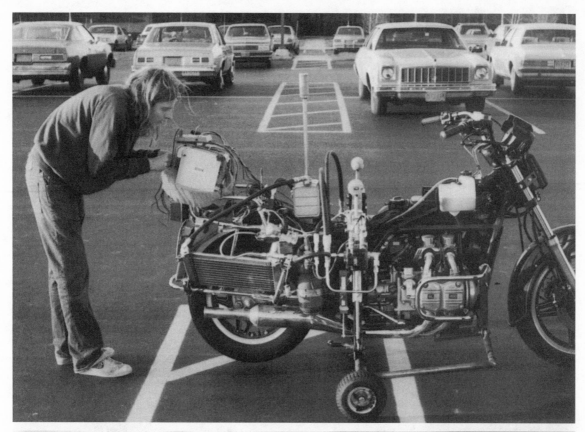

Fig. 26-9
At top, Peter Milliken adjusts the electronic control of the Moog outrigger vehicle. Bottom photo shows Peter Wright riding the Moog vehicle on the parking lot at Moog Inc.

interesting experiment, this was not deemed sufficient for producing a roll-stabilized vehicle.

For the third vehicle, Bill agreed to the use of small outrigger wheels whose positions relative to the vehicle were controlled by hydraulic cylinders to produce the desired bank angle. A Honda Goldwing was acquired as the test vehicle. The Moog pendulum was simulated by two accelerometers for ease of packaging, and an auxiliary gasoline engine powered the hydraulic system. The control system incorporated two control laws: the first simulated automobile control by producing a yaw rate and appropriate bank for an ideal turn, and the second simulated motorcycle control in which the bank is initiated by reverse steering. Considerable analysis was required for such a complex setup.

The machine was taken to the Moog plant for shakedown testing by Doug and Peter Milliken. On one run an electrical failure put Doug into a snowbank, which resulted in a lot of laughter but no harm done. Eventually the vehicle was demonstrated for Bill Moog on the parking lot. The day was overcast and the surface was wet. The system generally performed as planned, but "automobile" control felt very peculiar, and Peter Wright (who was in town) nearly collided with a lamp pole. Outrigger wheels not being in line with Bill Moog's original objective, the three-year project was discontinued.

Still, there were a number of good offshoots. Bill and I had hit it off, and I was invited to become a member of the Moog Inc. board of directors.

Lotus

My association with Lotus began late in 1981, following my first visit to the company. From London I had called ahead to Tony Rudd, taken

Fig. 26-10
As a member of the Moog Inc. board, I am talking here with Bill Moog at an annual meeting. Both Bill and I had worked at Cornell Aeronautical Laboratory.

a commuter flight from Heathrow to Norwich, and was met by a driver who chauffeured me to Hethel. Narrow country roads lined by hedges, thank-you-ma'ams, rural villages and farms was scarcely the milieu one would expect for an enterprise like Lotus. But from this bucolic scene we suddenly turned right at a sign listing the company's Formula I championships, and approached an airfield that had been a B-24 bomber base during WWII. All very modern, neat and landscaped, the airfield now served as a proving ground, and the engineering area beyond the lobby was one large open room adjoining the factory and production facilities in the back.

Lotus impressed me as a beehive of activity staffed with highly motivated engineers, well organized on a project basis and willing to tackle anything. I was escorted down to the small office area where Colin Chapman, Fred Bushell, Mike Kimberly, Tony Rudd, a couple of secretaries and the executive board room were located. Colin spent most of his time at "The Hall" with the Grand Prix team, and was not in evidence.

My acquaintance with Tony, who was corporate research director, had begun at the U.S. Grand Prix at Watkins Glen when he was heading up BRM and had turned the hat trick with Graham Hill. An engineer of vast experience who had begun as a Rolls-Royce apprentice, Tony had been involved in aircraft engine installation and tests during the war, and motor racing thereafter. Although unaware of the details of his career until publication of his best-selling autobiography *It Was Fun*, I did know he had single-handedly designed the BRM H-16 engine, and couldn't imagine how anyone could have designed such a complex powerplant. Asking how he laid out the project, Tony gave me an off-the-cuff tutorial starting with the cylinder head, the induction system and on down to the bottom end. I learned he had done much of the design on a drafting board in his kitchen!

After an hour of reminiscing, Tony introduced me to Peter Wright, who was working as a consultant to Lotus. At lunch he and I became deeply involved in a discussion of race cars and motor racing that continued well into the afternoon. I was aware of some of Peter's accomplishments, especially shaping the bottom of a race car to produce large amounts of aerodynamic downforce. This ultimately led to the first true ground-effect machine, the Lotus 78. This meeting was the beginning of a permanent friendship, and one of the most significant contacts in my technical career.

Peter hinted at a major forthcoming breakthrough, but trade secrecy prevented him commenting further. He did admit that increased aerodynamic downforce had led to horridly stiff suspensions that affected both drivers and handling on rough circuits, both issues of great concern.

Fig. 26-11
I first met Tony Rudd when I was chief steward of the U.S. Grand Prix at Watkins Glen. Tony later became research director for Lotus. He was very active at SAE in motor sports and we became close friends with his family.

Fig. 26-12
Peter Wright has had a remarkable career in motor sports. He is perhaps most famous for discovering how to develop aerodynamic downforce from a car's underbottom, and also for his work on active suspension. He was head of Team Lotus, and now is Technical Advisor to the FIA, FIA Foundation and FIA Institute. He is the author of two outstanding books on motor racing. We are close friends with Peter and his family.

Within two years MRA became involved with a new and fascinating Lotus technology. When Peter and I met again in London, he was able to tell me about their successful active-suspension prototype. Viewing the United States as its most promising market, Lotus wanted to take advantage of our contacts in the automobile industry. Fig. 26-13 gives the general agreement. Basically, MRA was to receive a percentage of the net sales price plus expenses, with any consulting fees compensated on an hourly basis.

Active Suspension

The concept was proposed by David Williams, head of the Flight Instrumentation Laboratory at the Cranfield College of Aeronautics, who had developed an in-car instrumentation system for Team Lotus. Among his earlier accomplishments were modifications to the Hawker Harrier control system after the Falkland experience, and the control systems for the first variable-stability aircraft in England.

The load control system devised by David and Peter was a major departure from CAL's variable-stability automobiles that used slip angle/yaw control and steer-by-wire. The Lotus scheme replaced springs and dampers with hydraulic actuators, Dowty valves (a licensee of Moog), a high-pressure oil supply and numerous sensors, all integrated in a feedback control system. The relatively low-frequency motions of the car body were sensed by lateral and longitudinal accelerometers on the body; the high-frequency motions of the unsprung masses were sensed by a vertical accelerometer near the wheel, and vertical position and velocity via a linear variable displacement transducer (LVDT). Wheel load cells also were provided. Thanks to frequency separation and inertial damping, some independent control of the sprung and unsprung masses was possible. The control algorithms converted the motions of the four wheels into four modes: heave, pitch, roll and warp.

Once our contractual relationship was established I was given a demonstration of the active prototype and a verbal rundown on the system. To interest potential customers I needed an overall understanding of the system and its capabilities, but was given no detailed knowledge of the algorithms.

Once the system was conceived, David and Peter approached Chapman who, I gather, agreed somewhat reluctantly to the use of an Esprit and a very modest budget. With this Lotus produced the demonstration prototype—a classic example of fundamental engineering thinking followed by lots of development and modification under full-scale on-road testing. The electronics were carefully analyzed, but no attempt was made to model the complete vehicle and control system, an approach typical of race car development.

As I was to discover, David and Peter had produced a remarkable ride system that also gave astounding control of vehicle handling and road-holding.

Let me describe some of its aspects. One could stiffen the heave mode and soften the pitch mode. You then could push down at the bumper and produce a pitch motion but no

Lotus Cars Limited
Norwich, Norfolk, NR14 8EZ, England
Telegrams: Lotus, Norwich   Telex: 97401
Telefax: Wymondham   (0953) 606884
Telephone Wymondham (0953)

21st July, 1983

Milliken Research Associates Inc.
245 Brampton Road,
Williamsville,
New York 14221
U.S.A.

Attn: William F. Milliken, Jr. - President

Dear Bill,

In accordance with our recent discussions, Lotus Cars confirms Milliken Research Associates as their sole representative in the U.S.A. in connection with the introduction and liaison of Active Control Systems based on Lotus' developments and Patent structure in this field.

This arrangement has been affected for the convenience of American companies interested in this technology and to bring into the Lotus Active Control enterprise the reputation and experience of Milliken Research Associates in automotive stability and control.

We look forward to a long and fruitful association in this new and exciting area of technology.

Yours sincerely,

A.C. Rudd
Corporate Research Director

Fig. 26-13
The agreement with Lotus Cars Limited to assist in selling prototype active suspension cars in the USA.

heave, or change the mode settings to enable no pitch but a soft heave mode, a weird feeling to say the least. By mixing modes the pitch axis could be moved fore and aft. Similarly, the roll behavior of the vehicle could be softened or stiffened and the lateral location of the roll axis varied.

The warp mode, if defined in terms of the vertical motions of the four wheels, was the sum of the left front and right rear, minus the sum of the right front and left rear. The modal scheme, which could also be applied to the load changes, was related to the use of antiroll bars, but being active was far more effective.

The driving demonstration was still more dramatic. On accelerating, pitch could be completely eliminated, or exaggerated, or made to pitch down. Similarly, on braking it could be eliminated or given exaggerated pitch down or, like a horse, pitch up. On cornering the car could be made to remain flat, or bank in or out. Contrary to expectation, most drivers preferred flat to banking inward, tentatively explained by the elimination of a roll transient. Road-holding on rough turns could be improved by softening the ride and increasing the damping.

Most dramatic was the control of over/understeer by the warp mode via a control on the dash. To ensure I would get the full treatment, Peter arranged for a Grand Prix driver to do the high-speed demo. As we charged down the straight, I reached over and turned the knob to full oversteer. The vehicle went into a violent spin, looping its way down the straight, while the driver sat there laughing.

The road-holding action of the wheels was fascinating. When a wheel encountered a bump, its vertical acceleration and load were sensed and the actuator was brought into play to maintain the static load on the wheel, i.e., to lift the wheel to follow the contour of the bump. The result was a remarkable smoothing out of a rough road. The use of the diagonal mode to control directional stability was very effective to the point of a wheel lift-off, far more than normally achieved by antiroll bars. The fully active and adjustable vehicle was effectively an on-road simulator and a tremendous learning tool.

Back home I put together a set of 25 vuegraphs and a dozen color photos of the Esprit system with the vehicle cornering. It was a simplistic picture of the technology, but it

Fig. 26-14
Dave Williams, formerly of Cranfield University, was in charge of instrumentation. He developed the first variable-stability airplane in England, and proposed the load approach to active suspension. With Peter Wright they developed the original active Lotus Esprit and the variety of active vehicles that followed. He is a highly original, self-taught control system engineer.

did show the ride, handling and road-holding potential. I also included a description of the Moog valve, which was not well known to automotive and tire engineers at that time.

My first targets were General Motors and Goodyear. The response was enthusiastic and resulted in a joint project between the two companies. Two GM C cars were equipped with the fully active system. Peter and David and, I believe, Martin Long came over for the final negotiation. Lotus introduced an additional technology fee that was accepted, specifications were defined and the project was underway. From the beginning of the active development Peter was assisted by Steve Green, who continued to be involved throughout.

For the next three years I placed a high priority on Lotus active suspension promotion, and particularly remember my next sale, an active Corvette prototype. Calling Corvette chief engineer Dave McLellan to arrange a hearing, I was somewhat surprised to find that the meeting place was a large auditorium and I had a substantial audience. Lotus made a video available.

According to my records, the following active suspension systems were sold under my original agreement with Lotus:

General Motors C Car
Goodyear C Car
Chevrolet Corvette
Chevrolet Cavalier
Chrysler Active
Chevrolet-Pontiac-Canada Show/Press Car
CPC Technology Demonstrator
CPC Production Active
CPC 4WD/4Wheel Steer
GM Project Trilby

The last-named was one of the most complex of the active series as a ride and handling research machine. It was named after Trilby, the girl who would do anything.

Upon learning that Chevrolet was considering a V-8 twin-cam 400-hp engine for a high-performance Corvette, I contacted Russ Gee (GM) and Tony Rudd, and Lotus obtained the contract for the LT-5, which went on for several years.

The servo valve was a key component of the active suspension system, and if the system went into production it would be advantageous for Lotus to work closely with a valve manufacturer. Introducing Lotus to Moog was an obvious step. The Lotus and Moog technical people and David Williams were compatible from the start, and by about 1986 a joint venture had germinated.

As a member of the Moog board of directors, I made two interesting trips to Europe, one involving a visit to the company's operations in Germany, France and England. The other was to the Paris Air Show where Moog had a pavilion. With the formation of Moog-Lotus my European travels increased in exciting and interesting ways. Dan Clark and I flew over to Lotus on Bill's personal twin-engine jet, leaving Buffalo, with a stop in Newfoundland, and putting down in England the next day. Dick Aubrecht, Bill's son-in-law, played a prominent role in the formation of Moog-Lotus, and the deal was formalized in London with Mike Kimberly leading the Lotus delegation.

Traveling with Bill Moog was a first-class experience. In London we stayed at the Savoy, where he was so well known that the manager greeted us personally and escorted Bill to his suite (which I understand had been occupied by General Eisenhower during WWII). Sir Stafford Cripps had arranged for Bill to become a member of the famous nightclub Annabel's, where we dined on several occasions.

One Saturday, Bill announced he would like to visit his British subsidiary, 75 miles or so away. While I was looking at our travel options Bill

suddenly remembered he had left a car in the hotel parking garage for just this eventuality. We went down, found the Porsche and made the trip in that.

Bill and I had many good laughs together. Returning to the States in his new jet, in which he had not yet flown, we chose seats in the rear opposite each other. The pilots, formerly of Philippine Airlines, made a spectacular takeoff, holding the airplane down and then doing a rapid pull-up. Like two ten-year-olds, we

Fig. 26-15
A standard-suspension Lotus Excel cornering at 70 mph. Note the roll angle and the inside wheels nearly lifting.

Fig. 26-16
This shows the active suspension Lotus Excel cornering with minimum roll. The Lotus system controls both the body and the unsprung masses, and improves both ride and road holding.

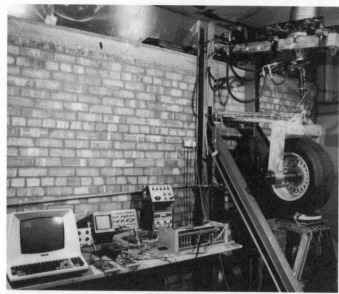

Fig. 26-17
This rig, for a single corner of the car, was installed at Cranfield and used by Dave Williams in developing the General Motors C car and later systems. Servo-controlled road input is shown under the road wheel tire. Above the wheel is the actuator with hydraulic lines leading to it. Oil flow is controlled by a Moog valve sensing various input from the "sprung and unsprung" masses: The "sprung mass" is represented by the weights on the upper A-frame. This rig proved to be an important design tool for an active suspension system.

Fig. 26-18
This shows the implementation at one wheel. The actuator is attached to the hub carrier (at the bottom) and to the chassis at the top. The hydraulic lines enter the actuator above and below the piston in the actuator cylinder. The Moog valve is shown at top left. The LVDT, the small vertical tube next to the actuator, gives the vertical wheel position and, differentiated, the wheel vertical velocity. A load cell on the top of the actuator gives the wheel load.

looked at each other as Bill exclaimed, "Gee, what an airplane!" We stopped at Iceland, bought a couple of fur coats and arrived in Buffalo the next day.

MRA promoted major systems, support and component contracts for Moog-Lotus as follows:

> CPC Servovalves and Energy
>   Conserving Modules
> CPC Front and Rear
>   Servoactuator
> GM Truck and Bus Active
>   Prototype
> Chrysler Active Support
> Cadillac Allante Active
>   Suspension
> Corvette, 200 Car Sets (Delco)
> Chrysler Rear Steer Car
> CPC Traction Control
> Chrysler Active to Production

GM, and to an extent Chrysler, moved toward incorporating active suspension in a production vehicle. General Motors tried absorbing the technology to incorporate the design into a production vehicle, but was not totally successful. To be the first to market, we had suggested a run of 200 active Corvettes. Lotus probably could have produced a prototype of sufficient reliability to sell in limited production; that GM could have produced one is questionable. In any event, an active production car was not realized at this time.

That cost constraints and other factors put the project on hold should not detract from the technical accomplishment. The Lotus system totally changed one's perspective of ride, handling and road-holding, demonstrating the extension of design possibilities inherent in active control. Despite issues of complexity and reliability, the enormous performance gains cannot be ignored. The situation parallels that of aircraft. CAL's early work with variable-stability aircraft and stability augmentation using servo control technology had led to my prediction in 1950 that we could anticipate the adoption of fly-by-wire and full-servo systems in military and large commercial aircraft. It took 30 years, but it was inevitable. Advances in computers and electronics already have led to advances in automotive engine and transmission control, antilock and antispin systems, semi-active ride and stability systems, fancy shock absorbers, etc. Active controls generalize the equations of motion by introducing many additional derivatives, non-linearities and the use of operating-point analysis.

MTS Systems Corporation

Early in 1983 John Beal, general manager of the MTS Driveline Dynamics Division, approached us about designing an indoor driving simulator based on the Flat-Trac Roadway units from their tire tester. The intent was to bring stability, control testing and development into the laboratory, with its obvious advantages over full-scale proving ground testing. Fiat, with whom MTS had been negotiating, had an interest in such a facility for its new Elisis research center in Naples.

The MTS design as originally proposed allowed the test vehicle to make limited excursions on wide Flat-Trac belts under the wheels, but Fiat questioned its ability to adequately reproduce the behavior of a real car on the road. Some time earlier we had performed a Moment Method analysis of a front-drive sports car for Alfa Romeo, the company in the interim having been acquired by Fiat. That the Moment Method might be useful in an improved design of the MTS machine was recognized, hence Beal's contact with us.

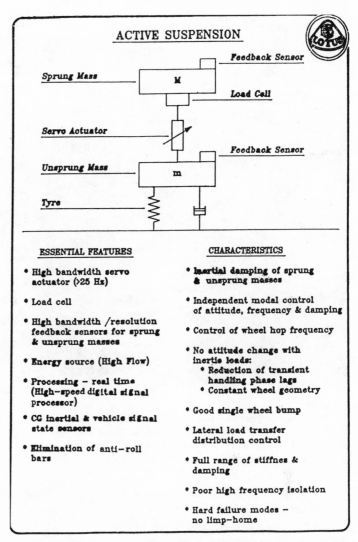

Fig. 26-19
This figure summarizes the features and characteristics of the installation. Peter Wright, who was in town when this was written, pointed out that in actual practice much effort was spent in isolating the high-frequency inputs from the servo strut to the car body and in eliminating compliances in the system.

For three decades those of us in Vehicle Dynamics at CAL had been interested in constrained testing. We had performed the "maypole" test on ice, followed Winchell's constrained test for the Corvair litigation and the MIRA tests in England. Using those experiences, we came up with the Constrained Vehicle Tester (CVT) concept and obtained multi-year contracts from GM to develop its theory and design. Installing a CVT in GM's new full-scale wind tunnel was halted for financial reasons, at which point we produced

Fig. 26-20
The MTS Flat-Trac Roadway Simulator, the first of which was installed at Fiat's research center in Naples. A Flat Trac Roadway unit may be seen under each wheel. The Moment Method system restrains the vehicle laterally, fore and aft, and in yaw. This leaves it free in heave, pitch and roll to yield appropriate tire loads.

a computer simulation. Thus we had a great deal of pertinent experience.

In any motion simulator, all the major forces and moments that produce the accelerations, velocities and displacements must be represented in some fashion, a requirement that the original MTS design did not meet. The small permitted motions of the test vehicle bore no relationship to a real vehicle because velocity and path curvature, hence centrifugal force, were completely absent.

The CVT used the d'Alembert principle to simulate the acceleration forces by reversing the effective inertia forces in the constraints. That is, the system was brought to rest by adding constraint forces equal and opposite to the forces that would accelerate the vehicle,

$$F - MA = 0$$

where F is the force in the constraint.

In simulating an automobile, it is paramount that the vertical forces on the four wheels (wheel loads) correspond to those existing on the real vehicle under similar

conditions; otherwise the tire slip angles, camber angles, suspension deflections, etc., are totally unrealistic. The wheel loads depend on the vertical acceleration (weight) and the longitudinal and lateral accelerations (weight transfers). The vehicle in the simulator cannot be restrained vertically, in pitch or roll, but must be free to adjust itself in terms of wheel loads. That is, it must accommodate itself to the d'Alembert forces in the lateral and longitudinal directions, and to the weight. In a steady turn the yawing moment is zero, i.e., the angular acceleration also is zero. To simulate maneuvering, control yawing moments can be applied.

Based on CVT experience we were able to propose a constraint system faithfully simulating real-life conditions that was adopted by MTS. A contract was worked out for its transfer, together with the Moment Method technology. Roy Rice and Dave Segal had independently proposed a scheme for performing constrained transients on the machine that also was adopted. We conducted a lecture series at MTS on vehicle dynamics, and over the course of our association transferred the complete mathematical basis of CVT. This also included a study of the lateral attachment problem, to achieve the best compromise between roll angle and lateral weight transfer.

With its substantial investment, MTS hoped to find other prospective buyers. I became involved in the sales activity and visited Fiat, General Motors and Ford. One trip was a grand tour of Europe. Headed by John Beal, our delegation first went to Paris to call on Peugeot, Renault and Valeo, where we examined the Odier machine, an early and much publicized device that failed to meet the CVT standards of simulation. At the Aerodynamic Institute at St. Cyr we met with director Menard, whose history with the institute dated back to early airfoil developments. This was a trip back in time for me, and I found his reminiscences absolutely fascinating.

After visiting Michelin in Clermont-Ferrand, we continued to England to see Lotus, Moulton and the Royal College of Science in Shrivenham, which had a constrained tester closely related in principle to the CVT.

These travels did not result in sales of Flat-Trac Roadway systems other than to Fiat, but after introducing MTS to the Chevrolet Vehicle Handling Facility (VHF), the company subsequently produced its own kinematics and compliance (K&C) machines and sold a number in its worldwide market. I worked on the first sale, to Ford.

I was at MTS during its check of the complete Fiat system before shipment to Italy, an impressive sight with seemingly miles of hydraulic lines, pumps, filter and accessories, as well as the roadway units and the constraint

Fig. 26-21
In addition to licensing our Moment Method technology to MTS, we also presented a series of lectures on vehicle dynamics. L-R: Bill Langer, WFM, Doug Milliken, John Beal (MTS), Dave Segal and Dr. Hugo Radt.

system. It is one thing to develop the theory and configuration, and quite another to see it in hardware.

As a small supplier with big ideas, MRA had its ups and downs working with large corporations, but John Beal (MTS) and I forged a permanent relationship of friendship and respect that I value highly.

Rolls-Royce

I first met Harry Grylls, chief engineer of Rolls-Royce, at the time of our IME presentations in London in 1956. He invited us to visit the factory in Crewe. Getting there proved to be a long drive with lots of lorry traffic, putting us in the vicinity of Crewe much later than planned. With no idea where the plant was, we asked a lady on the sidewalk who rattled off directions, ending with, "You can't get lost in Crewe." We were to think of that remark many times in our travels in England. Although late in the day, Grylls and other Rolls-Royce executives awaited us in the boardroom, and we were wined and dined that evening. It was the beginning of a long and productive relationship.

Rolls-Royce had more than a little interest in the handling qualities of its cars. Much of its testing was conducted in France, where one could cruise at high speed for hours at a time on Routes Nationale. Because Sir Henry Royce spent much of his life on the Riviera, I can imagine the run from Crewe to Le Canadel had an almost romantic aura. During one of my visits I was given a demonstration by a test driver on the country roads around Crewe. It was far from boring.

Grylls had followed our research and indulged in some unique experiments of his own. Among these was the installation of the driver's seat on an adjustable pivot to rotate against a centering spring under the action of centrifugal force. If the location of the pivot corresponded to the CG of the driver, the seat showed little tendency to rotate and was deemed neutral. If the pivot was forward, the seat rotated in the direction of the turn and was oversteer. For rear pivot, the seat rotated in the understeer direction. This "over/understeer seat" demonstrated that if the driver judged over/understeer by a tendency to plow or spin, it would be simulated or augmented by a driver rotation relative to the vehicle, perhaps a useful device for driver training. Some of Harry's non-automotive activities were raising conifers, devising sundials and throwing boomerangs. He was a brilliant and delightful individual. Before retirement Harry introduced us to his successor, John S. Hollings, who had been transferred from the turbine engine division.

The first contract research task we performed for the company was a subjective evaluation of the on-center handling characteristics of a Silver Shadow Standard Saloon. I already enjoyed an acquaintance with Rolls-Royce design chief MacCraith Fisher and Derek Coulson. Collecting the Shadow at the Rolls-Royce distributor in New Jersey, I met Ken Preece, Trevor Williams and Tom White. I was to work with Ken on subsequent contracts.

Having never driven a Rolls-Royce any distance, I carefully recorded my initial impressions. The general feeling the Silver Shadow created was one of ultimate quietness, smoothness, ease and precision. Maurice Olley

told me Sir Henry Royce insisted that special attention be paid to whatever one saw, heard, touched, felt or operated—in short, to the interface between the man and the machine. There was little I could detect in the Shadow that did not appeal to the senses in a satisfying way.

One time Doug was driving the Shadow into Buffalo at night. Layers of low-hanging fog came at us in the headlights. As usual, there was no perceptible road or engine noise. Doug suddenly looked over and said, "Are we on the ground or are we flying?" I shared the feeling that we were gliding noiselessly a few feet above the earth. Another moment of sheer elation happened while I was driving along the Hudson in brilliant sunshine, the car filled with music from the quadraphonic sound system. I had almost forgotten how fulfilling motoring could be.

In Buffalo we began our week of on-center handling evaluation. Roy Rice and Dennis Kunkel joined Doug and me, and Barbara gave the woman's point of view. In all, we put in 31 hours and some 1,500 miles, most of it in the 55–75 mph range, but some up into the 90s. Although the car was a production unit, the power steering system had been modified by Rolls-Royce. Any lost motion, slop, lash, flexibility or compliance was undetectable; the slightest movement of the steering wheel was reflected at the front wheels. No valve effects were noticeable near on-center, and the car was smooth and faultless in large lane changes. In general, we agreed the steering ratio was a very good compromise over the maneuvering and speed range.

The steering force level was very low, however, as was the force gradient to position change. Rim forces in the range of a pound or less, which followed the Rolls-Royce philosophy of minimizing driver effort, reminded us of the so-called "full-time" Chrysler power-steering system.

In general, humans are "designed" to use both motion and force in any action, whether it is slicing bread or driving a car. Rolls-Royce had produced a steering system that was nearly pure position control. Flight control systems tend to be dominated by forces as opposed to positions, since there are few visual references like the edge of a road.

We found that the low force level and lack of crisp centering made the Shadow difficult to trim in the on-center region, which we defined as plus and minus 0.05g lateral acceleration. The driver was continually trying to find the steering wheel position for straight running, with only visual feedback. In the process of seeking trim he or she was, in effect, continually disturbing the vehicle. We also deduced that the vehicle itself was susceptible to small road disturbances. It had been so well isolated from external disturbances that few cues were returned to the driver.

As a check on the driver/vehicle interactions, we artificially held the steering wheel in one position and carefully changed this fixed position until the path of the car aligned with the road. At that point everything settled down and the car began to bore along on a definite trim. Before artificial means were employed to get a definite trim, our evaluation comments were:

"The vehicle lacks directional sense."

"The vehicle feels squirrelly."

"I can't quite catch up with this car."

Our report provided a tutorial on the on-center problem and specific corrections for improving the Shadow. Driving the car back to New Jersey over wet and icy roads, and now accustomed to the handling, I could confidently operate near the limit and even let the tail drift out to approach a controlled slide, getting away with this until a mile from the distributorship, when I hit a curb with a rear wheel, blew a tire and bent the rim. No one at R-R seemed particularly disturbed about this, but instead were immensely pleased with my overall time from Buffalo to New Jersey.

Our next contract with Rolls-Royce, in late 1976, was to subjectively evaluate the handling of the Silver Shadow equipped with a rack and pinion steering gear. There had been general agreement between us on the evaluation of on-center handling, but R-R now thought the problems lay with the steering gear, and this had been confirmed by MIRA tests on its tethered rig. The first car we tested wore Avon fabric-belted radials, but the rack and pinion car had Avon steel-belted radials. Comparison between the two evaluations was complicated by this change.

Subjective evaluation of handling is extremely difficult because of driver experience and biases. Hoping to obtain a broader understanding of the on-center handling behavior, Doug and I decided to check out a variety of handling elements. Small effects can be important in this region. To this end we considered trim, fixed- and free-control stability, oscillation frequencies and dampings, control ratio, forces and gradients, centering and car and driver behavior in simple maneuvers and responses. This was a tall order to do subjectively, but we tried.

There was some "pull" that we concluded was due to the plysteer of radial tires. Our general observations were:

- The car was close to fixed-control neutral steer.
- The resonance natural frequencies of fixed and free control were about 1 Hertz (within the driver maneuvering range) and had low damping. Free-control oscillations persisted for two cycles after initiation. Fixed-control forced oscillation built up very rapidly near resonance, with the steering wheel out of phase with yawing and lateral motion.
- Control effectiveness was very high and could easily excite the oscillations.
- The steering force and gradient were very low and comparable to the standard Shadow. Centering was ill-defined, with no "detent" feel. Car felt "twitchy" or "squirrelly" near center. There was no breakout force at all.

Our impressions regarding the rack and pinion gear were:

- Very responsive with low, if any, compliance. The control effectiveness was so great that it tended to mask on-center problems, but could lead to overcontrol unless one was very alert. The overcontrol was facilitated by the low control force gradient.
- In evasive maneuvers it was difficult to judge control use; the car was dicey. In general, as control effectiveness increases, the control forces also should increase, but this was not true of this car.

We concluded that rack and pinion steering, with its positive control effectiveness, though desirable in itself, might not be desirable in the overall context of the other characteristics of the car. If the standard car exhibited an on-center "vagueness," the rack and pinion car was too "twitchy." Both these characteristics are driver/vehicle (closed loop) behavior, and would be improved by:

- Increasing the caster for more rapid, positive centering,
- Increasing the control force and gradient level beyond the effect of caster change,
- Increasing the damping of the free-control oscillation (through the steering system), and
- Reducing the steering ratio if necessary.

On both the standard and the rack and pinion car, the steering force gradient was about 4 to 5 lbs/g. General Motors' experience and ours (notably on MX-1) suggest 10 to 12 lbs/g as more reasonable. For a car like the Rolls-Royce, a better balance between ease of steering and control effectiveness would be closer to the American experience, even taking into account Great Britain's winding roads or the use of Rolls-Royces on long high-speed cross-country trips.

In a final program for Rolls-Royce we performed a Moment Method (MMM) analysis of the Shadow SE with Avon Turbosteel 235/70 HR15 tires, considering 30 different operating conditions of road load, dropped throttle, traction and braking. Tire data was measured on Calspan TIRF; suspension and compliance measurements were made on Chevrolet's vehicle handling machine. Roy Rice did the diagram calculations under subcontract to Calspan. Analysis of the MMM diagrams indicated that the tire was not well-matched to the vehicle's stability requirements, especially if tire pressures dropped below 20 psi. Any increase in gross weight resulted in a penalty in vehicle stability.

Compared with subjective testing, the MMM study yielded solid quantitative results. After our kinematics and compliance tests were completed at Chevrolet, two young Rolls-Royce engineers and I drove the SE back to Buffalo. Anxious to get home, I was cruising at 80-plus, to the consternation of my passengers, who had been briefed on the 55-mph limit and the horrifying penalties for exceeding it. They asked how I dared cruise at such a speed? Obviously I always was on the lookout for those who hand out speeding tickets, but to make my passengers more comfortable I explained that experienced American drivers developed an ESP as reliable as a radar detector. They accepted this explanation, which put the burden on me to prove it. Fortunately, the police were taking an evening off. We arrived in Buffalo in record time.

Active-Camber Corvette

In 1987 an interesting one-of-a-kind Chevrolet project for an active-camber car was initiated in Brian Decker's group, to be performed on a 1986 Indy Pace Car Corvette convertible equipped with 255VR50/16 tires. After MMM analysis the car was modified for static adjustment of camber. Doug ran a series of private tests at TRC Ohio and the results were encouraging, so the next phase was building an active prototype.

Increasing the max lateral over the measured 0.88g while maintaining neutral directional stability right up to the limit, or complete "spin-proofing," was the objective, Continuous control, unlike ABS or ESP, does not intervene. On performance cars like the Corvette, car magazine road testers emphasize the max lateral (a measurable parameter) and the characteristics at the limit.

Because of the work overload on Chevrolet supervisors, Doug Milliken became the de facto overall project manager, coordinating the control system design with Hugo Radt, and the build with Specialized Vehicles Inc., a fabrication shop in Troy, Michigan. Max Behensky, electronics engineer, hardware and software wizard at Atari games, and a contemporary of Doug's at MIT, was engaged to develop the IBM PC control and instrumentation system design and algorithms.

The system was designed to permit −10° to +5° of active camber on all four wheels. An active antiroll bar was provided on the rear, and the system was implemented with hydraulic servos and Moog valves. No attempt was made to control the weight which, with the mechanical mods and control additions, increased by 550 pounds (from 3,200 to 3,750). Despite this, and with only a week of development, the max lateral (corrected for the extra weight) was increased from 0.88 to 0.99 (12 percent). The vehicle was completely neutral-steer over the whole range, and spin-proof at the limit under all combinations of power on, power off and braking.

An early example of a successful stability system, perhaps the project was too early to continue as a production application.

Chrysler

As early as 1957 I met Otto Winkelmann, chief engineer of Chrysler, who had published a remarkably complete state-of-the-art analysis of car handling requirements. Although I had reviewed our IME papers in a talk at Chrysler, some years passed before we engaged in contract research for the corporation. In 1991 a request for a study of roll damping came through Don Van Dis of Small Car Vehicle Dynamics at Chrysler's Chelsea Proving Ground. The work was successfully accomplished by Dr. Hugo Radt using his simplified vehicle dynamics model (SVDM). Participation in a hands-on handling criteria exercise at Chelsea followed. Through Don we performed a series of research projects for Chrysler. He also introduced us to Dr. Choon Chon's SST initiative (Synthesis of Simulation Technologies, c. 1993), which resulted in a week-long workshop on MMM and "g-g" diagram technology. For several years we worked on driver modeling, simulators and on-center handling.

Realizing that aircraft handling is highly advanced, but related to vehicle handling, Don learned to fly. For years he had been interested in "force feel," a feature of aircraft control systems. He envisioned that it could be significant in the on-center steering of automobiles. By 1997 we became involved in a force-feel (or force control) model of a power steering system for Van Dis. Once the analysis and modeling were completed, the model was incorporated into VDS (Vehicle Dynamics Simulation). Developing this steering system model of small forces and motions (on-center) proved to be extremely challenging. Nevertheless, the model was completed before Don's retirement in 2002, but has yet to see extensive use.

Currently, MRA continues as a contractor to Chrysler.

Summary

As a small, family-owned and-operated business, MRA has survived for three decades and acquired an enviable reputation in its field. While I focused on the promotion and accomplishment of projects, Barbara has been a full partner, handling the financial records, secretarial work and general administration. Our daughter, Ann, became the artist in the family, but our sons, both with strong inclinations toward mechanical and electrical engineering, joined the family business. Assisted by Doug, Peter developed an early lap-time simulation and path optimizer program, and participated in Moog vehicle projects until he became a victim of multiple sclerosis. Doug, who has a remarkable physical sense of vehicle dynamics, took over the management of MRA about a decade ago.

I attribute MRA's successes to the following factors:

- Our roots in ground vehicle dynamics are deep, extending back into the early work at General Motors by Maurice Olley, Bob Schilling and associates, and into our GM-sponsored work for Bidwell. As our technical library attests, we have a strong sense of the historical.

- My aeronautical background has enabled us to take full advantage of the vast fund of technology from government-supported aircraft stability and control research, starting with the equation of motion and pioneering British research. MRA is unique in transferring aircraft technology to ground vehicles, including both statics (Moment Method) and dynamics.

- Over the years we have enjoyed our association with many highly experienced and gifted engineering associates and career vehicle dynamicists like Roy Rice, Fred Dell'Amico, Dr. Hugo Radt and Dave Segal. Their experience goes back to HVOSM and DK-4, early large-amplitude, non-linear models. Dave is a vehicle dynamicist and programmer of note, who programmed the Moment Method for the PC (first running under DOS and later under Windows). Dave also developed the post-processing techniques, and was responsible for creating the current Lap Time Simulation (LTS), which features a complex four-wheel vehicle model with detailed representation of aerodynamic downforce. Our youngest associate is Edward Kasprzak who currently is teaching the course in Vehicle Dynamics at the University of Buffalo, using *Race Car Vehicle Dynamics*, while working toward a PhD. Edward also was responsible for developing our VDMS, a vehicle dynamics program in Matlab.

- Our early recognition of the importance of tire data led to the major advances in tire testers at Calspan and Dr. Radt's conception of the non-dimensional scheme for improving tire data analysis. By facilitating its use in computer programs, this significantly reduced testing costs.
- Our policy is one of concentrating on the continual improvement of a small suite of highly developed and validated parameter-based vehicle dynamic programs aimed at producing real-world test results. To this end we have exhaustively analyzed the core mathematical models underlying these simulations.
- Our legacy of experience is incorporated in the series of books earlier noted.

In conclusion, MRA has been a good solution to my retirement problem, and a whole lot of fun!

Chapter 27

Full Circle

> "How can life grant us boon of living unless
> we dare?"
>
> – Amelia Earhart
> (*20 Hrs. 40 Min.*), 1928

By 1990, as I approached the age of 80, MRA became less of a demand on my time as Doug became more deeply involved. Why not try something new and exciting, I thought, like horseback riding? Actually this was not exactly new, but my last equine venture had been the Averills' pony in the early 1920s, and I was now thinking bigger. At Willow Creek Farm, a riding stable in Clarence Center 20 minutes away, the attractive young female trainer came straight to the point: "What's your objective?" Somewhat baffled, I replied, "Have you ever seen a Western movie? Well, turn me into one of those cowboys." So we started with a western saddle and all the fixings. Training went well. The horse chosen for me was an old jumper and we had just reached the jumping stage. But driving home one day, I passed a house with its own grass airstrip, a small hangar and an ultralight sitting in front. I went in to explore.

Larry Merkle, the owner of the facility, noted my interest and inquired if I had ever done any flying. I explained that although I held a commercial license at one time, I hadn't flown in recent years. To which he responded, "Get in and just taxi down the airstrip and see what you think." I didn't hesitate to accept the invitation.

The ultralight's twin 10-hp engines, each swinging a biplane propeller[1] to keep the diameter down, were mounted in the leading edge of the wing and pull-started by the pilot in a hammock seat below. The tail was an inverted vee. Getting in, I saw that the stick pivoted at the top instead of the bottom. This told me that for nose-down elevator one moved the handle back, which I still believe is logical, but the designer must have thought otherwise. As I taxied, a gust of wind gave the airplane some lift. I pulled the stick back, to keep the nose down, but instead found myself in the air. Everything I

[1] *Two propellers bolted on the same armature shaft.*

Goodwood 2002. On one occasion Dean and I wound up side by side in the staging area. Hard to beat that!

Fig. 27-1
Lazar twin-engine ultralight.

did increased the altitude. I remember thinking, "I better figure this damned thing out or I'll never get down." I finally made a rough landing at the far end of the field. One of my feet bounced off the rudder pedal and was run over by a landing gear wheel. When I arrived back, Larry was all smiles: "Gee, you did a great job, I didn't think you were going to fly it!" We soon became good friends and together bought another ultralight.

My days of horseback riding were over as I plunged into the delights of ultralight flying. There were few regulations, just stay off the airways. With friendly farmers in all directions you could land almost anywhere and shoot practice landings. Flying low and slow offered the warmth of the earth and the perspective of early pioneer pilots. In an ultralight you enjoyed the freedom of a bird.

On weekends a country-club atmosphere prevailed at the hangar. Larry also had a cabin job (an enclosed-cabin light plane) and a Pitts biplane that he used for aerobatic displays. Pilots from other local airstrips often flew in. His father-in-law had built a Christen Eagle and appeared frequently. A steady fixture at the airstrip was Larry's dog, Lindbergh, who took to aircraft like his namesake.

Early on I practiced stalls at an altitude of 500–600 feet. By throttling back one engine,

I also practiced single "engine-out" operation. The directional stability with the vee-tail and short tail length was marginal, but seemed adequate.

One afternoon, returning to the field at low altitude, an engine suddenly quit. Looking for a place to land, I gave full throttle to the one remaining. The rule is to put the dead engine high if you have to turn, but the best landing area I saw meant a turn with the dead engine low. By that time I was pretty well crossed-up and losing altitude fast. Before I had a chance to come up with an alternative, I flew into the tops of the trees, tripping the plane into a vertical attitude. After plunging nose-down some 40–50 feet through branches, the ultralight came to a sudden stop on the floor of a dense forest. The branches must have slowed us, because I unfastened the belt and fell out uninjured. After vainly trying to get through the underbrush for about a half hour, I had just decided to curl up and sort things out the next morning when it occurred to me to climb a tree to see which way to go. I hadn't climbed many trees in the last 40 years, but went up this one like a monkey and discovered that I had been going in the wrong direction. The hangar was only a couple of miles away, and I hiked back.

Because it was a small target standing on its nose, a good bit of time in another airplane was required to locate the ultralight the following day. Borrowing a small bulldozer, we made a rough woods road to the plane, discovered less damage than expected and retrieved it early the next morning. We were not anxious to alert the neighbors that airplanes could fall out of the sky and possibly land on them!

Post-accident analysis brought the following conclusions: ultralights are well designed for some kinds of crashes. In this case, the wing absorbed much of the energy on the way down through the trees. Had I tried to sideslip into a restricted area, the wing probably would have struck first, using up energy as it disintegrated. A twin-engine ultralight, however, is a bad idea. Ultralights are seldom maintained by professional mechanics, and two engines double the chance of an engine failure (a point noted by Lindbergh in preferring a single-engine machine). At the low power levels of an ultralight the likelihood of producing a twin-engine machine that flies well on one engine is minimal. If a single-engine ultralight quits, at least one has a nicely controllable glider, maneuverable in either direction. Even with both engines operating, however, the machine I was flying had marginal directional stability. Following Koppen's experience, it would have been better to have replaced the vee-tail with a larger vertical tail and longer tail length. In an airplane that knows where it wants to go, emergencies are minimized. A well-designed ultralight would be a delight to fly and safe to boot.

Back to Racing

Bridgehampton, 1996—FWD Miller
There is an old saying that one thing leads to another. Occasionally it can lead to a remarkable chain of events. Such was the case in early October 1996, when I received a phone call from a Dean Butler. I later learned that he was the founder of Vision Express, a European chain store offering prescription glasses on a walk-in/walk-out basis. He now owned the FWD Miller I had raced more than four decades earlier, and would be attending a private party of old race machines organized at Bridgehampton by Bob Rubin, a former owner of the car. "I'm sure the FWD would like to see you again," Dean said, "and in the driver's seat." As a further incentive, Griff Borgeson, author of the classic *The Golden Age of the American Racing Car*, would be there

because he was writing a book about the FWD Miller.

Of course I went. At the circuit I spotted the Miller, resplendent in the sun and just as I remembered it, next to a large transporter in back of the pit area. The small group around the car included Dean, Bob Rubin, Jim Himmelsbach (Dean's crew chief), Martin Walford and Griff Borgeson. Introductions barely over, Dean turned to me and smiled: "Jump in and drive it, Bill." I hesitated and asked its current worth, remembering that Harry Miller had delivered the car to the Four Wheel Drive Automobile Company for $15,000 or so in 1932. "Well," came the reply, "a guy offered me a million and a half and I just laughed at him." I gulped, "Wow, what if I bend it?" Dean said not to worry, he was self-insured, so I climbed in. Someone produced a crash helmet and Jim gave me a quick check of the controls.

It was the Miller I knew except for the accelerator pedal, now located between the clutch and brake pedals, a common arrangement on Italian Grand Prix cars of the 1920–30 era. The gear ratios in the box and rear end were exactly as we had run at Pikes Peak in 1948, with wide spacing between first and second gears requiring double- clutching down, and even up. I had practiced that relentlessly in the years I raced the car, and

Fig. 27-2
Bridgehampton, 1996. L to R: Bob Rubin, former custodian of the FWD-Miller, E. Dean Butler, current owner/custodian, and Bill Milliken. A happy trio.

more than 40 years later it all came back. After a lap or so the familiar sensations of the very stiff suspension, the go-where-you-point-it of four–wheel drive and the trailing throttle oversteer were all there, though I was far from utilizing the Miller's full cornering performance.

Later Dean and I took turns lapping the car. I mentioned that we always operated with locked center differential at Pikes Peak, and at Watkins Glen in 1949 when we anticipated a shower and a low coefficient of friction. So we made runs with both the unlocked and locked diff. With the latter, Dean reported the car felt "squirrely" under hard braking. I too felt uncomfortable under the same circumstances, but we had no explanation for this phenomenon.

Upon returning home, Doug and I came up with an explanation that I relayed to Dean: With the center diff operating, the car had some brake distribution between the front and the rear based on the leverage ratios in the mechanical brake system. We believed the braking was well biased toward the front because of the weight transfer forward when the car was braked on a dry, hard surface (high friction coefficient). When the center diff was

locked out, the front and rear wheel rotational speeds were forced to be the same. The "slip ratio" (ratio of the tangential speed at the bottom of the tire to the car speed) was then about the same front and rear. This said that the brake distribution had moved toward the rear, and the limiting friction circle would be reached at the rear first (where the wheel loads are lightest). In short, under heavy braking, the rears reached their limit first and the car became oversteerish or, as Dean said, "squirrely." This was not the last time I would be impressed with Dean's sensitivity to car control and tire behavior.

After Griff Borgeson made a couple of laps with me in the Miller, Dean suggested I make a round in his monoposto Maserati 8CTF, the type used by Wilbur Shaw in his Indy victories and by Louis Unser when he set a record at Pikes Peak in the forties. Indeed, Dean's 8CTF may be the one Unser drove. I had driven a few powerful cars in my career but this one was in a different league. Having negotiated the circuit with a bit of wheel spin here and there, my verdict was "what a bomb!"

Griff and I really hit it off because I appreciated his concerns for the various problems of our society. During the research period for his Miller book, we had established some rapport after he queried me about my FWD experiences. Griff's writings on race car history were landmarks, and he spent much time enlightening me on various aspects of auto sport. He mentioned an interest in republishing *The Golden Age of the American Racing Car*. I offered to approach SAE as a possible publisher, and also for his forthcoming 4WD Miller book.

A highlight of the Bridgehampton weekend was getting to know Dean Butler. Because of his interest in automobile racing, he had created an extensive reference library in his

Fig. 27-3
Bridgehampton, 1996. Griff and Dean. Dean commissioned Borgeson to write the history of the FWD Miller.

Fig. 27-4
Goodwood, 1997. Keith Chapman in discussion with Bill Milliken, with Tony Best assessing the engine.

restoration facility, Zakira's Garage in Fairfax, Ohio, near Cincinnati. His selective collection of race cars included Raymond Mays's ERA, the Type 51 Bugatti driven to victory by Louis Chiron in the 1931 Monaco GP, the 8CTF Maserati and the FWD Miller, among others. But most impressive was his detailed knowledge of the history of these machines from their inception to their race records to their drivers. I had never realized that the 255-cubic-inch engine in the FWD Miller was, in fact, the prototype Offy engine built to Miller's drawings and castings by FWD in its experimental shop when Miller was leaving his business and Offenhauser was taking over. Dean's intent, and an expression of his generosity, was to give his cars the greatest exposure so others could enjoy and learn from them. He wanted to see the machines used in historic racing events and in exhibits for educational purposes.

Dean is a shining example of realism and trust. He recognizes that anyone who steps into a race car takes on a responsibility for

risks to the machine and to himself. He knew my record of spills and accidents but never once uttered a cautionary word for either me or his cars. He never stepped over the line of one's personal responsibility. I found this one of Dean's most endearing characteristics and closely related to the early days of motor sport when you "took your chances and raced regardless."

Goodwood 1997—WD Miller

On the first day of February 1997, Dean Butler phoned to say the FWD Miller had been invited to the famous Goodwood Festival of Speed in England and "you gotta come over and drive it in the hill climb." It took me all of a millisecond to accept. This was vintage Dean: a good idea, an opportunity, swift and positive action, all guaranteed to create an enthusiastic response. The event was scheduled for June 20–22. He would arrange to transport the car to England, handle credentials and accommodations; all I had to do was to get to

England and back, find my way to the course, and bring a crash helmet, a driving uniform and a tux for the banquet.

In the Goodwood event, one had the option of parading up the hill or running for time. Naturally, the idea of loafing up the hill didn't appeal to me. In Buffalo we proceeded to prepare for the event. First was the installation of a "g-Analyst" in our Chrysler New Yorker so I could sharpen my cornering acceleration. In about a month I had worn out the new Goodyear Eagles on the front wheels. Obtaining a large-scale map of the Goodwood hill climb course, we made runs with our Lap Time Simulation computer program to get a feel for cornering speeds, and for what gears to use, by dividing the course into straights and turns, tabulated lengths, radii and elevation changes. We summarized the known and estimated data on the Miller's weight and center of gravity, engine torque and power, the gearing and the suspension characteristics that affected the ride and roll rates. Armed with these data, an assumed road surface friction (or cornering g's) and a redlined engine rpm, Doug entered these parameters into our Lap Time Simulation computer program. Five sets of runs were made, using different operating assumptions. But for learning purposes we used

the case of 0.8g cornering acceleration and 0.6g braking, with a redline of 5,800 engine rpm. These were conservative values for a dry surface. Plots of speed, lateral acceleration and engine rpm versus distance along the course were constructed. We concluded that after a standing start in first gear, most of the run could be made in second, with a possible use of third near the top.

Our good friend and business associate Tony Best offered to become part of the crew for the weekend, and to drive me to Goodwood, stopping by Southhampton on the way to visit the Schneider Trophy Supermarine Museum. At the paddock we met the crew Dean had assigned to our car: Keith Chapman, Martin Walford, Mark Turner and Paul Myatt. We needed all the help we could get. It rained incessantly over the weekend, the electricals got wet, and push-starting was required. With the FWD Miller and the center differential locked out, we had an ideal machine for wet weather. The calculations made with LTS were helpful, but turn No. 3 proved different from that used in the calculations (i.e., tighter than shown on the map, with a sort-of reverse on exit). Nevertheless we managed a second place in our category. On the last of my eight runs I was hoping for a really good time and a high speed through the trap near the top of the hill. But the timing system failed. Approaching 6,000 rpm in second, I must have been at 100-plus.

Goodwood was a spectacular show. Everything was first class, and it seemed that every interesting race car I had ever read about was there. The sights and sounds, the personalities, the color and the fanfare were capped by a garden party and dinner at the Earl of March's palace, Goodwood House, complete with three dance bands performing music of three eras. That

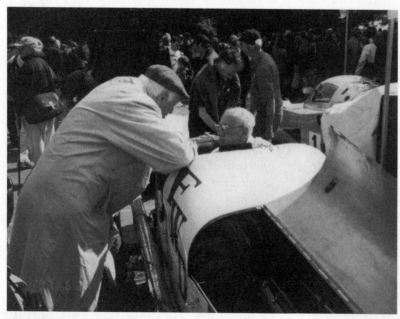

Fig. 27-5
Goodwood, 1997. Alex Moulton is well known for designing the suspension for the original Austin Mini, and for his bicycle designs.

weekend will always remain a four-star memory.

Griff Borgeson had planned to use Goodwood as the final chapter in his Miller book. But for health reasons he was unable to make the trip, and said that he would write the chapter from information we supplied. Griff was under considerable pressure to simultaneously finish *GA-2*, as he referred to *The Golden Age of the American Race Car,* and *The Last Great Miller.* Both of them involved SAE, although there had not yet been a firm commitment for the latter book. Because I had introduced Griff to SAE, I was drawn into the picture. Progress on the Miller book was delayed, but *GA-2* was published in a beautiful volume including a color portfolio of extant race cars of the "Golden Age." Griff had asked me to write the foreword to the book, which was a difficult task.

A day or two after writing him a long letter describing my impressions of running the Miller at Goodwood, I received a fax from his wife Jasmine: "With immense sadness, I must tell you that Griff is no longer with us. Sunday evening at 22 hours he had cardiac arrest that was immediate and irreversible. . ." His death came as a great shock to all his friends. He left a legacy of character, knowledge and historical writing that has enriched the lives of many people worldwide.

The problem of completing and publishing *The Last Great Miller* remained. At the time of Griff's death, there was still no firm commitment to publish from SAE. Early in July Dean Butler, who had assumed sponsorship of the book when he acquired the FWD Miller from Bob Rubin, asked me to inquire into its status, which I did. A few days later SAE agreed to publish. Dean's brother Don, together with his wife Dolores, took on the major task of finishing the book. Locating, proofing and inserting the figures in their proper sequence proved especially difficult. A preface was prepared with statements from Buck Boudeman

To Bill, thanks for a great weekend at the Goodwood Festival of Speed 1997 Martin Walford.

Fig. 27-6
Goodwood, 1997. Martin Walford, one of the FWD Miller crew. Martin is an outstanding race driver and business associate of Dean Butler. His enthusiasm is contagious!

(the Miller's owner before Rubin), Bob Rubin and Dean Butler. At Dean's request I wrote an epilogue on the Goodwood experience and our calculations of the performance on the hill.

An important aspect of the book was the correspondence between Harry Miller and Walter Olen of the Four Wheel Drive Automobile Company. Olen was totally devoid of automobile racing experience, while Miller was steeped in it. Their correspondence provides direct insight into the thinking of these two men, and their struggles to understand each other and successfully campaign the car. One gets a genuine feeling for what it was like to compete at Indianapolis in that era. The book was published in 2000.

Watkins Glen 50th Anniversary, September 11, 1998

In recent years the Village of Watkins Glen has celebrated the historic first road race of the postwar era with an annual Grand Prix Festival, including a re-enactment of the first laps of the 1948 event, a discussion session with race veterans, and an event for vintage race cars. For the 50th anniversary the village had hoped to attract cars that had actually raced on the old circuit, and I was approached by organizer

Fig. 27-7
Goodwood Hill Climb, 1997. Underway in the FWD Miller.

Fig. 27-8
Goodwood, 1997. In the rain.

I hadn't driven the Miller since Goodwood so I ran through the starting procedure before the event:

- Open diff., shift in neutral
- Air valve open
- Pump up tank
- Shut off air valve
- Fuel cock open
- Transmission oil line open
- Battery switch (in new location) on
- Spark retarded
- Hit the starter button and, with engine running,
- Advance the spark.
- Don't forget the throttle is now between the clutch and brake.

There's nothing like an Offy! Like a fine horse, that big four-banger was ready to go, and I enjoyed the vibrations as I revved it during warm-up. Since the main show didn't begin until noon, I decided to drive downtown. Sheri climbed into the mechanic's seat for the ride.

Franklin Street was crowded, just like the old days. We edged through and parked in front of Smalley's Garage, the Miller's headquarters in '49. For the next two hours we were surrounded by spectators and photographers, answering questions, autographing and reminiscing with a few old-timers who remembered, or had read about, the FWD Miller. Standing alongside, Barbara nudged my arm. I looked in her direction and saw Les Smalley in a wheelchair, but in fine voice and enjoying the occasion. He had been involved in the Grand Prix since the earliest days.

"The Legends Speak" is, I believe, an original with the Glen. The title exactly describes the event. The six "legends" sit at a long table, which was located this year at the state park entrance not far from the site of

Dave Wild, who wondered if the FWD Miller might be available. Answering my letter on the subject, Dean Butler said he could not attend but the Miller would be there, and he had the car delivered to the Glen together with Mike Yust, one of the top technicians at his restoration facility. Mike was accompanied by his wife Sheri; our entourage included Barbara, Ann, Doug and a number of friends.

the drivers' meeting in 1948, and included Stirling Moss, John Fitch, Phil Walters, Denise McCluggage, Denny Cornett and me. The whole thing was an enjoyable occasion, with brief talks by us and lots of questions from the audience.

Following various preliminaries late in the afternoon, the re-enactment began. After gridding, the cars were waved off for two laps of the old race circuit. Among the machines this anniversary year were the restored "Ardent Alligator" that had been driven to a Watkins Glen Grand Prix win by Miles Collier, several model Allards, a Type 35 Bugatti, Jags, Ferraris and MGs. We were up front in the Miller, and Doug was in the mechanic's seat with a hand-held video camera. All around us was a milling mob, many more people than I remember at the car's first race at the Glen.

Finally we started, and suddenly, what it had been like in 1949 all came rushing back to me. It was a thrill to be driving this re-enactment with Doug. He had heard plenty of stories about these early races and was now getting a firsthand idea of what it was like.

In the late forties, the Miller virtually flew over the railway grade crossing but today we took it at a more modest pace. As we approached Franklin Street, crowds lined both sides to give us a big hand as we slowed down. Doug was all smiles. It had been a great experience for both of us. After the weekend we received dozens of photographs from professional and amateur photographers. One of the best, taken by Mike Yust as we rolled into the first turn, was used on our Christmas card that December. (Figure 27-13).

Miller Club Event in Milwaukee, 1999

The annual Harry A. Miller Club Meet, founded by Dave Uihlein, was scheduled for July 10–11, 1999, at the

Milwaukee Mile track. Dean Butler and Jim Himmelsbach entered a 1926 Amilcar and the 1932 FWD Miller. Earlier my son Doug had suggested a "Salon" feature on the Miller to *Road & Track* magazine, and arrangements had been made for Kim Reynolds and photographer John Lamm to attend the Miller club weekend. A serious case of food poisoning kept Dean at home, but his brother Don represented him in Milwaukee. Our Buffalo contingent included Doug, Dave Kimball (a car enthusiast friend) and me. The entry list comprised more than

Fig. 27-9
Goodwood, 1997. More rain. Note my Goodyear helmet.

Fig. 27-10
Watkins Glen, 1998. Barbara and Lester Smalley at the Watkins Glen 50th Anniversary. Les Smalley was one of the organizers of the early Glen events. His service station was the site of race car inspections. We always kept our car at Smalley's facility.

34 cars and some 23 owners, with a substantial number of Miller-designed cars and engines.

A weak point in the FWD Miller was the transfer drive casting. It had cracked back in 1948 at Pikes Peak, and its replacement had cracked again. Dean reported, ". . .we pulled the car to bits and have now machined a new transfer case, which looks like the old one, from a solid billet of aluminum alloy. This case should be far stronger than the problematic castings which have been used in the past."

Fig. 27-11
Watkins Glen, 1998. Rounding the first turn off Franklin Street in the re-enactment.

Fig. 27-12
Watkins Glen, 1998. At Milliken's Corner. The Flat Iron Building now occupied by Glassart and beautifully restored inside.

The Milwaukee Mile track has been a staple in American racing for years, usually following the Indianapolis 500 in the schedule of Indy-car open-wheel races. When my son Doug was challenging human-powered vehicle records with a streamlined bicycle built around an English Moulton, he had used the track and an experienced RAAM rider in a 24-hour record attempt. Crosswind conditions prevented setting that record, but Doug's bike still holds the speed mark for bicycles with conventional seating, i.e., not prone or supine.

The Saturday night party at the Uihleins's home was a highlight. I had never seen Dave's historic race car collection. Two machines of particular interest to me were the single-seat centrifugally supercharged Duesenberg that Pete de Paolo drove to victory at Indianapolis, and the Wisconsin Special in which Sig Haugdahl unofficially achieved 180 mph at Daytona. Both of these date back to my teens, when I was just becoming interested in auto racing.

At the party was Duke Nalon, perhaps the only driver who mastered the Novi and justly deserves respect for that accomplishment.

It was a real pleasure to talk with him. When the Novi first ran at Indianapolis in 1946 I was a spectator. It was a sensational machine, difficult to handle but certainly the highest-powered front drive yet to appear at the Speedway. Its behavior brought to mind Reid Railton's comment about what to do if you get into trouble with a front drive: "Ease on the power but expect to get only temporary relief."

The *R&T* Salon session took place late on the second day when the sun was in a favorable position for photography. Asked to wear period clothing, I donned white coveralls and unearthed my leather Buco helmet and goggles from the thirties. The story appeared in *Road & Track*'s December 1999 issue.

MX-1 Restoration and Goodwood, 2002

In October 1999, Jim and Carol Himmelsbach paid us a visit while vacationing in Niagara Falls. He saw MX-1, took an immediate interest and thought Dean would be interested too. Jim offered to restore the car to running condition on his own time, a magnificent offer to which I enthusiastically agreed.

The following month we trailered the car to Zakira's Garage, Phil Henderson supplying the trailer and Dave Kimball the tow car. Don Butler turned over the motel suite attached to the garage to the three of us, and we put in a couple of days enjoying the cars, the shop

Fig. 27-13
Watkins Glen, 1998. Doug and Bill having a go on Franklin Street.

facilities and the extensive library. In addition to maintaining Dean's historic cars, Don does other restorations on a contract basis. The full shop capability includes NC machines, sheetmetal working machines (among them an English wheel), paint shop, spray booth, etc., and a highly experienced and talented staff of mechanics and craftsmen. When we arrived they were working on the HCS (for Harry C. Stutz) Special, the single-seat 122 Miller that Tommy Milton drove to victory in the 1923 Indy 500. Obviously the MX-1 had found a good temporary home.

I summarized our handshake deal in a November 1999 letter to Jim. The restoration of MX-1 to running condition would be done without major changes to the car, engine or chassis setup. There was no time schedule. I would pay for any purchased or manufactured parts, provide drawings and assist in any way I could. After storage for 18 years, I never imagined that I would see the car in running condition again.

In the MX-1's final high-negative-camber setup, all wheels tilted in to $-22°$ with a small amount of toe-out on front and rear. It rode on the Goodyear Eagle bias-ply tires used

for Harley-Davidson motorcycles that had been used through all of our development. With these tires we had achieved a cornering acceleration of 1.0g with the wheels cambered to $-22°$.

Because we had never publicized MX-1, the Butlers were somewhat surprised by the car, questioning us about the theory behind it. The following e-mail arrived from Dean in early December:

From: E. Dean Butler   12/3/99
cc: Zakira's Garage
Subject: Camber Car

Bill: Thanks a million for bringing down the camber car. This will be a fun project. . . . One thing I cannot figure out: with the wide contact patch of modern wide racing tires, grip is very significant. With the camber car setup, the contact patch is necessarily smaller. Does this not limit cornering power, and, in fact, restrict cornering power to limits considerably below what can be achieved with modern tires running in the conventional position?

I realize that wide tires have a wide contact patch which results in sudden break away—and that narrower tires have a contact patch significantly longer, in the relative sense, in the front to back direction—and that this makes drifting the car a lot easier. Maybe this would come into play with the camber car?

Dean had asked pertinent questions and started a train of thought that still involves me. Our camber car project had begun in 1960, a few years before Mickey Thompson came up with the small-diameter, flat-tread wide slicks for Indianapolis to reduce tire aero drag. This established the trend toward "low-aspect-ratio" flat wide tires that has continued ever since. It is impossible to draw simple comparisons between

Fig. 27-14
Miller Club event, 1999. At the Milwaukee Mile. Don Butler, left, with Doug and Bill. Don operates Zakira's Garage facility in Fairfax, Ohio, best known for its Miller restorations based upon original drawings and patterns.

our different approach and the current racing environment that uses high aerodynamic downforce and wide, flat-tread tires.

Extrapolating from the MX-1 tire tests, I attempted to answer Dean's e-mail (in eight typed pages), concluding there was a lot more to this comparison than "the amount of rubber on the road," or print size. One must look at the effective load sensitivity of a wheel pair with lateral load transfer, the reaction of the two approaches to aerodynamic downforce, the details of what goes on in the different print shapes on approaching the limit, the overall aerodynamic drag of cars designed for wide, low-aspect-ratio tires versus those with narrower tires on cambered wheels, etc. In my earlier chapter on the MX-1, I delved into more detail on the virtues of negatively cambered wheels.

The history of invention suggests that the first, most obvious, solution to a problem is often superseded by a more sophisticated scheme. One can cite digital versus analog computing. I feel sure the low-profile wide, flat, vertical tire solution is poor aerodynamically and on a number of other counts. The cambered technology is certainly more complex, but it has several fundamental advances not attainable with the wide tire design. For one thing, cambered wheels exhibit remarkable limit behavior.

Less of a conundrum was the MX-1 engine. Fortunately, we had been running the two-stroke on a higher oil/fuel ratio, as recommended by the manufacturer, even though it smoked and fouled the plugs. This excess oil probably kept it from freezing up during its long period of storage. Jim was able to turn the engine over and saw no

Fig. 27-15
Miller Club event, 1999. The *Road & Track* Salon was researched and photographed during the Miller Meet in Milwaukee. It appeared in the December 1999 issue of R&T by Kim Reynolds. I did the driving wearing period clothes and helmet.

Fig. 27-16
Preparing to transport the MX-1 camber car to Zakira's. Phil Henderson supplied the trailer and Dave Kimball the tow car.

reason for taking it apart. He planned to run it on modern two-stroke oil at a 50-to-1 ratio. He did, however, do a number of other necessary things on the engine including:

- Cleaned the carburetor jets and installed new parts from KN-10A kit.
- Repaired the fuel pump using type-50 fuel pump kit.

Fig. 27-17
Don Butler and the author discussing features of MX-1.

Fig. 27-18
Jim Himmelsbach, who restored MX-1 on his own time at Zakira's, discussing other restoration work.

- Replaced all fuel lines.
- Replaced electrical wiring.
- Flushed out engine cooling system.
- Installed new battery.
- Replaced oil in rear end.
- Replaced brake fittings and hoses. Bled brakes.
- Repaired leak in fuel tank.

Through our Dunlop connection in Buffalo we investigated the availability of tires that would fit our original 16 × 3 built-up rims; Dunlop's K591 rear bias/belted, sports performance motorcycle tire, 150/80 VB16TL, would do the job. This tire compared with the Eagle is shown in Table 27-1.

We used the old tubes with the new tubeless Dunlops as a precaution.

The restoration continued as Jim's time permitted until November of 2001, when an event occurred that gave the project a new direction and a higher priority. At the Tokyo Automobile Show that month, Mercedes-Benz showed the F400 Carving, an experimental research vehicle equipped with active computer-controlled camber in which the two outside wheels lean in while cornering as the inside wheels remain in normal position. Wide tires with asymmetrical tread and special wheels were featured. That a maximum camber of −20° on the outside wheels was used, while we ran −22°, was interesting. M-B claimed a 30 percent improvement in maximum lateral acceleration; we had measured around 25 percent on MX-1 using the ancient bias tires. Our passive system was obviously far simpler than their computer-controlled scheme and offered other advantages over the Carving, notably in the reduction of aerodynamic drag.

Dean decided to enter the MX-1 at Goodwood, and offered to transport the car and handle its entry. On March 11, 2002, Doug and I drove to Fairfax for the engine run-in and checkout. It started on the first attempt, which was a real thrill, and ran freely with no smoke on the 50-to-1 two-stroke oil. Revving

Table 27-1. MX-1 Camber Car Tire Comparison

	Dunlop	Eagle
Permissible rim	3.5′	3.0′
Overall tire diameter	25.25′	26.00′
Overall tire width	6.25′	5.00′
Tread	7/32′ depth	Notched tread
Max. load rating	761@42psi	710@30psi

to 7,000–8,000 rpm was without fuss, and the sound was that of a racing power plant. On the small go-kart track behind Zakira's Garage we took turns driving the car. Jim and Doug felt that they could get close to breakaway on the tail, so we decided to install a small antiroll bar on the rear track that would bring the car near neutral. We also decided to move the brake balance forward, so plow rather than spin would be promoted on hard braking. Other than for a few details, the machine was ready for Goodwood. It was shipped to England in April in a large container, together with Dean's Type 51 Bugatti, the Louis Chiron Monaco winner.

Meanwhile, assisted by Tim Cottam, Keith Chapman arranged for the transport of MX-1 to Goodwood from Mere Hall, Dean's new home in the Midlands. Barbara accompanied me on the trip. Tony Best and his wife Naemi offered to drive us down from Alex Moulton's place in Bradford on Avon. Dean and our crew arrived at the Norfolk Arms Hotel in Arundel on Thursday. The cars were already in the pits.

This Festival of Speed was nothing short of staggering. On the sloping hillside past the Earl of March's mansion were gathered many of the world's greatest race cars, past and present, as well as the men who raced them. Like tournaments of old, the place was dotted

Fig. 27-19
Jim Himmelsbach driving the Novi front-drive special after rebuild.

Fig. 27-20
Dean Butler's library at Zakira's Garage This is just one row of stacks. It is maintained by Don and Delores Butler.

I approached Goodwood with reverence for the creators of these memorable machines and for their drivers. Race cars are a form of mechanical art, conceived in the imagination but built within the constraints of scientific laws. The men who have consistently driven them to their limits have themselves achieved a balance between skill and risk. What other sport is so demanding of all of man's mental and emotional faculties?

In the pits, Dean's FWD Miller and the MX-1 were side by side. I experienced overpowering flashbacks: memories of the No. 1 Miller push car of my childhood to my experiences with the FWD Miller some 30 years later. Barbara had been in the pits on the latter occasion when I set a new record at Mt. Equinox, beating George Weaver's Maserati Poison Lil by more than a second.

with tents and pavilions of all shapes, sizes and colors. Viewing areas and stands lined the course, the pits were covered and a gigantic fan-like structure supporting full-sized race cars centered the activity in front of Goodwood House. Facilities and access roads showed the results of months of planning.

It was raining, a reminder of the Goodwood five years before when the electricals

Fig. 27-21
Checking out MX-1 on the go-kart track behind Zakira's Garage. Doug is driving. Body panels yet to be installed.

Fig. 27-22
Goodwood, 2002. Barbara in the pits with MX-1, surrounded by spectators as usual.

Fig. 27-23
Goodwood, 2002. MX-1, a good view of the extreme camber that handled well and cornered phenomenally.   627

got wet and every run was preceded by a push start. Today I got into second gear as quickly as possible after the start, revved up hard and stood on the brakes before the first turn in order to check the brake balance in the wet. After that I concentrated on handling, because this configuration had not been driven faster than 60 mph during its development on the highway. We had removed the tail body to help cooling, but there were no electrical problems and the engine revved easily to over 6,000. The spray from the cambered wheels was horrendous and I was soaked. Shifting into third proved awkward. Doug had done the best possible job of setting up the shift mechanism, but getting

Fig. 27-24
Goodwood, 2002. Driving my own car design at Goodwood was an unimagined experience.

across the gate had to be done with precision.

The car ran straight at the higher speeds and cornered on a rail. The Dunlop tires were vastly superior to the old Eagles. The cornering ability of this cambered configuration was greater than its driver's nerve, and I forced myself to enter the corners faster.

By Saturday good weather had returned, the fuel had been mixed, the battery was charged and the atmosphere was exhilarating. We were inundated with spectators. Some wondered if the car had been built with vertical wheels and then dropped. Serious onlookers sought a technical explanation. I tried all kinds of analogies: men and most machines lean in when cornering, so

Fig. 27-25
Goodwood, 2002. Well underway on the climb.

why not lean-in the controlling outside wheels? Or think of it as two motorcycles, one for cornering to the right, the other to the left.

As I drove to the staging area the curiosity seemed intense. Coming back from the turnaround, Stirling Moss, traveling the other way in a Jag, recognized me and yelled, "What the hell is it?" My Goodyear helmet with all the signatures also came in for a lot of comment.

Soon it was time for the second run of the day. As I slid down into the seat I had another flashback, this time to the mockup we used in designing the seat, and the interest shown in it by Doug and Peter. The seat and the whole cozy cockpit was a source of enjoyment. At the staging area I found Dean in the FWD Miller and parked next to him. He looked over, all smiles.

Sunday we were at the track early and met Phil and Alma Hill at breakfast in the large pavilion. On the first run I missed a shift from second to third. Because the small-engine MX-1 did not fit into a racing category we were not officially timed, and at 18 lbs/hp were hardly competitive. Nevertheless I decided to go all-out on the last run. Our Mercury outboard engine was very short-stroked, so at 8,000 to 9,000 rpm its piston speed was well within structural limits. Peak power was at 7,500 or more, so I decided to get into third, forget the revs, and go over the top flat out. I managed a clean shift into third before the last bend and was literally screaming as we passed the line. A best guess is we were doing 110, the fastest for MX-1 to date. Most gratifying was the handling with this extreme camber. The control forces were modest and the directional response fast and well damped.

The Earl of March presided at the awards ceremony, where magnums of champagne and trophies were handed out to the winners. We received a citation and a trophy sponsored by General Motors for the most innovative entry.

The next day we trailered MX-1 to the Long Cross proving ground south of London to give Mick Walsh a chance to drive it and interview us for an article in his magazine, *Classic and Sports Car*. At the same time Dean, Keith and Tim could have some time in the car. An excellent place to demo MX-1, Long Cross

Fig. 27-26
Goodwood, 2002. In the Winner's Circle for outstanding Innovation.

has all the features of GM's Milford facility on a smaller scale: a large flat "Black Lake" connected to run-in roads, high-speed straights, handling area, rough-surface roads, a steep hill, etc. When we arrived, two of the McLaren F1 "million dollar" road cars were running check tests before delivery.

Among the features of MX-1 is its limiting behavior. The car resists normal breakaway, either at the front or rear, because of the camber thrust induced by lateral load transfer. When set up neutral it also resists lateral drift. On this occasion each driver, using whatever maneuvers he preferred, was unable to produce

Fig. 27-27
Goodwood, 2002. L-R, Keith Chapman and Naemi and Tony Best.

Fig. 27-28
On the skid pad at Long Cross Proving Ground. The MX-1 is cornering at about 1.3g. The car is close to neutral steer at the limit and is very controllable. Much of the weight is transferred to the outer wheels.

anything that seemed like a conventional breakaway. In this respect, the car was very forgiving. Unfortunately, the g-Analyst failed to work with the electrical system, so no lateral g levels were measured, but all indications suggest 1.3g.

In building the car, we installed two ignition switches, one on the left dash, one on the right, which I regarded as a safety feature should I ever get upside-down in the car. Amusingly, the left-hand switch was moved onto "Off" and it took us a while to discover it.

Fig. 27-29
Dean's home, Mere Hall, completely restored and modernized but in a way that retains its long heritage.

From Long Cross we visited Dean, his wife Elena and their 13-month-old daughter Anya at Mere Hall. Built a hundred years before Columbus headed west, and lived in by one family for three centuries, the house has been restored and modernized by the Butlers without destroying a single historical feature. It is nothing short of breathtaking. A section of the old stables now garages Dean's classic race cars, with which he still competes in historical races around the world.

While there we were visited by Mike Evans, Rolls-Royce Heritage, Karl Ludvigsen, Martin Walford and a representative from Moog, England.

With the favorable publicity accruing from Goodwood, we look forward to future contacts and adventures with MX-1. Development continues. And all this because of a single phone call six years ago.

Fig. 27-30
A demo of the FWD Miller on the grounds of Mere Hall.

Epilogue

Through the ages the commandment "know thyself" has appeared as a noble objective but not one easy to attain. One virtue of writing an autobiography is the insight it can give the author into his own life. After reading an early chapter of this book my friend Peter Wright wrote, "I feel there is a philosophy of life in the offing." Now that the book is completed I am certain he was optimistic but I do have some impressions to share with the reader who has gotten this far.

As I look back I'm amazed at how much the environment and experiences of my childhood determined the course of my life. By the time I was five I had picked up on the idea of an adventurous life from my father, by ten my long-term interest in automobile racing was firmly established and by sixteen I had an equal fascination with aircraft. I have never encountered two finer individuals than my parents, who never failed to support my interests, and I was indeed fortunate in having as role models my cousin Ed Waterhouse, the race car enthusiast, and the pilots of the pioneering oceanic flights, exemplified by Charles Lindbergh.

I am also surprised that a single event can have a lifetime effect. The brief flight of my highly unstable homebuilt airplane created in me a career interest in vehicle stability and control. From the earliest days of flight, stability and control was a mysterious and controversial subject. My hectic firsthand encounter with it stirred my curiosity to the boiling point and has never left me.

The physical demands of race car driving and long distance flying suggested the value of a program of physical conditioning which was to become a regular feature of my life. My mother was also an exerciser and believer in preventive medicine. The subject of diet was brought to my attention by Don Brubaker, a pioneer of organic food and an avid proponent of physical health. For years my wife Barbara has maintained an organic vegetable garden and an interest in good nutrition.

For my particular interests, I could not have had a better education. Three years at the University of Maine grounded me in mechanical engineering, while the construction of the small wind tunnel, tutoring in propeller theory and the flight experience at the Boeing School accelerated my aeronautical objective. At MIT I was exposed to a phenomenal group of teachers in the forefront of education and research. Otto Koppen's course in airplane stability and control was the only one in the country that gave the full mathematical treatment, and Rauscher's aeronautical theory was outstanding. What an asset it was to have parents who supported my education in the middle of the Great Depression.

Working in the aircraft industry proved to be an exciting continuation of my academic education with a large dose of reality. Pursuing stability and control in the format of flight testing exceeded my fondest hopes for adventure, culminating in three great airplanes: the first pressurized transport, the B-307 Stratoliner; the last of the Clippers, the A-314; and the high-altitude B-17. With the XB-29 I was to know tragedy and face one of the most emotionally charged periods of my career. Earlier with my father's death I had been forced to realize that life can deal blows only survivable by an unrelenting discipline to fight to the finish. I think this philosophy got me through the B-29 period.

The demise of the XP-79 Flying Wing at Avion initiated a dramatic career change from a practitioner of stability and control to a researcher. There is a law of balance: if you take a lot out of something, there is a time to put something of equal value back. The research opportunity for advancing stability and control technology created a sense of continuity and purpose in my life as a whole. It also brought into focus the subject of creativity.

I have always thought of imagination as a unique characteristic of man—the ability to project onto the mental screen new ideas and concepts which lead to invention and increased understanding of our universe. My life has been gifted by contacts with creative people. Cornell Lab was a powerhouse of such individuals and they are also the mainspring of industry. No one knows exactly how new ideas are generated. Sometimes they appear after long concentration on a problem or through the interchange of views in a group. But we do know that entire technologies have followed from the glimmer of a single notion. I have derived immense satisfaction from participation in a few new ideas that have stood the test of time.

Considering my intense obsession with auto racing as a child, it was only a matter of circumstances before I would race as an adult. The opportunity coincided with the postwar revival at Watkins Glen. I was 37 years of age at that time and raced for 15 years. Automobile racing is a supreme form of sport involving all of man's mental, physical and emotional qualities in the engineering and the optimization of the driver/vehicle entity in the racing environment. Racing is all about trying to win; anything less is just going along for the ride. My team threw everything we could into fielding the most competitive vehicles, including extensive re-engineering and rigorous mechanical preparation. I took my share of risk, and had some great "goes." When we lost, which was frequently, no one could have been happier for the winners. Without racing, my CAL Flight Research department would never have become involved in stability and control research of ground vehicles and the halcyon years of trying to understand them that followed.

It seems to me everyone is entitled to some peak experiences in life. Like mountain tops, they are the events that stand out above the routine plateau of life and become part of a family's heritage. Some of my peak experiences are certainly associated with flying and auto racing. I think particularly of driving the MX-1 camber car at Goodwood in 2002.

There are the great questions about the origin of the universe and mankind's position in it. Many systems of belief have arisen, and in the absence of absolute certainty tolerance is necessary. The mystical, extrasensory belief in a personal god with heaven and eternal life offers solace and faith and is a beautiful concept. I believe life is the greatest gift and I love it dearly, but I also believe it is finite with a beginning and an end. If this is true, it places emphasis on living it to the fullest, and this implies taking risks. Accepting life as finite appeals to me as more courageous and heroic but also eternal in the sense of the memory of one's life. I have great confidence in science and its medical advances and burgeoning understanding of how man and nature work. I daily feel surrounded by the miracles it has produced. Adding it up, my philosophical orientation as developed in this book appears to be that of "exuberant existentialism," coined (after Sartre) by my friend Al Fonda.* It implies total responsibility by the individual for the meaning and values in his life.

---

*To quote Sartre, "Now I have the shattering awareness that by being totally free, I am totally responsible for my choices, totally responsible for what I am and do, totally responsible for giving meaning and value to my world. . . " This is existentialism. Fonda adds that if it is appealing, it would be exuberant existentialism.

'Tis not too late to seek a newer world.
Push off, and sitting well in order smite
The sounding furrows; for my purpose holds
To sail beyond the sunset, and the baths
Of all the western stars, until I die…

Tho' much is taken, much abides; ….
that which we are, we are;

One equal-temper of heroic hearts …
To strive, to seek, to find, and not to yield.

> — From *Ulysses*
> Alfred Lord Tennyson

Men turn, and see the stars, and feel the free
Shrill wind beyond the close of heavy flowers,
And through the music of the languid hours
They hear like Ocean on a western beach
The surge and thunder of the Odyssey.

> — From *The Odyssey of Homer*
> (translated by S. H. Butcher and A. Lang;
> originally reprinted in *The Glorious Adventure* by Richard
> Halliburton by permission of the Macmillan Company.)

Appendix I

Research and Innovations

Innovative research in CAL/Calspan Flight Research and Vehicle Dynamics Departments (1944–1956), Transportation Research Division (1963–1976) and Milliken Research Associates (1976–current)

Measure and Effect Dynamic Characteristics of Aircraft

- First frequency response measurements on aircraft (1947).
- Early variable stability fly-by-wire aircraft (Laura Tabor Barber Air Safety Award, 1967).
- First use of variable stability for flying qualities specifications and for test pilot training (1948).
- Pioneered fly-by-wire stability augmentation systems (1948–50).
- Extraction of stability and control derivatives from flight tests (1949).
- Automatic control of a stalled aircraft (1948–52).
- Early recognition that the conventional "fixed surface aerodynamic" aircraft is special case of electronically servoed augmented aircraft (1948).

Translation of Aircraft Dynamic Stability and Control Technology to the Automobile

- Initiated and directed ten-year research program that laid the foundation for vehicle handling analysis (1952).
- Presentation of "Research in Automobile Stability and Control and in Tyre Performance" series of technical papers to the Institution of Mechanical Engineers, London (1956).
- Development of linearized equation of motion, derivative notation (Leonard Segel, Crompton-Lanchester Medal, 1956).
- Development of several nonlinear sets of equations including HVOSM (Highway Vehicle Object Simulation Model) and DK-4 for high amplitude, multiple degrees of freedom, etc. The predecessors of numerous analytical developments (1963–73).
- First six-component on-road tire tester. Axis system and notation later adopted by SAE (1954).
- First variable control feel automobile (1953).
- First variable stability car (1956).
- Earliest patent on variable stability for automobiles (1956).
- First automobile frequency response measurements and calculations (1958).
- Development of automobile statics.
- Moment Method simulation of constrained testing (conceived 1952, implemented 1969 to present).
- Constrained Vehicle Tester (CVT), based on Moment Method (1973).
- MTS Flat-Trac Roadway Simulator for Fiat and recently for Aberdeen Proving Ground, based on Moment Method technology (1973 to current).

- First comprehensive (analog) study of skidding automobile (1960).
- Development of Calspan Tire Research Facility (TIRF), the first high-speed flat belt tester with traction/braking capability, large slip and camber angles, high loads, dry and wet surface testing, etc. Pioneered air and water bearings for belt support and method of lateral belt constraint (1973).
- Non-dimensional treatment of tire data potentially reducing testing time, improving data accuracy and consistency over load range (Hugo Radt).
- Developed MX-1, a high-camber, mechanically variable stability vehicle. Demonstrated the virtues of high negative camber (1968).
- Pioneered lap time simulation (LTS) in USA, and developed it over period of years using more complete vehicle models (1971).
- Developed new vehicle stability and control concepts, such as yaw damping, path curvature stiffness, stability index, etc. (1956 to current).
- One of pioneers of "g-g" diagram and made numerous measurements and calculated "g-g" diagram using complex vehicle model (1970).
- Developed spiral jump as filmed in James Bond movie *Man with the Golden Gun* (JM Productions, 1974).
- Vehicle dynamic model for driving simulator (Atari arcade game, police driving pursuit trainer, etc.)
- Active camber Corvette prototype car for GM (1987).
- Path optimizer computer program for automatically calculating racing line (1984).
- First installation of torque converter transmission in race car (1950).
- Control system analysis for Vehicle Dynamics Test Vehicle (VDTV) for NHTSA. Vehicle Dynamics Matlab/Simulink® program (VDMS).
- Analytically determined chassis setup for new design of race car for high-speed oval.
- Represented Lotus active suspension cars in USA (1981).
- Represented Anthony Best Dynamics K&C machine in USA.

Many individuals contributed to the above developments including Walt Breuhaus, Dave Whitcomb, Len Segel, Dan Clark, Graham Campbell, Ed Laitone, Al Fonda, Cliff Muzzey, Bill Close, Hugo Radt, Roy Rice, Fred Dell'Amico, Ray McHenry, Doug Roland, Ed Kidd, Bob Wolf, Pat Miller, King Bird, Dave Segal, Edward Kasprzak, Dennis Kunkel, Doug Milliken, Peter Milliken and Bill Milliken and many others at GM and other contractors.

Long-range Automotive Stability and Control Research Plan Outline

This proposed outline of a long-range research plan was the very beginning of our research in automobile stability, control and handling. It was based upon our knowledge of the history of aircraft stability and control.

Cornell Aeronautical Laboratory, Inc.
Buffalo, New York

Flight Research Department

Long-range Automotive Stability & Control Research Program
(11/30/52)

By W. F. Milliken, Jr.

I.   General Discussion of Research Area, Philosophy and Objectives.
II.   Development of Prediction Methods.
III.   Data for Handling Qualities Prediction.
IV.   Methods for Full Scale Stability and Control Measurements.
V.   Specific Handling Qualities Measurements.
VI.   Methods for Determining Desirable Handling Qualities.
VII.   Specification Research.
VIII. Improvement of Handling Qualities.

We did not follow this Long-range plan religiously but its logic proved useful guidance for over 50 years of activity in the field through my years at CAL Flight Research Department, Vehicle Dynamics Department, Calspan Transportation Research Division and Milliken Research Associates.

Appendix II

SCCA Positions and Contributions

Positions held by Bill Milliken in the Sports Car Club of America (SCCA) and in Watkins Glen Grand Prix races (WGGP), and additional contributions to the sport. (Compiled by Bill Green, Watkins Glen Grand Prix Historian)

1946	Joined SCCA.
1947–49	Founder and Region Executive of the SCCA Western New York Region
1948–50	WGGP Technical Committee Chairman
1949	SCCA Vice President
1950	SCCA Competition License No. 6
	SCCA Contest Board Chairman
	Introduced SCCA Competition Vehicle Registration and Dash Plaques.
	Initiated Photographic Timing & Scoring Equipment at 1950 WGGP.
1951–52	SCCA Contest Board Member
1952	WGGP Technical Committee Chairman
1955	Proposed to Watkins Glen Grand Prix Board to build a permanent circuit.
1956	Helped locate site and shape of permanent (2.3-mile) Watkins Glen circuit.
	Contacted Cornell University Civil Engineering department who agreed to design and lay out the 2.3-mile circuit
1957–76	Watkins Glen Grand Prix Corporation, Director
1958–60	Chief Steward, WGGP Formula Libre Races
1959	First SCCA Governor from Area 11 (currently Area 10)
1961–70	Chief Steward, U.S. Grand Prix at Watkins Glen
1971	Organized Computer Simulation of Watkins Glen rebuild of the fourth course.
1971–74	Technical Director for WGGP Corp. at U.S. Grand Prix
2004	Elected to SCCA Hall of Fame.

Fig. App. II-1
Meeting of SCCA Contest Board and Activities Committee in Washington, DC, 1950. L-R: S. Hempstone Oliver, Reggie Smith, Alec Ulmann, Russ Sceli, Nils Michelson, George Weaver, Miles Collier, Bill Milliken. Cam Argetsinger in Silverstone Healey.

June 28, 1948

To: Members and Subscribers of the Sports Car Club of America

Subject: Watkins Glen Road Races - Entry Blanks and Information.

         The plans for a series of real road races to be held at Watkins
Glen, New York, have previously been announced, and a general summary of
progress will appear in the next issue of SPORTS CAR. Suffice it to say
that things are materializing rapidly and that during a recent session at
Watkins Glen with the Mayor and the Chairman of the Chamber of Commerce,
basic decisions regarding the date, organization and nature of the events
were made by Alec Ulmann, SCCA Chairman of Activity. At that time
Cameron Argetsinger agreed to serve as Chairman of the Race Committee,
with the undersigned assisting as Chairman of the Technical Committee.

         The information and entry blanks which are enclosed have been
prepared at the Regional Headquarters in Buffalo with the collaboration of
Cam Argetsigner and have been approved by the Chairman of Activity. As
will be discussed further, a real attempt has been made to incorporate the
ideas and suggestions put forth at Indianapolis, and in correspondence, by
various club members. These are in many cases conflicting, and are also
subject to modification by actual conditions existing at the Glen, and by
the paramount necessity of insuring a maximum of safety. It is hoped that
by presenting in detail the plans to date, many further suggestions and
ideas will be forthcoming. This year's efforts should be viewed as a
start toward a significant annual event, which will as time goes by become
more and more representative of the interests of SCCA members as a whole.

         A date of Saturday, October 2, 1948, has been chosen. For the
first year it will be an advantage to hold the races after the summer
season. Also it gives a maximum of time for organization of the event and
preparation of the cars, and the weather is usually beautiful at that locale
in October. For many reasons the affair is being organized as essentially
a one-day meet. However, it will be an advantage to get to the Glen earlier,
and all entrants should arrive no later than Friday night. A social event
is scheduled for Sunday morning but the day is essentially available for
the return trip home unless conditions are extremely unfavorable on Saturday
and it becomes necessary to use Sunday as a "Rain Date."

         The enclosed material includes:

         1. Program of Events   -   This is a detailed "play-by-
play" account of activity from the time of your arrival at the Glen on
Friday, October 1. All arrangements are being designed with the idea of providing a maximum of assistance to the entrants in completing their final

Members and Subscribers of SCCA

car preparation, and in becoming familiar with the course by Saturday noon. However, this is a big order and as mentioned before the earliest possible arrival will be to your advantage. It is felt that two items should be included in the interest of safety, (a) an examination of all competing machines by a technical representative of the club, (b) a "drivers' meeting" just prior to the start, which would be presided at by the Chief Steward, and must would be attended by all those responsible for patrolling the course, running and competing in the events. All concerned would then be congizant of last minute details.

In order to simplify things from the contestants' standpoint, all places that he may be required to reach will be closely located on Franklin St. Thus, on arriving in town he reports at an Information Center at the Jefferson Hotel. This information center will be under the Chamber of Commerce, with help from the Club. It will have a bulletin board for all important notices. A variety of services will be provided for SCCA members at this Center.

From there it is just a step to the Fredericks Motor Company, where competing machines may be garaged together in a special space. Here the technical inspection can be completed. The various gas stations which will be assigned for servicing of the cars are conveniently grouped in a few blocks up and down the same street. For practice, and when not at the pits, a "paddock" will be available in the Glen entrance parking lot which is close to the START-FINISH line, and across the street from the County Court House where the "drivers' meeting" will be held. The pits will be near the START-FINISH line across the street from the Timers and Scorers Tables. The general arrangement of these places on Main Street is shown below:

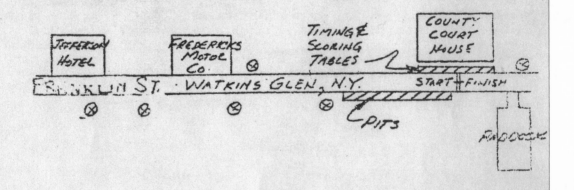

⊗ Gas stations (exact number not shown).

-3-

Members and Subscribers of SCCA

From the standpoint of the spectators, as well as in the best spirit of the sport, it is hoped that special attention will be directed toward the appearance of the equipé and the attire of the drivers and pits attendants. White coveralls are suggested.

The events will start with a concour d'elegance - a parade of sports cars around the course (or around the principal streets of the town). Town officials will be the guests of the Club in this parade. The scheduled races will then be run off during the afternoon, concluding with the "Grand Prix of America ."

Arrangements are being completed for a Victory Banquet for Saturday evening, at which time trophies and ribbons will be distributed. For the events tentatively proposed, it is suggested that the following prizes be considered:

Event
#1   Trophy for winner. Blue, red, and yellow ribbons for 1st, 2nd, and 3rd positions.

Event
#2   Trophy for "out and out" winner. Ribbons for 1st, 2nd, and 3rd positions in all classes.

Event
#3   Trophy for "out and out" winner. Ribbons for 1st, 2nd, and 3rd positions ("out and out"). Ribbons for 1st, 2nd, and 3rd positions in all classes.

Cam Argetsinger has already offered a crash helmet for the "out and out" winner of Event #2, and it is understood that Col. Felton is planning to present a trophy of some kind. While an "Awards" Committee will probably be appointed, those desiring to give a trophy should so indicate to Alec Ulmann (342 Madison Ave., New York City, Murray Hill 7-8790) immediately. Goggles, helmets, tools, accessories, racing books, stop watches, plaques and objects of art would make excellent trophies.

2.   Map of Course — This map of the course has been prepared with the idea of portraying all important features to the drivers. In arriving at this course, a comparison was made between a number of suggested ones in the vicinity, and they were rated on the basis of such factors as (a) safety to spectators and contestants, (b) difficulty of obtaining permission for use, (c) interest to spectators and contestants, (d) length, (e) surface conditions, etc. The course is not perfect, and

-4-

Members and Subscribers of SCCA

there is a short stretch of rough dirt and a RR crossing to be contended with, but in the aggregate it is the best compromise. The town officials have generously offered to attempt certain improvements, and will provide bales of hay etc. at strategic locations. It is not a difficult course to learn, and from the drivers' standpoint offers exciting prospects in cornering, shifting and driving judgment. The length (6.5 miles) offers the possibility of running a large number of machines at one time with comparative safety.

3.   The Organization Chart - The matter of improved organization of club events was discussed at some length at Indianapolis. The achievement of a smooth working organization which functions without previous practice for one weekend only must be regarded as a difficult task. In the hope of at least partially achieving this end, an organizational arrangement has been evolved, and is offered for the criticism and interest of the Club members. An attempt has been made to show the relationship of Club and Town officials. Many of the jobs which will have to be done are as yet unassigned, and the names of the individuals can be filled in as the assignments are made.

Cam Argetsinger, who is providing the principal liaison with the town, is planning to circularize the names of town officials, and their addresses, and their responsibilities so that "down the line" cross liaison can be initiated between club and town officials for the accomplishment of particular jobs.

At the risk of citing the obvious it is suggested that if each person assigned a job would do the following, the affair would go off safely, and with minimum strain:

(a) Establish exactly what he is responsible for.

(b) Establish whom he reports to on race day.

(c) Establish whom he should work with in the club and the town to accomplish his objectives.

This Regional Headquarters has been assigned the handling of all timing and scoring. A group from Cornell Aeronautical Laboratory engineers have agreed to handle the major burden, and should be able to adequately plan since the individuals live locally and can get together as often as is required beforehand. The timing and scoring group will report to a Chief Steward who will be a responsible club member, preferably a past or present officer of the club. On the day of the race the Chief Steward's word is final. As mentioned before, he will preside at the "drivers' meeting." The announcer at the START-FINISH line, who will call out the events, is responsible to the Chief Steward, as is the Starter.

- 5 -

Members and Subcribers of SCCA

The Town Officials with whom negotiations have been handled to
date are:

H. D. Erway   - Mayor of Village of Watkins Glen
Donald Brubacher   - President of Chamber of Commerce
John Osborne   - Secretary of Chamber of Commerce
Arthur Richards   - Chairman of Publicity for the Event

4.   Location of Watkins Glen - A brief description of how to get to
Watkins Glen is presented. It is approximately 300 miles from New York City.

5.   Entry Blanks - Entry blanks and instructions for completing them,
and race regulations, are attached. For the purposes of immediate planning,
three races are tentatively proposed for your consideration. A great deal of
discussion and effort has gone into the selection of these proposed events,
since the requirements are so numerous and complicated. In the first place,
three events are all that can be practically run in an afternoon. Second, we
arbitrarily eliminated any event for out and out race cars since we felt there
are so few of them, and it is difficult to define what is and what is not an
out and out racing machine. In this respect it appeared better to let them
compete with other cars. On the basis of discussion at Indianapolis it seemed
desirable to provide both a short and a long event, since there is such a diversity
of opinion. From the standpoint of scoring, etc, it has been felt advisable to
eliminate handicapping at least for this year. Naturally some members will desire
to enter their cars in more than one event, or enter two cars, and the proposed
selection enables this. The course has been chosen with the idea in mind of
equalizing the differences in performance of the various club machines. It is
entirely possible that events No. 2 and No. 3 could be won by a smaller displacement car. The advantage of having classes within the races is that under any
circumstances each individual will have a chance at competing with very similar
cars and receiving recognition for it if he does the best job.

In addition to the above, consideration of course has to be given
to safety, and spectator interest. The event must be successful from the latter
standpoint if we are to have repeat performances in the future.

6.   Insurance - Last but not least, this all important requirement has
been settled. A coverage of between $500,000 and $1,000,000 will be available.
The premium will be about $700 and will be covered by entry fees and the club
treasury.

With all best regards,

A.E. Ulmann   C.R. Argetsinger   W. F. Milliken, Jr.
Ch. of Activities SCCA   Ch. of Race Committee   Ch. of Technical Committee

WFM:fms

OFFICIAL ENTRY BLANK

(Return two (2) copies; keep one (1) copy)

Return on or before Aug. 7, 1948

1. Please enter my registered sports car as follows:

Event	Car Make	Type	Year	Body Style	Eng. Displ.	Blowers	No. Cyls.	Approx. Weight
No. 1								
No. 2								
No. 3								

2. If there are too many entrants it may be necessary for you to compete in either event No. 2 or No. 3 but not both. Please state preference _____

3. Check brand of service desired: SINCLAIR ____ SUNOCO ____ TEXACO ____ GULF ____ MOBIL ____ ATLANTIC ____ AMOCO ____ .

4. I will need garage accommodations for _____ competition cars, and _____ additional cars for the following dates _____.

5. I will need the following living accommodations. (State whether hotel, tourist home, tourist cabin; number of persons; twin, single, etc., and dates desired:)

   _____

   _____

   _____

6. Do not send these blanks in without:
   (a) Entry fee of $10.00 per car.
   (b) Glossy photograph of each car entered.
   (c) Your comments and suggestions on the proposed events, and interesting history of your cars. (Write this on back of this entry blank.)
   (d) Considering the possibility of contributing a trophy for one of the events!

7. This is an informal commitment on my part to show at the events with the cars indicated. I have read the rules and agree to abide by them.

   Signed _____

   Address _____

   Phone _____

   Return 2 copies of this blank to:

   W. F. MILLIKEN, JR.
   FLIGHT RESEARCH DEPARTMENT
   CORNELL AERONAUTICAL LABORATORY #2
   BUFFALO 21. NEW YORK

Appendix III

Al Reed

When I parted company with Al Reed, my former direct boss and head of flight test at Boeing, following Avion experience, Al went to work for Project Vista, a classified military project headquartered in Pasadena. For the next few years I kept in touch by occasional phone calls and Christmas cards and by correspondence with Orin Johnston, a friend of Al's who had worked in Flight Test at Boeing. Then in 1946 (or '47) a bizarre event occurred which is so well described in Bill Sears's autobiography, *Stories from a 20th Century Life,* that I quote directly,

> I was not in touch with Al in those days and was astounded to read in the newspapers, some time later, that he had "disappeared." He was, of course, described as a brilliant aeronautical specialist, privy to all of America's and the Allies' secrets; there was at least a suggestion that he might have been kidnapped by some enemy nation—or defected to them! I learned that, since the Avion days, he fathered a child. His wife was in financial need and was not well, the papers said. I also learned that Al had spent some years, during childhood, in Mexico, and was fluent in Spanish.
>
> I took no such stock whatever in the "defection" theory, or even the "kidnapping." Some of us wondered if he had had an unhappy marriage, and there was a rumor, among his acquaintances, that his wife's illness might have been psychosomatic and had been annoying to him, but some time after his disappearance the lady died of a heart ailment and the child had to be taken in by her mother. Still no sign of Al.
>
> After a year or so of disappearance, Al was found by the FBI by a strange fluke. He was working as a groom of racehorses at the Santa Anita racetrack, under an assumed name, living in the rude quarters provided for the grooms. There was some scandal about the horses being doped, and all the employees were being fingerprinted. He was unaware of his wife's death.

I, too, had read in the newspapers about Al's disappearance. When he was discovered the *Buffalo News* carried a picture of him and his race horse, mentioning the Santa Anita track. I immediately called the track and got Al on the phone. He sounded perfectly normal to me and noted that he had been cleared by the FBI after searching and tedious interviews. His son was living with relatives of Florence (his deceased wife) in Albany, New York, and he planned to come East to see him. A few weeks later he made the trip and on the way back stopped off in Buffalo and visited our Flight Research Department. Al was his usual discreet self and gave me no clue as to why he had disappeared, but he did say that the meeting with his son had not gone well, that they were unlikely to get together. He showed little emotion but I sensed this was a hard blow.

I followed the events of Al Reed's life until his death in 1995 from blood poisoning as the result of an automobile accident.

Appendix IV

Automotive Handling: Experiments and Results

Qualitative Definition of Desirable Automobile Handling

In the early 1960s we developed this definition of desirable automobile handling based on our racing and research experience. Although purely qualitative, it remains a good guide as to what to shoot for.

1. Basic response to steering fast and well damped
   a. Minimize roll mode, steady state roll angle and roll yaw coupling
2. Steering ratio appropriate for speed-range and adequate for emergency
3. Smooth control force curve with appropriate gradient in normal driving range
   a. Definite center feel and moderately fast spin-back
4. Minimum control backlash, springiness and shake
5. Minimum change in heading, pitching and control response with road roughness
6. Minimum change in heading with gust disturbance
7. Steady aerodynamic effects over speed range minimized or in favorable direction
8. High developable side force, or ultimate cornering adhesion
9. Satisfactory skidding characteristics
   a. Adequate skid warning
   b. Gradual rear breakaway
   c. Easy natural recovery
10. Minimum change in behavior with braking and acceleration.

Recorded Handling Experiences with Reference to Critical Situations Encountered in Racing

In the early days of postwar road racing, there were no driver training schools and chassis tuning was nonexistent. In order to become more proficient, I recorded my experiences after each event. Some examples are given below:

Turnpike Runs, Bugatti Type 35A (January–August 1947)

High-frequency vibration apparently due to wheel unbalance (at 100 mph+) led to failure of radiator hose.

Pikes Peak, Bugatti Type 35A (September 1, 1947)

Very high control forces on sharp corners (due in part to fast steering ratio); also stiction in steering box which reduced returnability.

Pikes Peak, FWD Miller (September 6, 1948)

Spins with unlocked center differential (improvement with locked center diff).

Desirability of fast steering ratio on dirt.

Watkins Glen, Bugatti Type 35A (October 2, 1948)

Spins at foot of hill with little warning when turn entered too fast.

Very high steering forces with stiction limited speed on Big Bend. Made accurate steering difficult.

Bridgehampton, Bugatti Type 35A (June 11, 1949)

Speed on back stretch limited by road roughness, harsh suspension and tendency to follow camber.

Steering still heavy on Country Club corner, although ratio had been lowered.

Watkins Glen, FWD Miller (September 17, 1949)

Speed on back stretch limited by tendency to follow camber and by lack of feeling of directional stability. (Fixed control neutral.)

Also by harsh suspension on rough road.

Also by brake grab and feeling brakes unequalized. particularly on Big Bend. (This feeling may be due to operating car with locked center differential on dry surface.)

Steering system poor—friction and slop.

Palm Beach Shores, Bugatti Type 51 (January 3, 1950)

This car felt good in all respects even in the rain, but the road was smooth.

Mt. Equinox, FWD Miller (May 22, 1950)

Nearly lost it due to trailing throttle oversteer.

Fast and good steering system made car maneuverable on rough ridge.

On standing start with all wheels spinning, the car slid sideways on road camber.

Bridgehampton, Bugatti Type 54 (June 10, 1950)

Spin out on right-angled corner in practice. Little warning and wheel jerked out of hand. (Big aligning torque effect.)

Humpback Bridge—pitched nose down on landing when speed too high.

A handful on rough back stretch.

Watkins Glen, Dynaflow Bugatti, Type 54 (September 23, 1950)

Very tiring on rough, wavy back stretch at high speed, bounced a lot and slow directional stability. Had control but very busy.

Lands nose down at RR tracks. This limited speed.

Braking would have been limited by front axle tramp without the parallelogram mechanism.

Spun out on Seneca Lodge corner due to excessive speed and limit on corner. Also nearly lost it on turn back to Franklin Street.

Sebring, 6 Hour MG TC (December 31, 1950)

This car always feels tail-heavy as if rear tires overloaded on turns.

Giant's Despair, Bugatti Type 54 (May 12, 1951)

A handful on rough road and big single bumps. Front end bounces off ground.

Mt. Equinox, FWD Miller (October 28, 1951)

Lowered rear tire pressure for starting traction and got real oversteer but still did allright.

In time trial on circuit through woods the day before, got a "pilot induced" oscillation with the 9-to-1 steering ratio (which is very fast). It occurred on the narrow dirt road but I slowed down and caught it.

Edenvale Airport, Canada, FWD Miller (May 25, 1952)

Fairly smooth. Used some different tire pressures and things felt fine.

Mt. Equinox, FWD Miller (June 15, 1952)

Lowered rear tire pressure for starting traction and got real oversteer but still did allright.

In time trial on circuit through woods the day before, got a "pilot induced" oscillation with the 9-to-1 steering ratio (which is very fast). It occurred on the narrow dirt road but I slowed down and caught it.

Watkins Glen, AJB/FWD (September 10, 1952)

Steering system very flexible, poor brakes, etc. Car spun at foot of hill, just after Milliken's Corner due to four-wheel-drive trim change and impossible steering.

Car also has a queer rotational motion at rear, probably due to Panhard rod location.

Pikes Peak, AJB/FWD (September 7, 1953)

The car lets go too easily on tail. Did not have the sidewise four-wheel drift of the FWD Miller at the Peak.

Neither this car nor the Miller had enough lock for the sharper turns.

Edenvale, AJB/FWD (June 18, 1955)

When rear Panhard rod broke have new idea of what lack of lateral fixity at rear feels like.

Generally car ran well with duals on rear which eliminated trailing throttle oversteer.

Giant's Despair, AJB/FWD (July 20, 1956)

Impossible on practice on rough stretch with high pressure in tires. Tremendous improvement on lowering tire pressure.

Car ran with single rears but no trouble power on and off. (Same also true at WG later.)

Watkins Glen (2nd circuit), AJB/FWD (September 15, 1956)

Car handled badly on rough wavy downhill leg. Lowering tire pressure helped but getting some differential tire pressure, and hence some directional stability, was a real improvement.

The lap times were still limited by speed on downhill leg. The car was floating some but not as bad as Austin-Healey. Any slop in steering was very noticeable.

Side wind gust tending to turn car up into wind was very noticeable and uncomfortable on hill.

Appendix V

Archie Butterworth Letter Regarding the FWD-AJB "Butterball"

BUTTERWORTH ENGINEERING CO., LTD.

Automotive Research & Development.
Racing Car Constructors.
Engine Builders.

RECEIVED
FLIGHT RESEARCH DEPARTMENT
W. F. MILLIKEN, JR.
MAY 5 1952
MR. _____
COMMENT   RETURN
FOLLOW UP   FILE

AIR MAIL:

Grove Gardens,
Frimley,
NR ALDERSHOT.

Dear Bill,

I am afraid I have let you down rather badly over
replying to this letter. It reached me during a time of
extreme flap just before Goodwood and I carried it round with
me for several days hoping to find half an hour to reply to you.
No paper got dealt with during that last week or so and
eventually I decided to take it away with me on a short holiday
in Cornwall immediately after the Goodwood meeting. When I got
down there, of course, I discovered I had left it behind.

I am glad to hear that the car arrived safely and was
decently packed. From hereon I shall answer your queries as
they come up.

Regarding the lengthening of the wheel base, I agree
that the best way would be to pull the front end forward
leaving the engine where it is. I have no precise location for
the C.G., and the only wheel weights I have refer to the car
when it had the old gearbox and are, consequently, much less
useful than what you can get by weighing it fore and aft in its
present condition. (It was deliberately made nose heavy in the
first instance to help it to run straight at high speed and at
that time I had a free wheel incorporated in the front drive
instead of an inter-axle differential so that the light back
end could not indulge in wheel spin by itself.
I always found the car much more manageable with the 25 gallon
tank in, so obviously I over-did the nose heaviness where fast
corners were concerned. With the inter-axle differential
something very near to a fifty fifty weight distribution seems
indicated and now that it has independent front suspension it
should be easy to avoid oversteer, or wander, on the straight.
I only drove the car for half a season with the independent
suspension and it was so very much better than the rigid axle
that at first it seemed perfect which, of course, does not make
for good analysis.

In road races on circuits like Winfield and Boreham
with the 25 gallon tank about half full, it had very few vices
indeed though possibly inertia was a little too concentrated.
With the small sprint tank in position it was still a little
difficult on slow corners (showing a tendency for the back end
to try and come alongside under hard braking and "power-off"
cornering but it still took fast smooth curves very well.
It still reacted very badly to undulating surfaces and after
my experience at Shelsley I was going to advise you never to
race it on bumpy surfaces with the small tank, except on low
speed courses. What happened at Shelsley appears to have been
that the independent suspension permitted me to get through the

649

Crossing bend about ten miles an hour faster than I had ever done before with the result that I hit those undulations at about ninety miles an hour. The feeling was as if one end of the back axle had been disconnected, the car swerved very wildly, got on to the grass and hit a cross gully which threw me out. I rejoined her at the bottom of a ravine very violently and broke all my ribs against the safety tube which went round inside the head fairing of the tail. There should be a laugh in that somewhere.

I think the mechanics of this occurrence were that the very hard rear springs allowed the rear axle to bounce clear of the road as the undulations got into phase with the pitch frequency and, having a free inter-axle differential, the back end probably speeded up to about twenty miles an hour. When the back wheels landed revving much too fast and, with the axle pushed down to the full re-bound position, the car would probably be largely under the control of rear steering effects. At all events it was no longer under the control of A.J. Butterworth.

I may be out of phase with your question at this point but I would like to say that the rear spring of this car was a very ad hoc affair. You will see, if you examine the chassis, that there was very little bump clearance. When I erected it first with very hard springs, this didn't much matter but to soften the springs I was faced with the alternative of accepting a considerable slope-down from the rear spring eyes to the axle, with consequent undesirable rear steering effects, or of using a flatter spring and occasionally bottoming on the chassis. The actual springs used were a compromise which was fairly satisfactory with the half full 25 gallon tank, but could occasionally be bottomed over severe bumps at high speed.
If you can do anything to give yourself more axle clearance, it would be well worth fitting softer springs to give phenomenal rear end frequency of around 100 to 120 cycles per minute.

Referring to the bottom of page 1. again, there was adequate under-steer on the straight and in general handling, and the steering was always quite light. It did not need winding into a corner in advance and, thinking back, I have the impression that the under-steer margin decreased as you put it into a corner under moderate power. There was no sign of a decrease of the under steer margin at high speed on the straight, but you would expect this, of course. in a nose heavy car.

The amount of power you used on a corner tended to be controlled by spin of the off-side track on a right hand bend and in the case of slow corners by the fact that to use a lot of power tends to complicate the straightening-out process unduly. My practice was to enter the corner as fast as I could, complete the tightest practical radius under a small throttle opening and get the car nearly straight before letting it off again under full throttle. This procedure, of course, applies only to tight turns. I did not get much experience of the tail coming out with the independent suspension as I was still learning how to drive the car when I crashed it. With the rigid suspension it was quite easy to get the tail out in a flick to the point where you couldn't tuck it in again. I have several times coasted back to the foot of Prescott on a practice run through trying a new way

of entering the Esses, only to find myself racing downhill again
very abruptly. As I say, she was very greatly improved by the
new suspension and I was rather feeling my way in finding how much
so I did not provoke the old girl more than I could help.

My experience of really powerful rear drive racing cars
is limited and on the very fast corners, where I could just hold,
say, my old 4½ litre Bentley in a four-wheel slide without quite
adequate power, I had to drive S.2 around feeding as much throttle
as the car would take without drifting off the line.
I find it hard to describe the limited amount of power it would
take on a fast curve as the behaviour was always different as
between a smooth and a bumpy curve. On really smooth right-hand
curves of the 100-110 mile an hour type, I was often limited by
adhesion of the off-side front tyre which lifts under torque and
could be made to spin at surprisingly high speeds if there was
lateral acceleration. On a bumpy curve one began to get a
feeling of unsafeness if the throttle was opened too far, which I
did not care to explore too thoroughly as the car was able to take

fast curves on equal terms with, for example, Tony Rolt in his
ERA engined-Delage. I have never run the car without the
differential axle operating except, of course, in the old days
when I had the free wheel arrangement as on a Land Rover.
Its behaviour with that arrangement was generally bad but how
far this was due to transmission I do not know. With all
differentials operating the tail always went first under heavy
power. Wheel spin on a straight racing start was heaviest on
the off-side front wheel and second heaviest on the off-side
rear wheel, but there was sufficient traction for a standing
¼ mile to be covered in 12.69 seconds as against 12.78 with the
solid front axle. A limited slip-differential in the front
and rear axles would certainly help the standing start and
probably also be of advantage in the centre differential.

The only criticism I had of the offset differential
at the front was the obvious one of the torque lifting that
wheel. This would be dealt with, of course, by a control type
differential. I got no steering reactions at all from this
arrangement, whereas with the rigid axle there was a high
frequency dither coming out of corners under power though this
rapidly stabilised with rising speed. My main criticism of the
present steering arrangement is that it is too springy and has
excessive back-lash. Sidney Allard's solution of running a
steering column straight down the Vee of the engine and using
a rack and pinion type steering gear, would be far more
satisfactory and if you are moving the front suspension further
from the engine, I think you should consider adopting some such
arrangement.

I was always in difficulty at the top of Shelsley,
where very rapid and slight corrections of direction are
necessary to keep you between the hedges at over 110 miles an
hour over quite severe bumps. I think the importance of complete
freedom from spring and back-lash in road racing steering gears
is not sufficiently realised. The geometry I used at the front
end was as follows:-

Camber   approx   2 degrees static

Castor $1\frac{1}{2}$ "

Static deflection of springs - 4 inches.

Tow-in - 1/16th of an inch at each side measured by straight edge or string from rear wheel to front wheel (the car now has a slight crab-track which makes the measurement of tow-in and alignment a little more difficult.)

        I varied the tyre pressures a lot for different conditions and always made them proportional to the actual weights on the wheels. Typical road racing figure on a dry day would be:-

L.H. Nearside front	32	C.G. = approx, 47%.
R.H. Off-side front	30	
Nearside rear	28	
Offside rear	26	

        For a wet sprint I might go down to:-

L.H. Nearside front	20	C.G, approx. 43%
R.H. Offside front	18	
Nearside rear	15	
Offside rear	14	

        I always use the same size tyres all round and nearly always 6" section. I never used bigger than this size though in its early days 5.50s were used quite successfully. An attempt to climb Prescott with 5.25 tyres fitted to alter the gear ratio (in the days of the old gearbox) was discontinued abruptly when I found the car completely uncontrollable with this tyre size.

Old Mac of Dunlops was immensely amused by this as he had told me my car was too powerful for this size of tyre and I could not see how this could be so as the course did not involve speeds greater than 80 miles an hour. I was most emphatically wrong about this and the car felt as if it was being driven on ice.

        Regarding the C.G. location again, I do not see any trouble that you can get into from moving it aft and I think this will be a considerable improvement. If you can get a De Dion arrangement in at the back I think it would be well worth while. I didn't have any very definite trouble with the back end which I could not trace to the hard springs, but it is difficult to soften these much without introducing rear steering effects. I would like a definition of your term "fitness ratio" as applied to springs. I would have liked to give the car an undamped natural frequency at the front end of 95 cycles per minute and at the rear end of 100 under mean load conditions, in the case of this car using the inherent "scrub" of the swing axle front suspension instead of a front anti-roll bar. I think this would have given a consistent flat ride, but there was no easy way to soften the rear springs as I have explained. The actual static deflections and frequencies in road racing form are

Front 4"   95 cycles
Rear 2½"   (at this point I went away to find the car's log book in which these figures were written down but have failed to do so, so the above is from memory. I think the rear end frequency was about 120 to 130, in any case much too high).

I never had any trouble on the straight on any reasonable road surface but some of the English hill climbs have dangerous undulations in them. Compared to Bira's old 3-litre Maserati, for example, in the braking area at the end of the Brighton Kilometre, she was very stable indeed. In fact I used to let the Maserati pass me and sit comfortably to watch its antics when the poor driver tried to brake at about 120 to 130 miles an hour (I had a lot of scraps with this car in sprints when Ken McAlpine was racing it; the only time he beat me was at Weston when I blew up at half distance).

I have already answered emphatically your question regarding the differences in handling as between the road racing tank and the sprint tank. The difference in weight is approximately 50 lbs. I have been more frightened by that piece of weight saving than by quite a lot of air raids. The small radius rods were desirable to prevent torque wind up of the rear springs and the function of the diagonal rod is to locate the axle positively at the end to which this rod is attached. You will see that the axle location, neglecting spring stiffness for the moment, is that a rigid right angled triangle formed by one radius rod and the diagonal; angular movement between chassis and axle being accommodated by independent oscillation of the other radius rod and spring.

The shock absorber characteristics which I used were as follows:-

Front bump   100 lbs at 15 inches per sec.
Front rebound   350 lbs at 15 inches per sec.
Rear bump   75 lbs
Rear rebound   250 lbs.

These shock absorbers seemed to give very satisfactory results to my way of thinking but I did no great experimentation so you may be able to improve on them. The calibration at 15 inches per sec is Newton & Bennett's standing practice and I cannot remember whether this is to be taken as average oscillating speed (as for piston speed) or instantaneous speed at the middle of the stroke, but probably your shock absorber people will be able to advise.

The present steering ratio represents an increase over the original figure which was too low. It is quite an arbitrary ratio, being the highest I could get by lengthening the drop arm when fitting the new suspension. I think you could profitably experiment with a higher ratio still as there is very little vice in the way of steering reaction. I have never felt that different ratios are needed for hill climbs or road races as I drive in much the same way in either instance.

-5-

Please do not re-arrange the radius rods as you suggest. If you visualise the suspension in plan you will see that there are two rigid pin joints, one each side of the front axle and that the two $\frac{1}{2}$-axles must be permitted to oscillate round an axis through those bearings. The present rear bearing at the back of the radius rods is a continuation of this axis and any attempt to make the suspension oscillate on ball joints attached to the chassis sides out of line with this axis, would cause fracture or cross binding of the pin joints astride the centre constant-velocity joint.

Apart from this mechanical point, which could probably be overcome by re-designing the split axle joints, I think it would be a retrograde step, from the purely suspension point of view, to make the $\frac{1}{2}$-axles swing on effective axes which were at an angle to the fore and aft axis of the car. Sidney Allard has been using such an arrangement for several years because of the difficulty of using a common axis behind the sump on his engines, and has now improved his cars considerably by arranging such a common axis a short distance in front of his front axles.

The swing axle type of front suspension only works, in my opinion, by a series of happy accidents. I should avoid provoking it if I were you.

I think you are right in locking out the centre differential for Pikes' Peak and probably the rear axle could be locked as well. I would not like to give an opinion about the effect of locking the front axle differential from the steering point of view. It would certainly be a big advantage from the point of view of traction, as I have already explained. I know that the Emeryson 500 cc front drive racing car uses no differential and seems to steer quite well.

There seem to be no signs of the swing axle as such leading to wheel spin on curves, apart from the torque effect mentioned already, but you will not, of course, be able to use much power on a loose surface on any curve on this car owing to the very high power-weight ratio. I think I have already dealt with the Shelsley accident.

Regarding the frame stiffness, I don't think any frame is sufficiently stiff, certainly not that of the A.J.B. I had it in mind to run diagonal tubes from the centre cross member towards the four spring supports, thus providing the chassis with a cruciform bracing stressed both in tension and compression, but I never made any close investigation of this plan though I recall that I had $1\frac{1}{8}$ inch by .048 inches steel tube in mind for the job, flattened locally where the tubes crossed under the main cross member.

It will be excellent if you can move the driver further aft but you will have to do something about the box section cross member at present in the way.

I see that we are in agreement about weight distribution and the increasing of the polar moment.

I shall be very interested indeed to hear how the car handles with these improvements. I was not troubled with over-heating of this engine in any conditions I met, though I have no doubt that the engine cowling could be improved by a more scientific approach. We always raced the car on 80% alcohol fuel and large jets which gave adequate cooling.

Oil temperature tends to get pretty close to 100° centigrade but
I don't think this matters. On the present gear ratio the car
does a standing ¼ mile in 12.69 secs (official Course record
Gosport Speed trials) and a standing kilometre in just over
23 secs (this is not an official figure, I think it would have
been if we had had a fine day for Brighton last year).

I have never had a chance to discover the terminal
velocity but on a fairly short runway 145 miles an hour came up
quite readily. When I was testing the car at Aldermaston, which
has a smooth surface, before the 1949 Brighton speed trials, we
readily reached 155 at the end of a standing start kilometre;
an average time for several runs in one direction was 24.1 secs
in those days. This was with the smaller inlet valve and the wide
ratio Steyr gearbox.

I am a little gloomy about the performance of the
engine on 90 to 100 Octane fuel as the cylinders are pitched
rather closely for cooling with hydrocarbon fuels. I think you
may have to take cowling problem rather seriously in these
circumstances and I personally would doubt whether you would get
away with the compression ratio much above 8½ to 1.
I can actually supply pistons giving the above ratio which I
have had made up for Sports versions of the Flat-Four. These
are in stock and you can have them at quite short notice if you
think they would suit your purpose. They are, of course, complete
with rings and piston pins.

We never had any structural failure on the car at
all. I used to inspect various critical welds and bolted
assemblies at intervals as a matter of routine but there was
never anything to see. All the jeep steering bell cranks that
I inspected seemed to have built-in crack in the sharp angle so,
after polishing this out, I braced the bell crank with the strut
that you can see. I would not advise using these bell cranks
without this stiffener. Fuel consumption on a fast road
circuit (Boreham) on 80% Methanol was 6.8 to 7 miles per gallon.
I have never used the car on any other compression ratio than
the present so can give you no data for 90 Octane.

Regarding the gearbox I found that the present ratio
would provide a gear for practically any imaginable set of
circumstances and in fact I never changed ratios from the time
I put it in. It is important to ensure that the gearbox oil
pump is working satisfactorily. I used to prime it until I
found that this was unnecessary if it was filled with oil to
just above the level of the gearbox floor, i.e. so that the oil
just runs out if one of the ¼" bolts securing the lower edge of
the steel back-plate of the gearbox is withdrawn.
It is advisable to run the car and corner it a bit for a few
miles and then top up and make this check again, as oil lodges in
various places. After that it is just a question of keeping
an eye on the gearbox thermometer which samples casing
temperature near the main shaft bearing. Failure of the oil
pump would be signalled by a sudden abrupt rise in temperature.
It would be very dangerous to go on driving the car after such
a signal. Using SAE 40 oil cut with 25% Redex, we found the
temperature stabilised at about 50 to 60 centigrade, but a
steady temperature of up to 90 centigrade would be quite safe.
Apart from this we had no trouble at all with the box; make
clean fast changes and you should never miss a gear. There is
a bit of a trick getting back into gear if you do.

I have now found the log book so I will amplify some of the points mentioned earlier. I see that the deflections of the rear springs are recorded as follows:-

Light	2.63 inches.
Periodicity	123 cycles a minute.
Average	2.8 inches.
Periodicity	112 cycles a minute.
Full tank	3.2 inches.
Periodicity	105 cycles a minute.

which is not quite as bad as I thought.

These were apparently with springs giving a free Camber on the offside of 3.05 inches and on the nearside of 3.35 inches, the rate being 114 lbs/inches.

The front springs by the way have different rates to suit the different weights on each side. They are both $7/16^{ths}$ wire diameter and 2 $9/16^{ths}$ mean diameter (OD 3 inches). The difference in rate is obtained by using $15\frac{1}{2}$ working coils on the offside and $13\frac{1}{2}$ on the nearside.

The offside rate is 197 lbs/inches. The nearside rate 225 lbs/inches. These are spring rates and not suspension rates, of course.

As a matter of interest I see that the car currently holds the following Course records –

Blandford Hill Climb	30.15 secs.
Gosport Speed Trials	12.69 secs.
Boreham Speed Trials	25.12 secs.

I have discovered a chart of speed in miles an hour on all the gears with the present 32 tooth transfer wheel and with 600.X 16 racing Dunlops fitted, which I am asking my Secretary to type out for you in full as it is a very useful ready reference. This chart takes the revs up to 5,500 but don't you dare! I normally limit myself to 4,900 and I think that 4,800 is actually safer.

I hope that you will be successful in getting the car back into action soon and that you have a lot of fun with it. Don't hesitate to call on me for any help that I can give at any time.

Yours sincerely,

Appendix VI

Awards and Honors

Some of the major citations awarded to Bill Milliken in his career.

SCCA Hall of Fame, 2004: For contribution to SCCA's 60th Anniversary Celebration and Historical Perspective.

GM Powered Spirit Award, 2002: For employing energy, creativity and spirit in pursuing significant automotive innovation. (Given for the MX-1 camber car at the 2002 Goodwood Festival of Speed).

Niagara Aerospace Museum Aviation Hall of Fame, 2000: For contributions to the aeronautical sciences.

SAE Edward N. Cole Award, 1985: For automotive engineering innovation. For outstanding creativity and achievement in the field of automotive engineering.

IME Starley Premium Award, 1983: For presentation of the Moment Method at the Conference on Road Vehicle Handling.

SAE Fellow, named 1980: For exceptional professional distinction by reason of outstanding and extraordinary qualification, experience and sustained accomplishment in automotive engineering.

Laura Taber Barbour Air Safety Award, 1967: For contribution to the development of concepts for the variable stability of the airplane.

MIT Boit Essay Awards, 1933, 1934: For essays on historical scientific subjects.

W. E. Boeing Scholarship Award (2nd place), 1932: For essay "Design in Relation to Speed of Aircraft."

Youth's Companion Y. C. Lab 49th Weekly Award, 1926: For Exelsior-powered three-wheeler.

Youth's Companion Y. C. Lab Special Award, 1928: For Aero-Triple-Cycle.

Editor's Note

Among the greatest pleasures of my career as an automobile historian has been collaborating on their personal stories with the people who have made that history. I am a Method editor, a vestige of college acting days. Trying to "inhabit" the person I'm working with makes for a better edit, and it's so much more rewarding. Years ago I began as Ralph Mulford, thundering the disintegrating dirt tracks in the 24-hour race marathons of pre–World War I America. This was followed at the close of the twenties by engineering the front wheel drive Ruxton as William Muller and designing the moderne body of the Marmon Sixteen as W. Dorwin Teague. As René Dreyfus in the thirties, I drove Bugatti, Alfa and Delahaye race cars and was National Champion of France. As Howard "Dutch" Darrin, I was the polo-playing, let's-make-merry designer who created dynamic automobile coachwork in Paris and in Hollywood. There have been many others.

I mention all this because I can say unequivocally that never have I enjoyed being anyone more than Bill Milliken. Beginning with the adolescent who was equal parts Peter Pan and Dennis the Menace, and who really hasn't changed much more than eight decades later, Bill's life has been one of unrelenting adventure, together with risk and innovation, as the subtitle to this book so aptly states. To Bill, risk was part of the adventure, with innovation as the logical successor.

There was a lot to learn editing the estimable Mr. Milliken. I'm better at math now, can fathom a bit of physics, and understand vehicle dynamics. Bill gave me my first chance to fly an airplane. I wind tunneled, experienced tail stall, and tested all sorts of marvelous aircraft. I had raced before, of course, but never in a four–wheel-drive Miller nor a Dynaflow Bug, nor had I spun out so dramatically at a certain corner in Watkins Glen. Nowadays I find camber really sexy. It's been a super ride.

–Beverly Rae Kimes

Index

A

Academy High School, *16*
active camber/active suspension
    active camber system (Corvette), 606–607
    active suspension Corvette prototype, 598
    GM "C" car development, 598, *600*
    Lotus Active Suspension, MRA promotion of,
      597, 598–599
    Lotus Eclat experimental suspension system,
      596–598
    Lotus Excel experimental suspension system, *599*
    Mercedes-Benz F-400 Carving, 520, 522, 524–
      525, *525,* 624
    MRA/Moog active-camber Corvette, 606–607
    production vehicles, active suspension in, 600–
      601
    See also MX-1 *for alternative approach*
Adams, John, 313
aerodynamics. *See* Dutch roll; dynamic stability and
    control project (C-W); MIT course curricula;
    stability *(various);* stall, dynamics of; wind
    tunnels. *See also specific aircraft*
Agatha, 36, *37*
Air Force/Cornell On-Road Tire Tester, *538,* 538–
    539, 570–571, *572*
airplanes, home-built. *See* Brown, Ralph; gliders;
    M-1 aircraft
airplanes, military and commercial. *See specific
    aircraft*
Allard, Sydney, 468, 470, *470*
Allen, Edmund T. (Eddie)
    biographical sketch of, 170, 176, 279
    offer letter to WFM, *171*
    and Boeing Stratoliner, *179,* 183–186, 188–190
    Boeing Clipper flight tests, 195–196, *203*
    B-17 flight tests, 212, *221,* 229
    Avro Lancaster evaluation, 234, 243
    and WFM transcontinental flight, 252, *264,*
      265–266
    B-29 taxi runs and hop tests, 280–281
    conflict with Al Reed (re B-29), 284–285, 289,
      292
    WFM removed from B-29 flight tests, 285, *297*
    fatal B-29 crash, 288–289, *290, 291,* 292
    WFM memorial to, 292
Alter, Dewey, 402, 467
Amundsen, Roald, 54
Anderson, Harvey, 329
Anthony Best K & N Machine, 589, *589*
Arendt, Rudi, 560
Argetsinger, Cameron
    biographical sketch of, 385
    at Bridgehampton (1950), 435
    at Indianapolis, 383, *384*
    and International Motor Racing Research Center,
      408
    and SCCA Great Controversy, 464
    at Sebring (1960), 481
    in Silverstone Healey (1950), *638*
    with Type 35A Bugatti, *416, 427*
    at Watkins Glen
      1948, 383–385, *395, 402*
      1949, 415
      1950, 437, 438, 451, *452*
      Watkins Glen permanent circuit, 465
Arnold, Gen. Henry (Hap), 113
Ascani, Fred, 320
Aubrecht, Dick, 599
Auriol, Jacqueline, *333*
autopilots
    advanced, for A-26 bomber, 325
    in B-25 frequency response tests, 316–319, *317–
      320,* 326
    and Bryan's equations of motion, 334
    early (Wiley Post), 337
    in F4U-5 variable stability program, 339
    WFM "Automatic pilot in flight test" proposal,
      351
    See also control augmentation
"average driver" study (CAL), 578–579
Averill, Lou, *246*
Averill, Rod, *93,* 95, *163*
Avion, Inc. *See* Northrop Avion flying wings
Avro Lancaster, 234, 243

B

B-25. *See* North American aircraft, B-25
B-29. *See* Boeing XB-29
B-26 Marauder, *335–336,* 340, 343–344, *344*
Babchek, Frank, 314, *376,* 382, 415, *427, 449, 483–484,* 526
Bajorek, Al, 526
Baker, Paul (at Chance Vought)
  Chief Engineer (Vought-Sikorsky), *153*
  Head of Flight Aerodynamics, *151–152,* 153–155, 157–159, 161
  and SB2U-1 flight test program, 155, 157–159, 161
  V-160 flaps and spoiler tests, 158–159, 161
  XOS2U-1 *Kingfisher* flight, tail stall tests, 158–161
Balchen, Bernt, 144, 145–146
Bangor
  Bangor and Aroostock steam train, 17
  See also Bangor, WFM flight to; transcontinental flight, F-22
Bangor, WFM flight to (1932)
  planning and departure, 134–136
  noseover at Augusta, 136–138
  WFM reconstruction and analysis, 138–139
Barris, William, 312–313
Bassett, Preston, *326*
Beal, John, 601, 603, *603*
Beilman, Jack, 315, *352*
Beisel, Rex, 152, 158
Bekker, M.G., 550
Bell, Larry, 333
Bellanca airplanes
  Green Flash, 81, *81*
  Roma, 63–65, *64, 65*
  Wright-Bellanca *Columbia,* 55–58, *56,* 65
Bennett, Floyd, 54, 56
Benton, Bud, *195, 196*
Bergensfjord, SS, 145, 146
Bernard 191 *Yellow Bird, 80,* 80–82
Berry, Jim, 467
Bertraud, Hill and Payne, 79, *79*
Besserdich, William, 378
Best, Tony, 589, *615,* 616, 625, *630*
bicycles (CAL studies)
  bicycle dynamics, 575–576
  bicycle/minibike safety, 579
Bidwell, Joe, 569, 578–579
Big Bug. *See* Bugatti Type 54 *(various)*
Bird, King, 559, *573,* 578

Blaine, Chuck
  Boeing high altitude testing, 219, 223, 222, *225, 229,* 231, 239
  B-29 transcontinental flight, 286
  fatal B-29 crash, 288
Blakemores, Jack and Cassa, 174
Boardman, George, 400
Boeing aircraft, early
  Model 247, 111
  Model 221 Monomail, *170, 175,* 176, 210
Boeing aircraft, WW II period. *See* specific aircraft (e.g., Boeing B-17)
Boeing Aircraft Company
  corporate culture, 177
  description of facility, 174–176, *175,* 194
  flight test difficulties and constraints, 181–182
  Flight Test section growth, 219–220, 222, *222*
  high altitude pressure chamber (*See* high altitude research)
  high speed subsonic tunnel, 113
  WFM at
    job offer and acceptance, 170, *171*
    trip to Seattle, 173–174
    meetings with Allen, Reed and Cook, 176–177
    settling in at Seattle, 180–181
    Christmas trip to Maine, 236–237
    lecture on Langley towing tank tests, 200, *200*
    tonsillectomy, 227, 229
    Dumas' musketeers and the B-17, 237
    fatal B-29 crash, 288–292
    B-29 crash, WFM reaction to, 291–292, 301
    engagement to Elizabeth Philips, 301
    (*See also* transcontinental flight; *specific aircraft*)
Boeing B-17
  origins and model designations, 210, 212
  altitude limitations of (initial), 213
  B-17/B-29 development testing timeline, *219*
  bailout crew (horizontal stabilizer failure), *232*
  blind flight over Seattle, 225–227
  control forces/tab control on, 208
  engine oil cooler failures, 225–226
  first flights to 35,000 feet, 234
  flight crew development, growth, 219–220, 222
  flight test crew roster, 222
  in-flight photographs of, *213, 242*
  instrument panel, ca 1940, 223
  jammed control cable, 221
  low temperature problems, 223
  Model 299 (B-17 prototype), 210, *211,* 212
  oxygen safety, rules and caveats, 215–216, 218–219, 227, *228,* 229–230

pressure carburetor failure, 230–231

propeller pitch control failure, 224–225

test program accomplishments, summary of, 231–233

transcontinetal flight, planning for, 285–287

turbocharger overspeed failure, 223–224

WFM flight tests on, 209, *221*, 223–227, 229–231, 234

WFM pilot's handbook (B-17E), 234, 244–245

wind tunnel model (Model 299 prototype), 210, *211*

winter flying suits, *229*

Wright engines in, 212

See also high altitude research

Boeing Clipper (A-314)

compass calibration, *203*, 204

Dutch roll problem, 176, 194–195

instability, directional, 194–196

instability, longitudinal, 202–203

internal configuration, 193–194

Pan American Airways flight test, 204

sea wings on, 196–197, *196–197*, 199–200, *199–201*

takeoff, flight photographs, *204, 205*

taxiing, *192–193*

towing tests, *198*, 199–200, *200–201*

triple-fin configuration, origin of, 194–196, *196*

WFM accolade for, 193, 206

WFM photographs with, *194–196*

wind tunnel models, 197, *197*

Wright Cyclone engines, 193–194

See also Boeing XPBB-1 patrol flying boat

Boeing Model 299 (B-17 prototype), 210, *211*, 212

Boeing School of Aeronautics

WFM at, 106–107, *106–108*

Boeing Stratoliner (Boeing 307)

CAA certification, 186–189, *187*

cabin explosive decompression, 178, 185–186, 188

carburetor icing, 190

flight tests, 178–183

forward section mockup, 181

fuel dump test, *186*, 188–189

fuselage fabrication, *168–169*

lost in the Cascades, 183–186

original configuration, *178*

pitot tube freeze up, danger from, 183–185

propeller failure, *184*

prototype crash, 178

stall-spin characteristics, 178–180, *179*, 190

"swiveling pitot" on, 182–183

TWA blind landing test, 189–190

wind tunnel models, *179, 180*

wing with plain flap deflected, *183*

Boeing XB-29

historical note and origins of, 275

first impressions, premonition (WFM), 272, 274

strategic bombing, origins of, 274–275

B-29/B-17 development testing timeline, 219

contrast with B-17, B-24, 276–277

engineering/manufacturing organization for, 275–276

design specifications and features, 277–278

in-flight photographs, *272–274, 280, 283*

side view, *277*

cockpit layout, *278*

Wright 3350 engine, problems with, 277, 283–284, 287–290, 292

initial flight plan, constraints and caveats for, 279–280

taxi runs and hop tests, 279–281, *293–296*

first flight test, 281–283

transcontinental flight, planning for, 285–287

crossed aileron cables on, 290

WFM demotion by Allen, 285, *287, 297*

fatal crash of, 288–290, *290*

WFM affidavit re B-29 crew composition, *298*

Eddie Allen, WFM memorial to, 292

See also Allen, Edmund T. (Eddie)

Boeing XPBB-1 patrol flying boat, 205–206, *205–206*

bomb, trailing, 155

Bonnier, Jo, 465

Boothby, Dr. Walter, 213, 214, *214*, 237, 238, 239, 241

Borgeson, Griff, 613–614, *614*, 617

Bowdoin, schooner, 53–54

Boyd, Albert, 320

brake tramp (Bugatti Type 54), *448*, 448–449

Breck, Bernice, 8

Breeze, Vance, 322

Breuhaus, Waldemar O. (Walt)

personal, technical qualifications of, 328

A-26 dynamic response project, 325–326

B-25 dynamic stability project, 318–319, 325

assistant to WFM at CAL, 328

variable stability aircraft monograph, 338

Laura Tabor Barbour Air Safety Award, 338

head of CAL Flight Research, 343, 346–356

and longitudinal stability study, 340

with Miller FWD, *376*

at Watkins Glen, 404, 415, *427*

at Bridgehampton (1950), *432*

Bridgehampton
  1949
    MG on hay bales, 415
    Type 35A Bugatti at, 412–415, *414–415,*
      425– 426, 642, 647
  1950
    Type 54 Bugatti at, *429,* 430–435, *431–435,*
      448–449, 642, 647
  1996
    MIller FWD at, *613–614,* 613–615
Brown, Eddie, *241,* 250, 252, 282
Brown, Ralph, 72–74, *73*
Brubaker, Don, 384, 402, *402*
Bryan equations of motion
  at MIT (Koppen), *119*
  at CAL, 318, 328, *334*
Bugatti
  Type 35A
    early history of, 356
    front wheel camber on, 493–494, *494*
    WFM acquisition, first drive, *357,* 357–358
    at CAL, 358
    Pike's Peak race, modifications for, *354–355,*
      361–363, *363*
    and René Dreyfus, 358, *358*
    at Garthwaite Trophy weekend, *359*
    Buffalo to Albany winter run, 371–375, *372,*
      374–375
    at Indianapolis Time Trials, *384*
    WFM in, *384*
    at Watkins Glen (1948), *398–399, 403–405*
    cockpit, engine compartment of, *400–401*
    at CAL before Glen race (1948), *401*
    at Bridgehampton (1949), 412–415, *414–415,*
      425–426
    Cam Argetsinger with, *416, 427*
    WFM winter run to Albany, 371–375, *372,*
      374–375
    (*See also* Pike's Peak)
  Type 51
    at Palm Beach Shores (1950), *419,* 419–420
  Type 54 (Bridgehampton, 1950)
    handling characteristics, 428–429, 432–434
    carburetion, supercharging, 430–431
    cranking, impossibility of, 433
    description, characteristics of, 430
    dropped at Le Havre, 430, 435
    gearbox, gear ratios, 430–431
    photos of, *429, 431–435*
    sound of, 433
    transmission case crack, failure, 430, 435

WFM race description, 434–435
  (*See also* Bugatti, Type 54 (Dynaflow
    conversion))
  Type 54 (Dynaflow conversion)
    Cliff Muzzey at wheel, *450*
    cockpit layout, *443*
    completed car (group photo), *449*
    con rods, replacement of, 441–442
    change from friction to hydraulic shocks,
      448–449
    Dynaflow unit, discussions with Buick about,
      439–440
    Dynaflow installation, 442–444, *444–445*
    dynamometer tests, 446, *446*
    Phil Hill driving, *461*
    race preparations and necessary rework, 441
    starter installation, *442*
    stripped down chassis, *438–440*
    tramp, discussion and modification for, *448,*
      448–449
    transmission, search for, 438
    typical T&S readings, *450*
    weight and balance summary, *446,* 447
    (*See also* Giant's Despair Hill Climb (1951);
      Watkins Glen)
Bulbulian, Dr. Arthur, 213, *214*
Bull, Giff, 343
Bullard, Lyman, 154, 160
Bundorf, Tom, *553*
Burnelli biplane, *64*
Burr, Maurice "Mossy," *27,* 28, *30*
Butler, Don, 619, 621–622, *622–623*
Butler, E. Dean, *613–614,* 613–615, 617–619,
  622, *626, 631*
Butterball FWD
  originally Butterworth S.1, 468, 470, *470,* 472,
    474
  Butterworth letter re FWD design, 652–659
  in hanger at CAL, *471*
  Butterball rebuild, 474–475, *475–475, 482*
  transmission design, 472, *473,* 474
  front-end configuration, *473*
  races/hill climbs
    Edenvale Airport (Canada, 1955), 478–479
    Giant's Despair (1955), *480*
    Holland Hill Climb (1957), *485*
    Mt. Equinox (1956), *468–469*
    Pike's Peak (1953), *477,* 478
  Watkins Glen
    1952, 475–476, *475–477, 482*
    1955, 479, *484*

1956, 479–480, *484*

1957, *484*

spinout at Milliken's Corner (1955), 475–476, *477*

competition history (table), *482*

See also Butterworth, Archie; Steyr [tank] engine

Butterworth, Archie

four-cylinder flat engine design, 474

letter to WFM re FWD-AJB, 649–656

S.1 FWD car design, 470, 472–474, *473*

See also Butterball FWD; Steyr [tank] engine

Byrd, Lt. Cmdr. Richard E.

Arctic exploration, 53–54

transatlantic flight, *55,* 55–65, 58–59, 144

C

C-W Junior. *See* Curtiss-Wright Corporation

CAL. *See* Cornell Aeronautical Laboratory

Caldwell, Frank, 109

Calspan

origins of, 584

summary of accomplishments, 638–640

See also Cornell Aeronautical Laboratory (CAL); Milliken Research Associates (MRA)

camber, wheel

active-camber Corvette (MRA), 606–607

Bugatti Type 35A, front wheel camber on, 493–494, *494*

camber cars, aerodynamic downforce of, 525

competition camber rear suspension, *496,* 497

leaning vehicles (tilters), *496,* 496–497

technical discussion of, 494, 496–497

WFM camber car patent disclosure, *495*

See also MX-1

Campbell, Donald, 553

Campbell, G.F., 318

"Car of the Year panel," WFM on, 581, *581*

Cardenas, Bob, 320–321

carrier aircraft

size, performance requirements for, 156

See also Chance Vought aircraft

cars, home-built. *See* home-built vehicles

Case, Bill, *487*

Ceresole, Paul, 356, 400

Cerra, John, 526

Chamberlain, Clarence, 57, 60, 65, 67

Chance Vought Corporation

history and description of, 152–153

flight test instrumentation at, 154–155

Fairchild 24 (V-160) flap/spoiler tests, 158

Flight and Aerodynamics Group, *152,* 153–154, 168

"Horse Feather" flap/aileron development, 156–157, *158,* 159–160, 171

See also Sikorsky *(various)*

WFM at

interview and job offer, 151

Hartford, 151–152, 164

responsibilities and resources, 153–154

flight instrumentation, primitive quality of, 154–155

Mt. Holyoke, flight to, 164, *165*

SB2U-1, WFM flight test in, 155

and Curtiss-Wright Junior, *160,* 161–164, *165*

decision to leave Vought, 168–170

Chance Vought aircraft

XF4U-1 Corsair

genesis of, 164–165

aerodynamics, design problems, 165–166

in-flight photo of, *167*

XF4U-5 Corsair

control augmentation flight test program, 339

flight flutter test program, 322–324, *323–324*

SB2U-1 Vindicator

in-flight photo of, *154*

trailing bomb, adventures with, 155

WFM test flight in, 155

XSB2U-1 wind tunnel model, 142, *154*

XOS2U-1 Kingfisher

carrier version, *155*

float plane version, *156*

"horsefeather" flap and aileron on, 156–157, *158,* 159

initial flight, 158–159

Sikorsky wind tunnel test, 156–157

stability/tail stall problems, 157, 159–161

wing spoilers on, 157–158

Chaparral, Winchell/Hall, 494, 566–568, *567*

Chapman, Colin, 466, 481, 595

Chapman, Keith, *615, 630*

Chapman, Ralph, 15–16, 96

Chayne, Charles, 439, 443, 457

Chevrolet Vehicle Handling Facility. *See* MX-1

Child, Lloyd, 310, 316, *350*

Chilstron, Ken, 320

Chon, Choon, 607

Chrysler roll-damping study (MRA), 607

Cierva, Juan de la, 173

Clark, Dan, 553, 557, 599

Clark, V.E. (Clark Y wing section), 82, 84, 105

Close, Bill

and Butterball rebuild, *474,* 474–475
at SCCA meeting (1947), 358
at Watkins Glen (1955), 466, 481, *484*
Close, Virginia, 466, *487*
Clough, Harry and Alice, 123–124
Cobb, John, 369–371
Cobean, Sam and Ann, 384
Cochran, Jackie, 214, *215*
Cole, Tommy, 434, 437
Collier brothers
at Palm Beach Shores (1950), 418–419
at Watkins Glen (1948), 400, 404–405
Miles
at SCCA Contest Board meeting (1950), *638*
and SCCA Great Controversy, 464
Sam
and Big Bug Dynaflow conversion, 450
death of, 454–456, 463
Sam Collier Memorial Grand Prix (Sebring), 462
Commercial pilot's license, WFM, 312–313, *312–313*
Constitution, U.S. Frigate, 8
control augmentation
CAL projects, 337–339
See also autopilots; dynamic stability and control project (C-W); stability, variable
Cook, Bill
biographical sketch of, 177, *177*
in Boeing Clipper, *201*
and B-29 development, 274, 277
with WFM and Barbara in Seattle, 268, 270
Cooper, John, 467
Corkille, Capt. John, 212, 230–231
Cornell Aeronautical Laboratory (CAL)
Flight Research Department
formation, mission of, 324–325, 535
WFM heads Flight Research, 327–328, *328*
A-26 automatic tracking control project, 325–326
air-supported building collapse, 344
automatic pilots (*See* autopilots)
B-25 lateral frequency response tests, *320,* 326
B-26 variable stability study, *335, 336,* 340, 343–344, *344*
Dynamic Stability & Control paper (WFM), 340, 342–343, *346–349*
flight dynamics and equations of motion, 318, 328, *334*
Full Scale Division, *342,* 343
Furnas administration of, 324–328, 535, 583
group photo (ca. 1948–49), *345*
history, technical contributions of, 344–347, *345*

Irv Statler contributions to, 352
NACA Subcommittee on Stability and Control, 333, 335
Northrop N9MB flying wing stability studies, 335–336
P-80A Shooting Star flight dynamics study, *310–311,* 328–329, *329–330*
PT-26 stalled flight project, *331–332,* 331–333
Walter Diehl at, 333–334
WFM presentation to aircraft manufacturers, 333
WFM with Taylorcraft, *327*
Wind Tunnel Department at, 326–327
(*See also* Curtiss-Wright Corporation, Flight Research Department)
early vehicle dynamics projects
introduction to, 535–536
Air Force/Cornell On-Road Tire Tester, *538,* 538–539, 570–571, *572*
equations of motion, formulating, *537,* 537–538
initial GM research contract, 536–537
long range automotive stability and control research, 540–541, *541–544,* 545, *546–547,* 637
variable stability system (Buick), 545, *546–547*
Vehicle Dynamics Department - initial concept, 541
writing, presenting IME papers, *542–543,* 542–544
Vehicle Dynamics Department
introduction to, 544–545
automatic control systems, 553
car, aircraft parameter measurements, 551
Conference on Dynamics and Stability (SAE), *553*
GM Corvette presentation, *551*
GM directional stability and control research, 545, *546–547,* 547
GM research report, list of, 545
Goodyear thump and roughness study, 548
highway safety projects, 553
human factors studies, 551–552
"man-amplifier" mechanical exoskeleton, 552
Motions of Skidding Automobiles (WFM), *549,* 549–550
road surface/road mechanics, 552–553
rough-water seaplane control augmentation, 550
safety conference participants (CAL), *552*
skid tester (Portland Cement Company), 547–584, *548*
stability and control of other vehicles, 550–551

Transportation Research Division
 formation, mission, structure, 557–558
 WFM transfer to, 557–558
 Antares Indy car, *568*
 Chaparral, Winchell/Hall, 494, 566–568, *567*
 Corvair litigation defense, 563–564
 crash research at, 560–561
 Highway Vehicle Object Simulation Model
   (HVOSM), 560–561, *561*
 Moment Method, formulating, 568–570,
   569–570
 Spiral Jump (Houston Astrodome), *556–557,*
   561–564, *562*
 Vehicle Experimental Research Facility (VERF),
   559, 559–560
Vehicle Research Department
 "average driver" study, 578–579
 DK-4 computer program, 570
 "g-g" diagram development, 574–575
 "gangster getaway" (NY State Police Training
   Academy), 576–577
 GM Saginaw steering simulation, 579
 minibike/bicycle safety study, 579
 MTS Flat-Trac Roadway Simulator, 569, *571,*
   573
 NHSTA handling standards study, 579–581
 Niagara raft ride, *577,* 577–578
 powered monocycle, 576
 tandem propeller submarine, 576
 WFM at (photos), *556–558, 561–562, 567–*
   568, 577, 581
 WFM highway safety paper, 580
 WFM on MT's "Car of the Year" panel, 581, *581*
 WFM brief retrospective, 581
 (*See also* GM Automotive Stability and Control
   project; Safety; tires)
the end of an era
 Cornell University dismantles CAL, 583–584
 Calspan formed, later sold, 584
 WFM retires (1976), 584
 summary of accomplishments, 635–637
 (*See also* Calspan)
Cornett, Denny, 404, 619
Corsair, Chance Vought. *See* Chance Vought aircraft
Corvair litigation defense, 563–564
Corvette
 active-camber system (MRA), 606–607
 active suspension in, 598, 600
 presentation to CAL, *551*
 SS racing team, WFM timing/scoring for, 480–481
crash research (CAL), 560–561

Cridland, Dorothy, 553
Cripps, Sir Stafford, 599
Critofen, Dick, 526
Crosby, Harry, 303, 305–306
Cunningham, Briggs
 at Palm Beach Shores (1950), 419
 at Watkins Glen (1948), 404, 408
Currie, Malcolm, 466
Curtiss, Walt, 588, *591*
Curtiss Aircraft Company
 Curtiss-Bleeker helicopter, 67, *68*
 Curtiss JN-4 (Jenny), 66, *72*
 Garden City facility, *66*
 wind tunnel at, 66, *67*
Curtiss-Wright Corporation
 aircraft
   Junior, *160,* 161–164, *165*
   P-40, 316, *350*
   SB2C Helldiver, 310, 317, 321–322, *322*
 Flight Research Department
   formation of, 310, 535
   WFM joins, 310, 312
   WFM assistant head, Flight Research
   Department, 314
   staffing of, 314–316, *315*
   Ira Ross at, 314, *314*
   B-25 longitudinal frequency response tests,
     316–319, *317–320*
   Dynamic Stability and Control paper, WFM,
     318, *319*
   flight dynamics project, 316–318
   F4U-5 Corsair flutter program, 322–324,
     322–324
   Glen Edwards, WFM commentary on, 321
   P-40, WFM check flight in, 316, *350*
   proposed Mt. Everest flight, 319
   SB2-C Helldiver stability project, 321–322, *322*
   test pilots, reminiscences about, 319–321
   WFM commercial pilot's license, 312–313,
     312–313
   WFM divorce, 314
   becomes Cornell Aeronautical Laboratory,
     324–325
   (*See also* Cornell Aeronautical Laboratory (CAL);
     dynamic stability and control project (C-W))
Cutter, Meryl, 101

D

Dalton, George, 526
Dansfield, Bob, 288

Davidson, Ken, 554

Davis, Jim, *577,* 578

Davis, S.C.H. "Sammy," 468

Day, Charles Healey, 66

Defechereux, Philippe, 404, 437

DeHavilland Moth, 250, *251*

Deleys, Norm, 561

dell'Amico, Fred, 569, *570,* 580

Denton, Everett, *233*

Dickerman, Fred, 152, 164

Diehl, Walter S., 333–334

Dole Derby (California to Hawaii), 58

Doolittle, Jimmy, 142, 167

Douglas DC-2, DC-3, 111

Douhet, Gen. Guilo, 274

Draper, Charles Stark "Doc," 147–148

Dreyfus, René, 358, *358*

Duesenberg Company letters from, *29,* 29–30

Dumont, Pierre, 429

Duryea, George, 526, 572

Dutch roll
    in Boeing Clipper, 176, 194–195
    in carrier fighter aircraft (F4U-5 tests), 338, 339
    in F4U-5 project, 339
    in M-1 aircraft, 99
    stability analysis of (for fighter aircraft), 348, 350
    in XP-79 flying wing, 305

Duvall, John, 467

Dye, Edward, 557

dynamic stability and control project (C-W)
    Wright Field support of, 316
    B-25 as test plane, 316–319, *317–320*
    longitudinal motion, first flight tests of, 317–319, *318*
    Statler research on high speed unsteady flow, 352
    WFM research papers
        Dynamic Stability & Control (RAS-IAS), 340, 342–343, *346–349*
        dynamic stability (IAS meeting), 318, *319*
    See also autopilots; control augmentation; stability, variable

E

Earhart, Ameila, 61, *61*

Earl, Harley, 481

early aircraft, specifications for, *77*

Eastern Steamship Lines, WFM employment at, 60–61

Easton, Archie, 378

Edenvale Airport (Canada)

Miller FWD at (1950), 470–471

Butterball FWD at (1955), 478–479, 648

Edighoffer, Earl, 315

Edwards, Glen
    B-25 longitudinal frequency response project, *317,* 317–319, *320*
    death of (in YB-49), *308,* 321, 335

Eichorn, John, 314, 362, 382, *401,* 412

Ellman, Joe, 526

engines, aircraft
    R-1820 (on B-17), 212
    R-2600 (on Boeing Clipper), 194, *194*
    R-3350, problems with (B-29), 277, 283–284, 287–290, 292
    Wright Gipsy, *248,* 256, 260

equations of motion. *See* Bryan equations of motion

Equestrian interlude, WFM, 611

Erway, A.D., 384, 402

Evans, Cap, 588

Ewers, Gerry, 526

Excelsior engines
    Excelsior-twin w/ direct drive propeller, *44, 74*
    See also home-built vehicles

Excelsior motorcycle. *See* motorcycles

F

Fabian, Jack, *416, 484,* 557

Faboni, Nick, 384

Fairchild aircraft
    F-22 (flight to Bangor), *132–133,* 134–135, *135, 138*
    F-22 (transcontinental flight), *246–253,* 247, 249–250, *262, 264–266*
    F-24 (V-160) flap/spoiler test bed, 158
    PT-26 stalled flight project, *331–332,* 331–333

Fangio, Juan-Manuel, 481, 564

Felton, George, 400, 404

Ferguson, Earl, 195

FIA (Fédération Internationale de l'Automobile)
    and Watkins Glen races, 437–438, 462, 464–465

Fina, Perry, 420

fires and major conflagrations (Old Town), 40–41

Fitch, John, 408, 448, 463, 481, *551–552,* 553, 573, 619

Flax, Al, *551*

flight data analysis
    early interest in, 111
    See also simulators, flight; stability *(various)*; stall, dynamics of

Flivver Plane (Ford), 117
Flying Banana, 404, *412–413*
flying wing aircraft. *See* Northrop Avion flying wings
Fokker, Anthony, 67–68
Fokker, "Wind Tunnel" Tony (nephew), 156–157, 171
Fokker aircraft
  fighter (WW I), 120
  single-engine *(Old Glory)*, *79,* 79–80
  tri-motor
    America (Byrd), *55,* 58, *61*
    Bird of Paradise, 58
    at Fokker factory, 68
    Friendship (Earhart), *61*
    Southern Cross, 59
Fonck, René, *54,* 55, 63
Fonda, Al, *496,* 496–497, 550–551, 574
Forbes, Danny, 321
Ford, Daniel, 318–319
Four wheel drive. *See* Butterball FWD; Four Wheel Drive Company; Miller FWD; Mt. Equinox Hill Climb; Pike's Peak, FWD Miller at (1948)
Four Wheel Drive Company
  history of, 378–379
  WFM letters to re racing Miller FWD, *392*
  agrees to purchase Butterball, 470
  lease agreement with WFM, *394*
  letters to WFM re Miller FWD, *378, 393*
  WFM letter to re Mt. Equinox Hill Climb, 420–424
  See also MIller FWD
Fraser, Jim, 222, 234, *235*
Frey, Bill, 314, *315,* 362, 382, *449,* 526
Friel, Walt "Madman," 364, *365,* 366
Furnas, C.C.
  conflict with Norton Moore, 310
  at Curtiss-Wright Research Laboratory, 310, 312, 314, 316
  at Cornell Aeronautical Laboratory (CAL), 324, 326–328, 332, *336,* 344
  and race car prep at CAL, 382
  leaves CAL, 557

G

g-Analyst , 616, 631
g-forces, parachute opening, 267
g-g diagram development, 574–575
GALCIT (Guggenheim Aeronautics Laboratory at Caltech, 111

Galliano, Chick, 561–563
"gangster getaway" (NY State Police Training Academy), 576–577
Gardner, Goldie, 553
Garsides, Joe, 134, 162
Garthwaite, Al (Garthwaite Trophy), 358–359
Gates, Don, *568*
Gee, Russ, 599
General Motors
  Corvair litigation defense, 563–564
  Corvette presentation (CAL), *551*
  directional stability and control research, 545, *546,* 547, *547*
  early research support by, 536–537
  GM research report list (CAL), 545
  long-range automotive stability and control program, 540–541, *541–544*
  Saginaw steering simulation project, 579
  See also Winchell, Frank
Gerstner, Ron, 526
Gerstung, Wally, 526
Giant's Despair Hill Climb
  1951
    anthracite sculpture, loss of, 460
    Big Bug at, 448, *458*
    course description, history, 457, 459–460
    fuel blend for, 457–458
    speeding ticket, 460–461
    WFM race description, 460
    (*See also* Holland Hill Climb; Mt. Equinox Hill Climb)
  1956
    Butterball at, 479, 482
Gieseke, Glen, 364, 366
Gifford, Len, 314, *449*
Gillespie, Bob (Milliken's Corner painting), *411*
Glemming, Dave, 588, *589–590,* 590–591
gliders
  early WFM designs (1924), 33–34
  MX-334 flying wing test vehicle, 303
Gluhareff, Mike, 130, 172
Godfrey, Cecil, *47,* 47–48
Goebel, Art, 63
Goett, Harry, *326*
Golden Age of the American Racing Car (Borgeson), 613, 614, 617
Goldschmidt, Erwin, 438, 455–456, *457,* 463–464
Goodwood
  1997
    Miller FWD at, *610–611,* 615–617, *615–619*
  2002

MX-1 at (photos), 626–630
(*See also* MX-1)
Goodyear thump and roughness study (CAL), 548
Goosen, Leo, 471
Gough, Eric, 553
Graham, Dunston, 339, *416,* 435
Grassel Fiberglass Boats, 526
Gray, Braley, 36, 47, 75
Gray, Capt. Harold, 204
Gray, Sam, 74, *75*
Great Northern Railway, 7–8
Green, Bill, 465
Green, Bob, 526
Green Archer, 42–43
Greene, Jim, 560
Grier, Bob, 438
Griswold, Frank, *409, 410*
Griswold, Roger, 156–157
Grosjean, Leon, 384
Grumman, Leroy, 333
Grylls, Harry, 603–604
Guggenheim Aeronautical Laboratory. *See* MIT
Gurney, Dan, 465
Gusakov, Ignaty, 526

H

Haldeman, George, 183, 185–190, 266
Hall, Jim, 566–567, *566–567*
Hammond, George, 389
handling
  aircraft
    aircraft handling qualities rating scale, 340, *341*
    (*See also* Dutch Roll; stability, aircraft; stall,
      dynamics of)
  automobiles
    desirable handling qualities, list of, 646
    handling experiences/critical incidents (various
      races), 646–648
    (*See also* Milliken Research Associates (MRA);
      MX-1; stability, vehicular (CAL))
Harmon, Col. Jake, 290
Hartz, Harry, *365,* 366, 378
Haselton, Ted, 550, 576
Hawker, Harry, 109
Hawker Hornbill, 120–123
Haynes, Bill, 554
Heinz, Rust, 404, *410*
Helck, Peter, 415, 467
Helen Hunt Junior High School, 19, *22,* 42, 47,
  72, 77–78

helicopters
  Curtiss-Bleeker helicopter, 67, *68*
  de la Cierva rotor head design, 173
  prototype Sikorsky helicopter, *172*
  Sikorsky design innovations, 172–173
Helldiver (Curtiss-Wright SB2C), 310, 317, 321–
  322, *322*
Henderson, Phil, 621, *623*
Henderson-Heath aircraft engine, 87–88, *87–88*
Herndon, Hugh Jr., 59, *60*
high altitude research
  aeroembolism, 215, 233
  B-17/B-29 development testing timeline, 219
  bailout oxygen equipment, 1940, 215 *218, 233*
  BLB oxygen masks, descriptions of, 213–214, 233
  Boeing Stratochamber, 220, *224, 226, 237*–240
  high altitude flight crew development, 219–220
  Mayo Clinic pressure chamber, 213–215
  Mt. Everest equivalence, 217, 234, 239
  oxygen
    as hangover cure, *214*
    oxygen deprivation, effect of, 215-216 *216,*
      229-230, 234
    oxygen masks, WFM wearing, *209, 218, 225–*
      226, 229–230
    safety rules and caveats, 215–216, 218–219,
      227, *228,* 229–230
  parachute jump (Lovelace), 222, 234–236, *235*
  pressure suit development, 237–242
  summary of accomplishments, 231–233
  See also Boeing B-17
Highway Vehicle Object Simulation Model
  (HVOSM), 560–561, *561*
Hill, Graham, 467
Hill, James J., 7
Hill, Ken, 404, *412–413*
Hill, Phil, *461,* 581, *581*
hill climbs. *See* Giants' Despair Hill Climb;
  Goodwood; Holland Hill Climb; Mt. Equinox
  Hill Climb; Pike's Peak
Himalayas, survey of, 319
Himmelsbach, Jim, 613, 619, 621, *624, 625*
Hinds, Vince, 352
Hinkler, Burt, 249–250, 251
Hirtreiter, Walt, 315, 451
Hodkin, Richard, 526
Holland Hill Climb (1957), *485*
Hollings, John, 553–554
home-built airplanes
  Milliken M-1 (*See* M-1 aircraft)
  Ralph Brown airplane, 72–74, *73*

home-built vehicles, WFM
  first push car, *28*
  No. 1 Miller (push car), *30–32,* 30–33
  Duesenberg No. 4 (push car), *27–28,* 28–29
  light vehicle, staged accident with, 30, *30*
  bicycle (with Shaw engine), 34
  No. 1 Miller (with Shaw engine), 34
  Excelsior-powered 3-wheeler (1926), 38–39, *38–40*
  Excelsior-powered Ski Mobile, 43–44, *43–44*
  Aero-Triple-Cycle No. 2, 48, *48–49*
  vehicle designs, list of (1921-1934), 49–50
  four-wheel cyclecar, 47
  See also gliders; home-built airplanes; motorcycles
Hoover, Bob, 320
Hopkins, Tex, 467
"Horsefeather" flap and aileron, 156–157, *158,*
    159–160, 171
Hospers, Jack, 159
Hughes, Howard, 261, 285
Hunsaker, Jerome, 105, 109, *326*
Hunt, George, 7
Hunt and Milliken Co., 7, *8*
Huntoon, George G., 418
Hutchinson, Charles (Chuck), *484,* 554
Hyde, Verne, 225–227
hydrostabilizers (on Boeing Clipper), 196–197,
    196–197, 199–200, *199–201*

I

IAS (Institute of Aeronautical Sciences)
  WFM research papers to (*See* research papers, WFM)
Indian Island Reservation, ferry, 15–17, *17*
Infanti, Nello, 343
Innocenti, Willie, 246, *253*
Institute of Aeronautical Sciences, WFM at, 468

J

Jaworski, Casey, 314–315, *315, 320,* 344, *485,* 526
Johns, Martin, 589
Johnson, Amy, 250, *251,* 257, 265–266
Jones, Ralph, 526
Jordan Lumber Company, 74–74
Junior, Curtiss-Wright. *See* Curtiss-Wright
    Corporation

K

Kamm, S.I.E. (Wunibald), 554
Kase, Paul, *317*

Kauffman, William (Bill), 338
Kayten, Jerry, 338
Kelly, Pat, 320
Kelsey, Lt. Ben, 142
Kidd, Ed, 558–559
Kidder, R.C., 318
Kimball, Dave, 619, 621, *623*
Kimes, Beverly Rae (Editor's Note), 658
Kingfisher, Chance Vought. *See* Chance Vought
    aircraft
Kingford-Smith, Charles E., 58–59, *60*
Knotts, Lewis, 346
Koegler, Dick, *484*
Koppen, Otto
  biographical sketch, 117–118, *117–118,* 120
  equations of motion tutorial, 119
  Hornbill stability analysis, 121–123
  Pratt & Whitney transport design, 143
  and XOS2U-1 stability analysis, 159
Ksayian, Haig, 404, *406,* 407–408
Kulok, Larry, 438
Kunkel, Dennis, 526, 569, 578

L

Laitone, Ed, 318
Lamb, Jim, 361
Lamson, Bob, 222
Landsberg, Dr. Fritz, 404
Langer, Bill, *603*
Langley Aerodrome, 72
Langley Field, towing test facility at, 196–198
Larson, Herman, 379
Larson, Lief, 343
Laura Tabor Barbour Air Safety Award, 338
Lawrence, T.E., 25
leaning vehicle (Fonda), *496,* 496–497
Lee, Walter, 588
Leith, Sandy, *357, 400*
Levine, Charles, 56
Liebfeld, Sam, *317*
Lindbergh, Charles A.
  with mother, 1927, *57*
  Pan American survey flights, 59
  to Ryan Aircraft for NYP airplane, 56
  transatlantic flight, *52–53,* 57
Lockheed aircraft
  Altair *Lady Southern Cross, 60*
  P-80A Shooting Star (F-80 predecessor), *310–*
    311, 328–329, *329–330*
  Vega *Yankee Doodle,* 63, *63*

locomotives, lateral instability of, 8–9

logging (on Penobscot River), 12–13, *13*

L'Oiseau Blanc (Levasseur biplane), 55

Long Range Flight Design (WFM), 126–127, *126–127*

Longfellow, Stevens, 9

longitudinal instability. *See* stability, aircraft

Lord, Francis, 19

Lotti, Armand, 80–82

Lotus Engineering
  initial contact with MRA, 595–596
  Eclat active suspension development, 596–598, *599*
  Excel experimental suspension system, *599*
  Lotus Active Suspension, MRA promotion of, *597*, 598–599
  Moog-Lotus joint venture, 599–600

Lovelace, Randolph, 213–215, 222, *235*, 235–236, *237*, 238, 241

Ludvigsen, Karl, *479*, *581*

Luplow, Ken, 213, *232*

Lytle, Charles, 402, *427*, 466–467, 480, *484*

M

M-1 aircraft
  design and construction
    introduction to, 70, 72
    completion: painting and assembly, 84
    conflict with schoolwork, 77–78
    design considerations, 76, 78–79
    engine mount, cowling, 88
    fuselage, details and views of, *70–71, 78,* 78–79, *82*
    Henderson-Heath aircraft engine, 87–88, *87–88*
    layout of, with modifications, *75*
    parental support for, 75–76, 78, 84
    preliminary design and preparation, 74–75
    Sam Gray's garage, 75, *76*
    stability, questions regarding, 88–89
    total cash outlay for, 76
    wing design and structure, 82, *82–84,* 84–85
  flight
    transporting M-1 to Pine Point, 90–92
    assembled aircraft, photos of, *91, 93, 97–100, 102*
    tent, configuration of, 90, *91, 93*
    severe storm at Pine Point, 92–94
    visitors, crew at Pine Point, *92–93*
    engine run-up before flight, *94, 98*
    first taxi run, *95*

noseover and broken propeller, 95–97, *96*
    first flight, *98,* 98–100, *100*
    stability problems with, 95–96, 99–100
    landing and noseover, 100, *100*
    newspaper coverage of flight, *99, 101*
    Abbie Milliken letter re flight, *102*
    restored M-1 at Owl's Head Museum, *102*

MacMillan, Donald, 53–54

Maeda, Teruo, 586

Maefs, Lee, *317, 352, 484*

Main, Reg, 553

Maitland and Hegenberger, 58

Mandale, Art, 314, *449,* 526

Marias Pass, discovery of, 7–8

Markham, John, 105, 141

Marsh Island, 11–12

Martin B-26 Marauder, *335–336,* 340-343, 344

Maserati V8R1 *(Poison Lil),* 404, *409,* 421–422, *422, 424,* 451, *471,* 475, *475*

Mayo clinic, 213– 214, 234, 238, 241

Mays, Raymond, 424

McCarthy, C.J., 158

McClellan, Dave, 598

McCluggage, Denise, 619

McGline, Dick, *209*

McHenry, Ray, 526, *560,* 560–561, *562,* 570

McKenzie, Wallter, *551*

McLaren, Bruce, 467

Mead, George, 143

Melton, James, 415, *427*

Mercedes-Benz F-400 Carving, 520, 522, 524–525, *525,* 624

Merkle, Larry, 611

Merrill, Elliott, 286

Metcalf, Walt, 526

Meulen, Jacob Vander, 272, 274

MG
  at Bridgehampton (1949), 415
  Cam Argetsinger in, 383
  MGTB, WFM acquisition of, 355–356, *356*
  O'Hare MG, *462,* 463, *464*
  at Palm Beach Shores (1950), 419
  Phil Milliken to Maine in, 356
  at Watkins Glen (1948), 403–404, *404*

Michael, Marvin, 222, *228, 232,* 264, *265,* 286

Michelson, Nils, 384, 402, 415, *427,* 453, *638*

Mikuma (Japanese cruiser), 155

Miller, Bill, 90, *92,* 95, 99, *100,* 101

Miller, Charlotte and Shirley, 90

Miller, Harry, 378–379, 472

Miller, Pat, 560

Miller, Ray ("Shorty"), 314, 343, *352*, 362, 382, 399, *408*, 526
Miller Club Meet, 619, 621, *622*
Miller FWD
  description and technical details
    before modifications, 379–380
    at CAL Flight Research, *377, 380, 471*
    checking understeer, *381*
    final drive and rear suspension, *382*
    forward cg, test with, *381*
    gear ratio chart, *383*
    gearbox, straight-cut, *382*
    handling (as received), 380–381
    The Last Great Miller (Borgeson), 617
    Maserati V8R1, comparison with, *422*
    Road & Track "Salon" feature, 619, *623*
    transmission and transfer case, *383,* 390, 620
  races
    Bridgehampton (1996), *613–614,* 613–615
    Edenvale Airport (Canada, 1950), 470–471
    Goodwood (1997), *610–611,* 615–617, *615–617, 619, 631*
    Indianapolis, configuration at (1932), *379*
    Miller Club Meet (1999), 619, 621, *622*
    Mt. Equinox Hill Climb (1950), *420,* 420–424
    Mt. Equinox Hill Climb (1952), 471 *471*
    Pike's Peak (1948) (*See* Pike's Peak)
    Watkins Glen (1949), *416–418*
  See also Four Wheel Drive Company
Milligan, Jay (J.M. Productions), 561–563, *562*
Millikan, Clark B., 111
Millikan, G.A., 240
Milliken, Abbie (mother)
  courtship, marriage, 4–5
  education and temperament, 4–5
  illness, pregnancy and childbirth, 5
  letter to Bill re M-1 flight, *102*
  marital difficulties, 10–11
  photographs of, *4–6*
  support of M-1 project, 84
  death of, 4
Milliken, Barbara (wife)
  at Bridgehampton (1950), 435
  at Goodwood (2002), *627*
  at Mt. Equinox (1952), *471*
  at Sebring, *487, 489*
  with WFM and Doug, *582–583*
  with WFM in Seattle, 268, 270
Milliken, Bill
  childhood and youth (*See* Milliken, Bill (early years) *below*)

education (*See* MIT (Massachusetts Institute of Technology))
employment (*See specific companies*)
equestrian interlude, 611
honors and awards, 657
racing (*See* racing, automobile; specific vehicles, race venues)
research papers (*See* research papers, WFM)
Ultralight adventures, 611–613, *612*
vehicle dynamics (*See* Cornell Aeronautical Laboratory (CAL); Milliken Research Associates (MRA))
epilogue: a look back, 632–633
Milliken, Bill (early years)
  Agatha, 36, *37*
  ballroom dancing, 21, 77–78
  Bellanca, high school oration on, 78
  childhood illnesses, 11
  with cousin Frank, *26, 38*
  Eastern Steamship Lines, job at, 60–61
  family conflicts, 10–11
  The Green Archer, 42–43
  hitchhiking to Long Island, 61–62
  Hunt & Milliken, work at, 17
  Lindbergh flight, emotional impact of, 53
  Milliken home (Old Town), *6,* 9–10, *11*
  upperclassmen, hazing by, 41
  WFM photo ca. 1924, *72*
  winter sports, 18–19
  YMCA summer camp, 31–32
  See also specific subjects (*e.g.,* home-built vehicles; M-1 aircraft; Old Town, Maine)
Milliken, Cooper (brother)
  architectural career of, 11
  flight with WFM in *Junior,* 162–163, *163*
  at Pine Point, *92*
Milliken, Doug (son)
  bicycle studies
    bicycle/minibike safety, 579
    human-powered record attempt, 621
  at Goodwood (2002), *627*
  at MRA, *582,* 584, *584,* 585, 590, 592, *593, 603,* 604–607
  and MX-1, 501, *501,* 503, 512–513, 515–517, 519, 526
  with WFM at Watkins Glen
    1958, *485*
    1998, *621*
    1959 trip to (in XK-120), 481
Milliken, Hugh (ancestor), 3
Milliken, Peter (son)

at MRA, 584, *584,* 585, 587–588, 592, *593–594,*
595, 607
and MX-1, 501, *501*
Milliken, "Phil" (wife). *See* Phillips, Elizabeth
Milliken, William F., Sr. (father)
western experiences of, 3–6, *4–6*
in Maine, ca. 1920, *4*
with infant Bill, *7*
Hunt and Milliken, 7, *8*
wild locomotive ride of, 8–9
marital difficulties of, 10–11
at Pine Point, *92*
reaction to WFM winning Boeing scholarship,
106
Milliken Research Associates (MRA)
formation, staffing of, 584–585, 588
books, list of, 587–588
categories of work, 586
client research projects
active-camber Corvette, 606–607
Chrysler, 607
Goodyear, *588,* 588–591, *590–591*
Lotus active suspension, 595–598, *597, 599*
Moog vehicles (*See* Moog, Inc.)
Nissan trim control sensitivity study, 591–592
Rolls-Royce *Silver Shadow* evaluation, 603–606
Doug Milliken at, *584*
educational lectures and workshops, 586
Lotus active suspension, MRA promotion of, *597,*
598–599
MRA logo, *585*
MRA research projects
computer programs, summary of, 586–587
"g-g" Diagram, 586
lap time simulation, 585
Moment method (MMM), 585, 587, *590,*
601–603, *602–603,* 606
Vehicle Dynamic Simulation (VDS), 586
Peter Milliken at, *584*
retrospective summary, WFM, 607–608
Milliken's Corner (Watkins Glen)
Type 35A Bugatti spinout (1948), 406, *406–408,*
408, *411*
Butterball wipeout (1952), 475–476, *477*
Miller FWD at (1998), *620*
See also Butterball FWD; Watkins Glen (1948)
Mills, Tony, 526
MIT (Massachusetts Institute of Technology)
course curricula
16.00: force/moment coefficients, airfoils,
110–111

16.01: laminar & turbulent flow, drag,
cowlings, 111
16.62, 16.63: ten wind tunnel experiments,
113–114, 128–130
equations of motion (Koppen), 119
M43, M44: Theoretical Aerodynamics
(Rauscher), 114–116
facilities
7-1/2 foot wind tunnel, *112*
5 foot wind tunnel, 111, 113
Daniel Guggenheim Aeronautical Laboratory,
104–105, 109–110
GALCIT (Guggenheim Aeronautics Laboratory
at Caltech, 111
WFM at
initial interview with John Markham, 105
Boston residences, 108, 143
transfer to Mathematics Department, 108–109
social life, 123–125
position as wind tunnel assistant, 127, 141–142
Nancy Overton, 133–134
Bangor, flight to, 134–139
with torpedo plane model, *147*
graduation, 127
(*See also* Boeing School of Aeronautics)
Mizen, Neil, 526
Moment Method
at CAL, 568–570, *569, 570*
at MRA, 585, 587, *590,* 601–603, *602–603,*
606
monocycle, powered, 576
Montana Central Railroad, 3
Monza Grand Prix (1951), 468
Moog, Inc.
as CAL spinoff, 583
active-camber Corvette, 606–607
active suspension Corvette, 598
GM steering and control systems, 539, *546,* 553
Moog-Lotus joint venture, 599
Moog-Lotus systems, MRA promotion of, 600
Peter Milliken at, *584*
two-wheel inertia-stabilized vehicles, 592, 595
two-wheel outrigger machine, *593–594,* 595
WFM on Moog board, *596*
Moore, Norton, 111, 310
Moran, Bill, 526
Moss, Stirling, 327, 465, 466–467, 481, 576, 619
motorcycles
1914 Excelsior, 35–38, *36–38*
Indian Scout (1927), 44–45
Moulton, Alex, *616,* 625

Mt. Equinox Hill Climb
1950
FWD MIller at, *420*
course comparison w/ Pike's Peak, *421*
FWD Miller and Maserati compared, *422*
final results (tabulation), *424*
prominent hill climb records compared, *424*
WFM race description (to FWD Co.), 420–424
1952
FWD MIller at, 470, *471*
1956
Butterball FWD at, *468–469,* 471, *471*
Mt. Everest altitude equivalence, 217, 234, 239
Mt. Holyoke, WFM flight to, 164
MTS Systems Corporation
Flat-Trac Roadway Simulator, 569, *571,* 573
Mueller, Robert, 110, *118,* 146–147
Mummert, Charles and Harvey, 382
Muncey, Joe, 66, 382, 526
Murphy, Jimmy, 27, 35
Musser, Jim, 566, *566*
Muzzey, Cliff
and Bugatti Dynaflow conversion, 439, 442, 443, *445,* 448, *449–450*
at CAL Vehicle Dynamics Department, 541, 544
and GM variable steering system vehicle, 539–540
at Watkins Glen (FWD MIller, 1948), 417
MX-1
design and development
aerodynamic downforce of camber cars, 525
bulkhead and control layout, *532*
on Chevrolet Vehicle Handling Facility, *492–493*
contributors, list of, 526
design/build approach, 499–501
development test program, 512–520
Doug/Peter Milliken contributions to, 501
engineering design drawings, *527–532*
frontal area reduction/aerodynamic drag, *524,* 524–525
LeMans car, comparison with, 525, *525*
limit behavior, 523–524
normalized lateral force, plots of, *523*
street-legal configuration, *526*
technical specifications, 497–499
tires, discussion of, 520–522, 525
vs. Mercedes-Benz F-400 *Carving,* 520, 522, 524–525, *525,* 624
(*See also* camber, wheel)
at Goodwood (2002)
with Miller FWD, *610–611*

restoration of, *610,* 621–625, *623–624, 626*
tires, analysis of, 622–623, *625*
Zakira's Garage, 621–622, *623, 624, 626*
Festival of Speed, description of, 625–628
"g-Analyst" in, 631
limit behavior, 623, 630, *630*
race description, *627–628,* 628–629
at Winner's Circle, *629, 630*
MX-334. *See* Northrop Avion flying wings

N

NACA
NACA cowling, 111
Subcommittee on Stability and Control, 333, 335
Nader, Ralph, 557
Newell, Joe, 141, 143
Niagara raft ride (CAL), *577,* 577–578
North, Vince, 222, 286
North American aircraft
B-25
hairy landing in snow squall, 326
lateral frequency response tests, *320,* 326
longitudinal frequency response tests, 316–319, *317–319*
F-86 Sabre
non-linear yaw dampers on, 352, *353*
Northrop, Jack, 302–303, 305, 307
Northrop, WFM at
move to Northrop, 301–302
Jack Northrop, personality of, 305
WFM responsibilities at, 303–305
proposal to Douglas Aircraft re flight test contract, 308
termination from Northrop, 306, *306*
decision to return to Northeast, 308–309
See also Northrop Avion flying wings
Northrop Avion flying wings
Avion, Inc., WFM introduction to, 302
magnesium wing, design and construction, 305–306
MX-334 glider, tests of, 303–304
MX-334 (XP-79 plywood test vehicle), 303–304
N9M/N9MB, 303, *304,* 335–336
scale model wind tunnel tests, 305
stall behavior, 303–304, 306–307, 321
technical legacy of, 307–308
yaw dampers on, 338
XB-35, 303, 307, *307,* 335
XP-79, 302–304, *303,* 307, 334
XP-79 fatal crash, 305–306

YB-49, *300–301,* 303, 307–308, *308,* 335, 338
YB-49 fatal crash, 321
Novi FWD Special, *625*
Nutt, Arthur, 282

O

Ober, Shatswell, *110,* 110–111
Oddo, Carl, 314, *449, 484*
Odlum, Floyd, *215*
Offenhauser, Fred, 379, 472
Offenhauser Special, 364, 390
O'Hare, Frank, *462,* 463, *464*
Old Orchard Beach
  and Milliken M-1 flight, 70, 87, 90
  transatlantic flight point of departure, *65,* 79–81,
    80
Old Town, Maine
  Academy Hill, 16
  Bachelor's Field, 17
  Carnegie Library, *21*
  circuses, gypsies and the Chatauqua, 21
  dancing in, 21
  fires and major conflagrations, 40–41
  local businesses, 15, **15**
  maps of, *14, 22*
  Old Town Trolley, *20*
  Universalist Church, 41–42, *42*
  winters and summers in, 18–20
Olen (Walter, Robert, Don), 378, 420
Oliver, Smith H., 377, 402–404, *639,* 467, *638*
Olley, Maurice, 74, 448, 536, *536,* 538, 542–543,
  545, 553, 565
Olmsted, John, 343
O'Malley, J.J., 465
Orteig, Raymond (Orteig Prize), 54–59
Oshei, John, 356, 358
Osofky, Irv, 526
Østby, Lt. Kristian, *144,* 144–145, *146*
Oswald, W. Bailey, 111
Overton, Nancy, 133–139
  See also Bangor, WFM flight to
Owl's Head Museum, 101, *102*
oxygen masks. *See* high altitude research

P

P-40, Curtiss-Wright, 316, *350*
P-80A Shooting Star, *310–311,* 328–329, *329–330*
Pacejka, Dr., *553*
Page, George, 333

Pair analysis, 522
Palm Beach Shores (1950), 418–420
Palmer, Dick, 302, 306
Pancho Villa, 6
Pangborn, Clyde, 59, *60,* 143, 234, 243
parachutes
  and B-17 crew bailout, *232*
  and bailout oxygen bottle, *218*
  Bill Talbott's homemade parachute, 236
  in Boeing Clipper flight tests, 193
  in Boeing Stratoliner flight tests, 178, 186
  Eddie Brown supplier of (for B-17 testing), *241*
  high-altitude parachute jump (Lovelace), 222,
    234–236, *235*
  opening g-forces, analysis of, 267
  on WFM cross-country flight, 252, *260*
Paris-to-America flight (Nungesser and Coli), 55
Parkinson, Jack, 199
Patton, Bob, **201**
Peavy Cantdog, 8, 13
Peck, Cam, 438, 442, 463–464
Penobscot River, *12,* 12–13, *13, 22*
Petre, Kay, 468
"Phantom Corsair," 404, *410*
Phillips, Elizabeth
  engagement to WFM, 301
  to Maine in MG, 356
  and Pike's Peak race (1947), 360, 365–366
  at Watkins Glen (1949), *416*
  separation, divorce, 314, 418
phugoid oscillation, 105, 318, 340
Pike's Peak
  Butterball at (1953), *477,* 478, *478*
  FWD Miller at (1948)
    FWD, advantages of, 377
    WFM mental practice for, 385–386
    modifications for, 381–382, *381–382*
    trial runs, difficulties with, 386–387
    WFM in Miller (still photo), *386*
    cornering during Time Trials, *387*
    center differential, locked *vs.* unlocked, 387–
      388
    to the peak — a good beginning, 388–389
    chart of daily activity, *388*
    transfer case failure, 389–390, 620
    cornering hairpin turn, *390*
    race report to FWD Co., *391*
  Type 35A Bugatti at (1947)
    course map, description, *360,* 361
    WFM practice runs, 363–364
    Walt "Madman" Friel, 364, *365,* 366

repairs to Bug fuel lines, distributor, 364–366
time trials, 364–365
race to the peak, 366–367, *367–368,* 369
rear drive cars, problems with, 377
(*See also* Bugatti, Type 35A)
Pillsbury, Winslow, 89, *89*
Pine Point. *See* M-1 aircraft
Pitcairn Mailwing, 68
"Poison Lil" (Maserati V8R1), 404, *409,* 421–422, *422, 424,* 451, *471,* 475, *475*
Pomeroy, Lawrence, 553
Poon, Yuck Poey and Fuey Poey, 142
Poore, Dennis, 468
porpoising, seaplane (Boeing Clipper), 202–203
Pottinger, Marion, *553*
Pratt and Whitney Aircraft Company
R-1690 engines (on B-17), 212
WFM summer job at, 143–144
pressure suit development (Boeing), *237,* 237–242
See also high altitude research
Propeller failure
on B-17, 224–225
on Boeing Stratoliner, *184*

quotations
Abzug and Larrabee, 105
Allen, Edmund T., 273
Anonynmous, 133, 301, 469, 557, 583
Argetsinger, Cameron, 399
Autocar Magazine (British), 355
Cook, William H., 141
Davis, S.C.H. (Sammy), 413
Dumont, Pierre, 429
Earhart, Amelia, 611
Gardiner, Bertha Lee, 193
Halliburton, Richard, 209, 247
Holmes, Oliver Wendell, 151, 493
Homer (*Odyssey*), 634
Lawrence, T.E., 25
Maurice Olley, 74
Moss, Stirling, 327
Pasteur, Louis, 535
Ross, Ira G., 311
Royce, Sir Henry, 476
Stevenson, Robert Louis, 3
Tennyson, Alfred Lord, 634
Turner, Nancy Byrd, 53
Wilcox, Bill, 377, 387
Winchell, Frank, 71, 565

racing, automobile
handling experiences/critical incidents (summary of), 646–648
See also specific vehicles, races
Radt, Hugo
and MX-1, 526
at CAL, 545, 549–550, 557, 574
at MRA, 589, 590, 592, *603,* 606–608
railroads
Bangor and Aroostock steam train, 17
Great Northern Railway and Marias Pass, 7–8
Locomotives, lateral instability of, 8–9
Montana Central Railroad, 3
serving Old Town, Maine, 13
Railton Mobil Special, 369–371, *371*
Rand, George C., 418, 419
rating scale, aircraft handling qualities, 340, *341*
Rauscher, Manfred, 114
Ray, Earl, 526
Reed, Albert C.
biographical sketch of, 176–177, 185
B-29 first flight, 281
blind B-17 flight over Seattle, 225–227
and Boeing Clipper, *195, 201*
conflict with Eddie Allen, 284–285, 289, 292
emotional stress at Boeing, 235
with Fraser, Lovelace and Gagge, *235*
at Northrop Avion, 301, 304, 306, 308–309
and Stratoliner flight tests, 178, 182, 183–186, 188–190
with WFM and B-17, *149, 208, 209, 220–221*
disappearance of, 645
research papers, WFM
Dynamic Stability & Control (RAS-IAS meeting), 340, 342–343, *346–349*
dynamic stability (IAS meeting), 318, *319*
"Flight Test Organization, Procedures and Crew Training" (IAS), 231
highway safety paper (CAL), 580
IME automotive stability papers, *542,* 542–544, *543*
Motions of Skidding Automobiles (SAE), *549,* 549–550
pilot's handbook (B-17E), 234, 244–245
Rice, Roy, 569, 570, *571,* 576, *577,* 578–579
Richards, Art, 384
Richardson, Erie, 442
Ripley, Millard, *et ux,* 481, *487, 488*
Robbins, Bob, 222

Robertson, Ted, 356
Rockefeller, Jim, 100
Rockefeller, W.C., 111, 302, 306, *306*
Roesch (Arline, Barbara), 435
Rogers, Al, 364–365, 367
Roland, R. Douglas, 467, *569,* 569– 570, 574–577
Rolls-Royce Silver Shadow evaluation (MRA), 603–606
Romeo, Dave, 560, 576, *577,* 578
Roos, Carl, 526
Rose, Mauri, 377, 554
Ross, Everitt, 526
Ross, Ira G.
   and F4U-5 flutter flight test, 323
   head of C-W Flight research, 314, *314*
   head of CAL wind tunnel, 326–327
   president of CAL, 557–558, 583
   quotation re derivatives, 311
   WFM relationship with, 314
Rossby, Carl-Gustav, 109, 142
Rouzer, Bill, 314, *317, 377,* 382, *431, 432, 449*
Royal Aeronautical Society, WFM at, 468
Royce, Sir Henry, 476
Rubin, Bob, 613, *613,* 617
Rudd, Tony, 467, *596, 597,* 599
Ryan Aircraft Company, 56, *56*

S

safety
   minibike/bicycle safety study (CAL), 579
   NHSTA handling standards study (CAL), 579–581
SB2C *Helldiver* (Curtiss-Wright), 310, 317, 321–322, *322*
SB2U-1 Vindicator. *See* Chance Vought aircraft
SCCA (Sports Car Club of America)
   Alec Ulmann expulsion from, 463, 464
   Argetsinger promotes Glen circuit (1948), 383, 384–385
   as closed "gentlemen's" organization, 438, 464
   Contest Board group photo (1950), *638*
   Garthwaite Trophy announced, 358–359
   Great Controversy (1951), 463–465
   Sam Collier Memorial Grand Prix (Sebring), 462
   WFM activities in
      appointed Western New York director, 358
      re closed "gentlemen's organization," 438, 456
      WFM joins, first meeting, 355–356, 358
      WFM positions and contributions to, 638, *638*
Sceli, Russ, 355–358, 400, *638*

Schairer, George S.
   B-29 development, 274, 277, 281, 284–285, 292
   biographical sketch, 176, *176*
   Boeing Clipper Dutch roll, 194–195
   Boeing Clipper towing tests, 196–197, 199
   Boeing XPBB-1 design refinements, 206
   and fatal B-29 accident, 288, 289
   seaplane porpoising, 202
   Stratoliner test flight loading, 188
Scher, Dr. Sam
   at Bridgehampton (1950), 428, 430, *432*
   at Palm Beach Shores (1950), 418–420
   at Watkins Glen 1950), 450, 456–457
Schilling, Bob, 536, *536,* 539, *541,* 553
Schoolfield, Bill, 153, 157
Schroeder, Ewald, 579
Schwartz, AL, *483–484*
Schwartz, Al, 526
sea sleds (Cecil Godfrey), *47,* 47–48
sea wings (on Boeing Clipper), *See* hydrostabilizers
seagulls, laminar flow test with, 148
Seal, John
   B-25J lateral response tests, 326
   F-86 Sabre, *352*
   F4U-5 flutter flight tests, 323–324
   Northrop N9MB flying wing tests, 335–336
   SB2C flight tests, 310, 317, 321–322, *322*
   WFM checkout in PT-26, 331
Seaman, Bob, *326*
seaplanes, longitudinal instability of, 202
Sears, Olga, 124–126
Sebring
   1950
      origin of, 461–462
      "Coefficient of Performance" formula, *462,* 462–463
      race description, 463
   1958
      Alfa Veloce, WFM in, *489*
      Barbara Milliken at, *487, 489*
      Cam, Jean Argetsinger at, *487–489*
      Jaguar XK-120M, WFM in, *486*
      Ripley's Elva, WFM in, *486, 488*
   1960
      WFM and Argetsinger at, 481
Seckel, Ed, *449*
Segal, Dave, 557, 561, *577,* 578, 588, 591
Segel, Leonard
   equations of motion, derivation of, *537,* 537–538
   GM Automotive Stability and Control project, 540–541, *541–544,* 545, *546–547*

GM technical research reports, 545, 547

IME paper presentation (1956), 542–543, *542–543*

at SAE dynamics and stability conference, *542, 553*

tire forces, analysis of, 549, *553,* 554

Seneca Cup races. *See* Watkins Glen

Seneca Lodge, 402, *409,* 417, 453, *454,* 465

sesquiplane, defined, 63

Sewell, James W. (and family), 15, 19

Shanahan, Florence, 385, *385*

Sharp, Hap, 566

Shaw, Wilbur, 415, *427,* 614

Shaw Speedster, *33–34,* 34

Shoemaker, Norris, 560

Shorr, Mel, 329

Showalter, N.D., 290

"Sidler" sideways parking device, 474

Sikorsky, Igor, 171–173

Sikorsky aircraft

at Curtiss Field (Garden City, LI), 63

prototype Sikorsky helicopter, *172,* 172–173

S-36, S-37 amphibians, 171

S-40, S-2 clippers, 171

S-43 *Valkyrien, 141,* 145, *148*

S-35 *Ville de Paris, 54,* 55, 63

seaplane wind tunnel model, 130, 142

See also Vought-Sikorsky

Sikorsky Aviation

early history of, 171

merger with Chance Vought, 152

See also Vought-Sikorsky

Silber, Sid, 222

Simonak, Dick, 430

simulators, flight

Boeing 777 flight simulator, 268

first analog (Mueller), 146–147

Skelly, Ed, 315

Skelton, Betty, *485*

Ski Mobile. *See* home-built vehicles

Small, Knowlton, 53, 54, *93,* 136

Smalley, Lester and Flossey, 400, *402, 619*

Smith, Archie, 402

Smith, Reggie, 461, *638*

Smith, Sheridan, 500–501

Snow, Ira, 87

Sockalexis, Andrew and Louis, 17

Sonnen, Henry, 314, *315,* 362, 381–382, *449, 483–484,* 526

Sperry, Elmer Jr., *326*

Spiral Jump (Houston Astrodome), *556–557,* 561–564, *562*

Spirit of St. Louis, 52–53, 56, 57

Spokely, Mildred, 250

Spruce, Paul "Peanut"

youthful experiences, 10, 18–19, *41,* 41–43

early glider flight, 33–34

and Indian Scout motorcycle, 44–45

and Aero-Triple-Cycle, 45–46

flight with WFM in *Junior,* 163

and M1 airplane, 90–91, 93–95

adult life and death, 43

stability, aircraft

CAL/Calspan summary of accomplishments, 635

early analysis of

Bryan's equations of motion, *119,* 318, 328, *334*

Fokker D-VII, 120

Hawker Hornbill (1932), 120–123

M-1 aircraft, stability problems with, 95–96, 99–100

(*See also* stall, dynamics of)

lateral instability

B-25 lateral frequency response tests, *320,* 326

longitudinal instability

of B-17, 208

B-25 longitudinal frequency response project, *317,* 317–319, *320*

of Boeing Clipper, 202–203

of Curtiss-Wright SB2C Helldiver, 310, 317, 321–322, *322*

of seaplanes, 202

variable stability

introduction to, 336–337

Dynamic Stability and Control Research (WFM paper), 340, 342–343, *348–349*

F4U-5 project, 338–339

Handling Qualities Rating Scale, 340, *341*

specifying stability and control (discussion), 339–340

T-33A variable stability aircraft, *342*

(*See also* autopilots; control augmentation; dynamic stability and control project (C-W))

stability, vehicular (CAL)

GM directional stability and control research, 545, *546,* 547, *547*

GM long-range automotive stability and control program, 540–541, *541–544,* 637

summary of accomplishments, 635–636

stall, dynamics of

introduction to, 120

Boeing 307 Stratoliner, 178–180, *179,* 190

control augmentation, importance of, 308, 329

flying wing stall behavior, 303–304, 306–307, 321

Hawker Hornbill analysis, 120–123

WFM PT-26 stall behavior project, 329–333, *331–332*

XB-29 stall behavior, 283

XOS2U-1 Kingfisher, stability/tail stall problems, 157–161

Stanley, Jean and Louis, 467

Statler, Irving, 352, *352*

Steiner, Jack, 222

Stevens, John. F., 3, 7–8

Stevenson, Bruce, *437*

Stevenson, Robert Louis, 3

Steyr [tank] engine, 472, *472, 478, 479, 483*

Stinson-Detroit airplanes, 58, 63

stowaway (on *Yellow Bird*), 81

Strang, Mr. (Mercury Outboard Company), 526

strategic bombing, origins of, 274–275

Stratochamber, Boeing, 220, *224, 237*–239

Stratoliner, Boeing. *See* Boeing Stratoliner (Boeing 307)

submarine study, tandem propeller (CAL), 576

Szekely engine, *161,* 161–163

T

Tacoma Narrows Bridge, collapse of, 210

tail stall (XOS2U-1 Kingfisher), *155,* 157, 159–161

Talbott, Bill, 220–222 *224,* 236, *253,* 295, *297*

Tapia, George, 526

Taruffi, Piero, 480, *485*

Taylor, Charles F., 109

Taylor, Edward S., 109

technical reports, WFM. *See* research papers, WFM

Teeter, Ermyl, 285, *286,* 301

Terdina, Frank, 170

test pilots

aircraft rating scale of (subjective), 340, *341*

in early Flight Test Division, 319–320

enthusiasm for automatic flight control, 316

personalities of, 320

toughness, training of, 325

See also specific aircraft, projects

Thayer, Bill, 553, 557

Thelin, Carl, 467, 560

Thompson, Mickey, 524

Three Musketeers (Dumas), 236–237

tilters (Fonda leaning vehicle), *496,* 496–497

tires

Air Force/Cornell On-Road Tire Tester, *538,* 538–539, 570–571, *572*

Camber Car tire comparison, 624, *625*

Goodyear thump and roughness study, 548

and MX-1 camber car, 520–522, 525

skid tester (Portland Cement Company), 547–548, *548*

tire force analysis (Segel), 549, *553,* 554

tire pressure (Pike's Peak, 1947), 363–364

Tire Research Facility (TIRF), 570–573, *573*

See also General Motors

towing tests

of Boeing Clipper, *198,* 199–200, *200–201*

Langley Field facility, 196–198

Townsend, Guy, 320

Trailing throttle oversteer, 380

transcontinental flight, B-29, 285–288

transcontinental flight, F-22

Fairchild F-22, views of, *246–253, 262, 264–266*

acquisition/overhaul of F-22, 246, 248

auxiliary fuel tank, installation of, 248–249

flight plan and compass deviation, 250, 252, 254

final check and departure, 252–255

frightening passage through narrow canyon, 255–256

Cascades landscape, views of, *269*

emergency landing at Terry, 257–258

fuel consumption, 260

runaway aircraft at Wheeling airport, 261

social interlude at Chambersburg, 261

fatigue and anxiety, 261–263

Pittsfield to Bangor (Doanes Field), 263–264

Old Town homecoming, 264–265, *266*

WFM return to Seattle, 265–266

Haldeman congratulatory note, 266

Allen presents flexible dividers, *265*

WFM review of flight, 266–268

WFM reprises trip with Barbara, 268–270

transoceanic flights, 58–60

Truscott, Starr, 198–199

Turner, Nancy Byrd, 53

Turner, Roscoe, 142

U

Ulmann, Alec, 384, 415, 437, 461, 463–465, *638*

Ultralight adventures, WFM, 611–613, *612*

Umpleby, Steve, 222

Universalist Church, organ adventure in, 41–42, *42*

University of Maine

WFM at, 78, 82

wind tunnel at, *86,* 86–87

Unser, Louis

Autocar quotation about, 355

at Bridgehampton (1966), 614
at Pike's Peak (1947), *359,* 360–361, 363–367, 422
unsteady flow, Statler research on, 352

V

V-160 (Fairchild 24) flap/spoiler test bed, 158
Valent, Henry, 400, 465
Van Dis, Don, 607
variable stability, studies of. *See* stability, variable
Vaughan, Mike, 400
Vehicle Experimental Research Facility (VERF), *559,* 559–560
Vindicator, SB2U-1. *See* Chance Vought aircraft
vintage aircraft. *See specific airplanes*
Voboril, Jan, *461*
von Karman, Theodore, 111, 210
Vought-Sikorsky
    consolidation at Bridgeport, Conn., *153,* 168, 171
    wind tunnel at, 156, *157*
    See also Sikorsky *(various)*

W

Wacker, Fred, *437, 453–455,* 455, 463
Wadsworth, General Peleg, 9
Walford, Martin, 613, 616, *617,* 631
Walters, Phil, 619
Warden, Pete, 320
Warner, Edward P., 66, 88–89, 109, 114, 117
Warner, Eugene, 526
Waterhouse
    Clara and Ruth, *246–247*
    Ed
        and Dumas' novels, 236–237
        early years in Maine, 24, *26–27, 30, 32,* 49, 62, 101
        at Hartford, 152, *163*
        MIT years, 107, 127
        and SCCA activities, 355, 372
        and WFM Pike's Peak run, *369*
    Frank, 24, *26,* 30–31, 36–37, *38,* 101
    William ("Uncle Willie"), 24, 57
Watkins Glen
    1948
        WFM trip to, 399–400
        Argetsinger promotes Glen circuit, 383–385
        Briggs Cunningham cars, 404, 408
        Bug crossing Franklin Street Bridge, *398–399*
        course description and corner names, 401–402
        diversity at (car and driver), 400
        entry blanks and information, 639–644
        first race, *403,* 404–408, *405–408*
        fixing speeding tickets, 400
        Griswold's winning Alfa, *409–410*
        "local formula libre" (first race), 404
        other contestants, Phantom Corsair" at, 404, *410*
        Strang's Garage, 402
        Weaver's Maserati, *409*
        WFM writes regulations for, 383–385
        WFM reprise of, 408
        (*See also* Milliken's Corner)
    1949
        start-finish line at, *413, 427*
        Race Committee, 415
        preparations for, 415, 417
        FWD Miller at, *416–418*
        race description, 417–418
    1950
        FIA regulations, conformity with, 437
        Goldschmidt win (Grand Prix), 456, *457*
        Grand Prix, photos of, *451–455*
        "Grand Prix Memories" (WFM retrospective), 466–467
        Milliken wipeout (Grand Prix), 455–456, *456*
        non-SCCA members, controversy over, 438
        Sam Collier, death of, 454–456
        timing and scoring (T&S) at, 449–450, *450*
        WFM race description (Grand Prix), 453–456
        (*See also* Bugatti, Type 54 (Dynaflow conversion); Giant's Despair Hill Climb)
    1955
        Butterball FWD at, 479–480
    1998
        FWD MIller at, *615,* 617–619, *619–620*
        "The Legends Speak," 618–619
    Permanent Circuit
        origination, development of, 465
        Butterball FWD at (1956), 479–480
    Seneca Cup race
        Butterball at (1952), 475–476, *475–477, 482*
        Goldschmidt win at (1950), 456
        as qualifier for Glen Grand Prix (1950), 438, 451, *452*
        WFM in Ferrari (with Doug, 1958), *485*
    handling experiences/critical incidents (summary of), 646–648
    Grand Prix memories (WFM), 466–467
Watts, Bob, 344

Weaver, George, 400, *638*
    See also "Poison Lil" (Maserati V8R1)
Weichel, Hans, 322
Wersebe, Ed
    B-17 flight and high-altitude tests, 204, 219, *225, 228–229, 233,* 239
    B-29 test program, 278, *297*
Whitcomb, Dave, 338–339, 402, *431, 449, 551,* 557
White, Graham, 274, 289–290
Wiggins Airways, 134, 138, 143
Wik, Elmer, 526
Wilcox, Bill, 526
    with Butterball prep crew (Glen, 1952), *484*
    and FWD Miller (Pike's Peak '48), 377, *377,* 381–382, 386–388, 390
    at Giant's Despair (1951), 458, *458*
    and MX-1 drive system assembly, 500, 526
    at Pike's Peak (1953), *477–478*
    with Steyr Butterball engine (1952), *479, 483*
    and Type 35A Bugatti, 358, 362, *401*
    and Type 51 Bugatti, 418
    at Watkins Glen
        1950, 439, *449,* 451, 453
        1952, 476, *476*
        1957, *484*
Williams, Dave, 596, *598,* 599, *600*
Wilson, Dud, *403*
Winchell, Frank, 494, 566–567, *567*
    and Chevrolet-Chaparral collaboration, 494, 566–567, *567*
    head of Chevrolet R&D, 526, 559
    head of Corvair defense team, 563–564
    support for CAL TIRF program, 569, 570, 572
    Vice President, GM Engineering, 509
    WFM biographical sketch of, 565
Winchell/Hall Chaparral, 494, 566–567, *567*
wind tunnels
    Boeing high speed subsonic tunnel, 113
    Cornell Aeronautical Laboratory, 326–327, 557
    Curtiss Aircraft Company, *66,* 67
    MIT 7-1/2 foot tunnel, *112*
    MIT 5 foot tunnel, 111, 113
    Sikorsky, 156, *157*
    University of Maine, *86,* 87
    WFM involvement with (table), 129
    Wright Field 20-foot tunnel, 113
    See also MIT; wind tunnel models

wind tunnel models
    Chance Vought XSB2U-1, 142
    Sikorsky seaplane, 142
    Stratoliner (Boeing 307), *179–180*
    torpedo plane (Østby), 145, *145–147*
    See also wind tunnels
wing spoilers (XOS2U-1 Kingfisher), 157–158
Winkelmann, Otto, 607
winter run to Albany (in Type 35A Bug), 371–375, *372, 374–375*
Wolf, Bob, 558
Woodman, Johnny, 17–18
Woods, Fred, 222
Wright, Burdette, 333
Wright, Peter, 525, *594,* 596, *596*
Wright Aeronautical, aircraft engines
    R-1820 Cyclone (on B-17), 212
    R-2600 Cyclone (on Boeing Clipper), 194, *194*
    R-3350 Cyclone (on XB-29), 277, 283–284, 287–290, 292
Wright-Bellanca *Columbia,* 55–58, *56,* 65
Wright Field 20-foot tunnel, 113
Wyer, John, 481

X

XB-35. *See* Northrop Avion flying wings
XP-79. *See* Northrop Avion flying wings

Y

Yaeger, Betty, 325
Yanecek, Steve, 526
Yates, Brock, 437
yaw dampers
    on F-86 Sabre, 352, *352*
    on Northrop Avion flying wings, 338
YB-49. *See* Northrop Avion flying wings
Yeager, Betty, 325
Youth's Companion (Y. C. Lab) Awards, *40, 46*
Yust, Mike, 618–619

Z

Zachow, Otto, 378
Zakira's Garage, 621–622, *623–624, 626*
Zimmerman, Charles, 152

Figure Credits

Foreword	International Motor Racing Research Center
Dedication	Milliken Collection

Chapter 1

Bernice Breck	1-1, 1-8a, 1-8b, 1-7
Milliken Collection	Figs. 1-2, 1-3, 1-4, 1-5, 1-6
Old Town Public Library	CO, 1-11, 1-12, 1-14 through 1-16, 1-18, 1-19
Robb Ramsey	1-13, 1-20
Ed Waterhouse	1-9, 1-10, 1-17a, 1-17b

Chapter 2

Braley Gray	2-33
Milliken Collection	2-8, 2-16, 2-17, 2-19, 2-24, 2-25, 2-32, 2-34
Old Town Public Library	2-26
Ed Waterhouse	CO, 2-1, 2-2 through 2-7, 2-9 through 2-15, 2-18, 2-20, 2-21, 2-22, 2-23, 2-27 through 2-31, 2-35, 2-36, 2-37

Chapter 3

Frederick Hemlen	3-12
Milliken Collection	3-3, 3-13, 3-14, 3-15, 3-16
National Air and Space Museum	3-2, 3-4, 3-5, 3-6, 3-7, 3-8, 3-9, 3-10, 3-11
San Diego Air Museum	CO
Sikorsky Archive	3-1

Chapter 4

Ralph Brown	4-3, 4-4
Cooper Milliken	4-8a
Milliken collection	CO, 4-1, 4-10 through 4-15b, 4-19 through 4-35
National Air and Space Museum	4-11
Robb Ramsey	4-6, 4-7, 4-8b, 4-9, 4-14, 4-15a, 4-16, 4-17, 4-18
Charles Reid	4-36
Ed Waterhouse	4-2, 4-5

Chapter 5

Milliken collection	5-1, 5-2, 5-3, 5-4, 5-10
MIT Museum	CO, 5-5, 5-6, 5-7, 5-8, 5-9
Robb Ramsey	5-11, 5-12, 5-13

Chapter 6

Experimental Aircraft Association	6-1
Milliken collection	CO, 6-2

Chapter 7

Milliken collection	all

Chapter 8

Paul Baker	8-1
Igor I. Sikorsky Historical Archives	8-3, 8-4, 8-5, 8-13
Milliken Collection	8-8, 8-9, 8-12
Robb Ramsey	8-6, 8-7
United Technologies Corporation Archive	8-2
Ed Waterhouse	CO, 8-10, 8-11

Chapter 9

Boeing Historical Archives	CO, 9-1, 9-4, 9-5, 9-6, 9-7, 9-8, 9-9, 9-10a, 9-10b, 9-10c, 9-11, 9-12, 9-13, 9-14, 9-15, 9-16
Igor I. Sikorsky Historical Archives	9-3
Milliken Collection	9-2

Chapter 10

Boeing Historical Archives	CO, 10-1, 10-18, 10-19, 10-20, 10-21
Milliken Collection	10-2 through 10-17

Chapter 11

Boeing Historical Archives	CO, 11-2, 11-6, 11-10, 11-14, 11-15, 11-16, 11-17, 11-18, 11-19, 11-20, 11-21, 11-22, 11-23, 11-24, 11-26, 11-27, 11-28, 11-33

Eddie Brown   11-32
Milliken Collection   11-1a, 11-1b, 11-1c, 11-4, 11-11, 11-12, 11-13, 11-25
Robb Ramsey   11-3, 11-5, 11-7, 11-8, 11-9, 11-29, 11-30, 11-31

Chapter 12
Experimental Aircraft Association   12-1, 12-2
Milliken Collection   12-7, 12-15, 12-16, 12-17, 12-18, 12-19
A. R. Payne   12-5, 12-6
Susan Pratt   CO, 12-13, 12-14
Robb Ramsey   12-8
Bill Talbott   12-3, 12-4, 12-9, 12-10, 12-11, 12-12

Chapter 13
Boeing Historical Archives   CO, 13-1, 13-2, 13-3, 13-4, 13-5, 13-6, 13-7, 13-9
Milliken Collection   13-8, 13-10, 13-11a, 13-11b, 13-11c, 13-11d, 13-12, 13-13

Chapter 14
Milliken Collection   14-1, 14-4
Northrop Grumman Archives   CO, 14-2, 14-3, 14-5, 14-6

Chapter 15
Cornell University   15-13
Curtiss-Wright Corporation   15-11, 15-12
Ralph Jones (CAL)   CO, 15-4, 15-5, 15-9, 15-10, 15-14, 15-17 through 15-25, 15-28, 15-29,
                                         15-30, 15-31, 15-36
Milliken Collection   15-1, 15-2, 15-3, 15-6, 15-7, 15-8, 15-15, 15-16, 15-32, 15-33, 15-34,
                                         15-35
Robb Ramsey   15-26, 15-27

Chapter 16
Autocar Magazine   16-5
Rene Dreyfus   16-3
Ralph Jones (CAL)   CO, 16-7, 16-13
Milliken Collection   16-1, 16-4, 16-8, 16-9, 16-10, 16-11, 16-14, 16-15, 16-16, 16-17
John Oshei   16-2
Pike's Peak Hillclimb   16-6
Ed Waterhouse   16-12

Chapter 17
Ralph Jones (CAL)   CO, 17-3, 17-4, 17-5, 17-6, 17-7, 17-8, 17-12
Four Wheel Drive Auto Company   17-2
Charles Lytle   17-11
Milliken Collection   17-1, 17-10, 17-13 through 17-22
Robb Ramsey   17-9

Chapter 18
Bob Gillespie   18-19
Ralph Jones   18-2
Harold Lance collection   18-8
Sandy Leith collection   18-1
Charles Lytle   CO, 18-5, 18-6, 18-7, 18-16, 18-17
Milliken Collection   18-4, 18-9 through 18-15, 18-18
Ed Waterhouse   18-3

Chapter 19
Ralph Jones   CO, 19-4, 19-5, 19-14, 19-15
Charles Lytle   19-6
Milliken Collection   19-2, 19-3, 19-7, 19-8, 19-9, 19-11, 19-13
John Oshei   19-1, 19-10, 19-12

Chapter 20
Cam Argetsinger   20-4
Pete De Beaumont   CO, 20-3, 20-5
Richard Thierry   20-1, 20-2

Chapter 21
Michael Argetsinger   21-18
Pete De Beaumont   21-27, 21-28, 21-31
Bill Close   21-32, 21-33
Grand Prix Graphics   21-34

Harry Harrs	21-26
Ralph Jones	21-1, 21-2, 21-3, 21-5, 21-6, 21-7, 21-8, 21-12 through 21-17
David Kyle	21-36
Charles Lytle	CO
Milliken Collection	21-4, 21-11, 21-19 through 21-25, 21-29, 21-30
Cliff Muzzey	21-9, 21-10
Robb Ramsey	21-35

Chapter 22

Bill Argetsinger	22-28, 22-33
Jean and Bart Brooks	22-11
Ralph Jones	22-3, 22-4, 22-5, 22-6, 22-8, 22-9, 22-10, 22-13, 22-17, 22-19, 22-20, 22-22
Ludvigsen Library	CO
Ozzie Lyons	22-18
Charles Lytle	22-12, 22-24, 22-25, 22-29, 22-30, 22-31, 22-32, 22-34, 22-35
Milliken Collection	22-1, 22-2, 22-15, 22-16, 22-21, 22-23, 22-26, 22-36
Robb Ramsey	22-7
Art Richard	22-14
Jess Woods	22-27

Chapter 23

Bill Close	23-9, 23-55, 23-56, 23-57, 23-58
Al Fonda	23-3
Ralph Jones	23-5, 23-6, 23-7, 23-12
Milliken Collection	CO, 23-1, 23-2, 23-4, 23-8, 23-11, 23-13, 23-17a,b,c,d through 23-44, 23-52, 23-53, 23-54, 23-59 through 23-65
Mercedes-Benz	23-51
Robb Ramsey	3-10, 23-14, 23-15, 23-16, 23-45 through 23-50

Chapter 24

Tom Bundorf	24-23
John Colt	24-15
Al Fonda	24-11
Ralph Jones	24-3, 24-4, 24-5, 24-6, 24-7, 24-8, 24-18, 24-19
Milliken Collection	CO, 24-1, 24-2, 24-9, 24-10, 24-17, 24-21, 24-22
Hugo Radt	24-20
Leonard Siegel	24-12, 24-13, 24-16

Chapter 25

JM Productions, Inc.	CO, 25-6, 25-7
Ludvigsen Library	25-5
Milliken Collection	25-1, 25-2, 25-3, 25-4, 25-6, 25-8 through 25-27
Petersen Publishing Company	25-28

Chapter 26

Walt Curtis	26-7
Goodyear Corporation	26-4, 26-5, 26-6
Ralph Jones	26-1, 25-20
Lotus Cars	26-15, 26-16, 26-18, 26-19
Milliken Collection	CO, 26-2, 26-3, 26-10, 26-12, 26-13, 26-14, 26-17
Moog, Inc.	26-8, 26-9
MTS Systems, Corp.	26-20, 26-21
Tony Rudd	26-11

Chapter 27

Dean Butler	CO, 27-2 through 27-9, 27-22 through 27-30
Don Butler	27-14, 27-19, 27-20, 27-21
Classic & Sports Car Magazine	27-28
Experimental Aircraft Association	27-1
Phil Henderson	27-17, 27-18
David Kimball	27-16
John Lamm	27-15
Mike Yust	27-10, 27-11, 27-12, 27-13

Appendix II

Milliken Collection	II-1

Selected Books and Repair Information From Bentley Publishers

Driving

Alex Zanardi - My Sweetest Victory
Alex Zanardi with Gianluca Gasparini
ISBN 0-8376-1249-7

The Unfair Advantage
Mark Donohue ISBN 0-8376-0073-1(hc);
0-8376-0069-3(pb)

Going Faster! Mastering the Art of Race Driving
The Skip Barber Racing School
ISBN 0-8376-0227-0

A French Kiss With Death: Steve McQueen and the Making of *Le Mans*
Michael Keyser ISBN 0-8376-0234-3

Sports Car and Competition Driving
Paul Frère with foreword *by Phil Hill*
ISBN 0-8376-0202-5

Engineering / Reference

Supercharged! Design, Testing, and Installation of Supercharger Systems
Corky Bell ISBN 0-8376-0168-1

Maximum Boost: Designing, Testing, and Installing Turbocharger Systems
Corky Bell ISBN 0-8376-0160-6

Bosch Fuel Injection and Engine Management
Charles O. Probst, SAE ISBN 0-8376-0300-5

Race Car Aerodynamics
Joseph Katz ISBN 0-8376-0142-8

Road & Track Illustrated Automotive Dictionary
John Dinkel ISBN 0-8376-0143-6

Scientific Design of Exhaust and Intake Systems
Philip H. Smith 0-8376-0309-9

Alfa Romeo

Alfa Romeo All-Alloy Twin Cam Companion 1954–1994
Pat Braden ISBN 0-8376-0275-0

Alfa Romeo Owner's Bible™
Pat Braden ISBN 0-8376-0707-8

Audi

Audi A4 Repair Manual: 1996–2001, 1.8L turbo, 2.8L, including Avant and quattro
Bentley Publishers ISBN 0-8376-0371-4

Audi A6 Sedan 1998–2004, Avant 1999–2004, allroad quattro 2001–2005, S6 Avant 2002-2004, RS6 2003-2004 Official Factory Repair Manual on CD-ROM
Audi of America ISBN 978-0-8376-1257-7

BMW

BMW Z3 Service Manual: 1996–2002, including Z3 Roadster, Z3 Coupe, M Roadster, M Coupe
Bentley Publishers ISBN 0-8376-1250-0

BMW 3 Series (E46) Service Manual: 1999–2005, M3, 323i, 325i, 325xi, 328i, 330i, 330xi, Sedan, Coupe, Convertible, Wagon
Bentley Publishers ISBN 0-8376-1277-2

BMW 3 Series (E36) Service Manual: 1992–1998, 318i/is/iC, 323is/iC, 325i/is/iC, 328i/is/iC, M3
Bentley Publishers ISBN 0-8376-0326-9

BMW 5 Series Service Manual: 1997–2002 525i, 528i, 530i, 540i, Sedan, Sport Wagon
Bentley Publishers ISBN 0-8376-0317-X

BMW 6 Series Enthusiast's Companion™
Jeremy Walton ISBN 0-8376-0193-2

BMW 7 Series Service Manual: 1988–1994, 735i, 735iL, 740i, 740iL, 750iL
Bentley Publishers ISBN 0-8376-0328-5

Bosch

Bosch Automotive Handbook 6th Edition
Robert Bosch, GmbH ISBN 0-8376-1243-8

Bosch Handbook for Automotive Electrics and Electronics
Robert Bosch, GmbH ISBN 0-8376-1050-8

Bosch Handbook for Diesel-Engine Management
Robert Bosch, GmbH ISBN 0-8376-1051-6

Bosch Handbook for Gasoline-Engine Management
Robert Bosch, GmbH ISBN 0-8376-1052-4

Chevrolet

Corvette Illustrated Encyclopedia
Tom Benford ISBN 0-8376-0928-3

Corvette Fuel Injection & Electronic Engine Management 1982–2001:
Charles O. Probst, SAE ISBN 0-8376-0861-9

Zora Arkus-Duntov: The Legend Behind Corvette
Jerry Burton ISBN 0-8376-0858-9

Chevrolet by the Numbers 1965–1969: The Essential Chevrolet Parts Reference
Alan Colvin ISBN 0-8376-0956-9

Ford

Ford Fuel Injection and Electronic Engine Control: 1988–1993
Charles O. Probst, SAE ISBN 0-8376-0301-3

The Official Ford Mustang 5.0 Technical Reference & Performance Handbook: 1979–1993
Al Kirschenbaum ISBN 0-8376-0210-6

Jeep

Jeep CJ Rebuilder's Manual: 1972-1986
Moses Ludel ISBN 0-8376-0151-7

Jeep Owner's Bible™ - Third Edition
Moses Ludel ISBN 0-8376-1117-2

Mercedes-Benz

Mercedes-Benz Technical Companion™
staff of The Star and members of the Mercedes-Benz Club of America ISBN 0-8376-1033-8

Mercedes-Benz E-Class (W124) Owner's Bible™: 1986–1995
Bentley Publishers ISBN 0-8376-0230-0

MINI Cooper

MINI Cooper Service Manual: 2002-2004
Bentley Publishers ISBN 0-8376-1068-0

Porsche

Porsche: Excellence Was Expected
Karl Ludvigsen ISBN 0-8376-0235-1

Porsche 911 Enthusiast's Companion™
Adrian Streather ISBN 08376-0293-9

Porsche 911 Carrera Service Manual: 1984–1989
Bentley Publishers ISBN 0-8376-0291-2

Porsche 911 SC Service Manual: 1978–1983
Bentley Publishers ISBN 0-8376-0290-4

Volkswagen

Battle for the Beetle
Karl Ludvigsen ISBN 0-8376-0071-5

Jetta, Golf, GTI Service Manual: 1999–2005 1.8L turbo, 1.9L TDI diesel, PD diesel, 2.0L gasoline, 2.8L VR6
Bentley Publishers ISBN 0-8376-1251-9

New Beetle Service Manual: 1998–2002 1.8L turbo, 1.9L TDI diesel, 2.0L gasoline
Bentley Publishers ISBN 0-8376-0376-5

New Beetle 1998–2005, New Beetle Convertible 2003-2005 Official Factory Repair Manual on CD-ROM
Volkswagen of America ISBN 978-0-8376-1265-2

Passat Service Manual: 1998–2004, 1.8L turbo, 2.8L V6, 4.0L W8, including wagon and 4MOTION
Bentley Publishers ISBN 0-8376-0369-2

Passat, Passat Wagon 1998–2005 Official Factory Repair Manual on CD-ROM
Volkswagen of America ISBN 978-0-8376-1267-6

Golf, GTI, Jetta 1993–1999, Cabrio 1995–2002 Official Factory Repair Manual on CD-ROM
Volkswagen of America ISBN 978-0-8376-1263-8

Jetta, Golf, GTI: 1993–1999, Cabrio: 1995-2002 Service Manual
Bentley Publishers ISBN 0-8376-0366-8

EuroVan Official Factory Repair Manual: 1992–1999
Volkswagen of America ISBN 0-8376-0335-8

BentleyPublishers™
.com

Automotive Reference

Bentley Publishers has published service manuals and automobile books since 1950. Please write to us at 1734 Massachusetts Ave., Cambridge, MA 02138, visit our web site, or call 1-800-423-4595 for a free copy of our catalog.